Around Mexico City
Pages 134–61

The Gulf Coast
Pages 242–59

The Yucatán Peninsula
Pages 260–91

Southern Mexico
Pages 216–41

Monterrey
Zacatecas
COLONIAL
ARTLAND
Guanajuato
Querétaro
Morelia
MEXICO
CITY
Puebla
Taxco
AROUND
MEXICO CITY
THE GULF
COAST
Oaxaca
Acapulco
SOUTHERN MEXICO
Tuxtla
Gutiérrez
Mérida
THE YUCATÁN
PENINSULA
Campeche
Chetumal

0 kilometers 250
0 miles 250

EYEWITNESS TRAVEL

MEXICO

DK

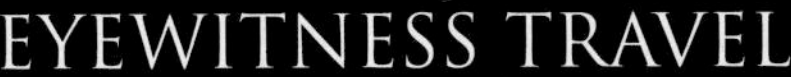

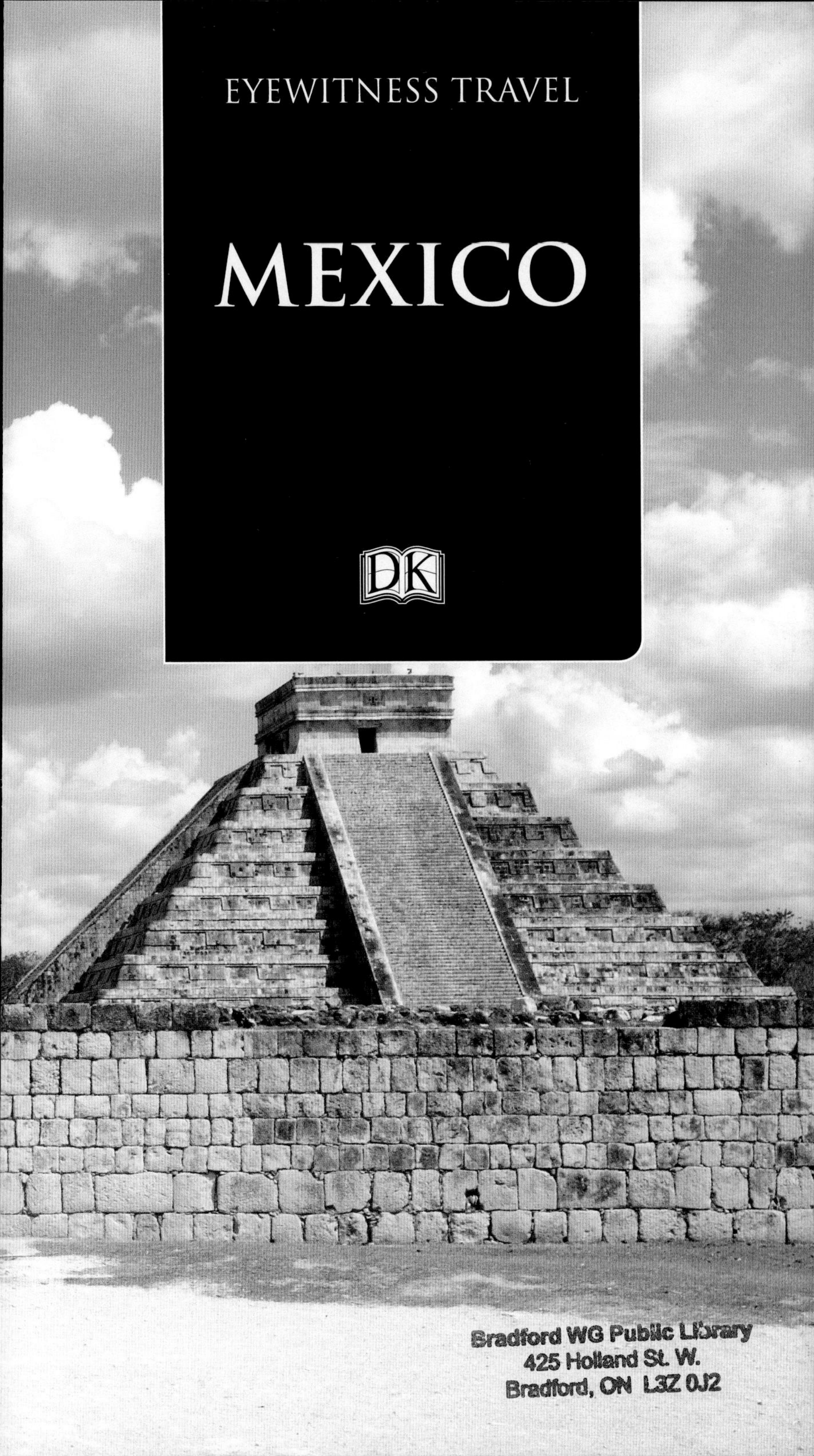

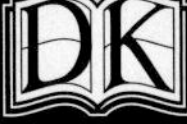

Project Editor Nick Inman
Art Editors Stephen Bere, Marisa Renzullo
Editors Elizabeth Atherton, Claire Folkard, Emily Green, Freddy Hamilton, Jane Oliver, Sophie Warne, Lynda Warrington
US Editor Mary Sutherland
Designers Gillian Andrews, Jo Doran, Paul Jackson, Tim Mann, Nicola Rodway
Map Co-ordinator David Pugh
Researcher Eva Gleason
Picture Researchers Monica Allende, Ellen Root
DTP Designers Maite Lantaron, Pamela Shiels

Main Contributors
Nick Caistor, Maria Doulton, Petra Fischer, Eduardo Gleason, Phil Gunson, Alan Knight, Felicity Laughton, Richard Nichols, Chloë Sayer

Consultants
Antonio Benavides, Simon Martin, Lourdes Nichols

Printed and bound in China

First American Edition, 1999
17 18 19 20 10 9 8 7 6 5 4 3 2 1

Published in the United States by
Dorling Kindersley Limited,
345 Hudson Street, New York, NY 10014

Reprinted with revisions 2001, 2002, 2003, 2006, 2008, 2010, 2012, 2015, 2017

Published in the UK by Dorling Kindersley Limited

A catalog record for this book is available from the Library of Congress.

ISSN 1542-1554
ISBN 978-1-46545-711-0

Throughout this book, floors are referred to in accordance with European usage, i.e., the "first floor" is the floor above ground level.

The information in this DK Eyewitness Travel Guide is checked regularly.

Every effort has been made to ensure that this book is as up-to-date as possible at the time of going to press. Some details, however, such as telephone numbers, opening hours, prices, gallery hanging arrangements and travel information, are liable to change. The publishers cannot accept responsibility for any consequences arising from the use of this book, nor for any material on third party websites, and cannot guarantee that any website address in this book will be a suitable source of travel information. We value the views and suggestions of our readers very highly. Please write to: Publisher, DK Eyewitness Travel Guides, Dorling Kindersley, 80 Strand, London WC2R 0RL, UK, or email: travelguides@dk.com.

Produced with the generous help of the Proyecto México, Dirección de Divulgación, Coordinación Nacional de Difusión, Instituto Nacional de Antropología e Historia, Córdoba 45, Col. Roma, Delegación Cuauhtémoc, CP 06700, Mexico

Front cover main image: The Palenque archaeological site in southern Mexico

Great pyramid with head of giant serpent, Chichen Itza

Guadalajara's Plaza de Armas and cathedral

Contents

Clay statue of an Aztec warrior in feathers, Templo Mayor Museum, Mexico City

Introducing Mexico

Mexico City

Virgin of Guadalupe, Mexico's patron saint

Mexico Region by Region

Mayan pyramid El Castillo at Chichén Itzá on the Yucatán Peninsula

Travelers' Needs

The classic Mexican egg dish, *huevos rancheros*

Survival Guide

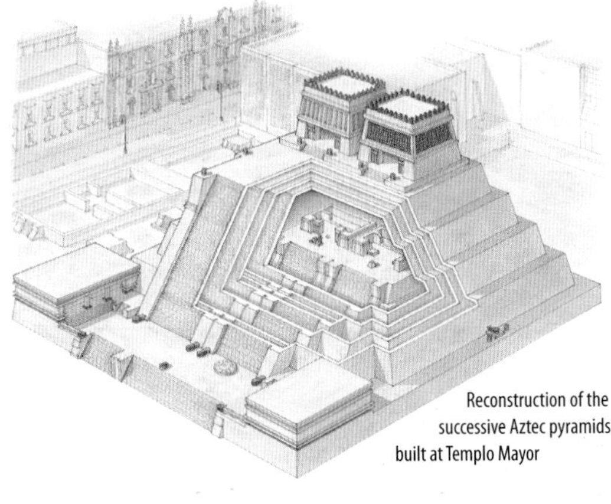

Reconstruction of the successive Aztec pyramids built at Templo Mayor

HOW TO USE THIS GUIDE

This guide helps you to get the most from your visit to Mexico. It provides detailed practical information and expert recommendations. *Introducing Mexico* maps the country and sets it in its historical and cultural context. The six regional sections, plus *Mexico City*, describe important sights, using maps, photographs, and illustrations. Features cover topics from food and wine to fiestas and native wildlife. Restaurant and hotel recommendations can be found in *Travelers' Needs*. The *Survival Guide* has tips on everything from making a telephone call to using local transportation.

Mexico City

This is divided into three areas, each with its own chapter. A final chapter, *Farther Afield*, covers peripheral sights. All sights are numbered and plotted on the chapter's area map. Information on each sight is easy to locate as it follows the numerical order on the map.

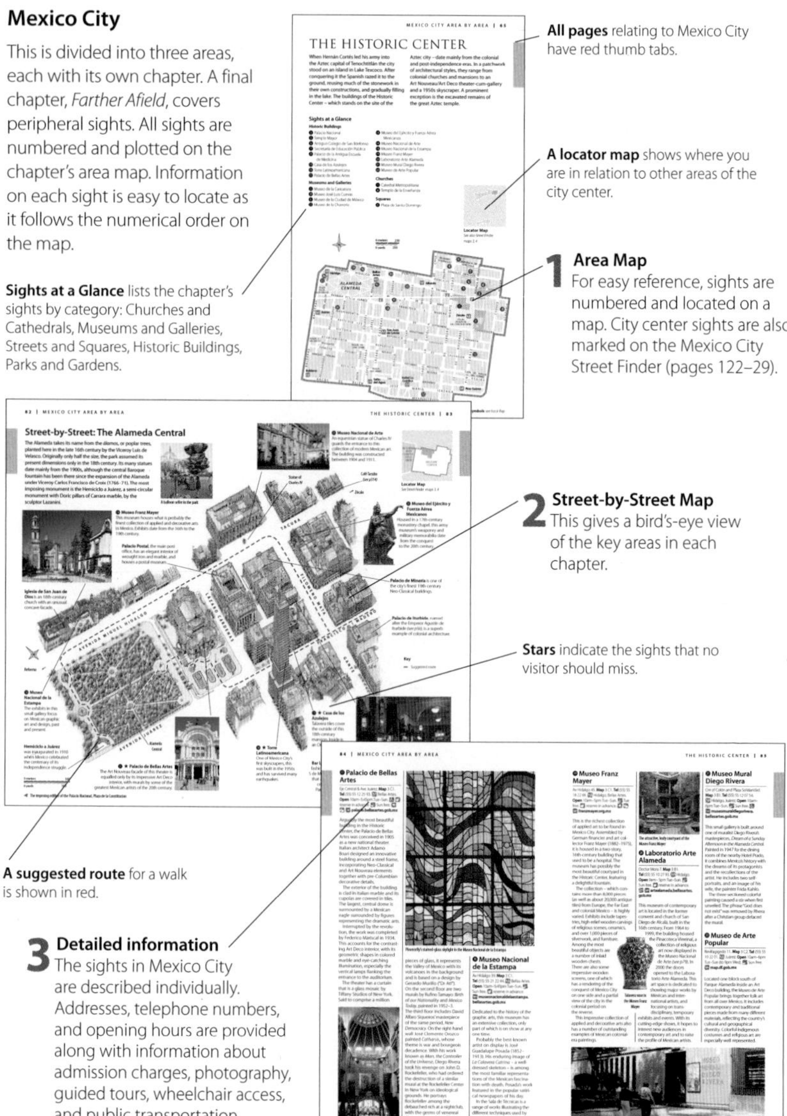

Sights at a Glance lists the chapter's sights by category: Churches and Cathedrals, Museums and Galleries, Streets and Squares, Historic Buildings, Parks and Gardens.

All pages relating to Mexico City have red thumb tabs.

A locator map shows where you are in relation to other areas of the city center.

1 Area Map

For easy reference, sights are numbered and located on a map. City center sights are also marked on the Mexico City Street Finder (pages 122–29).

2 Street-by-Street Map

This gives a bird's-eye view of the key areas in each chapter.

Stars indicate the sights that no visitor should miss.

A suggested route for a walk is shown in red.

3 Detailed information

The sights in Mexico City are described individually. Addresses, telephone numbers, and opening hours are provided along with information about admission charges, photography, guided tours, wheelchair access, and public transportation.

Mexico Region By Region

Apart from Mexico City, the country has been divided into six regions: Around Mexico City, Northern Mexico, the Colonial Heartland, Southern Mexico, the Gulf Coast, and the Yucatán Peninsula.

1 Introduction

The landscape, history, and character of each region is described here, showing how the area has developed over the years and what it has to offer the visitor today.

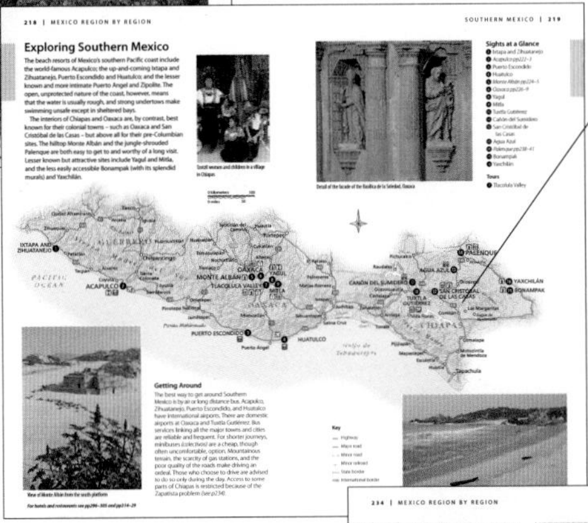

2 Regional Map

This shows the road network and gives an illustrated overview of the whole region. All interesting places to visit are numbered, and there are also useful tips on getting to, and around, the region by car and public transportation.

Each area of Mexico can be quickly identified by its color coding, shown on the inside front cover.

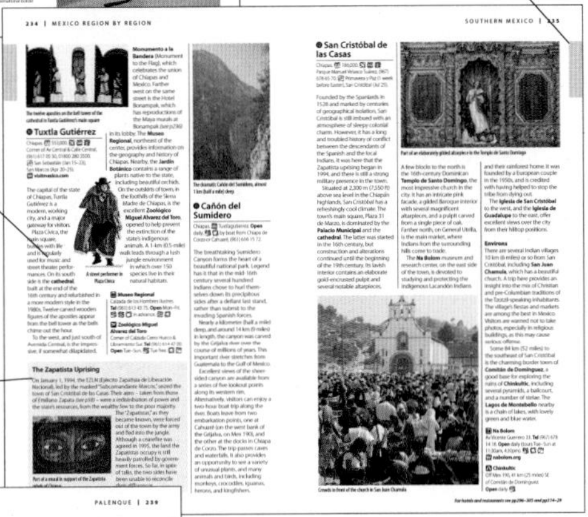

3 Detailed information

All the important towns and other places to visit are described individually. They are listed in order, following the numbering on the Regional Map. Within each town or city there is detailed information on important buildings and other sights.

Story boxes give background information on the region.

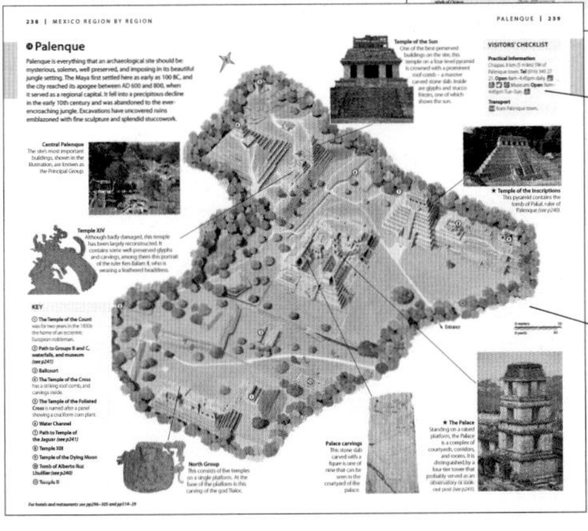

A Visitors' Checklist provides the practical information you will need to plan your visit.

4 Mexico's top sights

These are given two or more pages. Historic buildings are reconstructed or dissected to reveal their interiors. The most interesting sights are shown in a bird's-eye view, with features highlighted.

INTRODUCING MEXICO

DISCOVERING MEXICO

The following itineraries highlight the best Mexico has to offer. Ancient cultures, archaeological sites, colonial buildings, and modern Mexican life merge in the frantic and fascinating Mexico City. Two days here set you up beautifully for experiencing the rest of the country. Mexico is a big place, so break up long distances to keep things manageable and fun. The Northern, Central, and Southern Mexico itineraries all follow broad themes. On a ten-day tour of Southern Mexico most of the country's finest pyramid sites are linked, but there are also visits to Oaxaca's wonderful markets, the tropical colonial cities of Campeche and Mérida, and the diving reefs of Cozumel. A week in Central Mexico loops around the finest colonial cities, many with their rich roots in silver mining. Finally, a week in Northern Mexico is all about the beach, getting out into nature, and experiencing the Baja desert, plus riding El Chepe – the Copper Canyon railroad.

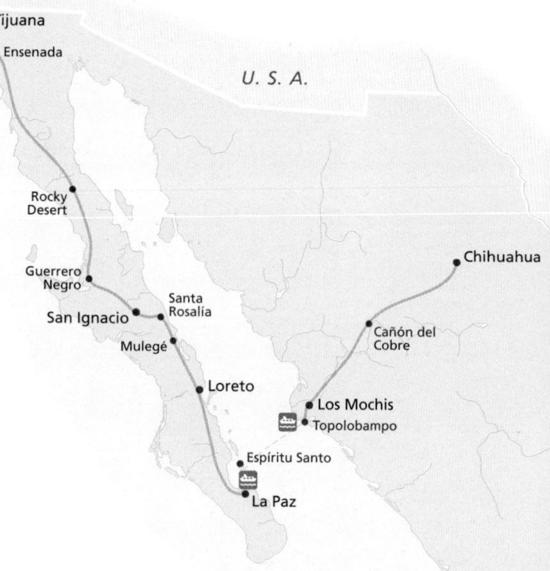

Key

- Northern Mexico tour
- Central Mexico tour
- Southern Mexico tour

One Week in Northern Mexico

- Spend a few hours off the coast of **Guerrero Negro** watching blue and California gray whales.
- See Baja cave art in the desert landscapes around the pretty oasis town of **San Ignacio**.
- Devote time to fishing or diving in **Loreto**, or just hang out at the beach.
- Spend the day around **Isla Espíritu Santo**, combining kayaking with snorkeling, diving among manta rays, and swimming with sea lions.
- Ride **El Chepe**, the magnificent railroad through the Cañón del Cobre (Copper Canyon) from the Pacific coast to the Chihuahua highlands.
- Set aside a few days to explore deeper into the **Cañón del Cobre** (Copper Canyon).

Guanajuato
Nestled below hills once rich in silver, this UNESCO World Heritage site has well-preserved streets packed with colonial architecture.

◀ Scenes from a religious ceremony in a reconstruction of a Mayan fresco from Bonampak

One Week in Central Mexico

- Sample some of central Mexico's best cuisine in the relaxed colonial setting of **San Miguel de Allende**.
- Wander through the tight network of alleys and tunnels in the compact silver town of **Guanajuato**.
- Visit historic **Zacatecas** with its fine cathedral and excellent museums, all wedged into a very tight valley.
- Get your head around the workings of Edward James's mind at his surreal jungle estate in **Las Pozas**.
- Check out the Orozco mural of colonial liberator, Hidalgo, in Mexico's second city, **Guadalajara**.
- Make a pilgrimage to the distilleries of **Tequila**, set amid agave plants.
- Sample Tarascan culture in the small villages that line **Lake Pátzcuaro**, and, if your timing is right, catch the country's best Day of the Dead celebrations.
- Marvel at the millions of monarch butterflies spending winter in the pine trees of the **Santuario El Rosario**.

Ten Days in Southern Mexico

- Spend a few hours in the colorful markets of **Oaxaca** and the nearby villages of the Tlacolula Valley.
- Visit the colonnaded mansions of 19th-century cotton and sugar barons, which make **Tlacotalpan** a wonderfully homogenous World Heritage site.
- Take time to appreciate the steamy jungle setting of the **Palenque** archaeological site.
- Spend a balmy evening on the streets listening to troubadours in the gracious capital of the Yucatán, **Mérida**.
- Wonder at the great pyramid, well-preserved ballcourt, intricate carvings, and sacred cenote at **Chichén Itzá**.
- Look down on the great beaches and warm waters of **Tulum** from clifftop Mayan sites.
- Don your snorkelling mask and dive into the Caribbean reef systems that surround **Cozumel**.

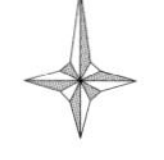

Two Days in Mexico City

Mexico's fascinating capital is packed with magnificent sights. Enjoy the busy and sprawling Mexico City by day and night.

- **Arriving** Mexico City's airport is 15 km (9 miles) from the city center. Pre-pay for a *sitio* (authorized taxi) or take the Metro or Metrobús into town.

Day 1

Morning Start in the Historic Center, the colonial heart of modern Mexico City. The vast **Zócalo** *(pp64–7)* is flanked on the north by the **Catedral Metropolitana** *(pp68–70)*, Latin America's biggest church. The distinct lean of its walls and columns attests to its vast weight. Have ID handy for accessing the nearby **Palacio Nacional** *(p71)* and the magnificent Diego Rivera murals around the main courtyard. The best decorates the staircase and depicts the country's long history from Quetzalcoatl to Pancho Villa, plus Rivera's wife, artist Frida Kahlo. Round off the morning at the **Templo Mayor** *(pp72–4)*, the foundations of the Aztec city of Tenochtitlán. Re-discovered in the 1970s, it remains an active archaeological site.

Afternoon Lunch on a rooftop terrace overlooking the Zócalo then spend the afternoon at the **Museo Nacional de Antropología** *(pp94–9)*. It can be overwhelming, so pace yourself and don't miss the Aztec Sun Stone or the reconstructions of sections of Maya temples. Try to secure tickets for the ballet or symphony at **Palacio de Bellas Artes** *(p84)* – the Art Deco interior is worth the price of a ticket. After the performance, catch a taxi to **Plaza Garibaldi** *(p113)* to hear street *mariachi* at its finest.

Day 2

Morning Beat the heat by heading out as early as possible to the pyramids 50 km (30 miles) north of the city at **Teotihuacán** *(pp138–41)*. You could easily spend the day here. To get a sense of the size, start by scaling either the Pyramid of the Moon, or the slightly taller Pyramid of the Sun (or both). Continue down the main avenue to the Citadel where the Temple of Quetzalcoatl is the star attraction. As the day heats up, spend half an hour in the museum before lunch.

Afternoon After resting your legs, head to **Coyoacán** *(pp100–9)*, in the south of the city. Once a separate village, it is now very much part of the metropolis. Visit **Museo Frida Kahlo/Casa Azul** *(see p107)*, once the home of artists Frida Kahlo and Diego Rivera, now a museum dedicated to Kahlo. Conveniently, Kahlo's sometime lover Leon Trotsky lived a few blocks away at what is now the **Museo Casa de León Trotsky** *(p107)*. Both museums offer superb insights into the lives of these fascinating characters. Coyoacán retains enough of a village atmosphere to justify staying for dinner and an evening stroll in the main square.

Frida Kahlo's former home, Casa Azul, now a museum

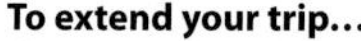

To extend your trip...
If you're in the city on the weekend, visit **Xochimilco** *(p116)* to be punted along the canals. Or spend a day or two in the colonial towns of **Taxco** *(pp150–51)* and **Cuernavaca** *(p152)*.

Ten Days in Southern Mexico

- **Arriving** Fly into Oaxaca airport, 10 km (6 miles) south of the city, or take one of the frequent and comfortable buses from Mexico City (6hr 30min). Fly out of Cancún airport, 20 km (12 miles) from town.
- **Transport** Due to the long distances, a car will get you around quicker but this itinerary can be completed using local bus services.

Day 1: Oaxaca

Just hanging out in **Oaxaca** *(pp226–9)* is a total delight, but the city does have sights worth seeking out. Make straight for the **Iglesia de Santo Domingo** *(see p226)*, probably the finest church in the city with its dazzling interior that draws on an array of architectural styles. Artifacts from some of the most important sites in southern Mexico fill the adjacent **Centro Cultural Santo Domingo** *(see p227)*, including some impressive gold pieces. Relax in the center's botanic garden before wandering along to **Casa de Juárez** *(see p227)*, former home of Mexico's great liberal reformer, Benito Juárez. The modern art inside the **Museo de Arte Contemporáneo** *(see p226)* brings a complete change of scene en route to lunch at one of the cafés around the central Plaza de Armas. Spend the afternoon at the markets. Closest is the **Mercado Juárez** *(p228)*, but leave time for the vibrant **Mercado de Abastos** *(p228)*, a great experience even if you're not buying, and busiest on Saturdays when Zapotec and Mixtec villagers come to trade.

For practical information on traveling around Mexico, see pp356–65

Pyramid from the late Classic period of Mayan civilization, Comalcalco

Day 2: Around Oaxaca
The Zapotec site of **Monte Albán** *(pp224–5)* command a superb mountain-top site on the outskirts of Oaxaca. Arrive early when fewer people crowd around the contorted carvings of Los Danzantes and the urn at Tomb 104. Don't miss the observatory and the well-preserved ballcourts. After lunch in Oaxaca, spend the afternoon driving the **Tlacolula Valley** *(pp230–31)*. Explore the pre-Columbian archaeological site at Mitla and ancient villages noted for their crafts.

Day 3: Tlacotalpan
If you're traveling by bus, plan ahead and start early for a long journey over the hills, probably with changes at Tuxtepec and Cosamaloapan. You'll want to reach **Tlacotalpan** *(p256)* with time to explore the colonnaded houses of this little-known UNESCO World Heritage site.

Day 4: Villahermosa and Comalcalco
Soak up the morning light in Tlacotalpan then make for **Villahermosa** *(pp258–9)* and have lunch overlooking the river in the **Museo Regional de Antropología Carlos Pellicer Cámara**. Spend the afternoon 60 km (37 miles) north of town at the Mayan site of **Comalcalco** *(p258)*, set among cacao plantations.

Day 5: Parque-Museo de La Venta and Palenque
View artifacts of the ancient Olmec civilization, which pre-dates the Mayans, in the lakeside setting of the **Parque-Museo de La Venta** *(p259)*, right in Villahermosa. Travel to **Palenque** *(pp238–41)* through the middle of the day then either relax or visit the archaeological site, one of the finest in Mexico and superbly set in the jungle.

To extend your trip...
From Palenque head to colonial **San Cristóbal de Las Casas** *(p235)* in the Chiapas highlands, or take a day trip to sheer-sided **Cañón del Sumidero** *(p234)*.

Day 6: Palenque and Campeche
Visit the ruins at Palenque. Even if you managed to visit at the end of the previous day, go again in the cool, especially if there is a little morning mist around. Linger, but leave time to travel to **Campeche** *(p264)* for a balmy evening stroll of the walled city, being sure to while-away some time in the pedestrianized main square, Parque Principal.

Day 7: Becal, Uxmal, and Mérida
Spend a couple of hours exploring the defensive bastions and colonial houses of Campeche before heading north, stopping at **Becal** *(p264)* to see "Panama" hats being made. If you're driving and not totally worn out, then detour west to see the superb late-Classic Maya site of **Uxmal** *(pp266–8)*. Otherwise press on to the gracious capital of Yucatán, **Mérida** *(pp274–5)*, where you can spend the evening being serenaded by *trovadores* in the **Plaza Grande**.

Day 8: Chichén Itzá and Tulum
Aim to get to the Mayan site at **Chichén Itzá** *(pp278–80)* as early as you can. It is a big site with lots to see, but don't miss the towering pyramid, El Castillo, the observatory, or the sacred cenote, reached by a jungle path. For a swim in a cenote make your way to **Cenote de Dzitnup** *(p282)*, illuminated by a natural skylight. Aim to make it to **Tulum** *(pp288–9)* in time for sunset at one of the beach bars.

Day 9: Tulum, Sian Ka'an, and Cozumel
Spectacular though they are, Tulum's archaeological sites are small and will only take an hour to explore. Divers and snorkelers should head, via the Playa del Carmen ferry, to the spectacular reef dive sites around **Cozumel** *(p286)*. If they don't appeal, you can book a night tour of **Sian Ka'an Biosphere Reserve** *(p290)*, spending an extra night in Tulum.

Day 10: Cancún
Spend your final morning relaxing on the beach at Tulum or Cozumel before traveling on to hectic **Cancún** *(p283)*, the Yucatán's frenetic resort city. It is a dramatic contrast from the rest of the peninsula with beaches backed by five-star hotels and all the watersports amenities you could ask for.

Swimming in the bright blue waters at Tulum beach

One Week in Central Mexico

- **Arriving** Flights from the US and Mexico City land at Del Bajío Airport, near Léon, 90 km (56 miles) west of San Miguel de Allende. Shuttle vans run between the two for a reasonable price; reserve in advance. A bus from Mexico City to San Miguel de Allende takes 4 hours. Morelia's domestic airport is 25 km (26 miles) from town.
- **Transport** Driving around Central Mexico is certainly feasible, but buses are fast, frequent, and comfortable.

Day 1: San Miguel de Allende
San Miguel de Allende *(pp202–3)* is the perfect introduction to Mexico – vibrant and colonial but very manageable and with great places to stay and eat. The sights play second fiddle to just ambling around, but visit the key churches and chapels – **La Parroquia**, **Santa Casa de Loreto**, and the **Oratorio de San Felipe Neri** – before settling in for a long lunch. Walk it off by strolling to the **Escuela de Bellas Artes**, calling in at **Casa Allende** and **Casa del Inquisidor** *(p202)* along the way.

Day 2: Guanajuato
It is only a short journey to wonderful **Guanajuato** *(pp206–9)*. The pleasure here is in exploring the maze of streets and alleys, perhaps calling in at the birthplace of Diego Rivera, **Casa Diego Rivera**, the **Museo Iconográfico del Quijote**, and the **Museo del Pueblo**. For lunch, head up to **La Valenciana** where there's a great restaurant opposite the magnificent church. Later, visit the macabre preserved bodies at the **Museo de las Momias**, or head to the monolithic former granary, **Alhóndiga de Granaditas**. Join the evening promenade around Jardín de la Unión, sit on the steps of the **Teatro Juárez**, and watch one of the bands of student minstrels strolling the streets.

Elaborate doorway of a Colonial mansion, San Miguel de Allende

To extend your trip...
Rent a car and explore the Sierra Gorda, heading for Edward James' fantasy world of **Las Pozas** *(p199)*.

Day 3: Zacatecas
If you're driving north you could call in at **Museo José Guadalupe Posada** *(p195)* in Aguascalientes to see the artist's skeletal engravings. It is too much trouble for bus travelers who should continue straight to **Zacatecas** *(pp196–7)*, another gem of a colonial city. Get a sense of its layout by taking a late afternoon walk up to the **Cerro del Grillo** *(p197)* and catching the cable car over the city to the **Cerro de la Bufa** *(p197)*. After dinner, visit a few bars then head back to Cerro del Grillo, where part of the silver mine operates as a nightclub.

To extend your trip...
Visit remote and quirky **Real de Catorce** *(p197)* and explore the restored ruins and surrounding desert.

Day 4: Zacatecas and Guadalajara
Spend the morning visiting **Ex-Templo de San Agustín** *(p196)*, **Museo Rafael Coronel** *(p197)*, or **Museo Francisco Goitia** *(p197)*. All are excellent, and varied enough to justify trying to squeeze them all in. An afternoon spent traveling to **Guadalajara** *(pp192–3)* should be rewarded by an evening strolling the streets of the colonial center, eating a good dinner, and visiting a bar or two.

The cable car in Zacatecas, linking Cerro de la Bufa to the city center

Day 5: Guadalajara
You don't have to walk far to see Guadalajara's key sights: the stately **Cathedral Basilica** *(p192)*, the **Palacio de Gobierno** *(p192)* with its powerful Orozco mural, and the **Instituto Cultural Cabañas** *(p192)*, Latin America's largest colonial building. Either grab lunch in Guadalajara, or head straight for **Tequila** *(p191)* for a distillery tour and to learn how Mexico's quintessential spirit is made. Several distilleries have restaurants: a full stomach is advisable before too much tequila tasting.

Day 6: Pátzcuaro
Much of the morning will be taken up getting to **Pátzcuaro** *(pp210–11)*. Though the **Basílica de Nuestra Señora de la Salud** *(p211)* is impressive, spend the afternoon soaking up the atmosphere around the Plaza Vasco de Quiroga and the adjacent Plaza Gertrudis Bocanegra. If you've timed your visit to coincide with the Day of the Dead, head out to **Isla Janitzio** *(p211)*, the main island in Lake Pátzcuaro, where a colorful night-time vigil takes place.

Day 7: Morelia
The local Tarascan people add color to Pátzcuaro, though you'll get a better sense of their way of life by driving around **Lake Pátzcuaro** *(p210)*. Continue to **Morelia** *(pp212–13)*, which has more colonial splendor, although in winter you should opt instead for the **Santuario El Rosario** *(p215)* to see millions of monarch butterflies.

For practical information on traveling around Mexico, see pp356–65

One Week in Northern Mexico

- **Arriving** Cross the US border from San Diego, or fly into Tijuana airport, 6 km (4 miles) east of downtown. From Chihuahua you can fly direct to Mexico City. Alternatively, connect with the Central Mexico itinerary by taking the bus to Zacatecas (12hr).
- **Transport** Drive or take public transport. Be aware though that buses in Baja are infrequent.
- **Booking** The Isla Espíritu Santo tours, the La Paz–Topolobampo ferry, and El Chepe railway should all be booked in advance.

The legendary train "El Chepe" crosses a viaduct in Cáñon del Cobre

Day 1: Guerrero Negro
If you're crossing the US border, start early to get through **Tijuana** *(p166)* and onto the **Transpeninsular Highway** *(p167)* – a long journey but the desert scenery makes it worthwhile. Drivers should break the journey where they can, though it might be a bit early in the day for sampling the wine of the *bodegas* at **Ensenada** *(p166)*. Stop at least briefly at **Rocky Desert** *(p167)*. Spend the night at the Baja's whale-watching capital, **Guerrero Negro** *(p168)*.

Day 2: Whale-watching and San Ignacio
If you hit the season, a few morning hours on the water spotting blue or California gray whales is essential – they're a magnificent sight. Refuel in Guerrero Negro before pushing on a couple of hours to the beautiful oasis and mission town of **San Ignacio** *(p169)*. It has a completely different feel from the rest of the peninsula, helped by the imposing mission church. Organize a permit for tomorrow's visit to the local cave paintings.

Day 3: Cave paintings and Loreto
The cool of the morning is best for visiting the cave paintings at **Cueva del Ratón** *(p169)*, and the spectacular desert landscape on the way makes it particularly worthwhile. You'll need your own transport. Continue south with brief stops (if you're driving) in **Santa Rosalía** *(p172)* with its Eiffel-designed Iglesia de Santa Bárbara, and pretty **Mulegé** *(p172)* with its excellent beaches. Stay in **Loreto** *(p172)* and relax on the beaches at Baja.

Day 4: Loreto to La Paz
Loreto's **Misión Nuestra Señora de Loreto** *(p172)* and the **Museo de las Misiones** *(p172)* shouldn't divert you long from a morning spent fishing, diving, or just lying on the beach. After a leisurely lunch, press on to **La Paz** *(p173)* in time for an early evening stroll along the *malecón*.

Day 5: Isla Espíritu Santo tour
Set aside a full day to visit **Isla Espíritu Santo** *(p173)*. Tour companies in La Paz offer something for everyone from snorkeling and swimming with sea lions to kayaking and dive trips on which manta rays and whale sharks may be seen.

Striking rock formations and fine snorkeling at Isla Espíritu Santo

Day 6: Ferry across Gulf of California to Los Mochis
Visit the **Museo Regional de Antropología e Historia** *(p173)* or spend time outside at one of La Paz's wonderful beaches. Grab an early lunch and leave plenty of time to catch the afternoon ferry (Mon–Fri only, *see pp360–61*) across the Gulf of California (also called the Sea of Cortés). On a calm day it can be a lovely crossing, though you won't get into Topolobampo until 9pm. You'll then need to catch a bus 24 km (15 miles) to Los Mochis, find a place to spend the night, and make sure you can get to the station in time for the 6am train.

Day 7: El Chepe railway to Chihuahua
Whether you call it Ferrocarril Chihuahua al Pacífico, **El Chepe** *(p180–81)*, or the Copper Canyon Railroad, this is one of the real highlights in northern Mexico. It takes a full day (6am–9pm) to wind up from Los Mochis, along the edge of the **Cañón del Cobre** *(pp180–81)* to **Chihuahua** *(p176)* – the ride is truly magnificent.

To extend your trip...
Spend several highly rewarding days exploring the **Cañón del Cobre** *(pp180–81)*. The best base is the former silver-mining town of **Batopilas** *(p179)*.

Putting Mexico on the Map

Geographically, Mexico is considered to be part of North, rather than Central, America. It covers an area of almost 2 million square kilometers (760,000 square miles) and has a population of around 121 million. Administratively, the country is divided into 31 states and a Federal District, in which stands the vast, sprawling capital, Mexico City.

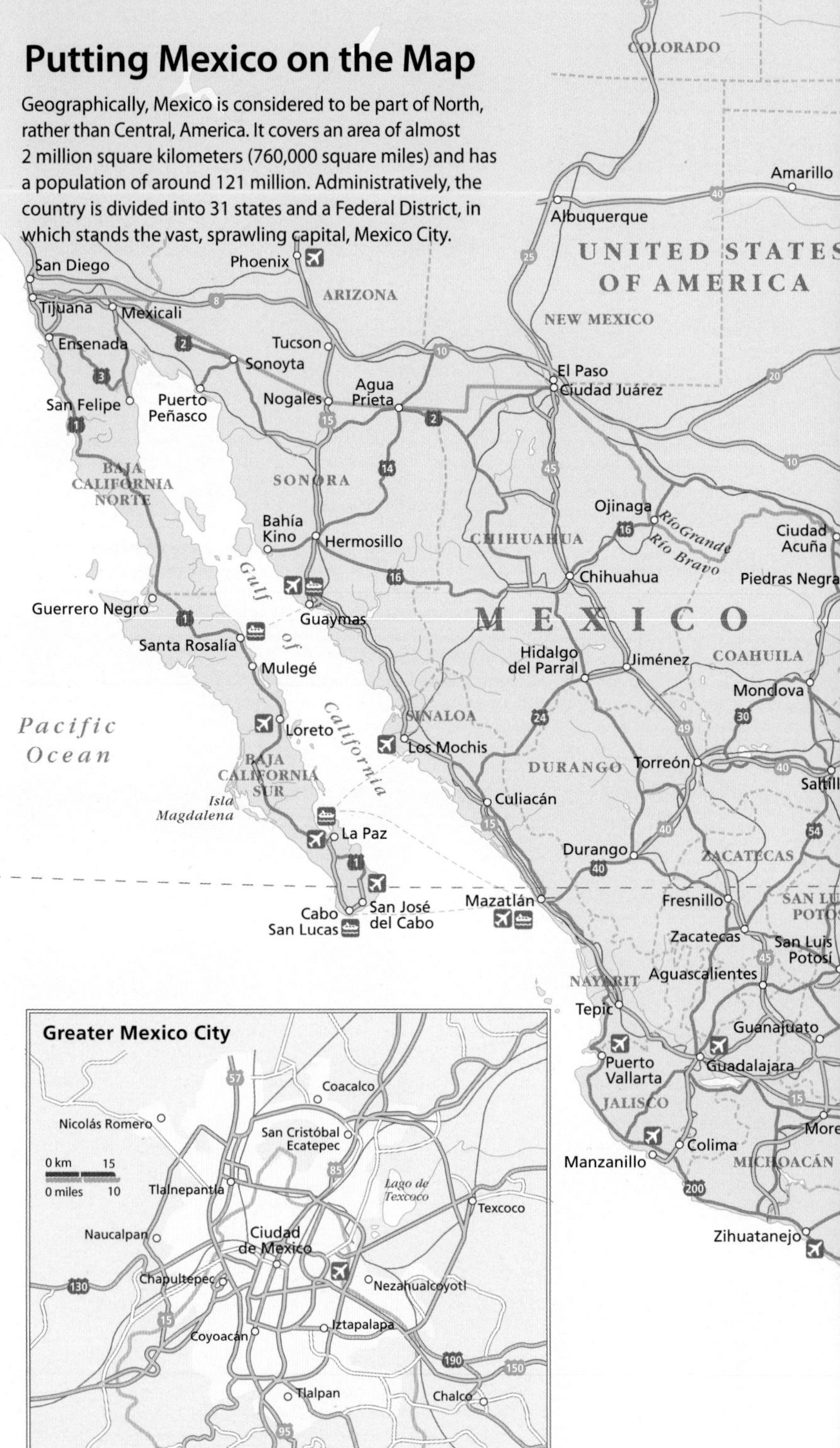

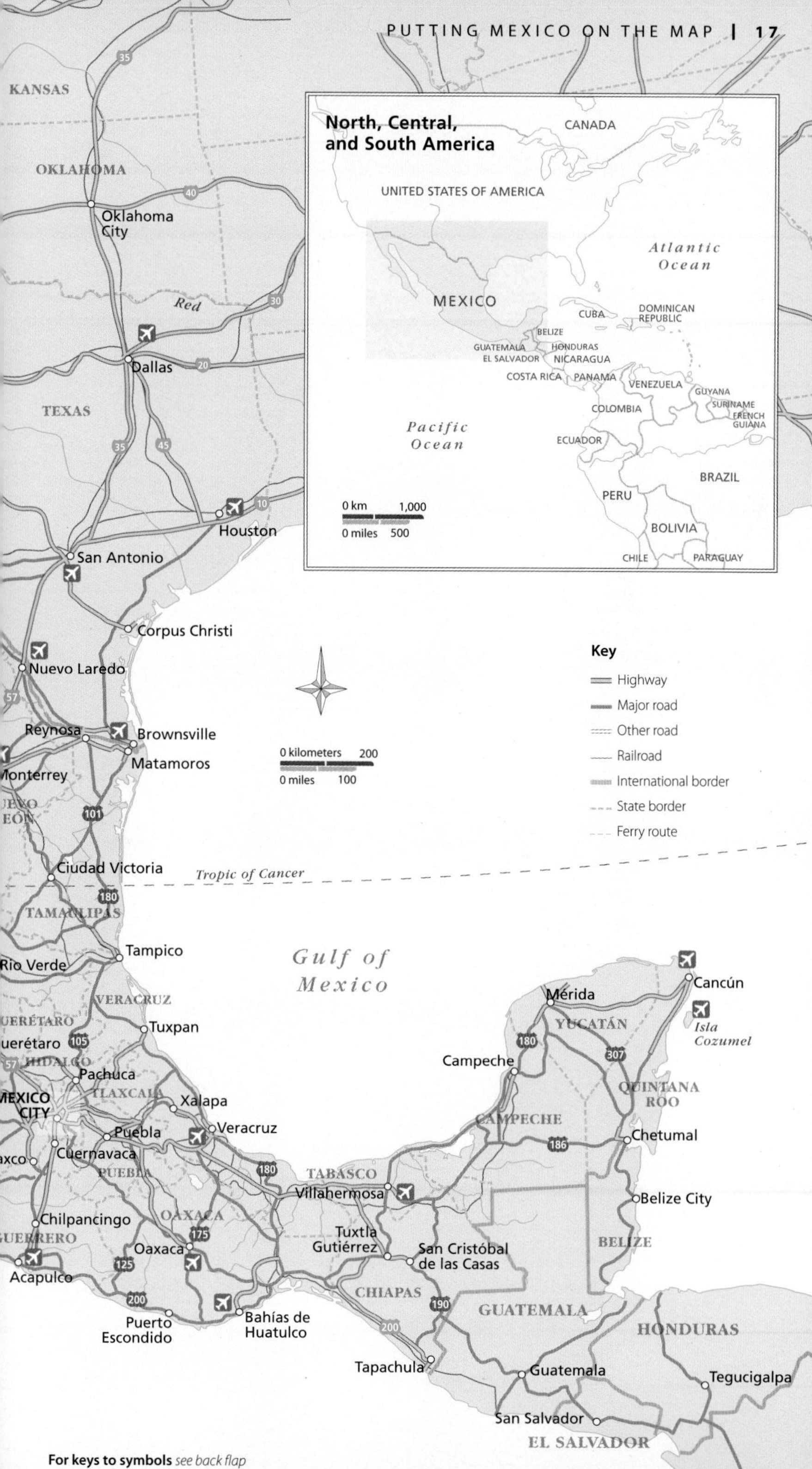

For keys to symbols *see back flap*

A PORTRAIT OF MEXICO

At once orderly and chaotic, Mexico assaults the senses with the sights and sounds, tastes, and smells of a unique mix of cultures and landscapes. Nowhere else in the Americas are ancient history and magic rituals so inextricably entwined with the routines of modern daily life.

Mexico's arid north abuts the US along a 3,140-km (1,950-mile) border, which has come to symbolize their complex, conflicted, and unbalanced relationship. To the south, Mexican territory ends amid tropical forest on the banks of the Usumacinta River, the border with Guatemala. North and south Mexico are starkly different. The northern states are wealthier, whiter, more urban, and industrialized. Although there are indigenous communities in the north, the southern states are home to the vast majority of the country's Indians, most of whom remain peasant farmers. Between these extremes there are many Mexicos to be seen. Modern agribusiness exists alongside pre-Columbian farming techniques. Rural Indian groups maintain their ancestral rites, while many urban Mexicans are swayed by Western consumerism.

For many travelers, Mexico seems both a known quantity and a mysterious place. The coastal communities and resorts, some of which were developed specifically for tourism by the government and public-private partnerships, are familiar to most tourists, while the vast, wildly diverse interior is less so. Those who make the effort to explore Mexico's heartland will find towns alive with rich cultural traditions and regions with unique identities that have made important contributions to Mexican history, cuisine, music, and way of life.

Mexico is a populous country. Of a total population of around 121 million, one fifth is crammed into the Valley of Mexico, around 2,100 m (7,000 ft) above sea level. The country is dominated by Mexico City. This vast, sprawling capital is one of the biggest cities in the world and its growth shows no sign of slowing down.

Palapa sunshades at Tukan Beach Club in the Yucatecan resort town of Playa del Carmen

◀ Tribal dancer at the Independence Day Parade

Decorative tiles in the city of Puebla

The Mexican Way of Life

The traditional Mexican view of the world can be thought of in terms of concentric circles. First comes the family, at the center of which is the venerated matriarch. Mother's Day is one of the most important dates in the Mexican calendar, and it is no coincidence that some of the harshest slang words and insults in Mexican Spanish incorporate variations on the word *madre*. Yet with the family under assault, as elsewhere in the world, from the forces of modernity, today this social fabric is being subjected to unprecedented strain. Loyalties outside the family are traditionally confined to an immediate circle of friends, who may be *compadres* or *comadres* (godparents to one's children), or simply *cuates* ("pals").

Wider society, as well as authority figures, tend to be regarded with suspicion, and although confrontations are usually avoided, compliance is often no more than lip service. Mexicans have a tendency (particularly in the south) to say "yes" even when they mean "no," and to regard rules as an unwarranted constraint. Yet Mexican society is far from homogeneous. Despite centuries of interbreeding between European settlers and native Mexican "Indians," 20 percent of Mexicans still consider themselves to be purely indigenous. The common culture of Mexico, as can be seen in the national cuisine, fiestas, and the arts and crafts, blends contributions from all quarters. Even so, in some regions pre-Columbian traditions, untouched by European influences, still survive.

Cycling, an inexpensive way of getting around town

Stalls in the market of San Cristóbal de las Casas

The Convento de la Santa Cruz in Querétaro

Religion

Almost eight out of ten Mexicans regard themselves as Catholic, The Church is said to be one of the three "untouchable" institutions (the others are the army and the presidency). Mexican Catholicism has incorporated many elements of pre-Christian religion. The most venerated figure, especially among the poor, is the Virgin of Guadalupe, the country's patron saint. The dark-skinned Virgin appeared, according to legend, in 1531 on a site once dedicated to the pagan mother-goddess Tonantzin. Shrines to the Virgin are to be found all over Mexico, even in remote places.

The state has had an uncomfortable relationship with the Catholic Church, as a result of the latter's support first for the Spanish colonial authorities and later for the Emperor Maximilian. Until the Salinas reforms of the 1990s, priests were forbidden to appear in public in their vestments and Mexico had no diplomatic relations with the Vatican. Paradoxically, the two great heroes of Mexican independence, Hidalgo and Morelos, were both priests.

In opposition to the Catholics, the influence of evangelical protestants is growing rapidly in Mexico. The evangelicals tend to be highly enthusiastic and regular practitioners of their religion.

The Arts and Sports

Mexico has a rich artistic tradition in the fields of painting, architecture, literature, and film.

Many of the murals of Diego Rivera, José Clemente Orozco, and David Alfaro Siqueiros, and the canvases of Frida Kahlo and Rufino Tamayo, are acknowledged masterpieces. Octavio Paz (1914–1998), the great contemporary interpreter of *mexicanidad* ("Mexican-ness") won a Nobel Prize for literature, and the novelist Carlos Fuentes (1928–2012) is world renowned.

Traditional mask

Mexican film had a heyday in the 1940s–50s, and the industry has since produced international hits regularly, such as *Like Water for Chocolate* (1992),

Festival in honor of the Virgin of Guadalupe, December 12

Charrería, a popular spectator sport, particularly in the north and in Guadalajara

Amores Perros (2000), *Y Tu Mamá También* (2001), and *Pan's Labyrinth* (2006). Almost more interesting than formal works of art are the expressions of folk art for which Mexico can be justifiably proud. *Mariachi* music has gained adherents as far away as Belgium and Japan. Mexican crafts, meanwhile, are testament to a limitless creativity.

Mexicans are sports mad. The most popular sports – soccer, boxing, bullfighting, and baseball – have been imported from other countries. Wrestling, *lucha libre*, is also an import but with a distinctive Mexican stamp in the form of masks worn by the combatants. A uniquely Mexican sport is *charrería*, which is somewhat akin to rodeo. It centers on competitions to test skills of horsemanship but has a whole culture of bright costume and festivity surrounding it.

Mariachis performing in Zacatecas

Masked wrestlers in *lucha libre*

Politics and Economics

Since the upheaval of the Revolution between 1910 and 1920, Mexico has been one of the most politically stable countries in Latin America. When the Soviet Union collapsed in 1991, the Institutional Revolutionary Party (PRI) inherited the title of the world's oldest political regime. Peruvian novelist Mario Vargas Llosa once described Mexico's system as "the perfect dictatorship" for its ability to change presidents – and even modify its ideology – every six years, while still retaining an iron grip on power.

The government of Carlos Salinas de Gortari (1988–94) swept away much of the economic control the PRI had formerly championed. His successor, Ernesto Zedillo (1994–2000), pursued the neo-liberal recipe with equal enthusiasm. The cost, however, was a widening gap between rich and poor.

In 1994 the Zapatista National Liberation Army (EZLN) burst onto the scene with the seizure of six towns in the state of Chiapas. The uprising coincided with Mexico's entry into the North American Free Trade Agreement (NAFTA) with the US and Canada, a treaty the guerrillas – almost all of them Maya peasants – saw as inimical to their interests. NAFTA was a bold attempt to overcome almost two centuries of suspicion between Mexico and its northern neighbor. But while the two economies are increasingly interlinked, the relationship remains delicate. The increasingly active opposition broke through in 2000, pushing the PRI from the presidency after 71 years in power. Changes were expected with the National Action Party (PAN), under Vicente Fox (2000–6) and then Felipe Calderón (2006–12), but political competition had done little to eradicate the endemic corruption that flourished during the PRI's bureaucratic monopoly. This had been boosted by the 1970s oil boom and the subsequent growth of crime syndicates who were able to buy political and police protection.

Mexico City's futuristic stock exchange building

Enrique Peña Nieto brought the PRI back to power when he was elected president in 2012, despite being widely disliked and even ridiculed. Regardless, he inherited all of the social, economic, and political challenges that preceded him, and he has had some success, including ambitious plans for economic and educational reform and the capture of several key figureheads from gangs that run the country's drug cartels. Despite the grand schemes, his tenure has been marred by a series of financial and human rights controversies.

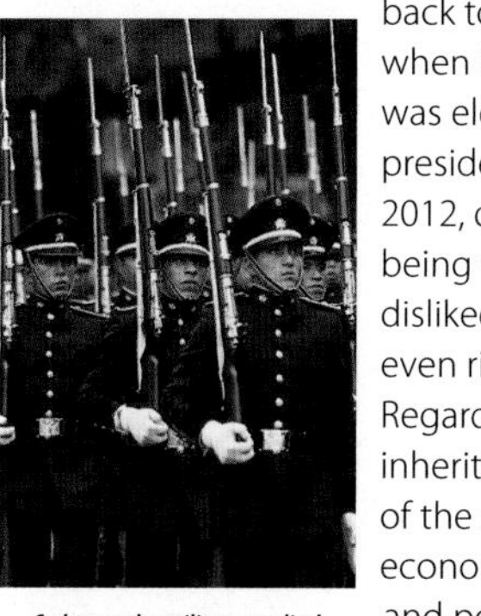

Cadets at the military medical school on parade

The thousands of undocumented migrants who annually cross the border in search of a better life – and the drug traffickers who exploit the same routes – remain major sources of friction, although emigration is now falling.

Mexico's rapid transformation from an agricultural to an industrial economy failed to resolve the employment problems of its growing population: over a million jobs per year are needed to keep pace with the new entrants to the job market, while the shortfall is provided by the precarious "informal" economy.

Partly as a legacy of the struggle for independence and the Revolution, and partly due to living next to a super- power, Mexicans are hugely patriotic. Their nationalism reaches its height each September 15, when Father Hidalgo's call or cry ("*El Grito*") for Mexican independence is repeated everywhere, from the Palacio Nacional in Mexico City to humble town halls. For visitors, witnessing this celebration and other expressions of Mexican patriotism is one of the most memorable experiences of a visit to this culturally rich country.

A political rally in the capital

The Landscape and Wildlife of Mexico

Despite serious threats to its environment, Mexico remains one of the three richest nations on earth in terms of the variety of its flora and fauna. With more than 30,000 plant species, over 500 different mammals, and over 1,000 types of bird – many of which are unique to Mexico – it is a naturalist's paradise. The reason for this natural wealth is the range of habitats, from snow-capped volcanoes to mangroves, deserts, and tropical forests, not to mention part of the Meso-American Reef, the second-longest barrier reef in the world.

The volcano Pico de Orizaba, Mexico's highest mountain

Deserts and Scrublands

Over half of Mexico's land is classified as arid, and another 30 percent as "semi-arid." The only true desert – where the annual rainfall is less than 25 cm (10 inches) – is the Desierto de Altar in northwest Sonora. The dry scrublands that cover much of northern Mexico, particularly Chihuahua, Sonora, and Baja California, conceal a surprising abundance of wildlife.

The desert tortoise is threatened with extinction due to the trade in wild animals. The Mapimi Biosphere Reserve *(see p177)* has been working to help the population rebound.

Cacti *(see p175)* have adapted to the harsh conditions of life in the deserts.

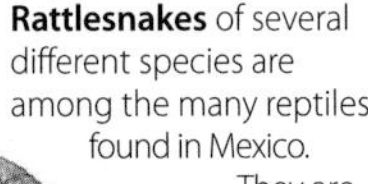
Rattlesnakes of several different species are among the many reptiles found in Mexico. They are typical of arid zones.

Wetlands

These habitats, which range from ponds to mangrove swamps and coastal lagoons, are fast disappearing through land reclamation, pollution, and urbanization. They are home to wading birds such as herons or egrets. The saline lagoons of the Yucatán Peninsula support colonies of flamingos *(see p276)*.

The leopard frog and its innumerable relatives fill the air of the wetlands with their chorus of croaking.

The sora, a member of the rail family, is a winter visitor found in reed beds across the country.

Mangroves grow along tropical coastlines in brackish water. They provide a habitat for wading birds and other fauna.

Coasts

Mexico's coastline totals over 10,000 km (6,250 miles) in length. On the Pacific, promontories and islets are common, while on the Atlantic side the coastline is sandy. A magnificent coral reef lies off the coast of Quintana Roo. Isolated beaches provide nesting grounds for species of sea turtle.

The sea fan is one of many fascinating species found on the coral reef *(see p287)*.

Whales, including the world's biggest, the blue whale, are seen off Baja California *(see p168)*.

Mountains and Canyons

Mexico is a land of mountains: more than half the country is over 1,000 m (3,200 ft) above sea level. Mountainsides are typically clad in pine or pine-oak forest. There are also arid mountains in the North, including the haunt of the endangered Mexican bighorn sheep, and areas of cloud forest and montane rainforest in the south.

Bighorn sheep, sacred to some pre-Columbian people, roam the remote, arid northwest mountains.

The bobcat is a medium-sized feline, sometimes glimpsed amid the thornscrub of northern Mexico.

Yellow-eyed junco is one of the most familiar birds of the Mexican mountains.

Tropical Forests

Rainforest is the earth's richest habitat in terms of the number of species it supports. Mexico's rainforest is on the Atlantic slope south of the isthmus of Tehuantepec, with isolated remnants in northern Oaxaca and southern Veracruz. These areas' rich wildlife includes jaguars, parrots, and the extraordinary quetzal, a bird sacred to the Maya *(see pp50–51)*.

The jaguar is Mexico's biggest cat, but it has suffered from the loss of its jungle habitat in the south and west.

The keel-billed toucan is unmistakable because of its huge, multicolored bill.

Armadillos defend themselves from predators by rolling into a ball.

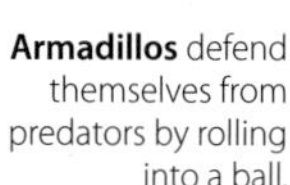

The Indigenous Peoples of Mexico

Mexico's indigenous inhabitants are probably more numerous today than at the time of the Spanish Conquest. However, the precise definition of "indigenous" is debatable. Official statistics show that more than one in ten of the population of 121 million belongs to one of the 62 Indian language groups. Some, like the Tarahumara, Huichol, and Lacandón *(see p236)*, retain much of their pre-Columbian way of life. Most, however, have abandoned traditional dress (at least in public) and ways of life, and are often indistinguishable from mixed-race Mexicans.

The Yaqui of Sonora perform their evocative Danza del Venado (Deer Dance) during Easter Week and on the Day of the Dead.

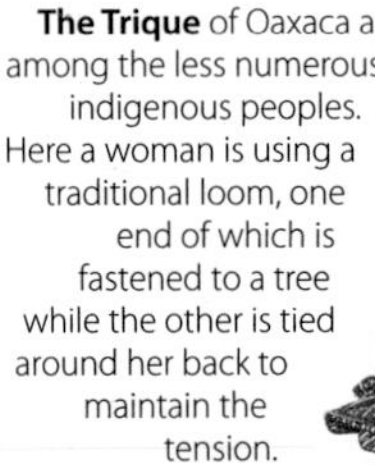

The Trique of Oaxaca are among the less numerous indigenous peoples. Here a woman is using a traditional loom, one end of which is fastened to a tree while the other is tied around her back to maintain the tension.

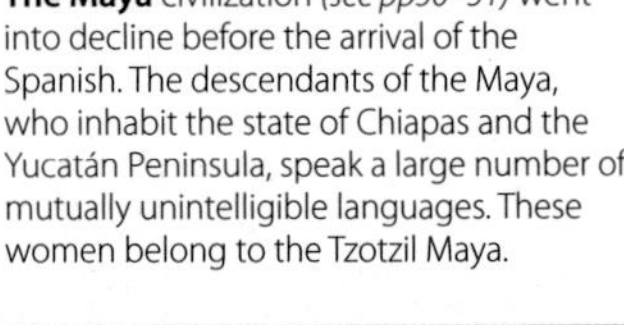

The Maya civilization *(see pp50–51)* went into decline before the arrival of the Spanish. The descendants of the Maya, who inhabit the state of Chiapas and the Yucatán Peninsula, speak a large number of mutually unintelligible languages. These women belong to the Tzotzil Maya.

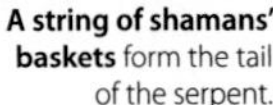

A string of shamans' baskets form the tail of the serpent.

Eight ancestors inhabit the second level of creation. They have no legs and cannot speak.

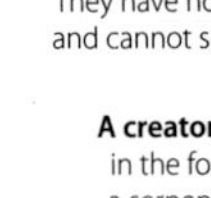

A creator god in the form of a serpent is at the heart of creation.

The mockingbird carries people's memories from the past to the present.

The Tarahumara *(see p178)*, who live in the area around Copper Canyon in Chihuahua state, play a tough endurance game called *rarajipari*, in which two opposing teams kick wooden balls around an improvised mountain course. The game can last for several days.

The Huichol *(see p188)* are known in Mexico for their dazzlingly colored handicrafts, especially beadwork. They cling precariously to the lands of their ancestors on the border of Jalisco and Nayarit states.

Where Mexico's Indigenous People Live

The indigenous population is concentrated mainly in the south, although some large groups – the Yaqui, Mayo, and Tarahumara – are in the north. The states of Oaxaca and Chiapas have the largest proportion of indigenous inhabitants. The five most widely spoken indigenous languages are Nahuatl (the language of the Aztecs), peninsular Maya, Zapotec, Mixtec, and Otomí.

The third or outer level of creation is the realm of plants, animals, and all other natural phenomena.

An open flower symbolizes life rising from the earth.

The sun is shown with a snake beneath it, which symbolizes its path across the sky.

An earth mother has a seed of corn in her chest and ears of corn to either side.

The shaman is a cross between a priest and a healer, with a vast knowledge of medicinal plants. There is no easy dividing line between magic, ritual, and traditional medicine in indigenous culture. However, all are rapidly being supplanted by "western" science and medicine.

Huichol Yarn Painting

Mexico's indigenous people make an extraordinary variety of crafts *(see pp332–3)*, usually in bright colors and based on striking, symbolic designs. This painting depicts the Huichol view of creation as divided into three phases or levels, each inhabited by different beings.

Catholicism in Mexico is for many a mixture of Christianity, brought by the Spanish, and lingering beliefs from ancient Mexico. The indigenous inhabitants of Mexico adapted their religion to that of their rulers without abandoning belief in their ancient gods.

Corn (maize) was unknown to Europeans before the conquest of the Americas. Along with beans, it is still the essential crop grown by Mexican peasants, although the agricultural way of life is increasingly threatened by the globalization of the world economy.

The tortilla *(see p308)*, a corn flour flat bread, is the staple food of both indigenous and mixed-race Mexicans. Here an Indian woman prepares tortillas the way it has been done for generations.

Architecture in Mexico

Most colonial houses in Mexico were highly functional, with an interior courtyard for privacy and wrought-iron grilles to protect the windows. The Baroque age introduced flamboyance, while local materials, such as Puebla tiles, led to the growth of regional styles. Neo-Classicism, fashionable after 1785, favored austerity, but French influence in the 1800s brought a return to ornamentation. In the 20th century, Modernism was embraced with enthusiasm.

Facade tiles on the Casa del Alfeñique, Puebla *(see p154)*

Early Colonial (1521–c.1620)

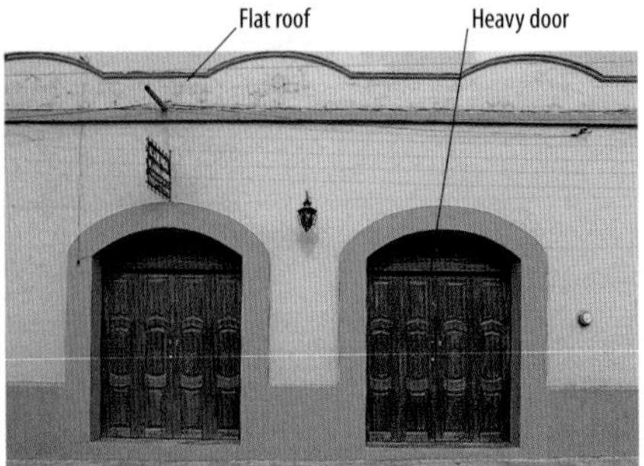

These houses in San Cristóbal de las Casas *(see p235)* have courtyards, flat roofs, and simple doorways.

Casa de Montejo (1543–9) in Mérida *(see p274)* has a Plateresque facade showing two conquistadors in full armor.

The Plaza Mayor

Mexican town-dwellers take pride in their *plaza mayor* (main square). Under Spanish rule, urban planning was strictly controlled, and towns were modeled on the capital. Straight streets led to a large plaza with civic and religious buildings, plus *portales* (arcades) for the merchants. Urban renewal in the late 1800s equipped the squares with statues, bandstands, and cast-iron lamps and benches.

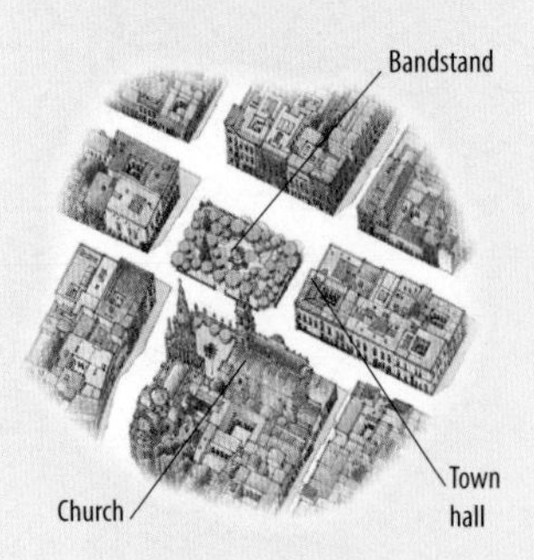

Baroque (c.1630–c.1800)

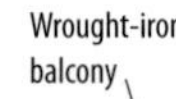

Palacio de Iturbide in Mexico City *(see p83)* was designed in about 1780 by Francisco Guerrero y Torres. The sumptuous former residence has an exuberant facade.

Casa de los Muñecos (House of the Figures; late 18th century), in Puebla *(see p154)*, has a façade adorned with locally made *azulejos* (blue glazed tiles).

Neo-Classical (1785–c.1880)

Stone statues portray eight of the nine Muses.

Upper balustrade

The portico has two rows of fluted columns.

Teatro Juárez in Guanajuato *(see p207)* was commissioned in 1873 and built by Antonio Rivas Mercado. It combines Neo-Classicism with lavish French styles of decoration.

Porfirian (1876–1911)

This late 19th-century stained-glass window showing a coat of arms is from the Museo Bello in Puebla *(see p156)*.

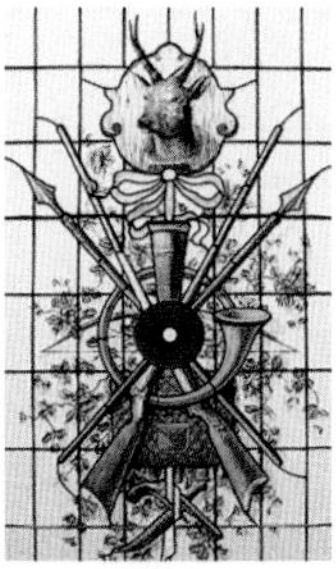

French-influenced ornamental stonework

Islamic-style window

This eclectic mansion in Guadalajara was completed in 1908. The era *(see p57)* freely combined Rococo, Neo-Classical, Neo-Baroque, and other styles.

Rural Architecture

Many Indian populations use local materials to build houses in styles particular to their region. Depending on geography and climate, houses may be square, rectangular, apsidal, or round. In regions with heavy rainfall, roofs are steep and often thatched with palm or grass, while overhanging eaves protect walls of poles or wattle-and-daub. Where trees are plentiful, wooden houses are common. In areas with low rainfall, builders use stone, bricks, or adobe (mud bricks).

Nahua house in Hidalgo, with log walls and a roof of *zacate* (grass)

Thatched Maya house of rubble masonry and plaster, in the Yucatán

Modern (c.1920–Present)

The outline emulates New York skyscrapers on a smaller scale.

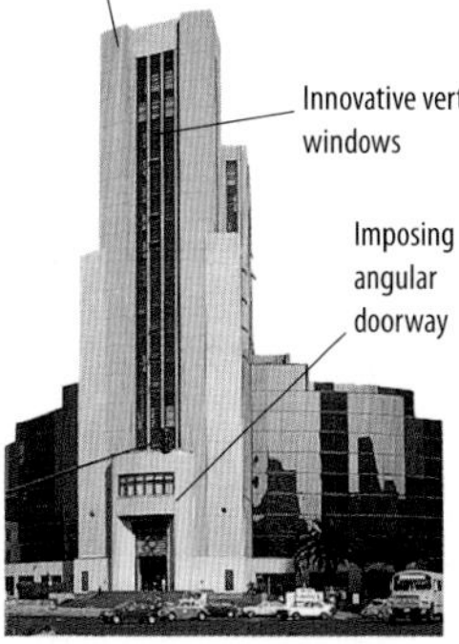

Innovative vertical windows

Imposing angular doorway

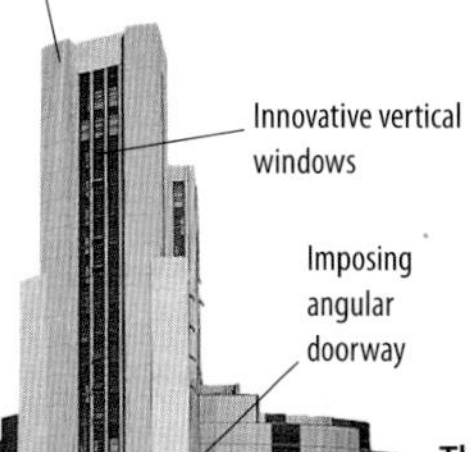

The Loteria Nacional *(see p89)* was built around 1936 by José A. Cuevas. Formality and symmetry give it an Art Deco appearance.

Museo Jumex is a strikingly modern building in Mexico City. Opened in 2012, its distinctive design houses a large private collection of Latin American art.

Saw-tooth roof

The imposing facade was made from locally sourced travertine.

Church Architecture

After the conquest, new towns were dominated by churches and cathedrals. Throughout the 16th century, missionary friars acted as architects, using Renaissance, Plateresque, and Mudéjar styles. Native carvers added details, and the result was *tequitqui*, a blend of Indian and European elements. The Baroque style of the 1600s became even more ornamented after 1750, with the Ultra-Baroque, or Churrigueresque.

Domes of Mitla church *(see pp230–31)*

Early Monasteries

As Spanish friars took their conversion work into remote territories, they established a network of missions. Each colonial monastery, with its church, was virtually self-sufficient, incorporating living quarters for the friars, a school, hospital, library, wells, and orchards. Crenellated stone walls and other defensive characteristics gave many missions a fortress-like appearance.

The Plateresque portal of San Agustín Acolman *(see p142)*, finished in 1560, contrasts with the monastery's overall severity. Beside the door are two pairs of garlanded columns on angel pedestals, with a saint set between each pair.

The mission church at Mulegé in Baja California *(see p172)* was built by the Jesuits in the 18th century. The simple, functional design is characteristic of remote missions.

Atrium

Izamal's Convento de San Antonio de Padua *(see p277)* was built on the site of a Maya religious center by the Franciscans between 1553 and 1561. The colonnade enclosing the large atrium was added in about 1618, the wall belfry in the 1800s.

The facade has detailed, exuberant carving. This scene shows the Baptism of Christ, surrounded by cherubs, spirals, and foliage. It is flanked by statues of St. Sebastian and St. Prisca.

Richly decorated *retablos* (altar-pieces) line the nave, adding to the cumulative splendor. This *retablo*, dedicated to St. Joseph, is adorned with cherubs, ears of corn, shells, and fruit.

The dome is covered with glazed tiles, probably from Puebla, and inset with eight rectangular windows. The dome's frieze reads: "Gloria a Dios en las alturas" ("Glory to God in the Highest"). External ribs lead to a tile-domed lantern, surmounted by a cross.

The sacristy is reached by a door beside the high altar.

Finials

The main retablo, conceived in high Churrigueresque style by Isidoro Vicente de Balbás, depicts the glory of the Christian Church. Heavily gilded, the carved wood conveys richness and splendor. *Estípite* (inverted) pilasters *(see p147)* replace the Classical columns of earlier times.

South entrance

Baptistery

Iglesia De Santa Prisca, Taxco

Begun in 1751, and finished in just seven years, the parish church of Taxco (see pp150–51) exemplifies the Churrigueresque style of Mexican architecture. The style is characterized by dazzling surface ornament that conveys flowing movement and obscures the form beneath. The huge costs of this church were borne by wealthy silver magnate José de la Borda.

Popular Baroque

San Francisco Acatepec *(see p153)*

Rural churches of the Baroque period often display enormous exuberance and charm. These eclectic, imaginative creations are aptly classified as *barroco popular*. In Puebla, the popular passion for ornamentation found expression in the glistening tiles that cover church facades with vivid patterning. Interiors exhibit a profusion of plaster figures, such as clusters of angels, cherubs, saints, animals, flowers, and fruit. These were accentuated with brilliant gold leaf and color.

Music and Dance

Across Mexico, celebrations are accompanied by music that owes its variety to a fusion of musical traditions. Pre-Conquest musicians played wind and percussion instruments. Today the reed-flute, conch shell, and *huehuetl* drum evoke the sounds of ancient Mexico. The Spanish introduced stringed instruments. Over time, Mexican music evolved into the *sones* (strains) of Jalisco, Veracruz, and other states. Mexico has also absorbed influences from the rest of Europe, and Africa, Cuba, and the US.

Man with accordion

Mariachi musician in traditional costume

Mariachis

Mariachi music originated in the state of Jalisco during the 19th century, when *mariachi* musicians (from the French word *mariage*) played music for weddings and balls. Suitors still often engage *mariachi* bands to serenade their girlfriends at home and in public places, such as parks.

A *mariachi* band can consist of between three and 15 musicians.

The guitar was introduced to Mexico by the Spanish.

The violin leads the *mariachi* melody.

Trumpets are a modern addition to *mariachi* music.

***Mariachi* bands** can be seen in the Plaza Garibaldi *(see p113)* in Mexico City, playing songs about love, betrayal, and revolutionary heroes.

Traditional Dances

Mexico has a vast range of regional dances performed only in their specific areas. During religious celebrations, they take place in squares and in front of churches. Dancers, who are usually male, communicate the storyline through dance steps, sign language, and sometimes words. Some dances hark back to pre-Columbian times and ancient rituals; others were introduced by Spanish friars and show European influence.

Tlaxcala Carnival dancers wear elaborate garments embroidered with sequins, and carved wooden masks with pale skin tones. Carnival is a time for revelry when dancers parody their ancient oppressors.

Quetzal dancers in Cuetzalan wear headdresses of reeds and colored paper, tipped with feathers. The steps of this Nahua dance relate to the passage of the sun.

Voladores

During this ancient Nahua and Totonac ritual, five men climb to the top of a pole often reaching as high as 30 m (100 ft). While one plays a drum and a reed-pipe on a tiny platform at the top, the other four "fly" to the ground, suspended on ropes.

Each *volador* circles the pole 13 times before reaching the ground, making a total of 52 turns. This symbolizes the 52-year cycles of the Mesoamerican calendar *(see p51)*. The central pole represents a vertical connection between the Earth, the heavens above, and the underworld below.

Totonac voladores wear velvet panels decorated with sequins and beads.

Headdresses are adorned with mirrors and plastic flowers.

Voladores perform regularly at El Tajín *(see pp246–7)*, outside the National Anthropology Museum in Mexico City *(see pp94–9)*, and in Puerto Vallarta *(see p189)*.

Tiger dancers perform during festivals in the state of Guerrero. These ancient dances reflect the preoccupations of farming communities and once featured jaguars or ocelots.

A *concher*o dancer performs for the Virgin of Guadalupe in Mexico City. Traditional instruments are used by *concheros*. Dance steps are also accompanied by the rattle of seed pods worn on the ankles.

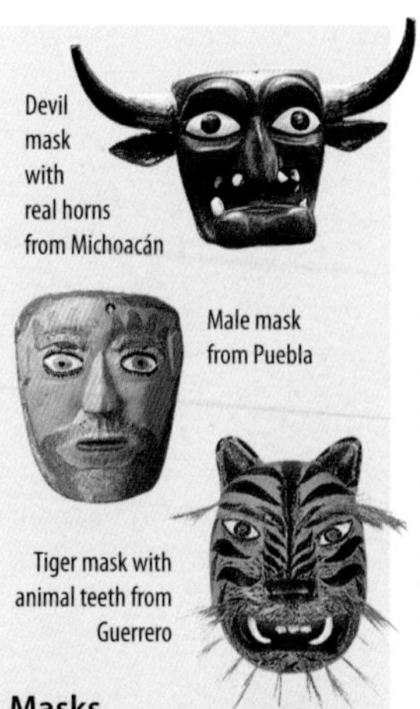

Devil mask with real horns from Michoacán

Male mask from Puebla

Tiger mask with animal teeth from Guerrero

Masks

Masks were worn for a range of dances in ancient Mexico and Spain. Today, Mexican masks represent men and women, supernatural beings, and birds and animals, and can be realistic or stylized. Wood is the most common material, but some mask-makers rely on leather, clay, paper, cloth, gourds, and even wax. Dancers look through slits above or below the painted eyes.

Dancehalls in the capital and Mexico's other major cities attract devotees of *danzón*, merengue, mambo, *cumbia*, salsa, rock, and other musical styles. Events in *Salón México* (1995), a remake of a classic movie, took place at the once famous dancehall of the same name in Mexico City, now closed to the public.

MEXICO THROUGH THE YEAR

In the words of Mexican poet Octavio Paz, "Fiestas are our only luxury." Indeed, every day is a saint's day or other cause for celebration somewhere in Mexico, with fireworks exploding, a band playing, and the population dancing. Some traditional fiestas derive from indigenous celebrations, while others were brought by the Christian Spanish conquistadors. Many now blend the two influences.

Most events are localized, but a few occasions are celebrated throughout the country – particularly Independence Day, the Day of the Dead, and the day honoring the Virgin of Guadalupe *(see p113)*. Each of these three holidays puts Mexicans' patriotism and faith on full display, and visitors are always welcome to celebrate alongside the locals.

If you're trying to decide when to visit based on the weather, consider the autumn; the weather is glorious, but not too hot for visiting archaeological sites. Winter is better for wildlife spotting. Keep in mind though that Mexico is a large country, with a variety of climates. Be sure to review average temperature and precipitation trends for the areas you're planning to visit *(see pp40–41)*.

Indigenous and Christian traditions mixed in an Easter procession

Spring

The temperate weather conditions of spring, just before the start of the rainy season, make this a perfect time to visit the coast. However, Easter Week is one of the busiest times, and transportation gets booked up in advance. At this time of year jacaranda and flame trees blossom in a riot of color in town squares all over the country. In late spring the weather is hot, and fruits such as mangos, mameys, pineapples, and papayas fill the markets. Migratory birds, particularly birds of prey, can be seen on the Gulf Coast as they fly along it when making their way north to their summer habitats.

Easter Week *(Semana Santa; Mar/Apr)* is celebrated all over Mexico but is particularly beautiful in the southern states and in the Colonial Heartland. Passion plays are performed in most regions, notably in Taxco (Guerrero), Pátzcuaro (Michoacán), San Cristóbal de las Casas (Chiapas), Ixtapalapa in greater Mexico City, and throughout Oaxaca state.

On Palm Sunday there are processions, and palm crosses are sold outside churches. Good Friday sees parades of women swinging incense holders and carrying flowers in front of images of Christ and the Virgin Mary. They are accompanied by solemn singing, torchbearers, and hooded penitents. On this day the steps of Christ along the route to his crucifixion are re-enacted. Participants include self-flagellating sinners, robed children, and Roman soldiers. Realistic re-enactments of the whipping and crucifixion of Christ may also be staged. In the evening and on Easter Saturday cardboard "Judases" are burned and fireworks let off. On the Saturday, it is also customary in some towns to throw water at passers-by.

The Tarahumara Indians *(see p26)* have evolved their own version of the Easter story featuring an annual running battle between wicked "pharisees" and "soldiers" guarding the Virgin.

Natalicio de Benito Juárez *(Mar 21)*. Wreaths are laid at monuments to the reforming president on his birthday, notably in Guelatao, near Oaxaca, where he was born.

A Cinco de Mayo parade, which celebrates the Battle of Puebla

One of the *voladores* taking part in a Corpus Christi display

Regata del Sol al Sol *(late Apr)*, Isla Mujeres (Quintana Roo). Fireworks, a basketball match, and parties mark the end of a boat race from St. Petersburg, Florida to the island.

Feria de San Marcos *(Apr/May)*, Aguascalientes. Cultural, sporting, and other events combine at this important fair *(see p189)*.

Labor Day *(Día del Trabajo; May 1)*. Marches organized by trade unions and political parties culminate with speeches in town squares.

Cinco de Mayo *(May 5)*. The commemoration of the Battle of Puebla, a Mexican victory over the invading French army in 1862, is celebrated with particular enthusiasm in Puebla state *(see p157)*.

Mother's Day *(Día de la Madre; May 10)*. Every *madre* in Mexico is honored on this day and, finances permitting, taken out to lunch, regaled with flowers, or serenaded by *mariachis (see p32)*.

St. Isidore's Day *(May 15)*. Seeds, agricultural implements, ox yokes, and animals are blessed before planting begins in rural Mexico.

Corpus Christi *(May/Jun)*. Church services and parades take place all over Mexico. In Papantla (Veracruz), there is a special performance by the *voladores*, or "flyers" *(see p33)*, whose ritual invokes fertility, communicating with the heavens, and honoring the sun.

Summer

With the arrival of the rains, summer is usually considered the off season in Mexico. However, the rain tends to fall in the afternoon, and the mornings are bright and clear. The high precipitation ensures the countryside is verdant, making this a good time to tour inland. The air in Mexico City is also at its cleanest. Markets everywhere are bursting with fruit and vegetables; and only in these months can visitors taste fresh *cuitlacoche* corn fungus *(see p311)*, Mexico's answer to truffles.

Navy Day *(Día de la Marina; Jun 1)*. Port towns organize events to honor the navy. Official festivities take place in Guaymas (Sonora) and include uniformed processions, regattas, and fleet parades.

Lienzo Charro *(Jun)*, Mexico City. There are displays of horsemanship *(charrería, see p78)* by riders in costumes and huge sombreros on most Sundays at the Lienzo Charro in the third section of Chapultepec Park *(see pp92–3)*. The main event is in June, when a national *charro* exhibition is held.

Horseman competing in the Lienzo Charro

Guelaguetza *(late Jul)*, Oaxaca. Regional indigenous dances are performed in full regalia at the main fiesta of Oaxaca state *(see p229)*.

Feast of the Assumption *(Dia de la Asunción; Aug 15)*. Church services and processions take place everywhere. In many towns, the streets are decorated with carpets of flowers, over which the procession of the statue of the Virgin passes. The most lively celebrations take place in Huamantla (Tlaxcala), where the Fiesta de la Virgen de la Caridad *(see p143)* lasts for nearly two weeks and ends with bulls being let loose in the streets of the town.

International Mariachi and Charrería Festival *(Encuentro Internacional del Mariachi y la Charrería; late Aug, early Sep)*, Guadalajara. Festival of *mariachi* music and horsemanship in the birthplace of *charrería*.

Public Holidays

Año Nuevo (New Year's Day; Jan 1)

Día de la Constitución (Constitution Day; Feb 5)

Natalicio de Benito Juárez (Birthday of Benito Juárez; Mar 21)

Jueves Santo (Easter Thursday)

Viernes Santo (Good Friday)

Día del Trabajo (Labor Day; May 1)

Cinco de Mayo (May 5)

Día de la Independencia (Independence Day; Sep 16)

Día de la Raza (Day of the Race; Oct 12)

Día de la Revolución (Revolution Day; Nov 20)

Día de la Virgen de Guadalupe (Festival of the Virgin of Guadalupe; Dec 12)

Noche Buena (Christmas Eve)

Navidad (Christmas Day)

Costumed dancer at the Guelaguetza

Costumed horsemen in an Independence Day celebration

Autumn

As the rainy season ends, the countryside is still green, the weather is warm, and days are long. Rivers are full, so the white-water rafting season begins in Veracruz and San Luis Potosí. Autumn is a good time to travel inland, especially with the added attraction of cultural events during the Festival Internacional Cervantino. The luxuriant vegetation of the Gulf Coast and Chiapas can also best be appreciated at this time of year, without heavy rains. In early and late autumn respectively, Mexico celebrates its two principal fiestas, Independence Day and the Days of the Dead.

Presidential Address *(Sep 1).* During the afternoon on this day people watch the president's speech on television or listen to it on the radio.

El Grito/Independence Day *(Día de la Independencia; Sep 15–16).* Father Miguel Hidalgo's "cry" to arms *(grito)* to free Mexico of Spanish rule in 1810 *(see p53)* is commemorated all over Mexico, particularly in Hidalgo del Parral *(see p177)*, Morelia *(see pp212–15)*, and Guanajuato *(see pp206–9).* Fiestas take place in every town square on the evening of September 15, including fireworks, music, and the throwing of eggshells filled with confetti. Later, local officials repeat Hidalgo's shout, while in Mexico City the president himself makes the cry from the balcony of the Palacio Nacional *(see p71).* The next day is an occasion for parades. Children, in particular, dress in national costume or as Independence heroes. The holiday's signature dish is the elaborate *chiles en nogada*, green chilies stuffed with ground meat and walnuts.

Festival Internacional Cervantino *(Oct)*, Guanajuato. Music, dance, and theater groups from all over the world gather in Guanajuato *(see pp206–9)* for the highlight of Mexico's cultural calendar. The festival is dedicated to the Spanish writer Miguel Cervantes, creator of *Don Quixote*. It began in the 1950s with Cervantes-inspired one-act plays staged by students here. Colonial buildings blend into stage settings for performances, which may feature period costumes and even horses.

A packed crowd witnesses a bullfight at Plaza México in Mexico City *(see p114)*

Día de la Raza *(Oct 12).* Originally the celebration of the discovery of the Americas, this day is now more of a homage to the peoples of ancient Mexico.

Black and Blue Marlin Tournament *(last week of Oct)*, Cabo San Lucas, Baja California Sur *(see p173).* A large cash prize for the biggest catch is on offer at this major international event.

Days of the Dead *(Días de los Muertos; Oct 31–Nov 2).* Mexico's most colorful fiesta *(see pp38–9).*

Baja 1000 *(1st week of Nov)*, Baja California, from Ensenada to La Paz or vice-versa depending on the year. Hundreds of motorcycles, beach buggies, and pickups from around the world take up the challenge of this grueling off-road race.

Bull-fighting season *(Nov–Mar).* The grandest bullrings include those in Mexico City, Aguascalientes, San Luis Potosí, and Zacatecas.

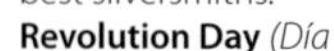

Days of the Dead decoration

International Silver Fair *(Feria Nacional de la Plata; Nov/ Dec)*, Taxco *(see pp150–51).* Stunning displays of silverwork can be admired at this fair, and prizes are awarded to the best silversmiths.

Revolution Day *(Día de la Revolución; Nov 20).* Small boys have black moustaches painted on them and wear red kerchiefs and boots. The girls are decked out as *lupitas* (female revolutionaries) in frilly skirts and loop earrings. There are also parades by sportsmen and women.

Día de Santa Cecilia *(Nov 22).* The patron saint of musicians is feted with much gusto. There are celebrations in the Plaza Garibaldi in Mexico City, Querétaro, and Pátzcuaro (Michoacán).

Puerto Escondido International Surf Tournament *(last week of Nov)*, Puerto Escondido, Oaxaca *(see pp220–21).* Surfers from all over Mexico and the US congregate in the sun to compete on Oaxaca's waves.

Winter

In all areas, temperatures drop at night in December, but, with the exception of Northern Mexico, the weather is still good enough for beach vacations. Over Christmas and the New Year, Mexicans and foreigners alike flock to the coastal resorts. In Mexico City, December brings the extravagant celebrations for Mexico's patron saint, the Virgin of Guadalupe. This is also the season when the first whales *(see p168)* reach Baja California and migratory monarch butterflies *(see p215)* arrive in Michoacán. In the markets, citrus fruit is in plentiful supply.

Día de la Virgen de Guadalupe *(Dec 12)*. The appearance of Mexico's patron saint in 1531 on the Cerro del Tepeyac hill is remembered in every town and village. Thousands of pilgrims flock to her shrine in Mexico City *(see p113)* to view her from a crowded moving walkway. In the rest of the country *las mañanitas* (an early-morning birthday song) is sung at dawn, and special church services are attended. Boys dress up as Juan Diego, the Indian who encountered the Virgin's apparition.

Posadas *(Dec 16–24)*. These parties re-enact the nativity story of Mary and Joseph seeking lodging, and take place over the course of nine nights in all parts of Mexico. The participants carry candles and lanterns and sing the *posadas* song. Each night culminates in a party at a different house. An essential part of any *posada* is the *piñata*, a papier-mâché figure filled with mandarin oranges, sugar cane, and candy and decorated with crepe paper, sometimes in the shape of comic heroes or animals. This is suspended overhead on a rope, and blindfolded children take turns swinging at it with a stick. In the end they crack it open and unleash a shower of candy and fruit.

The Night of the Radishes *(Noche de los Rábanos; Dec 23)*, Oaxaca. Radishes carved into fantastic shapes, including nativity figures, are put on display and offered for sale amid general festivities in the *zócalo (see p226)*, in the heart of the city.

A piñata, filled with sweets and fruit

Day of the Holy Innocents *(Día de los Inocentes; Dec 28)*. A day for practical jokes.

Epiphany *(Día de los Santos Reyes; Jan 6)*. Mexican children receive presents from the Three Kings in the morning and eat the traditional *rosca de reyes*, a ring-shaped cake filled with dried fruits and containing a hidden image of the baby Jesus.

A colorful carnival parade in the Yucatán Peninsula

An Indian in a headdress for the Día de la Virgen de Guadalupe

Most cities have processions to celebrate the arrival of the Kings. There are spectacular ones on Avenida Juárez and Xochimilco in Mexico City, in Querétaro, and in Campeche, Mérida, and Tizimín in the Yucatán Peninsula.

Candlemas *(Día de la Candelaria; Feb 2)*. Baby Jesus is lifted out of the nativity scenes across Mexico on this day. Streets are decorated with paper lanterns; in some villages there are bull runs and bullfights. Most towns have an outdoor fiesta in the main square with music, sideshows, fireworks, and dancing.

Zona Maco *(early Feb)*, Mexico City. Mexico's premier contemporary art fair that features excellent Mexican and Latin American art.

Flag Day *(Día de la Bandera; Feb 24)*. School children parade and pay homage to the flag. There are official ceremonies in the main squares of most towns of Mexico.

Carnival *(Feb/Mar)*. The days preceding the rigors of Lent are celebrated nationally with extravagant parades, floats, confetti, dancing, and the burning of effigies. The most spectacular partying takes place in port towns such as La Paz and Ensenada in Baja California, Acapulco, Mazatlán (Sinaloa), Campeche in the Yucatán, and, most famously, in Veracruz on the Gulf Coast.

The Days of the Dead

According to popular belief, the dead have divine permission to visit friends and relatives on Earth once a year. During the Days of the Dead, the living welcome the souls of the departed with offerings of flowers, specially prepared foods, candles, and incense. This is not a morbid occasion, but one of peace and happiness. Celebrations vary from region to region but in general the souls of children are thought to visit on November 1, in the evening, and those of adults on November 2, before departing for another year.

Skull masks and clothing painted with bones are sometimes worn by city children during the Days of the Dead. Carnival dancers may also take the role of Death, a familiar presence during Mexican festivals.

Sugar figures, bread, and other foodstuffs are temptingly displayed. The dead are believed to take the essence or the aroma of the offerings, which are themselves later consumed by the living.

A photo of the dead person is a common focal point for the Days of the Dead altars.

Candle sticks and incense burners

Altars for the Dead

Many families keep holy pictures and images of saints on a shelf or table. For All Saints' and All Souls' Days (November 1 and 2) these home altars carry offerings for the dead. In towns and cities, offerings may also be displayed in public places. Shown here is an altar in the Museo Anahuacalli (see p115)*, evoking the life and work of muralist Diego Rivera.*

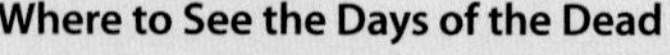

The marigold *(cempasúchil)*, often referred to in Mexico as "the flower of the dead," is used in profusion. Here Diego's name is spelled out among scattered marigold petals.

Where to See the Days of the Dead

Celebrations occur virtually everywhere in central and southern Mexico. Before the festival, market stalls sell an abundance of sugar figures, pottery, flowers, and skeleton toys. In Toluca *(see p148)* trestle tables are piled high with sweets. Most Mexicans visit cemeteries during the morning of November 2, but Purépecha villagers living around Lake Pátzcuaro hold a vigil on the night of November 1 *(see p211)*. In Tzintzuntzán *(see p210)*, masked villagers perform dances.

Isla Janitzio, an island in Lake Pátzcuaro, where the celebrations are particularly colorful

Personalized altars are set up in homes and adorned with the dead person's favorite foods and drinks, and other objects, such as children's toys.

Hand-made paper cuts, with the delicacy of lace, decorate many altars.

Papier-mâché skeletons are often displayed in public places. Like Posada's skeletons, they perform everyday activities.

Portrait of José Guadalupe Posada, from a mural by Diego Rivera *(see p85)*.

Fine textiles and articles of new clothing are sometimes set out on altars.

Calla lilies, which feature in many of Rivera's paintings, are included here among the offerings.

This child's grave in San Pablito, Puebla, with brightly colored flowers among the images painted on it, is typical of the highly personal style of decoration often used. Before the Days of the Dead, cemeteries throughout Mexico are tidied and graves repainted.

Arts and Crafts for the Days of the Dead

Death is portrayed with humor and even affection by craftspeople and artists. Skulls and skeletons are fashioned from sugar, tin, wood, paper, clay, and bone. Skeletons shown as bishops and shoe-cleaners participate side by side in the modern equivalent of the medieval dance of death. In the words of poet and essayist Octavio Paz, "The Mexican is familiar with death, jokes about it, caresses it, sleeps with it, celebrates it…." Many objects are made especially for the Days of the Dead; others are sold year round in galleries and craft shops.

This papier-mâché and wire skull, sporting skeletons and angels, was created by Saulo Moreno. The green growths of the apple tree stress the idea of regeneration.

Sugar skulls may be inscribed with the name of a person living or dead or, as here, with a fitting sentiment: "Amor Eterno" ("Everlasting Love").

Humorous miniature scenes, peopled with spectral figures, are made for the occasion. In this example skeleton gamblers of painted clay are depicted playing poker in a wooden, mirror-lined room.

La Catrina, by the engraver José Guadalupe Posada *(see p84)*, is widely associated with the Days of the Dead, and her image often appears in works by craftspeople.

The Climate of Mexico

Coastal influences and sharp variations in altitude both have an impact on Mexico's climate. The cold Californian current lowers temperatures and rainfall on the Pacific coast, and, along with the North Pacific anticyclone, contributes to the arid nature of northwestern Mexico. In sharp contrast, the Caribbean coast in the southeast, which faces warm waters, has a tropical climate. Inland, temperatures are much cooler in the central mountains.

CHIHUAHUA

month	Apr	Jul	Oct	Jan
Average daily maximum temperature °C (F)	28 (82)	32 (90)	28 (82)	18 (64)
Average daily minimum temperature °C (F)	11 (52)	18 (64)	11 (52)	3 (37)
Average daily hours of sunshine	9 hrs	8 hrs	8 hrs	6 hrs
Average monthly rainfall	2 mm	78 mm	19 mm	11 mm

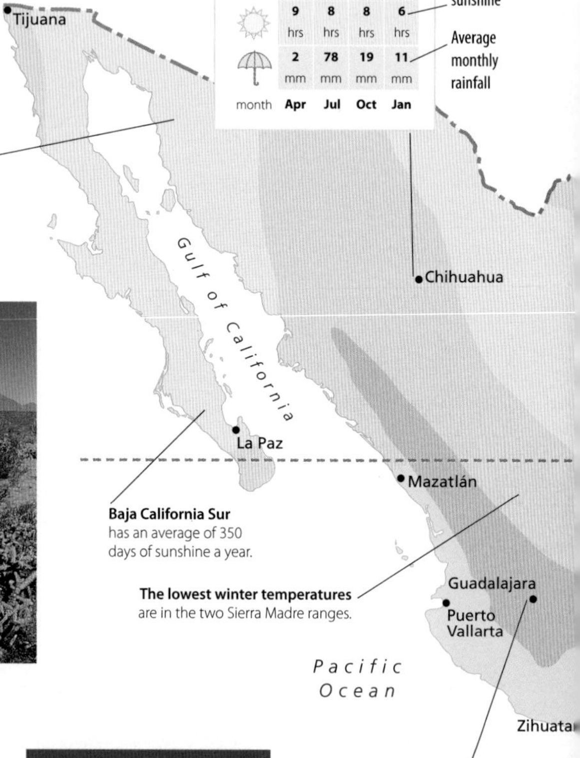

Tijuana

Gulf of California

Chihuahua

La Paz

Mazatlán

Guadalajara

Puerto Vallarta

Pacific Ocean

Zihuata

The highest temperatures in Mexico have been recorded in the Sonora Desert.

Baja California Sur has an average of 350 days of sunshine a year.

The lowest winter temperatures are in the two Sierra Madre ranges.

Stretch of desert landscape, typical of Baja California

GUADALAJARA

month	Apr	Jul	Oct	Jan
Average daily maximum temperature °C (F)	30 (86)	26 (79)	26 (79)	23 (73)
Average daily minimum temperature °C (F)	11 (52)	16 (61)	12 (54)	7 (45)
Average daily hours of sunshine	8 hrs	6 hrs	7 hrs	6 hrs
Average monthly rainfall	5 mm	263 mm	51 mm	16 mm

Climate Zones

- Desert regions: high temperatures and low rainfall
- Mountain and prairie areas with low rainfall; cold winters
- Temperate, savanna areas: warm with dry winters
- Warm weather all year round. Pronounced rainy season
- Warm, humid temperate regions often with hot summers
- Very hot and humid. Typical vegetation is tropical rainforest

Lago Arareco near Creel in winter *(see p178)*

MEXICO CITY

month	Apr	Jul	Oct	Jan
°C (F) max	27 (81)	23 (73)	22 (72)	21 (70)
°C (F) min	9 (48)	11 (52)	9 (48)	5 (41)
sunshine	8 hrs	6 hrs	6 hrs	7 hrs
rainfall	23 mm	160 mm	46 mm	8 mm

Banana plantation in the hot, humid state of Veracruz

0 kilometers 500
0 miles 300

Tabasco *(see pp258–9)* is the wettest part of the country with an average of over 2,500 mm (98 inches) of rain annually.

Hurricanes can hit the Caribbean and Pacific coasts in September and October.

Monterrey
Tropic of Cancer
Guanajuato
Gulf of Mexico
Cancún
Mérida
Caribbean Sea
MEXICO CITY
Veracruz
Villahermosa
Oaxaca
Acapulco
Tuxtla Gutiérrez

MÉRIDA

month	Apr	Jul	Oct	Jan
°C (F) max	33 (91)	32 (90)	30 (86)	28 (82)
°C (F) min	22 (72)	23 (73)	22 (72)	19 (66)
sunshine	6 hrs	6 hrs	5 hrs	5 hrs
rainfall	21 mm	129 mm	94 mm	28 mm

ACAPULCO

month	Apr	Jul	Oct	Jan
°C (F) max	31 (88)	32 (90)	32 (90)	31 (88)
°C (F) min	23 (73)	25 (77)	25 (77)	22 (72)
sunshine	8 hrs	7 hrs	7 hrs	9 hrs
rainfall	1 mm	282 mm	157 mm	8 mm

VERACRUZ

month	Apr	Jul	Oct	Jan
°C (F) max	28 (82)	31 (88)	29 (84)	24 (75)
°C (F) min	23 (73)	24 (75)	23 (73)	18 (64)
sunshine	6 hrs	7 hrs	6 hrs	5 hrs
rainfall	15 mm	384 mm	173 mm	20 mm

HISTORY OF MEXICO

Modern Mexico is the product of a collision of two cultures that occurred when the Spanish conquistadors defeated the Aztecs in 1521. In the following centuries, the ancient civilizations of Mexico fused with the Catholic European culture of Spain. After gaining its independence in the 19th century, Mexico set about forging its own identity, a process that continues today.

Mesoamerica, a region of which ancient Mexico formed a large part, had a history stretching back three millennia by the time the Spanish arrived in the early 16th century. Although powerful imperial states – especially that of the Aztecs – had developed, they were no match for the superior arms of the Spanish conquistadors, who overran the country and imposed their rule and religion on the indigenous population.

For the next 300 years Mexico was a colony of Spain. Hungry for silver, the Spaniards pushed into the arid north, founding new cities. In central and southern Mexico they lorded it over a subjugated Indian population, who worked on Spanish estates, paid tribute to the Crown, and worshiped the Christian God – albeit without completely abandoning old religious beliefs and practices. During the 18th century, however, Spain's grip on its colony weakened as it confronted rival imperial powers in the Americas and disgruntled colonial subjects in Mexico itself.

The Napoleonic Wars in Europe triggered a struggle for independence in Mexico that was finally accomplished in 1821. In the mid-19th century, however, the US expanded its territory southward, squeezing Mexico into its present-day borders.

Not until the mid-20th century, following the Revolution launched in 1910, did the country at last achieve stability and sustained economic growth. Nevertheless, social problems, some of them deriving from the colonial past, remain serious.

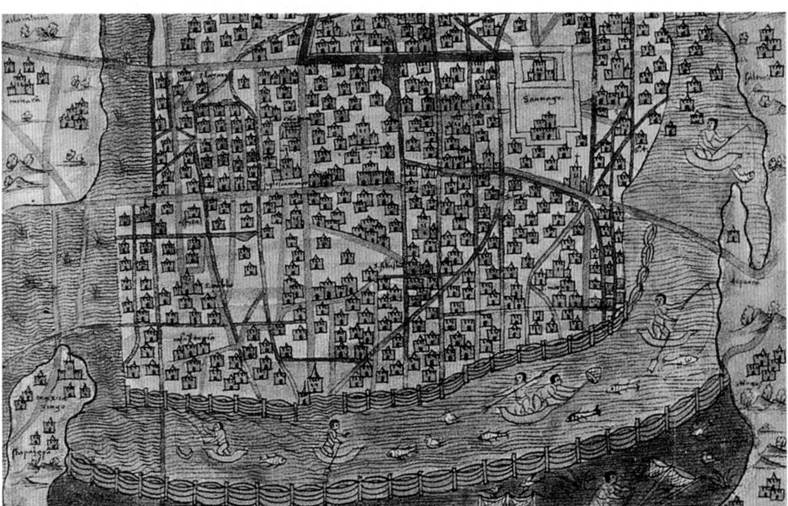

Map of the island city of Tenochtitlán (modern Mexico City), drawn by Alonso de Santa Cruz in 1560

◀ A well-preserved mural from Teotihuacán *(see p45)*

The Olmecs

Settlers arrived in Mexico having crossed the Bering landbridge from Asia to Alaska some 20 millennia ago. By the second millennium BC farming villages were springing up. Sometime around 1500 BC the first notable culture, that of the Olmecs, was established on the hot and humid Gulf coast, principally at San Lorenzo *(see p257)* and later at La Venta *(see p258)*. The Olmecs built ceremonial centers rather than cities, and their earthen pyramids suggest that they were governed by a central authority capable of mobilizing extensive manpower. They rafted heavy basalt blocks downriver and carved them into massive heads and other sculptures with stylized or feline ("were-jaguar") features. They also produced ceramics and exquisite jade figurines. During the first millennium BC, however, the Olmec centers declined. San Lorenzo was the scene of systematic destruction and desecration in around 900 BC – although by whom is uncertain – and Olmec civilization faded into obscurity.

Olmec stone figure

The Classic Maya

The Olmec "mother culture" inspired a series of successor cultures in the lowlands to the east and the highlands to the west. In the lowlands, dense Maya settlements, grouped around massive ceremonial centers, began to form in the Mexico-Guatemala border region by about 500 BC. Maya civilization reached its greatest flowering in the "Classic Period" of AD 200–900. Numerous cities developed in which elaborate temples were surrounded by elite residential quarters, and cultivated fields. The Classic Maya pursued a vigorous ritual life and practiced sophisticated art *(see p237)*. They also acquired remarkable mathematical and astronomical knowledge. This made it possible for them to do the elaborate calculations needed for the "Long Count" of their calendar, which spanned millennia *(see p51)*.

Once thought of as pacific, the Maya actually engaged in regular and ruthless intercity warfare. Glyphs *(see pp50–1)* on their

Carving in the palace of Palenque, one of the greatest cities of the Classic Maya

Colossal Olmec head carved in basalt

20,000 BC Migrants cross from Asia into the Americas and gradually spread south. The first known inhabitants of Mexico live in caves in the Valley of Mexico

20,000 BC

c.1500 BC First Olmec settlements established

1200 BC

c.900 BC Olmec city of San Lorenzo is destroyed and desecrated

800 BC

One of Los Danzantes carvings at Monte Albán

c.600 BC First settlement on the site of Monte Albán

400 BC

Wall painting in Tomb 105 at Monte Albán, the center of Zapotec civilization

stelae – carved stone obelisks – record the victories of great rulers, who warred, allied, intermarried, and patronized the arts in the same way as the princely families of Renaissance Italy. By around AD 800, however, the Classic Maya faced crisis: the population had outstripped available resources, and several centers were destroyed and abandoned.

The Rise and Fall of Teotihuacán

In the central highlands, meanwhile, other cities flourished. The population of the hilltop Monte Albán *(see pp224–5)*, for instance, climbed from 5,000 in 500 BC to around 25,000 in AD 700. When the city declined, Mitla *(see p230)* and other lesser towns sprang up to contest its power in the area around Oaxaca.

All these cities were over-shadowed, however, by the great Classic metropolis of Teotihuacán *(see pp138–41)*, built on an imposing site in an open valley to the north of what is now Mexico City. Teotihuacán rose to prominence around 200 BC and reached the height of its power in AD 400–500, when it dominated the valley and a wider hinterland beyond. Its influence stretched far to the south, into the Maya region. By this time it had become a vast city of some 125,000 inhabitants, making it one of the largest cities in the world.

During the 7th century disaster struck. Like the cities of the Classic Maya, Teotihuacán may have overstretched its resources.

Funerary mask from Teotihuacán

Poverty and discontent appear to have increased, and nomads from the arid north began to threaten the city. Around 650 the city was attacked and partially burned by these northern invaders, or local rebels, or both. It did not disappear suddenly but entered a long decline, as its population was leached away. The fall of Teotihuacán sent shock-waves throughout Mesoamerica.

Red coyote mural, Teotihuacán

c.200 BC Foundation of the city of Teotihuacán

AD 1

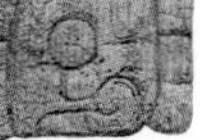

Maya glyph

c.400 Teotihuacán is at the height of its power

400

615–83 Reign of Pakal, king of Palenque

c.650 Fall of Teotihuacán

c.700 Population of Monte Albán reaches a high point of 25,000

799 Last recorded inscription at Palenque hints at the city's demise

800

c.800 Collapse of the Classic Maya civilization. Monte Albán abandoned at around the same time

The Toltecs

The collapse of Teotihuacán and decline of Monte Albán resulted in a phase of fragmentation and militarization in central Mexico. A series of successor states such as Cacaxtla *(see p160)*, and Xochicalco *(see p149)* carved out local fiefs. One, the Toltec state, built a loose hegemony between about 900 and 1100. Probably northern migrants, the Toltecs settled in the north of the Valley of Mexico. Here they built the city of Tula *(see p148)*, which may have had a population of 40,000. The Toltecs, who were keen traders dealing especially in obsidian, exacted tribute from dependent communities. They also developed a militarist culture, evident in the serried ranks of their Atlantes (stone warriors), gruesome friezes depicting war and sacrifice, skull racks, *chacmools* (reclining sacrificial statues), and military orders such as the Eagle and Jaguar Knights.

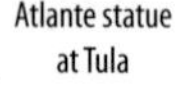

Atlante statue at Tula

Tula collapsed and was torched and desecrated around AD 1100, but its influence lived on. Some Toltecs are thought to have migrated to the Yucatán in the 10th century, where their influence is evident. Among them may have been a prince or leader called Quetzalcoatl (meaning the "Feathered Serpent"), who was later transformed into a god. Since the collapse of the Classic Maya cities, power had shifted to the northern part of the Yucatán Peninsula, especially Uxmal and the other cities of the Puuc hills. Around AD 1000 Toltec motifs – feathered serpents, Atlantes, and *chacmools* – began to appear, notably at Chichén Itzá. This city headed a regional confederacy until, in about 1200, it was overthrown by the nearby Mayapán, and Izamal, and by other rivals on the coasts of the Yucatán Peninsula.

The Aztec Empire

The last great Mesoamerican empire, that of the Aztecs (often called the Mexica), also arose in the Valley of Mexico, from where it went on to dominate much of the Mexican heartland. The Aztecs arrived as a poor, ill-equipped band, who had trekked overland from their distant northern homeland, Aztlán

The Aztec legend of the eagle perching on a prickly pear cactus, illustrated in the Codex Mendoza

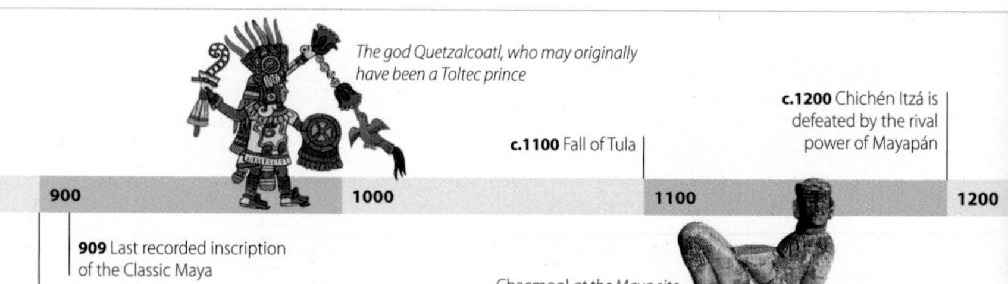

The god Quetzalcoatl, who may originally have been a Toltec prince

Chacmool *at the Maya site of Chichén Itzá*

(the location of which is unknown). They initially served as the menials and mercenaries of established cities. In around 1325, however, they were advised by their tribal god, Huitzilopochtli, to pitch their tents where they saw an eagle perched on a cactus, devouring a snake. This omen (depicted on Mexico's national flag) was seen on a lake-island, which thus became the site of the city of Tenochtitlán. Ruthless fighters with a sense of providential mission, the Aztecs gradually expanded their territory. At the same time they boosted agriculture by creating fertile *chinampas*, irrigated fields, to feed the urban population.

The Meeting of Cortés and Moctezuma, attributed to Juan Correa (c.1645–1716)

By the 1420s they had emerged as the dominant power in the Valley of Mexico. Their loose tribal organization gave way to an imperial system based on strict hierarchy, a warrior ethic, and a despotic emperor. Soon, their conquests spread to the rich lowlands of the south and east. Tribute poured in. At the same time, constant warfare provided prisoners, feeding the demand for human sacrifice to appease their gods – for only by feeding palpitating hearts to the gods could the fragile cosmos be maintained. Mass sacrifices – like those that which took place to mark the dedication of the rebuilt Templo Mayor *(see pp72–4)* in 1487, when 20,000 prisoners were said to have been immolated – served to terrorize enemies and bolster the empire.

Arrival of the Spanish

When the first Spanish voyagers made contact with Mesoamerica in the 1500s, the Aztec Empire was huge, populous, and dynamic. But it faced population pressures, internal dissidence, and resistance from outlying states: the Tarascan empire in present-day Michoacán, and the tough highland principality of Tlaxcala *(see p160)*, to the east.

Hernán Cortés landed on the coast of what is now Veracruz in 1519 and marched to Tenochtitlán. But first he defeated, then joined forces with, the Tlaxcalans who proved invaluable allies in the Spaniards' destruction of Aztec power. By means of such alliances, Cortés was able to confront and finally defeat the Aztec empire of Moctezuma II (1502–20). After a bloody and destructive siege, Tenochtitlán was conquered.

The Conquest of Mexico as depicted in a mural by Juan O'Gorman (1905–82)

Carving of the Aztec goddess Coyolxauhqui in the Templo Mayor, in Mexico City

1300 | 1400 | 1500

c.1325 The Aztecs found Tenochtitlán (modern Mexico City) on a lake-island

1426–40 The Aztecs take control of the Valley of Mexico under Emperor Itzcoatl

1500s Aztec wars with Tlaxcala, to the east, which later becomes a Spanish ally

1502 Accession of Moctezuma II as Aztec emperor

1519 Cortés lands on the coast of Veracruz

1520 On July 1, the so-called Noche Triste ("Sad Night"), the Spanish are defeated by the Aztecs

1521 The Spanish capture Tenochtitlán and the Aztec Empire falls

Mesoamerica

The term Mesoamerica refers to a geographical region whose people shared a broadly similar culture before the arrival of the Spanish *(see p47)*. It covers what is now central and southern Mexico, Belize, Guatemala, and parts of Honduras and El Salvador. The people of Mesoamerica had many things in common, including gods, a calendar, and building practices, but had different languages and customs. The civilizations are normally divided into "highland" (especially the Valley of Mexico) and "lowland," such as the Maya.

Chacmool
These carved reclining figures can be seen at central Mexican and Maya archaeological sites. The stone dishes often found on their stomachs are said to have held sacrificial offerings, but there is no evidence for this.

Ballgame
The ballgame, played with a rubber ball *(see p281)*, was a feature of most civilizations of Mesoamerica. This stone disk shows a Maya player.

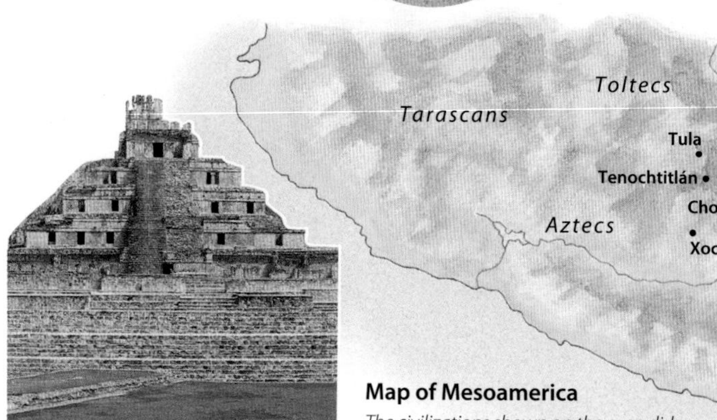

Pyramids
Mesoamerican pyramids are stepped and, like this one at Edzná *(see p265)*, crowned with a temple. The Aztecs used them for human sacrifices, while for the Maya they were usually funerary buildings. They were often built on top of earlier pyramids.

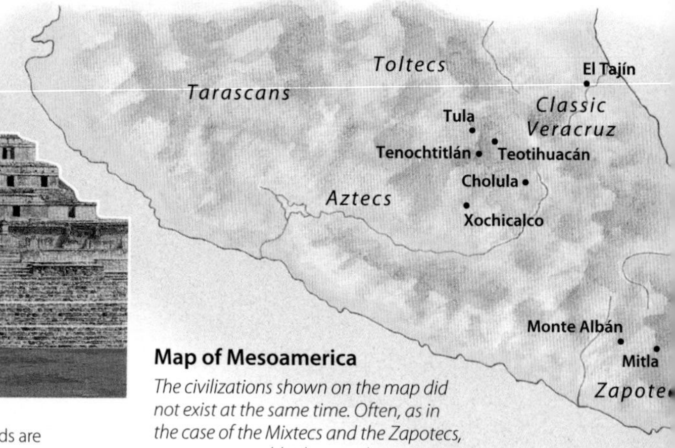

Map of Mesoamerica
The civilizations shown on the map did not exist at the same time. Often, as in the case of the Mixtecs and the Zapotecs, one group would take over the territories of its predecessors.

Human Sacrifice
The need to appease gods with human blood was a strong belief in ancient Mexico, particularly to the Aztecs. This codex illustration shows Aztec priests killing victims, whose bodies are then thrown down the steps of the temple.

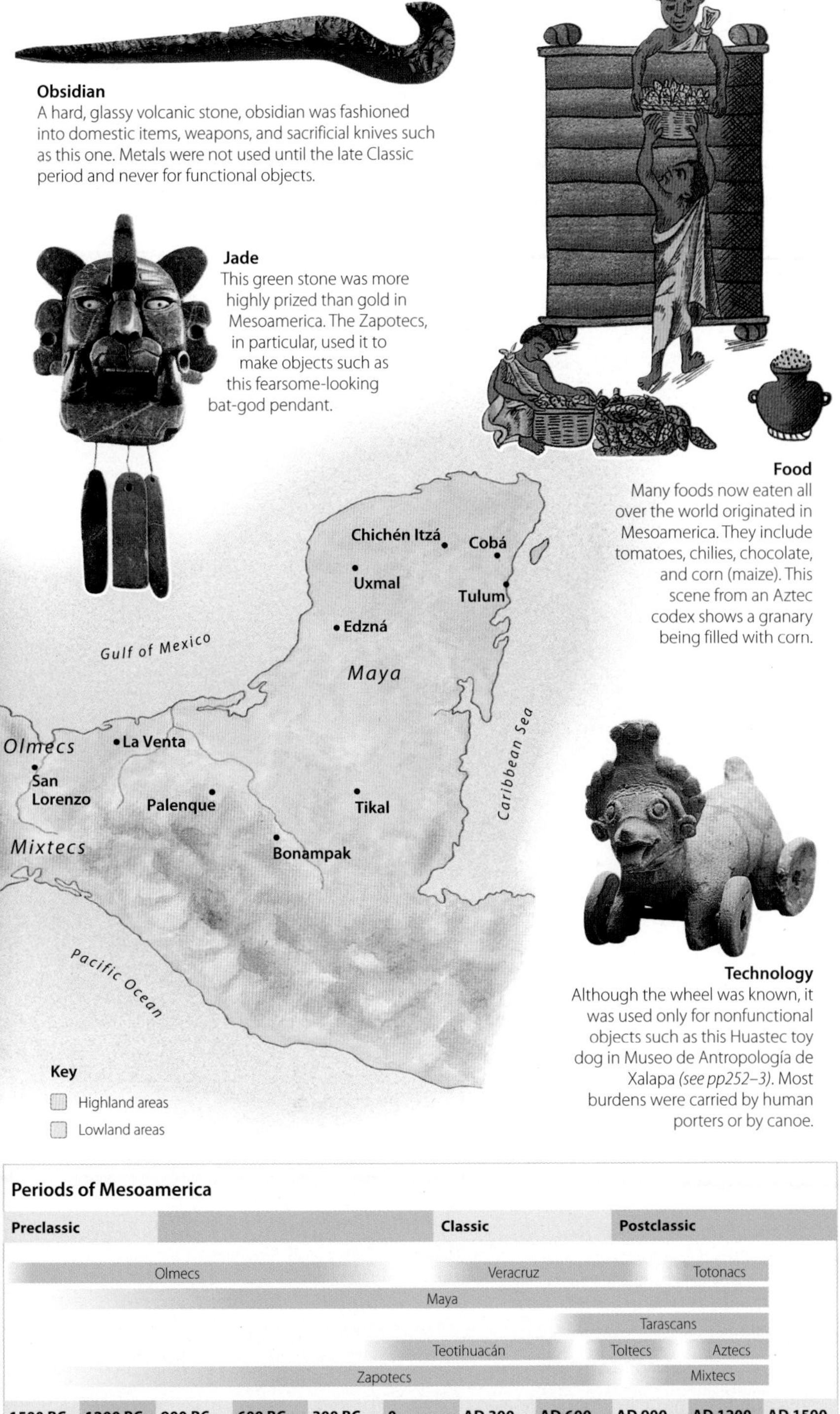

Obsidian
A hard, glassy volcanic stone, obsidian was fashioned into domestic items, weapons, and sacrificial knives such as this one. Metals were not used until the late Classic period and never for functional objects.

Jade
This green stone was more highly prized than gold in Mesoamerica. The Zapotecs, in particular, used it to make objects such as this fearsome-looking bat-god pendant.

Food
Many foods now eaten all over the world originated in Mesoamerica. They include tomatoes, chilies, chocolate, and corn (maize). This scene from an Aztec codex shows a granary being filled with corn.

Technology
Although the wheel was known, it was used only for nonfunctional objects such as this Huastec toy dog in Museo de Antropología de Xalapa *(see pp252–3)*. Most burdens were carried by human porters or by canoe.

Periods of Mesoamerica

Preclassic | **Classic** | **Postclassic**

Olmecs
Veracruz
Totonacs
Maya
Tarascans
Teotihuacán
Toltecs
Aztecs
Zapotecs
Mixtecs

1500 BC | **1200 BC** | **900 BC** | **600 BC** | **300 BC** | **0** | **AD 300** | **AD 600** | **AD 900** | **AD 1200** | **AD 1500**

The Maya

Unlike the other peoples of Mesoamerica, the Maya did not develop a large, centralized empire. Instead they lived in independent city-states. This did not impede them in acquiring advanced knowledge of astronomy and developing sophisticated systems of writing, counting, and recording the passing of time. The Maya were once thought to have been a peaceful people, but they are now known to have shared the lust for war and human sacrifice of other pre-Columbian civilizations.

Locator Map

Extent of Maya Territory

Mural from Bonampak
The Maya were the finest artists of Mesoamerica. Their talent for portraiture can be seen especially in the extraordinary series of murals painted in a temple at Bonampak *(see p236)*.

Architecture
Pyramids, palaces, and other great works of Maya architecture can be seen at such sites as Palenque *(see pp238–41)*, Chichén Itzá *(see pp278–80)*, Cobá *(see p288)*, and Tulum *(see pp288–9)*. This detail is from Uxmal *(see pp266–8)*.

In the Tzolkin or Sacred Round
20 day names were combined with 13 numbers to give a year of 260 individually named days.

Glyphs

Other Mesoamerican civilizations developed writing systems, but none was as complete or sophisticated as that of the Maya. They used about 800 different hieroglyphs (or simply "glyphs"), some representing whole words, others phonetic sounds. Some glyphs were understood as early as the 1820s, but the major advances in decipherment really began in the 1950s.

A Maya glyph can represent either a whole word, or the sounds of which it is composed. Some words were written in several ways. Above are two ways of writing the name Pakal, the ruler of Palenque. Pakal means "shield," depicted by the left glyph.

The Observatory at Chichén Itzá

Astronomy

The Maya had a knowledge of astronomy that was very advanced for their time. They observed and predicted the phases of the moon, equinoxes and solstices, and solar and lunar eclipses. They knew that the Morning and Evening Star were the same planet, Venus, and calculated its "year" to 584 days, within a fraction of the true figure (583.92 days). It is almost certain that they calculated the orbit of Mars as well. Remarkably, they achieved all this without the use of lenses for observing distant objects, instruments for calculating angles, or clocks to measure the passing of seconds, minutes, and hours.

The Maya Calendar

The Maya observed the 52-year "Calendar Round." This resulted from two calendar cycles, the Haab and the Tzolkin, which acted simultaneously but independently. For periods longer than 52 years the Maya used a separate system called the Long Count.

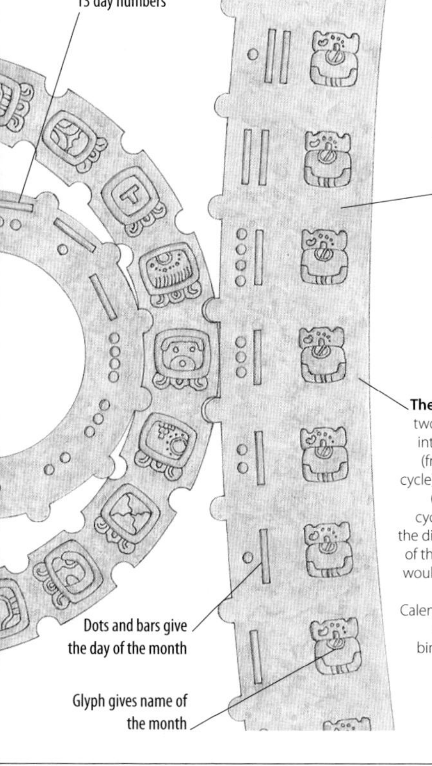

The Haab consisted of 365 days organized into 18 months of 20 days – with 5 unlucky days added at the end.

The date here has two names which interlock: 4 Ahaw (from the Tzolkin cycle) and 8 Kumk'u (from the Haab cycle). Because of the different lengths of the two cycles, it would take another 52 years (the Calendar Round) for this date combination to come around again.

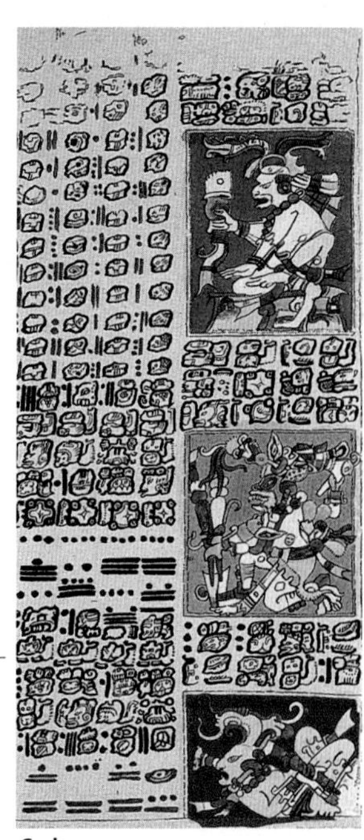
Codex
Maya books, codices, were created by writing on both sides of a thin sheet of bark, which was then folded like a concertina. Only four have survived, including the Dresden Codex, a replica of which is shown above.

Numbers

Mesoamerica used a vigesimal counting system, that is they worked to base 20 rather than base 10. The Maya represented numbers with dots (units) and bars (fives).

0	1	2	3	4
5	6	7	8	9
10	11	12	15	20

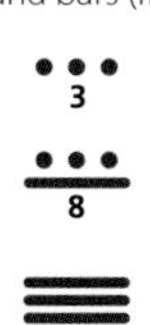
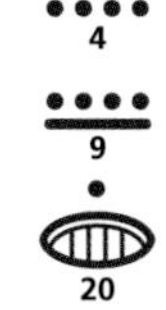

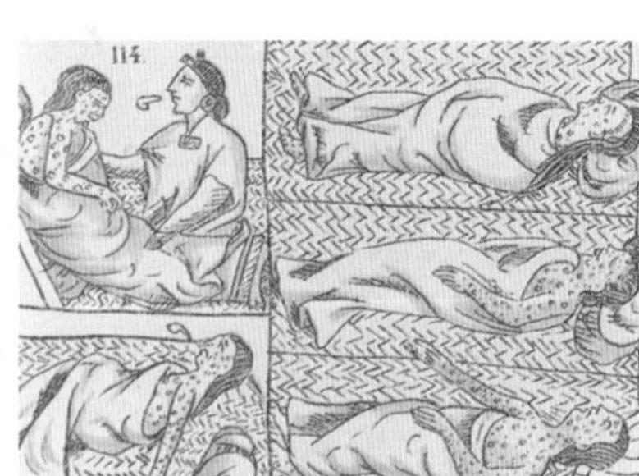
Indians suffering from smallpox, a disease introduced to Mexico by the Spaniards

Colonial Mexico

Following their defeat of the Aztecs, the conquistadors entrusted the Indian population to Spanish *encomenderos*. These quasi-feudal seigneurs were expected to protect and convert their charges, who, in return paid them tribute. Spanish expeditions probed the outer reaches of Mesoamerica – Oaxaca, Chiapas, and the Yucatán Peninsula. Lured by the promise of silver, they also penetrated the Gran Chichimec, the region to the north, beyond the boundaries of Aztec and Tarascan domains, to reach distant Zacatecas and beyond. Hand in hand with this military conquest in search of booty went a spiritual conquest. Franciscan and Dominican friars tirelessly preached to, converted, and baptized the Indians. European diseases such as smallpox produced massive Indian mortality.

Mexico in the 17th Century

During the 17th century, the institution of the hacienda *(see pp54–5)* was established by rich Spaniards looking for the good life of the hidalgo in the colonies. The distant Crown, represented by the Viceroy, managed to exert only a loose control over these settlers who came to farm and mine, and the colony enjoyed a measure of independence. Nevertheless, "New Spain" remitted huge quantities of bullion to its European overlord.

As the colonial economy matured, the settlers produced a Mexican-born, Creole elite, proud of their new homeland. Indians, whose numbers had begun to recover, learned how to cultivate European crops and raise cattle. The mixing of Spanish-born settlers with Indians created intermediate castes. The wealthy white elite financed grandiose haciendas, great town residences, and lavish churches *(see pp30–31)*. Creole accomplishments were also evident in Mexico City's flourishing University (the oldest in the Americas) and the literary output of the Baroque age, notably the plays and poems of Sor (Sister) Juana Inés de la Cruz. Compared to Europe, 17th-century Mexico was a tranquil place. The authority

The administrator and his clerks do business at the Hacienda Peotildas during the 1880s

1531 An apparition initiates the cult of the Virgin of Guadalupe *(see p112)*

The Virgin of Guadalupe

1546 Zacatecas *(see p196)* founded following the discovery of silver deposits

1550

1571 The Spanish Inquisition arrives in Mexico. The first auto-da-fé (act of faith) is held three years later

1600

1629 A major flood hits Mexico City and takes five years to subside

1650

1651 Birth of Sor Juana Inés de la Cruz

Sor Juana Inés de la Cruz

of the Church, combined with the lack of a regular army, created an underlying stability for the colony.

The Coming of Independence

In the 18th century, however, the new Bourbon dynasty in Spain sought to emulate French colonialism in clawing back Mexico's partial autonomy, centralizing royal power, weakening the Church, creating a regular army, boosting bullion remittances, and extracting more taxes. Relations between Spain and Mexico worsened as Creoles increasingly resented the interference of Spanish officials. Indians and lower castes suffered from higher taxes and – as the population grew and shortages of basic goods recurred – lower living standards. The old alliance between Crown and Church weakened: in 1767 the Jesuits were expelled.

Hidalgo shown in a mural by Juan O'Gorman in Castillo de Chapultepec *(see p92)*

International events compounded these tensions. Repeatedly involved in European wars, Spain was short of cash and incapable of controlling the sea-lanes to Mexico. To the north, the French and British threatened the colony's far-flung frontiers, which embraced the present southern United States, from Florida to California. The American Revolution of 1776 afforded an example of colonial rebellion, and Napoleon's overthrow of the Bourbon monarchy in 1808 provoked a crisis in the colonial government. On September 16, 1810, a parish priest, Miguel Hidalgo, gave his famous call to arms in the cause of independence, *El Grito* ("The Cry"). The revolt failed, however, and Hidalgo was executed. A second revolt four years later, led by another priest, José María Morelos, was similarly crushed. But repression could not shore up a tottering empire. Guerrilla resistance continued. In 1821, shortly after the army had seized power in Spain, Mexico's Creole elite proclaimed the country's independence. Spain lacked the will or ability to fight on, and its principal American colony became the independent nation of Mexico.

Independence leader José María Morelos (1765–1815)

1692 Riots in Mexico City caused by food shortages and ethnic tensions

King Charles III of Spain

1700 The Bourbon dynasty ascends the throne of Spain

1759–88 Reign of the reformist King Charles III

1765 Bourbon "reforms" tighten Spain's hold on Mexico

1767 Expulsion of the Jesuits from Mexico

1810 On Sep 16 Miguel Hidalgo launches a popular revolt against Spanish rule. The rebels are defeated. Hidalgo is executed the following year

1814 José María Morelos leads a second attempt at Mexican independence. He is captured and executed in 1815

1820 Liberal military coup takes place in Spain

1700 | 1750 | 1800

The Hacienda

Mexico's haciendas, or country estates, evolved during the colonial and post-colonial era. Production was determined by what the land and climate could offer. Some estates were given over to cattle, or to corn and wheat; others grew sugar cane or agave for making the alcoholic drink *pulque*. Landowners in the Yucatán grew rich cultivating *henequen* (sisal), whereas those in mountainous areas, such as Zacatecas, often ran silver mines. The 1910 Revolution brought about the destruction of many haciendas, but some have been preserved or restored, and a few now serve as hotels *(see p294)*.

Laborers on a Porfirian hacienda where, by 1910, many rural Mexicans lived and worked

A Typical Hacienda

This illustration shows an idealized 19th-century hacienda. Under Porfirio Díaz, many estates experienced their most prosperous phase. To make up for their isolation, haciendas were often self-sufficient, with dairies, brick kilns, orchards, and other facilities.

Lookout and defensive tower

Gardens offered an escape for the landowner from the working life of the hacienda.

Casa Grande (Main House)
This spacious and comfortably furnished building lay at the heart of the hacienda. During the Porfirian era, houses were often remodeled to resemble European castles or English stately homes. Landowners rarely lived on their estates, preferring to make brief visits from the city.

Worksheds
Each hacienda incorporated special buildings and work areas. The men shown above are breaking ore at a mining estate in Guanajuato.

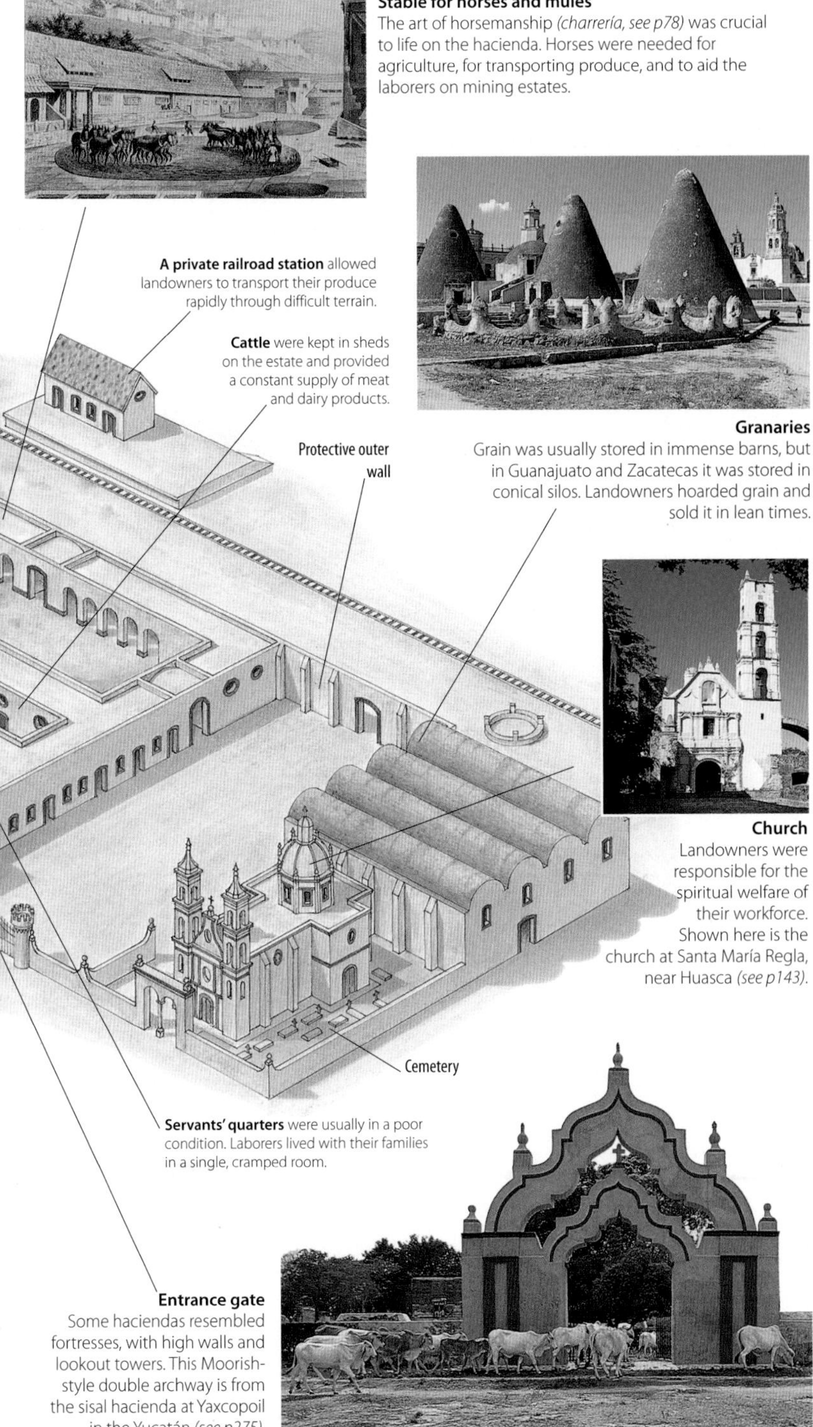

Stable for horses and mules
The art of horsemanship *(charrería, see p78)* was crucial to life on the hacienda. Horses were needed for agriculture, for transporting produce, and to aid the laborers on mining estates.

A private railroad station allowed landowners to transport their produce rapidly through difficult terrain.

Cattle were kept in sheds on the estate and provided a constant supply of meat and dairy products.

Granaries
Grain was usually stored in immense barns, but in Guanajuato and Zacatecas it was stored in conical silos. Landowners hoarded grain and sold it in lean times.

Church
Landowners were responsible for the spiritual welfare of their workforce. Shown here is the church at Santa María Regla, near Huasca *(see p143)*.

Servants' quarters were usually in a poor condition. Laborers lived with their families in a single, cramped room.

Entrance gate
Some haciendas resembled fortresses, with high walls and lookout towers. This Moorish-style double archway is from the sisal hacienda at Yaxcopoil in the Yucatán *(see p275)*.

The New Nation

Mexico achieved its independence at great cost. The economy was ravaged, and Spanish capital fled the country. After a brief imperial interlude – when Agustín de Iturbide made himself Emperor Agustín I (1821–3) – Mexico became a republic. But political consensus proved elusive. Mexico's elites were roughly divided into liberals, who favored a progressive, republican, free-trading secular society, and conservatives, who preferred a centralized, hierarchical state, backed by Church and army, possibly capped by a monarchy. Administrations came and went: 30 presidents governed in the 50 years following 1821. The army absorbed the bulk of revenue and generated a host of *caudillos* (military leaders) who built up their retinues and contested for power, often without principle or ideology. Prominent among them was Antonio López de Santa Anna, whose opportunism and shifting alliances with Church, army, and financiers enabled him to attain the presidency 11 times.

Monumento a los Niños Héroes *(see p93)*

War with Texas

Texas broke away from the rest of Mexico in 1836. Victorious at the Alamo, Santa Anna's forces were crushed by the Texans a month later at San Jacinto. Ten years after this, Texas' decision to join the US sparked a war where the US invaded Mexico by land and sea. Mexican resistance, though dogged, was ill-coordinated. The capital fell after fierce fighting, during which a group of cadets (the Niños Héroes – Boy Heroes) died defending Chapultepec Castle rather than surrender. The war ended with the Treaty of Guadalupe Hidalgo (1848), in which Mexico lost nearly half its territory – the vast area stretching from Texas to California – to the US.

Locator Map

- Mexican territory before 1848
- Modern Mexico

The Reform

Defeat in the war against the US provoked political reassessment and polarization. A new generation of liberals, led by the Indian lawyer Benito Juárez, advocated radical reforms to modernize the country. In 1854 they ousted Santa Anna and

Benito Juárez, the popular leader who steered Mexico through the period of the Reform

1820 | 1830 | 1840 | 1850 | 1860

1821 Mexican independence declared under Agustín de Iturbide

1824 Federal republic created

General Antonio López de Santa Anna

1836 Rebellion of Texas. Santa Anna victorious at the Alamo but defeated at San Jacinto

1840–46 War of the Castes: Maya revolt in the Yucatán

1846–8 Mexican-American War

1848 In the Treaty of Guadalupe Hidalgo, Mexico loses nearly half its territory, and the present-day border along Río Grande to the north is established

1857 Liberal democratic constitution

1858–61 War of the Reform: liberal victory under Juárez

1860 Reform laws

1862 May 5: Mexican forces defeat French invaders at Puebla

The Execution of Emperor Maximilian by the French painter Édouard Manet

embarked on a radical program, known as La Reforma (The Reform). In the 1857 democratic constitution they separated Church and state; sold off Church and other corporate-owned lands; and made all citizens equal before the law.

The Church and the army resisted these measures, but in the ensuing War of the Reform (1858–61) the liberals were victorious. In 1864, however, the conservatives struck a deal with Maximilian of Hapsburg, who assumed the Mexican throne, backed by the French bayonets of Napoleon III. Maximilian, a liberal, humane, but naive ruler, found himself depending on repression to maintain his crown. The liberals wore down the French and their conservative allies in a guerrilla struggle. In 1866 Napoleon III withdrew his troops and a year later, Maximilian was cornered at Querétaro, captured, and executed by a firing squad. Mexico's last monarchy had fallen; the republic under the national hero, Juárez, was restored.

Porfirio Díaz

After Juárez's death in 1872 the liberal leaders jockeyed for succession. A young general, Porfirio Díaz, hero of the war against the French, seized power in 1876. A canny politician, Díaz placated the Church and marginalized or eliminated his rivals. Consolidating his hold on government in the 1880s, he ruled as an authoritarian president until 1911. During the so-called *porfiriato*, Mexico prospered and became more centralized than ever before. Communications improved; cities expanded. But by the 1900s the elderly dictator had alienated the peasantry, who had lost their fields to commercial haciendas. The middle class, meanwhile, chafed under the political restrictions of the regime and yearned for genuine democracy. The scene was set for the Revolution of 1910.

Detail of a mural by Juan O'Gorman showing Porfirio Díaz (seated) and some of his ministers

1864–7 French occupation under Emperor Maximilian

1876 Porfirio Díaz assumes power and becomes president. He remains in office until 1911, except 1880–84, a period known as the porfiriato

1894 A railroad connecting Mexico's Gulf and Pacific coasts is inaugurated

1870 | 1880 | 1890 | 1900

1867 On June 19 Maximilian is executed at Querétaro *(see p200-1)*

1887 José Guadalupe Posada *(see p84)* settles in Mexico City and begins his prolific output of satirical engravings

Window of Palacio Postal, Mexico City

1907 Palacio Postal, Mexico City's main post office *(see p82)*, built

General Francisco "Pancho" Villa, the great northern revolutionary leader

The Revolution

In 1910 Francisco I. Madero, an idealistic young landlord, opposed Díaz's seventh reelection to the presidency and called for a national uprising. The ensuing revolution, which brought together disaffected peasants and urban middle class progressives, induced the aged dictator to negotiate and resign. Madero was elected president, but he could not meet popular demands for agrarian reform and greater democratization and at the same time satisfy conservatives who preferred Díaz's authoritarian rule. In Morelos, south of Mexico City, Emiliano Zapata led a fresh rebellion, championing the cause of villagers who – like his own family – had lost land to the sugar plantations. Madero, however, was not ousted by such popular movements but by the military, who assassinated him in February 1913. The ruthless Victoriano Huerta formed a new regime so unpopular that the opposition united against it. Zapata allied with the great northern revolutionary leader Pancho Villa *(see p177)*, who had built up a formidable army on the prairies of Chihuahua, and in a second period of civil war (1913–14), these and other supporters of the constitution defeated Huerta and destroyed the regular army.

Villa and Zapata could not stomach the authority of their nominal chief, the dour provincial landlord Venustiano Carranza. A revolutionary convention, at Aguascalientes, failed to broker a peace. In a third and final bout of civil war, in 1915, Carranza's leading general, Álvaro Obregón, defeated Villa, reducing him to an outlaw. Zapata and others fought on, but it was clear that Carranza's faction had won, and in 1917 they promulgated a radical new constitution.

Aftermath of Revolution

Mexico was exhausted after the Revolution. Over a million people had died during it, or emigrated because of it. The currency had collapsed, and the country's infrastructure was in tatters. Carranza's coalition, dominated

Poster of the revolutionary leader Emiliano Zapata

1910

1910 Mexican Revolution is launched by Madero

1911 Madero becomes president but is assassinated in 1913

1917 Mexico's current liberal, revolutionary constitution is passed

1919 Assassination of Zapata

1920 Military revolt ousts and kills Carranza

Venustiano Carranza

1923 Pancho Villa is assassinated

1928 Assassination of Obregón

1929 Partido Nacional Revolucionario formed

1930

1934 Cárdenas becomes president

1938 Nationalization of the oil industry

1940 Assassination of Trotsky in Mexico City *(see p107)*

1941–5 Mexico allies with the US during World War II

1950

1956 The Torre Latinoamericana is built in Mexico City *(see p79)*

by reformers such as Obregón and Plutarco Elías Calles, was shaky. Carranza was ousted and killed in 1920. In the following years, the infant revolutionary regime battled to survive against pressures from the Church, fearful of its anticlericalism, and from the US, which disapproved of such a radical constitution. In 1928, Obregón was assassinated. Calles responded to the crisis this caused by organizing a new national party, the Partido Nacional Revolucionario (PNR), the forerunner of the party which, under different names (PRM, PRI), governed Mexico until 2000.

Union poster in support of the reforms instituted by President Cárdenas

Modern Mexico

President Cárdenas (1934–40), confronting the depression, implemented a sweeping agrarian reform, boosted the rights of organized labor, and nationalized the foreign-owned oil industry. Subsequent leaders, typified by President Alemán (1946–52), favored the private sector, which became the motor of an "economic miracle" – the sustained growth of the 1950s and 60s.

The miracle eventually ended. In 1968, on the eve of the Mexico City Olympics, student protests were bloodily repressed, tarnishing the regime's legitimacy. Seeking to recoup prestige, while reorienting the economy, the governments of the 1970s borrowed and spent, partly on the basis of the oil boom. Inflation quickened and, in 1982, the economy slumped. President Salinas (1988–94) privatized state enterprises, cut protective tariffs, and concluded the North American Free Trade Agreement. Shortly after Salinas left office, Mexico suffered a recession. Mexico's problems in the 1990s were compounded by armed rebellion in Chiapas *(see p234)*.

Economic woes and social unrest led to victory for the center-right Partido Acción Nacional (PAN) in the 2000 elections. In 2006, Felipe Calderón, also of PAN, was elected. His administration was marked by a struggle to contain the country's drug war. In 2012, the PRI returned to power when Enrique Peña Nieto was sworn into office. He faces many challenges, including continued problems with drug cartels, but has met with some success – wanted cartel leaders have been captured. His ambitious reform agenda, however, has been marred by a number of fiscal and human rights scandals.

Parade during the opening ceremony of the 1968 Olympic Games, staged in Mexico City

2005 Yucatán Peninsula hit by Hurricane Wilma

2009 Swine flu outbreak

1985 On September 19 an earthquake hits Mexico City, killing an estimated 9,000 people

1988 President Salinas begins a series of Neo-Liberal reforms

2010 Country celebrates its bicentennial

2014 Government is implicated in disappearance of 43 students in Guerrero, sparking national outrage

2000 PAN wins presidential elections

1970 | **1990** | **2010** | **2030**

1968 Olympic Games in Mexico City. Student protest repressed

President Salinas

1994 Zapatistas overrun San Cristóbal de las Casas (Chiapas). In 12 days of fighting, 145 people die

2012 Enrique Peña Nieto becomes President despite a widespread student protest

2007 Chichén Itzá is named one of the New Seven Wonders of the World

INTRODUCING MEXICO CITY

Mexico City at a Glance

Mexico City is a huge, hectic, and overpopulated metropolis, as well as the center of commerce and government for the country. Yet despite the problems of modern city life, the oldest capital of the New World is rich in both indigenous and colonial history. The aptly named Historic Center was the site of the Aztec capital, while the elegant Paseo de la Reforma is lined with colonial architecture and striking contemporary buildings. Allow at least two or three days to explore the city in full.

Locator Map

The National Anthropology Museum *(see pp94–9)* is considered one of the finest museums of its kind in the world. It explores Mexico's prehistory; the lives and beliefs of the Maya, Aztecs, and other great civilizations; and the way of life of the country's present-day indigenous people.

Bosque de Chapultepec *(see pp92–3)* is Mexico City's largest park. Once a summer vacation spot for the Aztecs, it still offers a relaxing respite from the bustling city.

San Ángel *(see pp102–5)* is a lively district that preserves some of the finest colonial architecture in the capital. It is also known for its Saturday craft fair.

RÍO SAN JOAQUÍN

REFORMA AN
CHAPULTEPE
(see pp86–99)

PASEO DE LA REFORMA

AV. CONSTITUYENTES

0 meters 500
0 yards 500

AV. NSURGENTES SUR

PERIFÉRICO

RÍO CONSULADO CIRCUITO INTE

SAN ÁNGE
COYOA
(see pp100-

◀ Catedral Metropolitana at twilight overlooking the city's main square, the Zócalo

AV INSURGENTES NORTE
PASEO DE LA REFORMA NORTE
THE HISTORIC CENTER
(see pp64–85)
VIADUCTO
MIGUEL ALEMÁN
AV. CUAUHTÉMOC
AV. DR. JOSÉ MARIA VERTIZ
CALZADA DE TLALPAN

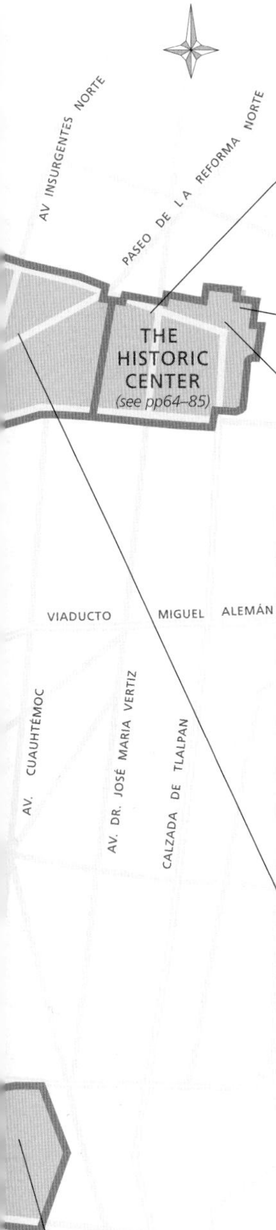

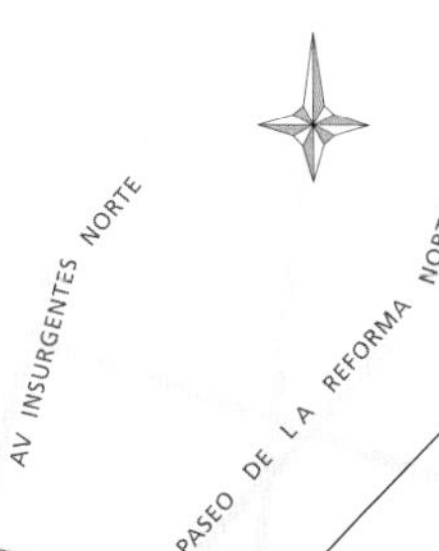

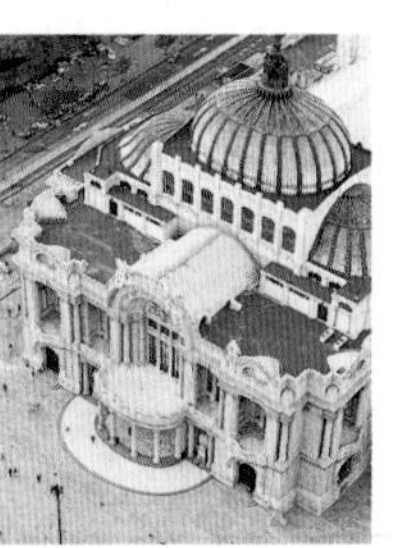

Palacio de Bellas Artes *(see p84)*, the city's hub of fine arts, is a grand early 20th-century building overlooking the Alameda Central. Inside, it is decorated with works by Mexico's greatest muralists. It is home to the popular dance group, Ballet Folklórico.

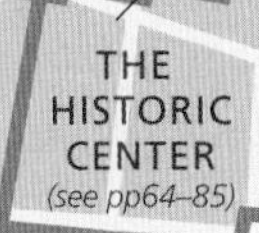

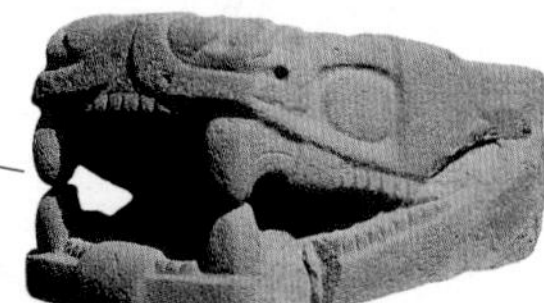

Templo Mayor *(see pp72–4)* is the site of the Aztec *teocalli* (sacred city) that formed the heart of Tenochtitlán, their capital. The first stone was discovered in 1978; later digs have uncovered spectacular finds.

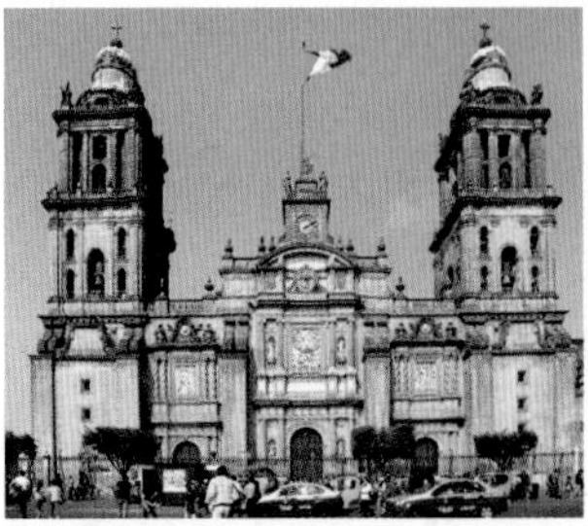

Catedral Metropolitana *(see pp68–9)* was completed in 1813 after almost 300 years construction. Latin America's largest church, it dominates the main square of the city. Its Baroque altars and side chapels are magnificently ornate.

Coyoacán *(see pp108–9)* has an atmosphere distinct from the rest of the city, with peaceful plazas and charming streets.

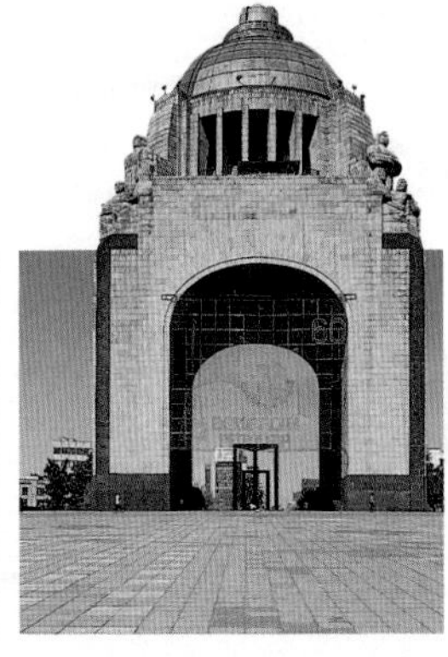

Monumento a la Revolución *(see p90)* is dedicated to the 1910 Revolution. Intended as the start of a new senate building, in 1932 it was made into a monument, and revolutionary heroes were buried beneath the pillars. A museum of the Revolution is housed at its base.

PALACIO DE BELLAS ARTES

THE HISTORIC CENTER

When Hernán Cortés led his army into the Aztec capital of Tenochtitlán the city stood on an island in Lake Texcoco. After conquering it the Spanish razed it to the ground, reusing much of the stonework in their own constructions, and gradually filling in the lake. The buildings of the Historic Center – which stands on the site of the Aztec city – date mainly from the colonial and post-independence eras. In a patchwork of architectural styles, they range from colonial churches and mansions to an Art Nouveau/Art Deco theater-cum-gallery and a 1950s skyscraper. A prominent exception is the excavated remains of the great Aztec temple.

Sights at a Glance

Historic Buildings

- 2 Palacio Nacional
- 3 Templo Mayor
- 4 Antiguo Colegio de San Ildefonso
- 7 Secretaría de Educación Pública
- 9 Palacio de la Antigua Escuela de Medicina
- 15 Casa de los Azulejos
- 16 Torre Latinoamericana
- 17 Palacio de Bellas Artes

Museums and Galleries

- 5 Museo de la Caricatura
- 10 Museo José Luis Cuevas
- 11 Museo de la Ciudad de México
- 12 Museo de la Charrería
- 13 Museo del Ejército y Fuerza Aérea Mexicanos
- 14 Museo Nacional de Arte
- 18 Museo Nacional de la Estampa
- 19 Museo Franz Mayer
- 20 Laboratorio Arte Alameda
- 21 Museo Mural Diego Rivera
- 22 Museo de Arte Popular

Churches

- 1 Catedral Metropolitana
- 6 Templo de la Enseñanza

Squares

- 8 Plaza de Santo Domingo

Locator Map
See also Street Finder maps 3, 4

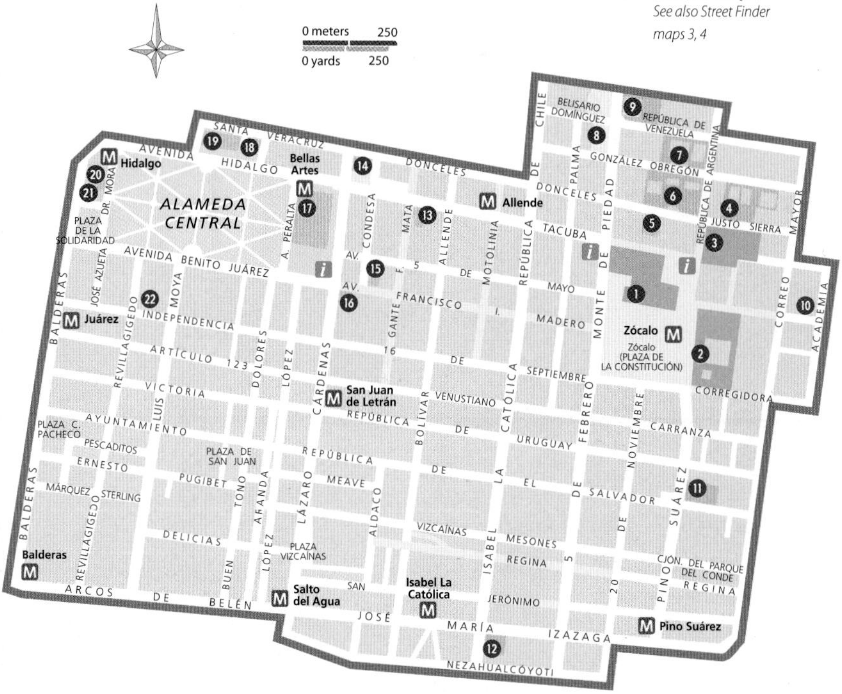

◀ Neo-Classical facade of Palacio de Bellas Artes

For keys to symbols *see back flap*

Street-by-Street: Zócalo

The Plaza de la Constitución, invariably known as the Zócalo, is one of the biggest public squares in the world. A giant national flag flies in the middle of this vast paved space, which is dominated by two buildings, the cathedral and the Palacio Nacional. On the square stand other public buildings, restaurants, shops, and hotels. At one corner are the sunken remains of the Aztecs' principal temple complex. A good view of the Zócalo can be had from the terrace of the Best Western Hotel Majestic *(see p296)*.

5 Museo de la Caricatura
A caricature of singer David Bowie is among the works of cartoon art in this 18th-century building.

6 Templo de la Enseñanza
A dazzling gold altarpiece is the main feature of this late 18th-century Baroque church, which was built as a convent chapel.

Nacional Monte de Piedad, a government-run pawn shop, occupies a historic building dating from the 16th century.

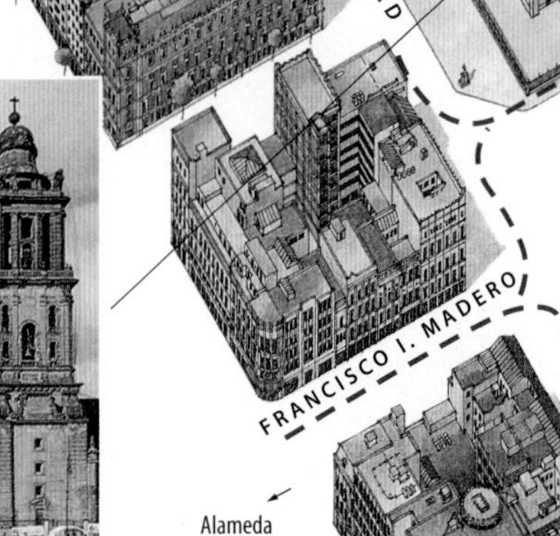

1 ★ Catedral Metropolitana
Although damaged by the subsidence affecting the center of Mexico City, this is still one of the greatest religious buildings in Latin America.

Sagrario Metropolitano

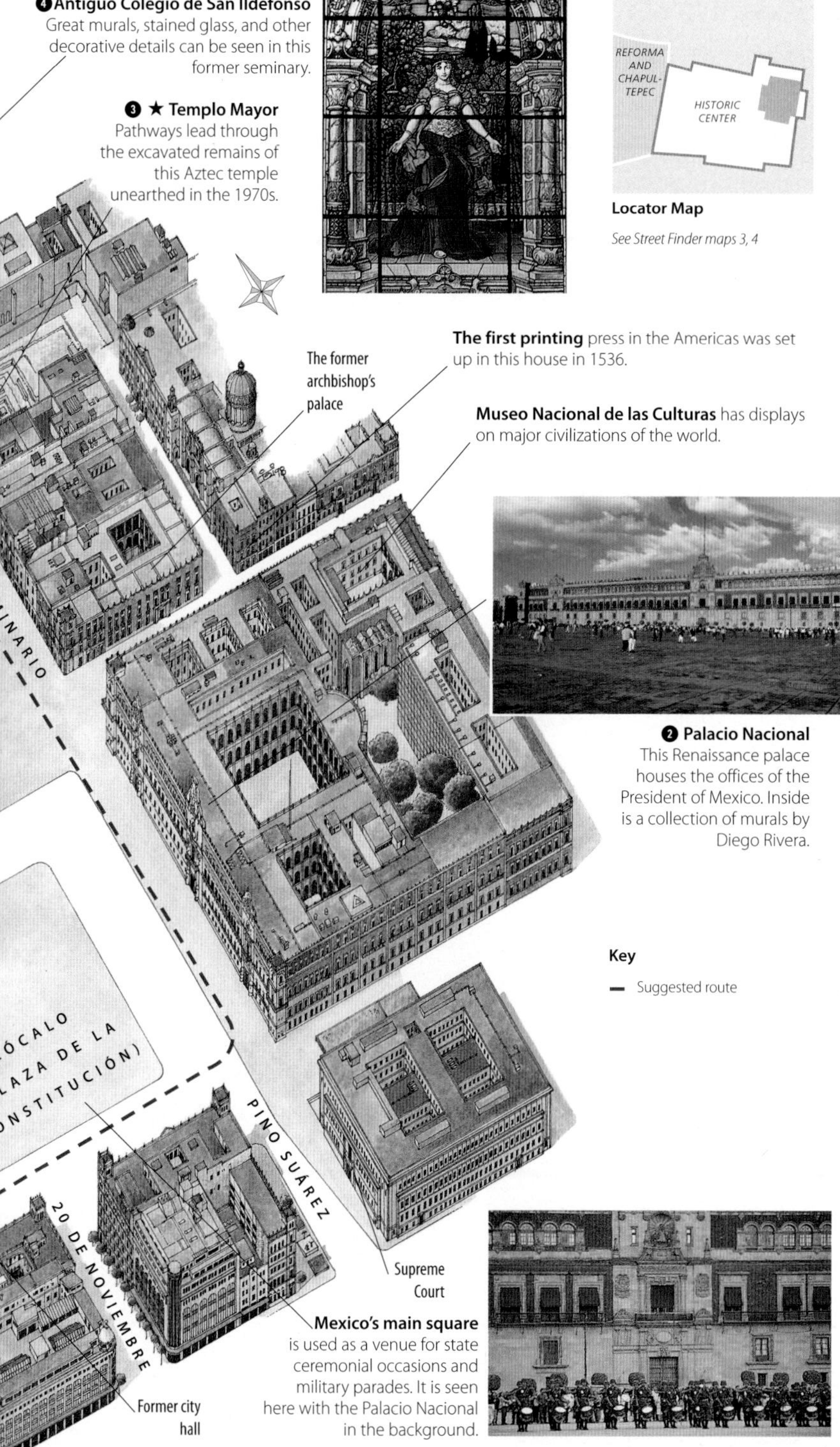

4 Antiguo Colegio de San Ildefonso
Great murals, stained glass, and other decorative details can be seen in this former seminary.

3 ★ Templo Mayor
Pathways lead through the excavated remains of this Aztec temple unearthed in the 1970s.

Locator Map

See Street Finder maps 3, 4

The first printing press in the Americas was set up in this house in 1536.

Museo Nacional de las Culturas has displays on major civilizations of the world.

2 Palacio Nacional
This Renaissance palace houses the offices of the President of Mexico. Inside is a collection of murals by Diego Rivera.

Key

— Suggested route

Mexico's main square is used as a venue for state ceremonial occasions and military parades. It is seen here with the Palacio Nacional in the background.

❶ Catedral Metropolitana

The biggest church in Latin America, Mexico City's cathedral is also at the heart of the world's largest Catholic diocese. Its towers rise 67 m (220 ft) above the Zócalo, and it took almost three centuries – from 1525 to 1788 – to complete. This extraordinarily long period is reflected in the multiple styles of its architecture and internal decoration, ranging from Classical through Baroque and Churrigueresque to Neo-Classical. It has five principal altars, and 16 side chapels containing a valuable collection of paintings, sculpture, and church furniture.

Sacristy
The sacristy contains 17th-century paintings and items of carved furniture such as this decorated cabinet.

★ Altar de los Reyes
The two oil paintings on this Baroque masterpiece are the *Adoration of the Kings* and the *Assumption of the Virgin*, both by Juan Rodríguez Juárez.

Side entrance

Kings and Queens
The sculptures adorning the Altar de los Reyes are of kings and queens who have been canonized.

Capilla de San José
This side chapel is one of 16 dedicated to saints and manifestations of the Virgin, all exquisitely decorated with statues and oil paintings.

KEY

① **The high altar** is a block of white marble carved with images of saints.

② **The clock tower** is decorated with statues of Faith, Hope, and Charity.

③ **The facade** is divided into three and flanked by monumental bell towers.

The Sinking Cathedral
The cathedral is sinking into the soft clay of what was once the bed of Lake Texcoco. Restoration work, mostly carried out underground, has prevented its collapse.

VISITORS' CHECKLIST

Practical Information
Zócalo.
Map 4 E2. **Open** daily (avoid visiting during mass).
Choir: **Open** 10am–3pm.
Sacristy: **Open** 11am–2pm.

Transport
M Zócalo.

Sagrario Metropolitano
Built in the mid-18th century as the parish church attached to the cathedral, the Sagrario has a sumptuous high Baroque facade adorned with sculpted saints.

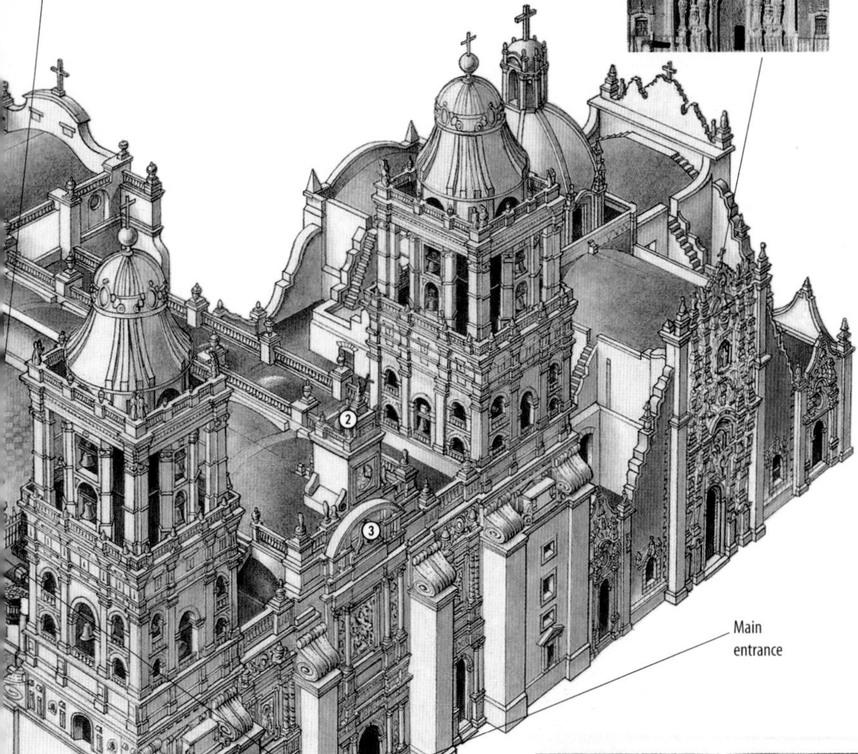

Main entrance

★ Choir
With its gold-alloy choir-rail imported from Macao, superbly carved stalls, and two magnificent organs, the choir is a highlight of the cathedral.

Architecture of the Catedral Metropolitana

The building of this vast cathedral took over 260 years, from the first decades after the conquest to the last years of Spanish rule, including long periods when construction virtually came to a halt. The result is the work of many different architects, artists, and sculptors at different times, incorporating a variety of styles, mostly from Spain but also elements that were distinctly Mexican. Despite this mixture, it all combines to form an enormously impressive whole.

Bell tower, built between 1660–1813

The Early Colonial Church

Mexico City's first cathedral, begun by Cortés in 1525, was just south of the modern one, near Avenida 5 de Mayo (the remains of some columns can still be seen). It was soon determined to be too small, however, and orders to build a new cathedral were issued in 1536 and 1552, though work did not actually begin until 1573. The basic plan, with three huge vaulted naves, was the work of Claudio de Arciniega, but his design was altered by other architects. Much of the first walls were built by Juan Miguel de Agüero, who was principal architect of Mérida Cathedral in the Yucatán. Only after the sacristy was finished, in 1626, was the first cathedral demolished.

Baroque Architecture

The greater part of the cathedral was completed in the mid-17th century, and consecrated in 1656. The oldest sections, such as the sacristy, are in the restrained Spanish Baroque style known as Plateresque, so named because its sculptors were said to reproduce the effects of silverware *(plata)* in stone. The three portals of the main facade, from 1670–90, are grander, with elegant columns framing statues of saints.

Carved estípites on the facade of the Sagrario Metropolitano

Churrigueresque

Spanish late Baroque architecture was dominated by the ornate style named after the Churriguera family of architects. A hallmark was the use of estípites – square-sided relief columns, like upturned obelisks, used as bases for elaborate designs. They are prominent in the choir, chapels, and the extraordinary Altar de los Reyes by Jerónimo de Balbas, built between 1710–37, which inspired similar designs throughout Mexico. Outside, the foremost example of Churrigueresque is the Sagrario Metropolitano's facade, built by Lorenzo Rodríguez in 1740–68.

Neo-Classical

In the 1780s the task of completing the still-unfinished upper levels was given to José Damién Ortiz de Castro – the only Mexican-born architect to work on the cathedral. He added the bell towers and upper stories of the façade. Additional touches were made by another Spaniard, Manuel Tolsá, who in 1813 added the clock tower and rebuilt the dome in a more austere Neo-Classical style.

Subsidence

The cathedral's huge weight has caused it to sink into the soft subsoil since it was first built, but this problem became acute after the 1985 earthquake. A massive rescue project to stabilize the structure was completed in 2000. This has ensured the cathedral will not fall down, and the now erratic angles of its columns, and the slope of the floor, are among its most striking features.

Elaborate altar inside the Capilla de las Reliquías

❷ Palacio Nacional

Plaza de la Constitución s/n.
Tel (55) 91 58 12 59. Ⓜ Zócalo.
Open 9am–4:30pm daily. book in advance, (55) 36 88 12 61.

Filling the whole east side of the Zócalo, this imposing building occupies the site of the palace of Aztec emperor Moctezuma, and later the home of the Conquistador Cortés *(see p47)*. The present palace was begun in 1562 in an austere Baroque style typical of Spanish architecture of the time, as the residence of Mexico's viceroys and the center of government.

It has had an eventful history, and was attacked by rebels in 1624 and 1692. After independence in 1821 it became the residence of the presidents of Mexico, and the offices used by President Juárez in the 1860s are open to the public. In the 1920s a third story was added, in harmony with the original style.

Today the Palacio Nacional still contains the offices of the President of Mexico and the Finance Ministry, but its greatest attractions are the extraordinary murals around the staircase of the main patio. These were painted by Diego Rivera in 1929–35, in the aftermath of the 1910 Revolution. His aim was to celebrate Mexico's turbulent history, from its ancient past to the potential future released by the Revolution, including an astonishing gallery of portraits of historical figures. The main murals above the great staircase present a dynamic panorama of Mexican history. On the right-hand wall is an idealized vision of ancient indigenous Mexico before the arrival of the Spaniards. Filling the bottom of the central panel are the bloody battles of the Conquest, with Cortés rearing up on a white horse, and Cuauhtémoc, the last Aztec emperor, shown holding a spear. The horrors of the Conquest are also depicted just above to the left, with priests torturing heretics, but across to the right priests such as Bartolomé de Las Casas, who protected Indians, are also shown.

Independence forms the centerpiece of the main panel, with heroes like Hidalgo and Morelos. Foreign invasions, by the United States in 1847 and France in the 1860s, are shown in the far right and left panels of the main wall respectively. The inner right panel refers to Juarez's Reform Laws of 1857, while the 1910 Revolution appears on the upper left, with Porfirio Díaz, Madero, and a host of other identifiable faces. The Revolution also crowns the central panel with peasant hero Zapata (with moustache) behind a banner demanding *Tierra y Libertad* ("Land and Liberty"). On the left wall is the astonishing *Mexico Today and Tomorrow*, an exuberant portrayal of the promise of the Revolution. Further murals with idealized images of life in pre-conquest Mexico and Aztec Tenochtitlán from 1941–51 continue around the first floor.

The main courtyard of the Palacio Nacional

Statue in the palace gardens

Plan of the Mural by Diego Rivera

Key

① Quetzalcoatl and the Ancient Indian World
② The Foundation of Tenochtitlán (c.1325)
③ The Conquest of Mexico (1521)
④ The Colonial Era
⑤ Mexican Independence (1821)
⑥ The US Invasion of Mexico (1847)
⑦ The Reform Laws (1857–60)
⑧ The French Occupation and Execution of Maximilian (1867)
⑨ The Mexican Revolution (1910)
⑩ Mexico Today and Tomorrow

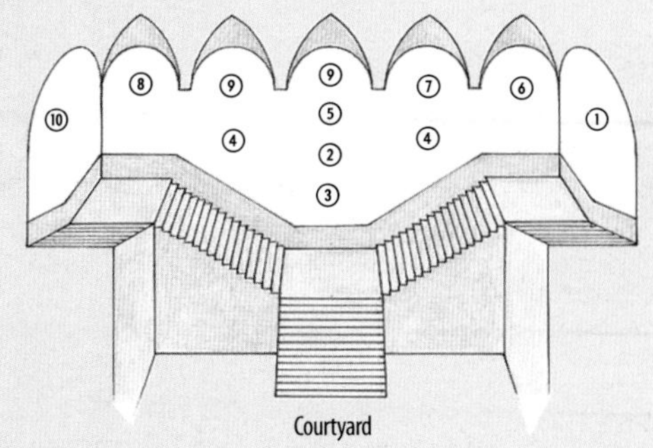

❸ Templo Mayor

This Great Temple, built by the Aztecs in the 14th and 15th centuries, stood at the heart of Tenochtitlán. The temple complex was almost completely destroyed by the Spaniards after their conquest of the Aztec capital. The chance discovery of the extraordinary Coyolxauhqui carving in 1978 prompted excavations that uncovered the remains of superimposed temples denoted by the stage of construction to which they belong. Stage I is not visible as it is buried beneath Stage II.

View of the Templo Mayor archaeological site

Chacmool
This reclining figure may have been an intermediary between god and man. Offerings were placed in the bowl it holds.

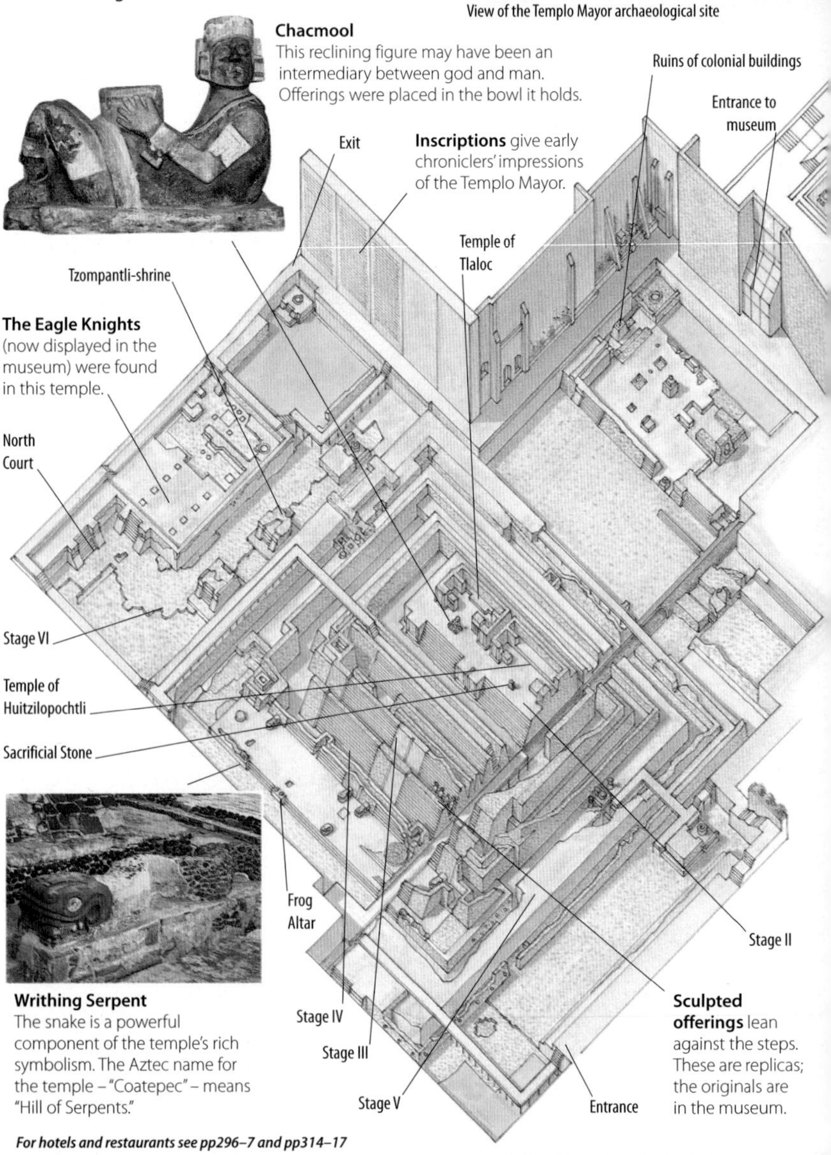

Ruins of colonial buildings

Entrance to museum

Exit

Inscriptions give early chroniclers' impressions of the Templo Mayor.

Temple of Tlaloc

Tzompantli-shrine

The Eagle Knights (now displayed in the museum) were found in this temple.

North Court

Stage VI

Temple of Huitzilopochtli

Sacrificial Stone

Frog Altar

Stage II

Writhing Serpent
The snake is a powerful component of the temple's rich symbolism. The Aztec name for the temple – "Coatepec" – means "Hill of Serpents."

Stage IV

Stage III

Stage V

Entrance

Sculpted offerings lean against the steps. These are replicas; the originals are in the museum.

Side Elevation of the Museum

4th Floor
Entrance
3rd Floor
2nd Floor
1st Floor
Ground Floor
Basement

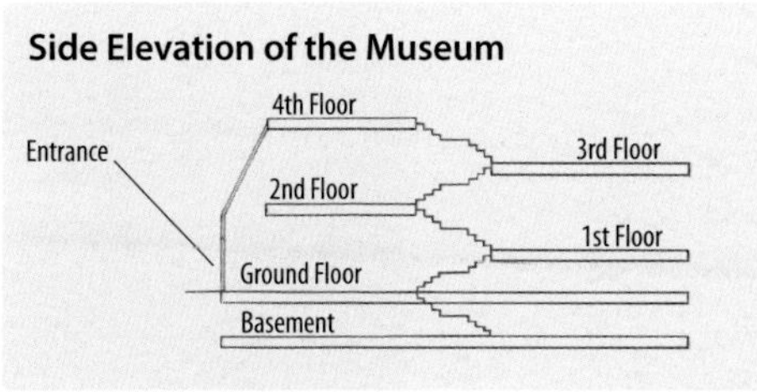

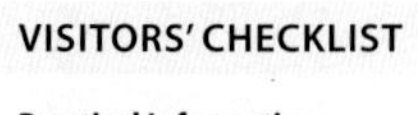

VISITORS' CHECKLIST

Practical Information
Seminario (off Zócalo).
Map 4 F1. **Tel** (55) 40 40 56 00.
Open 9am–5pm Tue–Sun.
(museum).
templomayor.inah.gob.mx

Transport
Zócalo.

★ Coyolxauhqui
This circular stone carving portrays the dismembered body of the Aztec goddess Coyolxauhqui *(see p74)*.

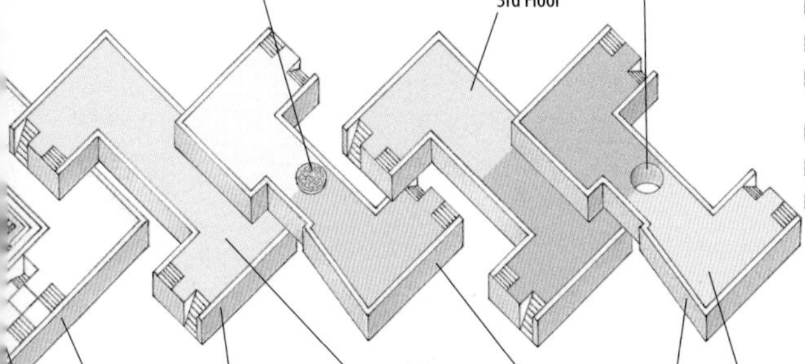

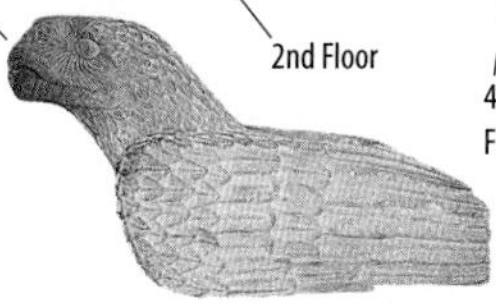

Hole in the floor to view Coyolxauhqui
3rd Floor
2nd Floor
Ground Floor
1st Floor
4th Floor

Key

- Room 1 Background
- Room 2 Ritual and Sacrifice
- Room 3 Tribute and Trade
- Room 4 The God of War
- Room 5 The God of Rain and Water
- Room 6 Flora and Fauna
- Room 7 Agriculture
- Room 8 Historical Archaeology

Museum Guide

The eight rooms are visited in order. Turn right at the entrance and take the stairs to Room 1. Continue up the stairs to Rooms 2, 3, and 4. Rooms 4 and 5 are interconnected. From the latter, stairs lead down again to Rooms 6, 7, and 8.

A model shows how the Templo Mayor complex would have been when the Spaniards first saw it.

Stone Eagle
This sculpted eagle symbolizes the sun and Huitzilopochtli. The hearts of sacrificial victims were placed in the hole in its back.

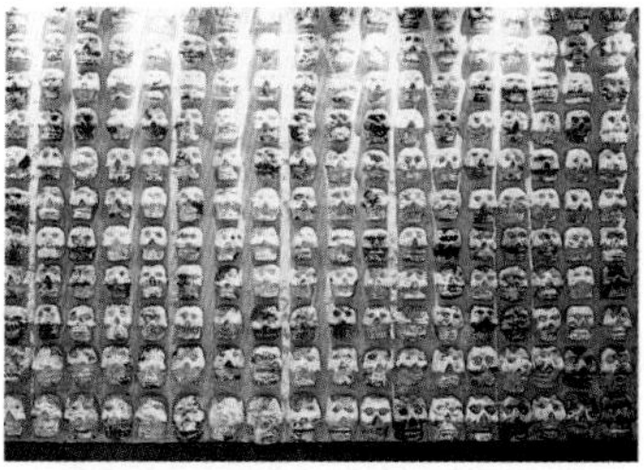

Tzompantli-shrine (Wall of Skulls)
This panel made of rows of human skulls covered with stucco is a copy of the original, which can be seen on the site.

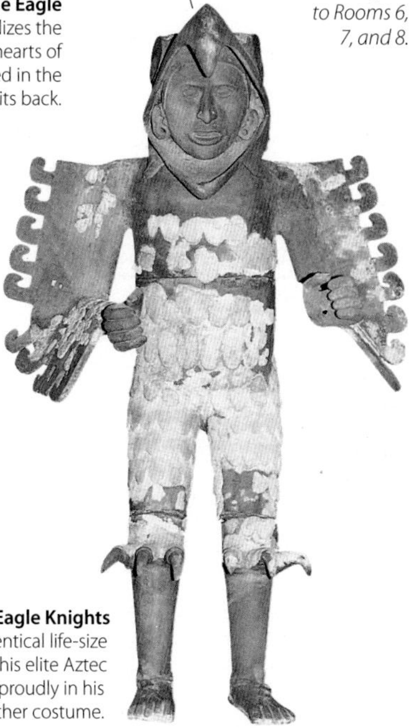

★ Eagle Knights
One of two identical life-size clay statues, this elite Aztec warrior stands proudly in his eagle feather costume.

The Building of the Templo Mayor

The Aztecs erected their most important religious building on the spot where – in fulfilment of a prophecy *(see p47)* – they had seen an eagle perched on a cactus devouring a snake. The first temple was built some time after 1325, according to Aztec sources, but it was enlarged many times over the course of the next two centuries. The twin temples on its summit were dedicated to the god of war, Huitzilopochtli, and the god of rain and water, Tlaloc. Aztec chronicles tell that both deities were frequently appeased with human sacrifices.

The site of the temples today

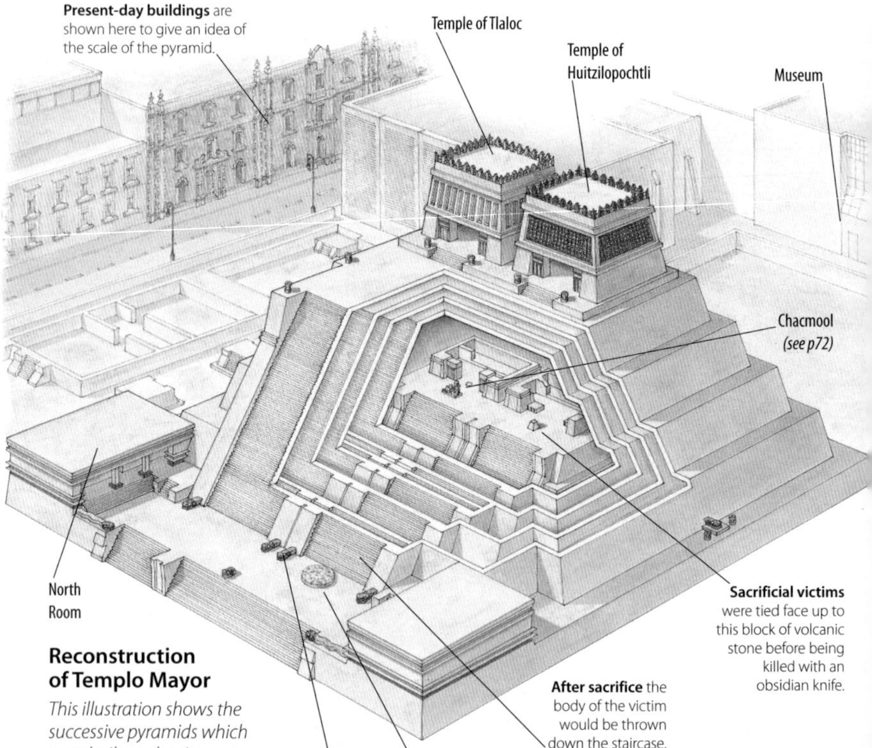

Present-day buildings are shown here to give an idea of the scale of the pyramid.

Temple of Tlaloc

Temple of Huitzilopochtli

Museum

Chacmool *(see p72)*

North Room

Sacrificial victims were tied face up to this block of volcanic stone before being killed with an obsidian knife.

After sacrifice the body of the victim would be thrown down the staircase.

Reconstruction of Templo Mayor

This illustration shows the successive pyramids which were built on the site, one on top of the other.

Two snake heads guard the foot of the main staircase. They indicate that the temple was built as a symbolic re-creation of Coatepec – "the Hill of the Serpent" – a sacred place in Aztec mythology.

A carved round stone shows the separated head, limbs, and torso of the Aztec goddess Coyolxauhqui. According to legend she was slain and dismembered by Huitzilopochtli, her brother, because she had killed their mother, Coatlicue. The stone is now in the museum *(see p73)*.

The colonial Antiguo Colegio de San Ildefonso, now home to an impressive collection of Mexican murals

❹ Antiguo Colegio de San Ildefonso

Justo Sierra 16. **Map** 4 F1. **Tel** (55) 57 02 29 91. Ⓜ Zócalo, Allende. **Open** 10am–5:30pm Tue–Sun (to 7:30pm Tue). Tue free. reserve in advance. **sanildefonso.org.mx**

This 16th-century building, originally a Jesuit seminary, is an outstanding example of Mexican civil architecture from the colonial era. It was remodeled in the 18th century, and the greater part of the present-day building dates from 1770–80. The facade on Calle San Ildefonso, however, which combines Baroque and Neo-Classical styles, is original.

Today the building belongs to the national university and serves as a museum. Its star attraction is the collection of murals from the earliest years of the Mexican muralist movement – including masterful works by Rivera, Siqueiros, and Orozco. In fact, San Ildefonso is regarded as the birthplace of the movement. The first murals commissioned included those of David Alfaro Siqueiros, who in 1922–4 painted four works around the stairwell of the Colegio Chico, the oldest of the three patios which make up the San Ildefonso complex. Perhaps the best-known of these is *The Funeral of the Sacrificed Worker*. At around the same time, José Clemente Orozco was painting a series of murals on the north wall of the Patio Grande with equally universal themes – among them motherhood, freedom, and justice and the law. These include *Revolutionary Trinity* and *The Strike*. Arguably the most dramatic piece, however, is *The Trench*. The Orozco works to be found on the staircase – including a nude study of Cortés and his indigenous mistress La Malinche – relate mostly to the theme of *mestizaje*, or the mixing of the races that formed the Mexican nation. The Anfiteatro Simón Bolívar contains an early work by Diego Rivera, *The Creation*. The other murals in this hall were painted by Fernando Leal between 1930 and 1942.

The conference room to the north of the Patio Grande, known as El Generalito, is furnished with 17th-century carved wooden choir stalls.

Courtyard of the Museo de la Caricatura, formerly the Colegio de Cristo

❺ Museo de la Caricatura

Donceles 99. **Map** 4 E1. **Tel** (55) 57 04 04 59. Ⓜ Zócalo. **Open** 10am–6pm daily. reserve in advance. **museodelacaricatura.org**

With its intricate and finely preserved Baroque facade, the former Colegio de Cristo is one of the best examples in Mexico City of an upper-class 18th-century dwelling. Originally conceived in 1610 as an educational foundation for poor students, it was rebuilt in the 1740s, and later became a private house. The tiny patio and the broad staircase with its low, stone archway are among the highlights. In the 1980s, the building was restored to house the collection of the Mexican Society of Cartoonists. This includes contemporary cartoons and works by the influential political satirist and engraver José Guadalupe Posada (1852–1913).

The gold main altarpiece of the Templo de la Enseñanza

❻ Templo de la Enseñanza

Donceles 102. **Map** 4 E1. **Tel** (55) 57 02 18 43. Ⓜ Allende, Zócalo. **Open** 11am–1pm & 4–8pm Mon, Tue, Thu & Fri.

One of the most remarkable churches in Mexico City, the Templo de la Enseñanza has an extremely narrow and ornate facade sloping backward slightly from ground level. The atrium is tiny and the interior decoration the height of late 18th-century "ultra-Baroque."

Built as a convent church, La Enseñanza was vacated by the nuns as a result of the 19th-century anti-clerical Reform Laws. It was later used by government bodies, including the Ministry of Education.

The dazzling gold main altarpiece is studded with the sculpted figures of saints. It rises up to the roof of the church, its height enhancing its vertical dimensions, and it is flanked by huge paintings. The vault above is adorned with a fresco of the Virgin of El Pilar, to whom the church is dedicated. In the lower choir, which is situated to either side of the altar, are lattice-work screens intended to hide the nuns from the gaze of other worshipers.

❼ Secretaría de Educación Pública

República de Argentina 28. **Map** 4 E1. **Tel** (55) 53 28 10 97. Ⓜ Zócalo, Allende. **Open** 9am–6pm Mon–Fri. **W sep.gob.mx**

This former convent building, dating from 1639, is renowned for its large series of murals by Diego Rivera. Painted between 1923 and 1928, they reflect Rivera's diverse influences: Italian frescoes, French cubists, and pre-Columbian Mexico.

The ground floor of the first patio is dedicated to the glorification of labor, a highlight being a mural showing a country schoolmistress giving a lesson. On the staircase is a series of Mexican landscapes, while on the third floor, in a panel called *The Painter, The Sculptor and the Architect*, is a well-known self-portrait. The first-floor walls contain monochrome *grisailles* depicting scientific, artistic, and intellectual labor, and on the top floor are portraits of workers' heroes, such as Zapata. The second patio, on the ground floor, features panels of popular fiestas, of which *The Day of the Dead* is particularly noteworthy. The third floor draws on revolutionary songs (*corridos*) for its subject matter and includes a panel, *The Arsenal*, in which the artist Frida Kahlo hands out guns to revolutionaries.

In stark contrast to the style of Rivera is a striking mural by David Alfaro Siqueiros, *Patriots and Parricides*. This is located on the staircase in a part of the building which used to be a customs house (the Ex-Aduana), near the República de Brasil entrance.

❽ Plaza de Santo Domingo

Map 4 E1. Ⓜ Allende.

Tower of the church of Santo Domingo

Second only in importance to the Zócalo itself, the Plaza de Santo Domingo (officially called Plaza 23 de Mayo) is steeped in history. The Dominicans built a convent here – the first in New Spain – in 1527, of which all that remains today is a restored chapel, the Capilla de la Expiación. Most of the other buildings that flank the square date from the 18th century. The church of Santo Domingo, with its sober facade partly covered in red volcanic *tezontle* stone, was erected between 1717 and 1737. Its tower is capped by a pyramidal pinnacle covered with Talavera tiles. The interior of the church contains statues of saints thought to date from

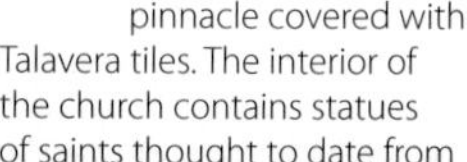

Siqueiros mural of *Patriots and Parricides* in the Secretaría de Educación Pública

Facade of the Capilla de la Expiación in the Plaza de Santo Domingo

the 16th century, as well as oil paintings by Juan Correa and Alonso López de Herrera. The antique organ and the 18th-century cedar-wood choir stalls with carved images of the saints are among the treasures. The side altars are impressive for their gold embellishments.

The uneven subsidence that led to the demolition of previous churches on this site is widely evident in the square. From the door of the church, the undulation of the Tuscan-style *portales*, or arcade, which runs down the west side of the square, is noticeable. Under the arcade sit scribes, who, for a small fee, will fill out official documents using old manual typewriters.

9 Palacio de la Antigua Escuela de Medicina

Brasil 33, cnr of Venezuela. **Map** 4 E1. **Tel** (55) 56 23 31 23. M Zócalo, Allende. **Open** 9am–6pm daily. W **pem.facmed.unam.mx**

Now home to the Museum of Medicine of the National University (UNAM), the Palacio de la Inquisición stands on the site of the building in which the Holy Inquisition carried out its fearsome interrogations from the late 16th- century onward. The building today dates from the 18th century and underwent restoration in the 1970s. It is notable for its Baroque facade – unusually set on the corner of the building – and for its graceful main courtyard. There are "hanging" arches in each corner of the courtyard, with the supporting pillars set into the wall behind. A typical 19th-century apothecary's store, transferred in its entirety from Oaxaca, is one of the museum's more unusual features. It has displays on the history of Mexican medicine from pre-Columbian times, including sacred and medicinal plants and their uses.

10 Museo José Luis Cuevas

Academia 13. **Map** 4 F2. **Tel** (55) 55 42 61 98. M Zócalo. **Open** 10am–6pm Tue–Sun. Sun free. reserve in advance. W **museojoseluiscuevas.com.mx**

Formerly the cloisters of the Santa Inés convent, this 17th-century jewel was converted to private dwellings in the 19th century and declared a national monument in 1932. Since 1988 it has housed an art gallery reflecting the personal tastes of Mexican painter and sculptor José Luis Cuevas.

The exquisite patio is dominated by the massive bronze sculpture of *La Giganta* (*The Giantess*), which Cuevas created specifically for this space. A number of smaller bronzes by the artist are dotted around the ground floor. The galleries contain paintings by Cuevas and other Mexican artists, including a number of portraits of him and

Statue of *The Giantess* in the patio of the Museo José Luis Cuevas

his wife Bertha. There are also temporary exhibits by foreign artists. At the entrance to a small "dark room" dedicated to Cuevas' works of erotica, visitors are warned, tongue-in-cheek, of the dangers they pose to those of a puritan upbringing.

The doors of the ex-convent church of Santa Inés, next door to the museum, are carved with reliefs showing scenes from the life of the saint (including her beheading) and portraits of the founders of the convent kneeling in prayer.

Nearby, on the corner of La Santísima and Moneda, is the 18th-century **Iglesia de la Santísima Trinidad** (Church of the Holy Trinity), worth a visit for the paintings of the martyrs in the nave, two wooden sculptures representing the Trinity, and a crucifix inlaid with bone and precious woods.

Doorway of the Iglesia de la Santísima Trinidad

Facade of the Museo de la Ciudad de México

⓫ Museo de la Ciudad de México

Pino Suárez 30, cnr of República del Salvador. **Map** 4 E3. **Tel** (55) 55 22 99 36. Ⓜ Zócalo. **Open** 10am–6pm Tue–Sun. Wed free.

The palace of the counts of Santiago de Calimaya, long renowned for their ostentatious lifestyle, is regarded as one of the most outstanding 18th-century buildings in the city. Built in 1781, the palace is faced with red volcanic *tezontle* stone. Its Baroque portal and magnificent carved wooden doors convey the social standing of its former inhabitants. At the foot of the southwest corner, the builders incorporated a stone serpent's head, which was taken from a wall made up of similar heads that surrounded the Aztecs' ceremonial center.

The first courtyard is noteworthy for the fountain with its carving of a mermaid holding a guitar, and for the trilobate arches near the staircase. Also outstanding is the richly carved stone doorway to the first-floor chapel.

In the early 20th century, the painter Joaquín Clausell lived in the building. The walls of his studio, on the third floor, are covered with an unusual mural, consisting of a collage-like set of scenes influenced by the Impressionists that Clausell met when he was in France.

The building has been occupied by the Museum of Mexico City since the 1960s. However, at present the collection is limited mostly to furniture and carriages associated with the house and temporary exhibits.

⓬ Museo de la Charrería

Isabel la Católica 108, cnr of José María Izazaga. **Map** 4 D3. **Tel** (55) 57 09 47 93. Ⓜ Isabel la Católica. **Open** 10am–7pm Mon–Fri. reserve in advance. **fmcharreria.com**

Dedicated to the Mexican art of horsemanship, this museum is located in what was once a Benedictine chapel dedicated to the Virgin of Monserrat. The remains of the chapel date from the 18th century, and its facade is still intact.

Inside, the museum displays the fancy, silver-trimmed costumes of the *charro* and his female equivalent, along with a wide variety of artifacts associated with the culture of *charrería*. Included in the collection are ornate saddles, spurs, and guns, as well as several of the impressive competition trophies awarded to the most successful *charros*. Watercolors of *charrería* events, a model of a *charro* stadium *(lienzo)*, and brief historical descriptions of the development of the art help to put the collection in context.

⓭ Museo del Ejército y Fuerza Aérea Mexicanos

Filomeno Mata 6, cnr Tacuba. **Map** 4 D1. **Tel** (55) 55 12 32 15. Ⓜ Allende, Bellas Artes. **Open** 10am–6pm Tue–Sat, 10am–4pm Sun & hols. reserve in advance.

Housed in what was once the chapel of a 17th-century Betlemitas hospital, this museum is notable for the three dramatic relief sculptures in metal on the wall facing Calle Filomeno Mata. They were created for the Paris Exposition of 1889 by Jesús F. Contreras and represent the indigenous chieftains Izcóatl, Nezahualcóyotl, and Totoquihuatzin.

Inside the museum is another statue worthy of note, depicting the last Aztec emperor, Cuauhtémoc. The museum itself is dedicated to the long and eventful history of the Mexican armed forces from the Conquest to the 20th century. Exhibits include chain mail, horse armor, and a fascinating array of weapons.

Nearby, on Calle Tacuba, is the Café Tacuba *(see p314)*, a restaurant renowned for its excellent Mexican cuisine.

Charrería

Charrería is the Mexican art of horsemanship and the culture associated with it. The *charro* is akin to a US cowboy. He dresses in traditional costume and proves his skill and daring in the saddle at *charreadas* (rodeos), wielding a lasso on horseback. But *charros* are seldom working cowboys. More often they are well-off landowners who can afford their fancy costumes. *Charrería* is more than a display of equestrian talent, however, and a *charro* event is a social occasion in which food, drink, and music also play an important role.

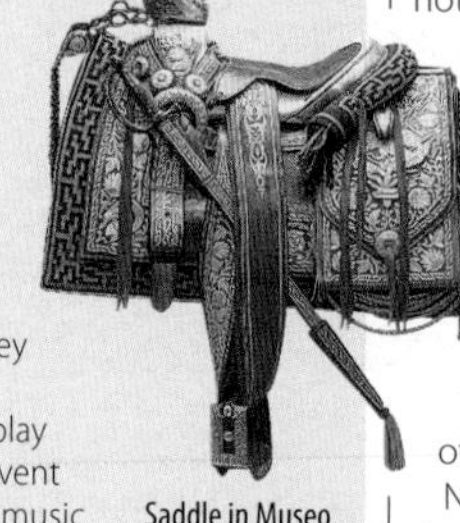

Saddle in Museo de la Charrería

⓮ Museo Nacional de Arte

Tacuba 8. **Map** 4 D1. **Tel** (55) 86 47 54 30. Ⓜ Allende. **Open** 10am–5:30pm Tue–Sun. reserve in advance. **munal.com.mx**

Created in 1982, the Museo Nacional de Arte is worth a visit for the building alone. An imposing, Neo-Classical piece of architecture, it was completed in 1911 as the Ministry of Communications and Public Works. Its double staircase, in bronze and marble, is enclosed by a semi-circular window three stories high. The interior, with its intricate ironwork and many candelabra, is sumptuous.

The museum's galleries encompass Mexican art from the 16th century to 1954. The collection includes commercial engravings, political cartoons, and folk art, as well as paintings. Much of the collection of religious art from the 16th to early 19th century resulted from confiscations following anti-clerical reform laws in the 1800s *(see p56)*. As well as works by the great muralists – Rivera, Siqueiros, and Orozco – the outstanding pieces include a series of landscapes by 19th-century painter José María Velasco. One room is devoted to portraits, including a depiction of the art-lover María Asúnsolo by David Alfaro Siqueiros.

Right in front of the museum is the Plaza Manuel Tolsá, centering on one of the city's favorite monuments – *El Caballito* (The Little Horse) is in reality a massive equestrian statue of Charles IV of Spain by Manuel Tolsá (1802).

Staircase in the Museo Nacional de Arte

⓯ Casa de los Azulejos

Francisco I. Madero 4. **Map** 4 D2. **Tel** (55) 55 12 78 24. Ⓜ Bellas Artes, Allende. **Open** 8am–10pm daily.

The 16th-century "House of Tiles" was originally the palace of the counts of Orizaba. The blue-and-white tiled exterior is attributed to a 1737 remodeling by the 5th countess, who is said to have imported the style from the city of Puebla, where she had been living previously. Now occupied by the Sanborns store *(see p119)* and restaurant *(see p314)* chain, the lovingly restored building conserves much of its original Mudéjar interior. The main staircase is decorated with waist-high tiling, and there is a mural on the first floor landing by José Clemente Orozco, entitled *Omniscience*, which was painted in 1925. On the upper floor it is worth taking note of the mirrors surrounded by elaborate gold frames containing the figures of angels and cherubs.

Window of Casa de los Azulejos

Across the street is the Iglesia de San Francisco, once part of the largest convent in New Spain, which had been built on the site of the Aztec Emperor Moctezuma's zoo. The church is entered via the Capilla de Balvanera, a chapel with a Churrigueresque facade and a decorated interior, but there is little left of interest inside.

Torre Latinoamericana at dusk

⓰ Torre Latinoamericana

Eje Central Lázaro Cárdenas and Francisco I. Madero. **Map** 4 D2. **Tel** (55) 55 18 74 23. Ⓜ Bellas Artes. **Open** 9am–10pm daily. **torrelatino.com**

Once Mexico's tallest building, this skyscraper rises 44 floors and its 183-m (600-ft) height boasts the best view of Mexico City – smog permitting. Completed in 1956, it has survived a number of earthquakes, notably that of 1985. In 30 seconds, its express elevators whisk visitors to the 37th floor. On the 38th floor is an exhibition devoted to the history of the tower. Two floors down, the Museo del Bicentenario covers post-colonial Mexico. A second elevator rises to a 42nd-floor viewing platform and a café. From here a spiral staircase leads to the open-air cage below the TV mast.

Street-by-Street: The Alameda Central

The Alameda takes its name from the *álamos*, or poplar trees, planted here in the late 16th century by the Viceroy Luis de Velasco. Originally only half the size, the park assumed its present dimensions only in the 18th century. Its many statues date mainly from the 1900s, although the central Baroque fountain has been there since the expansion of the Alameda under Viceroy Carlos Francisco de Croix (1766–71). The most imposing monument is the Hemiciclo a Juárez, a semi-circular monument with Doric pillars of Carrara marble, by the sculptor Lazanini.

A balloon seller in the park

⑲ Museo Franz Mayer
This museum houses what is probably the finest collection of applied and decorative arts in Mexico. Exhibits date from the 16th to the 19th century.

Palacio Postal, the main post office, has an elegant interior of wrought iron and marble, and houses a postal museum.

Iglesia de San Juan de Dios is an 18th-century church with an unusual concave facade.

LÁZARO CÁRDENA

AVENIDA MIGUEL HIDALGO

Reforma

⑱ Museo Nacional de la Estampa
The exhibits in this small gallery focus on Mexican graphic art and design, past and present.

AVENIDA JUÁREZ

Alameda Central

Hemiciclo a Juárez was inaugurated in 1910 when Mexico celebrated the centenary of its independence struggle.

0 meters 100
0 yards 100

⑰ ★ Palacio de Bellas Artes
The Art Nouveau facade of this theater is equalled only by its impressive Art Deco interior, with murals by some of the greatest Mexican artists of the 20th century.

◀ The imposing edifice of the Palacio Nacional, Plaza de la Constitucion

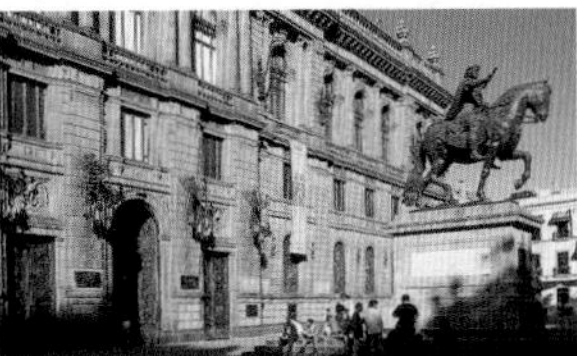

⓮ Museo Nacional de Arte
An equestrian statue of Charles IV guards the entrance to this collection of modern Mexican art. The building was constructed between 1904 and 1911.

REFORMA AND CHAPULTEPEC PARK
HISTORIC CENTER

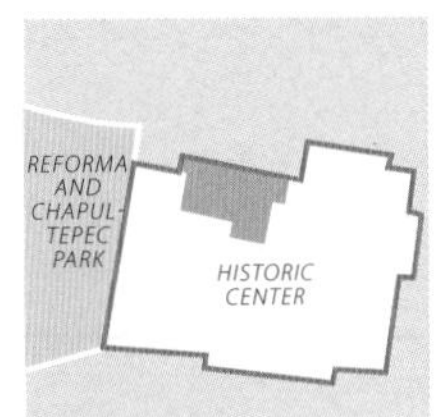

Locator Map
See Street Finder maps 3, 4

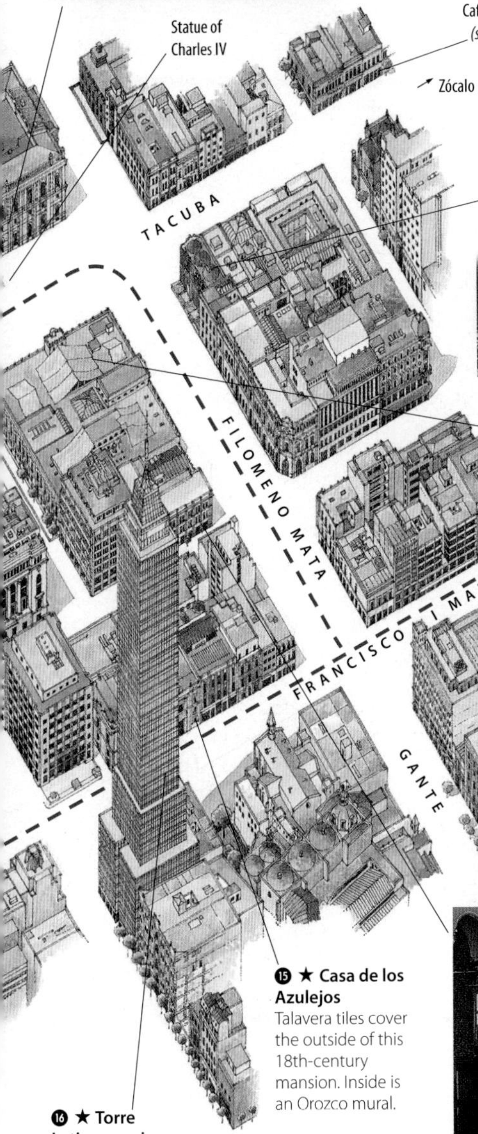

Statue of Charles IV
Café Tacuba
(see p314)
Zócalo
TACUBA
FILOMENO MATA
FRANCISCO I MADERO
GANTE

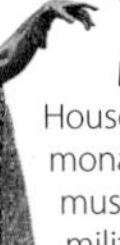

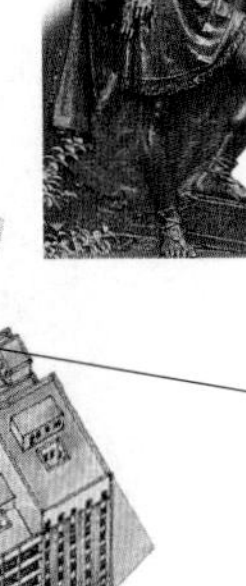

⓭ Museo del Ejército y Fuerza Aérea Mexicanos
Housed in a 17th-century monastery chapel, this army museum's weaponry and military memorabilia date from the conquest to the 20th century.

Palacio de Minería is one of the city's finest 19th-century Neo-Classical buildings.

Palacio de Iturbide, named after the Emperor Agustín de Iturbide *(see p56)*, is a superb example of colonial architecture.

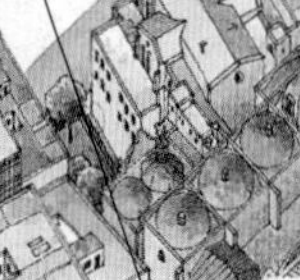

Key

— Suggested route

⓯ ★ Casa de los Azulejos
Talavera tiles cover the outside of this 18th-century mansion. Inside is an Orozco mural.

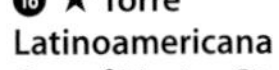

⓰ ★ Torre Latinoamericana
One of Mexico City's first skyscrapers, this was built in the 1950s and has survived many earthquakes.

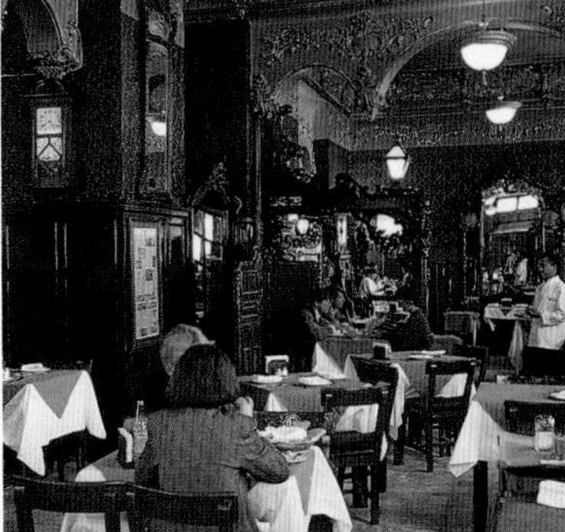

Bar La Ópera is an old-fashioned restaurant on 5 de Mayo. A legend says that a bullet hole in the ceiling was made by Pancho Villa *(see p58)*.

⓱ Palacio de Bellas Artes

Eje Central & Avenida Juárez. **Map** 3 C1. **Tel** (55) 55 12 25 93. Ⓜ Bellas Artes. **Open** 10am–5:45pm Tue–Sun. reserve in advance. Sun free. **w museopalaciodebellasartes.gob.mx**

Arguably the most beautiful building in the Historic Center, the Palacio de Bellas Artes was conceived in 1905 as a new national theater. Italian architect Adamo Boari designed an innovative building around a steel frame, incorporating Neo-Classical and Art Nouveau elements together with pre-Columbian decorative details.

The exterior of the building is clad in Italian marble and its cupolas are covered in tiles. The largest, central dome is surmounted by a Mexican eagle surrounded by figures representing the dramatic arts.

Interrupted by the revolution, the work was completed by Federico Mariscal in 1934. This accounts for the contrasting Art Deco interior, with its geometric shapes in colored marble and eye-catching illumination, especially the vertical lamps flanking the entrance to the auditorium.

The theater has a curtain that is a glass mosaic by Tiffany Studios of New York.

The impressive Art Deco interior of the Palacio de Bellas Artes

Pinoncelly's stained-glass skylight in the Museo Nacional de la Estampa

Said to comprise a million pieces of glass, it represents the Valley of Mexico with its volcanoes in the background and is based on a design by Gerardo Murillo ("Dr Atl"). On the second floor are two murals by Rufino Tamayo: *Birth of our Nationality* and *Mexico Today*, painted in 1952–3. The third floor includes David Alfaro Siqueiros' masterpiece of the same period, *New Democracy*. On the right-hand wall José Clemente Orozco painted *Catharsis*, whose theme is war and bourgeois decadence. With his work known as *Man, the Controller of the Universe*, Diego Rivera took his revenge on John D. Rockefeller, who had ordered the destruction of a similar mural at the Rockefeller Center in New York on ideological grounds. He portrays Rockefeller among the debauched rich at a nightclub, with the germs of venereal disease above them. The building also houses the Museo de Arquitectura.

⓲ Museo Nacional de la Estampa

Avenida Hidalgo 39. **Map** 3 C1. **Tel** (55) 55 21 22 44. Ⓜ Bellas Artes. **Open** 10am–5:45pm Tue–Sun. Sun free. reserve in advance. **w museonacionaldelaestampa.bellasartes.gob.mx**

Dedicated to the history of the graphic arts, this museum has an extensive collection, only part of which is on show at any one time.

Probably the best-known artist on display is José Guadalupe Posada (1852–1913). His enduring image of *La Calavera Catrina* – a well-dressed skeleton – is among the most familiar representations of the Mexican fascination with death. Posada's work featured in the popular satirical newspapers of his day.

In the Sala de Técnicas is a range of works illustrating the different techniques used by print artists. The building itself has a 1986 stained-glass skylight by Salvador Pinoncelly.

⓳ Museo Franz Mayer

Avenida Hidalgo 45. **Map** 3 C1. **Tel** (55) 55 18 22 66. Ⓜ Hidalgo, Bellas Artes. **Open** 10am–5pm Tue–Fri, 10am–7pm Sat & Sun. Tue free. reserve in advance. **ingles.franzmayer.org.mx**

This is the richest collection of applied art to be found in Mexico City. Assembled by German financier and art collector Franz Mayer (1882–1975), it is housed in a two-story, 16th-century building that used to be a hospital. The museum has possibly the most beautiful courtyard in the Historic Center, featuring a delightful fountain.

The collection – which contains more than 8,000 pieces (as well as about 20,000 antique tiles) from Europe, the Far East and colonial Mexico – is highly varied. Exhibits include tapestries, high-relief wooden carvings of religious scenes, ceramics, and over 1,000 pieces of silverwork, and furniture. Among the most beautiful objects are a number of inlaid wooden chests. There are also some impressive wooden screens, one of which has a rendering of the conquest of Mexico City on one side and a partial view of the city in the colonial period on the reverse.

Talavera vase in the Museo Franz Mayer

This impressive collection of applied and decorative arts also has a number of outstanding examples of Mexican colonial-era paintings.

The attractive, leafy courtyard of the Museo Franz Mayer

⓴ Laboratorio Arte Alameda

Doctor Mora 7. **Map** 3 B1. **Tel** (55) 86 47 56 60. Ⓜ Hidalgo. **Open** 9am–5pm Tue–Sun. Sun free. reserve in advance. **artealameda.bellasartes.gob.mx**

This museum of contemporary art is located in the former convent and church of San Diego de Alcalá, built in the 16th century. From 1964 to 1999, the building housed the Pinacoteca Virreinal, a collection of religious art now displayed in the Museo Nacional de Arte *(see p79)*.

In 2000 the doors opened to the Laboratorio Arte Alameda. This art space is dedicated to showing major works by Mexican and international artists, and focusing on trans-disciplinary, temporary exhibits and events. With its cutting-edge shows, it hopes to interest new audiences in contemporary art and to raise the profile of Mexican artists.

㉑ Museo Mural Diego Rivera

Cnr of Colón and Plaza Solidaridad. **Map** 3 B1. **Tel** (55) 15 55 19 00. Ⓜ Hidalgo, Juárez. **Open** 10am–6pm Tue–Sun. Sun free. **museomuraldiegorivera.bellasartes.gob.mx**

This small gallery is built around one of muralist Diego Rivera's masterpieces, *Dream of a Sunday Afternoon in the Alameda Central*. Painted in 1947 for the dining room of the nearby Hotel Prado, it combines Mexico's history with the dreams of its protagonists and the recollections of the artist. He includes two self-portraits, and an image of his wife, the painter Frida Kahlo.

The three-sectioned colorful painting caused a stir when first unveiled. The phrase "God does not exist" was removed by Rivera after a Christian group defaced the mural.

㉒ Museo de Arte Popular

Revillagigedo 11. **Map** 3 C2. **Tel** (55) 55 10 22 01. Ⓜ Juárez. **Open** 10am–6pm Tue–Sun (to 9pm Wed). Sun free. **map.df.gob.mx**

Located one block south of Parque Alameda inside an Art Deco building, the Museo de Arte Popular brings together folk art from all over Mexico. It includes contemporary and traditional pieces made from many different materials, reflecting the country's cultural and geographical diversity. Colorful indigenous costumes and religious art are especially well represented.

The Museo Mural Diego Rivera – home to the artist's great *Dream of a Sunday Afternoon in the Alameda Central*

PASEO DE LA REFORMA AND BOSQUE DE CHAPULTEPEC

In the 1860s, during the short-lived reign of the Emperor Maximilian *(see p57)*, a grand avenue was laid out between the City of Mexico and the Bosque de Chapultepec. This broad, elegant, tree-lined boulevard, the Paseo de la Reforma, is now flanked by tall modern office buildings. Little evidence remains of the mansions with which Reforma was lined at the turn of the century, but statues and fountains still adorn the avenue, including the golden Angel of Independence, the symbol of Mexico City.

South of the Paseo is the Zona Rosa, a lively area of cafés and nightclubs, popular with the gay and lesbian community. Beyond the Zona Rosa are Roma and, farther south, La Condesa, trendy residential neighborhoods with art galleries, hip restaurants, and boutiques.

Once the residence of the Aztec emperors, the Bosque de Chapultepec, at the western end of the avenue, has been a public park since 1530. The castle on the top of the hill at its northeastern end was also Maximilian's home. Today, with its lakes, zoo, and cafés, the Bosque de Chapultepec is a very pleasant place to escape the city. Just north of the park is the upscale neighborhood of Polanco, the place for high-end shopping and restaurants.

Sights at a Glance

Historic Buildings

3 Monumento and Museo de la Revolución
8 Castillo de Chapultepec

Museums and Galleries

2 Museo Nacional de San Carlos
4 Museo de Cera and Museo Ripley
5 Sala de Arte Público Siqueiros
6 Museo Rufino Tamayo
7 Museo de Arte Moderno
10 Museo Nacional de Antropología

Parks

9 Bosque de Chapultepec

Streets

1 Paseo de la Reforma

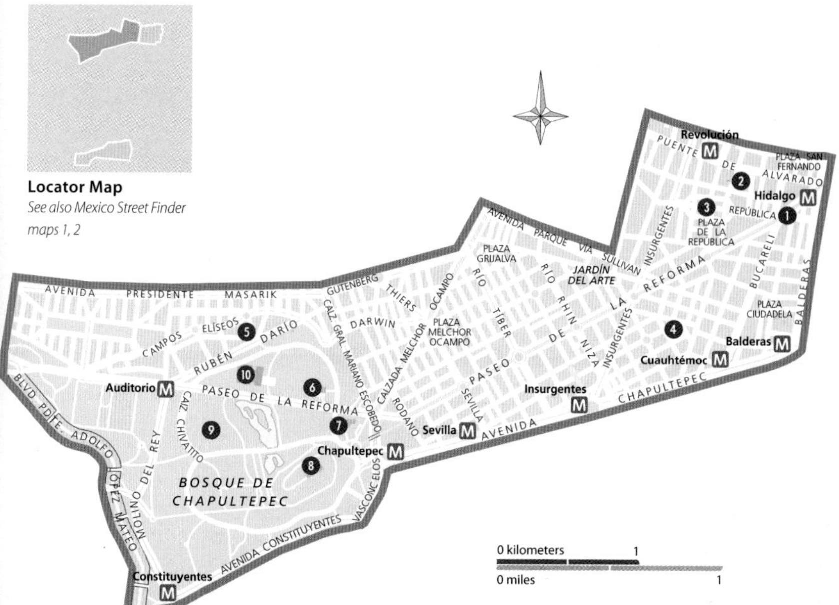

Locator Map
See also Mexico Street Finder maps 1, 2

◀ Stained Glass Gallery at Chapultepec Castle in Mexico City

For keys to symbols *see back flap*

❶ Paseo de la Reforma

The 3.5-km (2-mile) stretch of Reforma, which links the center of the city with Chapultepec, was once lined with beautiful houses. These have now given way to less stately hotels and office blocks, as well as to the Torre Reforma skyscraper, the tallest building in Mexico. Paseo de la Reforma remains, however, an outstanding city street. The monuments that adorn its *glorietas*, or traffic circles, have a special place in the affection of the locals. Between the Caballito and the Angel is a series of smaller statues, commissioned in the 19th century, which commemorate prominent Mexicans from each state. A number of contemporary installations also line the street, including some works that double as benches.

Monumento a la Independencia
Popularly known as the Angel of Independence, this figure was created by Antonio Rivas Mercado and was erected in 1910. It commemorates the heroes of the struggle against Spanish colonial rule *(see p53)*.

Diana Cazadora
The bronze figure of Diana the huntress, by Juan Fernando Olaguíbel (1896–1971), was once thought to offend public decency. At the request of the city authorities she was covered up, but only temporarily.

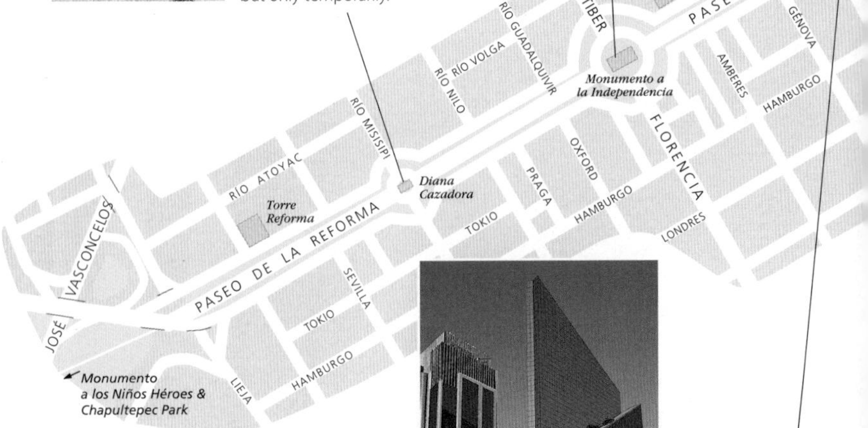

Río Rhin
Río Sena
US Embassy
Hotel Sheraton
Paseo de
Río Tiber
Génova
Río Guadalquivir
Río Volga
Río Nilo
Monumento a la Independencia
Amberes
Hamburgo
Río Misisipi
Florencia
Oxford
Río Atoyac
Diana Cazadora
Praga
Torre Reforma
Hamburgo
Paseo de la Reforma
Tokio
Londres
José Vasconcelos
Sevilla
Tokio
Hamburgo
Lieja
Monumento a los Niños Héroes & Chapultepec Park

Bolsa de Valores
Mexico City's stock exchange is in a futuristic building, which has a glass-domed dealing floor. This is flanked by a pencil-slim glass tower which houses offices.

0 meters 250
0 yards 250

San Hipólito
Built on the site of a 16th-century chapel, the Baroque church of San Hipólito is decorated with relief sculptures in the Mudéjar style.

Monumento a la Revolución
Porfirio Diaz's unfinished congress building was turned into a monument to the Revolution by those who ousted him *(see p57)*.

Cámara Nacional de Comercio

Monumento a Cuauhtémoc
A fusion of Classical and pre-Columbian styles, this monument honors the struggle of the last Aztec emperor against the Spanish invaders. Dating from 1887, it was designed by Francisco Jiménez.

El Caballito
The Caballito (Little Horse), a sculpture beside the Torre del Caballito, is one of the city's landmarks.

Zona Rosa
A triangle of partly pedestrianized streets south of Reforma, the "Pink Zone" is the hub of the gay and lesbian scene and packed with bars and nightclubs.

Lotería Nacional
The National Lottery building, designed by José A. Cuevas and completed around 1936, includes details of Art Deco craftsmanship *(see p29)*.

❷ Museo Nacional de San Carlos

Puente de Alvarado 50. **Map** 3 A1. **Tel** (55) 86 47 58 00. Ⓜ Hidalgo, Revolución. **Open** 10am–6pm Tue–Sun. Sun free. reserve in advance. **W mnsancarlos.com**

Occupying an imposing 19th-century Neo-Classical edifice, this museum has the largest collection of European art in Mexico. The bulk of the collection consists of paintings spanning the 14th to the early 20th century, including notable examples of the Flemish, French, Italian, and Spanish schools. Among the highlights are engravings by Goya and sculptures by Rodin. The collections were assembled by the San Carlos Academy of Mexico, established by the Spanish King Charles III in 1783.

Galleries on the upper floor house the permanent collection. Pride of place at the entrance is given to *La Encarnación*, a stunning gilded altarpiece dating from 1465, by Pere Espallargues.

At one time the building was home to a "museum of strange objects," but this was later moved to the Museo del Chopo, a twin-towered Art Nouveau structure. Built between 1903 and 1905, toward the end of the dictatorship of Porfirio Díaz *(see p57)*, this steel-framed museum was known for many years as the "crystal palace," because of its resemblance to the famous London building of that name.

The impressive Monumento a la Revolución in the Plaza de la República

❸ Monumento and Museo de la Revolución

Plaza de la República. **Map** 3 A1. **Tel** (55) 55 92 20 38. Ⓜ Revolución. **Open** noon–8pm Mon–Thu, noon–10pm Fri & Sat, 10am–8pm Sun. reserve in advance. **W mrm.mx**

The striking dome-topped cube that is the Monumento a la Revolución was originally designed as part of a parliament building under the dictator Porfirio Díaz. Due to unanticipated problems with the marshy ground, it was never completed. Then, in 1932, as an alternative to demolishing it, the architect Carlos Obregón Santacilia proposed that it be converted into a monument celebrating the 1910 revolution that put an end to the *porfiriato*. Stone cladding and sculptures were added, and the remains of revolutionary heroes such as Francisco Villa were interred at the base of the columns. The austerity of the monument's functional and Art Deco styling is relieved by details in bronze. The statues, sculpted by Oliverio Martínez de Hoyos, represent independence, the 19th-century liberal reform, and the post-revolutionary agrarian and labor laws.

At the base of the monument is a museum dedicated to the 50-year period from the expulsion of the French in 1867 to the 1917 revolutionary constitution. The exhibits on display range from photographs, documents, and reproductions of period newspapers to carriages, clothing, and contemporary artifacts.

Rear facade and gardens of the Museo Nacional de San Carlos

❹ Museo de Cera and Museo Ripley

Londres 6. **Map** 2 F3. **Tel** (55) 55 46 37 84. Ⓜ Insurgentes, Cuauhtémoc. **Open** 11am–7pm daily. **W** **museodecera.com.mx**

Housed in a striking Art Nouveau mansion that was designed by architect Antonio Rivas Mercado, the Museo de Cera (wax museum) is an entertaining trip through Mexican history and culture. One room contains effigies of every Mexican president since 1920. Other rooms feature personalities as diverse as Emiliano Zapata, the comedian Mario Moreno (Cantinflas), and soap opera star Verónica Castro. A robot of tenor Plácido Domingo sings an operatic aria, while in the dungeons below the torture victims groan and scream.

A sports car covered in coins in the Museo Ripley

Adjacent is the Ripley's Believe it or Not! museum of the bizarre, containing everything from a copy of the Mona Lisa made from pieces of toast to the ever-popular calf-with-two-heads. Those of a delicate disposition should avoid the tunnel that imitates the physical effects of an earthquake.

❺ Sala de Arte Público Siqueiros

Tres Picos 29. **Map** 1 A3. **Tel** (55) 86 47 53 40. Ⓜ Auditorio, Polanco. **Open** 10am–6pm Tue–Sun. Sun free. reserve in advance. **W** **saps-latallera.org**

This was the home and studio of the celebrated Mexican muralist David Alfaro Siqueiros. Just weeks before his death in 1973 he bequeathed it, with all its contents, to the nation. The painter's life and work are represented here by a collection that includes finished works as well as drawings, plans, models, and photo-montages of his many murals. There is also a selection of photographs and documents charting the events of Siqueiros' life, which was singularly eventful. It included two prison terms, one of which was for his part in a plot to kill Leon Trotsky *(see p107)* – Siqueiros had been a supporter of Stalin. In spite of this, his painting was popular, and in the 1940s and 1950s the state commissioned him to produce several works.

The ground-floor gallery is the site of the 1970's mural entitled *Maternity*, which was originally designed for a school. A ramp leads to the upper floor and the galleries which contain paintings by Siqueiros. The second-floor gallery is devoted to the work of other artists, both foreign and contemporary Mexican.

Murals on display at Sala de Arte Público Siqueiros

Modern interior of the Museo Rufino Tamayo

❻ Museo Rufino Tamayo

Cnr of Paseo de la Reforma & Gandhi. **Map** 1 B4. **Tel** (55) 52 86 65 19. Ⓜ Chapultepec. **Open** 10am–6pm Tue–Sun. Sun free. reserve in advance. **W** **museotamayo.org**

The outstanding collection of modern painting and sculpture assembled by one of Mexico's foremost 20th-century artists, Rufino Tamayo, and his wife Olga, occupies a stunning futuristic, concrete-and-glass building which is set among the trees of Chapultepec Park *(see pp92–3)*. The building was designed by renowned Mexican architects Teodoro González de León and Abraham Zabludovsky, and was awarded the National Prize for Architecture in 1981.

Sculpture at the Museo Rufino Tamayo

Housed within this light and airy gallery are some 800 paintings in all, as well as drawings, sculptures, and graphic art. There are also a number of paintings by Rufino Tamayo himself. Among the many other modern artists in the collection are Willem de Kooning, Andy Warhol, Salvador Dalí, and René Magritte. The museum also has a variety of temporary exhibitions.

❼ Museo de Arte Moderno

Cnr of Paseo de la Reforma & Gandhi. **Map** 1 B4. **Tel** (55) 86 47 55 30. Ⓜ Chapultepec. **Open** 10:15am–5:30pm Tue–Sun. Sun free. **W museoartemoderno.com**

A wide range of 20th-century Mexican painting and sculpture is housed in this gallery of modern art. The collection includes works by all the well-known figures – Rufino Tamayo, Diego Rivera, David Alfaro Siqueiros, and Frida Kahlo – as well as artists who do not belong to the mainstream established by the muralists and others since the Revolution. Foreign artists, such as Leonora Carrington, who have worked in Mexico, are also represented.

The museum has a fine array of oils by Tamayo and several works by Francisco Toledo, his fellow Oaxacan. Among the other highlights are Frida Kahlo's *The Two Fridas*, Diego Rivera's portrait of Lupe Marín, and *Las Soldaderas* by José Clemente Orozco. Contemporary artists in the collection include Alberto Castro Leñero, Irma Palacios, and Emilio Ortiz.

Sculptures are exhibited in the gardens, and the adjacent circular gallery has temporary exhibitions of modern Mexican and international art.

❽ Castillo de Chapultepec

Bosque de Chapultepec. **Map** 1 A5. **Tel** (55) 40 40 52 14. Ⓜ Chapultepec. **Open** 9am–5pm Tue–Sun. Sun free for Mexican citizens and residents, children, teachers, and seniors. **W mnh.inah.gob.mx**

The hill that forms the highest point of the Bosque de Chapultepec once stood on the lake shore across the water from Tenochtitlán *(see p98)*. On its summit stands this 18th-century castle, now housing the Museo Nacional de Historia. A crucial battle was fought here in 1847, when army cadets died trying

❾ Bosque de Chapultepec

A favorite weekend recreational spot for residents of Mexico City, Chapultepec has been a public park since the 16th century. Its tree-shaded paths are lined with vendors selling everything from Mexican snacks to balloons and cotton candy for children. Its attractions include a zoo, a boating lake, a number of museums and galleries, and often, live, open-air entertainment. There is also a botanical garden that dates from the earliest days of the republic. It is well worth making the climb up to the castle terrace, from which the view across the city is stunning.

① **Auditorio Nacional** Mexico's national concert hall is a favored venue for arts events. In front of it stands this contemporary sculpture by Juan Soriano.

Boaters on Lago Chapultepec

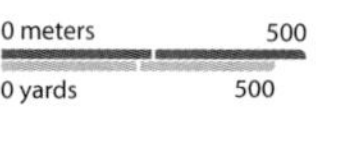

⑨ **"Papalote" Museo del Niño** This children's museum has over 400 interactive exhibits, organized into five themes: the human body, expression, the world, "Con-science," and communication. A giant video screen shows educational movies. There is also an Internet room.

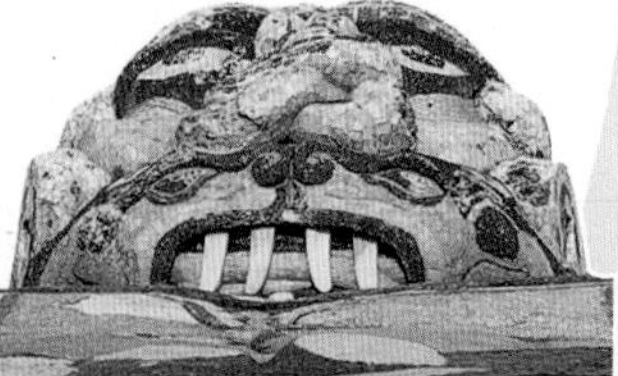

⑧ **Fuente de Tláloc** This fountain was designed by muralist Diego Rivera. Tlaloc was the central Mexican rain deity *(see p269)*, and one of the most important gods in the pantheon.

The historic Castillo de Chapultepec

to defend the fortress against invading US troops. In the 1860s, the castle became the palace of Emperor Maximilian *(see p57)*. Subsequently it was an official residence for presidents of the republic. The museum covers Mexican history from the Conquest to the Revolution; exhibits include items relating to historical figures. The eyeglasses of Benito Juárez and the rifles used in the execution of Maximilian are all on display.

The walls of the museum are decorated with large murals showing historical events. The most striking of these is Siqueiros' *From the Porfiriato to the Revolution*.

In the castle's grounds is the Galería de Historia, known as the Museo del Caracol (the "Snail Museum") because of its shape. In it, the visitor is guided through a series of dioramas illustrating scenes from the struggle for independence up to the Revolution.

② Sala de Arte Público Siqueiros
The house of muralist David Alfaro Siqueiros is now a museum displaying his paintings, and documents relating to his life *(see p91)*.

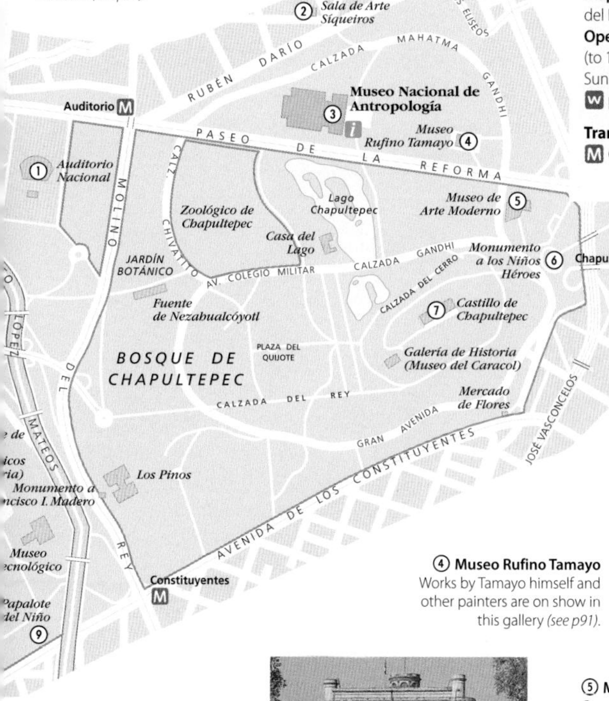

② *Sala de Arte Siqueiros*
CAMPOS ELISEOS
MAHATMA GANDHI
CALZADA
RUBÉN DARÍO
Auditorio
③ **Museo Nacional de Antropología**
Museo Rufino Tamayo ④
PASEO DE LA REFORMA
① *Auditorio Nacional*
MOLINO
CALZ. CHIVATITO
Zoológico de Chapultepec
Lago Chapultepec
Casa del Lago
Museo de Arte Moderno ⑤
Monumento a los Niños Héroes ⑥
Chapultepec
JARDÍN BOTÁNICO
AV. COLEGIO MILITAR
CALZADA GANDHI
CALZADA DEL CERRO
⑦ *Castillo de Chapultepec*
Fuente de Nezahualcóyotl
BOSQUE DE CHAPULTEPEC
PLAZA DEL QUIJOTE
Galería de Historia (Museo del Caracol)
Mercado de Flores
CALZADA DEL REY
GRAN AVENIDA
JOSÉ VASCONCELOS
AVENIDA DE LOS CONSTITUYENTES
Los Pinos
Monumento a Francisco I. Madero
Museo Tecnológico
Papalote Museo del Niño ⑨
Constituyentes
LÓPEZ MATEOS
DEL REY

VISITORS' CHECKLIST

Practical Information
Map 1 B4. "Papalote" Museo del Niño: **Tel** (55) 52 37 17 73.
Open 9am–6pm Mon–Fri (to 11pm Thu), 10am–7pm Sat, Sun.
papalote.org.mx

Transport
Chapultepec.

③ Museo Nacional de Antropología One of the city's main attractions, this museum has a world-famous collection of ancient relics. Several hours are needed to do it justice *(see pp94–9)*.

④ Museo Rufino Tamayo
Works by Tamayo himself and other painters are on show in this gallery *(see p91)*.

⑤ Museo de Arte Moderno
Opened in 1964, this museum has a collection of works by 20th-century Mexican artists.

⑥ Monumento a los Niños Héroes
This monument honors the army cadets ("boy heroes") who died defending the castle in 1847 *(see p56)*.

⑦ Castillo de Chapultepec
Once the residence of Mexican rulers, including the Emperor Maximilian and the president Lázaro Cárdenas, this castle enjoys views of the park and of the Paseo de la Reforma.

⑩ Museo Nacional de Antropología

Inaugurated in 1964, the vast and airy National Museum of Anthropology by Pedro Ramírez Vázquez is a just setting for a world-renowned collection of finds from Mexico's pre-Columbian cultures. The museum's large, central patio is almost entirely covered by an 84-m (275-ft) long canopy which is balanced on an 11-m (36-ft) pillar. This canopy is considered to be the largest concrete structure in the world supported by a single pillar.

The courtyard with bronze conch shell sculpture beside the pond

★ Olmec Heads
Two of the massive, basalt heads for which the Olmecs *(see p258)* are best known stand close together in the Gulf Coast gallery. Found at San Lorenzo *(see p257)*, they may be portraits of high-ranking people.

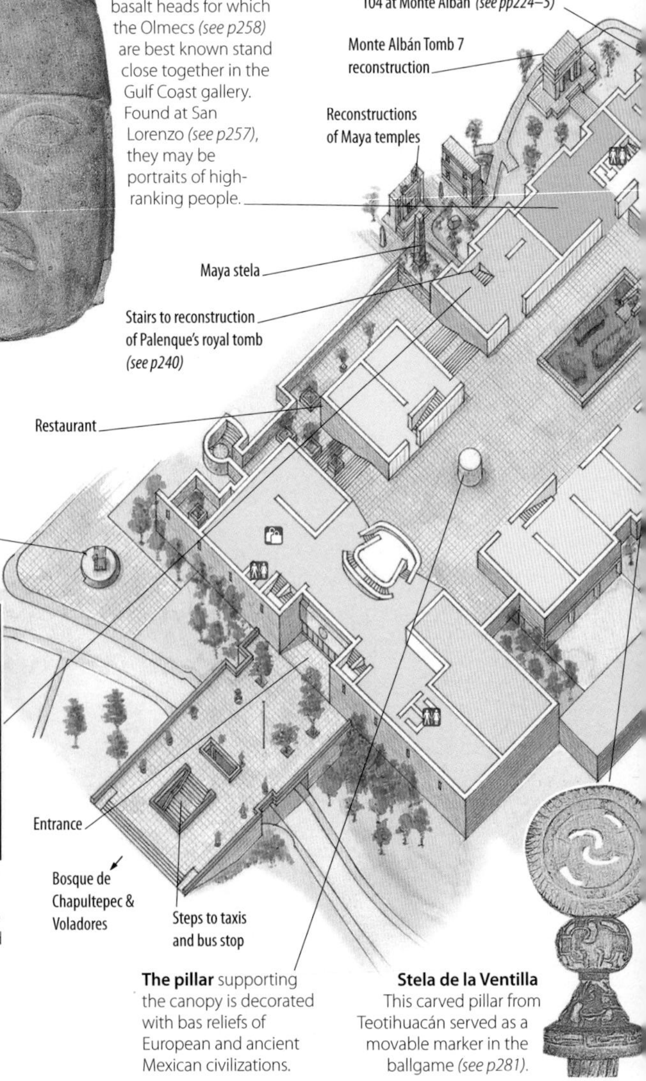

Stairs to reconstruction of Tomb 104 at Monte Albán *(see pp224–5)*

Monte Albán Tomb 7 reconstruction

Reconstructions of Maya temples

Maya stela

Stairs to reconstruction of Palenque's royal tomb *(see p240)*

Restaurant

A giant statue of a rain deity, either Chalchiuhtlicue or Tlaloc *(see p269)*, stands near the museum's entrance.

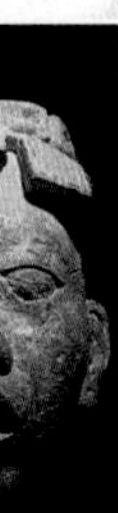

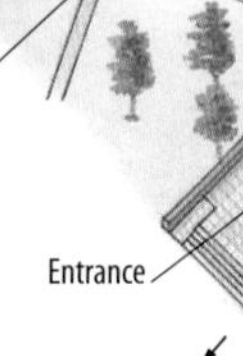

Entrance

Bosque de Chapultepec & Voladores

Steps to taxis and bus stop

Head of a young man from Palenque
This distinctive, life-size carved head was found among offerings in the tomb at the base of the Temple of the Inscriptions at the Classic Maya site of Palenque.

The pillar supporting the canopy is decorated with bas reliefs of European and ancient Mexican civilizations.

Stela de la Ventilla
This carved pillar from Teotihuacán served as a movable marker in the ballgame *(see p281)*.

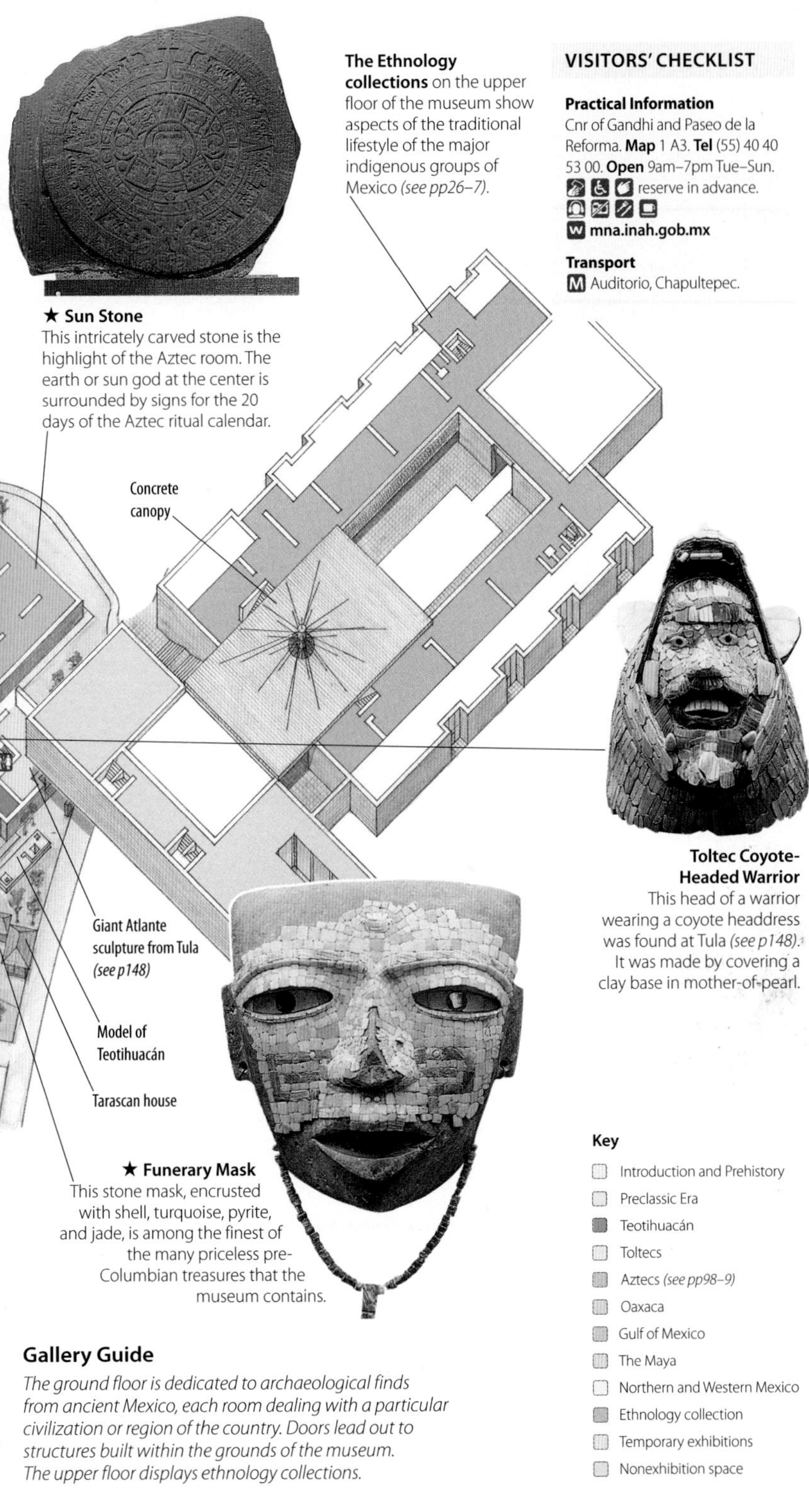

The Ethnology collections on the upper floor of the museum show aspects of the traditional lifestyle of the major indigenous groups of Mexico *(see pp26–7)*.

★ Sun Stone
This intricately carved stone is the highlight of the Aztec room. The earth or sun god at the center is surrounded by signs for the 20 days of the Aztec ritual calendar.

Toltec Coyote-Headed Warrior
This head of a warrior wearing a coyote headdress was found at Tula *(see p148)*. It was made by covering a clay base in mother-of-pearl.

★ Funerary Mask
This stone mask, encrusted with shell, turquoise, pyrite, and jade, is among the finest of the many priceless pre-Columbian treasures that the museum contains.

VISITORS' CHECKLIST

Practical Information
Cnr of Gandhi and Paseo de la Reforma. **Map** 1 A3. **Tel** (55) 40 40 53 00. **Open** 9am–7pm Tue–Sun.
reserve in advance.
mna.inah.gob.mx

Transport
Auditorio, Chapultepec.

Gallery Guide

The ground floor is dedicated to archaeological finds from ancient Mexico, each room dealing with a particular civilization or region of the country. Doors lead out to structures built within the grounds of the museum. The upper floor displays ethnology collections.

Key

- Introduction and Prehistory
- Preclassic Era
- Teotihuacán
- Toltecs
- Aztecs *(see pp98–9)*
- Oaxaca
- Gulf of Mexico
- The Maya
- Northern and Western Mexico
- Ethnology collection
- Temporary exhibitions
- Nonexhibition space

Exploring the Museo Nacional de Antropología

The twelve galleries on the ground floor are all accessible from the central patio, so that a tour can begin wherever the visitor likes. Although the first seven galleries are in chronological order, covering the history of the central plateau, the following five galleries visit the various regions of Mexico, including one dedicated to the great civilization of the Maya. The upper floor is devoted to a collection of costumes, houses, and artifacts of the 56 surviving indigenous cultures in Mexico as well as exploring aspects of their religion, social organization, and festivals.

Detail from the reconstruction of the Temple of Quetzalcoatl facade

Introductory Galleries

The first three galleries present an introduction to the study of anthropology, and an outline of the historical development of Mesoamerica *(see pp48–9)*, which ran from what is now northern Mexico down to western Honduras and El Salvador. An account of the prehistoric origins of the indigenous Mesoamerican cultures helps set the rest of the museum in context.

Preclassic Era

Beginning with the earliest agricultural settlements in the central plateau around 1700 BC, the Preclassic gallery illustrates the rise of more complex cultures, shown in particular detail through the development of the ceramic arts. Outstanding among the collection are a number of figures influenced by the Olmecs *(see p258)* from the Gulf of Mexico, including the "jaguar-boy" found at Tlapacoya in Mexico state. There is also a reconstruction of an intact burial site from Tlatilco in Mexico state, in which the skulls exhibit the cranial deformation and filed teeth that are typical of that period.

Teotihuacán

Centered on the mysterious, ancient city that the Aztecs dubbed "the place where men became gods," the culture of Teotihuacán *(see pp138–41)* was among the most important of the Classic era in Mesoamerica.

Imposing geometric sculpture of the water-goddess Chalchiuhtlicue

The gallery is dominated by the huge stone statue of the water-goddess, Chalchiuhtlicue. Along one wall a reconstruction of the facade of the Temple of Quetzalcoatl, reproduces the original blues and reds with which it was painted. Colorful murals of Teotihuacán life adorn the gallery's side walls.

Some of the finest pieces are less monumental. They include a wide variety of pottery vessels for domestic use, such as grain and water storage urns, figurines, and funerary masks showing a talent for lapidary, and obsidian carvings. The inhabitants of Teotihuacán, whose culture reached its height between 100 BC and AD 800, were experts in fashioning shiny black obsidian knives. There are also statues that illustrate aspects of the religious way of life in Teotihuacán.

Toltecs

As Teotihuacán declined, other cities of the central plateau, Tula in particular, rose to prominence. The founders of Tula *(see p148)* were the Chichimecas from the north, who adopted the name Toltecs, meaning "artists." They soon acquired a reputation as specialists in the military arts. The most noticeable exhibit is a gigantic stone warrior figure known as an Atlante, with which the Toltecs are most commonly associated. These figures were used as pillars in their temples.

The Toltec gallery also includes items from other cities of the Postclassic period, including Xochicalco in Morelos, which more properly belong to the Teotihuacán

One of the original Atlantes sculptures from Tula *(see p148)*

Crude Toltec pottery work

tradition. Notable among these exhibits are stone carvings dedicated to the god Quetzalcoatl, and the stylized head of a macaw, which was perhaps used as a ball-court marker. Xochicalco's most famous monument, the serpent frieze around the base of the temple of Quetzalcoatl, is beautifully illustrated with a photographic mural.

Oaxaca

Following on from the Aztec Hall *(see pp98–9)*, this is the first gallery dedicated to the regions of Mexico. It presents the artifacts of the two great peoples of Oaxaca: the Zapotecs, builders of the hilltop city of Monte Albán, and their neighbors and successors the Mixtecs, who created Mitla, with its stone friezes.

On display are polychrome ceramic pieces from both cultures. In the garden is a reconstruction of a Monte Albán tomb. Both peoples were skilled in the art of jewelry, and there are many examples here.

Gulf of Mexico

Among the most spectacular, and the best-known of all the museum's exhibits are the extraordinary colossal stone heads from the Preclassic Olmec culture, which flourished from 1200 to 600 BC. The Olmecs also produced smaller, but equally remarkable, sculptures of heads and figures in a variety of types of stone, most of them with the characteristic Olmec features of broad, flat-nosed faces and thick lips, curled downward.

Huastec sculpture of the god Xilonen

The Olmecs share this gallery with the Totonacs from central Veracruz and the Huastecs from the northern shores of the Gulf. The best-known creations of the Totonacs are the carved stone "yokes," the purpose of which is still not fully understood. The Huastecs were some of the finest artists of Mesoamerica, particularly in their use of clay, bone, and shell.

Stela from Yaxchilán showing a Maya ruler, circa AD 800

The Maya

There is no doubting the special hold of the Maya on the imagination of visitors to Mexico, whether because of the intricate beauty of their great stone cities in the jungle, such as Palenque in Chiapas *(see pp238–41)*, or the continuing mystery of their sudden decline, before the arrival of the Spanish conquistadors.

Among the highlights of the Maya gallery are carved stelae, such as the one from Yaxchilán, lintels from the Classic period, and a particularly outstanding carved head of a young man, found at Palenque. A small, underground gallery contains a reconstruction of the royal tomb of Pakal found beneath Palenque's Temple of the Inscriptions. It also displays artifacts from the site, including high-quality stucco heads. The outside garden features several reconstructions of Maya ceremonial buildings, together with a group of other sculptures and stelae.

Northern and Western Mexico

The sparsely inhabited northern deserts never produced the great civilizations characteristic of central and southern Mexico. Nonetheless, the ceramic art from Paquimé *(see p174)* – the most notable of the so-called Oasis cultures – has a distinctive elegance, with its geometric patterns, smooth-polished surfaces and adornments such as copper or turquoise. The gallery also contains examples of metalwork, and models of the unique multi-story adobe houses of Casas Grandes.

At the height of the Aztec (Mexica) empire, the Tarascans (Purépechas), the dominant culture of the Pacific coast, retained their independence, and with it a distinctive artistic tradition. This gallery provides evidence of their skill in metal-working (they were among the first in the region to use gold, silver, and copper for jewelry and utensils), and in pottery.

Other items of particular note include the polished earthenware from Classic-era Colima, and the ceramics of the cloisonné technique using different colored clays, which is thought to have originated there.

Colima earthenware

Ethnology Collection

The eleven interconnected galleries on the top floor of the museum, beginning with Gallery 13, are devoted to all aspects of Mexican ethnology, including housing, costumes, artifacts, religions, social structures, and the festivals of the 58 surviving indigenous cultures of Mexico.

The Aztec Hall

The largest gallery in the museum displays the treasures of the Mexica culture – better known as the Aztecs. When Hernán Cortés and his conquistadors arrived in 1519 *(see p47)*, the Aztecs ruled most of what is now Mexico, either directly or indirectly. This gallery gives the visitor a strong sense of the everyday culture of the Aztec people, the power and wealth of their theocratic rulers, and their enormous appetite for blood, sacrifice, war, and conquest.

Realistic stone head, possibly representing the common man

Large Sculptures

The entrance landing and central section of the gallery are devoted to large stone sculptures. Near the entrance is the Ocelotl-Cuauhxicalli, a 94-cm (3-ft) high stone vessel in the form of a jaguar-eagle. It was used as a receptacle to hold the hearts of human sacrificial victims. A statue of Coatlicue, the mother of Coyolxauhqui and later of Huitzilopochtli *(see p74)*, is one of the few representations of the goddess in Aztec art. This statue shows her with eagle's claws, a dress made of snakes, and a necklace of hearts and hands. She has been decapitated, and two serpents emanate from her neck to symbolize blood.

Other large sculptures here are of the goddesses Coyolxauhqui and Cihuateteoa, small-scale representation of a *teocalli* or temple, and a *tzompantli*, an altar of skulls from the Templo Mayor. On the wall opposite the door, dominating the gallery, is the Sun Stone.

The Aztec People and their History

The section to the right of the entrance describes the Aztec people, their physical appearance and their history. The most conspicuous piece here is a carved round stone, known as the Stone of Tizoc, which records the victories of

The Lake City of Tenochtitlán

The Aztecs' capital city, Tenochtitlán, was built on an island in a shallow lake. Stone causeways connected the city to the shore of the lake, and an aqueduct brought fresh water. Temples and other civic and ceremonial buildings stood at the center of the city (sacred precinct), around what is now the Zócalo *(see pp66–7)*. This area was surrounded by a great wall.

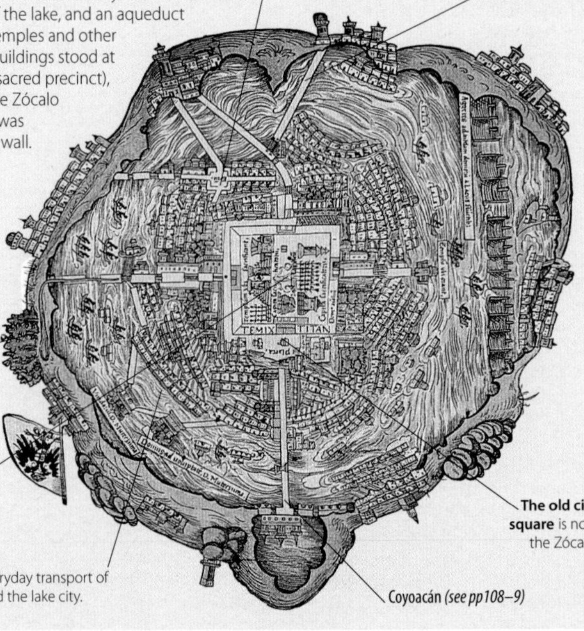

Tlatelolco and the Plaza de las Tres Culturas *(see p112)*.

Causeways connected the city to the lake shore.

Bosque de Chapultepec *(see pp92–3)*

Ceremonial center and Templo Mayor

The old city square is now the Zócalo.

Canals were used for everyday transport of goods and people around the lake city.

Coyoacán *(see pp108–9)*

Tizoc, the seventh ruler of the Aztecs (1481–6). This trachyte stone was found in the Zócalo. Another object of interest is a stone head with inset teeth and eyes to add to its realism. It is thought to represent the common man. Other sculptures represent everyday Aztec people, including a statue of a Mexica noble dressed in robes appropriate to his rank.

This part of the museum includes a model of the temple complex that stood at the center of Tenochtitlán. Surrounded by a wall, the complex focused upon the Templo Mayor topped by its twin shrines. The rounded temple in front of the Templo Mayor was dedicated to the god Quetzalcoatl. Above the model hangs a large painting by Luis Covarrubias showing the city as it may have looked when first seen by the Spanish.

The Sun Stone

Often mistakenly referred to as the Calendar Stone, this basaltic disk was unearthed in the Zócalo in 1790. The carvings describe the beginning of the Aztec world and foretell its end. The Aztecs believed they were living in the fifth and final "creation" of the world. Each creation was called a sun. The stone is 3.6 m (12 ft) in diameter and weighs 24 tonnes.

The central god could be the sun god Tonatiuh or the earth god Tlaltecuhtli.

The 20 days of the Aztec month are shown on the inner band.

Two fire serpents run around the rim of the stone, their tails meeting at the date of creation.

Four square panels around the center indicate that the previous suns (creations) were destroyed by jaguars, wind, rain, and water.

Polished obsidian statue of a monkey god

Sacred Objects

The display cases to the left of the entrance show items used for religious purposes by the Aztecs. One of the most interesting pieces is a vase in the form of a pregnant monkey, carved out of obsidian, a hard black, volcanic stone akin to glass. This vase symbolizes the wind loaded with black rain clouds which will engender growth and fertility. Also on display here is the stone altar on which human sacrificial victims were stretched in order to remove their hearts. Other items include solar disks, sacrificial knives, and representations of various deities.

Other Exhibits

Aspects of Aztec daily life are described in other parts of the hall. There are notable collections of craft objects. The ceramics section shows plates, vases, masks, and other items, many with decorative work. Pieces of Aztec jewelry made out of bone, gold, wood, crystal, and shells are displayed, while their clothing includes animal skins and feathers. The musicality of the Aztecs is shown with a range of instruments, such as flutes and whistles. A wooden drum *(huehuetl)* is finely carved with a warring eagle and vulture.

Along the back wall are documents and drawings explaining the system of tribute that sustained the Aztec economy. Here there is also a diorama of the market in Tlatelolco, part of Tenochtitlán, showing a scene of pots, food, and other goods being bought and sold.

Aztec shield made out of animal hide and feathers

SAN ÁNGEL AND COYOACÁN

At the time of the Spanish conquest, Coyoacán ("place of the coyotes") was a small town on the shore of Lake Texcoco. It was connected to the Aztec capital of Tenochtitlán, an island in the lake, by a causeway. After conquering Tenochtitlán, Hernán Cortés set up his headquarters here in 1521 while the city was rebuilt along Spanish lines.

Nearby San Ángel was then a village called Tenanitla, where Dominican and Carmelite friars chose to settle after the conquest. It became known as San Ángel in the 17th century, after the foundation of the convent-school of San Angelo Mártir. Its official name today is Villa Álvaro Obregón, but this is rarely used.

Until the 20th century both San Ángel and Coyoacán were rural communities well outside Mexico City. The growth of the metropolis has since swallowed them up, but both retain a good deal of their original colonial architecture. Much favored as a place of residence by artists and writers, many of whom prefer the relative tranquillity of San Ángel and Coyoacán to the bustle nearer the city center, they are also popular with families for weekend day trips.

Some of the area's famous inhabitants in the past have included Diego Rivera, Frida Kahlo, and Russian revolutionary Leon Trotsky. The latter was assassinated in Coyoacán in August, 1940. The former homes of all three are among the area's attractions, along with a number of museums and art galleries. Restaurants and specialty shops abound, and there are popular weekend craft markets in the Jardín Centenario (in Coyoacán) and the Plaza San Jacinto (in San Ángel).

Sights at a Glance

Museums and Galleries

3 Museo de El Carmen
4 Museo Estudio Diego Rivera
5 Museo de Arte Carrillo Gil
8 Museo de la Acuarela
9 Museo Frida Kahlo/La Casa Azul
10 Museo Casa de León Trotsky

Churches

6 Iglesia de San Antonio Panzacola

Streets and Squares

2 Plaza San Jacinto
7 Avenida Francisco Sosa
11 *Coyoacán* *see pp108–9*

Walks

1 *San Ángel to Coyoacán* *see pp102–3*

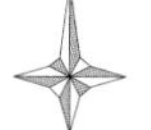

Locator Map

0 meters 500
0 yards 500

Key

••• Walk route

◀ Sculpture of saint surrounded by colorful handmade tiles, Coyoacán

❶ A Walk from San Ángel to Coyoacán

Few parts of Mexico City can boast a domestic architecture of the colonial and pre-revolutionary eras as well-preserved as that of Coyoacán and San Ángel. This walk connects the two squares at the heart of these districts, both of which are well-known in the city for their weekend craft fairs. The walk often follows tree-lined, cobbled streets. Along the way are churches, museums, art galleries, and monuments, as well as some picturesque places to stop for a meal.

The domes of the Museo de El Carmen in San Ángel

Iglesia de San Jacinto, on the main square of San Ángel

Sights on Walk

① Plaza San Jacinto
② Museo de El Carmen
③ General Álvaro Obregón
④ Plaza Federico Gamboa
⑤ San Antonio Panzacola
⑥ Avenida Francisco Sosa
⑦ Museo Nacional de la Acuarela
⑧ Plaza Santa Catarina
⑨ Jardín Centenario

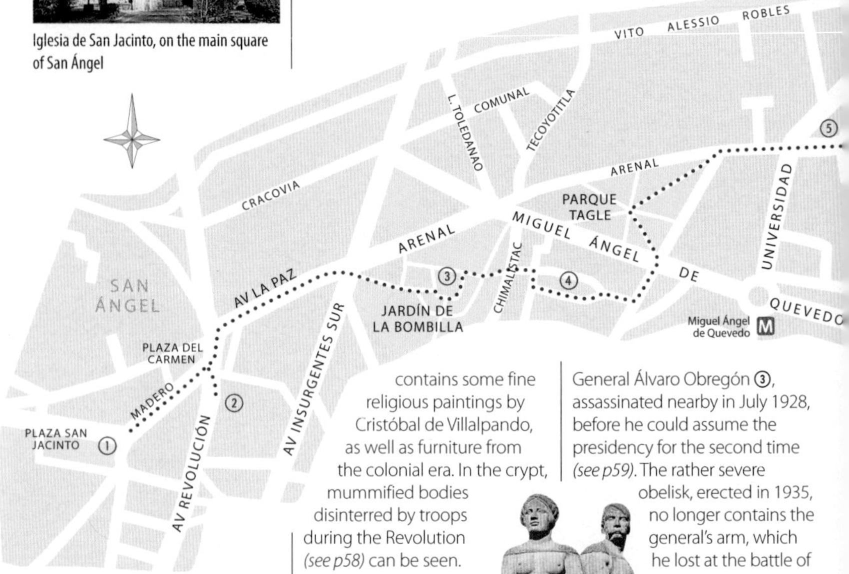

VITO ALESSIO ROBLES
COMUNAL
L. TOLEDANAO
TECOYOTITLA
CRACOVIA
ARENAL
PARQUE TAGLE
MIGUEL ÁNGEL DE QUEVEDO
UNIVERSIDAD
CHIMALISTAC
JARDÍN DE LA BOMBILLA
Miguel Ángel de Quevedo
SAN ÁNGEL
AV LA PAZ
PLAZA DEL CARMEN
MADERO
PLAZA SAN JACINTO
AV REVOLUCIÓN
AV INSURGENTES SUR

San Ángel

Leave Plaza San Jacinto ① *(see p104)*, a pleasant square with numerous restaurants, by Calle Madero. At the end of this road you will pass the Centro Cultural San Ángel on your right. On reaching Avenida Revolución, turn right and cross over to reach the Museo de El Carmen ② *(see p104)*. The church of this former monastery has three tiled domes that are the symbol of San Ángel. The museum contains some fine religious paintings by Cristóbal de Villalpando, as well as furniture from the colonial era. In the crypt, mummified bodies disinterred by troops during the Revolution *(see p58)* can be seen. On leaving the church, turn right and walk along Revolución then right again into the cobbled street of Avenida La Paz where there are some good but rather pricey restaurants.

Chimalistac

Cross Avenida Insurgentes and will you come to the Jardín de la Bombilla, the small, wooded park that surrounds the monument to General Álvaro Obregón ③, assassinated nearby in July 1928, before he could assume the presidency for the second time *(see p59)*. The rather severe obelisk, erected in 1935, no longer contains the general's arm, which he lost at the battle of Celaya. The granite sculptures that flank the monument are the work of Ignacio Asúnsolo (1890–1965). Cross Calle Chimalistac and walk along a lane to Plaza Federico Gamboa ④. This square (which is also known as Plaza Chimalistac) is named after a writer and politician of the *porfiriato (see p57)*. The chapel of San Sebastián

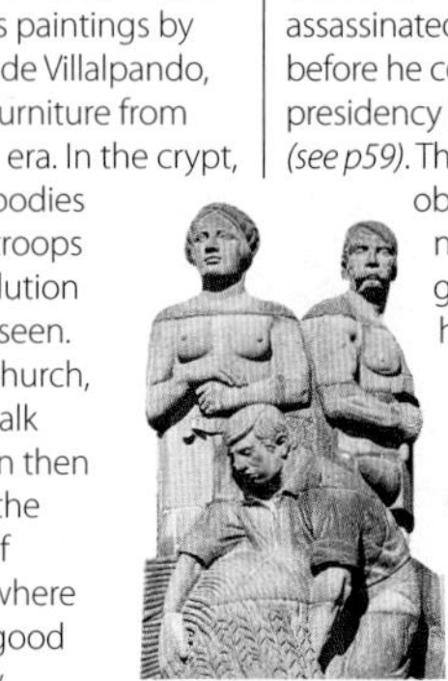
Detail of Monumento a Álvaro Obregón

Chimalistac, dating from the 17th century, sits crosswise in the square. It is notable, among other things, for a stunning Baroque altarpiece with 18th-century religious paintings. San Sebastián was one of the few open chapels in Mexico City. The atrial cross which stands in front of it is a relic of the days when mass was celebrated in the outdoors.

Jazz by Angel Mauro Rodríguez in Museo de la Acuarela

On leaving the square, turn left and walk along Ignacio Allende, a narrow street, until you reach Miguel Ángel de Quevedo. Cross this to stroll in Parque Tagle. Once through the park, bear right into Calle Arenal. Walk along this quiet street until you reach the bustling Avenida Universidad.

Avenida Francisco Sosa

Directly across Universidad stands the chapel of San Antonio Panzacola ⑤ *(see p105)*, a tiny jewel of a church dating from the 17th century. Next to the chapel is an old stone bridge over a tributary of the Río Magdalena. Cross this and you come to one of the prettiest streets in the city. Avenida Francisco Sosa ⑥ *(see p106)* is also one of the oldest colonial streets in Latin America. Take the first turn on the right down Calle Salvador Novo for a short detour to visit a gallery of watercolor paintings, the Museo Nacional de la Acuarela ⑦ *(see p106)*. Halfway along Francisco Sosa you come to the enchanting Plaza Santa Catarina ⑧ where story-tellers gather on Sunday lunchtimes. The main building on the square is a lovely yellow church with a triple-arched façade. Opposite the chapel is the Casa de la Cultura Jesús Reyes Heroles, a university arts center with a beautiful, leafy garden. At the end of Francisco Sosa you arrive at the twin arches of what was once the gateway into the convent of San Juan Bautista. This then leads into the pleasant square of Jardín Centenario ⑨ at the heart of Coyoacán *(see pp108–9)*.

Tips for Walkers

Starting point: Plaza San Jacinto, San Ángel. **Length:** 3.5 km (2 miles)
Places to eat: Plaza San Jacinto, Avenida La Paz, Plaza Santa Catarina, Jardín Centenario.
Metro station: Miguel Ángel de Quevedo.

Archway on Jardín Centenario, in the center of Coyoacán

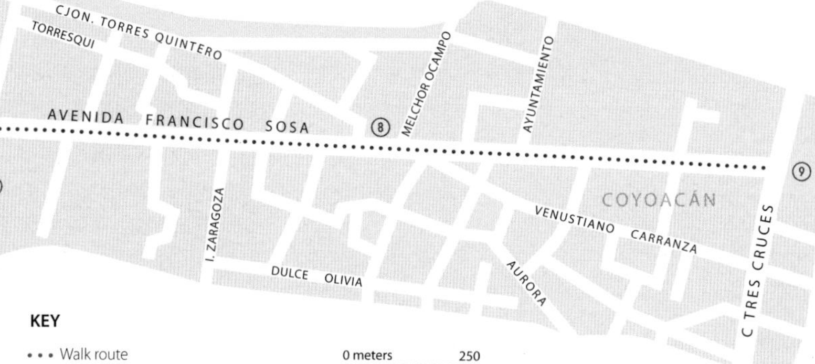

KEY

• • • Walk route

M Metro station

0 meters 250
0 yards 250

The charming Iglesia de Santa Catarina on the square of the same name

❷ Plaza San Jacinto

San Ángel. Ⓜ Miguel Ángel de Quevedo.

On Saturdays this square, which forms the center of San Ángel, is an excellent place to shop for Mexican handicrafts, either at the outdoor stalls or in the El Bazaar Sábado, which is located in a 17th-century house in the northwest corner.

The 16th-century Iglesia de San Jacinto, just off the square, was originally annexed to a Dominican monastery of the same name. The church has a fine dome. In the interior, the carved wooden screen, and the onyx font in the nave are both worth seeing.

The most impressive building on the north side of the square is the Casa del Risco, also known as the Casa del Mirador, a well-preserved, 18th-century house built for the Marqués de San Miguel de Aguayo and donated to the nation in 1963. Constructed around an interior courtyard with an extravagant fountain, the house contains a wealth of colonial furniture and decor.

On the square's west side is a plaque commemorating the soldiers of the Irish-American San Patricio batallion who died fighting for Mexico against the United States in 1846–7.

Courtyard of the Museo de El Carmen

❸ Museo de El Carmen

Avenida Revolución 9. **Tel** (55) 56 16 11 77. Ⓜ Miguel Ángel de Quevedo. **Open** 10am–5pm Tue–Sun. Sun free. **museodeelcarmen.gob.mx**

The Carmelite monastery-school of San Angelo Mártir, built in 1615, gave its name to the San Ángel district. The three beautiful domes that rise above it, elaborately decorated with colorful tiles, are still a symbol of the area. Later the monastery and its church became known as El Carmen. Today it serves as a museum of furniture, paintings, and other artistic and historical objects from the colonial period. Much of the original interior is preserved, including the monks' cells. In the crypt a dozen mummified bodies, which were disinterred by troops during the Revolution *(see p53)*, are displayed in glass-topped coffins. Decorative details include Talavera tiles from Puebla and carved, painted ceilings. The chapel on the first floor contains an 18th-century gold-painted altarpiece inset with oil paintings of saints. Other highlights to look out for in the museum are a series of religious paintings by the 18th-century master Cristóbal de Villalpando and a richly carved door with symbols representing the Virgin Mary.

Dazzling main altarpiece in the church of the Museo de El Carmen in San Ángel

Diego Rivera's workshop, surrounded by a cactus hedge

❹ Museo Estudio Diego Rivera

Corner of Calle Diego Rivera and Altavista. **Tel** (55) 86 47 54 70. Ⓜ Viveros, Barranca del Muerto. **Open** 10am–6pm Tue–Sun. Sun free. for a fee. **estudiodiegorivera.bellasartes.gob.mx**

One of the most outstanding 20th-century architects of Mexico, Juan O'Gorman, built these twin houses in 1931–2 for two of the country's most distinguished painters, Diego Rivera and Frida Kahlo. Surrounded by a cactus hedge, the houses are connected by a rooftop bridge, over which Frida used to take Diego his meals. *The Two Fridas* and several other of her renowned works were painted here. Behind her house is a building her father used as a photographic studio.

The large living room/studio in Rivera's house contains an assortment of his personal belongings, from paintbrushes to huge, papier-mâché skeletons and pre-Columbian pottery. Other rooms are devoted to temporary exhibitions.

Located across the street is the San Ángel Inn *(see p317)*, an elegant restaurant, with a beautiful garden popular with Mexico's elite. Built in 1692, it was originally a Carmelite monastery. After 1915 it was turned into a restaurant and today it is known for its excellent Mexican cuisine and its string of famous patrons, among them Brigitte Bardot, Henry Kissinger, and Richard Nixon.

❺ Museo de Arte Carrillo Gil

Avenida Revolución 1608. **Tel** (55) 55 50 62 60. Ⓜ Miguel Ángel de Quevedo. **Open** 10am–6pm Tue–Sun. Sun free. reserve in advance.
museodeartecarrillogil.com

This light and airy gallery on three floors has temporary exhibitions and sometimes shows the collection of art that embraces some of the finest 20th-century Mexican artists. Founded in 1974, the collection was assembled by Dr. Alvar Carrillo Gil and his wife and includes works by Diego Rivera, José Clemente Orozco, and David Alfaro Siqueiros. Among the Rivera canvases are a number of works from the artist's Cubist period. Less well-known, but equally interesting, are paintings by Austrian Wolfgang Paalen (1905–1959) and German Gunther Gerzso, a contemporary artist.

Dr. Carrillo, who studied medicine in Paris, began supporting avant-garde artists in his native Mexico from the late 1930s onward, by purchasing their works and through published criticism. He was himself a painter of some note, and a close friend of Orozco.

Not far from the museum, near the corner of Revolución and La Paz, is the well-known San Ángel flower market. You can pick up anything here, from an extravagant arrangement to a single rose at any time of the day or night. It is an especially fine sight at night, when the flowers glow under the artificial lights.

The red facade of the Capilla de San Antonio Panzacola

Colorful display of blooms on a stall in the San Ángel flower market

❻ Iglesia de San Antonio Panzacola

Corner of Avenida Universidad and Avenida Francisco Sosa. Ⓜ Miguel Ángel de Quevedo, Viveros.

This tiny 17th-century chapel originally belonged to the nearby parish church of San Sebastián Chimalistac *(see p102)*. It sits next to a miniature stone bridge over a stream at the end of Avenida Francisco Sosa *(see p106)*. Painted a striking dark red color, with reliefwork in a contrasting creamy white, its facade includes a niche containing a statue of St. Anthony. Above the arched entrance is a relief sculpture of St. Sebastian the martyr. The arch is flanked by pilasters supporting a molded entablature. The undulating roofline ends in twin towers and has a cross in its center.

The frontage of Casa Alvarado, one of the residences on Avenida Francisco Sosa

❼ Avenida Francisco Sosa

Between San Ángel and Coyoacán.
Ⓜ Miguel Ángel de Quevedo.

Mexico City's most attractive street is also one of the oldest colonial streets in Latin America. Running approximately 1.5 km (just under a mile) between Avenida Universidad and the Jardín Centenario in Coyoacán *(see pp108–9)*, it is lined with handsome residences.

At the beginning of it stands the quaint, 17th-century chapel of San Antonio Panzacola *(see p105)*. Continuing down the street there are a number of very attractive residences including the Casa de la Campana (No. 303) and No. 319, which has a replica Atlante *(see p148)* outside it. No. 383 is another interesting colonial house, thought to have been constructed in the 18th century by Pedro de Alvarado, the Spanish conqueror of Mexico and Guatemala. The house next door belonged to his son. About halfway along the avenue is the pleasant Plaza Santa Catarina. On this square stand a church and the Casa de la Cultura Jesús Reyes Heroles, a pleasant colonial-style building with patios and well-tended gardens. It houses a cultural center for art and literary events. A short way farther along is the cultural department of the Italian embassy. At the end of the street, on the corner of Jardín Centenario in Coyoacán, is the 18th-century Casa de Diego de Ordaz.

❽ Museo Nacional de la Acuarela

Salvador Novo 88. **Tel** (55) 55 54 18 01
Ⓜ Miguel Ángel de Quevedo.
Open 10am–6pm daily.
acuarela.org.mx

Dedicated primarily to some of the finest works by Mexican watercolor artists from the 19th century to the present day, this museum is located in a small, two-story house set in a pretty garden.

The larger part of the collection consists of works by contemporary artists, including many winners of the Salón Nacional de la Acuarela annual prize for watercolors. Embracing a wide range of styles and subject matter, it may surprise those who think of watercolors primarily in terms of delicate landscapes. Two outstanding canvases are *La Carrera del Fuego* and *Jazz,* both by Ángel Mauro Rodríguez, which can be seen on display on the ground floor of the museum.

There is an international room containing a selection of paintings by artists from all over the Americas, as well as Spain and Italy, including US artists Robert Wade and Janet Walsh. A separate gallery in the garden outside houses temporary exhibitions.

The Museo Nacional de la Acuarela, home to a collection of watercolors

Frida Kahlo (1907–54)

Arguably Mexico's most original painter, Frida Kahlo led a troubled life. A childhood bout of polio left her right leg slightly withered. Then, when she was 18, she broke her back in a traffic accident which rendered her incapable of having children. The pain she suffered for much of her life is reflected in many of her often violent and disturbing paintings, particularly her self-portraits. In 1929 she married the muralist Diego Rivera. Rivera was a notorious womanizer but Frida too had affairs, with both women and men – including Leon Trotsky. She and Rivera divorced in 1939, remarried the following year but thereafter lived separately.

Bronze statue of Frida Kahlo

9 Museo Frida Kahlo/La Casa Azul

Londres 247. **Tel** (55) 55 54 59 99. Coyoacán. **Open** 10am–5:45pm Tue, Thu–Sun, 11am–5:45 Wed. ground floor only. reserve in advance.
museofridakahlo.org.mx

Better known as Casa Azul (Blue House), this is where painter Frida Kahlo was born, lived much of her life, and died. She painted some famous works here, many inspired by the pain she suffered as a result of breaking her back.

This house is a treasure trove, not only of Frida's paintings, but also of many artifacts associated with her life and that of her lover Diego Rivera, with whom she shared the house. Donated to the nation by Rivera in 1955, not long after Frida's death, it is preserved much as it was when they lived there.

On display are letters and diaries as well as ceramics and other everyday items. A hand-written accounts book shows the couple's earnings and outgoings for March/April 1947, including the fee earned by Frida Kahlo for the famous painting *The Two Fridas*. One wall is covered with Rivera's collection of "*retablos*": small paintings created as religious offerings in gratitude for prayers answered. There are also giant paper "Judas" figures, burned on Easter Saturday as a symbolic destruction of evil forces *(see p34)*, as well as pre-Columbian art collected by Rivera. Frida's wheelchair and one of the corsets she had to wear constantly because of her disability are also on display.

The Assassination of Trotsky

The intellectual Leon Trotsky was born Lev Davidovich Bronstein, in Russia, in 1879. He played a leading role in the Bolshevik seizing of power in 1917 and in forming the Red Army to fight the Russian Civil War of 1918–20. But Lenin's death in 1924 led to a power struggle within the ranks of the victorious revolutionaries, and in 1927 Trotsky was forced into exile by his rival, Joseph Stalin. He was granted asylum in Mexico in 1937 but even across the Atlantic he was not safe from Stalin's purge of all his opponents. His house was assaulted in May 1940 by Mexican Stalinists led by the muralist David Alfaro Siqueiros and machine-gunned for 20 minutes. Then on August 20, 1940, he was fatally wounded by another assassin, Ramón Mercader, who pierced his skull with an icepick.

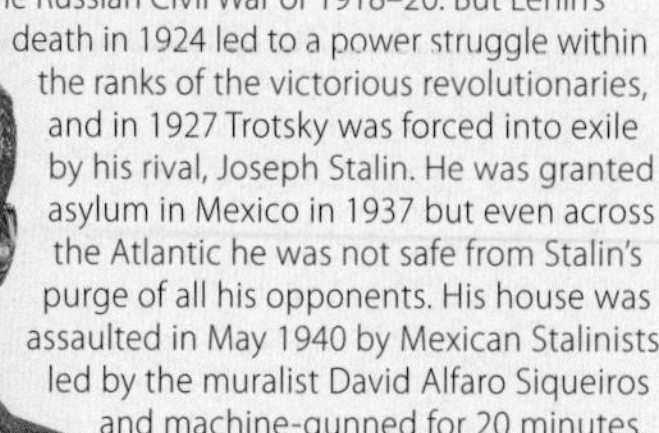
Bust of Leon Trotsky

10 Museo Casa de León Trotsky

Avenida Río Churubusco 410. **Tel** (55) 55 54 06 87. Coyoacán. **Open** 10am–5pm Tue–Sun.

Leon Trotsky, the Russian revolutionary, lived in this house from 1939 until his assassination in 1940. Before moving here he lived with the artists Diego Rivera and Frida Kahlo.

To frustrate would-be assassins, Trotsky fitted the windows and doors with armor-plating, raised the height of the surrounding wall, and blocked off most of the windows that overlooked the street, among other things. All this foiled one attempt on his life: about 80 bullet holes can still be seen in the outer walls.

However, these precautions did not stop Ramón Mercader, a regular visitor to the house, who had won his victim's confidence. The room where the murder took place is just as it was, complete with the chair and table where Trotsky was sitting when he died.

Trotsky's typewriter, books, and other possessions can be seen where he left them. One of the photographs on display shows him on his arrival in Mexico in 1937, standing on the quay in Tampico with his wife Natalia and Frida Kahlo.

Frida Kahlo's brightly colored kitchen with pottery on display

⓫ Street-by-Street: Coyoacán

Once the haunt of conquistador Hernán Cortés and his Indian mistress "La Malinche," the atmospheric suburb of Coyoacán is an ideal place for a stroll, especially on the weekend, when a lively craft fair operates in its two main squares, Jardín Centenario and Plaza Hidalgo. Packed with cafés, restaurants, and cantinas, its narrow streets retain much of their colonial-era charm. Calle Felipe Carrillo Puerto, heading south out of the plaza, is a good place to shop for curios. Coyoacán is also known in Mexico City for its delicious ice cream.

Casa de Cortés
The north side of Plaza Hidalgo is taken up by this distinctive 15th-century building, now used as government offices.

Indoor craft bazaar (open at weekends)

Cantina La Coyoacana *(see p120)*

FELIPE CARRILLO PUERTO

CABALLOCAL

ORTEGA

Avenida Francisco Sosa
This narrow, pretty street *(see p106)* leading to nearby San Ángel is a delight to stroll along. It is lined with handsome, well-maintained mansions which were built by wealthy families in colonial times.

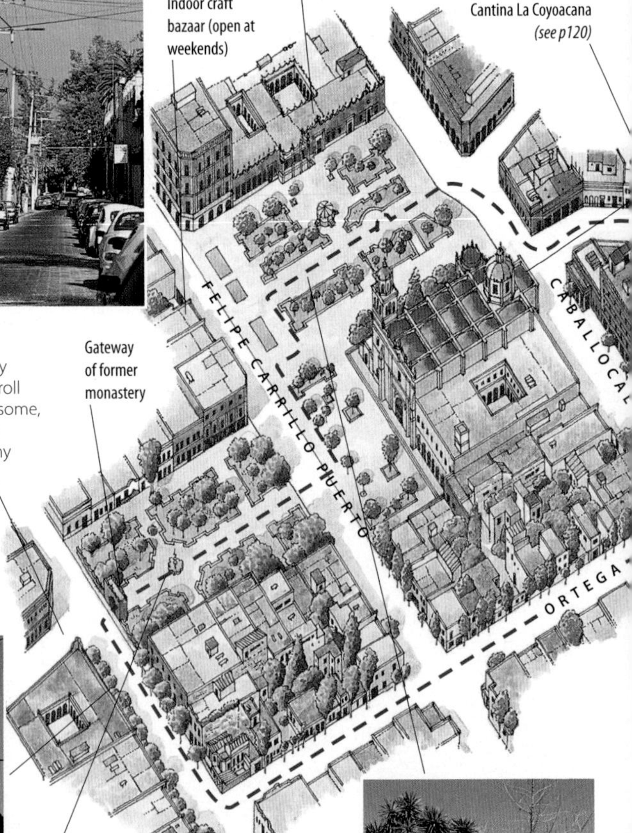

Gateway of former monastery

Jardín Centenario
was once the atrium of the monastery of San Juan Bautista, of which only the church remains.

Casa de Diego de Ordaz
While named after the conquistador Diego de Ordaz, the house dates only from the 18th century. At one corner is this ornate niche with a statue of the Virgin Mary.

Plaza Hidalgo
The Casa de Cortés faces the church of San Juan Bautista across this spacious square centering on a bandstand.

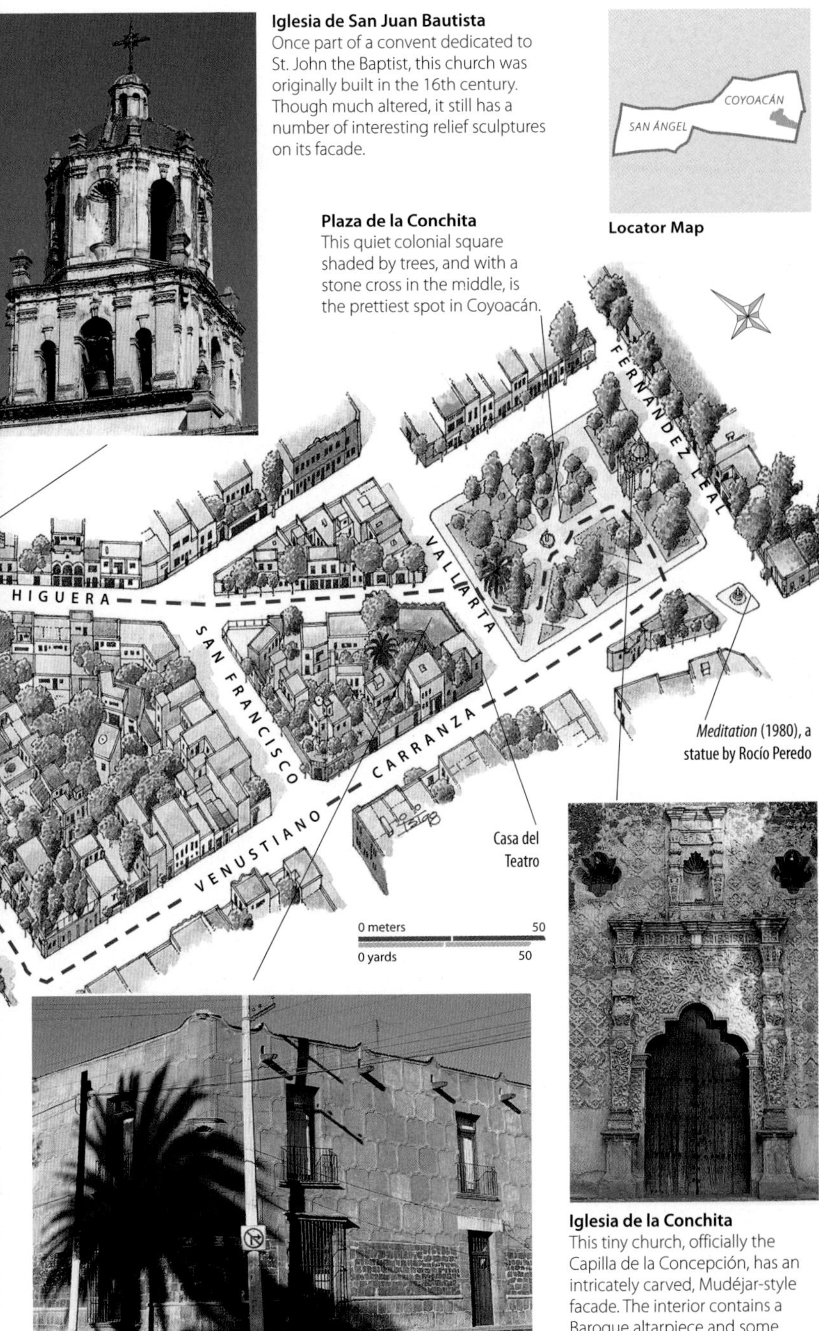

Iglesia de San Juan Bautista
Once part of a convent dedicated to St. John the Baptist, this church was originally built in the 16th century. Though much altered, it still has a number of interesting relief sculptures on its facade.

Locator Map

Plaza de la Conchita
This quiet colonial square shaded by trees, and with a stone cross in the middle, is the prettiest spot in Coyoacán.

Meditation (1980), a statue by Rocío Peredo

Casa del Teatro

Iglesia de la Conchita
This tiny church, officially the Capilla de la Concepción, has an intricately carved, Mudéjar-style facade. The interior contains a Baroque altarpiece and some outstanding colonial paintings.

Casa de la Malinche
Traditionally associated with Cortés' mistress "La Malinche," this 16th-century house was probably built for Ixtolinque, a local chieftain. Today it is the home of two well-known Mexican artists, Rina Lazo and Arturo García Bustos.

Key

▬ Suggested route

ROSITA
MARIA FERNANDA
ARTURITO
DIANA
MARIA
XOCHIMILCO
MAGICO

FARTHER AFIELD

There is plenty worth discovering in this massive, sprawling city beyond the Historic Center. Head north to the Plaza Garibaldi and you can be serenaded by *mariachis* or explore the nearby archaeological site of Tlatelolco, Tenochtitlán's twin city. The Basílica de Santa María de Guadalupe, the largest shrine to the Virgin Mary in all of the Americas, is even farther north, on the site where legend says she appeared in 1531. In the south, Xochimilco preserves the only remnant of Lake Texcoco and its pre-Columbian floating gardens. Boatmen will ferry you around its tree-lined canals. The 2,500-year-old pyramid of Cuicuilco, meanwhile, is thought to be the city's oldest structure.

Sights at a Glance

Museums and Galleries

6 Museo Nacional de las Intervenciones
7 Museo Anahuacalli
12 Museo Dolores Olmedo

Public buildings

8 Universidad Nacional Autónoma de Mexico (UNAM)

Squares and Markets

3 Plaza Garibaldi
4 Mercado de La Merced

Churches

1 Basílica de Santa María de Guadalupe

Historic Sites

2 Tlatelolco and Plaza de las Tres Culturas
9 Pirámide de Cuicuilco

Suburbs

10 Tlalpan
11 Xochimilco

Streets

5 Avenida Insurgentes Sur

Key

Main sightseeing areas
Parks and open spaces
Greater Mexico City
Highway
Major road
Minor road

0 kilometers 4
0 miles 4

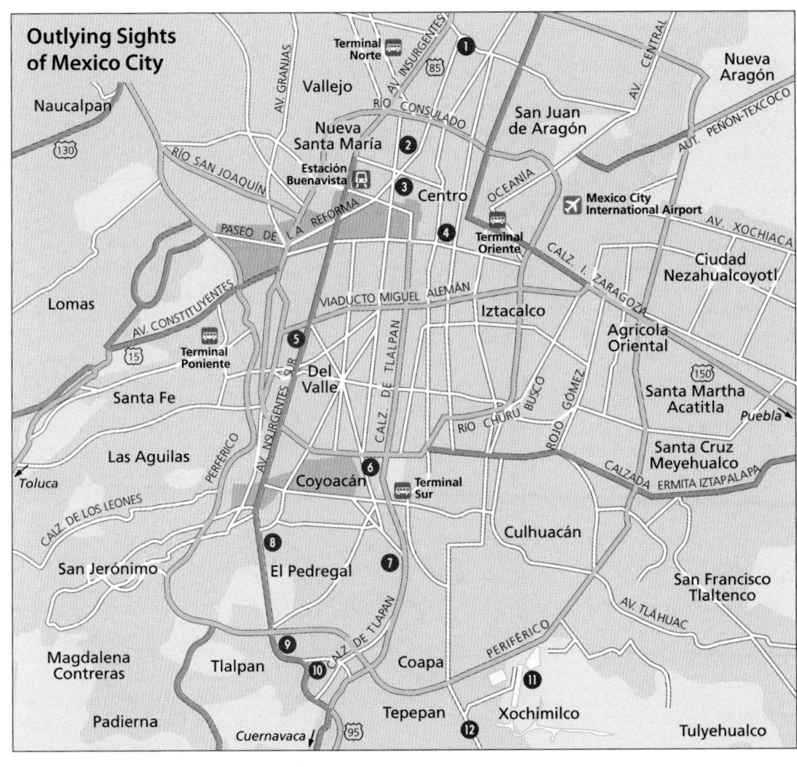

◀ Colorfully decorated *trajineras* in the floating gardens of Xochimilco

For keys to symbols *see back flap*

The beautiful Antigua Basílica de Santa María de Guadalupe, with its Baroque twin towers

❶ Basílica de Santa María de Guadalupe

Plaza de las Americas 1. **Tel** (55) 51 18 05 00. Ⓜ La Villa. **Open** 6am–9pm daily.
virgendeguadalupe.org.mx

The richest and most visited Catholic shrine in the Americas is a complex of buildings at the foot of a hill, the Cerro del Tepeyac. Legend says it was here that a brown-skinned Virgin Mary miraculously appeared to the Indian Juan Diego in 1531. She is named after the Virgin of Guadalupe in Extremadura, Spain.

The Antigua Basílica was built in the early 1700s. Twin towers flank its Baroque facade, which features relief carvings of the Virgin. It is overshadowed by the circular, modern church that now stands beside it, which can hold up to 10,000 worshipers. An object of veneration inside it is Diego's tunic on which the image of the Virgin was supposedly imprinted as proof of the miracle he witnessed.

The impressive Capilla del Pocito is a late 18th-century chapel regarded as one of the finest achievements of Mexican Baroque architecture. The Virgin is supposed to have appeared four times in all. This chapel was constructed on the site of her fourth appearance. It is roughly elliptical in shape and its domed roof is faced with dazzling blue and white Talavera tiles *(see p157)*.

Next door to another chapel, the Capilla de Indios, is a house in which Juan Diego is said to have lived after the Virgin's first appearance until his death in 1548.

Each year on December 12 hundreds of thousands of people assemble at the shrine to celebrate the anniversary of the appearance of the Virgin.

Tiles on the Capilla del Pocito, near the Basílica de Guadalupe

❷ Tlatelolco and Plaza de las Tres Culturas

Eje Central & Ricardo Flores Magón. **Tel** (55) 55 83 02 95. Ⓜ Tlatelolco, Garibaldi. **Open** 8am–6pm Mon–Sun.
tlatelolco.inah.gob.mx (Spanish only)

The remains of the ceremonial center of Tlatelolco form a major part of the Plaza de las Tres Culturas. The square gets its name ("The Three Cultures") from the mix of modern, colonial, and pre-Columbian architecture that have developed around it.

Tlatelolco, the "twin city" of the Aztec capital, Tenochtitlán, was the most important commercial center of its day. The site here has a "templo mayor" similar to that of Tenochtitlán *(see pp72–3)*. There are also smaller temples including the "calendar temple," dedicated to the god of the wind. It owes its name to the glyphs adorning three of its sides, which represent dates in the Aztecs' ritual calendar. In the northwest corner of the archaeological zone, the remains of the carved "wall of serpents" can be seen, which marked the boundary of the ceremonial center.

The Spanish erected their own temples on the site, particularly the Templo de Santiago, a

Catholic church in a severe, almost militaristic, style. Built by the Franciscan order in 1524, and reconstructed in 1609, the church has twin towers flanking the main door. Over the side door are statues of the apostles. The original font can still be seen inside. It is said that Juan Diego, who witnessed the appearance of the Virgin of Guadalupe, was baptized here. Beside the church is a Franciscan monastery, built in 1660.

The modern era is represented by several buildings, particularly the concrete-and-glass foreign ministry tower. Scattered around the plaza are sculptures by Federico Silva. Between the monastery and the nearby residential tower block is a 1944 mural by David Alfaro Siqueiros. Entitled *Cuauhtémoc Against the Myth*, it combines sculpture with alfresco painting. Cuauhtémoc was the last Aztec emperor, killed by the Spanish under Hernán Cortés. In front of the Templo de Santiago is a plaque that reads: "On 13 August 1521, heroically defended by Cuauhtémoc, Tlatelolco fell into the hands of Cortés. It was neither triumph nor defeat, but the painful birth of the *mestizo* nation that is Mexico today."

In October, 1968, the Plaza de las Tres Culturas was the scene of another painful moment in Mexican history, when the military opened fire on student protesters.

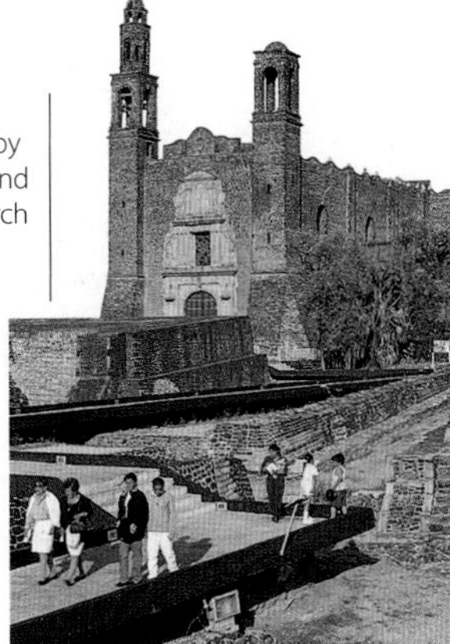

The entrance of the Templo de Santiago in the Plaza de las Tres Culturas

❸ Plaza Garibaldi

N of the Alameda, off Lázaro Cárdenas. El Museo del Tequila y el Mezcal: **Tel** 55 29 12 38. **Open** 1pm–10pm Sun–Wed, 1pm–midnight Thu–Sat. **mutemgaribaldi.mx**

The Plaza Garibaldi is the home of *mariachi* music *(see p32)*. Dressed in their tight-trousered costumes, *mariachi* musicians can be seen scouting for work among the traffic of the nearby Eje Central. *Mariachi* music was born in the area around Guadalajara in Jalisco. In the first two decades of the 20th century there was heavy migration from Jalisco to the capital, and the Plaza del Borrego (later renamed the Plaza Garibaldi) became the *mariachis'* home from around 1920 onward. Today the area abounds with bars and restaurants serving a staple fare of tacos and tequila. *Mariachi* bands can be hired per song or by the hour, and rates vary depending on the size of the band and its musical prowess.

The modern cultural space MUTEM Garibaldi houses **El Museo del Tequila y el Mezcal**, where visitors learn about the two spirits and perhaps have a taste.

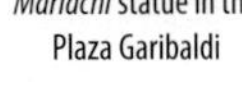

Mariachi statue in the Plaza Garibaldi

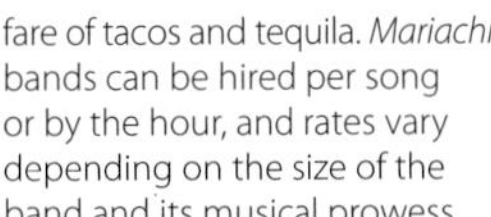

❹ Mercado de La Merced

Anillo de Circunvalación & Calle Callejón de Carretones. Merced. **Open** daily.

Said to be one of the biggest markets in the Americas, La Merced has over 5,000 stalls. It occupies the spot on which an Aztec market stood prior to the conquest by the Spanish.

La Merced is divided into seven sections, six of which specialize in different types of merchandise, while the seventh is a traditional market. The market is good for food, especially chilies, fruits, and fresh vegetables.

The northern section of the market used to be occupied by the Convento de la Merced. The restored 17th-century Moorish-style cloister of the monastery can still be seen on the other side of the Anillo de Circunvalación at República de Uruguay 170. It is noted for the richness of its carved stone-work. The Mercado is well known for prostitution, and it can be a dangerous area at night.

The Virgin of Guadalupe

On December 12 each year, hundreds of thousands of pilgrims flock to the Basílica de Santa María de Guadalupe to commemorate the apparition of Mexico's patron saint on the Cerro del Tepeyac. Acts of veneration also take place in every town and village throughout the country. Birthday songs, *las mañanitas*, are sung at dawn. Special services are then held, followed by dancing and music in town squares, with children dressed in local costumes. As often in Mexico, a Catholic tradition has merged with pre-Columbian influence: the cult of the Virgin of Guadalupe has distinct parallels with that of Tonantzin, a Mesoamerican mother-goddess.

The Virgin of Guadalupe, patron saint of Mexico

Spectators watching the action at the enormous Plaza México – Mexico City's bullring

5 Avenida Insurgentes Sur

South from Glorieta de Insurgentes. M San Antonio, Barranca del Muerto.

The Avenida de los Insurgentes runs just over 30 km (18 miles) from the capital's border with Mexico State in the north to the start of the highway to Cuernavaca in the south, and is said to be the longest street in Latin America.

Its southern (Sur) stretch has several sights of interest. Just a few blocks south of its junction with the Viaducto Miguel Alemán stands the World Trade Center, formerly the Hotel de México. This is without doubt one of the most prominent buildings on the Avenida. Its slim, glass tower is surmounted by a huge circular section that has a revolving floor.

The Polyforum Siqueiros, one of Mexico City's most audacious works of modern architecture, is next door to the World Trade Center. Its upper floor, which is reached by twin, circular staircases, is topped by an octagonal dome. This is decorated by one of David Alfaro Siqueiros' finest works, *March of Humanity*, one of the largest murals in the world.

At Eje 6 Sur and Insurgentes is the Ciudad de los Deportes, which includes a soccer stadium and the Plaza México *(see p121)*, reputedly the world's largest bullring. It seats up to 60,000 people and is surrounded by statues commemorating the great bullfighters, including Manuel Rodríguez ("Manolete"), who was in the arena's inaugural program in 1946.

Just before the junction with Barranca del Muerto is the Teatro de los Insurgentes, built in the early 1950s by architect Alejandro Prieto. The curved facade is adorned with an allegorical mural by Diego Rivera on the theme of theater in Mexico. Completed in 1953, the mural centers on a huge pair of hands holding a mask, around which are gathered significant revolutionary and independence heroes.

6 Museo de las Intervenciones

Cnr of General Anaya & Calle 20 de Agosto. **Tel** (55) 56 04 06 99. M General Anaya. **Open** 9am–6pm Tue–Sun. Sun free.

This former convent still bears the bullet holes from a battle that took place here between US and Mexican forces in 1847. Today it is a museum dedicated to the foreign invasions of Mexico since its independence in 1821. The collection consists of weapons, flags, and other

Cloister in the Museo de las Intervenciones

The carriage of Benito Juárez in the Museo de las Intervenciones

artifacts, including a throne and saber belonging to Agustín de Iturbide *(see p56)* and a death mask of the Emperor Maximilian *(see p57)*, as well as paintings, maps, and models.

Adjoining the museum is the former convent church, which has gilded altarpieces, as well as religious paintings from the 16th to the 18th century. These include *La Asunción* by the 16th-century painter Luis Juárez and the 17th-century work *La Virgen y San Ildefonso* by Manuel de Echave.

Rear facade of the unusual, pyramid-shaped Museo Anahuacalli

❼ Museo Anahuacalli

Museo 150. **Tel** (55) 56 17 43 10. **Open** 11am–5pm Wed–Sun. **Closed** public hols. ground floor. reserve in advance. **museoanahuacalli.org.mx**

This museum was conceived and created by muralist Diego Rivera to house his collection of pre-Columbian art. It was completed after his death by architects Juan O'Gorman and Heriberto Pagelson, and Rivera's own daughter, Ruth. Built of black volcanic stone, it takes the form of a pyramid. The collection consists of some 2,000 pieces, representing most of the indigenous civilizations of Mexico. There are funerary urns, masks, and sculptures from the ancient culture of Teotihuacán. The studio, although never actually used by Rivera, has been set up as if it were, with his materials and half-finished works on display. A smaller gallery next to the pyramid contains an exhibition of papier-mâché sculpture relating to the Days of the Dead, celebrated October 31 to November 2 *(see pp38–9)*.

Image of the Goddess of Maize in the Museo Anahuacalli

❽ Universidad Nacional Autónoma de México (UNAM)

Ciudad Universitaria. **Tel** (55) 56 22 55 72. Universidad, Ciudad Universitaria. **Open** 7am–9:30pm daily. **Closed** public hols. **unam.mx** Museo Universitario de Arte Contemporáneo: **Tel** (55) 56 22 69 72. **Open** 10am–6pm Wed, Thu & Sun, 10am–8pm Fri & Sat. **muac.unam.mx**

Latin America's largest university is also a UNESCO World Heritage site. It occupies a vast campus in the south of the city. Many of the most interesting buildings are concentrated in a relatively small area close to Avenida Insurgentes. To the west of the avenue is the striking Olympic stadium, the symbol of the 1968 Mexico Olympics. Over the main entrance is a high-relief mural by Diego Rivera. Facing the stadium, on the east side of Insurgentes, is the rectory tower, adorned with dramatic murals by David Alfaro Siqueiros. The theme of the mural on the south wall is the recurring struggle of the Mexican people to forge an independent identity, while on the north wall is a mural of glass mosaic tiles depicting the functions of the university. Nearby is the Biblioteca Central, one of the university's most spectacular buildings. Its tower is covered with mosaics by Juan O'Gorman. Each wall illustrates a period of Mexican history and the scientific achievements it produced.

A separate complex of buildings farther south on Insurgentes includes one of the city's major centers for performance arts, the Sala Nezahualcóyotl *(see p120)*. The Espacio Escultórico, a huge concrete circle, contains some modern sculpture. The **Museo Universitario de Arte Contemporáneo (MUAC)**, housed in an angular, modern building flooded with light, exhibits the largest collection of contemporary art in the country.

Close to the Olympic stadium is the university's Jardín Botánico. As well as its cactus collection, the garden has an arboretum and a section devoted to jungle plants. Located in the Pedregal ecological reserve, home to a unique volcanic ecosystem, the garden also has a noted collection of Mexican medicinal plants.

Mosaic on the Biblioteca in the University, depicting the scientific achievements of Mexican history

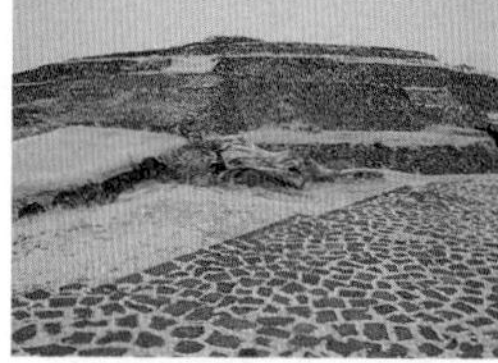

Unusual remains of the circular Pirámide de Cuicuilco

9 Pirámide de Cuicuilco

Avenida Insurgentes Sur & Periférico. **Tel** (55) 56 06 97 58. **Open** 9am–5pm daily. reserve in advance.

This pyramid belongs to the earliest known urban civilization in the Valley of Mexico, founded around 600 BC. It is all that is left of the ceremonial center of a settlement thought to have comprised as many as 20,000 inhabitants at its peak. The surviving structure is a truncated, layered cone, just 25 m (82 ft) high but 100 m (328 ft) across. The eruption of a nearby volcano, Xitle, forced the inhabitants of the area to flee around AD 100. The solidified lava, which can be as much as 8 m (26 ft) deep, makes excavation of the area difficult. However, a museum on the site exhibits the pottery, tools, and spearheads that have been found.

Another pre-Columbian ceremonial site within the urban area is the Cerro de la Estrella (southeast of the city), which was inhabited from AD 1000 until the arrival of the Spanish.

10 Tlalpan

Mex 95. 25 km south of city center.

In the age of the Spanish viceroys, Tlalpan was a favorite country retreat both for ordinary Mexicans and the nobility. As a result, a large number of elegant mansions and haciendas were built here from the early 18th century onward.

Visitors to the old town, now the seat of Mexico City's largest *delegación* (suburban area), can stroll along narrow streets and admire the beautiful architecture, which dates from the 17th to the 20th century. The 18th-century Casa Chata, the Casa del Marqués de Vivanco, and the Casa del Conde de Regla are among some of the outstanding buildings here.

In the central Plaza de la Constitución, with its *porfiriato*-era bandstand and busts of national heroes scattered around, is the Capilla del Rosario, a 17th-century chapel with a Baroque facade. Nearby is the 16th-century Dominican church of San Agustín, which has a large courtyard. In the same square stands the tree from which 11 patriots, who rebelled against the French occupation under the Emperor Maximilian, were hanged in 1866. Maximilian's wife, the Empress Carlota, occupied the Casa de Moneda (on the corner of Juaréz and Moneda), which was later used as a military barracks.

Carved wooden doorway of the Casa Chata

The garden of the Hacienda de Tlalpan, now a restaurant

On Avenida San Fernando, the church of Santa Inés has a plaque commemorating the brief detention of independence hero José María Morelos here in 1815.

The former country house of General Antonio López de Santa Anna, the victor of the Alamo, stands at the corner of San Fernando and Madero. He was named president of Mexico 11 times. On the Calzada de Tlalpan, what was once the old Hacienda de Tlalpan is now an elegant restaurant *(see p317)*, with restful fountains and colorful peacocks in its garden.

The yellow facade of the church of San Agustín in Tlalpan

11 Xochimilco

Prolongación División del Norte. 20 km SE of city center. M Embarcadero.

Known as "the place of the flower fields" in Nahuatl, the language spoken by the Aztecs, Xochimilco was once a lakeside village connected to Tenochtitlán by a causeway. Today it is the only part of Mexico City still to have the canals and semi-floating flower and vegetable gardens, or *chinampas*, built by the Aztecs.

The Iglesia de San Bernardino in the main square of Xochimilco

Originally created on a base of aquatic roots that were then covered with soil, the *chinampas* remain an important source of flowers and vegetables to Mexico City even today.

A favorite weekend pastime, popular with tourists as well as *chilangos* (the city's inhabitants), is to rent one of the many flower-decked punts *(trajineras)*, which have roofs and a table down the middle. A local boatman poles the punt along between banks shaded by willows. Waterborne *mariachis* will provide entertainment while smaller boats sell typical Mexican snacks. An optional stop provides an opportunity to haggle for rugs or other handicrafts at a local craft market.

On land, Xochimilco has a village-like atmosphere that is far removed from the bustle of the historic center of Mexico City. One of the architectural highlights in the main square is the Iglesia de San Bernardino. A fortified monastery built by the Franciscans in the late 16th century, it has a Classical-style facade with some hints of early Baroque. The magnificent main altarpiece contains paintings and sculptures of the apostles and other saints. Other altarpieces contain beautiful paintings by colonial-era masters such as Cristóbal de Villalpando and Juan Correa.

Near San Bernardino is the Capilla del Rosario, a pretty chapel built in 1768. It is completely covered in a profusion of high-relief mortar-work and Puebla-style tiles.

A row of colorful boats in Xochimilco

⓬ Museo Dolores Olmedo

Avenida México 5843. **Tel** (55) 55 55 12 21. Ⓜ La Noria. **Open** 10am–6pm Tue–Sun. Tue free. reserve in advance.
w **museodoloresolmedo.org.mx**

This is the largest private collection of works by artists Diego Rivera and Frida Kahlo. It is housed in a beautiful 17th-century mansion in Xochimilco known as the Finca Noria, which was gifted to the nation in 1994 by the wealthy collector and friend of Rivera, Dolores Olmedo.

As well as 137 works by Rivera, there are also 25 by Frida Kahlo and more than 600 pre-Columbian artifacts. The Rivera collection spans many periods of the artist's life. It includes several self-portraits as well as studies for large works. The excellent portrait, *The Mathematician*, was painted in 1919. Among the best-known of the Kahlo works here are *Self-Portrait with a Monkey, The Broken Column*, and *The Deceased Dimas*. There are also some pieces on display by Angelina Beloff, Rivera's first wife. A separate part of the collection is dedicated to Mexican popular culture.

The landscaped grounds of the mansion contain animals and plants native to Mexico, including the Mexican hairless dog, or *xoloitzcuintle*.

SHOPPING IN MEXICO CITY

The beauty of shopping in Mexico City is the vast range and accessibility of goods. Strolling around the city, visitors will stumble upon a dizzying number of vibrant street markets, selling anything from quality crafts and fresh flowers to rice-grain sculptures and witchcraft accessories. Those looking for contemporary designs and artist-run boutiques should try the Condesa and Roma neighborhoods. For high-end fashion chains head to Avenida Presidente Masarik in Polanco. Visitors in search of everyday essentials, as opposed to a hectic shopping experience, will fare better with neighborhood markets and grocery stores, or the convenience of one of the city's many comprehensive department stores.

A craft stall in the Plaza de San Jacinto, part of El Bazaar Sábado

Crafts and Gifts

The most complete selection of Mexican crafts *(see pp332–5)* can be found at **FONART**, a state-run chain. Prices here are above average, but all items are genuine crafts. The staff know the origins of every piece and can arrange international shipping.

A pleasant place to shop for unusual and original handicrafts is **El Bazaar Sábado** (Saturday Market) in the Plaza de San Jacinto in San Ángel *(see p104)*. Stalls are open only on Saturdays between 10am and 2pm. The heart of the market is the cluster of stalls around the fountain of an indoor patio belonging to a colonial building. The stalls sell a wide variety of crafts and gift items, including jewelry, clothing, Tiffany lampshades, gilt work, embroidered pillows, rice-grain sculptures, candles, wall hangings, and paper flowers. Shoppers can also enjoy a buffet breakfast to the accompaniment of *marimba* players.

The **Mercado de Londres** (also known as Mercado Zona Rosa or Mercado de Artesanías Insurgentes) in the Zona Rosa specializes in silver jewelry, painted papier-mâché trays and picture frames, and also embroidered shawls and waistcoats.

There is a large selection of crafts from all over the country in the **Mercado de la Ciudadela**. Prices are very reasonable here, although this is often reflected in the fact that many of the articles are not of the finest quality.

The artisan market **Mercado de Artesanías de San Juan** features wood, leather, and silver work, as well as pottery. Note that there's a popular food market nearby, also called San Juan.

Art and Antiques

Art and antique outlets in Mexico City tend to be concentrated in Polanco, the Zona Rosa, San Ángel, and Roma. In Polanco, **Galería López Quiroga**, **Oscar Román**, and the **Galería Misrachi** specialize in contemporary Mexican art. The antique shops in the Zona Rosa are concentrated around the shopping complex **Plaza del Ángel**, where an antique market is also held on Saturday mornings. Some of the best known galleries in Roma include **Galería OMR** and **Casa Lamm**. Downtown, the **Monte de Piedad** *(see p66)* is a pawnshop selling secondhand jewelry that is well worth a visit.

Books and Newspapers

Local newspapers can be purchased from street vendors, whereas international papers and magazines are sold at Sanborns, the department store, top hotels, and the charming **La Torre de Papel**.

Mexican bookstore chain **Librería Gandhi** has more than a dozen stores around the city. **El Péndulo**, frequented by artists and intellectuals, has locations in Polanco and Condesa. The English-language bookstore **Under the Volcano** is popular among expats.

Sweets

Mexicans tend to have a very sweet tooth. The city's many good quality pastry shops include downtown's **Dulcería de Celaya**. Another classic sweet spot is **Pastelería Ideal**, which has been selling cakes and classic Mexican pastries and breads since 1927.

The Dulcería de Celaya pastry shop, which attracts business from all over the city

A stall selling fresh produce in the Mercado de la Merced

Cigars

For cigar aficionados the best specialty shops are **La Casa del Habano** and **Hábano 2000**, which both stock a wide range of national and imported cigars, as well as pipe tobaccos. Genuine *Habanos* (Havanas) can be bought here quite reasonably.

Markets

Each neighborhood has its local market, and there are also several larger and more specialized markets. All of these are regular shopping places for Mexico City's residents, and give an insight into their daily life. Beware of pickpockets in all markets.

The **Mercado de Sonora** is a sprawling covered market specializing in seasonal wares, such as Christmas decorations and Easter candy. It also has permanent sections selling herbs, toys, and witchcraft accessories. It makes a heady combination of the kitsch and the occult for the few tourists who come here.

Close by is the huge **Mercado de La Merced** *(see p113)*, one of the largest markets, which operates daily. Of the thousands of stalls, the greatest proportion is devoted to fruit, vegetables, and flowers. The remainder sell a variety of other items.

A branch of the Liverpool chain store

Department Stores

The two largest department store chains in Mexico are **El Palacio de Hierro** and **Liverpool**, both of which have branches in most of the city's American-style shopping malls. Here shoppers can find anything and everything they might need. Each branch has large collections of international designer fashions, alongside local designs and the store's own brands. For English-language books, reasonably priced souvenirs, photographic equipment, and toiletries, any branch of **Sanborns** is a good bet. In addition, these stores provide a choice of restaurants. Though influenced by Mexican cuisine, they also serve international "fast food" sure to suit all tastes *(see p306)*.

DIRECTORY

Crafts and Gifts

El Bazaar Sábado
San Jacinto 11, San Ángel.
Tel (55) 56 16 00 82.
W elbazaarsabado.com

FONART
Av Juárez no. 89, Col Centro. **Map** 3 B1.
Av Paseo de la Reforma no. 116 Planta Baja, Col Juárez **Tel** (55) 55 21 01 71.
W fonart.gob.mx

Mercado de Artesanías de San Juan
Ayuntamiento near Buen Tono, Centro. **Map** 3 C2.
Tel (55) 55 21 78 46.

Mercado de la Ciudadela
Balderas, cnr of Emilio Dondé. **Map** 3 B2.

Mercado de Londres
Londres 154, Zona Rosa.
Map 2 E4.
Tel (55) 55 33 25 44.

Art and Antiques

Casa Lamm
Álvaro Obregón 99A.
Map 2 F5.
Tel (55) 55 25 39 38.

Galería López Quiroga
Aristóteles 169, Polanco.
Tel (55) 52 80 17 10.
W lopezquiroga.com

Galería Misrachi
Campos Eliseos 218, Polanco. **Tel** (55) 52 81 51 21. **W galeria misrachi.com.mx**

Galería OMR
Córdoba 100, Colonia Roma. **Map** 2 F4.
Tel (55) 55 11 11 79.
W galeriaomr.com

Monte de Piedad
Monte de Piedad 7. **Map** 4 E2. **Tel** (55) 55 21 10 70.

Oscar Román
Julio Verne 14, Polanco.
Tel (55) 52 80 04 36.

Plaza del Ángel
Londres 161. **Map** 2 E3.
Tel (55) 52 08 98 28.

Books and Newspapers

Librería Gandhi
Av Juárez 4. **Map** 3 C1.
Tel (55) 26 25 06 06.
W gandhi.com.mx

El Péndulo
Alejandro Dumas 81, Col Polanco. **Tel** (55) 52 80 41 11. **W pendulo.com**

La Torre de Papel
Filomeno Mata no. 6A, Col Centro Histórico. **Map** 4 D1. **Tel** (55) 55 12 97 03.
W latorredepapel.com

Under the Volcano
Celaya 25, Col Condesa.
W underthevolcano books.com

Sweets

Dulcería de Celaya
Cinco de Mayo 39. **Map** 4 D2. **Tel** (55) 55 21 17 87.
W dulceriadecelaya.com

Pastelería Ideal
Av 16 de Septiembre 18, Col Centro. **Map** 4 D2.
Tel (55) 55 21 22 33.

Cigars

La Casa del Habano
Av Presidente Masarik 393, Polanco. **Map** 1 A2.
Tel (55) 52 82 10 46.
W casahabanomexico. com.mx

Hábano 2000
Hamburgo 66. **Map** 2 F3.
Tel (55) 52 07 68 59.
W habano2000.com

Markets

Mercado de La Merced
Anillo de Circunvalación & Callejón de Carretones.

Mercado de Sonora
Av Fray Servando Teresa de Mier, cnr of Circunvalación.

Department Stores

Liverpool
Venustiano Carranza 92.
Map 4 D2. **Tel** (55) 51 33 28 00. **W liverpool.com. mx/tienda**

El Palacio de Hierro
Av 20 de Noviembre 3.
Map 4 E2. **Tel** (55) 52 29 31 85. **W elpalaciode hierro.com**

Sanborns
Francisco I. Madero 4.
Map 4 D1.
Tel (55) 55 18 01 52.
W sanborns.com.mx

ENTERTAINMENT IN MEXICO CITY

Mexico City offers a wide variety of entertainment. In the evenings you can choose between salsa music joints or traditional *cantinas*. On a Sunday, you can experience folk ballet at the Palacio de Bellas Artes, watch the *charros* *(see p337)* in their dazzling costumes on horseback, or attend a bullfight in the world's largest bullring. There is also always an excellent range of dance, classical music, and opera. There is a full cultural calendar year round in the city, but the main annual event is the Festival del Centro Histórico, which is usually held before Easter, in March or April.

The Palacio de Bellas Artes, home of the Mexican National Symphony Orchestra

Entertainment Guides and Tickets

For information in English on events, *The News* has a "What's on" section on Fridays and Saturdays, and the local paper *Reforma* has daily listings. The weekly Spanish guides, *Time Out México*, *Chilango*, and *Dónde Ir* have complete information including a restaurant guide, sports events, and activities for children.

Tickets for almost all events can be bought through **Ticketmaster**, which charges a commission as well as a delivery charge. Sanborns *(see p119)* have Ticketmaster counters where charges are lower. Most theaters and sports stadiums in the city also sell tickets directly. The **Instituto Nacional de Bellas Artes** (INBA) operates several theaters and auditoriums, and has its own ticket booths and information service.

Classical Music, Dance, and Theater

The National Opera and the National Symphony Orchestra perform alternate seasons at the **Palacio de Bellas Artes**. The building is also host to a wide range of other music and dance events, including the Amalia Hernández Ballet Folklórico. Large scale classical and contemporary music events are held at the **Auditorio Nacional**. The **Centro Cultural Ollin Yoliztli** and the **Sala Nezahualcóyotl** in the UNAM university complex also play host to a range of events.

At the **Consejo Nacional de Artes (CENART)**, an arts complex, the Auditorio Blas Galindo is fast becoming an important concert hall for the city.

Contemporary and classical dance programs are held at the **Teatro de la Danza**. The National Dance School performs at the Teatro Raúl Flores Canelo at the CENART. The **Insurgentes, Hidalgo** and **Centro Cultural** theaters feature national and international companies.

Cantinas

Mexico's answer to the local bar is the *cantina*, which is both a simple lunchtime restaurant and a meeting place in the evenings. *Cantinas* were originally frequented exclusively by men, and some still display the sign outside that bans women, children, and men in uniform. *Cantinas* close around midnight, and on Saturdays and Sundays open only at lunchtime.

The lavishly decorated **Bar La Opera**, in Centro Histórico, is popular with locals and tourists alike. **La Coyoacana**, *(see p108)* in the Coyoacán neighborhood, is also worth visiting.

Bars, Clubs, and Rock Music

Many bars are reviving the downtown area of Mexico City, with those in Juárez and Condesa popular with the young crowd. Nightclubs range from the trendy to the glamorous. Rock concerts are held at the **Auditorio Nacional** or at various smaller venues around the city.

Latin American Music and Mariachis

Though many of Mexico City's grand dance salons have disappeared in recent years, a few are hanging on, offering visitors an authentic experience of live music and dancing with a crowd that is comprised almost exclusively of locals. Chief among them is **Salón Los Ángeles**,

Dancing to authentic Latin American music at a dance hall

which opened in 1937. "The person who doesn't know Salón Los Ángeles, doesn't know Mexico," so the saying goes, and even if you don't adore dancing, the Salón makes for an excellent night of people-watching – everyone's dressed to the nines.

For Cuban music including salsa, *cumbia*, and *bachata*, head to **Mama Rumba**. Capable instructors are on hand to offer on-the-spot lessons.

Plaza Garibaldi *(see p113)* is a traditional last stop for a night out, where *mariachi* musicians compete to be heard above each other. Listen to the music in comfort at **Salón Tenampa**, or one of the other bars around the square.

Mariachis playing in a café on Plaza Garibaldi

Entertainment for Children

Bosque de Chapultepec *(see pp92–3)* has a number of attractions that will keep children entertained, especially **La Feria Chapultepec Mágico** (an amusement park), "Papalote" Museo del Niño, **Six Flags**, and the **Zoo**.

Spectator Sports

Mexicans are avid sports fans and soccer is a national passion. Matches can be seen at the **Estadio Azteca** and at the **Estadio Olímpico**. Baseball, played at the **Foro Sol**, also has a large following. Boxing matches and typical Mexican masked wrestling, called *lucha libre*, can be experienced at the **Arena Coliseo** and at the **Arena México**. Bullfights take place at the **Plaza México** on Sunday afternoons *(see p114)*. *Charreadas*, trials of traditional equestrian skills *(see p78)*, are held at the **Rancho del Charro**. For more information on spectator sports, see page 337.

Footballers in action in Mexico City's Estadio Azteca

DIRECTORY

Ticket Sales

Instituto Nacional de Bellas Artes
Av Hidalgo 1.
Tel (55) 52 82 19 64.
W bellasartes.gob.mx

Ticketmaster
Tel (55) 53 25 90 00.
W ticketmaster.com.mx

Classical Music, Dance, & Theater

Auditorio Nacional
Paseo de la Reforma 50.
Tel (55) 91 38 13 50.
W auditorio.com.mx

Centro Cultural
Av Cuauhtémoc 19.
Tel (55) 52 37 99 99.
W ocesa.com.mx

Centro Cultural Ollin Yoliztli
Periférico Sur 5141.
Tel (55) 56 06 85 58.

Consejo Nacional de Artes (CENART)
Río Churubusco 79.
Tel (55) 41 55 00 00.
W cenart.gob.mx

Palacio de Bellas Artes
See Instituto Nacional above.

Sala Nezahualcóyotl
Insurgentes Sur 3000.
Tel (55) 56 22 71 25.
W musica.unam.mx

Teatro de la Danza
Campo Marte, Paseo de la Reforma. **Tel** (55) 52 83 46 00. **W ccb.bellas artes.gob.mx/recintos/ deladanza**
(Spanish only)

Teatro Hidalgo
Av Hidalgo 23. **Map** 3 C1.
Tel (55) 53 26 54 45.

Teatro Insurgentes
Av Insurgentes Sur 1587.
Tel (55) 56 11 42 53.
W teatroinsurgentes. com.mx

Cantinas

Bar La Opera
Av 5 de Mayo 10, Centro Histórico. **Map** 4 D1.
Tel (55) 55 12 89 59.
W barlaopera.com

La Coyoacana
Higuera 14, Coyoacán.
Tel (55) 56 58 53 37.
W lacoyoacana.com
(Spanish only)

Latin American Music/Mariachis

Mama Rumba
Querétaro 230.
Tel (55) 55 64 69 20.
W mamarumba.com.mx

Salón los Ángeles
Lerdo 206, Col Guerrero.
Tel (55) 55 97 51 81.
Open 6–11pm Tue, 5pm–1am Sun.
W salonlosangeles.mx

Salón Tenampa
Plaza Garibaldi 12.
Tel (55) 55 26 61 76.
W salontenampa.com

Entertainment for Children

Chapultepec Zoo
Bosque de Chapultepec.
Tel (55) 55 53 62 63.
W sedema.df.gob.mx/ zoo_chapultepec

La Feria Chapultepec Mágico
Bosque de Chapultepec.
Tel (55) 52 30 21 21.
W laferia.com.mx

Six Flags
Carretera Picacho–Ajusco 1500. **Tel** (55) 53 39 36 00.
W sixflags.com.mx

Spectator Sports

Arena Coliseo
Perú 77.
W cmll.com

Arena México
Dr. Lavista 189. **Map** 3 A4.
Tel (55) 55 88 29 95.
W arenamexico.com.mx

Estadio Azteca
Calzada de Tlalpan 3465.
Tel (55) 54 87 31 00.
W estadioazteca. com.mx

Estadio Olímpico
Av Insurgentes Sur s/n, Universidad Nacional Autónoma de México.
Tel (55) 56 16 20 45.
W unam.mx

Foro Sol
Av Viaducto Rio de la Piedad y Rio Churubusco s/n. **Tel** (55) 52 37 99 99.
W ocesa.com.mx

Plaza México
Augusto Rodin 241.
Tel (55) 56 11 44 13.
W lamexico.com

Rancho del Charro
Av Constituyentes 500.
Tel (55) 49 86 65 85.

MEXICO CITY STREET FINDER

The map below shows the area covered by the city center street map on the following pages. The map references given in the text for centrally located places of interest, hotels, restaurants, shops, and entertainment venues refer to these maps. Sights in San Ángel and Coyoacán are located on the map on page 101, and more distant attractions in Mexico City can be found on the Farther Afield map on page 111. Opposite is a map showing the main highways used for crossing, or getting around, the vast and potentially confusing area that is greater Mexico City.

Key

- Major sight
- Place of interest
- Other building
- Metro station
- Tourist information

- Hospital
- Police station
- Church
- Pedestrian street

Scale of Maps 1–4

0 meters 300

0 yards 300

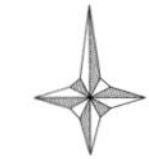

0 kilometers 1

0 miles 1

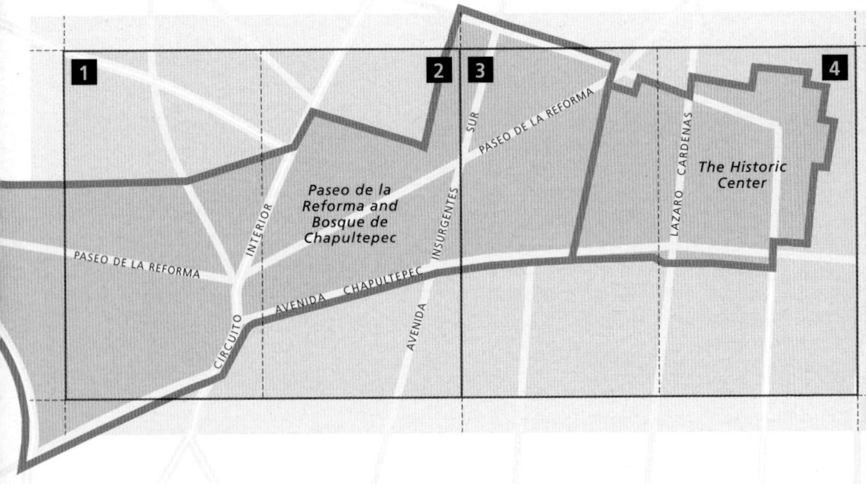

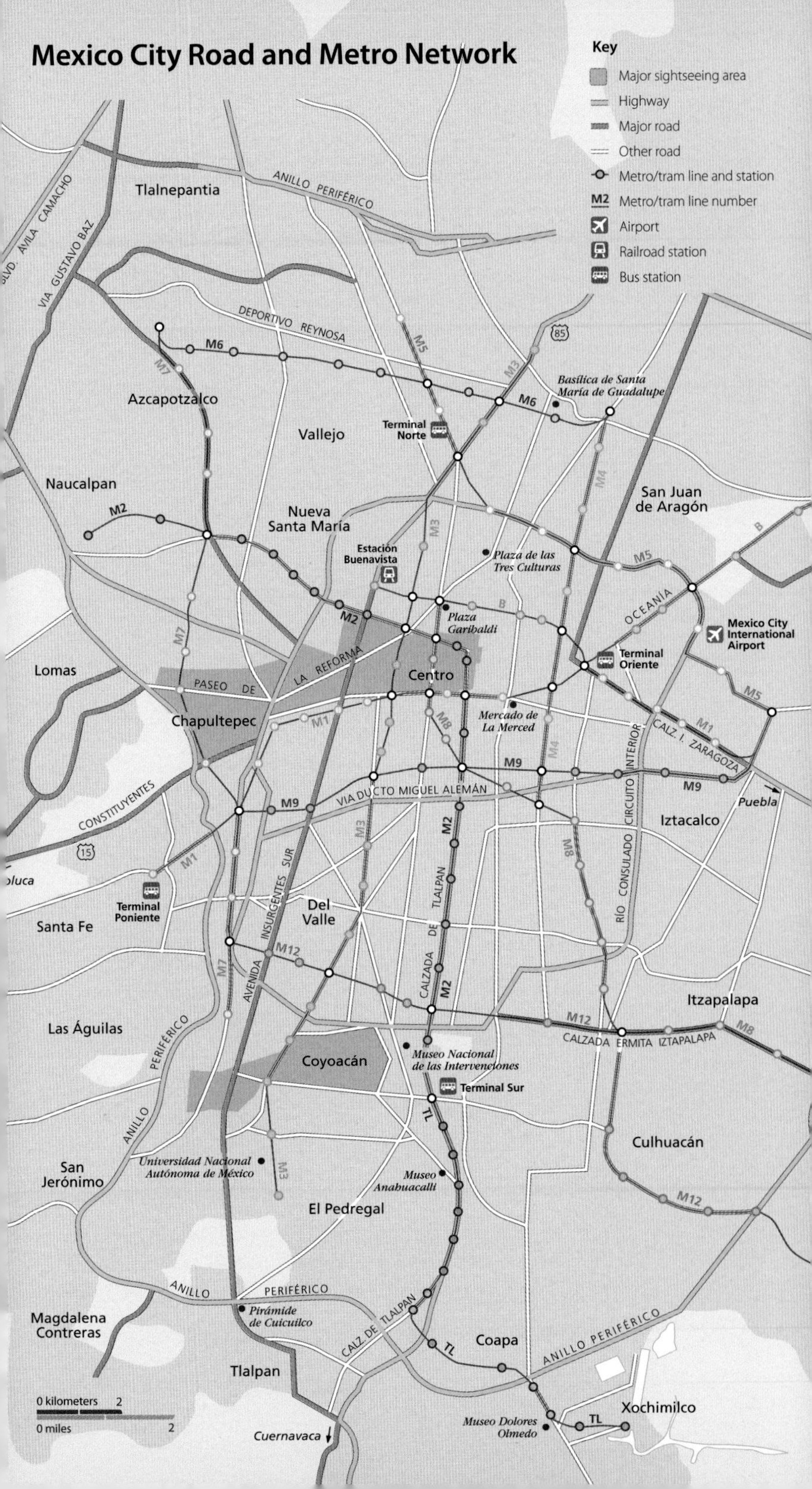

Mexico City Road and Metro Network
Key
Major sightseeing area
Highway
Major road
Other road
Metro/tram line and station
M2 Metro/tram line number
Airport
Railroad station
Bus station
Tlalnepantia
ANILLO PERIFÉRICO
BLVD. ÁVILA CAMACHO
VIA GUSTAVO BAZ
DEPORTIVO REYNOSA
M6
M7
M5
M3
85
Azcapotzalco
Vallejo
Basílica de Santa María de Guadalupe
Terminal Norte
Naucalpan
M2
Nueva Santa María
San Juan de Aragón
M4
Estación Buenavista
Plaza de las Tres Culturas
B
OCEANÍA
Mexico City International Airport
Plaza Garibaldi
Terminal Oriente
Lomas
PASEO DE LA REFORMA
Centro
Chapultepec
M1
M8
Mercado de La Merced
CALZ. I. ZARAGOZA
CIRCUITO INTERIOR
M9
Puebla
CONSTITUYENTES
VIADUCTO MIGUEL ALEMÁN
Iztacalco
15
Toluca
INSURGENTES SUR
CALZADA DE TLALPAN
RÍO CONSULADO
Terminal Poniente
Del Valle
Santa Fe
M12
AVENIDA
Itzapalapa
Las Águilas
PERIFÉRICO
CALZADA ERMITA IZTAPALAPA
Museo Nacional de las Intervenciones
Coyoacán
Terminal Sur
TL
ANILLO
Culhuacán
Universidad Nacional Autónoma de México
Museo Anahuacalli
San Jerónimo
El Pedregal
ANILLO PERIFÉRICO
Pirámide de Cuicuilco
CALZ. DE TLALPAN
Magdalena Contreras
Coapa
Tlalpan
Xochimilco
0 kilometers 2
0 miles 2
Museo Dolores Olmedo
Cuernavaca

Mexico City Street Finder Index

1
A
B
C
BOSQUE DE CHAPULTEPEC
Museo Nacional de Antropología
Museo Rufino Tamayo
Sala de Arte Siqueiros
Museo de Arte Moderno
Casa del Lago
Monumento a los Niños Héroes
Castillo de Chapultepec
Galería de Historia (Museo del Caracol)
Mercado de Flores
Torre Mayor
Plaza Melchor Ocampo
Chapultepec
PASEO DE LA REFORMA
CALZADA GENERAL MARIANO ESCOBEDO
CALZADA MELCHOR OCAMPO
JOSÉ VASCONCELOS
AVENIDA CONSTITUYENTES
AV PRESIDENTE MASARIK
CAMPOS ELÍSEOS
RUBÉN DARÍO
LAGO ALBERTO
AVENIDA MARINA NACIONAL
AVENIDA LAGO
CALZADA MAHATMA GANDHI
CALZADA DEL CERRO
CALZADA DE LOS POETAS
CALZADA DE LOS FILÓSOFOS
CALZ. DE LOS ARTISTAS
CALZADA DEL REY
GRAN AVENIDA
AVENIDA MAZATLÁN
VERACRUZ
AGUSTÍN MELGAR
JUAN DE LA BARRERA
JUAN ESCUTIA
GUTENBERG
THIERS
DARWIN
HOMERO
HORACIO
SCHILLER
NEWTON
TAINE
SUDERMANN
TASSO
PETRARCA
FRANCISCO
TORCUATO
EULER
KEPLER
HERSCHEL
LEIBNIZ
BRADLEY
SHAKESPEARE
DESCARTES
MILTON
GOETHE
COPÉRNICO
LAFAYETTE
CUVIER
COMTE
MICHELET
HERODOTO
RENAN
VICTOR HUGO
DANTE
TOLSTOI
RÍO RODANO
RÍO ELBA
RÍO DUERO
RÍO DE LA PLATA
RÍO HUDSON
TOKIO
BURDEOS
TAMPICO
ACAPULCO
PUEBLA
SINALOA
DURANGO
GUADALAJARA
SALVATIERRA
ZAMORA
PACHUCA
MATEHUALA
ANTONIO SOLA
JOAQUÍN ARGÁEZ
13 DE SEPTIEMBRE
CADETES DEL 47
GRAL PEDRO A DE LOS SANTOS
2
3
4
5

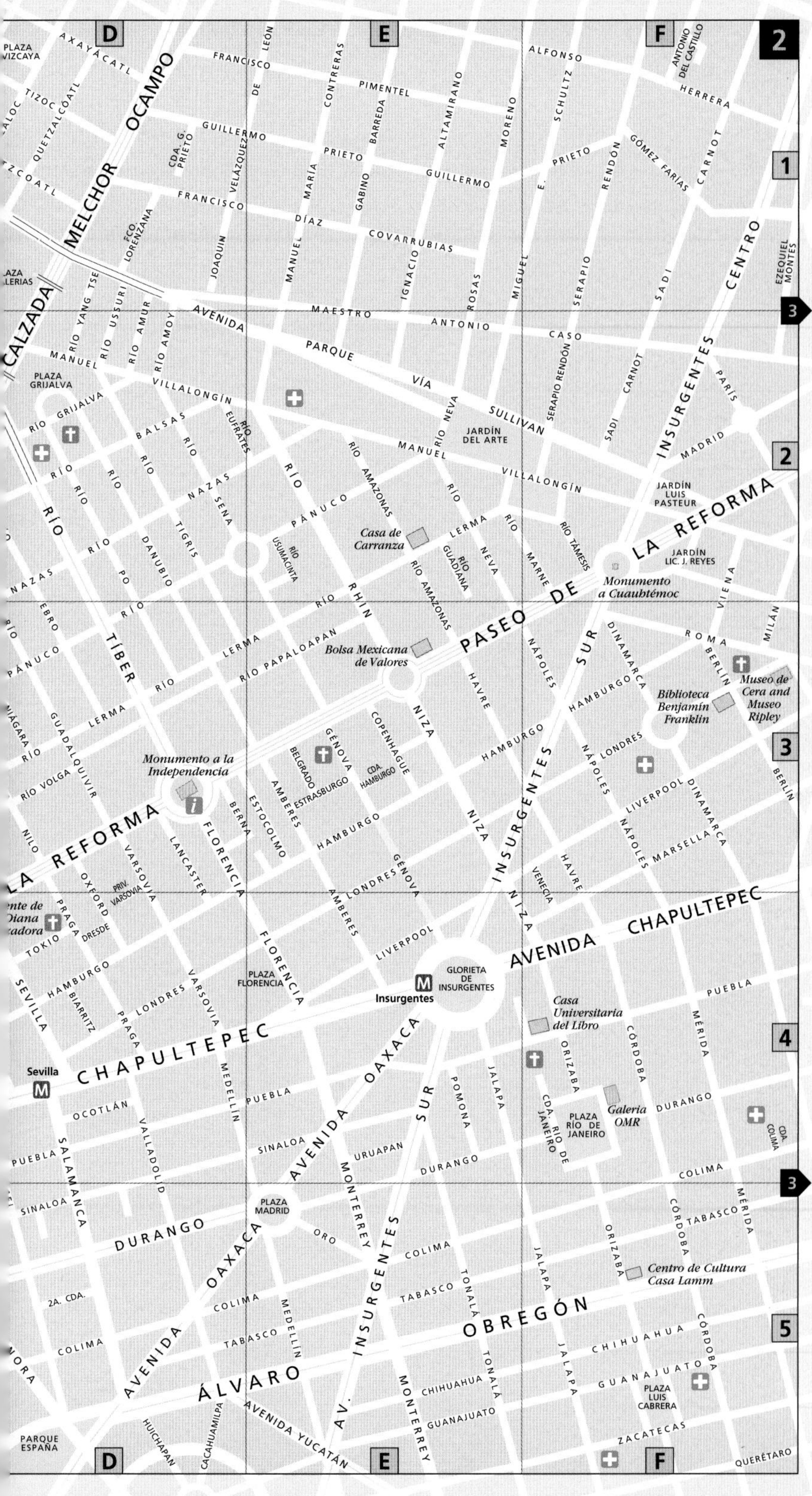
D
E
F
2
1
2
3
4
5
3
3
PLAZA VIZCAYA
AXAYÁCATL
FRANCISCO
LEÓN
DE
VELÁZQUEZ
CONTRERAS
PIMENTEL
ALTAMIRANO
MORENO
SCHULTZ
ALFONSO
ANTONIO DEL CASTILLO
HERRERA
TIZOC
QUETZALCÓATL
MELCHOR
OCAMPO
GUILLERMO
CDA. G. PRIETO
MARÍA
BARREDA
PRIETO
GABINO
GUILLERMO
E.
PRIETO
RENDÓN
GÓMEZ FARÍAS
CARNOT
FRANCISCO
DÍAZ
COVARRUBIAS
FCO. LORENZANA
JOAQUÍN
MANUEL
IGNACIO
ROSAS
MIGUEL
SERAPIO
SADI
CENTRO
EZEQUIEL MONTES
CALZADA
RÍO YANG TSE
RÍO USSURI
RÍO AMUR
RÍO AMOY
AVENIDA
MAESTRO
ANTONIO
CASO
PARQUE
VÍA
SULLIVAN
SERAPIO RENDÓN
CARNOT
SADI
INSURGENTES
PARÍS
MANUEL
PLAZA GRIJALVA
VILLALONGÍN
RÍO GRIJALVA
BALSAS
RÍO EUFRATES
JARDÍN DEL ARTE
RÍO NEVA
MADRID
RÍO AMAZONAS
MANUEL
VILLALONGÍN
JARDÍN LUIS PASTEUR
RÍO
NAZAS
SENA
TIGRIS
DANUBIO
PO
RÍO USUMACINTA
PÁNUCO
Casa de Carranza
LERMA
RÍO GUADIANA
RÍO AMAZONAS
NEVA
MARNE
RÍO TÁMESIS
LA REFORMA
JARDÍN LIC. J. REYES
Monumento a Cuauhtémoc
DE
PASEO
VIENA
NAZAS
EBRO
RÍO
RHIN
RÍO
PÁNUCO
TÍBER
LERMA
RÍO PAPALOAPAN
Bolsa Mexicana de Valores
NÁPOLES
SUR
DINAMARCA
ROMA
MILÁN
BERLÍN
HAVRE
Museo de Cera and Museo Ripley
Biblioteca Benjamín Franklin
HAMBURGO
NIZA
GUADALQUIVIR
LERMA
NIÁGARA
RÍO
RÍO VOLGA
GÉNOVA
COPENHAGUE
BELGRADO
CDA. HAMBURGO
ESTRASBURGO
HAMBURGO
LONDRES
NÁPOLES
LIVERPOOL
DINAMARCA
BERLÍN
Monumento a la Independencia
i
BERNA
ESTOCOLMO
AMBERES
HAMBURGO
NIZA
INSURGENTES
NÁPOLES
MARSELLA
HAVRE
VENECIA
NILO
REFORMA
LA
VARSOVIA
LANCASTER
FLORENCIA
OXFORD
PRIV. VARSOVIA
LONDRES
GÉNOVA
AMBERES
NIZA
CHAPULTEPEC
AVENIDA
Diana Cazadora
PRAGA
DRESDE
TOKIO
FLORENCIA
LIVERPOOL
GLORIETA DE INSURGENTES
M
Insurgentes
SEVILLA
HAMBURGO
BIARRITZ
VARSOVIA
LONDRES
PLAZA FLORENCIA
PUEBLA
Casa Universitaria del Libro
CÓRDOBA
MÉRIDA
PRAGA
CHAPULTEPEC
MEDELLÍN
OAXACA
JALAPA
POMONA
ORIZABA
Sevilla
M
PUEBLA
SUR
CDA. RÍO DE JANEIRO
PLAZA RÍO DE JANEIRO
Galería OMR
DURANGO
CDA. COLIMA
OCOTLÁN
VALLADOLID
AVENIDA
SINALOA
URUAPAN
DURANGO
PUEBLA
SALAMANCA
MONTERREY
COLIMA
SINALOA
PLAZA MADRID
CÓRDOBA
MÉRIDA
TABASCO
DURANGO
OAXACA
ORO
INSURGENTES
COLIMA
ORIZABA
Centro de Cultura Casa Lamm
JALAPA
TONALÁ
2A. CDA.
COLIMA
MEDELLÍN
TABASCO
OBREGÓN
CÓRDOBA
COLIMA
TABASCO
AVENIDA
AV.
CHIHUAHUA
ÁLVARO
TONALÁ
MONTERREY
JALAPA
CHIHUAHUA
GUANAJUATO
PLAZA LUIS CABRERA
AVENIDA YUCATÁN
GUANAJUATO
ZACATECAS
PARQUE ESPAÑA
HUICHAPAN
CACAHUAMILPA
MONTERREY
QUERÉTARO

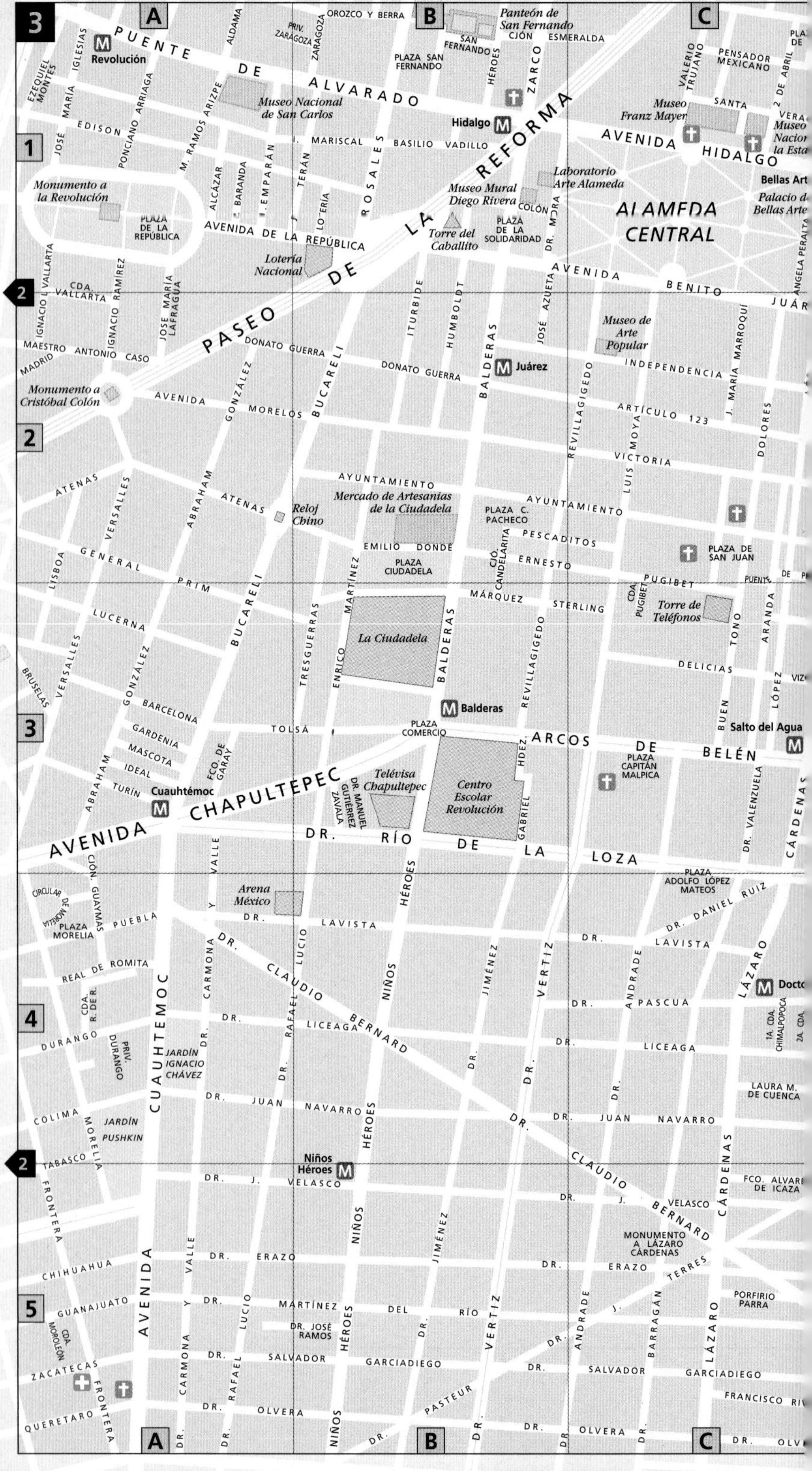

3
A
B
C
1
2
3
4
5
2
2
Revolución
Hidalgo
Juárez
Balderas
Cuauhtémoc
Salto del Agua
Niños Héroes
Doctores
Bellas Artes
PUENTE DE ALVARADO
PASEO DE LA REFORMA
AVENIDA HIDALGO
AVENIDA BENITO JUÁREZ
AVENIDA CHAPULTEPEC
ARCOS DE BELÉN
DR. RÍO DE LA LOZA
AVENIDA CUAUHTEMOC
AVENIDA DE LA REPÚBLICA
AVENIDA MORELOS
BUCARELI
BALDERAS
INDEPENDENCIA
ARTÍCULO 123
VICTORIA
AYUNTAMIENTO
DONATO GUERRA
EMILIO DONDÉ
ERNESTO PUGIBET
MÁRQUEZ STERLING
DELICIAS
REVILLAGIGEDO
LUIS MOYA
DOLORES
J. MARÍA MARROQUÍ
LÓPEZ
ARANDA
BUEN TONO
DR. VALENZUELA
CÁRDENAS
LÁZARO CÁRDENAS
ATENAS
GENERAL PRIM
LUCERNA
BARCELONA
GARDENIA
MASCOTA
IDEAL
TURÍN
TOLSÁ
VERSALLES
LISBOA
BRUSELAS
ABRAHAM GONZÁLEZ
TRESGUERRAS
ENRICO MARTÍNEZ
ITURBIDE
HUMBOLDT
JOSÉ AZUETA
DR. MORA
ZARCO
HÉROES
ROSALES
TERÁN
LOTERÍA
J. EMPARÁN
BARANDA
ALCÁZAR
M. RAMOS ARIZPE
ALDAMA
PRIV. ZARAGOZA
ZARAGOZA
OROZCO Y BERRA
SAN FERNANDO
CJÓN. ESMERALDA
PLAZA SAN FERNANDO
Panteón de San Fernando
Museo Nacional de San Carlos
Museo Franz Mayer
Museo Nacional de la Estampa
PENSADOR MEXICANO
VALERIO TRUJANO
2 DE ABRIL
SANTA VERA
I. MARISCAL
BASILIO VADILLO
EDISON
PONCIANO ARRIAGA
JOSÉ MARÍA IGLESIAS
EZEQUIEL MONTES
Monumento a la Revolución
PLAZA DE LA REPÚBLICA
Lotería Nacional
Torre del Caballito
Museo Mural Diego Rivera
Laboratorio Arte Alameda
COLÓN
PLAZA DE LA SOLIDARIDAD
ALAMEDA CENTRAL
Palacio de Bellas Artes
ÁNGELA PERALTA
IGNACIO VALLARTA
CDA. VALLARTA
IGNACIO RAMÍREZ
JOSÉ MARÍA LAFRAGUA
MAESTRO ANTONIO CASO
MADRID
Monumento a Cristóbal Colón
Museo de Arte Popular
Reloj Chino
Mercado de Artesanias de la Ciudadela
PLAZA C. PACHECO
PESCADITOS
CJÓ. CANDELARITA
PLAZA CIUDADELA
La Ciudadela
CDA. PUGIBET
Torre de Teléfonos
PLAZA DE SAN JUAN
PUENTE DE PERALVILLO
VIZCAÍNAS
PLAZA COMERCIO
FCO. DE GARAY
DR. MANUEL GUTIÉRREZ ZAVALA
Televisa Chapultepec
Centro Escolar Revolución
HDEZ. GABRIEL
PLAZA CAPITÁN MALPICA
PLAZA ADOLFO LÓPEZ MATEOS
DR. DANIEL RUIZ
Arena México
CJÓN. GUAYMAS
CIRCULAR DE MORELIA
PLAZA MORELIA
PUEBLA
REAL DE ROMITA
CDA. R. DE R.
DURANGO
PRIV. DURANGO
JARDÍN IGNACIO CHÁVEZ
DR. LAVISTA
DR. CLAUDIO BERNARD
DR. LUCIO
DR. RAFAEL LUCIO
NIÑOS HÉROES
DR. JIMÉNEZ
DR. VERTIZ
DR. ANDRADE
DR. PASCUA
DR. LICEAGA
DR. CARMONA Y VALLE
DR. JUAN NAVARRO
LAURA M. DE CUENCA
1A. CDA. CHIMALPOPOCA
2A. CDA.
COLIMA
MORELIA
JARDÍN PUSHKIN
TABASCO
FRONTERA
DR. J. VELASCO
FCO. ALVAREZ DE ICAZA
MONUMENTO A LÁZARO CÁRDENAS
CHIHUAHUA
DR. ERAZO
DR. J. TERRES
PORFIRIO PARRA
GUANAJUATO
CDA. MOROLEÓN
DR. MARTÍNEZ DEL RÍO
DR. JOSÉ RAMOS
DR. BARRAGÁN
ZACATECAS
DR. SALVADOR GARCIADIEGO
FRANCISCO RIVAS
PASTEUR
QUERÉTARO
DR. OLVERA

4
D
E
F
1
2
3
4
5
PLAZA CONCEPCIÓN
Asamblea de Representantes
Teatro de la Ciudad
Museo Nacional de Arte
Senado
Allende
Palacio de la Minería
Museo del Ejército y Fuerza Aérea
Correo Central
Casa de los Azulejos
Torre Latinoamericana
Palacio de Iturbide
San Juan de Letrán
PLAZA DE SANTO DOMINGO
Palacio de la Antigua Escuela de Medicina
Antigua Aduana
Secretaría de Educación Pública
Templo de la Enseñanza
Antiguo Colegio de San Ildefonso
Museo de la Caricatura
Templo Mayor
Nacional Monte de Piedad
Catedral Metropolitana
Ex-Palacio Arzobispal
Casa de la Primera Imprenta
Museo José Luis Cuevas
Zócalo
ZÓCALO (PLAZA DE LA CONSTITUCIÓN)
Palacio Nacional
Museo de las Culturas
PLAZA LORETO
Suprema Corte de Justicia
PLAZA DE LA ALHÓNDIGA
San Agustin
Iglesia de San Felipe Neri
Museo de la Ciudad de Mexico
Ex-Convento de la Merced
Iglesia de Jesús
Colegio de las Vizcaínas
Isabel La Católica
Convento de San Jerónimo
Pino Suarez
Museo de la Charrería
PLAZA SAN PABLO
PLAZA SAN SALVADOR EL SECO
PLAZA SAN SALVADOR EL VERDE
PLAZA TLAXCOAQUE
La Concepción Tlaxcoaque
PLAZA SANTA CRUZ
San Antonio Abad
REPÚBLICA DE CUBA
DONCELES
TACUBA
AVENIDA 5 DE MAYO
AVENIDA FRANCISCO I. MADERO
16 DE SEPTIEMBRE
VENUSTIANO CARRANZA
REPÚBLICA DE URUGUAY
REPÚBLICA DE EL SALVADOR
MESONES
REGINA
SAN JERÓNIMO
JOSÉ MARÍA IZAZAGA
SAN PABLO
NEZAHUALCÓYOTL
DR. RÍO DE LA LOZA
FRAY SERVANDO TERESA DE MIER
CHIMALPOPOCA
CJÓN. SAN ANTONIO ABAD
20 DE NOVIEMBRE
PINO SUÁREZ
SAN ANTONIO ABAD
CALZADA DE LA VIGA
REPÚBLICA DE BOLIVIA
COLOMBIA
VENEZUELA
SAN ILDEFONSO
JUSTO SIERRA
REPÚBLICA DE GUATEMALA
MONEDA
SOLEDAD
CORREGIDORA
LORENZO BOTURINI
DR. CLAUDIO BERNARD

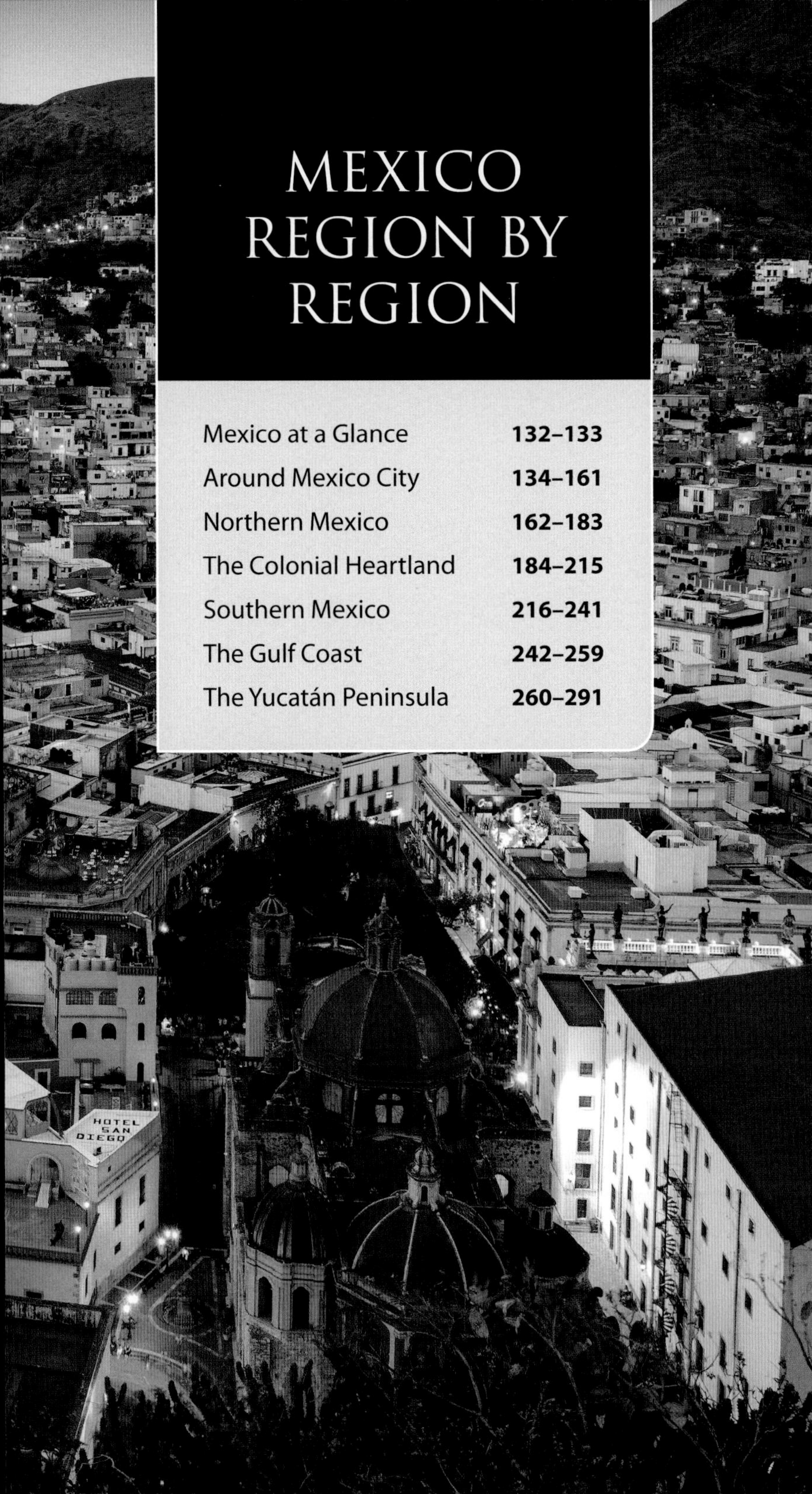

MEXICO REGION BY REGION

Mexico at a Glance

Mexico is an enormously varied country, and traveling from one part to another can seem like crossing between different worlds. The north is characterized by its deserts, and great mountains and canyons, with the Baja California peninsula as a place apart. The area northwest of the capital has the country's finest colonial architecture. Central and Southern Mexico, and the Gulf Coast region, are most visited for their pre-Columbian ruins.

Cañón del Cobre *(see pp180–81)*, a spectacularly deep and scenic canyon, can be viewed from one of the world's most extraordinary railroads.

Baja California *(see pp166–9)* is popular with visitors from the USA who head especially for the beaches and resorts on its southern tip. In the winter months, whales can be seen off the shores of "Baja."

Guadalajara *(see pp192–3)* is dominated by its 16th-century cathedral. It is the largest of the colonial cities to the northwest of Mexico City. Also worth visiting are San Miguel de Allende, Morelia, and Guanajuato.

◀ Aerial view of the historic city of Guanajuato, a UNESCO World Heritage site

El Tajín *(see pp246–7)* was home to the Totonac civilization between AD 700 and 900. It is one of the best places in Mexico to see voladores dancers perform *(see p33)*.

Teotihuacán *(see pp138–41)* was once the most powerful city of the New World. Its people left behind a fascinating legacy, including the towering Pyramids of the Sun and the Moon.

Palenque *(see pp238–41)* is notable for its fine stucco carvings. Beneath its main temple, the Temple of Inscriptions, is the only known Maya crypt, which was created for Pakal, the ruler of Palenque.

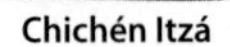

Chichén Itzá *(see pp278–80)* is the best preserved of Mexico's Maya sites, with temples, an observatory, and the largest ballcourt in Mexico. It flourished from the 11th to the 13th century.

Oaxaca *(see pp226–9)* is an elegant colonial city with a number of churches and museums, and two lively markets. This relief of the Virgin is found over the main door to the cathedral.

AROUND MEXICO CITY

Guerrero (North) · Hidalgo · Mexico State · Morelos Puebla · Tlaxcala

Snowcapped volcanoes, among them Mexico's highest peaks, tower over the country's central plateau – a series of vast plains and broad valleys at altitudes of around 2,000 m (6,550 ft). Centered on the Valley of Mexico, the country's heart for over two millennia, this region has an unparalleled collection of stunning pre-Columbian and colonial monuments, set against dramatic natural backdrops.

These highlands were densely populated even before the arrival of the Spanish in 1519. Great civilizations flourished here and built extensive cities and awesome ceremonial sites such as Tula and Teotihuacán. Spanish missionaries fanned out from here to explore and pacify the vast territories later consolidated as New Spain. They dotted the region with fortress-like convents and opulent churches such as San Francisco Javier in Tepotzotlán. Puebla, the provincial capital east of Mexico City, with its exuberant ecclesiastical and secular architecture, was one of the colony's most important cities. Meanwhile, the discovery of precious metals sparked the development of mining towns, most notably the picturesque Taxco. Today, busy highways radiate from Mexico City to burgeoning cities in the neighboring states. So far, however, the incursions of modern Mexico into the region have not significantly disturbed the area's natural beauty, protected in part by a series of national parks.

A rich volcanic soil accounts for the region's endless fields of crops – rice and sugar cane at lower altitudes in the south, grain and vegetables elsewhere. The land once belonged to huge estates, run from imposing haciendas. After the Revolution, much of it became communal, and it remains the principal means of subsistence for the region's rural population, many of whom are Nahua and Otomí Indians, the two largest of Mexico's indigenous groups.

The ruins of the great city of Teotihuacán, one of the most fascinating pre-Columbian sites in Mexico

◀ Detailed facade of the 16th-century Ex-Convento Dominico de la Natividad, Tepoztlán

Exploring Around Mexico City

The routes north of Mexico City lead to a colonial treasure trove at the Museo Nacional del Virreinato, and to the pyramids of Tula and Teotihuacán, the latter Mexico's most visited pre-Columbian site. To the east, beyond Popocatépetl and Iztaccíhuatl volcanoes, is the splendid colonial city of Puebla, a good base for visiting isolated Cantona and the ancient murals at Cacaxtla. The western part of the region has cool forests and scenic lakes, while to the south warmer weather attracts visitors to busy Cuernavaca and beautiful Taxco, famed for its silversmiths and Churrigueresque church.

Dome of the Iglesia de la Compañía in Puebla

Sights at a Glance

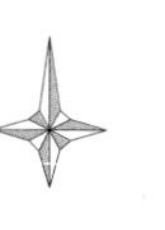

The Pyramid of the Sun, the largest structure at Teotihuacán

For hotels and restaurants see pp297–8 and pp317–19

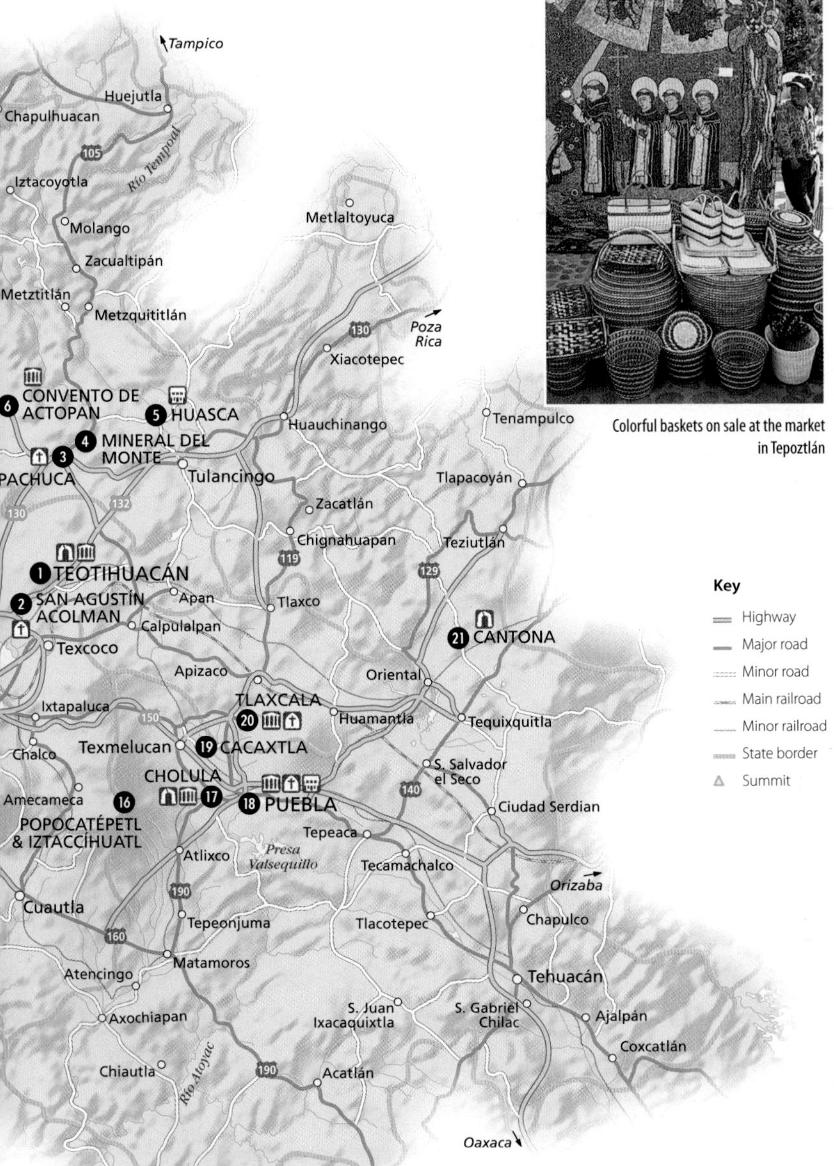

Colorful baskets on sale at the market in Tepoztlán

Key

- Highway
- Major road
- Minor road
- Main railroad
- Minor railroad
- State border
- Summit

Getting Around

Modern toll highways lead out of Mexico City in all directions, and signs indicating them are being improved. Two highways, the Periférico and Circuito Interior, partially circle the capital, while the Viaducto cuts across it from west to east. A network of mostly paved roads connects the outlying towns and cities. Frequent express buses serve the cities, and bus services from here to smaller towns are highly efficient. However, a car or taxi is needed for remote sights such as Cantona. The few trains still running no longer take passengers.

For keys to symbols *see back flap*

❶ Teotihuacán

Teotihuacán is one of the most impressive cities of the ancient world. Founded before the Christian era, this colossal urban center once housed up to 125,000 people and covered over 20 sq km (8 sq miles). It dominated life in the region for 500 years before being destroyed (possibly by its own people) and abandoned, around AD 650. Later, the site was held sacred by the Aztecs, who believed it had been built by giants. The ceremonial center, with its temples, palaces, and pyramids, bears witness to the city's splendor. However, the inhabitants' origin, way of life, and even demise remain a mystery. Teotihuacán is an active archaeological site, with new discoveries made regularly.

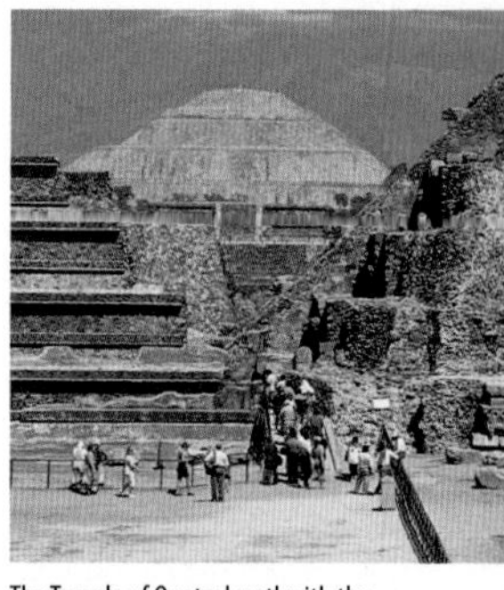

The Temple of Quetzalcoatl with the Pyramid of the Sun behind

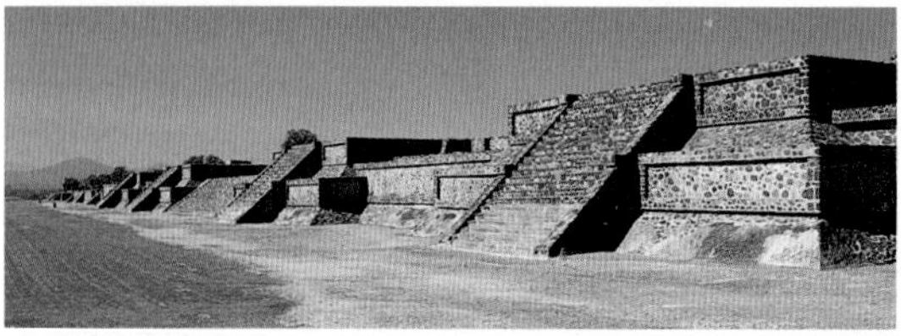

Avenue of the Dead
This wide avenue runs the length of the present site but once stretched much farther toward the south. It was named by the Aztecs who mistakenly believed that the buildings lining it were royal tombs.

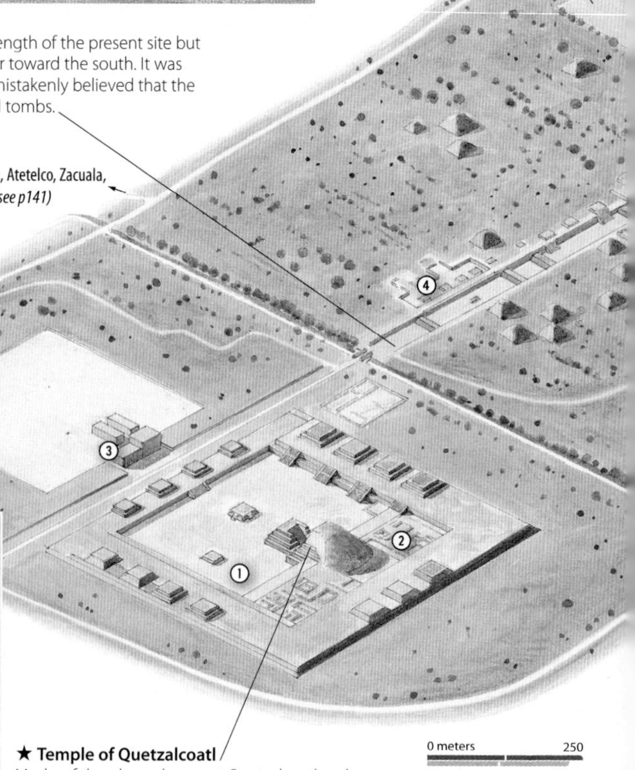
Entrance 2
Palaces of Tetitla, Atetelco, Zacuala, and Yayahuala *(see p141)*
Entrance 1
Mexico City
①
②
③
④
0 meters 250
0 yards 250

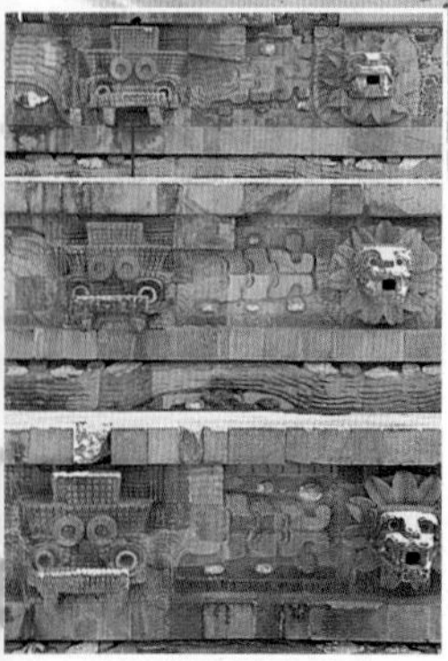

★ Temple of Quetzalcoatl
Masks of the plumed serpent Quetzalcoatl and a god sometimes identified as rain god Tlaloc decorate this temple. Built around AD 200, it was later covered by a pyramid, which has now been partially removed.

For hotels and restaurants see pp297–8 and pp317–19

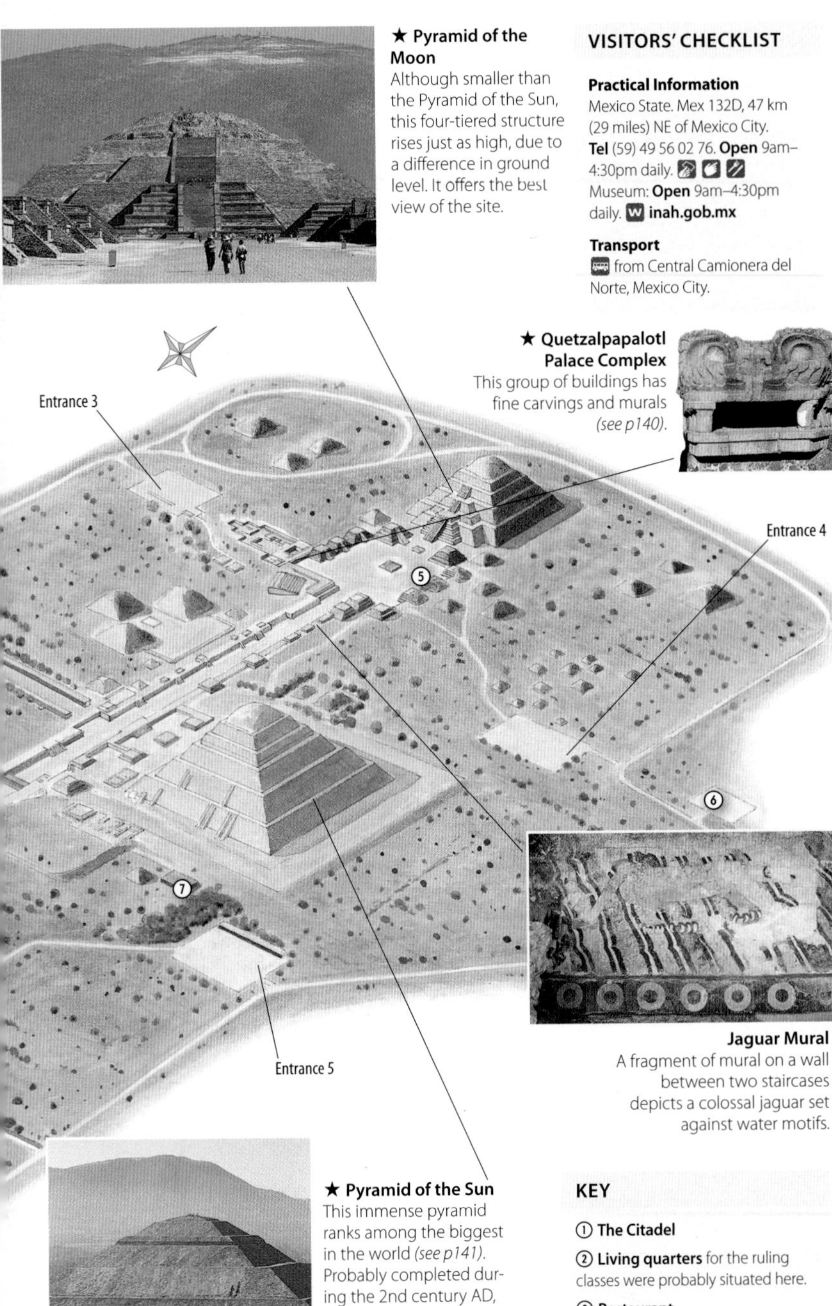

★ Pyramid of the Moon
Although smaller than the Pyramid of the Sun, this four-tiered structure rises just as high, due to a difference in ground level. It offers the best view of the site.

★ Quetzalpapalotl Palace Complex
This group of buildings has fine carvings and murals *(see p140)*.

Jaguar Mural
A fragment of mural on a wall between two staircases depicts a colossal jaguar set against water motifs.

★ Pyramid of the Sun
This immense pyramid ranks among the biggest in the world *(see p141)*. Probably completed during the 2nd century AD, it is made of adobe bricks and earth, covered with gravel and stone. This would have been coated with brightly painted stucco. Chambers and a tunnel have been found beneath the structure.

VISITORS' CHECKLIST

Practical Information
Mexico State. Mex 132D, 47 km (29 miles) NE of Mexico City.
Tel (59) 49 56 02 76. **Open** 9am–4:30pm daily.
Museum: **Open** 9am–4:30pm daily. **inah.gob.mx**

Transport
from Central Camionera del Norte, Mexico City.

KEY

① **The Citadel**

② **Living quarters** for the ruling classes were probably situated here.

③ **Restaurant**

④ **The Superimposed Buildings *(Edificios Superpuestos)***

⑤ **Plaza of the Moon**

⑥ **Palace of Tepantitla** *(see p141)*

⑦ **Museum** *(see p141)*

Quetzalpapalotl Palace Complex

This maze of residential and temple structures grew slowly over several centuries. The last part to be built was probably the elegant Palace of Quetzalpapalotl, uncovered in 1962 and reconstructed with mostly original materials. It sits atop the now buried Temple of the Feathered Conches (2nd–3rd century AD). The Jaguar Palace, just to the west, has a large courtyard faced by a portico and a stepped temple base.

The Palace of Quetzalpapalotl is named for the mythological creatures (bird-butterflies) carved into its courtyard pillars. They have obsidian eyes and are surrounded by water and fire symbols.

Murals in the Jaguar Palace show plumed jaguars playing musical instruments made from feathered shells.

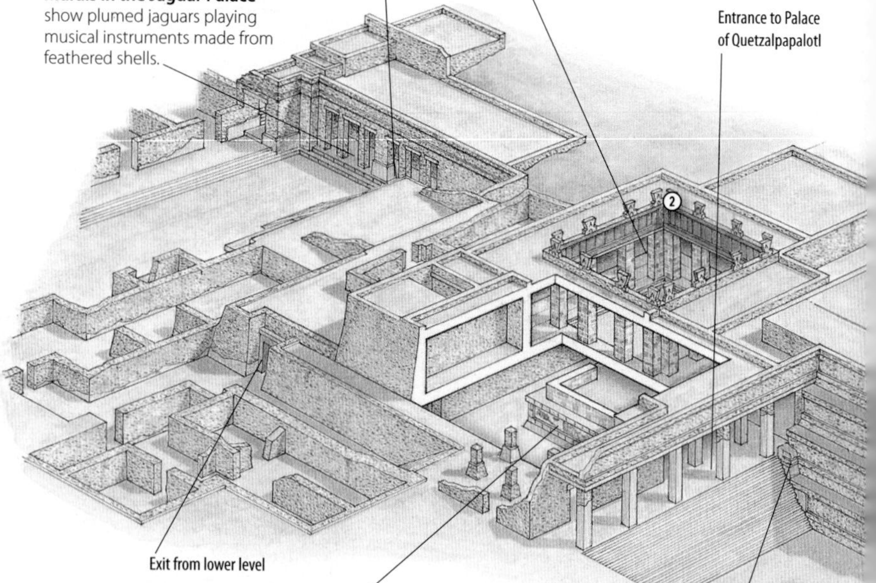

Entrance to lower level

Entrance to Palace of Quetzalpapalotl

Exit from lower level

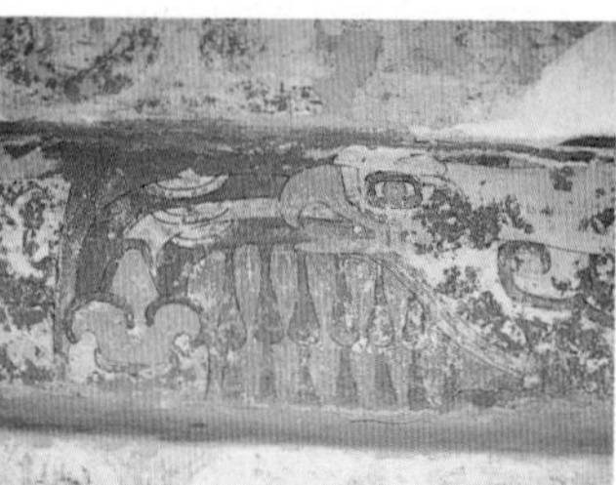

The Temple of the Feathered Conches is an older structure that archaeologists discovered buried beneath the Palace of Quetzalpapalotl. It sits on a platform adorned with brilliantly colored murals such as this one, which depict green parrot-like birds spewing water from their beaks. Reliefs of feathered conches and four-petaled flowers decorate the temple facade.

A stone serpent's head of enormous proportions juts out from the top of a steep staircase and guards the porticoed entrance to the Palace of Quetzalpapalotl.

KEY

① **Plaza of the Moon**

② **Decorative merlons** symbolizing the calendar crown the courtyard.

For hotels and restaurants see pp297–8 and pp317–19

Exploring Teotihuacán

In order to appreciate the grandeur and colossal scale of this awesome site, visitors should be prepared for long walks over uneven ground and stiff climbs up steep stairways – all at an altitude of 2,300 m (7,550 ft) and often under a hot tropical sun. Comfortable shoes, a hat, and sunblock are a must, plus basic rain gear in summer.

Partially restored mural depicting feathered coyotes, at Atetelco

The Museum

The on-site museum is located just south of the Pyramid of the Sun. It displays artifacts found at Teotihuacán, explanatory maps and diagrams, and, beneath the glass floor of its main hall, a scale model of the city. The shady gardens outside are a good place to rest during a tour of the site. They are planted with botanical species native to the area and decorated with original Teotihuacán sculptures.

Outlying Palaces

Several ancient dwelling complexes are situated beyond the fence and road that ring the site. Some 500 m (0.3 miles) east of the Pyramid of the Sun lies the **Palace of Tepantitla**, which contains the most important and colorful murals discovered so far at Teotihuacán. These include representations of elaborately dressed priests, the rain god Tlaloc, and his carefree paradise, Tlalocan, where miniature human figures frolic in an Eden-like setting.

Bird spewing water, in the museum

Just west of the site, and best reached by car, are four other palaces: Tetitla, Atetelco, Zacuala, and Yayahuala. **Tetitla** is a maze-like complex of more than 120 walls, showing remnants of refined frescoes depicting birds, jaguars, priests, and various deities. **Atetelco** is distinguished by a miniature altar in one courtyard and, in another, stunning red murals of jaguars and coyotes with feathered headdresses. **Zacuala** and **Yayahuala** are extensive complexes with sophisticated drainage systems, and vestiges of wall paintings in their many rooms, corridors, courtyards, and porticoes.

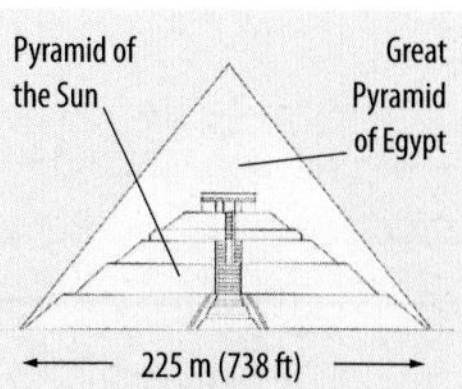

Two Pyramids

The Pyramid of the Sun stands on a base of very similar dimensions to that of the Great Pyramid of Egypt, but it is only half the height – 65 m (213 ft), as against 144 m (472 ft). It consists of about 2.5 million tonnes of stone and earth, compared with the Great Pyramid's 6.5 million.

The Unearthing of Teotihuacán

Bones found on the site

For more than 1,000 years after its decline, the crumbled ruins of Teotihuacán remained hidden below a thick layer of earth and vegetation. Despite being venerated by the Aztecs, the site was never noticed by Cortés and his men when they passed by during their retreat from Tenochtitlán in 1520. The structures visible today, a mere tenth of the city, were excavated at digs that began in 1864 and continue to this day. Early 20th-century reconstructions partially destroyed and distorted some of the principal edifices, but since then more systematic explorations have resulted in the unearthing of the Temple of Quetzalcoatl in the 1920s and the Palace of Quetzalpapalotl 40 years later. Chambers were discovered under the Pyramid of the Sun in 1971, and in 1998 archaeologists found human remains and offerings inside the Pyramid of the Moon.

Bird fresco at Tetitla, excavated in the 1950s

The Plateresque facade of the church of San Agustín Acolman

❷ San Agustín Acolman

Mexico State. Acolman, off Mex 85, 38 km (24 miles) NE of Mexico City. Acolman. **Open** 10am–5pm daily. **inah.gob.mx/paseos/exacolman**

One of Mexico's oldest monasteries, San Agustín Acolman was founded in 1536 by Augustinian monks sent here to convert the local Indians. It is notable for its atrium, a Christian version of the pre-Columbian ceremonial plaza, where crowds of Indian disciples would gather to hear the new religion preached from a chapel balcony above. The fortress-like building, now housing colonial paintings and sculptures, is typical of New Spain's early monasteries.

The forbidding aspect of the monastery is softened, however, by the adjoining church's beautiful Plateresque facade, which is characterized by classic Italian Renaissance columns, richly decorated door arches, and a choir window replicating the portal below. The sparse interior of the 57-m (187-ft) nave is notable only for its apse, which boasts Gothic fan vaulting and is adorned with rich frescoes.

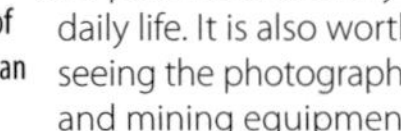

Detail on facade of San Agustín Acolman

❸ Pachuca

Hidalgo. 268,000. Avenida Madero 702, (771) 715 14 41. Feria Regional de Pachuca (Oct).

Pachuca, capital of Hidalgo state, lies in the heart of one of Mexico's richest mining areas. The center of town, with its steep, narrow lanes and small squares, retains some buildings from the two mining booms of the 16th and 18th centuries.

Undoubtedly, the most significant colonial complex is the late 16th-century **Ex-Convento de San Francisco** and its adjoining church. The church contains the remains of the 3rd-century martyr St. Columba, whose mummified body was brought here in the 18th century. Part of the massive monastery building houses the **Fototeca Nacional** (National Photographic Archive) and the **Museo de Fotografía**. The latter has exhibits on the history of photography and shows selections from the 1 million photos on file. One section is dedicated to the Casasola Archive, an outstanding chronicle of the Mexican Revolution and post-Revolutionary daily life. It is also worth seeing the photographs and mining equipment at the **Museo de Minería** and the mineral samples at the **Museo de Mineralogía**. The tower in the main plaza, the 40-m (130-ft) Neo-Classical **Reloj Monumental** (Monumental Clock), has an eight-bell carillon made by the creators of Big Ben in London.

Environs

The hills of **El Chico**, a vast national park north of Pachuca, are very popular with hikers, fishermen, and rock climbers.

Fototeca Nacional and Museo de Fotografía
Casasola. **Tel** (771) 714 36 53. **Open** 10am–6pm Tue–Sun. reserve in advance.

Museo de Minería
Mina 110. **Tel** (771) 715 09 76. **Open** 10am–6pm Tue–Sun. Sun free.

Museo de Mineralogía
Abasolo 600. **Tel** (771) 717 20 00, ext. 1302. **Open** 8am–4:30pm Mon–Fri (10am–1pm during holidays).

❹ Mineral del Monte

Hidalgo. 14,000. Rubén Licona Ruiz 1, (771) 797 05 10.

Better known as Real del Monte, this mining town, at an altitude of 2,700 m (8,800 ft), used to be the richest in the area. Gold and silver were discovered here before the Conquest *(see p47)*, and the Spanish started mining in the mid-1500s. The mines were later abandoned, but reopened in the late 1730s under Pedro Romero de Terreros.

The town's steep streets, stairways, and small squares are lined with low buildings, some dating

The charming colors of houses on the central plaza in Mineral del Monte

Fresco at the Convento de San Nicolás de Tolentino de Actopan

back to colonial times. The houses with high sloping roofs and chimneys indicate a Cornish influence, the legacy left by the 350 Cornishmen employed by the English company that ran the mines between 1824 and 1848. They are also responsible for *pastes*, a local specialty based on the Cornish pasty, as well as for introducing soccer to Mexico.

5 Huasca

Hidalgo. 17,000. to Pachuca. Plaza Principal, (771) 792 07 47. San Sebastián (Jan 20).

The picturesque village of Huasca is best known for its *haciendas de beneficio*, haciendas where mineral ores were refined. One of the most visited is **San Miguel Regla**, 3 km (2 miles) northeast of town. It is now a hotel *(see p297)* and offers guided tours of its *beneficio* installations. More impressive is **Hacienda Santa María Regla**, a little farther away, which has vaulted cellars, and patios with stone drag mills and melting ovens. From here visitors can access the spectacular 15-km (9-mile) canyon **Prismas Basálticos**, whose walls are made up of red and ocher basalt hexagons.

Hacienda Santa María Regla
7 km (4.5 miles) NE of Huasca. **Tel** (55) 59 38 48 58. **Open** daily.
haciendaderegla.com.mx

6 Convento de San Nicolás de Tolentino de Actopan

Hidalgo. Actopan, 36 km (22 miles) NW of Pachuca. Actopan. **Open** 9am–5pm Tue–Sun. reserve in advance.

The imposing Convento de San Nicolás de Tolentino de Actopan, built in the 1550s, is one of Mexico's most remarkable and best preserved 16th-century fortress-monasteries. Even more spectacular than its Plateresque church facade, square Moorish tower, and vaulted open chapel are its frescoes, which are considered the most beautiful and extensive from this era in Mexico. The finest include the portraits of saints on the main stairs and the depiction of hermits in the De Profundis hall, in a style reminiscent of native codices. Perhaps most impressive are the naive scenes of heaven and hell in the open chapel.

Adam and Eve fresco, Convento de Actopan

Environs
In Ixmiquilpan, 40 km (25 miles) farther north, is the **Ex-Convento de San Miguel Arcángel**. Now a museum, it displays some fine frescoes that incorporate Indian warriors, Biblical scenes, and pre-Columbian figures.

Ex-Convento de San Miguel Arcángel
Av Angeles, Ixmiquilpan. **Open** daily.

Fiestas Around Mexico City

Chalma Pilgrimages *(Jan 6, Easter week, May 3, Jul 1)*, Chalma *(see p149)*. Hordes of pilgrims, laden with colorful flowers, can be seen making their way to the shrine of El Señor de Chalma – by foot, on their knees, by car, bicycle, or bus. Pentecost celebrations on May 3 include traditional dances by the splendidly attired Concheros dancers.

Chalma pilgrims armed with bunches of flowers

Fiesta de los Tiznados *(Jan 21)*, Tepoztlán *(see p152)*. Revelers smear themselves with ash in remembrance of the ancient Tepoztec king, who fled his enemies disguised as a peasant.

El Día de la Batalla de Puebla *(May 5)*, Puebla *(see pp154–7)*. The 1862 Mexican victory over the French at the Battle of Puebla is celebrated with re-enactments, military parades, and fireworks. Also called Cinco de Mayo.

Fiesta de la Virgen de la Caridad *(mid-Aug)*, Huamantla *(see p161)*. On the first Sunday of the fiesta the image of the Virgin is carried over 5 km (3 miles) of sawdust carpet, and her church is decorated. The following Sunday, bulls run through the streets as part of the *Huamantlada*.

Reto al Tepozteco *(late Aug–mid-Sep)*, Tepoztlán *(see p152)*. Following tradition, local villagers race one another up Tepozteco Hill, before consuming copious quantities of *pulque (see p313)*.

❼ Museo Nacional del Virreinato

The country's most complete collection of colonial art and artifacts, one of its finest Baroque churches, and a splendid former Jesuit college built in the 17th and 18th centuries together make up this stunning museum covering Mexico's viceregal era. The church and college buildings, a vast complex with courtyards and gardens in the quaint village of Tepotzotlán, were nearly complete when the Jesuits were expelled from New Spain in 1767. They were extensively restored and opened as a museum in 1964. Exhibits include treasures preserved in situ as well as pieces brought here from other collections around the country.

Gardens
Formerly an orchard, the peaceful gardens have a chapel and an aqueduct.

Claustro de los Naranjos
This courtyard, once a place of meditation for novices, is filled with orange trees.

Stairs to lower level

Ivory Statues
These figures of the Virgin Mary and Christ show the Asian features characteristic of religious carvings created in the Orient. They were probably brought to New Spain from the Philippines.

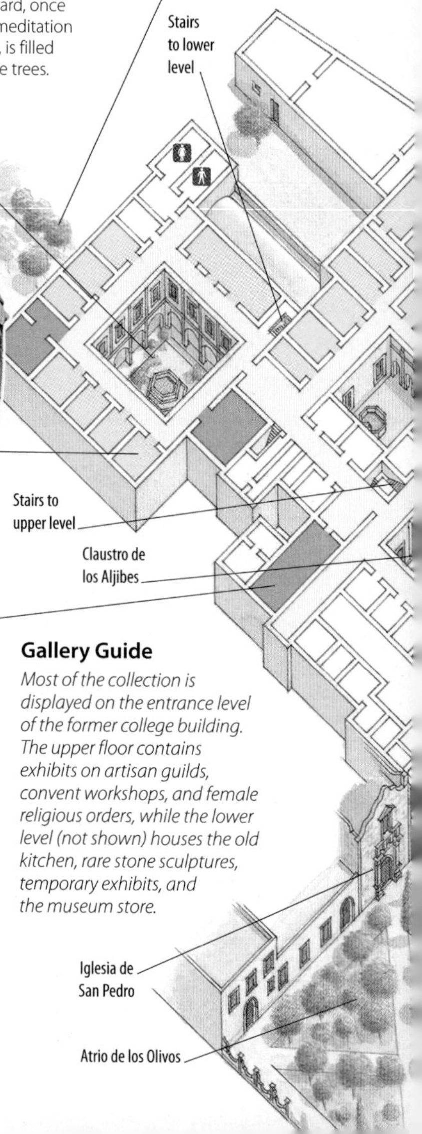

Stairs to upper level

Claustro de los Aljibes

Gallery Guide

Most of the collection is displayed on the entrance level of the former college building. The upper floor contains exhibits on artisan guilds, convent workshops, and female religious orders, while the lower level (not shown) houses the old kitchen, rare stone sculptures, temporary exhibits, and the museum store.

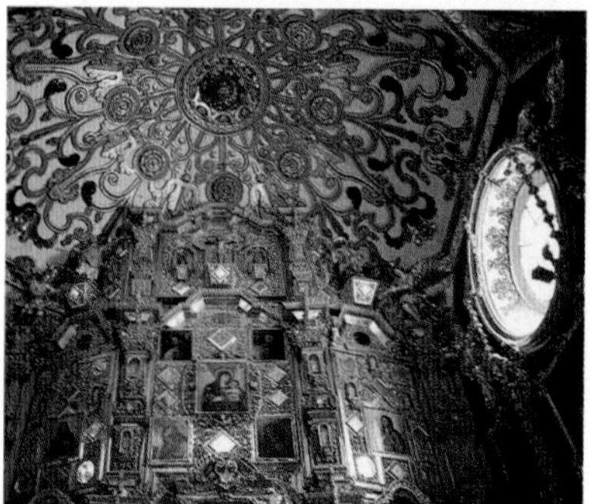

★ Capilla Doméstica
The chapel was for the exclusive use of college residents. Profuse decorations include paintings, statuettes, reliquaries, mirrors, and polychrome plasterwork, all effective means of inspiring religious awe in the students during services.

Iglesia de San Pedro

Atrio de los Olivos

VISITORS' CHECKLIST

Practical Information
Plaza Hidalgo 99, Tepotzotlán, 44 km (27 miles) N of Mexico City.
Tel (55) 58 76 27 70. **Open** 9am–6pm Tue–Sun. Sun free. in advance.
virreinato.inah.gob.mx

Transport
from Central Camionera del Norte, Mexico City.

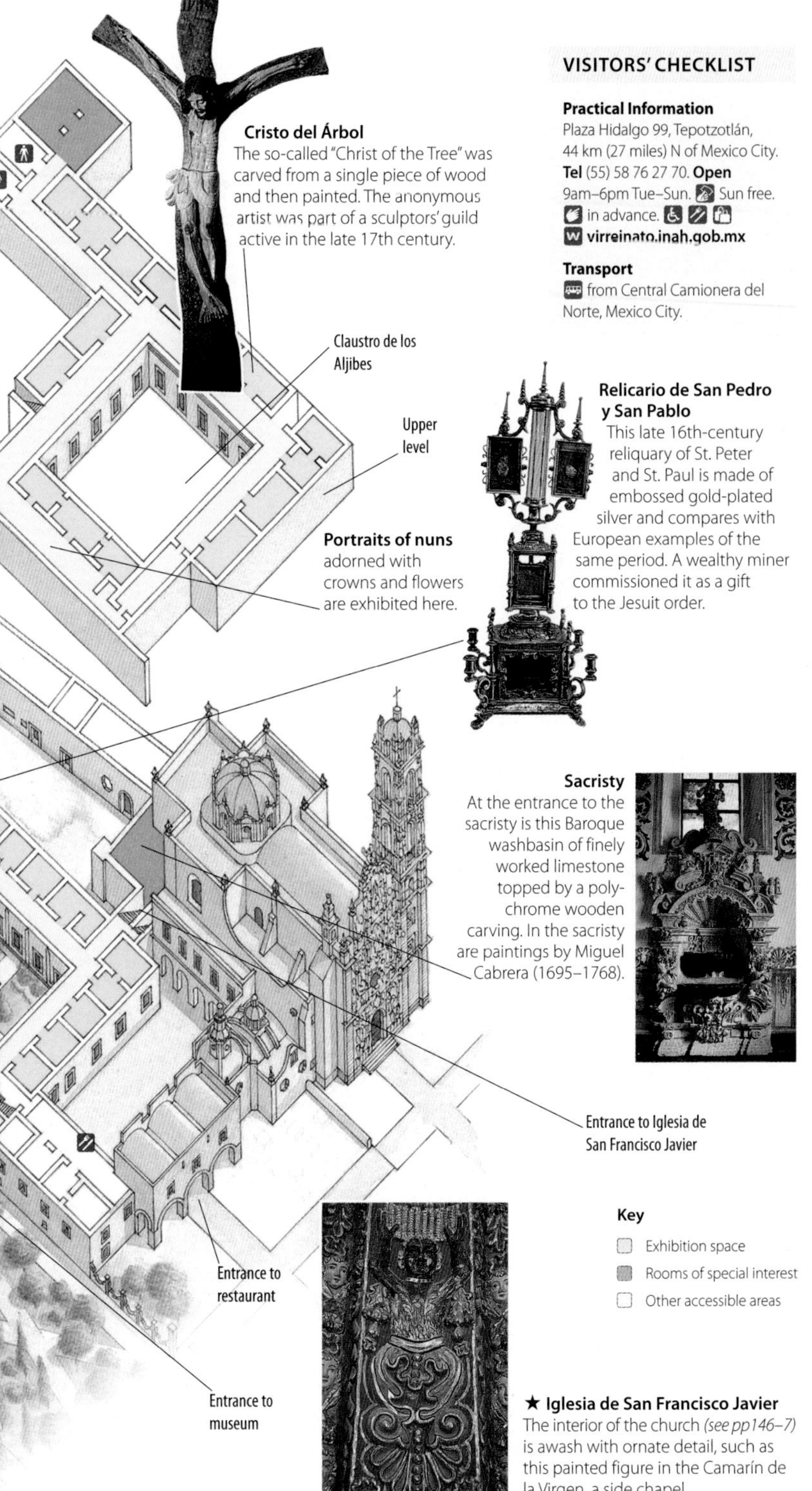

Cristo del Árbol
The so-called "Christ of the Tree" was carved from a single piece of wood and then painted. The anonymous artist was part of a sculptors' guild active in the late 17th century.

Relicario de San Pedro y San Pablo
This late 16th-century reliquary of St. Peter and St. Paul is made of embossed gold-plated silver and compares with European examples of the same period. A wealthy miner commissioned it as a gift to the Jesuit order.

Portraits of nuns adorned with crowns and flowers are exhibited here.

Sacristy
At the entrance to the sacristy is this Baroque washbasin of finely worked limestone topped by a polychrome wooden carving. In the sacristy are paintings by Miguel Cabrera (1695–1768).

★ Iglesia de San Francisco Javier
The interior of the church *(see pp146–7)* is awash with ornate detail, such as this painted figure in the Camarín de la Virgen, a side chapel.

Iglesia de San Francisco Javier

Constructed in the late 1600s, this majestic Baroque church is famous for its splendid 18th-century additions: the richly decorated Churrigueresque facade and tower, the exuberant gold altars, a trio of unusual chapels on one side, and the Miguel Cabrera murals in the chancel and cross vaults. The facade and interior are both prime examples of Mexican High Baroque. Together they form a harmonious whole equaled only by Santa Prisca in Taxco *(see p151)* and San Cayetano near Guanajuato *(see p209)*.

★ Main Altar
The most imposing of the altars in the church is dedicated to St. Francis Xavier, patron saint of the Jesuit college.

Entrance from museum

★ Relicario de San José
Built to house relics revered by the Jesuits, this chapel resembles the inside of a treasure chest.

KEY

① **Corridor**

② **The Casa de Loreto** is said to be a replica of the Virgin Mary's Nazareth home, which angels moved to Loreto in Italy when the Muslims invaded the Holy Land. A 17th-century image of the Virgin of Loreto adorns the gold altar in the otherwise sober interior.

③ **The altar to the Virgin of Guadalupe** centers on a Miguel Cabrera painting of the patron saint of Mexico.

④ **The altar to St. Stanislaus Kostka** honors a Polish Jesuit who served as a model to the novices and students of the institution.

⑤ **The altar to St. Ignatius Loyola** shows the founder of the Jesuits holding a book displaying the order's crest and motto.

⑥ **The bell tower** has 13 bells hanging on three levels under a tiled dome topped by a filigreed iron cross.

⑦ **Pulpit**

★ Camarín de la Virgen
This profusely decorated octagonal chamber once served as a dressing room for the Virgin of Loreto – the statue's vestments and jewels were changed regularly. The beautiful dome is shaped like a papal tiara.

Dome
The dome rising above the intersection of the Latin Cross nave is best seen from a viewpoint in the museum *(see pp144–5)*.

Altar to the Virgen de la Luz
A multitude of cherubs and angels surrounds the central image of the Virgin and Child; one proffers a basket containing souls from purgatory. The pulpit (beside the altar) is from a church in Mexico City.

Facade
The imagery and style of the frontispiece echoes that of the altars inside, while the abundance of finely carved limestone prepares the visitor for the brilliant interior.

Estípite Pilasters
So-called *estípite* pilasters form the verticals of the altars. Inspired by the proportions of the human figure, *estípites* taper off at the base, thus appearing to be upside down. Many are decorated with faces.

The towering Atlantes, standing guard on the Pyramid of the Morning Star at Tula

8 Tula

Hidalgo. Off Mex 57, 85 km (53 miles) N of Mexico City. Tula de Allende then taxi. **Tel** (773) 100 36 54. **Open** daily.

The most important Toltec site in Mexico, Tula flourished as a great urban center from AD 900–1200, after the decline of Teotihuacán *(see pp138–41)* and prior to the rise of Tenochtitlán *(see pp45–6)*. At its peak, the city covered up to 16 sq km (6 sq miles) and had an estimated population of 40,000. Then inner strife, invasions, and fire destroyed the Toltec empire and this, its capital. Only remnants of the main palaces, temples, and ballcourts survive on a windswept hill overlooking the small town of Tula de Allende.

The site is most famous for its giant stone sculptures, the Atlantes. At a height of 4.6 m (15 ft), these four warrior figures in battle gear crown the Pyramid of Tlahuizcalpantecuhtli, or the Morning Star. Together with a massive serpent and other pillars, they probably once supported an ornately carved roof. (Note that parts of the sculptures are reproductions.) The base of the temple and the Coatepantli, or Serpent Wall, on its northern flank, are decorated with carved friezes of serpents, eagles, and jaguars, some devouring human hearts.

Certain stylistic elements at Tula – such as the column-filled Palacio Quemado (Burnt Palace), the *chacmool* sculptures, and the huge size of Ballcourt No. 2 – underline the site's similarity to the Maya city of Chichén Itzá *(see pp278–80)*. Legend tells that Toltec king Topiltzín was driven out of Tula and fled to the Yucatán Peninsula where he ushered in a cultural renaissance. Recent theories dispute this, however, suggesting that the similarities are a result of Maya influence on Tula, not vice versa.

9 Valle de Bravo

Mexico State. 62,000. Antiguo Palacio Municipal, (726) 269 62 00 or 01800 69 69 696 (toll free). Santa Cruz (May 3), San Francisco (Oct 4). **valledebravo.gob.mx**

Set among pine-covered volcanic mountains, this pretty colonial town traces its origins back to the earliest days of Spanish rule. It achieved popularity after the construction of an artificial lake in the 1950s. "Valle" offers an equable climate, a wide range of sports (especially hang gliding, horseback riding, and waterskiing), and stunning scenery. The landscape around the town and lake is perfect for hiking, and trails wind past mountain streams, cornfields, and patches of wildflowers.

Easy access from Mexico City and a lively nightlife make the town a favorite weekend destination for the capital's elite, but during the week peace returns to the cobbled streets.

The lake at Valle de Bravo, popular with watersports enthusiasts

The pastel tones of Templo de la Santa Veracruz in Toluca

10 Toluca

Mexico State. 820,000. 1st de Mayo corner Robert Bosch, (722) 276 19 00. Virgen del Carmen (Jul 16). **toluca.gob.mx**

The capital city of Mexico State is, at 2,680 m (8,790 ft) above sea level, the highest state capital in the country.

Founded by the Spaniards in the late 17th century, Toluca is full of fine buildings. In the city center, near Plaza de los Mártires, are the 18th-century **Templo de la Santa Veracruz** and the 19th-century **Portales**, a series of arched walkways lined with cafés and shops. To the north is the **Museo de Bellas Artes**, which exhibits Mexican art from the last four centuries. Nearby, the **Cosmovitral Jardín Botánico** shows botanical specimens in the beautiful old market, its walls and ceiling ablaze with colorful stained glass. Every Friday, Toluca plays host to what is thought to be the country's largest market.

To the southeast, the suburb of **Metepec** is famous for its brightly colored, ceramic *árboles de la vida* (trees of life; *see pp332–3)*, loosely based on the story of Adam and Eve; examples can be purchased.

Environs

Just 8 km (5 miles) west of Toluca is the **Centro Cultural Mexiquense**, a large complex of museums devoted to modern art, local history, and regional crafts.

The extinct, snow-capped **Nevado de Toluca** volcano, Mexico's fourth highest mountain at 4,690 m (15,387 ft), is a 45-km (28-mile) drive southwest. A dirt road leads almost to the top, and hikers can descend into the crater.

The hilltop ceremonial center of **Teotenango** is 25 km (16 miles) south of Toluca. Dating from AD 900, the extensive site features several restored pyramids, plazas, a ballcourt, and a museum.

Museo de Bellas Artes
Santos Degollado 102, Poniente. **Tel** (722) 215 53 29. **Open** 10am–6pm Tue–Sun. Wed free.

Cosmovitral Jardín Botánico
Juárez & Lerdo s/n. **Tel** (722) 214 67 85. **Open** 9am–6pm Tue–Sun.

Centro Cultural Mexiquense
Blvd Jesús Reyes Heroles 302. **Tel** (722) 274 12 72. **Open** 10am–6pm Tue–Sat (to 3pm Sun).

The stained-glass ceiling of Cosmo Vitral Jardín Botánico in Toluca

View of the town below from the lofty ruins of Malinalco

11 Malinalco

Mexico State. Off Mex 55, 70 km (43 miles) SE of Toluca. 26,000. **malinalco.gob.mx**

This charming town is nestled in a valley, surrounded by steep volcanic hills. An Aztec ceremonial center sits on a narrow ledge 20 minutes' climb above town. Begun in 1501, it was still unfinished at the time of the Spanish conquest.

Its main structure, the House of the Eagle, is carved entirely out of the rock. The doorway represents the fanged mouth of a serpent, and the circular chamber inside has integrated sculptures of jaguars and eagles. The building is thought to have been used for initiation ceremonies of high-ranking Aztec knights. Behind it stand the remains of the Temple of the Sun and the Tzinacalli Edifice, where the bodies of knights killed in combat were burned and deified.

Environs

Chalma, a small village in a deep gorge 12 km (7 miles) east of Malinalco, attracts crowds of pilgrims all year *(see p143)*. They venerate an image of Christ that is said to have miraculously replaced a pagan statue in 1533.

12 Taxco

See pp150–51.

13 Xochicalco

Morelos. Off Mex 95, 40 km (25 miles) SW of Cuernavaca. Alpuyeca then taxi. **Tel** (737) 374 30 91. **Open** daily.

The extensive ruins of Xochicalco, an important city-state in pre-Columbian times, lie on a plateau with splendid views. The city rose to prominence after the decline of Teotihuacán and flourished from AD 700 to 900, before being eclipsed by the rise of the Toltecs.

Pyramid of the Plumed Serpent at Xochicalco

About 30 per cent of the site has been unearthed, including three ballcourts and the remains of several pyramidal structures. An on-site museum displays artifacts found during archaeological work.

The Pyramid of the Plumed Serpent, excavated between 1777 and 1994, is considered one of the most beautiful monuments in the country. It shows remarkably well-preserved bas-reliefs featuring serpents, figures carved in a distinctly Maya style, and glyphs. One theory suggests that the pyramid commemorates a meeting of astronomers from throughout Mesoamerica.

Another highlight is the Observatory, a large underground cave with a narrow shaft bored 8 m (26 ft) through the rock. Twice a year, on May 14–15 and July 28–29, the sun casts the hexagonal image of the shaft on the chamber floor.

⓬ Street-by-Street: Taxco

Set against a spectacular rugged mountainside, 1,800 m (6,000 ft) above sea level, Taxco is one of the least spoiled colonial towns in Mexico. The Spaniards were drawn to the area in 1522 by Aztec tales of rich mineral deposits, and the subsequent silver boom lasted for 100 years. The town's fortunes have been revived twice since, with the discovery of new lodes by José de la Borda in the 18th century, and the arrival of William Spratling in 1932, who established it as a center for silversmiths. There are fine views of the town from the *teleférico* (cable car).

View across the tiled roofs of Taxco

Casa Borda
Overlooking the main square, this house was built by the Borda family in 1759 for the parish priest. Today, it holds exhibitions by local artists.

Plaza Borda
This intimate and lively square is lined with charming old buildings. There are numerous restaurants and bars nearby. In addition, the area abounds with silver shops, filled with the high-quality pieces for which Taxco's many silversmiths are famous.

PLAZUELA DE BERNAL

PLAZA BORDA

OJEDA

CUAUHT

Acapulco

Casa Figueroa was built for the Count of Cadena. It has a dark and interesting history involving subterfuge and murder.

Key

— Suggested route

0 meters 25

0 yards 25

For hotels and restaurants see pp297–8 and pp317–19

★ Museo de Arte Virreinal (Casa Humboldt)
This beautifully maintained building is named after Baron von Humboldt, the German naturalist, who spent a night here in 1803. It contains a well-organized museum.

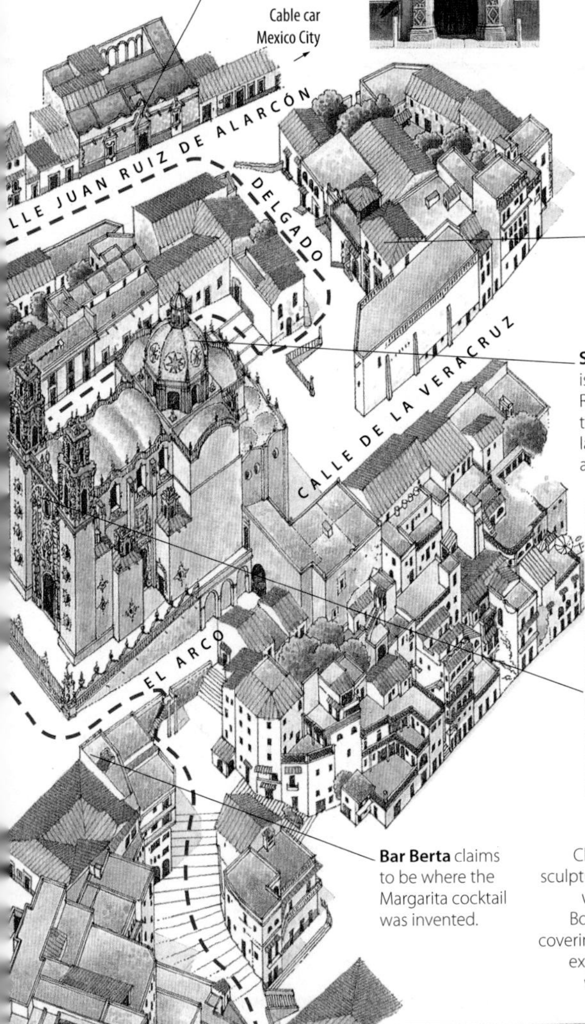

Cable car Mexico City

CALLE JUAN RUIZ DE ALARCÓN

DELGADO

CALLE DE LA VERACRUZ

EL ARCO

VISITORS' CHECKLIST

Practical Information
Guerrero. 48,000. **Tel** (762) 622 01 31. Avenida de los Plateros 126, (762) 622 07 98. Santa Prisca y San Sebastián (Jan), Feria Nacional de la Plata (Nov/Dec). Museo de Arte Virreinal (Casa Humboldt): **Tel** (762) 622 55 01. **Open** Tue–Sun. Museo Guillermo Spratling: **Tel** (762) 622 16 60. **Open** 9am–6pm Tue–Sat (to 3pm Sun). Sun free.

Transport
Avenida de los Plateros 310.

Museo Guillermo Spratling contains William Spratling's collection of pre-Columbian artifacts and works of art from around the world.

Santa Prisca's octagonal dome is covered with colorful tiles. Rising behind the church's twin towers, it is an unmistakable landmark that can be seen from all over the city.

★ Iglesia de Santa Prisca
This magnificent church, with its Churrigueresque facade and ornate sculptures, dominates the Plaza Borda. It was paid for by José (Joseph) de la Borda, who made his fortune by discovering important deposits of silver. No expense was spared in construction, which took seven years (1751–58).

Bar Berta claims to be where the Margarita cocktail was invented.

Local Market
Off the south side of the Plaza Borda is Taxco's bustling market. Stalls laden with fresh produce, basketware, and local crafts crowd the narrow steps.

The imposing facade of the Catedral de la Asunción

⓮ Cuernavaca

Morelos. 365,000. Avenida Morelos Sur 187, (777) 329 55 00. Feria de la Flor (late Mar–mid-Apr), Feria de Tlaltenango (late Aug–early Sep). **cuernavaca.gob.mx/turismo**

Cuernavaca, inhabited since 1200 BC, is one of the oldest cities in the country. Originally called Cuauhnáhuac ("Place of the Whispering Trees"), it was renamed Cuernavaca ("Cow's Horn") by the Spanish. Today it is a popular weekend destination for visitors from Mexico City.

The **Palacio de Cortés** was built by the Spanish on the site of the Aztec pyramids they had destroyed. It served as Cortés's residence until his return to Spain in 1540. Known for a series of 1930 Diego Rivera murals depicting Mexico's history, it also contains the Museo Regional Cuauhnáhuac, a fine collection of archaeological and historical artifacts.

The fortress-like **Catedral de la Asunción**, dating from the 1520s, has refurbished murals thought to have been painted by artists brought over from China or the Philippines in the early days of Spanish trade. The **Museo Robert Brady**, situated in a former cloister of the cathedral, holds the extensive art and craft collection of this American artist.

The well laid-out **Jardín Borda**, created by the former silver magnate José de la Borda *(see pp150–51)* in the 18th century, became a popular retreat for the Emperor Maximilian and his wife *(see p57)*.

To the east is **La Tallera**, the refurbished studio of the great Mexican muralist David Alfaro Siqueiros. Revolutionary politics shaped his life and work, and fired the revolutionary aesthetic behind his ambitious projects. The museum is part of the Proyecto Siqueiros, along with the Sala de Arte Público Siqueiros *(see p91)*.

Environs

About 25 km (16 miles) northwest of the town is the beautiful **Lagunas de Zempoala Park**, with its six lakes fringed by dense forests. Only 10 km (6 miles) of the 70 km **Cacahuamilpa Caverns** have been explored. Around 20 of the majestic chambers, many more than 40 m (120 ft) high, are illuminated.

Palacio de Cortés
Avenida Leyva 100. **Tel** (777) 312 69 96. **Open** Tue–Sun. reserve in advance.

Museo Robert Brady
Netzahualcóyotl 4. **Tel** (777) 318 85 54. **Open** 10am–6pm Tue–Sat (to 5pm Sun).

Jardín Borda
Avenida Morelos 271. **Tel** (777) 318 10 38. **Open** Tue–Sun. Sun free.

La Tallera
Venus 52, Jardín de Cuernavaca. **Tel** (777) 16 01 11 90. **Open** 10am–6pm Tue–Sun. Sun free.
saps-latallera.org

⓯ Tepoztlán

Morelos. 42,000. Los Tiznados (Jan 20 & 21), Carnival (Feb/Mar), Reto al Tepozteco (Sep 8).

Lying in a lush green valley, Tepoztlán is surrounded by spectacular volcanic rock formations. A tiring but worthwhile climb above the town stands the **Santuario del Cerro Tepozteco**, a shrine dedicated to Tepoztecatl, the ancient god of pulque – an alcoholic beverage made from the agave plant *(see p313)*. The dominant building in the town itself is the massive, fortified 16th-century **Ex-Convento Dominico de la Natividad**, whose austere cloister still has delightful mural fragments in the cloisters, though the building is in a state of disrepair. For lovers of pre-Columbian art, the **Museo Carlos Pellicer** holds a small but interesting collection, the legacy of the Tabascan poet and anthropologist Carlos Pellicer, who lived in Tepoztlán *(see p259)*.

Environs

The town of **Cuautla**, 27 km (17 miles) to the southeast, is the site of the last resting place of Emiliano Zapata, one of the heroes of the Revolution *(see p58)*.

Museo Carlos Pellicer
González. **Tel** (739) 395 10 98. **Open** 9am–5pm Tue–Sun.

Surviving murals in the Ex-Convento Dominico de la Natividad, Tepoztlán

⑯ Popocatépetl and Iztaccíhuatl

Mexico State. Off Mex 115, 14 km (9 miles) E of Amecameca.
Tel (597) 978 38 29 (updated reports).
Amecameca then taxi.
iztapopo.conanp.gob.mx

The snow-capped volcanoes of Popocatépetl, or Popo, ("Smoking Mountain") and Iztaccíhuatl ("Sleeping Lady") are the second and third highest peaks in Mexico, standing at 5,465 m (17,930 ft) and 5,230 m (17,160 ft) respectively. On a clear day, they are two of Mexico's most awesome sights.

According to legend, the warrior Popocatépetl fell in love with Iztaccíhuatl, an Aztec princess. To win her hand, he defeated a great rival in battle. Wrongly believing him to be dead, the princess herself then died of a broken heart. In his grief, Popocatépetl turned himself and his princess into these two adjacent mountains. The outline of Iztaccíhuatl bears an uncanny resemblance to that of a sleeping woman.

The **Paso de Cortés**, a saddle between the two peaks accessible by car, is an ideal base for walks on Iztaccíhuatl, but ascents of the peak itself should be left to the very fit and those who have hired a guide. Such services are offered by the park; see the website above. Access to Popocatépetl is currently not permitted due to the threat of volcanic activity.

Nuestra Señora de los Remedios, with Popocatépetl behind

The arcade on the western side of Cholula's *zócalo*

⑰ Cholula

Puebla. 100,500. Portal Guerrero 3, 4 Norte, (222) 261 23 93. Carnival (Feb/Mar), Virgen de los Remedios (1st week of Sep).

Before subjecting it to one of the bloodiest massacres of the Conquest, Cortés described Cholula as "the most beautiful city outside Spain." In pre-Columbian times it had been a sacred city – a place of pilgrimage – and a large and important commercial center.

The arcade on the west side of Cholula's large *zócalo* (main square) shelters restaurants and cafés. Opposite is the fortified, Franciscan **Convento de San Gabriel**. Founded in 1529 on the site of a temple to Quetzalcoatl *(see p269)*, the main church has a single nave with rib vaulting and Gothic tracery. Visitors can tour the monastic kitchen, dining rooms, cloisters, and sleeping areas. On the left of the atrium is the **Capilla Real**, built for Indian converts. It acquired its 49 mosque-like domes in the early part of the 18th century.

The impressive double gateway of San Gabriel, Cholula

To the east is the **Zona Arqueológica**, a site which is dominated by the remains of the largest pyramid ever built in Mesoamerica, at 65 m (213 ft) high. Since the 1930s, archaeologists have dug 8 km (5 miles) of tunnels through this Great Pyramid, identifying at least four stages of construction between 200 BC and AD 800. Visitors enter the tunnels on the north side, and emerge several hundred meters later on the east.

Opposite the entrance to the tunnel is a museum with a large cut-away model of the pyramid and artifacts from the site. Digs on the south side have revealed the **Patio de los Altares**, an area of astounding acoustics, used for public ceremonies and probably the sacrifice of children. On top of the pyramid sits the 1874 church of **Nuestra Señora de los Remedios**. The wonderful view from the atrium takes in Puebla *(see pp154–7)*, the volcanoes, and Cholula's many other churches.

Environs

The extraordinary folk-Baroque church of **Santa María Tonantzintla**, 5 km (3 miles) south of Cholula, has an interior that is bursting with colorful saints, fruit, angels, and cherubs. Begun in the 16th century, it took its Indian craftsmen 200 years to complete. The church of **San Francisco Acatepec** *(see p31)*, 1.5 km (1 mile) farther south, has a facade entirely covered in colorful, handmade Talavera tiles *(see p157)*.

Convento de San Gabriel
Corner of Calle 2 Sur & Avenida Morelos. **Open** daily.

Zona Arqueólogica
Avenida Morelos. **Tel** (222) 247 90 81. **Open** daily.

⓲ Street-by-Street: Puebla

Mexico's fourth-largest city, Puebla is best known for the beautiful Talavera tiles that adorn its walls, domes, and interiors; for *mole poblano* *(see p309)*, the thick sauce enriched with chocolate that originated here; and for being the site of an important battle on May 5, 1862 *(see p56)*. The streets of the compact city center are lined with churches, mansions, and other handsome old buildings and are a delight to stroll around.

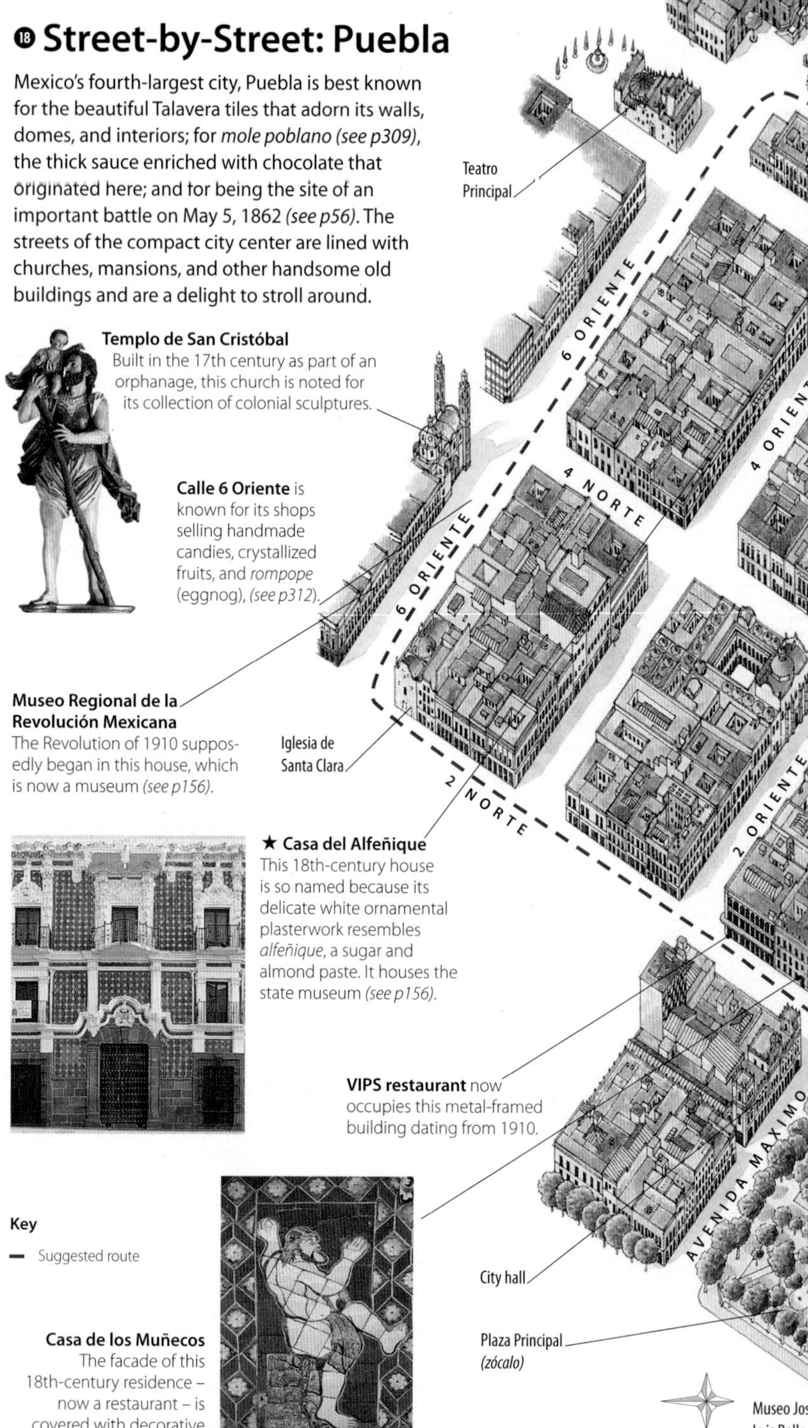

Templo de San Cristóbal
Built in the 17th century as part of an orphanage, this church is noted for its collection of colonial sculptures.

Calle 6 Oriente is known for its shops selling handmade candies, crystallized fruits, and *rompope* (eggnog), *(see p312)*.

Museo Regional de la Revolución Mexicana
The Revolution of 1910 supposedly began in this house, which is now a museum *(see p156)*.

★ Casa del Alfeñique
This 18th-century house is so named because its delicate white ornamental plasterwork resembles *alfeñique*, a sugar and almond paste. It houses the state museum *(see p156)*.

VIPS restaurant now occupies this metal-framed building dating from 1910.

Key

— Suggested route

Casa de los Muñecos
The facade of this 18th-century residence – now a restaurant – is covered with decorative red tiles. Several panels show dancing figures.

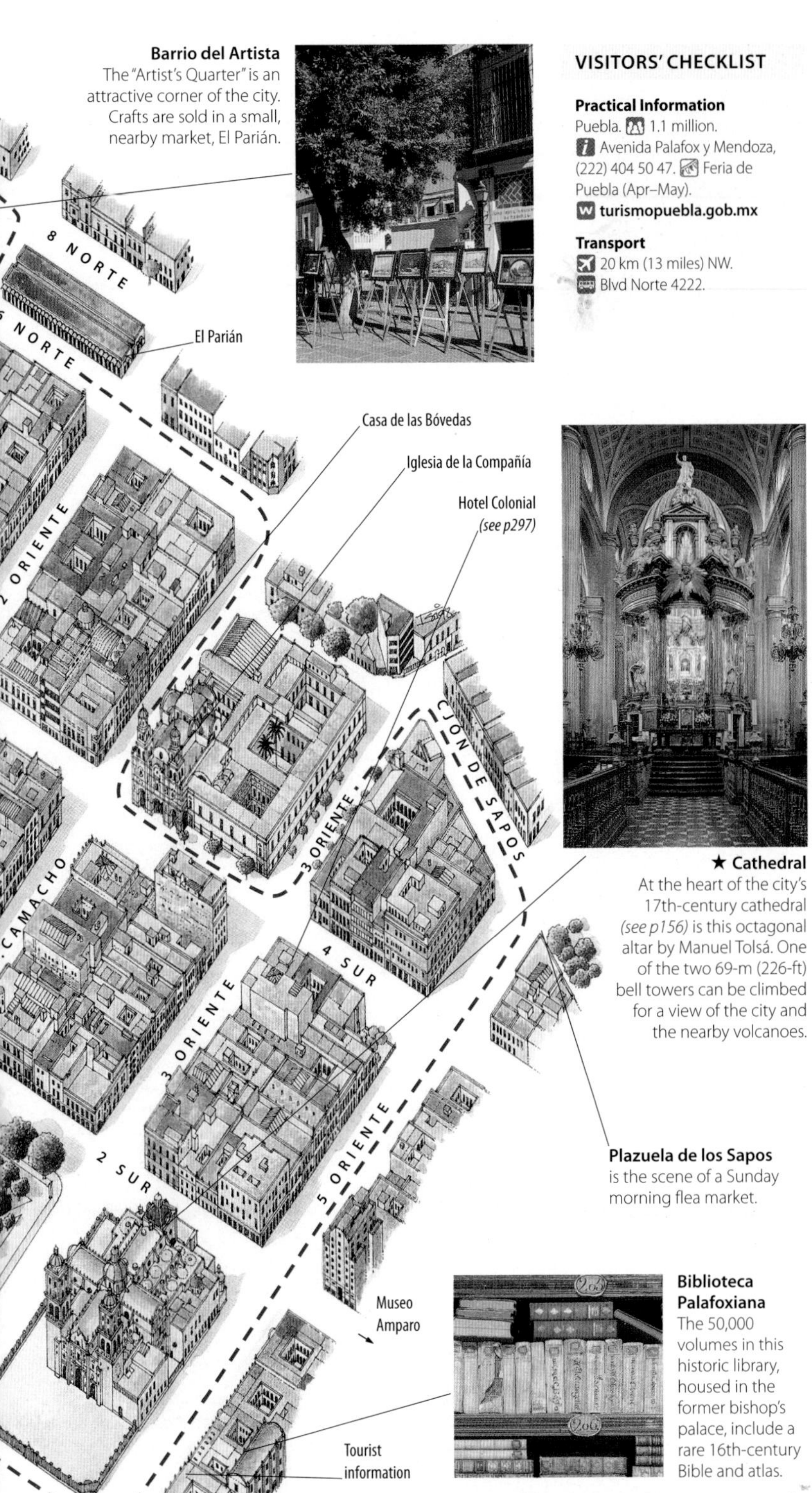

Barrio del Artista
The "Artist's Quarter" is an attractive corner of the city. Crafts are sold in a small, nearby market, El Parián.

VISITORS' CHECKLIST

Practical Information
Puebla. 1.1 million.
Avenida Palafox y Mendoza, (222) 404 50 47. Feria de Puebla (Apr–May).
turismopuebla.gob.mx

Transport
20 km (13 miles) NW.
Blvd Norte 4222.

★ Cathedral
At the heart of the city's 17th-century cathedral *(see p156)* is this octagonal altar by Manuel Tolsá. One of the two 69-m (226-ft) bell towers can be climbed for a view of the city and the nearby volcanoes.

Plazuela de los Sapos is the scene of a Sunday morning flea market.

Biblioteca Palafoxiana
The 50,000 volumes in this historic library, housed in the former bishop's palace, include a rare 16th-century Bible and atlas.

Exploring Puebla

Founded in 1531, Puebla was the first settlement in Mexico to be laid out on a grid pattern by Spanish colonialists, rather than elaborating on an existing settlement. Modern Puebla is a state capital and university city that has preserved its rich heritage of colonial architecture. In recent decades many of its finest buildings have been transformed into museums displaying collections of colonial art and regional crafts, as well as historical and archaeological finds from all over Mexico.

Ornate onyx washbasin situated in the sacristy of the city's cathedral

Cathedral

Juan de Palafox, Bishop of Puebla, consecrated the city's cathedral (the second largest in Mexico after the one in the capital) in April 1649. It is built in a combination of Renaissance and Baroque styles.

The pillars around the large atrium – the plaza in front of the building – are surmounted by statues of angels, symbols of the town whose full name is Puebla de los Angeles ("People of the Angels").

Inside there are five naves and 14 side chapels. The main altar, known as the *ciprés*, was designed by Manuel Tolsá in 1797. Standing on an octagonal base, it consists of two superimposed "temples" supported by eight pairs of Corinthian columns, crowned by a tiled dome in imitation of that of St. Peter's in Rome. Behind the *ciprés* is the Altar de los Reyes whose dome was painted in 1688 by Cristóbal de Villalpando.

Museo Regional de la Revolución Mexicana (Casa de Aquiles Serdán)

6 Oriente No. 206. **Tel** (222) 242 10 76. **Open** 10am–5pm Tue–Sun. Sun free.

The event said to have sparked the 1910 Mexican Revolution took place in this house. Aquiles Serdán, his family, and about 17 others who opposed Porfirio Díaz's dictatorship *(see p57)* resisted arrest and were killed by soldiers. The house is now a museum of revolutionary memorabilia.

Casa del Alfeñique

4 Oriente No. 416. **Tel** (222) 232 04 58. **Open** 10am–5pm Tue–Sun. Tue free.

Puebla's state museum now occupies this Baroque mansion. Exhibits include carriages, paintings, costumes, and ornately furnished rooms.

Museo Amparo

2 Sur No. 708. **Tel** (222) 229 38 50. **Open** 10am–6pm Wed–Mon (to 9pm Sat). Mon free. for a fee. **museoamparo.com**

Occupying a restored 18th-century hospital, this museum houses one of the finest collections of pre-Columbian and colonial art in the country.

The first section is devoted to pre-Columbian art. An introductory room includes a timeline comparing Mesoamerican cultures *(see pp48–9)* with contemporary cultures from around the world. A multilingual audiovisual system gives information on the artistic techniques employed, and the significance of the pieces in these rooms. The first section ends in an area dedicated to the collection's finest pieces, such as a Huasteca necklace of 17 tiny skulls carved out of bone, an Olmec statue known as *The Thinker*, and a Maya altar from Palenque.

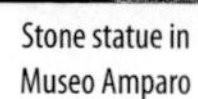

Stone statue in Museo Amparo

In the second section, the rooms are filled with colonial pieces, starting with a painting of the Virgin of Guadalupe in a silver frame. Other exhibits include Manuel Tolsá's model for the altar in the cathedral, and an unusual 18th-century statue of St. Anthony of Padua. A tradition in Puebla is for girls searching for a partner to turn the statue on its head; when they get married, they turn him back on his feet.

Museo José Luis Bello y Zetina

5 de Mayo 409. **Tel** (222) 232 47 20. **Open** 10am–4pm Tue–Sun. **Closed** Jan. **museobello.org**

Without ever leaving his beloved city of Puebla, 19th-century industrialist José Luis Bello, owner of cigar and textile factories, assembled this eclectic collection. There are some 2,500 pieces, and the emphasis is on variety rather than a particular theme. Exhibits include a collection of locks and keys; Chinese porcelain and ivory; gold and silver pocket watches; European furniture; and 16th- to 18th-century Talavera pottery in colorful, earthy designs.

One of the exquisitely ornate rooms in the Museo Bello

Taller Uriarte Talavera

4 Poniente No. 911. **Tel** (222) 232 15 98. **Open** daily. Mon–Fri. uriartetalavera.com.mx

This Talavera pottery workshop offers guided tours to visitors. The production process can be seen through from the early purifying of the clay, to the painting, glazing, and final firing of the piece.

Iglesia de Santo Domingo de Guzmán

Corner of 5 de Mayo and 4 Poniente. **Tel** (222) 242 36 43. **Open** daily.

One of the most elaborately decorated chapels in Mexico is contained in this Baroque church. Built in the second half of the 17th century, the **Capilla del Rosario** is a riot of gilt carving. Along the walls, grotesque heads spew golden vines whose tendrils twist and twine to form the frames of six paintings depicting the mysteries of the rosary. The dome is no less ornate with saints, cherubs, dancing angels, and a heavenly choir. The main church has a fine onyx pulpit.

Highly decorated dome of the Capilla del Rosario

Centro Cultural Ex-Convento de Santa Rosa

14 Poniente No. 305. **Tel** (222) 232 77 92. **Open** Tue–Sun. Tue free.

Six blocks north of the city center, in Puebla's market area, is the 17th-century convent of Santa Rosa. The building has served at different times as an Augustinian nunnery, hospital for the mentally ill, and tenement for more than 1,500 people. It was salvaged in 1968 and converted into a museum to display crafts produced in the state of Puebla.

Exhibits here include the huge tree of life from Izúcar de Matamoros, which represents an Indian interpretation of the story of Adam and Eve. There are also brightly colored embroideries, carnival masks, and furniture finely inlaid with mother-of-pearl, malachite, and bone.

The highlight of the Santa Rosa museum, however, is the vaulted kitchen, which is entirely covered with tiles. Tradition has it that the famous *mole poblano* *(see p309)* was invented by the Augustinian nuns in this atmospheric room.

Kitchen of the former convent of Santa Rosa, now a museum

Museo de Arte Religioso de Santa Mónica

18 Poniente No. 103. **Tel** (222) 232 01 78. **Open** 10am–5pm Tue–Sun. Sun free.

Built around a pretty tile-and-brick cloister, the 17th-century Convento de Santa Mónica was used to hide nuns during the years of clerical persecution after the 1857 Reform Laws. With the help of hidden doors and concealed passages, the nuns lived here in secret until 1933, when they were finally evicted. The building is now the Museum of Religious Art. As well as paintings, sculptures, and ecclesiastical artifacts, there is a macabre collection of instruments and clothing that were used by the nuns for the purpose of self-mortification.

Cerro de Guadalupe

2 km (1.5 miles) NE of city center.

This large park, which contains two forts and several museums, marks the site of the historic Battle of Puebla. On May 5, 1862 a small Mexican army under General Ignacio Zaragoza defeated a much larger French army that had invaded Mexico. The victory proved short-lived, but the day has still become one of national celebration.

Talavera Pottery

The colorful, glazed pottery so characteristic of Puebla is a fusion of Arabic, Spanish, Italian, and Chinese influences. The earliest pieces, with cobalt blue designs on a white background are typically Moorish. The technique was brought to Mexico in the 16th century by Dominican monks from Talavera de la Reina, Spain. New colors, such as green, black, and yellow, were introduced from Italy in the 17th century, while pieces imported from China and the Philippines inspired floral and animal designs. It takes six months to produce an authentic piece of Talavera pottery.

Talavera jars for sale in Puebla

⓳ Cacaxtla

Tlaxcala. Off Mex 119, 30 km (19 miles) NW of Puebla. **Tel** (246) 416 00 00. from Tlaxcala. **Open** daily.

Meaning "the place where rain dies in the earth," Cacaxtla was the capital of the Olmeca-Xicalanca, a Gulf Coast group who dominated this area from the 7th–10th centuries AD. Some of Mexico's best preserved murals, probably painted by Maya artists, were discovered here in 1974.

The 22-m (72-ft) *Mural de la Batalla* depicts a violent battle between jaguar and eagle warriors, with no fewer than 48 human figures in vibrant colors. Glyphs *(see pp50–51)* are inserted among the characters.

Two other extraordinary murals are in Edificio A. The *Hombre-jaguar* represents a lord dressed in a jaguar skin standing on a "jaguar-snake." Surrounding him is a border of sea creatures. Also in Edificio A, the *Hombre-ave* is a "bird-man" painted in black with an eagle headdress. He holds a blue serpent staff and stands on a plumed snake. Heads of corn around the edge have small human faces.

Environs

Just 2 km (1 mile) away is another Olmeca-Xicalanca site, **Xochitécatl**, whose platforms and pyramids date from about 1000 BC.

The vivid and well-preserved *Hombre-ave* mural at Cacaxtla

The richly gilded interior of the Basílica de Ocotlán, near Tlaxcala

⓴ Tlaxcala

Tlaxcala. 90,000. Cnr of Avenida Juárez & Lardizábal, (246) 465 09 00. Carnival (Feb/Mar), Virgen de Ocotlán (3rd Mon of May). **turismotlaxcala.com**

Often seen as a provincial backwater, the city of Tlaxcala is, in fact, one of the country's colonial treasures. Its seclusion is partly due to the historical independence of the local people, the Tlaxcaltecas. During the Conquest they took up arms against their old enemy, the Aztecs, joining Cortés to conquer Tenochtitlán.

The so-called Ciudad Roja (Red City) is dominated by earthy tones of terracotta and ocher. In the center is the spacious tree-filled *zócalo* (main plaza) with its bandstand and fountain, the latter given by King Philip IV of Spain in 1646.

The colorful and richly decorated brick, tile, and stucco façade of the **Parroquia de San José** dominates the northwest corner of the square. At the entrance to this church two fonts have pedestals depicting Camaxtli, the ancient Tlaxcalan god of war and hunting, and the Spanish imperial coat of arms. Beside the altar is a 17th-century painting showing the baptism of a Tlaxcalan chief, watched by Cortés and his mistress, La Malinche.

The 16th-century **Palacio de Gobierno** flanks the north side of the *zócalo*. Exterior details include the French-style stucco added at the start of the 20th century. Inside, murals by artist Desiderio Hernández relate the history of Tlaxcala.

Across Plaza Xicoténcatl to the south, a path leads uphill to the **cathedral**, which has a stunning Moorish-style coffered ceiling and contains the font used to baptize the four local chiefs who allied with Cortés. The **Museo Regional**, in the cloisters next door, has a collection of pre-Columbian

The ornate bandstand in Tlaxcala's shady and peaceful *zócalo*

◀ Rich stuccowork in the dome of the *camarín* at Basílica de Ocotlán, just outside Tlaxcala

Decoration in Basílica de Ocotlán

pieces, including a large stone figure of Camaxtli, the god of war. The two rooms upstairs are dedicated to colonial art.

The **Museo Vivo de Artes y Tradiciones Populares de Tlaxcala** (west of the *zócalo*) is a living museum. Here artisans demonstrate their techniques.

Environs
On a hill above the city, the twin-towered **Basílica de Ocotlán** is one of the most lavish Churrigueresque churches in Mexico, comparable with those in Tepotzotlán *(see pp144–7)* and Taxco *(see pp150–1)*. The 18th-century façade combines hexagonal brick and white-stucco decoration. The interior and adjoining *camarín* are an explosion of Baroque giltwork. Pilgrims flock here in May for the procession of the Virgin.

Nearby villages include **Santa Ana Chiautempan**, known for its embroidery and weaving, and **Tizatlán**, where a 16th-century chapel with frescoes stands beside the remains of a pre-Columbian palace.

In **Huamantla**, 45 km (28 miles) east of Tlaxcala, the 16th-century Convento de San Francisco has a polychrome Churrigueresque altarpiece dedicated to the Virgin of Charity. The Virgin is celebrated at a fiesta held in August *(see p35)*.

Museo Regional
Ex-Convento de San Francisco, off Plaza Xicoténcatl. **Tel** (246) 462 02 62. **Open** 10am–6pm Tue–Sun. Sun free.

Museo Vivo de Artes y Tradiciones Populares de Tlaxcala
Blvd Emilio Sánchez Piedras 1. **Tel** (246) 462 57 04. **Open** 9am–6pm Tue–Sun. reserve in advance.

㉑ Cantona

Puebla. 30 km (19 miles) NE of Oriental via 4 km (2.5 miles) of unpaved road from Tepeyahualco. tours from Puebla. **Open** daily.

The remains of what was once a major city occupy a vast area of low hills beside a lava field. Only ten per cent of the well-maintained site, which is dotted with yuccas and pine trees, can be visited.

Little is known about the history of Cantona but it was probably inhabited from about AD 700–950. One of the most built-up of all Mesoamerican cities, it may have supported a population of 80,000.

A full visit will take at least two hours. A signposted route from the parking lot sets off on one of the **calzadas**, or cobbled streets, which connect the various parts of Cantona. This leads past the ruins of houses and patios before climbing to the **Acrópolis**, the cluster of public buildings at the heart of the city. Soon the route reaches the first of 24 **ballcourts** excavated here – more than at any other site in Mexico. Of these, 12 are unusual in that they form parts of complexes with a pyramid at one end and the playing area at the other.

The path reaches the **Plaza Oriente** and then loops back to **El Palacio** and the **Plaza Central**. The return to the parking lot is along a second *calzada*.

Platforms and a pyramid at Cantona, interspersed with yucca plants

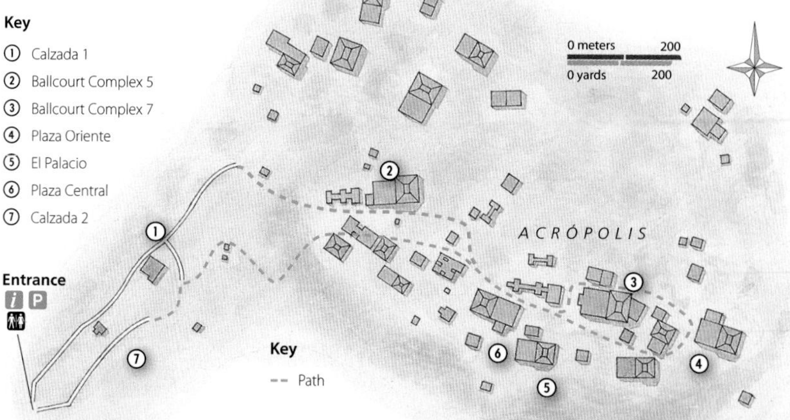

For keys to symbols *see back flap*

NORTHERN MEXICO

Baja California Norte · Baja California Sur · Chihuahua · Coahuila Durango · Nuevo León · Sinaloa · Sonora · Tamaulipas

With its stark mountains and arid plains, giant cacti and men on horseback, the North is the Mexico of popular imagination. Sparsely populated and occupying over half the country's landmass, it stretches from the magical beaches of Baja California to the marshes and islands of the Gulf of Mexico.

Two mountain ranges, the eastern and western Sierra Madre, cross this great territory from north to south. Between them lies the vast Chihuahuan Desert, the largest in North America. To the northwest is the Sonoran Desert, which extends down the beautiful 1,300-km (800-mile) long peninsula of Baja California. It is here that the North's best beaches are located.

Although often austere, the mountains conceal beautiful places where cool pine forests, placid lakes, and thunderous waterfalls can be found. The Sierra Tarahumara holds forested ravines deeper than the Grand Canyon, which are traversed by one of the world's most spectacular railroads.

Though no great pre-Columbian civilization ever developed in this region, the superb pottery and unique architecture of the Paquimé culture and the mysterious cave paintings of Baja California hold their own fascination. Present-day indigenous survivors, like the Tarahumara people of the Sierra Madre Occidental, cling to a traditional way of life quite apart from modern Mexican society.

The region is delimited to the north by the 1,950-mile (3,140-km) border with the United States, which for much of its length follows the Rio Grande (known as the Río Bravo in Mexico). Receiving influences from the cultures on either side of it, the border region is almost a third country, defined by its unique blend of languages, music, and food.

Even as far south as Monterrey, Mexico's industrial heartland, the influence of the gringo is still strongly felt. But here the accumulated wealth and economic power – enshrined in the glass and concrete of bold modern architecture – are purely and soberly Mexican in character.

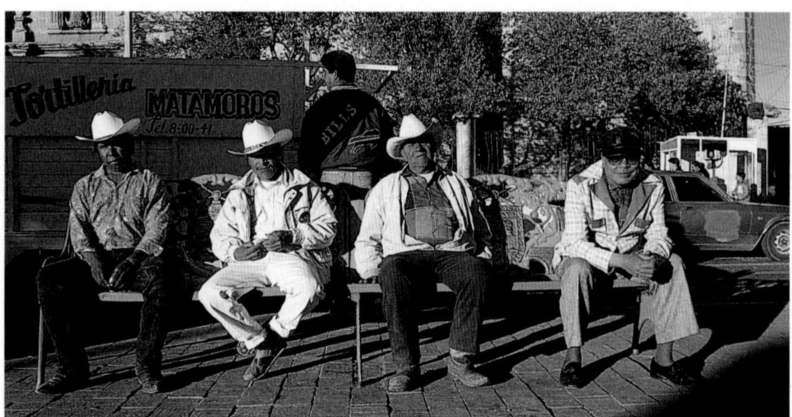

Local men in the town of Hidalgo del Parral

◀ Aerial view of Cabo San Lucas, Baja California

Exploring Northern Mexico

Distances involved when traveling between sights in the region should not be underestimated. Sun worshipers will find some of Mexico's finest beaches on the 800-mile (1,300-km) peninsula of Baja California, which also has spectacular desert scenery and varied wildlife, including the gray whale. On the mainland, Mazatlán is a popular retreat from northern winters. Inland, the vertiginous gorges of the Copper Canyon are great for hiking. Elsewhere, you can walk the streets of western film sets near Durango or take in the culture and nightlife of modern cities such as Tijuana and Monterrey.

Wildflowers and cactus, common in Northern Mexico

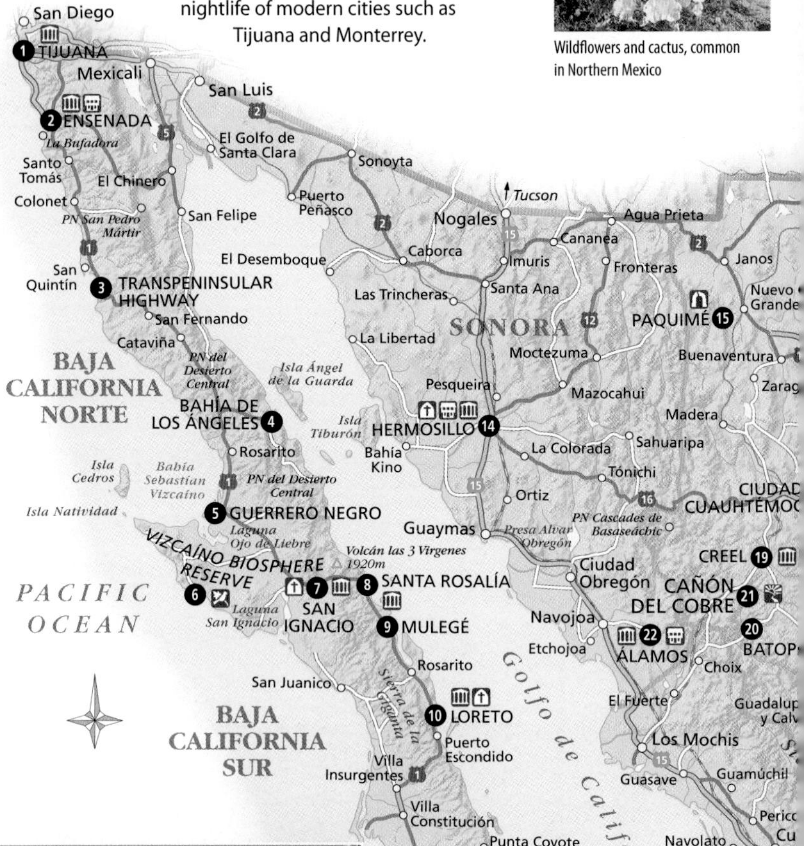

Lovers' Beach at Cabo San Lucas, cut off by rocks and accessible only by boat

For hotels and restaurants see pp298–9 and pp319–21

Sights at a Glance

1. Tijuana
2. Ensenada
3. Transpeninsular Highway
4. Bahía de los Angeles
5. Guerrero Negro
6. Vizcaíno Biosphere Reserve
7. San Ignacio
8. Santa Rosalía
9. Mulegé
10. Loreto
11. La Paz
12. San José del Cabo
13. Cabo San Lucas
14. Hermosillo
15. Paquimé
16. Chihuahua
17. Ciudad Cuauhtémoc
18. Hidalgo del Parral
19. Creel
20. Batopilas
21. *Cañón del Cobre pp180–81*
22. Álamos
23. Mazatlán
24. Durango
25. Saltillo
26. Monterrey

Getting Around

The region's road network is generally good, but distances can be huge and toll roads expensive. Avoid nighttime driving and beware of deteriorations in the road surface and *vados* (fords), which – even when dry – require a slower speed. Buses offer an alternative to pricey air travel and are usually comfortable. One of the few passenger train services still running is the spectacular Chihuahua al Pacífico, also known as El Chepe *(see p180)*. Several car-ferry services link mainland Mexico with Baja California.

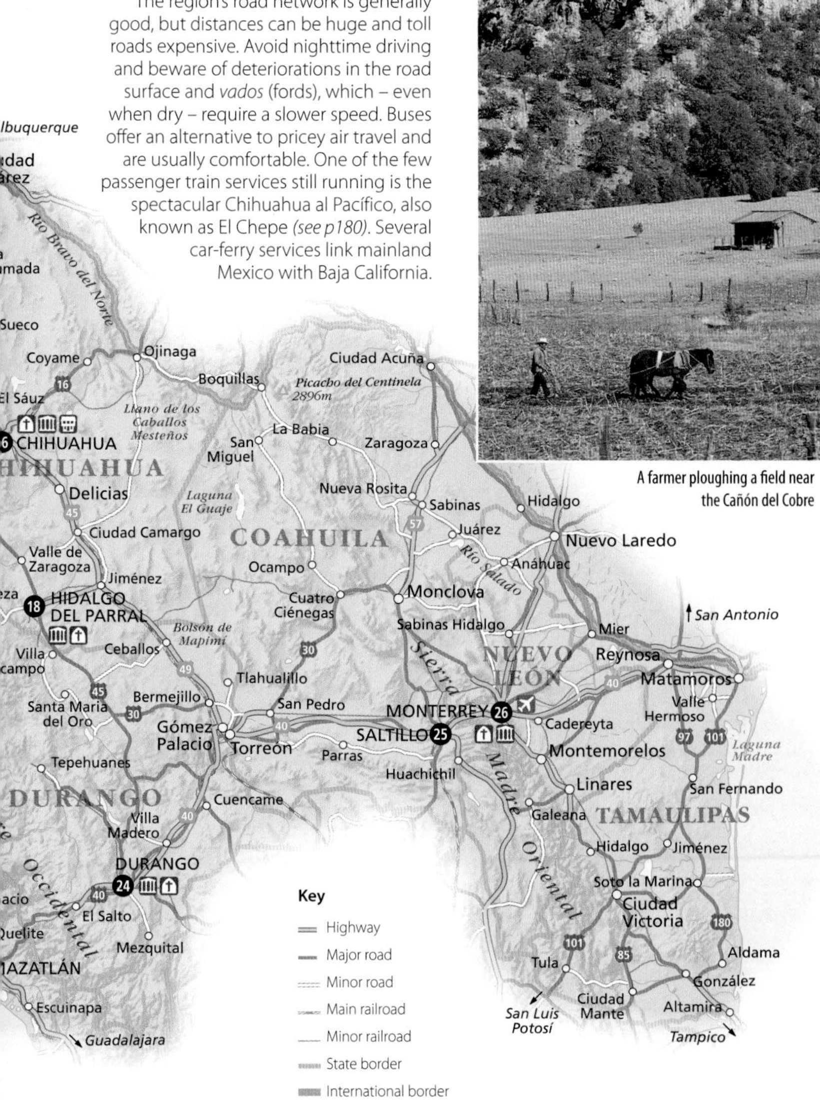

A farmer ploughing a field near the Cañón del Cobre

The Domo IMAX theater at the Centro Cultural Tijuana

❶ Tijuana

Baja California Norte. 1,560,000. Paseo de los Héroes 10289, (664) 973 70 00. Aniversario de Tijuana (Jul). **tijuana.gob.mx**

Just over the border from San Diego (California), Tijuana is the quintessential border city and claims to be the world's busiest crossing, with 300,000 hopping over the line daily.

Towering skyscrapers and massive shopping malls are a measure of its modernity. Most people come here to shop or party. The best shopping is in the quiet bazaars on either side of Avenida Revolución. Painted pottery, leather boots, silver jewelry, mezcal, and tequila are the most popular buys. Customers are encouraged to barter with the stallholders. The vibrant nightlife is also centered on Avenida Revolución, where there are plenty of restaurants and cafés.

Tijuana also has a few cultural attractions, the main one being the futuristic **Centro Cultural Tijuana** beside the river. Concerts and art exhibitions are held here, and there is an Domo IMAX theater that shows movies about nature and Mexico.

Centro Cultural Tijuana
9350 Paseo de los Héroes. **Tel** (664) 687 96 00. **Open** daily. movies. **cecut.gob.mx**

The Mexico–US Border

The US and Mexico are separated by a land border that runs for 3,140 km (1,950 miles) between the Pacific Ocean and the Gulf of Mexico. There are 47 crossings between Tijuana in the west and Matamoros in the east. Most US citizens who cross the border are on day-trips for a taste of the exotic, to shop, or to enjoy themselves in a country where their dollar goes further. For some Mexicans, the border is the gateway to "El Norte," the promised land of high salaries and consumer goods. The meeting of the two worlds creates a vibrant mix of cultures, but it has its down-side – most visible in the steadily lengthening and constantly patrolled "wall" – the barrier erected by the US to deter illegal immigrants.

Signs and a souvenir stall mark the Mexico-US border crossing at Tijuana

❷ Ensenada

Baja California Norte. 467,000. Blvd Lázaro Cárdenas 609, (646) 178 85 88. Carnival (Feb/Mar), Vendimia Wine Festival (Aug). **enjoyensenada.com**

This busy port and cruise-ship destination is popular with fishermen, surfers, and divers. The scenic drive from Tijuana takes just 90 minutes, past bays and red bluffs that hint at the spectacular desert landscape farther south. A lookout just before the city offers a view over the bay.

City sights include the twin-towered church of **Nuestra Señora de Guadalupe** and the giant sculpted heads of three national heroes – Juárez, Hidalgo, and Carranza – on the Plaza Cívica. The **Riviera del Pacífico**, near the waterfront, was a hotel in the 1930s but now houses exhibitions. In the lobby is a remarkable 3-D mural showing the 18th-century Jesuit missions of the Californias. **Bodegas de Santo Tomás**, which makes some of Baja's finest wine from grapes grown in vineyards south of town, offers daily tours and wine tasting.

Ensenada's small but lively "party district" clusters around the old-fashioned **Hussong's Cantina** on Avenida Ruíz. This bar was founded in the 19th century by the German Hussong family, still a powerful force in the city. Visitors can buy a Hussong's T-shirt in the Hussong mall.

Environs

The beaches in town are not recommended, but a few miles south are the clean and pleasant **Playa El Faro** and **Playa Estero**, both of which have superb sunsets. Farther south is **La Bufadora**, where a cleft in the rock produces a spout of sea foam, especially when the waves swell in windy weather. The best diving in the area is here.

About 90 km (56 miles) inland of Ensenada is **Parque Nacional Constitución de 1857**, reached by a winding road among hills made of huge boulders. Here, surrounded by pine trees, is tranquil **Laguna Hanson**, a haven for birds.

The heads of three national heroes on Plaza Cívica in Ensenada

Riviera del Pacífico
Blvd Lázaro Cárdenas 1421. **Tel** (646) 176 43 10. **Open** 8am–7pm daily.

Bodegas de Santo Tomás
Av Miramar 666. **Tel** (646) 174 08 19. **Open** Mon–Fri.
santo-tomas.com

❸ Transpeninsular Highway

Baja California Norte and Sur. Mex 1, Tijuana to Cabo San Lucas. serving the whole highway.

The two extremes of Baja California are linked by one highway, the two-lane Mex 1, which runs 1,700 km (1,060 miles) from Tijuana to Cabo San Lucas *(see p173)*. There are few places worth stopping for on the long drive, but the desert landscapes of the north do have an austere beauty. The **Parque Nacional Sierra de San Pedro**, reached via a side road 140 km (87 miles) south of Ensenada, includes the 3,095-m (10,154-ft) snowcapped peak, Picacho del Diablo. Farther south, near the truck stop of Cataviña, is the so-called **Rocky Desert**, with its jumble of massive boulders and wide variety of cactus species.

❹ Bahía de los Angeles

Baja California Norte. 450.

Located on the beautiful bay of the same name, and reached by a paved, if rather rutted, 68-km (42-mile) spur road off Mex 1, Bahía de los Angeles is a peaceful spot even by Baja standards. Popular with sportfishing enthusiasts, it also offers opportunities for diving and kayaking around the numerous islands in the bay. Other attractions include a sea turtle conservation project and trips across a spectacular desert landscape to see Indian rock paintings and the well-preserved San Borja mission. Boats are available to visit various offshore islands.

Brown pelicans perched on a rock at the picturesque Bahía de los Angeles

Fiestas of Northern Mexico

Easter *(Mar/Apr)*, Cusarare and Norogachi (Chihuahua). The most important ceremony of the Tarahumara Indians re-enacts the Crucifixion story as a battle between "soldiers" and evil "pharisees," the latters' bodies often painted with white clay. It is accompanied by singing and dancing.

Tarahumara Indians, taking part in Easter celebrations

Carnival *(Feb/Mar)*, La Paz. Thought by some to be the best in Mexico, the carnival consists of six days of parades, feasting, music, and cockfights. Mazatlán and Veracruz also host a spectacular party.

Fiesta de las Flores *(1st week of May)*, Nogales (Sonora). As this festival coincides with the anniversary of the Battle of Puebla (May 5), floats display both flowers and battle motifs.

Día de la Marina *(Jun 1)*, Guaymas (Sonora). Mock naval battles and fireworks commemorate the Mexican navy.

Nuestra Señora del Refugio *(Jul 4)*, Durango. The highlight here is the fascinating Matachines dance, performed by men wearing long animal-skin tunics, feathers in their hair, and wooden-soled sandals.

Vendimia Wine Festival *(Aug)*, Ensenada. Growers and producers show off their wares in Mexico's principal wine region.

❺ Guerrero Negro

Baja California Sur. 10,000.

Guerrero Negro, "Black Warrior," is named after a whaling ship that ran aground in a lagoon near the town in the middle of the 19th century. The lagoon is the main breeding ground of the California gray whale – which most visitors come here to see. It also provides the raw material for the world's largest sea-salt operation, which environmentalists say may threaten the long-term future of the whales, only recently brought back from the brink of extinction. Seven million tons of salt per year is produced from thousands of evaporation ponds south of the town, and barges take the washed salt to the island of Isla Cedros, where it is transferred to ocean-going ships. The island itself remains almost unspoiled and supports unusual plant species and the endangered Cedros mule deer. Isla Cedros can be reached from Guerrero Negro by a light aircraft that makes the crossing twice a week.

Sea salt leaving the evaporation works south of Guerrero Negro

Horse and rider, Sierra de San Francisco

❻ Vizcaíno Biosphere Reserve

Baja California Sur. Mex 1, S of Guerrero Negro. Guerrero Negro.

Covering 25,000 sq km (9,600 sq miles), this preserve is claimed to be the largest protected natural area in Latin America. It stretches from the Peninsula de Vizcaíno across Baja California to the east coast. The whale sanctuaries of Laguna Ojo de Liebre and Laguna San Ignacio fall within its boundaries, as do the islands of Natividad, Asunción, and San Roque, part of the Sierra de San Francisco, and – in the east – the triple volcano of Las Tres Vírgenes.

Ranging from coastal mangroves and sand dunes to arid upland plateaus and the occasional freshwater oasis, the preserve's ecosystems harbor a wide variety of species. Apart from the whales, other interesting animals are the endangered bighorn sheep (*borrego cimarrón*), the pronghorn antelope,

Whale-Watching in Guerrero Negro

Two dozen species of cetaceans are found off the coasts of Baja California, from the small, endangered *vaquita*, confined to the northern reaches of the Sea of Cortés, to the world's largest animal, the blue whale. The best place to see these magnificent creatures is at Guerrero Negro, where the most common species, the California gray whale, can be seen in February and March, either from the shore or, better still, from a small boat.

A curious whale approaching two boatloads of enthusiasts, Guerrero Negro

The California gray whale (Eschrichtius robustus), makes one of the longest migrations of any mammal. After a 9,500-km (6,000-mile) trip from Alaska, it calves in the warm lagoons of Mexico's Pacific coast. Once almost extinct, the species has recovered, and its numbers are now rising.

How to See the Whales

The whales can be viewed with binoculars from several vantage points on the shore, such as the one reached by a dirt road from Mex 1 approximately 8 km (5 miles) south of Guerrero Negro. A better option is to go on an organized dinghy trip lasting 2–3 hours. Choose a reputable company that will not approach the whales too closely. One such is Malarrimo, which has an office next to its restaurant *(see p320)*. An alternative is to strike a deal with a local fisherman to take you out in his boat. Farther south in Baja California you can often see whales at Laguna San Ignacio, Bahía de Magdalena, on the eastern side of the peninsula between Loreto and La Paz, and at Cabo San Lucas.

Ancient Cave Paintings of Baja California

The cave paintings of Baja California have been compared with the aboriginal art of Australia and prehistoric paintings in the caves of France and Spain. When 18th-century Jesuit missionaries asked about the origin of the paintings, the local Cochimi Indians attributed them to a race of giants who had come from the north. It is now thought that ancestors of the Cochimi themselves painted the images. Their exact age is unknown, but some may date from 1200 BC.

The complexity of the beliefs suggested by the paintings has led to a reassessment of the supposedly "primitive" hunter-gatherer society encountered by the Spanish on their arrival.

Cave Paintings The images, usually in black and red, depict human figures with their arms raised, various animals, and abstract designs of unknown significance.

Painting of hunters and prey in a cave near San Ignacio

elephant seals, and several kinds of sea turtle. The Laguna San Ignacio (reached from the town of San Ignacio) holds what is believed to be the densest breeding colony of ospreys in the world. Herons, egrets, brown pelicans, and various other seabirds can also be spotted here.

Much of the interior of the preserve, with its strangely-shaped *cirio* (or "boojum") trees and giant Mexican cereus *(see p175)*, is practically inaccessible, but a passable road leads up the Peninsula de Vizcaíno to Bahía Tortugas.

⑦ San Ignacio

Baja California Sur. 750.

Standing among thousands of date palms, the church at San Ignacio is one of the most imposing and best-preserved missions in Baja California. Although originally founded by Jesuits in 1728, before their expulsion from Spanish America, the church seen today was actually built in 1786 by Dominicans, with money from the queen of Spain. Its whitewashed Baroque facade, with masonry details in reddish lava stone, holds four polygonal windows and four niches containing carvings of saints. St. Peter and St. Paul flank the main door, with its intricately carved lintel. The interior has original furniture and altarpieces, as well as a beautiful main altar decorated with 18th-century oil paintings.

In the canyons near San Ignacio are the ancient Indian cave paintings. The **Cueva del Ratón** (Cave of the Mouse) is the easiest to reach, via a turn off to San Francisco de la Sierra, 45 km (28 miles) north on the Transpeninsular *(see p167)*. However, the most spectacular and best-preserved paintings are to be found in the **Cueva de las Flechas** (Cave of the Arrows) and the **Cueva Pintada** (Painted Cave). You must be accompanied by an approved guide – a visit to the last-named sites in the San Pablo canyon involves a two- or three-day camping trip with mules. The **Museo de las Pinturas Rupestres de San Ignacio** has exhibits on the cave paintings.

The 18th-century mission church at San Ignacio

Museo de las Pinturas Rupestres de San Ignacio
Prof. Gilberto Valdivia Péna. **Tel** (615) 154 02 22. **Open** Oct–Mar: 8am–5pm daily; Apr–Sep: 8am–5pm Mon–Sat.

The spectacular view over the Cañón del Cobre (Copper Canyon) ▶

8 Santa Rosalía

Baja California Sur. 10,500. Avenida Carranza and Plaza Santa Rosalía, (615) 152 23 11. Santa Rosalía (Sep 4).

This small town was founded by a French copper-mining company in the 1880s. The copper ran out, and the company moved on in the 1950s, but engines and rolling stock from the mine railroad, along with some of the mine installations, can still be seen.

Santa Rosalía has many two-story timber buildings with verandas, which give it a Caribbean look. Another curiosity is the **Iglesia de Santa Bárbara**, a prefabricated church designed by Gustave Eiffel, of Eiffel Tower fame, and shipped here in 1895. The waterfront walk, the Andador Costero, is a pleasant place for a stroll. Overlooking the town is a mining museum, the **Museo de Historia de la Minería de Santa Rosalía**.

Museo de Historia de la Minería de Santa Rosalía
Jean-Michel Cousteau 1. **Tel** (615) 152 29 99. **Open** 8am–3pm Mon–Sat.

Santa Rosalía's Iglesia de Santa Bárbara, designed by Gustave Eiffel

9 Mulegé

Baja California Sur. 4,000. Santa Rosalía (Sep 4).

This pretty town has a lovely church, founded by Jesuit missionaries. Set on a bluff, it has superb views of the Santa Rosalía River below. Not far away is the **Museo Mulegé**, which has displays on the town's history. It is housed in an old whitewashed prison building, complete with tiny, crenellated towers. Mulegé is popular with scuba divers, but for some of the best beaches in Mexico take the road south out of Mulegé, past the **Bahía Concepción**. The water here changes dramatically from deep blue to an intense green.

A view across to the Bahía Concepción, the bay to the south of Mulegé

Museo Mulegé
Cananea. **Open** 8am–2pm Mon–Fri. Donations.

10 Loreto

Baja California Sur. 17,000. Corner of Francisco Madero and Salvatierra, (613) 13 50 411. Virgen de Loreto (Sep 8), San Javier (Dec 3).

Once the capital of the Californias (made up of present-day California and Baja California), Loreto is now better known as a magnet for the sportfishing fraternity. The heart of the town is the area around Plaza Cívica and the superbly restored **Misión Nuestra Señora de Loreto**. The mission, the first in the Californias, was damaged by a hurricane and earthquake in the 19th century. The original stone building (1699) survives as a side chapel to the main church. From here, 18th-century Jesuit missionaries embarked on a campaign to evangelize (and hence peacefully subdue) the indigenous population. The **Museo de las Misiones** in the mission explains how this was accomplished and displays period artifacts, including huge cooking pots that the priests used in their attempts – initially more successful – to influence the Indians by way of their stomachs. In the museum courtyard is a colonial, horse-driven *trapiche* (sugar mill).

In addition to fishing, there is good diving, kayaking, and snorkeling, especially around the offshore islands of **Isla del Carmen** and **Coronado**.

Museo de las Misiones
Salvatierra 16. **Tel** (613) 135 04 41. **Open** 9am–12:45pm & 1:45–6pm Tue–Sun. Sun free.

Fishing boats moored at the small marina near the center of Loreto

For hotels and restaurants see pp298–9 and pp319–21

⓫ La Paz

Baja California Sur. 252,000. Carretera Transpeninsular, km 5.5, (612) 121 68 70. Carnival (Feb/Mar), Fundación de La Paz (May 2–7). **lapaz.gob.mx**

The capital of the state of Baja California Sur, La Paz sits beside the largest bay on the Sea of Cortés, at the foot of a peninsula endowed with some excellent, and often half-deserted, beaches. Its curving, 5-km (3-mile) *malecón* (waterfront promenade) is lined with palm trees, hotels, and restaurants and is a lovely place for a stroll. Sit on a bench and enjoy the sunset, or walk along the dilapidated pier. A few blocks farther south is the main square, Plaza Constitución.

La Paz owes its foundation, by the conquistador Hernán Cortés, to the abundance of pearls in nearby waters, and its fortunes have often risen and fallen with those of the pearl industry. It dominated the international market in the 19th century, but in the 1940s a combination of disease and over-exploitation wiped out the oyster beds. Nowadays, in addition to its government offices and port facilities, its economy increasingly relies on tourism and on its status as one of the premier sportfishing destinations in the world.

La Paz's well laid-out **Museo Regional de Antropología e Historia** has interesting displays on pre-Columbian rock paintings and other aspects of Baja's indigenous heritage, as well as on its struggle for independence.

The nearby islands are popular with divers for their reefs, caves, and shipwrecks, and many also have fine beaches. **Isla Espíritu Santo** offers fantastic sailing opportunities and the chance to swim with wild sea lions.

Museo Regional de Antropología e Historia
Corner of 5 de Mayo and Altamirano. **Tel** (612) 122 01 62. **Open** 8am–6pm daily. Sun free.

Spectacular El Arco at Lovers' Beach, Cabo San Lucas

⓬ San José del Cabo

Baja California Sur. 70,000. Plaza San José, (624) 142 33 10. San José (Mar 13–21). **loscabos.gob.mx**

Situated at the tip of the Baja peninsula, the pleasant town of San José del Cabo is centered around the shady Plaza Mijares. On weekends there is an arts and crafts market. Farther inland is the old town, while to the south of Plaza Mijares, the streets slope downward to the beachfront boulevard with its modern tourist hotels, resort complexes, and condominiums. On the east side of the town is a palm-fringed estuary, said to be home to over 200 different species of birds, including flocks of migrant ducks, which find refuge here from the northern winter. A few kilometers farther east is the village of **Pueblo la Playa**, which has beautiful white-sand beaches, often deserted.

Pelicans at Cabo San Lucas

⓭ Cabo San Lucas

Baja California Sur. 68,450. Día de San Lucas (Oct 18). **Tel** (624) 146 96 28. **loscabos.gob.mx**

A miniature Acapulco, where it often seems that the official language is English, Cabo San Lucas is famous for its romantic "Lovers' Beach." Accessible by boat, the beach is set among the jagged rocks known as Los Frailes (The Friars), which seem to form the tip of the peninsula. The beach is framed by a rock archway considered to link the waters of the Pacific with those of the Sea of Cortés.

One of the world's best game-fishing locations, the town has a sizable marina and a waterfront strip crowded with bars, discos, and restaurants. Farther inland, much of the old town remains intact.

Beach activities are concentrated on the long **Playa El Medano**, where the swimming is safest and jet-skis can be rented. The diving is excellent around Los Frailes, where there is an immense underwater canyon.

Between Cabo San Lucas and San José del Cabo are several top-class golf courses and some stunning beaches.

A colorful building on one of the streets around Plaza Constitución in La Paz

Ruins of the ancient adobe buildings at Paquimé, northern Mexico's most interesting archaeological site

⓮ Hermosillo

Sonora. 785,000. Calle Comonfort, (662) 289 30 00 or 01800 716 25 55 (toll free). Wine Festival (Jun), San Francisco (Oct 4).
hermosillo.gob.mx

Sonora's busy, thriving capital city – where cattle ranchers rub shoulders with car workers – has a quieter, prettier side too. Centered on the **Plaza Zaragoza**, with its lacy white bandstand, its outstanding feature is the 19th-century **cathedral** with its twin towers and pale yellow dome, each surmounted by a cross. The cathedral's dazzling white facade is a blend of architectural styles, with Neo-Classical predominating. It is remarkably harmonious considering it took over a century to build.

The Neo-Classical **Palacio de Gobierno** contains frescoes painted in the 1980s by three artists whose inspiration ranged from indigenous creation myths to the Mexican Revolution. In a beautifully restored building, that was once the state penitentiary, is the **Museo de Sonora**, with galleries on the geology and ecology of the state and its development from prehistoric times to the present.

The brilliant white facade of Hermosillo cathedral

Palacio de Gobierno
Calle Comonfort y Doctor Paliza.
Tel (662) 213 11 70. **Open** Mon–Sat.
reserve in advance.

Museo de Sonora
Jesus García Final. **Tel** (662) 217 27 14.
Open 10am–6pm Tue–Sat, 9am–4pm Sun. reserve in advance.

⓯ Paquimé

Chihuahua. 8 km (5 miles) SW of Casas Grandes. from Chihuahua.
Open daily.

The most important archaeological site in northern Mexico, Paquimé is an extraordinary complex of adobe buildings, quite unlike central and southern Mexican sites. Set on a plateau overlooking the Casas Grandes River, it flourished between the 10th and 14th centuries and probably housed over 3,000 people. Its partial destruction by fire in about 1340 and the disappearance of its inhabitants before the arrival of the Spanish have yet to be fully explained.

Walls of packed earth, up to 1.5 m (5 ft) thick, a mazelike construction, and "apartment buildings" as much as five floors high with internal staircases are among the site's characteristic features. The houses also contain stoves for heating and beds in the form of alcoves. Low doorways in the shape of a thick "T" may have been partly for defence purposes. An impressive network of channels brought spring water from 8 km (5 miles) away for filtration and storage in deep wells. From here it was channeled to domestic and agricultural users, while another system of conduits drained away the waste. The inhabitants of Paquimé, whose language and ethnic origin are unknown, raised macaws for ceremonial purposes. The low, adobe pens with circular entrances, in which the birds were kept, remain intact. Other architectural elements seen here, including ballcourts, suggest cultural influence from Mesoamerican societies farther south.

Modern, colorful Paquimé pot

Unique to Paquimé, however, is a particularly fine type of pottery, distinguished by a high polish and geometric or anthropomorphic designs. The most typical colors are black and reddish brown on a buff background. The style has been revived by local potters, some of whom command high prices for a single piece. More modestly priced examples can be bought in the nearby town of Casas Grandes Viejo. The site museum contains original ceramics as well as a model of the city as it would have looked in its heyday.

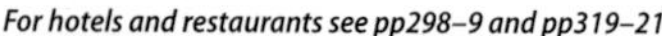

For hotels and restaurants see pp298–9 and pp319–21

The Cactuses of Northern Mexico

The landscapes of Northern Mexico are characterized by the extraordinary variety of cactuses that grow there. About 300 species of cactus exist in the Sonoran Desert, the most diverse desert in the world. They are superbly adapted to retain water and withstand fierce climatic extremes. Their fleshy stems, often protected by spines, are filled with water-storing tissue and surrounded by a thick, waxy layer to help retain moisture. Cactuses can remain dormant for long periods and then burst into bloom after a brief downpour. In Mexico, cactuses are used for food and drink, for roof coverings, and to make fish hooks and pot scourers.

Prickly pears *(Opuntia species)*, the largest cactus group, are also called Indian figs. Many have edible red, green, or purple fruits.

The desert landscapes of the North have a certain stark beauty.

The giant Mexican cereus *(Pachycereus pringlei)* is a tall, treelike cactus. They are often planted close together in rows to form fences.

The saguaro *(Carnegiea gigantea)* can grow to 16 m (52 ft) tall, taking nearly 150 years to reach its full height. Large specimens can hold several tons of water.

Agaves are used to make tequila *(see p313)* and henequen *(see p277)*. Some species take up to 50 years to flower.

The boojum tree *(Idria columnaris)* is an extraordinary sight. It is seen mainly in the deserts of Baja California.

The barrel cactus *(Ferocactus)* derives its name from its rounded shape. Mexico has nine species of barrel cactus.

Succulents

Most cactuses store water in fleshy stems, but many other succulents, such as the agaves, store moisture in their leaves. Succulents grow very slowly to reduce their need for water, and many have shallow, but very extensive, root systems.

⑯ Chihuahua

Chihuahua. 820,000. Palacio de Gobierno, (614) 429 33 00. Santa Rita (May 22). **chihuahua.gob.mx**

The ghosts of two Mexican heroes, Pancho Villa and Father Miguel Hidalgo *(see p53)*, seem to haunt the streets of Chihuahua. Set among rugged hills in a semi-desert landscape, it owes its foundation to the rich veins of silver discovered nearby in the colonial period. The city's **aqueduct**, referred to by locals as "los arquitos" (the arches), dates from that era. Its best-preserved section is at the intersection of Calle 56 and Calle Allende. Today Chihuahua relies mostly on automobile manufacturing and cattle-ranching.

The Plaza de Armas, the main square of Chihuahua, is dominated by the **cathedral**. This impressive, twin-towered building in rose-colored stone dates from the 18th century. Its 1920s altar of Italian marble is particularly fine. A side chapel contains a museum of religious art, open on weekdays.

The **Palacio de Gobierno** on Plaza Hidalgo (to the northeast of the main square) is a late 19th-century building. Its courtyard features striking murals by Aarón Piña Mora that illustrate episodes from Chihuahuan history. There is also an eternal flame commemorating Independence hero Father Hidalgo – it marks the spot where he was executed by firing squad in 1811 after leading a rebellion against the Spanish crown. Two blocks away, on Avenida Juárez, the **Palacio Federal** preserves within its walls the remains of the church tower that served as Hidalgo's cell. It contains a few poignant reminders of the priest's incarceration and fate, including a tiny lantern with which he illuminated the last few nights of his life.

The Art Nouveau Quinta Carolina, on the outskirts of Chihuahua

Undoubtedly the best-known Chihuahuan resident was Francisco "Pancho" Villa, the mustachioed hero of the 1910–20 revolutionary war *(see p58)*. The **Museo Histórico de la Revolución** features the bullet-riddled Dodge at whose wheel he met his end in 1923. The museum is situated in his former house, and much of his furniture and other household goods are still here. The galleries behind the house recount the story of the Revolution. There is also a death mask of Villa, taken just hours after his assassination.

Perhaps the finest house in the city is the Quinta Gameros, to the southeast of the Plaza de Armas, which now houses the **Centro Cultural Universitario Quinta Gameros**. It is worth paying the admission price to this exquisite Art Nouveau mansion just to see the dining room with its fantastic wood carvings. The rooms upstairs house permanent exhibitions, including paintings and sculptures by Mexican artist Luis Aragón.

A beautifully preserved section of Chihuahua's aqueduct, which dates from colonial times

Environs

Around 20 km (12 miles) to the southeast of Chihuahua is the mining town of **Santa Eulalia**. A stroll through its cobbled streets is enjoyable, particularly on a Sunday, when bands play in the town plaza. The **Cumbres de Majalca National Park**, situated about 70 km (43 miles) to the northwest of Chihuahua, offers opportunities for hiking, rock-climbing, and wilderness camping among forested canyons and peaks.

Statue on the façade of Chihuahua cathedral

Museo Histórico de la Revolución
Calle 10a 3010. **Tel** (614) 416 29 58. **Open** 9am–1pm & 3–7pm Tue–Sat, 9am–5pm Sun. ground floor.

Centro Cultural Universitario Quinta Gameros
Paseo Bolivar 401. **Tel** (614) 410 54 74. **Open** 11am–7pm Tue–Sun.

⑰ Ciudad Cuauhtémoc

Chihuahua. 155,000. Cnr of Allende and Agustín Melgar, (625) 581 34 88. San Antonio (Jun).

The industrious Mennonite farmers who have made Cuauhtémoc what it is today arrived in 1921 at the invitation of President Obregón. Originally from the Netherlands, these fundamentalist Christians had settled in Canada but came into conflict with the authorities there when they resisted the draft for World War I. This is

Pancho Villa (c.1878–1923)

A member of a bandit group as a young man, Francisco "Pancho" Villa became an influential leader of the Revolution after joining the campaign to depose Porfirio Díaz in 1910 *(see p58)*. His excellent military strategies and charismatic leadership inspired great loyalty in his División del Norte army and made him a folk hero, particularly around Chihuahua where he had his headquarters. In 1920 Álvaro Obregón took power and encouraged Villa to retire to a hacienda in Canutillo (Durango). Three years later, on a trip into Hidalgo del Parral, he was assassinated. About 30,000 people attended his funeral.

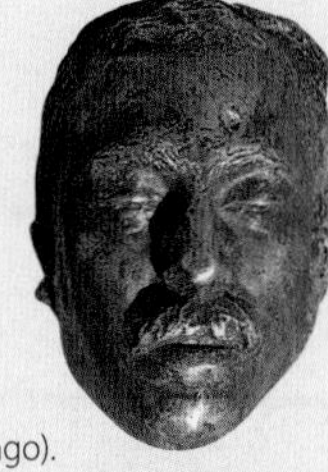
The death mask of Pancho Villa

the largest Mennonite group in Latin America. Their self-sufficient farms, known as camps, stretch north and south from Cuauhtémoc. Often blond and blue-eyed, the Mennonites stand out from their Mexican neighbors and have remained culturally distinct. Although they have embraced some modern technology, they still have a very traditional way of life. Their pitched-roofed, woodframe houses and barns give this part of Mexico a strangely European aspect.

A Mennonite man in traditional dress

Mennonite men, with their trademark denim overalls, usually speak Spanish, but many of the women speak only the Low German dialect of their ancestors. The easiest way to meet them is to buy some of the excellent cheese, which is their best-known product. The cheese factory at Camp 6½ (all the camps are numbered, not named) is open to visitors, except on Sundays, when everything apart from the churches closes down.

⓲ Hidalgo del Parral

Chihuahua. 107,100.
Mina La Prieta, (627) 525 44 00.
Francisco Villa (Jul 20).

Most famous as the site of Pancho Villa's murder, Parral (as it is usually known) was founded in 1631. It owes its existence to the gold and silver mines, and at the end of the 19th century it was one of the most opulent cities in Mexico. Its churches are noted for the chunks of ore that went into their construction.

The La Prieta mine-head still overlooks the town. Nearby is the **Templo de la Virgen de Fátima**, the church dedicated to the miners' patron saint. Built at the end of the 19th century, it has small pieces of metal from the mines, including silver and gold, set into its walls. In place of traditional pews are stools shaped like claim markers.

Another outstanding building is a 19th-century church, the **Parroquia de San José**. Situated on the town's main square, it has an unusual diamond pattern on its walls.

Farther to the west, at the corner of Calle Primo de Verdad and Riva Palacio, is the splendid **Casa de Alvarado**. It was built at the start of the 20th century for the Alvarado family, whose fortune came from La Palmilla – believed at the time to be the richest silver mine in the Americas. Notice the anguished face over the main door, which is said to be that of an Indian mine worker. Nearby, over one of the bridges that span the Parral River (in winter just a dry arroyo), is the **Museo Casa Francisco Villa**. It is housed in the building from which Villa's assassins fired the fatal shots, and a bronze starburst on the pavement outside marks where he died. The building is now a library, with the Villa museum on the first floor. It includes photos taken after the murder and a model of the scene.

Environs

Parral can be used as a southern gateway to the rugged landscape of the Sierra Tarahumara, which stretches away to the northwest, while 15 minutes' drive east of town are the hot mineral springs of **El Ojo de Talamantes**, in the lush Valle de Allende.

Farther to the east is a stark, inhospitable desert region, the **Bolsón de Mapimí**, which encloses a remote area called the "Zone of Silence." Rumored to be a landing site for UFOs or a kind of Mexican Bermuda Triangle, it gets its name from the popular theory that radio waves cannot enter or leave it. A few kilometers east is the massive **Mapimí Biosphere Reserve**, home to rare desert plants and animals.

Museo Casa Francisco Villa
Juárez 11. **Tel** (614) 416 29 58.
Open 9am–7pm Tue–Sat (to 4pm Sun) (daily in holidays). ground floor. reserve in advance.

The Templo de la Virgen de Fátima, the miners' church in Hidalgo del Parral

The beautiful Lago Arareco, high in the mountains of the Sierra Madre Occidental

⓳ Creel

Chihuahua. 5,100. Privada Tecnológico 1504, (635) 429 33 20. Carnival (Feb/Mar).

Redolent of wood smoke and fresh mountain air, the small logging town of Creel is the main road and rail gateway to the largely unspoiled Sierra Tarahumara and the Copper Canyon *(see pp180–81)*. It is an excellent place to join the spectacular El Chepe railroad *(see p361)*, or to disembark and spend a few days exploring the pine-clad mountains.

Near the railroad station are the town plaza and Creel's main street, Calle López Mateos. Two churches stand on the square along with the Tarahumara Mission shop, which gives informal advice to visitors as well as selling Indian artifacts and books about the surrounding sierra. On the other side of the railroad tracks is the **Casa de las Artesanías**, a government-run museum and craft shop. It tells the story of railway tycoon Enrique Creel (after whom the town is named) and includes exhibits about the numerous Jesuit missions in the area and the culture of the Tarahumara Indians. One glass case contains mummified bodies found in the nearby hills.

The best spot around the town for a gentle stroll or a picnic is at **Lago Arareco**, just 5 km (3 miles) to the south. The U-shaped lake is surrounded by unusual rock formations and a fragrant pine forest. A few kilometers farther along the same road is the start of a 4-km (2.5-mile) trail that winds through a scenic canyon to **Cascada Cusárare**, a 30-m (100-ft) waterfall. Other attractions within easy reach of Creel include the hot springs at **Recohuata**, the weird, mushroom-shaped rocks of the **Valle de los Hongos**, and **El Divisadero**, the viewpoint over the breathtaking Copper Canyon. El Chepe trains stop here briefly, but there are also minibus tours to the viewpoint for those who wish to spend longer contemplating the magnificent view. Tours to various sights, including helicopter trips over the canyons, are available in town.

Environs

A three- or four-hour drive northwest of Creel is the dramatic **Cascada de Basaseáchic**. At almost 300 m (1,000 ft) high, this is the third highest waterfall in North America. The towering falls are surrounded by 57 sq km (22 sq miles) of national park, with excellent walking trails and campgrounds. The park also contains several other waterfalls.

Casa de las Artesanías
Avenida Ferrocarril 178. **Tel** (635) 456 00 80. **Open** 9am–6pm daily (to 1pm Sun).

The Tarahumara Indians

A very private people, the Tarahumara Indians moved up into the mountains of the Sierra Madre Occidental about 400 years ago to avoid the Spanish missionaries. Since then, they have kept themselves very much apart from the rest of Mexico, preferring to live in small self-sufficient farming communities. They call themselves the Raramuri (Runners) and are superb long-distance athletes. The traditional tribal sport, *rarajipari (see p26)*, involves teams of runners kicking a wooden ball for huge distances across rugged mountain slopes. Participants wear sandals on their feet, and matches can last for several days.

A Tarahumara Indian woman and her children in traditional dress

The Hacienda Batopilas, built by a wealthy silver baron

⓴ Batopilas

Chihuahua. 14,500.

Barely more than a single street wide, and clinging to the riverbank at the bottom of a 1.5-km (1-mile) deep canyon, Batopilas is one of Mexico's hidden treasures. And it was treasure, in the form of silver, that brought the Spanish, and later the noted US politician Alexander Shepherd, to this remote spot. Not the least remarkable fact about this extraordinary place is that it was built when the only way in and out was by mule train over the mountains. Today, it can still take three hours to traverse the 60 km (37 miles) of dirt road that link Batopilas with the Creel-to-Guachochi highway. As it descends, the road drops over 2,100 m (7,000 ft) down the canyon wall via a hair-raising sequence of bends.

Batopilas was the birthplace of Manuel Gómez Morín, who formed PAN (Partido de Acción Nacional), the main opposition party to the long-running PRI *(see p59)*. There is little more than a plaque and a bust to mark the fact, but monuments to another former resident, Alexander Shepherd, abound. Shepherd, the last governor of Washington DC, created the Batopilas Mining Company in the 1890s. The ruins of his home, the **Hacienda San Miguel**, now overgrown with wild fig and bougainvillea, lie just across the river from the town entrance. Much of the aqueduct he built is still intact, and his hydroelectric plant, which made Batopilas the second electrified town in Mexico, is working again. The **Hacienda Batopilas**, now a popular hotel, is another noteworthy edifice with fantastic domes and arches.

Environs

Farther down the canyon, remote **Satevó** has a domed church, a testament to the zeal of the Jesuits who brought the Gospel here.

㉑ Cañón del Cobre

See pp180–81.

㉒ Álamos

Sonora. 26,000. Guadalupe Victoria 5, (647) 428 04 50. Virgen de Concepción (1st Sun of Dec).

A colonial jewel, set on the western edge of the Sierra Madre Occidental, Álamos owed its fame and fortune to the silver discovered here in the 17th century. However, its restoration is largely due to the community of people who have moved here from the US.

On the main plaza is the Baroque **Parroquia de la Purísima Concepción**, built between 1783 and 1804. Its bell tower has china plates, allegedly donated by local women, embedded in its walls. Sadly, most of the plates were broken in the Revolution. Also on the square is the **Palacio Municipal** (1899), which has a square tower and iron balconies. Nearby, the **Museo Costumbrista** charts the local history.

Decorative wall tiles in Alamos

However, it is the restored Sonoran mansions, with their interior patios and large windows with wrought-iron grilles, that give the town its flavor. Tours of some of these homes take place every Saturday.

Museo Costumbrista

Guadalupe Victoria 1. **Tel** (647) 428 00 53. **Open** 9am–6pm Wed–Sun. reserve in advance.

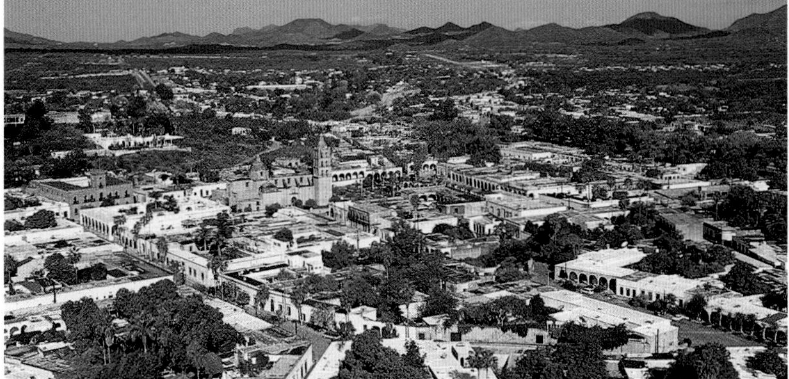
The attractive colonial town of Álamos, centered on the Parroquia de la Purísima Concepción church

㉑ Cañón del Cobre (Copper Canyon)

Bigger by far than the Grand Canyon, yet nowhere near as well known, Mexico's Copper Canyon region is one of the great undiscovered wonders of North America. Here, rivers have carved half-a-dozen canyons into the volcanic rock of the Sierra Madre Occidental. Amid the pine forests are spectacular waterfalls, weird rock formations, and tranquil lakes, some of which can be seen from the awe-inspiring railroad that winds across the northern part of the region. Thinly populated, the canyons are home to the Tarahumara Indians *(see p178)* and also contain evocative relics of past mining booms.

The spectacular Cañón del Cobre, over 1.5 km (1 mile) deep and 50 km (31 miles) in length

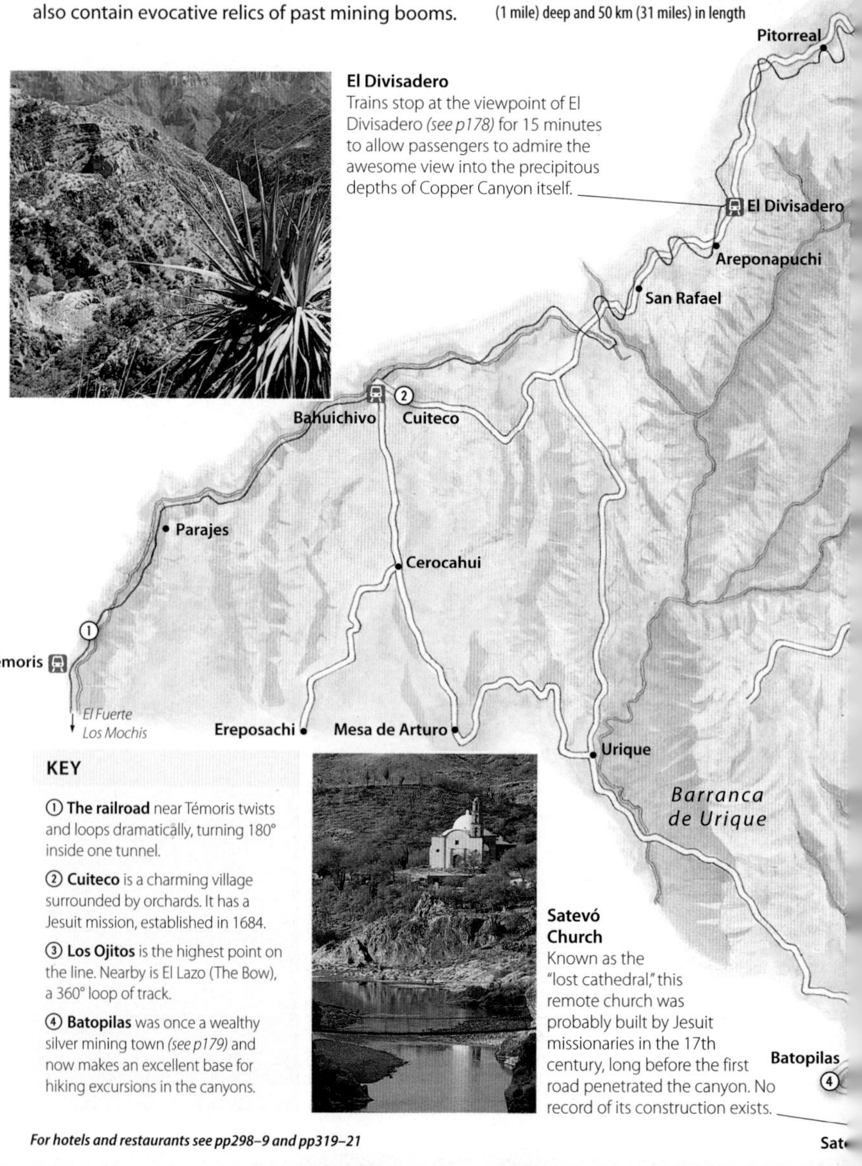

El Divisadero
Trains stop at the viewpoint of El Divisadero *(see p178)* for 15 minutes to allow passengers to admire the awesome view into the precipitous depths of Copper Canyon itself.

Pitorreal
El Divisadero
Areponapuchi
San Rafael
Bahuichivo
② Cuiteco
Parajes
Cerocahui
① Témoris
El Fuerte
Los Mochis
Ereposachi
Mesa de Arturo
Urique
Barranca de Urique
Batopilas ④
Sat

KEY

① **The railroad** near Témoris twists and loops dramatically, turning 180° inside one tunnel.

② **Cuiteco** is a charming village surrounded by orchards. It has a Jesuit mission, established in 1684.

③ **Los Ojitos** is the highest point on the line. Nearby is El Lazo (The Bow), a 360° loop of track.

④ **Batopilas** was once a wealthy silver mining town *(see p179)* and now makes an excellent base for hiking excursions in the canyons.

Satevó Church
Known as the "lost cathedral," this remote church was probably built by Jesuit missionaries in the 17th century, long before the first road penetrated the canyon. No record of its construction exists.

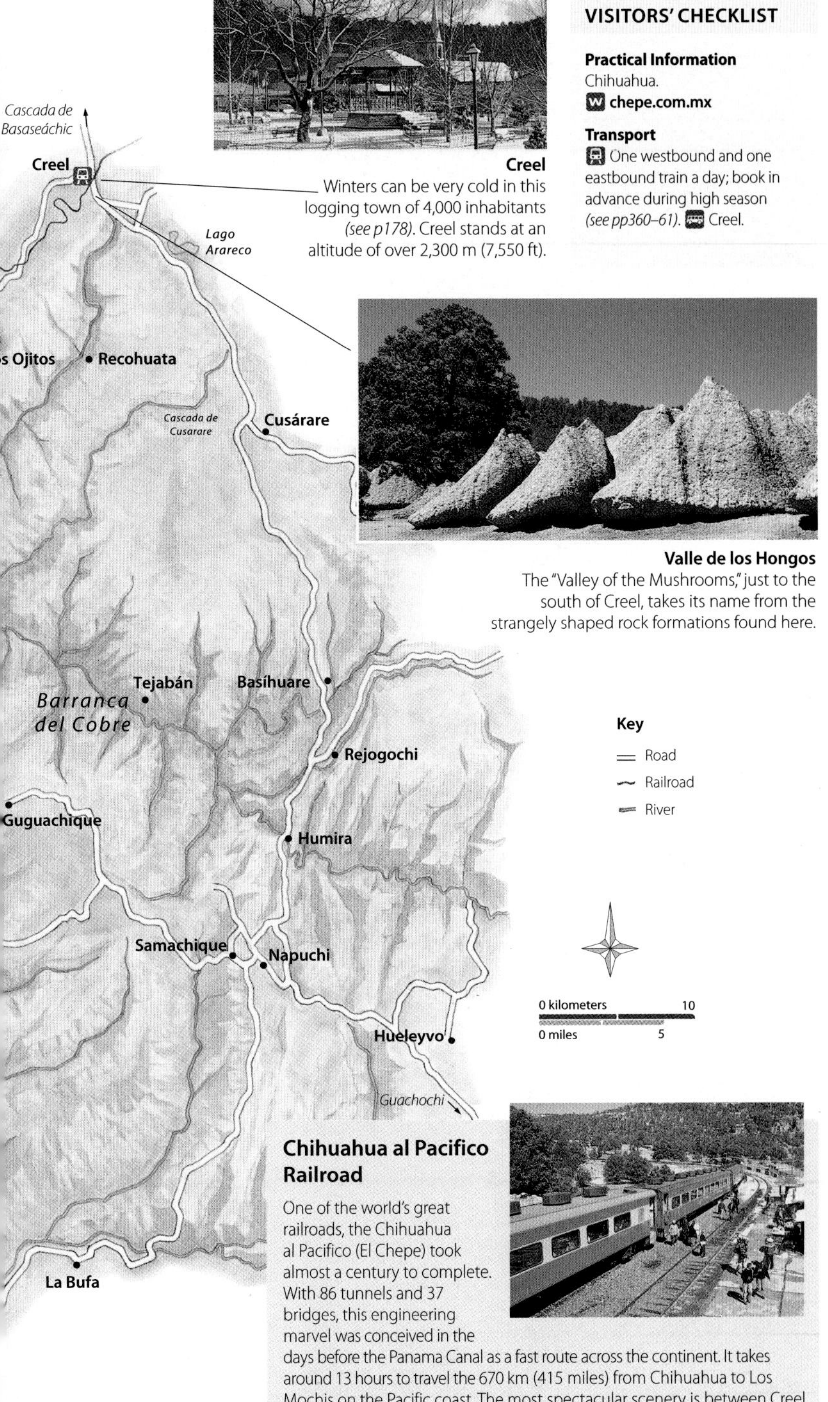

Creel
Winters can be very cold in this logging town of 4,000 inhabitants *(see p178)*. Creel stands at an altitude of over 2,300 m (7,550 ft).

Valle de los Hongos
The "Valley of the Mushrooms," just to the south of Creel, takes its name from the strangely shaped rock formations found here.

VISITORS' CHECKLIST

Practical Information
Chihuahua.
chepe.com.mx

Transport
One westbound and one eastbound train a day; book in advance during high season *(see pp360–61)*. Creel.

Chihuahua al Pacifico Railroad

One of the world's great railroads, the Chihuahua al Pacifico (El Chepe) took almost a century to complete. With 86 tunnels and 37 bridges, this engineering marvel was conceived in the days before the Panama Canal as a fast route across the continent. It takes around 13 hours to travel the 670 km (415 miles) from Chihuahua to Los Mochis on the Pacific coast. The most spectacular scenery is between Creel and El Fuerte, a stretch that drops more than 2,000 m (6,550 ft).

Fishing boats on Mazatlán's peaceful beachfront, the Playa del Norte

㉓ Mazatlán

Sinaloa. 438,000.
Carnaval 1317, (669) 981 88 83. Carnival (Feb/Mar).
gomazatlan.com

Situated just south of the Tropic of Cancer, Mazatlán is one of Mexico's most northerly major resorts. An agreeable climate and almost 20 km (12 miles) of beaches make it extremely popular. Another attraction is the Mazatlán carnival, claimed to be the third largest in the world, after those of Rio and New Orleans.

A waterfront boulevard connects the narrow streets and 19th-century architecture of the old town with the expensive beach hotels of the touristic Zona Dorada (Golden Zone). Of the offshore islands, **Venados, Lobos**, and **Pájaros** all offer an enticing combination of wildlife and uncrowded, sandy beaches, and are easily and cheaply reached by small boats. The misleadingly named **Isla de la Piedra**, however, is not actually an island but a peninsula across the estuary. Famous for its sandy beaches fringed with coconut palms, it is the site of one of Mexico's largest tourist developments, the Estrella de Mar.

Historic Mazatlán is worth visiting for its beautifully restored, Italianate **Teatro Ángela Peralta**, named after a famous Mazatlán-born opera singer, and its intriguing **cathedral** – Neo-Gothic on the outside, exuberantly Baroque on the inside, and noted for its gilded altar. Both buildings date from the late 19th century. However, Mazatlán's oldest church is the **Iglesia de San José**, built in 1842 on the slopes of the Cerro de la Nevería (Icebox Hill). The Cerro, which offers a spectacular view of the city by day or night, acquired its name from the 19th-century practice of storing imported ice in a tunnel carved into the hillside. The country's biggest aquarium, the **Acuario Mazatlán**, has more than 250 species of fish and other marine creatures.

Environs

Sinaloa is one of the few areas where the pre-Columbian ballgame known as *hulama* is still played *(see p281)*. The town of **El Quelite**, 50 km (31 miles) north of Mazatlán along Mex 15, holds matches on Sundays.

Acuario Mazatlán
Avenida Deportes 111. **Tel** (669) 981 78 15. **Open** daily.
acuariomazatlan.com

Detail of a mural at Durango's Palacio de Gobierno

Durango's Baroque cathedral, with its impressive twin towers

㉔ Durango

Durango. 582,000.
Florida 1106, Barrio del Calvario, (618) 811 21 39. Feria Nacional (Jul 8). durangoturismo.com

This city's main attraction is its association with the movie industry, particularly Westerns. Many of its restaurants and shops have cowboy themes.

There are also several important buildings. On the north flank of the Plaza de Armas stands the impressive **cathedral**. Begun in 1695, it has a Baroque façade and a fine choir with gilded stalls featuring figures of saints. A few blocks west of the plaza is the **Palacio de Gobierno**, the seat of the state government, known for its striking set of 20th-century murals painted by Francisco Montoya de la Cruz, Guillermo Bravo, and Guillermo de Lourdes. The **Casa del Conde de Suchil**, a late 18th-century mansion east of the plaza, now houses a museum where the original interior can still be seen. The exquisite Art Nouveau **Teatro Ricardo Castro**, built in 1900, holds what is reputedly the country's largest hand-carved relief made from a single piece of wood.

Environs

There are several movie locations outside the city, most notably **Villa del Oeste**. Nearby is the village of **Chupaderos**, which was probably Durango's most used Hollywood location.

For superb views of mountains and canyons, head west on Mex 40, which reaches around 2,600 m (8,530 ft) above sea level. The highlight is the **Espinazo del Diablo** (Devil's Backbone), a winding 9-km (6-mile) stretch along a narrow ridge about 130 km (81 miles) west of Durango.

Villa del Oeste
Mex 45, 12 km (7 miles) N of Durango. **Tel** (618) 137 43 86. **Open** Tue–Sun.

Saltillo cathedral's pulpit, with its gold-leaf decoration and saintly figurines

25 Saltillo

Coahuila. 725,000.
Avenida Universidad 205, (844) 416 48 80. Ferias (Jul–Aug).
saltillo.gob.mx

Dubbed "the city of columns" because of the number of buildings characterized by Neo-Classical colonnades, Saltillo is also famous for what is probably the most beautiful **cathedral** in northeast Mexico. Dominating the old Plaza de Armas, the Churrigueresque facade of this 18th-century building has six columns richly embellished with carved flowers, fruit, and shells.

Inside, visitors can climb the smaller of the two towers, and view the Spanish 16th-century wooden cross in the Capilla del Santo Cristo, which is located in the main body of the church. The cathedral also holds a large collection of colonial oil paintings, but its principal treasure is the silver front of the side altar dedicated to San José. So fine is the silverwork, in fact, that the piece is often exhibited elsewhere and replaced in the cathedral by a photograph.

On the opposite side of the plaza is the state government headquarters, the **Palacio de Gobierno**, which contains a mural charting the history of Coahuila. The other building of note in the center, which stands out both for its history and for its attractive, tiled cupola, is the **Templo de San Esteban**. This church served as a hospital for injured Mexican troops during the US invasion of Mexico *(see p56)*.

Saltillo also has a unique museum dedicated to the birds of Mexico. The **Museo de las Aves de México** contains a collection of stuffed birds, covering over 670 different species. The **Museo del Desierto** aims to promote a greater understanding of the biodiversity of desert ecology.

Museo de las Aves de México
Calle Hidalgo 151. **Tel** (844) 414 01 67. **Open** 10am–6pm Tue–Sat, 11am–7pm Sun.

Museo del Desierto
Carlos Abedrop Dávila 3745. **Tel** (844) 986 90 00. **Open** 10am–5pm Tue–Sun.

26 Monterrey

Nuevo León. 1.1 million.
Washington 648 Oriente, 01800 832 22 00 (toll free). Virgen de Guadalupe (Dec 12). **nl.gob.mx**

One of Mexico's largest cities, Monterrey is a thriving industrial center with some striking 20th-century architecture like the **Planetario Alfa**, which houses science exhibitions and a planetarium, and the **Basílica de la Purísima**, finished in 1946. In the Gran Plaza **MARCO**, (Museo de Arte Contemporáneo) houses Latin American modern art. A monumental sculpture, the **Faro del Comercio**, towers above Monterrey's cathedral. The city's historical museum **3Museos** offers five floors of exhibits from the prehistoric era to the present.

Environs

Occupying an area of mountainous semidesert west of the city is the **Parque Nacional las Cumbres de Monterrey**. Two of its most accessible sights are the 25-m (82-ft) Cola de Caballo falls and the spectacular Grutas de García caves.

Planetario Alfa
Avenida Roberto Garza Sada 1000. **Tel** (81) 83 03 00 01. **Open** 2:30–7pm Tue–Fri, 10:30am–7pm Sat & Sun. half price Wed.

MARCO
Cnr Zuazua & Jardón. **Tel** (81) 82 62 45 00. **Open** 10am–6pm Tue–Sun (to 8pm Wed). Wed free. in advance. **marco.org.mx**

3Museos
Dr Coss 445. **Tel** (81) 20 33 98 98. **Open** Tue–Sun.

Monterrey's massive scientific exhibition space, the Planetario Alfa

Hollywood in Mexico

Clear blue skies and magical, semidesert landscapes made Durango for many years a favorite location for the movie industry, especially for Westerns. The stars who have filmed here range from John Wayne and Kirk Douglas to Anthony Quinn and Jack Nicholson. Some of the best-known movies shot near Durango include John Huston's *The Unforgiven* and Sam Peckinpah's *The Wild Bunch* and *Pat Garrett and Billy the Kid*. A few Hollywood locations can be visited, including the Villa del Oeste (officially called Condado Chávez) and Chupaderos.

The dusty village of Chupaderos, one of Durango's Wild West movie locations

THE COLONIAL HEARTLAND

Aguascalientes · Colima · Guanajuato · Jalisco · Michoacán Nayarit · Querétaro · San Luis Potosí · Zacatecas

Charming, well-preserved towns built during colonial times characterize the states to the north of Mexico City, where sun-drenched coastlines and humid jungles adjoin cactus-strewn mesas and snow-capped volcanoes. Indian villages, bustling cities, and beach resorts also form part of this vast and varied territory.

Following the fall of the Aztec empire *(see p47)*, Spanish soldiers marched north to conquer the nomadic Indian tribes of this region. Missionaries also came, to spread the Gospel, and adventurers to seek their fortune, some exploiting the veins of precious metal in the area's arid hills, others its fertile plains.

Soon opulent, Spanish-style cities, brimming with palaces, churches, and convents, were founded in the area. Zacatecas, Guanajuato, and San Luis Potosí boomed as a result of being the principal suppliers of silver and gold to the Spanish royal family. Aguascalientes, San Miguel de Allende, and Querétaro were all important stopovers on the silver route to the capital. The city of Morelia established itself as the cultural and social hub of New Spain's western province, and Guadalajara rose to prominence as the gateway to the Pacific ports of Manzanillo and San Blas. In the early 19th century, general discontent with Spanish rule began to simmer in Querétaro, and nearby colonial strongholds. The plotting, and first armed uprising, by rebels here earned the region the title "the Cradle of Independence." Ferocious battles were fought in the cities of Guanajuato and Morelia, until Mexico declared its independence from Spain in 1821 *(see p53)*.

Today, the Colonial Heartland of Mexico remains a relatively prosperous region, thanks to its rich agricultural lands, thriving industry (which includes the production of tequila), and increasingly popular tourist attractions.

A volcano rises above fertile plains in Nayarit state, where agriculture is the main source of income

◀ The Plaza de Armas gardens and Neo-Classical facade of the Cathedral Basílica, Guadalajara

Exploring the Colonial Heartland

Beaches and colonial cities are the tourist magnets of this region. Big, booming Puerto Vallarta and the smaller, less hectic Manzanillo are resort cities on the long, beautiful Pacific coastline. Inland, Guadalajara is a modern metropolis notable for its majestic colonial core. The old towns of Zacatecas, San Luis Potosí, Aguascalientes, Guanajuato, San Miguel de Allende, and Querétaro were constructed with fortunes amassed from silver. Pátzcuaro and Morelia are colonial jewels in Michoacán. Off the beaten track in Riviera Nayarit are Huichol and Cora Indian villages in the Sierra Madre Occidental, the ghost town of Real de Catorce, isolated missions in the untamed Sierra Gorda, and the majestic waterfalls of the lush Huasteca Potosina.

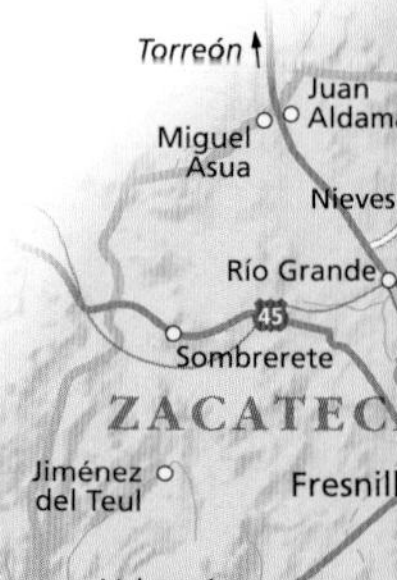

Indian pottery on sale at a market in Pátzcuaro

Sights at a Glance

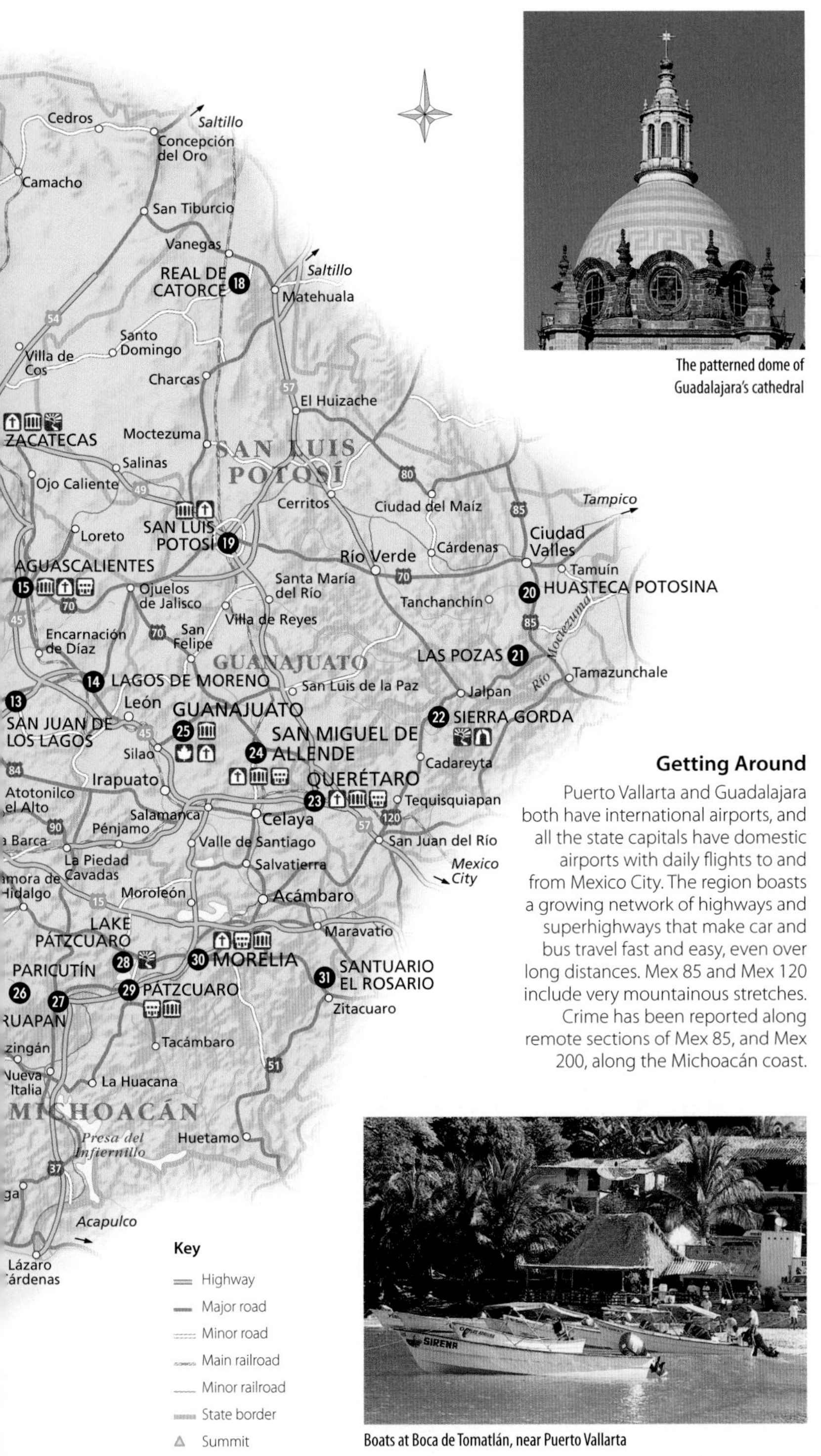

The patterned dome of Guadalajara's cathedral

Getting Around

Puerto Vallarta and Guadalajara both have international airports, and all the state capitals have domestic airports with daily flights to and from Mexico City. The region boasts a growing network of highways and superhighways that make car and bus travel fast and easy, even over long distances. Mex 85 and Mex 120 include very mountainous stretches. Crime has been reported along remote sections of Mex 85, and Mex 200, along the Michoacán coast.

Boats at Boca de Tomatlán, near Puerto Vallarta

For keys to symbols *see back flap*

❶ Mexcaltitán

Nayarit. 900. Fiesta de San Pedro y San Pablo (Jun 28–9).

This tiny island, its name meaning "Place of the Moon Temple," is no more than 400 m (1,310 ft) across. It sits in a lagoon in Mexico's largest mangrove swamp area, and in the rains of August and September the streets become canals. According to legend the Aztecs slept here on the way to their promised land.

Although no Aztec artifacts have been found here, the archaeological pieces on display in the **Museo del Orígen**, located in the former town hall, nonetheless emphasize the importance of the island of Mexcaltitán as "The Cradle of Mexicanism."

Museo del Orígen
Porfirio Díaz 1. **Tel** (311) 131 56 27. **Open** 9am–2pm & 4–6pm Tue–Sun.

❷ San Blas

Nayarit. 43,000. José María Mercado 29. Día de San Blas (Feb 2), Carnival (Feb/Mar), Día de la Marina (Jun 1).

Little remains from San Blas' colonial heyday, when it was a thriving seaport, an important shipbuilding center, and a garrison for the Spanish Armada. The only visible legacies are the ruins of an 18th-century Spanish fort and church, and a large, crumbling 19th-century customs house. Today San Blas is a sleepy fishing village of palm groves and mangrove-fringed estuaries. It is the state's oldest developed resort, with a few hotels and palm-thatched restaurants catering to the swimmers and surfers attracted by the 19 km (12 miles) of golden beaches around the Bay of Matanchén. Beware of the mosquitoes that descend at sunset.

Environs

For boat trips through the lush jungle estuaries teeming with wildlife, head to the jetties east of town, on the road to Matanchén. The most popular destination is **La Tovara**, a freshwater spring and swimming hole adjacent to a crocodile farm.

Boats awaiting intrepid jungle adventurers

The panoramic view of the serene Bay of Matanchén near San Blas

The Huichol Indians

There are still some 44,000 Huichol Indians living in Mexico, mostly in villages in the Sierra Madre Occidental mountains. They are known for their secret religious rites. An indispensable ingredient in these ceremonies is the hallucinogenic *peyote* cactus, which grows miles away in the state of San Luis Potosí. Every September, Huicholes go to their sacred mountain near Real de Catorce *(see p197)* to gather the plant. Huichol traders are known for their colorful *nierika* yarn paintings and *chaquira* beadwork.

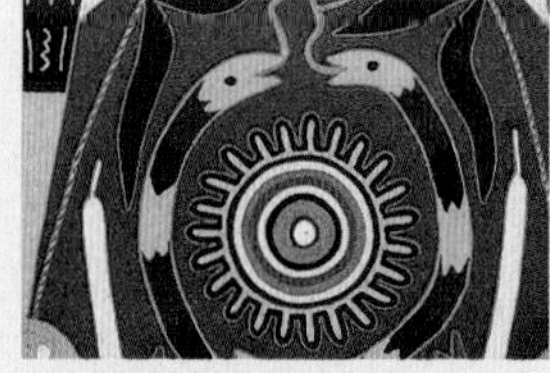

Part of a brilliantly colored yarn painting by the Huichol Indians

❸ Tepic

Nayarit. 390,000. Cnr of Avenida México and Calzada del Ejército Nacional, (311) 214 80 71. Feria Nacional de Tepic (Feb 25–Mar 21). **rivieranayarit.com**

A provincial town with an agreeable climate, Tepic was founded in the foothills of an extinct volcano. Not far from the Plaza Principal and the **cathedral** is the **Museo Regional de Nayarit**, where you will find shaft-tombs and displays about the Cora and Huichol Indians. The **Centro Estatal de Culturas Populares e Indígenas de Nayarit** has exhibits about the Huicholes, Tepehuanos, Mexicaneros, Coras, and mestizo people of the region; some of whom flock to Tepic on May 3 to visit the grass cross at the **Templo y Ex-Convento de la Cruz de Zacate**.

Environs

In the hills 30 km (19 miles) southeast of Tepic is the **Santa María del Oro** lake, popular with hikers and birdwatchers.

Museo Regional de Nayarit
Avenida México 91 Norte. **Tel** (311) 212 19 00. **Open** 9am–6pm Mon–Fri (to 3pm Sat). in advance.

Centro Estatal de Culturas Populares e Indígenas de Nayarit
Avenida México 105, Tepic. **Tel** (311) 212 17 05. **Open** 10am–2pm & 4–7pm Tue–Sat.

❹ Puerto Vallarta

Jalisco. 256,000. Plaza Marina 144–6, (322) 221 26 76. Día de Guadalupe (Dec 12).
visitpuertovallarta.com

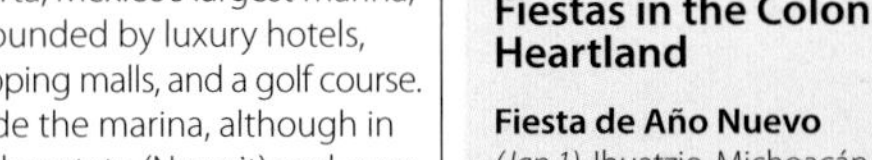

Hollywood stars discovered the tropical paradise of Banderas Bay in the 1960s. Since then, Puerto Vallarta has become one of Mexico's top Pacific resorts. Now 1.5 million tourists flock here annually to savor the beautiful beaches, the year-round pleasant climate, and the vibrant nightlife.

The various resort towns stretch for more than 40 km (25 miles) around the bay, but at the heart is Puerto Vallarta's old town, **Viejo Vallarta**. This area has managed to conserve some of the quaintness of a Mexican village, with its white-washed, tile-roofed houses and stone-paved streets stretching toward the jungle-clad mountains. The small **Isla Río Cuale**, an island in the river dividing the town, is the location for boutiques, cafés, and a botanical garden.

Head to the *malecón*, the waterfront boardwalk, for water taxis serving other parts of the bay, such as the Zona Hotelera, the main hotel strip which extends to the seaport in the north. Farther north is Marina Vallarta, Mexico's largest marina, surrounded by luxury hotels, shopping malls, and a golf course. Beside the marina, although in another state (Nayarit) and even another time zone, is **Nuevo Vallarta**. This is the most recent development on the bay, and its miles of beach, river, and estuary frontage reach as far as the town of **Bucerías**. The tourist infrastructure then peters out, leaving a string of small, pristine beaches that stretch to the bay's northernmost point, **Punta Mita**.

The southern, more scenic arc of Banderas Bay begins with **Playa de los Muertos** (Dead Men's Beach), the old town's most popular section of coastline. From here, the road winds past villa-dotted cliffs and sparkling blue coves to **Mismaloya**, before turning inland. Beyond this point, the exotic coves and superb swimming and snorkeling beaches are accessible only by boat.

Environs

To the north of Puerto Vallarta are some of the area's most famous diving sites, including **Las Marietas**, **Corbeteña**, and **El Morro**. Trips to the forests, canyons, and villages of the hinterland are also easily arranged.

Sailboats moored in the calm waters of Puerto Vallarta's marina

Fiestas in the Colonial Heartland

Fiesta de Año Nuevo *(Jan 1)*, Ihuatzio, Michoacán *(see p210)*. Purépecha Indians perform traditional masked dances to music and Pirecua songs. For the dance of "Los Viejitos" (The Old Men), originally dedicated to the elderly pre-Columbian god Huehuetéotl, dancers hobble around wearing masks and woollen shawls.

Masked Indian dancing at the Fiesta de Año Nuevo

Easter Week *(Mar/Apr)*, Tzintzuntzán *(see p210)* and Tarímbaro, Michoacán. A realistic crucifixion of Christ is re-enacted by a volunteer, who is flogged and carries his own wooden cross. Traditional processions also take place in San Miguel de Allende *(see pp202–3)* and Guanajuato *(see pp206–9)*.

Feria de San Marcos *(Apr/May)*, Aguascalientes *(see p195)*. At Mexico's largest fair, up to 100,000 people jam the town day and night to see exhibitions, parades, and fireworks, listen to concerts, and cheer at bullfights, cockfights, and *charreadas*, the riding and rodeo shows.

Day of the Dead *(Nov 1–2)*, Pátzcuaro and Isla Janitzio, Michoacán *(see p211 and pp38–9)*. Dead relatives and ancient gods are remembered, and traditional masked dances are performed, including "The Fish," in which fishing nets symbolically haul in a fish-masked dancer.

A sheltered, tranquil bay at the northern end of the Costalegre

5 Costalegre

Jalisco. Chamela, Barra de Navidad, Cihuatlán. Jalisco 67, Barra de Navidad, (315) 355 51 00. **costalegre.com**

Jalisco's beautiful "Happy Coast" stretches for more than 200 km (125 miles), south from Puerto Vallarta *(see p189)* to the border with Colima state. The Mex 200 highway runs parallel with the coastline but mostly inland, taking in lush green mountain ranges and the occasional banana plantation. Most of Costalegre's white-sand beaches are accessible only to hotel guests or from the ocean. The luxury resorts – some with golf courses, polo fields, and airstrips – are shielded by gates and guards and can be reached only by private roads.

Set on a beautiful bay 165 km (102 miles) south of Puerto Vallarta, the resort of **Careyes** was developed in the late 1960s by an Italian entrepreneur. The colorful mix of Mediterranean and Mexican architecture, featuring open living areas and palm-thatched roofs, or *palapas*, has become known as the "Careyes Style." If money is no object, some of the dream houses perched on the soaring cliffs can be rented.

Somewhat more affordable are the lodgings found on the bays of Chamela, Tenacatita, and Cuastecomate. Swimming here is much safer than on the open-ocean beaches, which are subject to dangerous waves and treacherous currents. The southernmost of the bays on the coast is **Bahía de Navidad**, where the family resort of **Melaque** and the fishing village of **Barra de Navidad** are found. Most of Barra's small restaurants and modest hotels are squeezed onto a narrow sandbar, which enjoys sunsets over the Pacific Ocean and views of a peaceful lagoon to the east. Small boats from Barra ferry customers to the rustic eateries of **Colimilla**, a lagoon-side hamlet at the foot of a towering wooded peninsula. The peninsula is now dominated by the massive Isla Navidad resort, which has an ecological preserve and a 27-hole golf course.

6 Manzanillo

Colima. 161,000. Blvd Miguel de la Madrid 875A, (314) 333 22 77. Fiestas de Mayo (May 1–10), International Sailfish Fishing Tournament (1st week of Nov). **colima.gob.mx**

Mexico's main west coast shipping center, Manzanillo is also Colima state's foremost beach resort and calls itself "The Sailfish Capital of the World." The colorful houses of the old port cling to a hill overlooking the main harbor, while the newer part of town covers a sandbar separating the lagoon from the ocean. Most of Manzanillo's restaurants and hotels are located along the white sands of **Las Brisas** and **Playa Azul**.

Separating the Bahía de Manzanillo from the Bahía de Santiago is a peninsula, site of **Las Hadas** ("The Fairies"), a luxury Moorish-style hotel with a golf course which opened in the 1970s. Hotels now line most of the Bahía de Santiago, from La Audiencia to Playa Miramar.

Environs

Natura Camp is an eco-adventure park near Manzanillo, where visitors can swoop along zip lines, among other activities. You can make a day trip, or rent a cabin or campsite to stay longer.

Natura Camp
Carretera Manzanillo, Minatitlán km 1.6. **Tel** (314) 332 19 21. **Open** 9am–6pm Mon–Sat.

7 Cuyutlán

Colima. 940. Fiesta de la Santa Cruz (May 2–3).

Cuyutlán is a traditional resort on the central part of Colima's coast. It is characterized by black volcanic sand, pounding surf, and the Mexican tourists who descend on the town on weekends. It is at the tip of the immense Cuyutlán Lagoon, which extends south for 32 km (20 miles) from Manzanillo.

Salt from the area provided an essential ingredient for ore processing in colonial times. The tiny Museo de la Sal gives an insight into the salt economy, its workers, and harvesting methods. A spectacular springtime phenomenon seen on the coast here

Manzanillo's grand Las Hadas resort

Volcán de Fuego, seen from the road heading out of Colima toward Guadalajara

is the ola verde, when glassy green waves up to 10 m (33 ft) in height gleam with phosphorescent marine organisms.

Museo de la Sal
Juárez. **Tel** (312) 326 40 14.
Open 10am–6pm Tue–Sat.

Bandstand in the tropical Jardín de Libertad, Colima

8 Colima

Colima. 147,000. Palacio de Gobierno, (312) 312 20 21. San Felipe de Jesús (Feb), Feria de Todos los Santos (Oct 27–Nov 11).
colima.gob.mx

The graceful provincial town of Colima, capital of one of Mexico's smallest states, was the first Spanish city on the west coast. It has been rebuilt several times since 1522 because of earthquakes, but the center still boasts Neo-Classical buildings, several museums, and tropical parks, such as the **Jardín la Libertad**.

La Campana archaeological site on the outskirts of town was an important pre-Columbian settlement between AD 700 and 900, with the earliest remains dating back as far as 1500 BC. While its size and scale does not compare to some of Mexico's better-known pre-Hispanic sites, La Campana makes for an interesting excursion. Major exploration in the mid-1990s unearthed several monumental plazas and structures. Ceramic vessels and human and animal figurines from early shaft-tombs can be seen in the **Museo de las Culturas de Occidente. The Museo Universitario de Artes Populares** exhibits regional and national folk art, covering both pre-Columbian and more recent periods.

Environs
The route heading north out of the city offers impressive views of the active **Volcán de Fuego** and the taller, dormant **El Nevado de Colima** behind. The foothills of both provide wonderful hiking opportunities.

Museo de las Culturas de Occidente
Corner of Galván & Ejército Nacional.
Tel (312) 313 06 08. **Open** Tue–Sun.

Museo Universitario de Artes Populares
Manuel Gallardo Zamora 99.
Tel (312) 312 68 69. **Open** 10am–2pm & 5–8pm Tue–Sat (to 1pm Sun).
Sun free.

9 Tequila

Jalisco. 41,000. José Cuervo 33. Fiesta Septembrina (Sep 16), Feria Nacional del Tequila (Dec 1–12).

Everything in Tequila reminds the visitor of Mexico's most famous drink *(see p313)*, especially the scent from the distilleries. Plantations of *Agave tequilana weber* surround the town, the cores, or *piñas*, of which have been used to make tequila since the 16th century. The town is the country's largest producer and exports to nearly 100 countries. Take a distillery tour followed by a tasting session. The biggest and oldest factories are La Perseverancia and La Rojeña, which displays original equipment and a cooking pit.

Harvesting the *Agave tequilana weber*, in fields near Tequila

⑩ Guadalajara

Until just a few decades ago, the capital of the state of Jalisco was a placid provincial city. Then an industrial boom swiftly transformed Guadalajara into a modern metropolis second only to Mexico City. A broad industrial belt and sprawling suburbs now ring the historic center. However, the traditional flavor of the "Pearl of the West" or "City of Roses" lingers on in the vast series of squares, lined with majestic colonial buildings, that make up the core of the city. Distinctive and once separate communities such as Zapopan, with its sacred basilica, and Tlaquepaque ***(see p194)*** **have their own attractions and are now suburbs of the city.**

Guadalajara's imposing cathedral, seen from the Plaza de Armas

Cathedral Basílica

Construction of this monumental cathedral began shortly after Guadalajara was founded in 1542. However, it was not finished until the early 17th century, and then in a medley of styles. Two earthquakes, in 1750 and 1818, destroyed the original facade and towers. They were replaced in the mid-19th century by the present yellow-tiled twin spires, which soon became the recognized symbol of the city.

More than a dozen mostly Neo-Classical altars grace the otherwise somber interior. Among the 18th- and 19th-century paintings in the sacristy is *The Assumption of the Virgin*, which was painted by the Spanish artist Bartolomé Esteban Murillo.

Museo Regional de Guadalajara

Calle Liceo 60. **Tel** (33) 3614 99 57. **Open** Tue–Sun.

A lovely former seminary dating from 1699 is now the home of the Museo Regional de Guadalajara. The ground-floor galleries have displays on palaeontology, prehistory, and archaeology. Among exhibits here are a complete mammoth skeleton found in the state, and a replica of a shaft tomb discovered in Zapopan. Upstairs are ethnographic displays about Indian tribes, a gallery on local history since the Conquest, and paintings by colonial and contemporary Jalisco artists.

Open, horse-drawn carriages can be hired at the museum entrance for a ride through the city's historic center.

Palacio de Gobierno

Cnr of Moreno & Av Corona. **Tel** (33) 3668 18 02. **Open** daily.

Finished in the Baroque style in 1774, the Palacio de Gobierno is today the seat of the Jalisco state government. Murals by José Clemente Orozco adorn the main staircase, the dome of the former chapel, and the upstairs congress chambers. They celebrate Independence hero Miguel Hidalgo, who proclaimed the abolition of slavery in Mexico here in 1810. The wooden main door is intricately carved with nude female busts. Originally made for the cathedral, the door was deemed inappropriate and later installed here.

The Plaza de Armas, outside the building, has an ornate bandstand where concerts are staged on Thursday and Sunday evenings.

Teatro Degollado

Belén s/n, corner Morelos. **Tel** (33) 36 14 47 73. **Open** daily.

Eight Corinthian columns topped by a triangular frieze depicting Apollo and the Muses make up the portico of this 1,400 seat Neo-Classical theater. The red-and-gold five-tier interior boasts chandeliers and a dome with a fresco showing scenes from Dante's *Divine Comedy*. The theater has been remodeled several times since its 1866 inauguration.

Instituto Cultural Cabañas

Cabañas 8. **Tel** (33) 3668 16 47. **Open** 10am–6pm Tue–Sun. Tue free. **hospicio cabanas.jalisco.gob.mx**

Founded by Bishop Juan Cruz Ruiz de Cabañas in 1805 and now a UNESCO World Heritage site, this former hospice is the largest colonial edifice in the Americas and one of Mexico's finest Neo-Classical buildings. The structure, with its large central dome and 22 courtyards, was the work of Manuel Tolsá.

Sculpture on Plaza de Armas

For most of its history, the site was an orphanage, housing up to 3,000 children. In 1979 it was restored and turned into an exhibition center and a school for the performing and fine arts.

Frescoes by José Clemente Orozco, executed in the late

Mural of Miguel Hidalgo, painted by José Clemente Orozco, in the Palacio de Gobierno

Frog-shaped fountains in the pedestrianized Plaza Tapatía

1930s, cover the interior of the former chapel, with the central *Man in Flames* in the dome. These masterworks take as their themes the Conquest, political terror, and the dehumanization of modern man.

The Plaza Tapatía, fronting the building, marks the end of a nine-block pedestrian zone extending from the cathedral. Nearby is the **Mercado Libertad**, one of Latin America's largest covered markets.

Churches

There are many fine colonial churches within easy walking distance of the cathedral. The **Templo de San Juan de Dios**, with its vivid gold, white, and blue interior, backs onto a square where *mariachi* musicians and fans congregate.

To the south is the **Templo de San Felipe Neri**, which has a beautiful Plateresque facade. This church and the **Capilla de Aranzazú**, across the street, used to be part of a Franciscan monastery. The chapel contains three ornate Churrigueresque altars.

The lateral facade of the **Templo de Santa Mónica**, to the northwest, is an excellent example of Baroque styling.

Basílica de Zapopan

Zapopan, 7 km (4 miles) NW of center. **Tel** (33) 3633 66 14. **Open** daily.

The early 18th-century Basílica de Zapopan is home to one of the most revered religious relics in Mexico, the Virgen de Zapopan. The small corn-paste statue was presented to the Indians of the region by a Franciscan friar in the 16th century and is believed to bring relief from natural catastrophes. To the right of the basilica's entrance is a small museum displaying Huichol Indian crafts *(see p188)*.

VISITORS' CHECKLIST

Practical Information
Guadalajara. 1.5 million. Morelos 102, (33) 3668 16 00. Virgen de Zapopan (Oct 12).

Transport
17 km (11 miles) S. Carretera libre a Zapotlanejo and Carretera Tonalá, (33) 3600 03 91.

An ornate Baroque side entrance to the Templo de Santa Mónica

Guadalajara City Center

1. Cathedral Basílica
2. Museo Regional de Guadalajara
3. Palacio de Gobierno
4. Teatro Degollado
5. Instituto Cultural Cabañas
6. Mercado Libertad
7. Templo de San Juan de Dios
8. Templo de San Felipe Neri
9. Capilla de Aranzazú
10. Templo de Santa Mónica

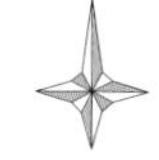

0 meters 300
0 yards 300

For keys to symbols *see back flap*

⓫ Tlaquepaque

Jalisco. 609,000. Guadalajara. Ayuntamiento, (33) 3562 70 50. Fiestas de Tlaquepaque (Jun).

Once a separate potters' village and stylish weekend retreat for the residents of Guadalajara *(see pp192–3)*, Tlaquepaque is now effectively a suburb of the city. However, it retains a village atmosphere.

The overwhelming selection of pottery, blown glass, textiles, metal, wood, and papier-mâché items cluttering the crafts shops is the main factor that attracts large numbers of visitors to come here.

There are also many restaurants. A favorite meeting spot off the appealing, flower-filled central square is El Parián. Hailed as the world's biggest cantina, it gathers about 20 eating and drinking establishments around its giant courtyard. In the center of the courtyard is a bandstand where *mariachi* musicians often play.

The best ceramics pieces from Tlaquepaque and the surrounding region can be appreciated at the **Museo Regional de la Cerámica**. Located in a beautiful old mansion, the museum counts a 16th-century kitchen among its most interesting exhibits. Many of the items sold in Tlaquepaque are in fact made in workshops in the neighboring suburb of Tonalá. Like Tlaquepaque, this was once a village outside Guadalajara, and was originally an Indian settlement. Its streets become an open-air craft market on Thursdays and Sundays.

Mariachi statuettes in a shop in Tlaquepaque

A view of the Laguna de Chapala, Mexico's largest lake

Museo Regional de la Cerámica
Independencia 237. **Tel** (33) 36 35 54 04. **Open** Mon–Sat.

⓬ Laguna de Chapala

Jalisco. Chapala, Ajijic. Madero 407 Altos, Chapala, (376) 765 31 41.

Mexico's largest natural lake, the Laguna de Chapala, supports a popular resort area, the Ribera, along its northwestern shore. However, the lake is drying up, mainly because of the increasing water needs of the burgeoning population and industry of nearby Guadalajara.

The built-up Ribera has a near-perfect climate, and its proximity to Mexico's second city has for decades resulted in streams of foreign visitors. It stretches for 21 km (13 miles) from the old-fashioned resort of **Chapala**, where writer D.H. Lawrence stayed, to the village of Jocotepec at the western end of the lake. **Ajijic**, an artists' colony with cobblestone streets, crafts shops, galleries, and a 16th-century chapel, is the most picturesque village of the Ribera. Farther west, the spa resort of **San Juan Cosalá** offers the attractions of public swimming pools and a natural geyser.

Boat trips from Chapala head for two islands: the tree-covered **Isla de los Alacranes**, with its fish restaurants; and **Mezcala**, with the ruins of a 19th-century fort where independence fighters held out for four years before surrendering to the Spanish in 1816.

The scenic road along the mostly undeveloped southern shore opens up splendid views of the lake.

A candy stall on Calle de Independencia, Tlaquepaque

⓭ San Juan de los Lagos

Jalisco. 65,000. Fray Antonio de Segovia 10, (395) 785 09 79. La Candelaria (Jan 25–Feb 2), Fiesta de la Primavera (late May).

The imposing 18th-century cathedral in San Juan de los Lagos is one the most important Catholic sanctuaries in Mexico. An estimated nine million pilgrims travel here every year to venerate the Virgen de San Juan de los Lagos,

For hotels and restaurants see pp299–302 and pp321–5

a small 16th-century corn-paste statue enshrined in an altar originally made for the church of Santa Maria degli Angeli in Rome.

The cathedral, which reaches a height of 68 m (223 ft), has a sumptuous interior. In its vast sacristy is a group of large 17th- and 18th-century paintings, six of which have been attributed to Rubens. Touching votive pictures, expressing gratitude to the Virgin for favors granted, line the walls of a room beside the sacristy.

Many colonial buildings have been lost from the town's narrow streets, but the **Capilla de los Milagros** and **Casa de la Cultura**, both dating from the 17th century, are fine examples that have survived.

A colorful mural depicting life in Mexico, San Juan de los Lagos

⓮ Lagos de Moreno

Jalisco. 154,000. Feria de Agosto (late Jul–early Aug).

Tourists rarely stray into this architectural jewel, which boasts many 18th- and 19th-century buildings and is known as the "Athens of Jalisco."

In colonial times, Lagos de Moreno was on the silver road between Zacatecas and Mexico City. The magnificent Baroque **parish church**, the more sober **Templo y Ex-Convento de Capuchinas**, and a bridge with Neo-Classical decoration all date from this era. The town peaked as a prosperous cattle-ranching center in the late 1800s, when it was enhanced by the charming **Teatro Rosas Moreno**. Two stately Neo-Classical residences from the same time are still here and look out onto the central park. These buildings now house the **Palacio Municipal** and the **Hotel de París**.

The arcaded main courtyard of the Palacio de Gobierno, Aguascalientes

⓯ Aguascalientes

Aguascalientes. 797,000. Palacio de Gobierno: Plaza de la Patria, (449) 910 20 00. Feria de San Marcos (mid-Apr–mid-May), Las Calaveras (early Nov).

Named after its hot springs, Aguascalientes still attracts visitors to its thermal baths but is today best known for its popular spring fair, the Feria de San Marcos *(see p189)*.

The colonial red and pink **Palacio de Gobierno** has a spectacular maze of arches, pillars, and staircases around its main courtyard. A series of murals inside were painted by Oswaldo Barra Cunningham, a pupil of Diego Rivera. Across the Plaza de la Patria is the 18th-century **cathedral**, with a gallery of colonial paintings, and the Neo-Classical **Teatro Morelos**. The **Museo de Arte Contemporáneo** displays prize-winning contemporary works, and the **Museo José Guadalupe Posada** has engravings by Mexico's best known satirical cartoonist. In contrast, **Museo Interactivo de Ciencias y Tecnología** is an interactive science museum.

The 18th-century cathedral on Plaza de la Patria in Aguascalientes

Museo de Arte Contemporáneo
Morelos and Primo Verdad. **Tel** (449) 918 69 01. **Open** 10am–6pm Tue–Sun. Sun free.

Museo José Guadalupe Posada
Jardín del Encino s/n. **Tel** (449) 915 45 56. **Open** 11am–6pm Tue–Sun. Sun free. in advance.

Museo Interactivo de Ciencias y Tecnología
Avenida San Miguel. **Tel** (449) 913 70 15. **Open** 9am–6pm Tue–Fri, 11am–7pm Sat & Sun.

⓰ La Quemada

Zacatecas. Mex 54, 57 km (35 miles) SE of Zacatecas. from Zacatecas. **Tel** (492) 922 50 85. **Open** daily.

The archaeological site at La Quemada stretches over a steep hill rising from a wide, arid valley. From around AD 350, La Quemada was an important religious and political center and the focal point for trade between the area and Teotihuacán *(see pp138–41)*. After AD 700, La Quemada seems to have substituted trade with more bellicose activities. In around 1100, it apparently suffered a violent end, despite an 800-m (2,600-ft) long and 4-m (13-ft) tall defensive wall on its northern slope.

It takes about two hours to explore the site by following the steep, rocky path that leads from the lower Main Causeway and Hall of Columns all the way up to the Citadel.

The Churrigueresque facade of the cathedral in Zacatecas

⓱ Zacatecas

Zacatecas. 139,000.
Avenida Hidalgo 403, (492) 922 34 26. La Morisma (Aug), Feria de Zacatecas (1st two weeks of Sep).
zacatecas.gob.mx

Founded in 1546, shortly after the discovery of metal deposits in the area, Zacatecas was soon supplying silver to the Spanish crown. The city is remarkable for its Baroque limestone buildings that fill a narrow valley between steep, arid hills. Aristocratic patrons built many stately mansions, convents, and churches.

Cathedral

The profuse decoration on the impressive three-tiered facade of the city's cathedral is considered the prime example of the Churrigueresque, or Ultra-Baroque architectural style *(see pp30–31)* in Mexico. Apostles, angels, flowers, and fruit adorn the pillars, pedestals, columns, and niches in dizzying excess. This exuberant exterior of the cathedral contrasts strangely with an interior whose treasures were lost in the turmoils of the Reform *(see p56)* and, later, the Revolution *(see p58)*. Most of the building was constructed between 1730 and 1775, but the northernmost of the two towers was not completed until 1904.

The cathedral's two lateral facades are both comparatively sober. A crucified Christ adorns the one that faces north toward the Plaza de Armas and its 18th-century palaces. On the east side of the plaza is the most striking of these palaces, the Palacio de Gobierno, which now contains offices.

The Palacio de Gobierno, one of the mansions on the Plaza de Armas

Ex-Templo de San Agustín

Plazuela de Miguel Auza. **Tel** (492) 922 80 63. **Open** Tue–Sun.

This large Augustinian church and its adjoining convent were tragically sacked during the Reform years *(see p56)*. Their Baroque splendor suffered further when they were later turned into a hotel and casino. Presbyterian missionaries from the US purchased the church in the 1880s and proceeded to strip it of its Catholic decoration, tearing down the tower and ripping out the main facade. Only the splendid Plateresque side entrance was spared. Ornate blocks from the exterior are now piled up like giant jigsaw pieces inside, a stark reminder of the former grandeur that is now a blank, white wall.

These days the church is used as an exhibition and convention center, while the former convent is now the seat of the Zacatecas bishopric.

Museo Pedro Coronel

Plaza de Santo Domingo. **Tel** (492) 922 80 21. **Open** 10am–4:30pm Mon–Wed, Fri–Sun.

The Zacatecan painter and sculptor, Pedro Coronel, is responsible for this unique art collection spanning a number of civilizations and continents, from Egyptian mummy cases to works by Goya and Hogarth. All this is housed on the upper floors of a former Jesuit seminary. There is also a library of 25,000 volumes dating from the 16th to the 19th century. Next to the museum stands the Templo de Santo Domingo, with its gilded Baroque side altars.

Sculpture by Pedro Coronel

Museo Rafael Coronel

Corner of Abasolo and Matamoros. **Tel** (492) 922 81 16. **Open** 10am–5pm Thu–Tue.

Another Coronel collection, this one by Pedro's brother Rafael, is held in the restored ruins of the Ex-Convento de San Francisco. An artist and a lover of folk art, Rafael Coronel amassed 10,000 ritual and dance masks from all over the country. About one-third of them are exhibited alongside a mass of other fine examples of Mexican popular art, pre-Columbian and colonial pottery, and architectural drawings and mural sketches by Diego Rivera.

Some of the many masks on display in the Museo Rafael Coronel

Museo Francisco Goitia

Enrique Estrada 102. **Tel** (492) 922 02 11. **Open** 10am–5pm Tue–Sun.

Paintings, silkscreens, and sculptures by the Coronel brothers and other Zacatecan artists are exhibited in a Neo-Classical villa. Until 1962 the house was the official residence of state governors. Its formal gardens overlook the Parque Enrique Estrada. This hilly park drops down to the remains of an 18th-century aqueduct and the Quinta Real hotel *(see p302)*, which is built around the city's old bullring.

Cerro de la Bufa

The hill northeast of the city center was the scene of a bloody battle in 1914. A museum at the summit exhibits items from the victory won by Francisco "Pancho" Villa *(see p177)*. There are splendid views from the cable car, which stretches 650 m (2,130 ft) from here to the Cerro del Grillo.

Cerro del Grillo

This hill's main attraction is a tour of three of the seven levels of the legendary Eden silver mine, which includes a ride in a mine train through 600 m (2,000 ft) of tunnel.

Zacatecas's aqueduct and old bullring, near the Museo Francisco Goitia

Museo Regional de Guadalupe

Jardín Juárez Oriente, Guadalupe. **Tel** (492) 923 20 89. **Open** 9am–6pm Tue–Sun. Sun free.

Just 10 km (6 miles) east of the city center lies the town of Guadalupe, whose imposing Franciscan church and ex-seminary house a museum of colonial religious art second only in importance to that of Tepotzotlán *(see p152)*. The treasures include works by Miguel Cabrera, Rodríguez Juárez, Cristóbal Villalpando, and Juan Correa. Beside the church is the jewel-like Capilla de Nápoles, built in the 19th century and considered to be the paragon of Mexican Neo-Classical expression.

Environs

About 45 km (28 miles) south-west of Zacatecas lies the historic town of **Jerez**, with its uncrowded streets, quiet squares, and authentic 18th- and 19th-century buildings.

View of Zacatecas, from the summit of the Cerro de la Bufa

⓲ Real de Catorce

San Luis Potosí. 1,400. Presidencia Municipal, (488) 887 50 71. Feria de San Francisco de Asís (Sep/Oct). **realdecatorce.info**

The crumbling structures and ghost-town atmosphere of Real de Catorce testify to the rapidly changing fortunes of Mexican silver-mining centers. Hidden high in the mountains of the Sierra Madre Oriental, it is accessible only through a 2.5-km (1.5-mile) tunnel.

In the early 20th century the town boasted a population of 40,000, served by several newspapers, a theater, a grand hotel, and an electric tramway. Then, drastically hit by falling silver prices, its fortunes slumped until only a few families remained. Its eerie, semi-deserted feel has made it the chosen set for several Mexican cowboy films.

Only the Neo-Classical church, the **Parroquia de la Purísima Concepción**, with its reputedly miraculous statue of St. Francis of Assisi and its large collection of votive pictures, was maintained for the sake of the pilgrims who flood the town once a year. Opposite the church is the dilapidated **Casa de Moneda** (closed Mon, Tue), a former silver warehouse and mint dating back to the 1860s. The town's former glory can also be seen in the shells of ornate mansions, the ruined bullring, and an octagonal cockfighting ring.

Real de Catorce's fortunes look set to rise and at least one of the surrounding mines is being tested as a possible source of precious metals. Ironically, the arrival of modern amenities is reducing the town's touristic appeal.

⓳ San Luis Potosí

San Luis Potosí. 773,000. Manuel José Ottón 130, (444) 812 99 39. San Luis Rey de Francia (Aug 25). **slp.gob.mx**

The mining wealth that the city of San Luis Potosí accumulated in the 1600s is evident in the historic buildings and three main squares at its core. The most central square, the **Plaza de Armas**, is dominated by the cathedral and **Palacio de Gobierno**, which was the seat of Benito Juárez's government when he denied clemency to Emperor Maximilian in 1867 *(see p57)*. Behind it stands the **Real Caja**, or Royal Treasury, whose wide staircase enabled pack animals to reach the storage chambers above.

The second square is the **Plaza de los Fundadores**, the site of a former Jesuit college and two 17th-century churches, the **Iglesia de la Compañía** and the graceful **Capilla de Loreto**. On the eastern side of town is the third main square, the **Plaza del Carmen**, on which stand the church of the same name, the imposing **Teatro de la Paz**, and the Museo de la Máscara.

Museo Nacional de la Máscara

Villerías 2. **Tel** (444) 812 30 25. **Open** 10am–6pm daily (to 5pm Sat, to 3pm Sun & Mon). Tue free. **museonacionaldelamascara.com**

The walls of a restored, former mansion are adorned with over 1,000 decorative and ritual masks.

The Capilla de Aranzazú in the Ex-Convento de San Francisco

Templo del Carmen

This Churrigueresque church, built in the mid-1700s, is by far the most spectacular religious structure in the city. The impressive exterior has a three-tiered main facade, an ornate tower, and multi-colored domes. Even more fabulous is the interior, not least for its Baroque side altars and Francisco Eduardo Tresguerras' main altar. The real highlight, however, is the exuberant Altar de los Siete Príncipes, which is not actually an altar but a floor-to-ceiling interior facade enclosing the entrance to a side chapel, the Camarín de la Virgen. Its white-stucco surface is dotted with polychrome statues of angels.

Ex-Convento de San Francisco

Plaza de Aranzazú. **Tel** (444) 814 35 72. **Open** Tue–Sun. Sun free. ground floor only.

The Franciscans, the first religious order to arrive in San Luis Potosí, began work in 1686 on this ambitious convent and church complex, which took over a century to complete. The extensive former convent now contains the Museo Regional Potosino, which has colonial and pre-Columbian exhibits, including displays on the Huastec culture of southeastern San Luis Potosí state.

Upstairs is the splendid Capilla de Aranzazú, the lavish private chapel for the former occupants. A unique Baroque jewel despite the garish colors chosen by its restorers, it has a rare covered atrium and a carved wooden portal. Behind the convent, on the Plaza de San Francisco, is the Templo de San Francisco. Beyond its classic Baroque facade lies a richly furnished main nave, several side chapels, and an original domed sacristy. The sacristy and the adjoining Sala de Profundis are filled with valuable paintings. Also notable is the church choir, where there are more paintings and the remains of a monumental Baroque organ.

Detail of Templo de San Francisco

Environs

In the arid hills 27 km (17 miles) to the east lies the ghost town of **Cerro de San Pedro**, whose mines were the source of the city's wealth. To the southeast, around 45 km (28 miles) from San Luis Potosí, is **Santa María del Río**, known for its hand-woven silk and silk-like *rebozos*, or shawls. Traditional dyeing, weaving, and fringe-knotting can be observed in the Escuela del Rebozo. Around **Villa de Reyes**, 57 km (35 miles) south of San Luis Potosí, former haciendas show visitors the architecture of a social system that engendered, and ended with, the Revolution *(see p58)*.

Corner of the late 18th-century Baroque Real Caja

⓴ Huasteca Potosina

San Luis Potosí. Ciudad Valles. Carretera Tamazuchale.

The southeastern part of San Luis Potosí state is an area of stunning natural beauty known in pre-Columbian times as Tamoanchán, or "Earthly Paradise." It boasts tropical valleys, lush mountains, clear rivers, and majestic waterfalls. The most spectacular cascade is Tamul, which plunges 105 m (344 ft) into a canyon and is up to 300 m (1,000 ft) wide in the rainy season. It is reached by boat from Tanchanchín, southwest of Ciudad Valles.

Of the area's many archaeological sites, the most notable is **El Consuelo**, near Tamuín to the east. It has remnants of a polychrome altar and stepped ceremonial platforms.

㉑ Las Pozas

San Luis Potosí. Off Mex 120, 3 km (2 miles) NW of Xilitla. Xilitla then taxi. **Open** 9am–6pm daily. **xilitla.org**

Flowering, a concrete sculpture by Edward James at Las Pozas

High in the mountains south of Ciudad Valles, near the spectacularly situated town of Xilitla, is this extraordinary, dreamlike jungle estate created by the British artist, eccentric, and millionaire Edward James. He first used the property to grow orchids and then as a private zoo. Later, with the help of local workers, sometimes numbering up to 150 at a time, he set about producing this architectural fantasy, which took over 30 years to complete. Many of the hundreds of Surrealist metal and concrete sculptures are unfinished or already disintegrating. They are scattered amid thick subtropical vegetation, springs, waterfalls, and pools. Slippery paths weave between the massive structures, which include the *Homage to Max Ernst*, *Avenue of the Snakes*, and *Toadstool Platform*.

Sculpted hands, one of the many Surrealist creations at Las Pozas

Edward James (1907–84)

The creator of the Las Pozas complex was, according to his friend Salvador Dalí, "crazier than all the Surrealists put together. They pretend, but he is the real thing." Edward Frank Willis James, born into a wealthy English family, was himself a moderately successful poet and artist, but excelled as a patron of the arts. He published books, founded ballet companies, financed large exhibitions, and amassed paintings by Dalí, Picasso, and Magritte, whose social circle he shared. His only marriage, to a Hungarian ballet dancer, ended in a scandalous divorce. In his later years, his private life revolved around the family of his long-time Mexican employee and companion Plutarco Gastelum Esquer, who had helped him create his jungle paradise at Las Pozas. When James died Esquer's children inherited the estate.

Eccentric Edward James relaxing at his Surrealist rain forest home

㉒ Sierra Gorda

Querétaro. Cadereyta, Jalpan.

One of the largest untamed regions in central Mexico, the semi-arid mountain range of the Sierra Gorda rises northeast of the city of Querétaro *(see pp200–1)* to over 3,000 m (10,000 ft). The lush green of its foothills is interrupted only by the massive monolith **La Peña de Bernal**, which towers 445 m (1,460 ft) above the village of Bernal.

In the mountains beyond **Cadereyta**, with its square of brightly colored churches, are the archaeological sites of **Toluquilla** and **Las Ranas**. These two sites are located on the rugged ridges near San Joaquín, to the east of Mex 120. Both feature fortress-like pre-Columbian ceremonial structures built between the 7th and 11th centuries AD. Continuing north into the mountains, Mex 120 gets even steeper before descending to **Jalpan**. This town is the site of one of five Franciscan missions founded in the mid-1700s to convert the Indians of these mountains. The missions – the others are in Concá, Tilaco, Tancoyól, and Landa de Matamoros – all have scenic settings, and distinctive facades with strong Indian touches in their profuse mortar decorations.

㉓ Querétaro

The modern suburbs of Querétaro hide its central colonial treasures, which UNESCO added to its protected World Heritage List in 1996. The city's location brought it prosperity in New Spain, but from the early 1800s Querétaro fell into decline, a trend interrupted only in 1848, when invading US troops briefly made it Mexico's capital. It was here that the treaty ceding half of Mexican territory to the United States was signed, and here also that Emperor Maximilian *(see p57)* faced the firing squad.

Plaza de Armas

With its austere colonial fountain, bougainvillea-covered garden, and stately old mansions, this intimate 18th-century square is a corner of Spain transplanted to Mexico. Most of the former residences on the plaza, among them the sumptuous **Casa de Ecala**, now house government offices, including the state congress and court. The only white facade, with plain moldings and sober balconies, is the **Casa de la Corregidora**, which was built in 1700 for Querétaro's royal representatives. Completely restored in 1981, it is now the seat of the state government. A few prison cells have been preserved in its rear courtyard. The bronze statue crowning the square's fountain honors the Marqués de la Villa del Villar, the city's early 18th-century patron.

Facade of a colonial mansion on the Plaza de Armas

Museo Regional

Corregidora Sur 3. **Tel** (442) 212 48 88. **Open** 9am–6pm daily. Sun free. ground floor only.

The state's regional museum is housed in the former convent of San Francisco, a building noted for its cloisters, domes, and stone columns. The ethnographic, archaeological, and colonial sections are on the ground floor. The second floor exhibits weapons, furniture, and photographs tracing Querétaro's pivotal role in Mexican history since the fight for independence.

Both the convent and its adjoining church, the **Templo de San Francisco**, were begun by Franciscan missionaries in 1540, and the complex was finished in a blend of styles in 1727. The church has *trompe l'oeil* murals and the city's tallest tower.

The tower of the convent church of San Francisco, Querétaro's tallest landmark

Templo de Santa Clara and Templo de Santa Rosa

These two 18th-century churches of former nunneries (at some distance apart) rival one another with the exuberance of their Churrigueresque interiors. Each has profusely carved altarpieces that form a floor-to-ceiling tapestry of foliage, shells, cherubs, and clouds. The naves are closed off by double choirs where the nuns once attended mass behind screens of delicately forged iron and gilded lattice. Both interiors are the work of Francisco Martínez Gudiño. Santa Rosa is also notable for its sacristy with life-size statues of Christ and the twelve apostles. A short walk from Santa Clara is the peaceful Jardín Guerrero, with its Fuente de Neptuno (Neptune Fountain).

Museo de Arte

Allende Sur 14. **Tel** (442) 212 23 57. **Open** 10am–6pm Tue–Sun. arrange in advance. **museodeartequeretaro.com**

This vast collection of 17th to 19th-century Mexican paintings is displayed alongside temporary art exhibitions and a smattering of contemporary paintings and photographs. They are housed in the 18th-century Ex-Convento de San Agustín, whose church captures the eye with its finely sculpted Plateresque facade and octagonal blue- and white-tiled dome. The real treasure here, however, is the supremely elegant Baroque main cloister, considered the finest of its kind in the Americas. Its richly carved details include caryatids supporting the arches.

Convento de la Santa Cruz

Independencia & Felipe Luna. **Tel** (442) 212 02 35. **Open** daily.

This plain convent has a long history. It started life in 1531 as a hermitage, on the site of the last battle between the Chichimecs and the Spanish. A 450-year-old stone replica of the cross that miraculously appeared in the sky, inducing the Indians to surrender and embrace Christianity, is mounted over the main altar of the small church. By 1683, the hermitage had become the first

The fortress-like Convento de la Santa Cruz, east of the city center

VISITORS' CHECKLIST

Practical Information
Querétaro. 1.8 million. Luis Pasteur Nte 4, (442) 238 50 67. Fundación de Querétaro (Jul 25), Fiestas de Diciembre (Dec).

Transport
Prolongación Luis Vega y Monroy 800, (442) 229 01 81.

missionary college in the Americas, and in 1848 the US invaders made the convent their headquarters. A sparsely furnished cell was Emperor Maximilian's prison before he was led to his death in 1867.

Los Arcos

Financed by the Marqués de la Villa del Villar in the 18th century, this is one of the world's largest aqueducts. It has 74 arches up to 23 m (75 ft) high and is 8 km (5 miles) long.

Cerro de las Campanas

The barren hill where Emperor Maximilian was executed with two of his officers on June 19, 1867, is now a tree-filled municipal park. A broad stairway leads to the Neo-Gothic chapel that was donated by the emperor's family to commemorate the renewal of diplomatic relations between Mexico and the Austro-Hungarian Empire in 1900. Inside, three marble slabs mark the spot where the executions took place. The painting on the altar is a copy of Maximilian's wedding gift from his mother. The cross over the altar is made from wood from the frigate that first brought him to Mexico and later returned his body to Europe. Nearby is a small museum with exhibits on the fall of the Second Mexican Empire. The whole site is dominated by a massive statue on the hilltop of the Mexican hero Benito Juárez, Maximilian's nemesis *(see pp56–7)*.

Environs

San Juan del Río, 47 km (29 miles) southeast, is known for its crafts and gemstones. The town's oldest buildings are the hospital and convent of San Juan de Dios, founded in 1661, and the 1690 convent of Santo Domingo.

Just 22 km (14 miles) northeast of San Juan del Río lies the quaint spa town of **Tequisquiapan**. Its cobbled lanes and arcaded main square make it a popular retreat.

Querétaro City Center

1. Plaza de Armas
2. Casa de Ecala
3. Casa de la Corregidora
4. Museo Regional
5. Templo de San Francisco
6. Templo de Santa Clara
7. Museo de Arte
8. Templo de Santa Rosa
9. Convento de la Santa Cruz

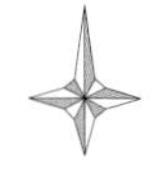

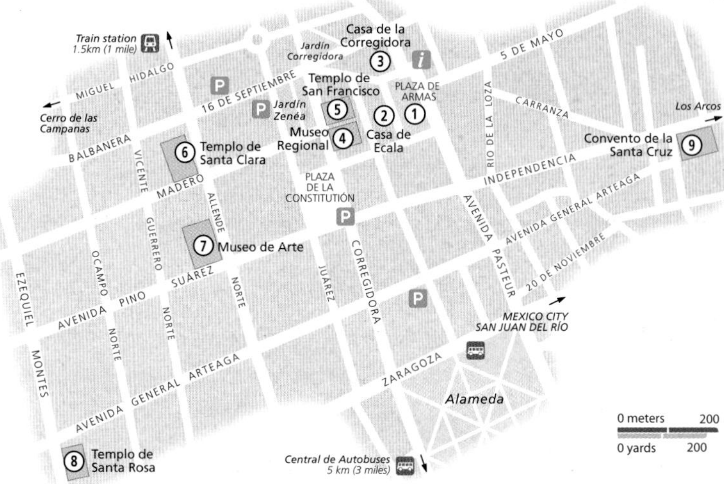

㉔ Street-by-Street: San Miguel de Allende

A delightful colonial town, San Miguel de Allende is filled with opulent mansions and handsome churches, all connected by narrow, cobbled streets. Now a popular tourist destination, it was once an important crossroads for mule trains, which carried silver and gold to the capital and returned with European treasures. The town's active cultural life combines traditional charm with the cosmopolitan air of the large non-Mexican population.

Templo de la Concepción
A huge dome from 1891 towers over the gilded altar of this church.

Escuela de Bellas Artes
This art school, in a former convent, has an unfinished 1940s mural painted by David Alfaro Siqueiros.

Casa del Mayorazgo de la Canal, the town's most sumptuous mansion, has Neo-Classical and Baroque styling.

Casa Allende, now a historical museum, was the birthplace of Ignacio Allende, a hero of Mexican Independence.

Casa del Inquisidor once housed visiting representatives of the Spanish Inquisition. Built in 1780, the house has fine windows and balconies.

Casa de la Inquisición served as the prison of the Inquisition.

★ La Parroquia
Notable for its fantastic Neo-Gothic exterior, this parish church was remodeled by self-taught local architect Zeferino Gutiérrez in the late 19th century.

For hotels and restaurants see pp299–302 and pp321–5

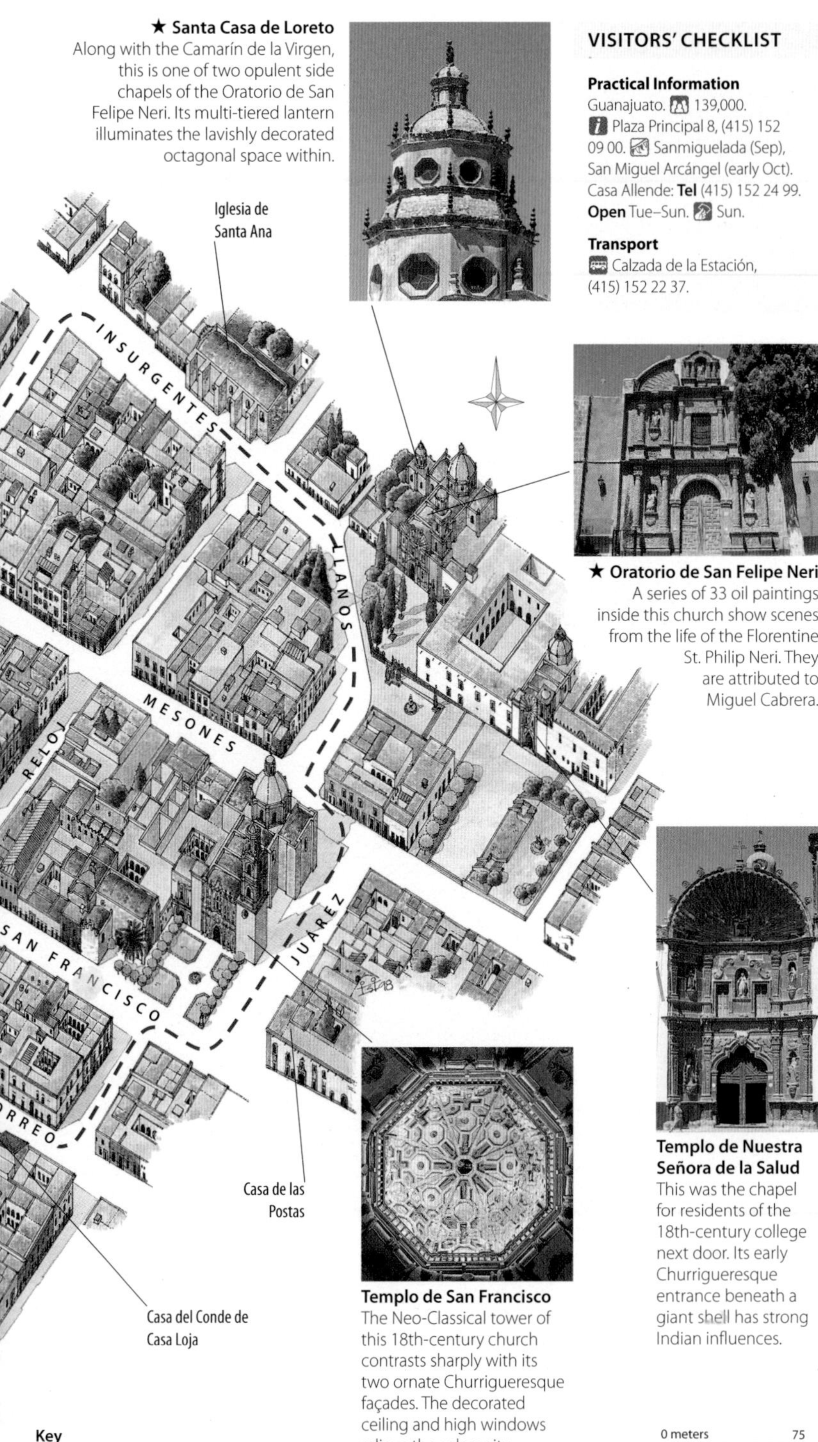

★ Santa Casa de Loreto
Along with the Camarín de la Virgen, this is one of two opulent side chapels of the Oratorio de San Felipe Neri. Its multi-tiered lantern illuminates the lavishly decorated octagonal space within.

VISITORS' CHECKLIST

Practical Information
Guanajuato. 139,000.
Plaza Principal 8, (415) 152 09 00. Sanmiguelada (Sep), San Miguel Arcángel (early Oct). Casa Allende: **Tel** (415) 152 24 99. **Open** Tue–Sun. Sun.

Transport
Calzada de la Estación, (415) 152 22 37.

★ Oratorio de San Felipe Neri
A series of 33 oil paintings inside this church show scenes from the life of the Florentine St. Philip Neri. They are attributed to Miguel Cabrera.

Templo de Nuestra Señora de la Salud
This was the chapel for residents of the 18th-century college next door. Its early Churrigueresque entrance beneath a giant shell has strong Indian influences.

Templo de San Francisco
The Neo-Classical tower of this 18th-century church contrasts sharply with its two ornate Churrigueresque façades. The decorated ceiling and high windows relieve the solemnity of the interior.

Key
— Suggested route

0 meters 75
0 yards 75

25 Street-by-Street: Guanajuato

One of Mexico's most beautiful silver cities climbs out of a rugged ravine and up bald hills that once supplied a quarter of New Spain's silver output. Mine owners studded Guanajuato's narrow twisting streets and charming plazas with stately mansions and imposing churches. A later bonanza added splendid late 19th-century touches, and modern engineers burrowed an ingenious tunnel network under the city to help overcome its crazy geography. The unique result is a center devoid of traffic lights and neon signs that was made a UNESCO World Heritage site in 1988.

A typical city street with overhanging balconies

Casa Diego Rivera
The house where Rivera was born in 1886 is now a museum exhibiting over 100 samples of his work, including sketches of his murals *(see p208)*.

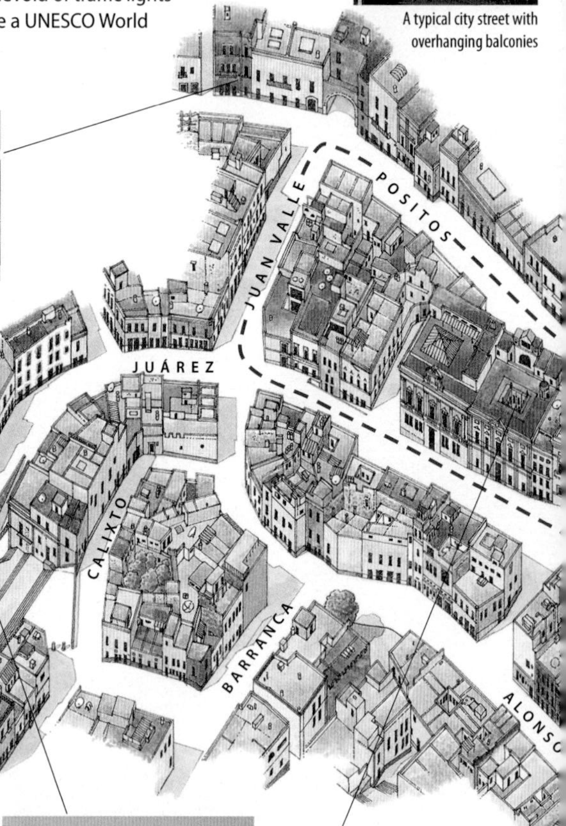

Plaza de los Angeles is a popular spot for students to gather.

Callejón del Beso (Alley of the Kiss) is only 69 cm (2 ft) wide in places. Legend tells of the tragic death of secret lovers who were caught exchanging kisses from opposing balconies.

Casa Rul y Valenciana, a beautiful late 18th-century mansion, is now the courthouse.

Calle Hidalgo
Converted from a river-bed in 1965 to alleviate traffic problems, this subterranean street winds under the city center. It is very dangerous and not recommended for visitors.

Key

▬ Suggested route

◀ Plaza de la Paz overlooked by Basílica de Nuestra Señora de Guanajuato

★ Templo de la Compañía
The Neo-Classical dome of this Jesuit church replaced one that had collapsed in 1808. It is now a city landmark. The façade is an early example of the Churrigueresque style.

VISITORS' CHECKLIST

Practical Information
Guanajuato. 172,000. Plaza de la Paz 14, (473) 732 15 74. San Juan y Presa de la Olla (Jun), Festival Cervantino (Oct).

Transport
32 km (20 miles) W. 7 km (4 miles) SW, (473) 733 13 40.

Museo del Pueblo houses a collection of regional art in a 17th-century mansion *(see p208)*.

The University was remodeled in Moorish style in 1945. It was originally a Jesuit seminary, founded in 1732.

★ Jardín de la Unión
Laid out in 1861, this laurel-shaded plaza is the heart of the city and a favorite meeting place. The municipal band plays here several times a week.

Plazuela del Baratillo was once a busy marketplace. The fountain was a gift from Emperor Maximilian.

0 meters 50
0 yards 50

Iglesia de San Diego

Basílica de Nuestra Señora de Guanajuato has an ornate statue of the Virgin Mary *(see p208)*.

★ Teatro Juárez
Doric columns, giant statues, and an auditorium hung with velvet set the tone at this lavish theater *(see p208)*.

Exploring Guanajuato

Most of Guanajuato's main sights are located near the center of the city, and one of the pleasures of visiting this colonial gem is strolling around its twisting streets on foot, marveling at the ornate architecture. A range of local buses will take you to sights outside the center, and tours are available from the tourist office.

Madonna statue in the Basílica de Nuestra Señora de Guanajuato

Basílica de Nuestra Señora de Guanajuato

This 17th-century church facing the Plaza de la Paz contains a bejeweled sculpture of the city's patron saint, the Virgin Mary, on a solid-silver pedestal. The statue was given to the city by Charles I and Philip II of Spain in 1557. Reputed to date from the 7th century, it is considered the oldest piece of Christian art in Mexico. The church interior is especially striking in the evening, when it is lit by Venetian chandeliers.

Teatro Juárez

Sopena s/n. **Tel** (473) 732 25 21. **Open** Tue–Sun.

Statues of the Muses crown the facade of this Neo-Classical theater. Below them a wide stairway flanked by bronze lions leads up to a stately foyer and Moorish-style auditorium. This is the main venue for the Festival Cervantino *(see p36)*.

Museo del Pueblo

Positos 7. **Tel** (473) 732 29 90. **Open** 10am–7pm Tue–Sat (to 3pm Sun).

The former home of a wealthy mine owner is one of the city's finest buildings. It now exhibits art pieces from pre-Columbian to modern times, concentrating on colonial religious objects.

Casa Diego Rivera

Positos 47. **Tel** (473) 732 11 97. **Open** 10am–7pm Tue–Sat (to 3pm Sun). on second floor.

The house where Diego Rivera was born is now a museum dedicated to his life and art. His work fills the upstairs rooms, while the ground floor preserves the family living area with its late 19th-century furniture and mementos.

Alhóndiga de Granaditas

Mendizábal 6. **Tel** (473) 732 11 12. **Open** 10am–6pm Tue–Sat (to 3pm Sun). Sun free.

This former granary, built at the end of the 18th century, was the site of the first major rebel victory of the War of Independence. In 1810, revolutionaries burned down the gates and killed most of the government troops barricaded inside. Reminders of the battle are the bullet-scarred walls and the hooks dangling from the building's four top corners, where the heads of four rebellion leaders were later hung.

The huge building is now a regional museum covering art, ethnography, and archaeology. The staircase is decorated with murals depicting the city's history by José Chávez Morado.

Imposing facade of the historic Alhóndiga de Granaditas

Museo Iconográfico del Quijote

Manuel Doblado 1. **Tel** (473) 732 67 21. **Open** Tue–Sun. Tue free.

Art pieces relating to Don Quixote, from postage stamps to murals, are displayed here. The unusual collection includes works by Dalí, Picasso, and Daumier.

Pyramid-style walls of La Valenciana mine, backed by the Templo de San Cayetano

La Valenciana

5 km (3 miles) N of city center. **Open** daily.

Silver and gold mining began here in the mid-1500s and boomed two centuries later after prospectors struck it rich at a shaft just to the west. The Bocamina de Valenciana, the original 1557 entrance shaft, is cut 100 m (330 ft) straight down into the rock. Visitors can climb down to half its depth on steep stairs over which miners once hauled up loads of ore-rich rocks on their backs. A small museum at the entrance tells the mine's history.

Templo de San Cayetano

Tel (473) 732 35 96.

Near La Valenciana mine is the city's most spectacular church. Also known as "La Valenciana," it was built between 1765 and 1788 with funds donated by the Count of Valenciana, owner of the nearby mine. Its pink limestone facade abounds with Churrigueresque pilasters. The Baroque interior has three splendid gold and polychrome altars and a pulpit inlaid with tortoiseshell and ivory.

Museo de las Momias

Explanada del Panteón. **Tel** (473) 732 06 39. **Open** daily.
momiasdeguanajuato.gob.mx

Southwest of the center is this macabre museum, which owes its popularity to the Mexican obsession with death. In cavernous rooms it exhibits over 100 mummies disinterred from a nearby cemetery where they had mummified naturally.

Museo Ex-Hacienda de San Gabriel de la Barrera

Marfil, 2.5 km (1.5 miles) SW of city. **Tel** (473) 732 06 19. **Open** daily.

This restored hacienda was built in the late 17th century as an ore-processing center. It is now a museum displaying European furniture from the 17th to the 19th centuries. The grounds have been converted into 16 gardens, each landscaped differently.

Environs

In the small town of **Dolores Hidalgo**, 54 km (34 miles) northeast of the city, the battle for independence from Spain began with Father Miguel Hidalgo issuing his famous *Grito*, or "cry" to arms *(see p53)*, from the parish church.

Elegant garden of the Hacienda de San Gabriel de la Barrera

Church half buried by solidified lava from Paricutín volcano

26 Paricutín

Michoacán. 38 km (24 miles) NW of Uruapan. Angahuan.

One of the youngest volcanoes in the world, Paricutín erupted in February 1943. Amid thunderous explosions, its cone grew to more than 330 m (1,100 ft) within one year. Ash and lava flows buried two villages and, while nobody was killed by the eruptions, more than 4,000 people had to flee their homes. The volcano's activity lasted until 1952, leaving behind a barren cone rising 424 m (1,391 ft) from a sea of black frozen lava. The total elevation above sea level is 2,575 m (8,448 ft).

The *mirador* (lookout) at Angahuan offers a dramatic view of the 25 sq-km (10 sq-mile) lava field and Paricutín behind it. The church tower that can be seen above the lava belongs to the buried village of San Juan Parangaricutiro. For a closer look, walk 3 km (2 miles) or hire a guide and a horse to take you down the steep cliff and through the lava rock formations. The stiff 30-minute climb to the crater rim is rewarded with stunning views of the double crater and surrounding lunar landscape.

The town of **Angahuan** has preserved its native character despite the influx of visitors to Paricutín. Most of the people speak Purépecha, the Tarascan language, and the women wear colorful traditional clothing.

27 Uruapan

Michoacán. 315,000. Juan Ayala 16, (452) 524 71 99. Coros y Danzas (late Oct).

Michoacán's second-biggest city, Uruapan is a busy agricultural center. Nestling against the Sierra de Uruapan, it links the cold upland region (*tierra fría*) to the humid lowlands (*tierra caliente*) that stretch toward the Pacific. Its subtropical climate supports exuberant vegetation, including vast avocado plantations.

The Spanish monk Juan de San Miguel founded the town in 1533 and divided it into nine neighborhoods (*barrios*), which still preserve their own traditions. He also built **La Huatápera**, a chapel and hospital that now houses a fine museum of Michoacán crafts.

La Huatápera

Plaza Morelos. **Tel** (452) 524 34 34. **Open** Tue–Sun.

㉘ A Tour Around Lake Pátzcuaro

The road around this idyllic lake bedded in rolling hills passes colonial and pre-Columbian architectural gems, and towns with rich craft traditions. Pátzcuaro, Tzintzuntzán, and Quiroga are popular destinations, but the western shore and marshlands to the south see fewer visitors. Yet here the winding road offers spectacular vistas of the lake and rare glimpses of Purépechan (Tarascan) Indian village life.

② Tzintzuntzán
The *yácatas*, multilevel temple bases, near this town reveal its history as the former Tarascan capital. Also noteworthy are the 16th-century Franciscan convent and the crafts market.

③ Quiroga A busy market town, Quiroga sells agricultural and handicraft products from all over Michoacán. Lacquerware, such as wooden bowls and trays painted with bright flowers, is a typical local product.

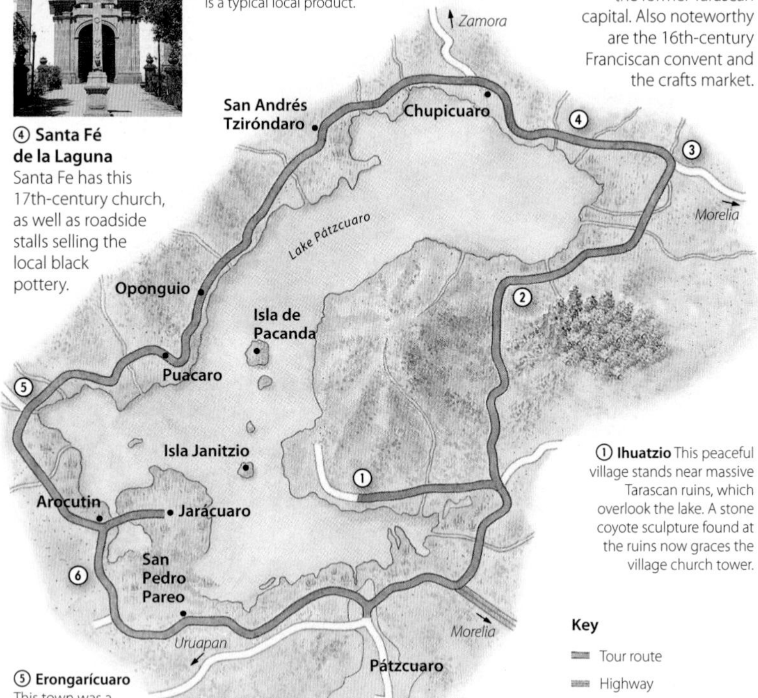

④ Santa Fé de la Laguna
Santa Fe has this 17th-century church, as well as roadside stalls selling the local black pottery.

Zamora
San Andrés Tziróndaro
Chupicuaro
Morelia
Lake Pátzcuaro
Oponguio
Isla de Pacanda
Puacaro
Isla Janitzio
Arocutin
Jarácuaro
San Pedro Pareo
Uruapan
Morelia
Pátzcuaro

① Ihuatzio This peaceful village stands near massive Tarascan ruins, which overlook the lake. A stone coyote sculpture found at the ruins now graces the village church tower.

Key
- Tour route
- Highway
- Other roads

⑤ Erongarícuaro
This town was a favorite hideaway of French Surrealist André Breton.

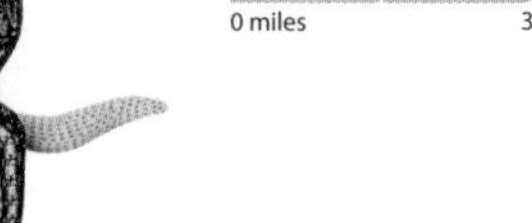

0 kilometers 5
0 miles 3

⑥ Tocuaro Famous for its prize-winning wooden masks, Tocuaro has a number of unmarked workshops selling these fantastic creations.

Tips for Drivers

Tour length: 89 km (55 miles)
Stopping-off points: There are plenty of places to eat in Pátzcuaro *(see p323)* and traditional family-run *cocinas* in Santa Fé de la Laguna. The small beach near Chupícuaro is good for picnics.

View of Isla Janitzio, the most important of the six islands on Lake Pátzcuaro

29 Pátzcuaro

Michoacán. 88,000.
Ahumada 9, (434) 342 12 14.
Año Nuevo Purépecha (late Jan), Day of the Dead (Nov 1–2).

Set amid the pastures and pine forests on Lake Pátzcuaro's southern shore, this historic town was once an important religious and political center of the Tarascan people. Its colonial splendor owes much to Michoacán's first bishop, Vasco de Quiroga, who temporarily turned it into the civic, religious, and cultural seat of the state.

The **Basílica de Nuestra Señora de la Salud**, an ambitious Vasco de Quiroga project, was to boast five naves and accommodate tens of thousands of people. However, only one nave was completed. Fires and earthquakes ravaged the building over the centuries, and the church was finally finished in a jumble of styles in 1833. Devout Indians flock here to visit the bishop's tomb.

Just to the south is the **Museo de Artes Populares**, a craft museum installed in the 16th-century Colegio de San Nicolás. The museum's collection includes a cabin-like *troje*, with typical Purépecha furnishings, that sits on a former pyramid platform.

The town's other architectural highlights include the Baroque **Templo del Sagrario** and an 18th-century Dominican nunnery. The latter is now the **Casa de los Once Patios**, a crafts center with workshops and stores. Its most attractive section is a small arcaded cloister where a nun and her servants lived.

The courtyard of the Museo de Artes Populares

Huge ash trees shade the quiet, elegant **Plaza Vasco de Quiroga** with its large fountain and statue of the town's benefactor. Many of the colonial mansions that face the square have been converted into shops, restaurants, and hotels, but the real commercial hub of the town is the nearby **Plaza Gertrudis Bocanegra**. Named after a local Independence heroine, it gives access to the covered market. On Fridays, the streets toward the Neo-Classical **Santuario de Guadalupe** church (1833) fill with stalls, and pottery is sold in the Plazuela de San Francisco.

Environs

Tours to the islands on Lake Pátzcuaro leave docks north of town. **Janitzio**, with its monument to Morelos *(see p53)*, is the most popular.

Museo de Artes Populares
Corner of Enseñanza and Alcantarilla.
Tel (434) 342 10 29. **Open** Tue–Sun.
in advance.

Casa de los Once Patios
Madrigal de las Altas Torres.
Tel (434) 342 43 79.
Open daily.

The 17th-century Templo del Sagrario in Pátzcuaro

Day of the Dead

Although Mexicans all over the country commune with the dead on the night of November 1 *(see pp38–9)*, the ceremonies on the island of Janitzio and in the villages around Lake Pátzcuaro are particularly impressive. This is largely because of their deep indigenous roots and unique settings. Throughout the night boats decorated with candles and flowers and laden with chanting people travel between Pátzcuaro docks and the island. The air is filled with wafts of incense and the ringing of bells. In the bustling cemeteries, each grave is covered with private tokens – special foods, photographs, and toys – intended to summon back the dead in celebration.

Wooden skeleton

㉚ Street-by-Street: Morelia

Capital of the state of Michoacán, Morelia was founded in the mid-1500s under the name of Valladolid on fertile territory once ruled by Tarascan kings. The first settlers were Spanish nobility and religious orders, who laid out a city of magnificent palaces, convents, and churches, along flagstone avenues and around plazas. The historic center has retained its Spanish character over the centuries; even new buildings sport colonial façades in pink limestone. The city's name was changed in 1828 to honor José María Morelos *(see p53)*, the native son instrumental in leading Mexico toward Independence.

★ Conservatorio de las Rosas
The peaceful courtyard of this former Dominican nunnery is enhanced by the sounds of practicing music students *(see p214)*.

★ Palacio Clavijero
Government offices now surround the courtyard of this former Jesuit college *(see p214)*. The austere Baroque building was named after a historian who taught here in the 1700s.

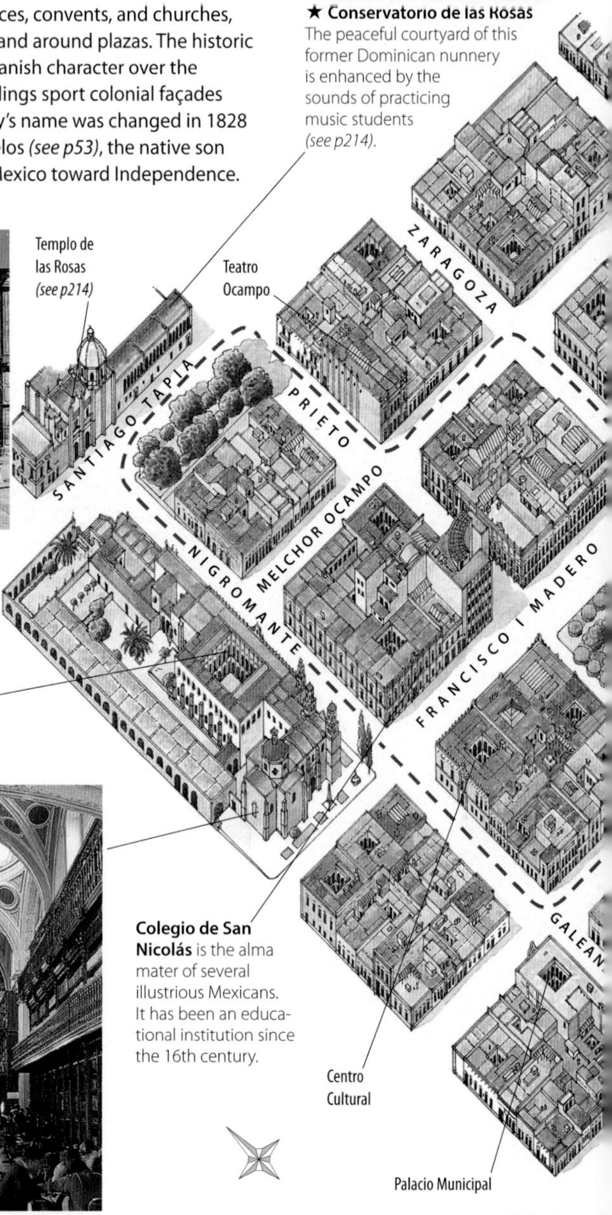

Templo de las Rosas *(see p214)*

Teatro Ocampo

ZARAGOZA

SANTIAGO TAPIA

PRIETO

MELCHOR OCAMPO

NIGROMANTE

FRANCISCO I MADERO

GALEANA

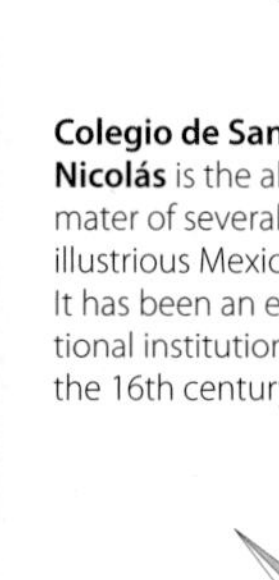

Templo de la Compañía de Jesús
This church was built in the 17th century for the adjoining Palacio Clavijero. Since 1930 it has been home to the Public Library.

Colegio de San Nicolás is the alma mater of several illustrious Mexicans. It has been an educational institution since the 16th century.

Centro Cultural

Palacio Municipal

Key

— Suggested route

0 meters 50
0 yards 50

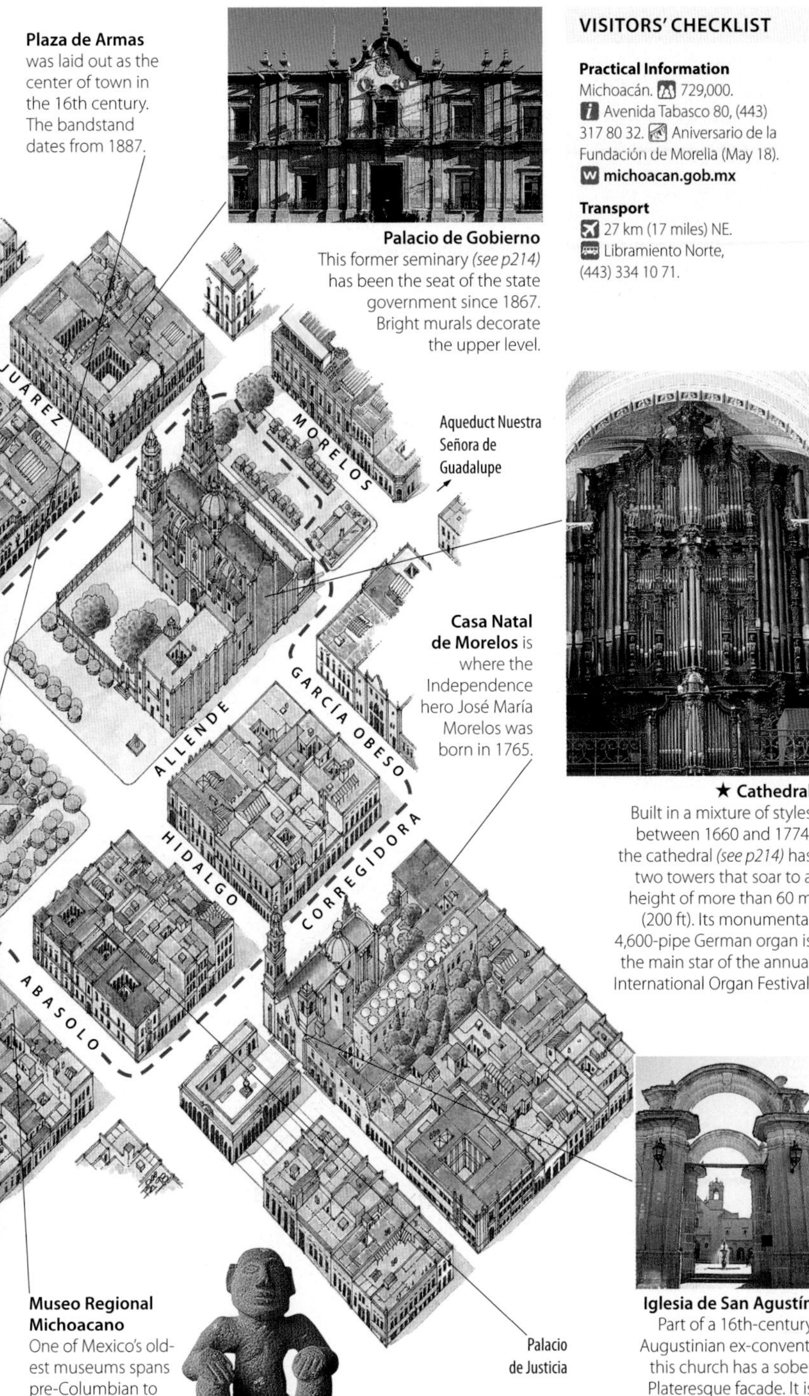

Plaza de Armas was laid out as the center of town in the 16th century. The bandstand dates from 1887.

Palacio de Gobierno
This former seminary *(see p214)* has been the seat of the state government since 1867. Bright murals decorate the upper level.

Aqueduct Nuestra Señora de Guadalupe

Casa Natal de Morelos is where the Independence hero José María Morelos was born in 1765.

★ Cathedral
Built in a mixture of styles between 1660 and 1774, the cathedral *(see p214)* has two towers that soar to a height of more than 60 m (200 ft). Its monumental 4,600-pipe German organ is the main star of the annual International Organ Festival.

Museo Regional Michoacano
One of Mexico's oldest museums spans pre-Columbian to modern eras *(see p214)*. This figure dates from the Classic Period.

Palacio de Justicia

Iglesia de San Agustín
Part of a 16th-century Augustinian ex-convent, this church has a sober Plateresque facade. It is seen here through the arches of the courtyard in front of it.

VISITORS' CHECKLIST

Practical Information
Michoacán. 729,000.
Avenida Tabasco 80, (443) 317 80 32. Aniversario de la Fundación de Morelia (May 18).
michoacan.gob.mx

Transport
27 km (17 miles) NE.
Libramiento Norte, (443) 334 10 71.

Exploring Morelia

Starting from Avenida Francisco I. Madero or the Plaza de Armas, almost all of Morelia's important sights are within short walking distance. The colonial-style streets and captivating Spanish architecture make this a pleasant city to stroll around. A short bus or taxi ride will take you east of the center, to the impressive aqueduct that runs alongside the city park.

Cathedral

This majestic structure in pink trachyte stone was begun in 1660 but not completed until a century later. The resulting blend of styles – Neo-Classical, Herreresque, and Baroque – can be seen in the twin towers that dominate the surrounding historic city center. Among the remnants of past splendor are the silver baptismal font in a side chapel and the 16th-century corn-paste statue of the Señor de la Sacristía. The statue's gold crown was a gift from Philip II of Spain.

Ornately carved stonework on Morelia's cathedral

Palacio de Gobierno

Avenida Francisco I. Madero 63. **Tel** (443) 313 07 07. **Open** daily.

This colonial edifice opened in 1770 as the Tridentine Seminary, which was attended by several key figures of the Independence *(see p53)* and Reform *(see pp56–7)* movements. It later became the seat of state government. In the 1950s, renowned artist Alfredo Zalce adorned the staircase and first floor with murals on local themes.

Alfredo Zalce's mural above the grand staircase of the Palacio de Gobierno

Templo y Conservatorio de las Rosas

Tapia 334. **Tel** (443) 312 14 69.

Dominican nuns came here in 1590, but most of their original buildings were replaced in the 17th and early 18th centuries with the convent and church that now face the Jardín de las Rosas. The Baroque facade of the church has twin portals, a typical feature of nunneries. Also notable are the gargoyles in the form of crocodiles, and the three gold altars. The convent was later converted into an orphanage and has housed a music school since 1904.

Palacio Clavijero

Nigromante 79. **Tel** (443) 312 04 12. **Open** 10am–6pm Tue–Sun.

The grand proportions and Baroque styling of the former Colegio de San Francisco Javier, a 17th-century Jesuit college, are best appreciated from its vast main courtyard. Elegant arcades on the ground floor contrast with a closed upper cloister where 28 windows with sober moldings replace the arches below. Geometrical patterns in the stone pavement imitate the layout of gardens that once surrounded the octagonal central fountain. The building now houses government offices, including the state tourist information bureau.

Museo Regional Michoacano

Allende 305. **Tel** (443) 312 04 07. **Open** 9am–5pm Tue–Sun. in advance.

For more than a century, the Regional Museum has collected objects relating to the state's ecology and history from pre-Columbian to modern times.

About one fifth of its treasures are on public display in the Baroque mansion where Emperor Maximilian *(see p57)* lodged during his visits. Highlights include Indian codices, a rare 16th-century Bible written in three languages, and a celebrated early 18th-century painting entitled *Traslado de las Monjas (The Moving of the Nuns)*. One of the few realistic portrayals of Mexican colonial society, it depicts the 1738 procession of nuns from one convent to another. They are escorted by dignitaries and observed by elegantly dressed ladies, dancing Indians, and black musicians.

Casa de Artesanías

Fray Juan de San Miguel 129. **Tel** (443) 312 24 86. **Open** daily.

The 16th-century Convento de San Buenaventura was restored in the 1970s and is now a showcase for Michoacán's rich craft tradition. The rooms around the arched courtyard contain a selection of items for sale, including pottery, textiles, and lacquerware. In the upstairs rooms visitors can observe artisans at work.

Aqueduct and Calzada Fray Antonio de San Miguel

Avenida Acueducto.

Water once flowed along this 18th-century aqueduct from a well 8 km (5 miles) away to the city's 30 public fountains and 150 private outlets. The final 1.5-km (1-mile) stretch consists of 253 arches, some of which

The vividly decorated dome of Santuario de Nuestra Señora de Guadalupe

reach a height of 10 m (33 ft). It is especially stunning when lit up at night.

The aqueduct was built by Bishop Fray Antonio de San Miguel, who also created the *calzada* (avenue) that bears his name. This pedestrian esplanade leads from the city end of the aqueduct to the Guadalupe Sanctuary. With its ash trees, Baroque benches, and 18th-century mansions, it recalls a long-gone era.

Las Tarascas fountain, where the aqueduct meets the *calzada*

Santuario de Nuestra Señora de Guadalupe

This 18th-century church at the far end of Calzada Fray Antonio de San Miguel has a sober Baroque facade but a remarkable interior. Molded clay rosettes and other floral motifs in bright colors and gold cover the walls, ceiling, and dome. These decorations were added in the early 1900s and combine Baroque, Art Nouveau, and folk-art styles.

Environs

North of Morelia there are two wonderfully preserved 16th-century Augustinian monasteries that can be explored on a leisurely day trip. The first monastery is in **Cuitzeo**, a pleasant fishing village 34 km (21 miles) from Morelia at the end of a causeway across a vast, shallow lake. The second is in **Yuriria**, an additional 32 km (20 miles) to the north. Both feature beautiful, Indian-influenced Plateresque façades, Gothic vaulting, and elegant cloisters. Fortress-like Yuriria was described by a chronicler in the 1620s as "the most superb building imaginable."

31 Santuario El Rosario

Michoacán. Off Mex 15, 13 km (8 miles) E of Ocampo. **Tel** (715) 153 50 55. Ocampo. **Open** Nov–Mar: daily. **mariposamonarca.semarnat.gob.mx**

The UNESCO World Heritage site Santuario El Rosario is one of two sanctuaries open to the public in the Monarch Butterfly Biosphere Reserve in the mountains west of Mexico City. The 160-sq-km (60-sq-mile) preserve is the winter home of an estimated 100 million monarch butterflies, which migrate here each year from the northern US and Canada. The mystery of where monarchs overwinter was solved by Canadian zoologist Fred Urquhart, who found the isolated roosts in the 1970s.

The best time to visit is late February when rising temperatures encourage the insects to search for flowers or begin their journey back north. The hiking route is well marked.

Environs

The nearby **Sierra Chincua Monarch Butterfly Sanctuary** sees fewer visitors than El Rosario, but is easier to reach and offers horses for its more rustic trails. Guides will accompany visitors on request.

Sierra Chincua Monarch Butterfly Sanctuary

Llano de las Papas, 9 km (6 miles) NE of Angangueo. **Open** Nov–Mar: daily.

Migration of the Monarch Butterfly

The annual migration of the monarch butterfly (*Danaus plexippus linneo*) begins in the northern parts of North America in early autumn. It is then that a special generation hatches, with a life cycle of up to nine months, four times that of spring and summer butterflies. These autumn-born individuals fly south in groups of several hundred to escape the winter. They cover up to 300 km (190 miles) a day and within a month reach the *oyamel* fir forests of central Mexico where they spend the winter. In spring they mate and head north again. En route, the females lay about 500 eggs each. Their offspring take up the baton and continue north to arrive in early June. None of the original migrants will survive to return to Mexico the following year.

Monarch butterfly

SOUTHERN MEXICO

Chiapas · Guerrero (South) · Oaxaca

With attractions ranging from the world-class beach resort of Acapulco to magnificent colonial cities and monumental pre-Columbian sites, Mexico's southern states could be a microcosm of the whole country. The region is also home to many of the country's indigenous communities, whose language, customs, and costume animate rural villages and city markets.

Southern Mexico's mild climate and fertile soils attracted some of the earliest recorded settlements in Mesoamerica, with the Oaxaca Valley first inhabited in the 7th century BC. Three centuries later, the Zapotecs built their capital at Monte Albán, which dominated the valley for hundreds of years, before giving way to other, smaller cities. Meanwhile, in the east, the Maya were reaching their cultural peak and building the magnificent city of Palenque.

The Spanish Conquest in the 16th century had a massive, and often destructive, impact but resulted in a unique fusion of pre-Columbian and colonial cultures. This is seen in the lives of the local Indians, whose dress, cuisine, fiestas, crafts, and markets rank among the best in the country. Only their languages remained immune, and Spanish is still a minority tongue outside the major towns. This integration has not been achieved without difficulties, however. Long-standing grievances have resulted in rising levels of crime and the emergence of the Zapatista revolutionaries in Chiapas, certain areas of which cannot now be visited.

Geographically, the South is dominated by the mountains of the Sierra Madre del Sur, which make travel difficult but provide spectacular scenery. The Pacific coast is mostly unspoiled. Its sandy beaches are lined with palm trees and pounded constantly by surf.

Peaceful and colorful Plaza Santo Domingo in the attractive colonial city of Oaxaca

◀ Carvings at the pre-Hispanic city of Monte Albán, near Oaxaca

Exploring Southern Mexico

The beach resorts of Mexico's southern Pacific coast include the world-famous Acapulco; the up-and-coming Ixtapa and Zihuatanejo, Puerto Escondido and Huatulco; and the lesser known and more intimate Puerto Angel and Zipolite. The open, unprotected nature of the coast, however, means that the water is usually rough, and strong undertows make swimming unsafe except in sheltered bays.

The interiors of Chiapas and Oaxaca are, by contrast, best known for their colonial towns – such as Oaxaca and San Cristóbal de las Casas – but above all for their pre-Columbian sites. The hilltop Monte Albán and the jungle-shrouded Palenque are both easy to get to and worthy of a long visit. Lesser known but attractive sites include Yagul and Mitla, and the less easily accessible Bonampak (with its splendid murals) and Yaxchilán.

Tzotzil women and children in a village in Chiapas

View of Monte Albán from the south platform

Getting Around

The best way to get around Southern Mexico is by air or long distance bus. Acapulco, Zihuatanejo, Puerto Escondido, and Huatulco have international airports. There are domestic airports at Oaxaca and Tuxtla Gutiérrez. Bus services linking all the major towns and cities are reliable and frequent. For shorter journeys, minibuses *(colectivos)* are a cheap, though often uncomfortable, option. Mountainous terrain, the scarcity of gas stations, and the poor quality of the roads make driving an ordeal. Those who choose to drive are advised to do so only during the day. Access to some parts of Chiapas is restricted because of the Zapatista problem *(see p234)*.

Detail of the facade of the Basílica de la Soledad, Oaxaca

Sights at a Glance

1 Ixtapa and Zihuatanejo
2 *Acapulco pp222–3*
3 Puerto Escondido
4 Huatulco
5 *Monte Albán pp224–5*
6 *Oaxaca pp226–9*
8 Yagul
9 Mitla
10 Tuxtla Gutiérrez
11 Cañón del Sumidero
12 San Cristóbal de las Casas
13 Agua Azul
14 *Palenque pp238–41*
15 Bonampak
16 Yaxchilán

Tours

7 Tlacolula Valley

Key

- Highway
- Major road
- Minor road
- Minor railroad
- State border
- International border

One of the many deserted beaches on southern Mexico's coast

For keys to symbols *see back flap*

❶ Ixtapa and Zihuatanejo

Guerrero. 70,000. at Zihuatenejo. Ayuntamiento (755) 544 83 50. **visitmexico.com/en/ixtapa-zijuatanejo**

Ixtapa and Zihuatanejo are actually two resorts in one. Ixtapa, 10 km (6 miles) to the northwest of its smaller neighbor, is a glitzy modern resort, full of luxury high-rise hotels. It is set along an attractive curving 4-km (2.5-mile) beach, Playa Palmar, which backs onto a very broad, palm-lined avenue packed with restaurants, shops, and nightclubs.

Zihuatanejo, in contrast, is low-rise and intimate, and still has the feel of a close fishing community. Set in a scenic, sheltered bay, fishermen come here to sell their daily catch.

Both Ixtapa and Zihuatanejo offer world-class deep-sea fishing, and some of the best scuba diving on Mexico's Pacific coast. They are also a good starting point from which to explore the spectacular, deserted beaches along the surrounding coast.

The magnificent beach at Zihuatanejo

❷ Acapulco

See pp222–3.

❸ Puerto Escondido

Oaxaca. 45,000. Blvd Benito Juárez, (954) 582 01 75. Surfing festival (end of Nov). **visitmexico.com/en/puerto-escondido**

Puerto Escondido, literally the "undiscovered port," lived up to its name until discovered by hippies in the 1970s and has

The Beaches of Oaxaca

Although blessed with some of the country's best beaches and lagoons, the coast of Oaxaca was untouched by tourism until the 1970s. Since then, limited development has taken place, but with 480 km (300 miles) of coast and only a couple of significant resorts, the area still retains a sense of undisturbed charm. The coast has some remarkable flora and fauna, especially in the freshwater lagoons west of Puerto Escondido. The ocean along this stretch of coast is inviting, but swimming is dangerous as the undertow can be very strong. Crime is also a problem in the region, particularly on the beaches and roads after dark.

Laguna Manialtepec, "the place of spring-fed waters," is a natural lagoon. Encircled by mangroves, it is home to a wide range of plant, animal, and bird life. It also has some beautiful beaches, accessible by boat.

Acapulco
Santiago Jocotepec
San Gabriel Mixtepec
Parque Nacional Lagunas de Chacahua
Rio Grande
200
Laguna Manialtepec
Bajos de Chila
Puerto Escondido

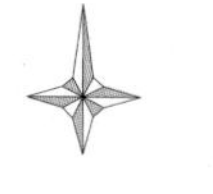

0 kilometers 20
0 miles 10

The Parque Nacional Lagunas de Chacahua is an ecological preserve with deserted beaches and a few small fishing communities. A crocodile sanctuary can also be visited on a tour from Puerto Escondido.

Puerto Escondido strikes a happy medium between the simplicity of the smaller resorts on Oaxaca's coast and the expensive luxury of Huatulco. It is especially popular with surfers.

since become a significant tourist destination. Although showing some signs of the strain of development, it retains much of the fishing village character that originally made it popular.

Playa Marinero, the main beach, is popular with locals and tourists alike. Shaded by palm trees, it faces a small cove dotted with fishing boats and fed by an endless supply of gentle surf. Playa Zicatela is a larger beach to the west and is very popular with surfers, especially in the late summer months when the waves are at their highest.

At the end of November, the town comes alive for an international surfing festival. A popular local fiesta with music and dancing takes place at the same time. Puerto Escondido is also a good base for trips to the nearby freshwater lagoons, such as Laguna Manialtepec.

❹ Huatulco

Oaxaca. 25,000. Blvd Benito Juarez, Bahía de Tangolunda, (958) 581 01 76. **visitmexico.com/en/huatulco**

Following the success of Cancún *(see p283)*, the Mexican government looked for an equivalent on the Pacific coast. The result was Huatulco, which was – until resorts sprang up in the 1980s – virtually unknown beyond the locals. Based around nine bays and 35 km (22 miles) of beaches, the resort now includes a small international airport, a golf course, and a marina. Beautiful, largely unspoiled, and relatively undiscovered.

Boats moored in the Santa Cruz marina in Huatulco

The Centro Mexicano de Tortuga, established in 1991, is dedicated to the preservation and study of endangered turtle species, several of which lay their eggs along nearby beaches. Visitors can see these beautiful creatures at various stages of their development.

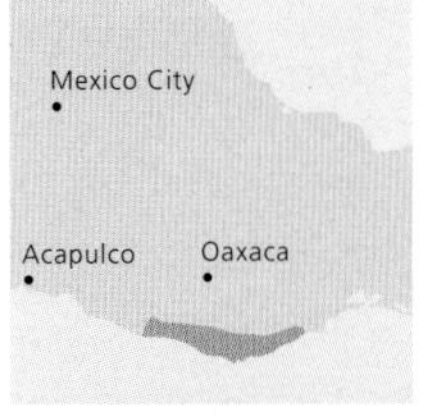

Puerto Ángel is a small, sleepy fishing village – ideal for simply relaxing on the lovely beach or sampling the excellent local seafood.

Zipolite, possibly the most relaxed resort in Mexico, has a bohemian atmosphere and is one of the few places where nude bathing is tolerated. However, crime is a problem here.

Huatulco, a refuge for pirates in colonial times, now draws holiday-makers to its stunning beaches. A wide range of water sports are offered here.

❷ Acapulco

Fringing one of the most beautiful bays on Mexico's Pacific coast, Acalpulco is the country's most famous resort. The Spaniards founded the city in the 16th century, and for the next 300 years it served as the country's main gateway to the Far East. Continued prosperity was guaranteed in the 1940s when the then president, Miguel Alemán, selected Acapulco as Mexico's first tourist resort. Hollywood celebrities such as John Wayne, Errol Flynn, and Elizabeth Taylor arrived shortly afterward, and the high-rise hotels soon followed.

View across Acapulco Bay from the southeast headland

Acapulco Bay

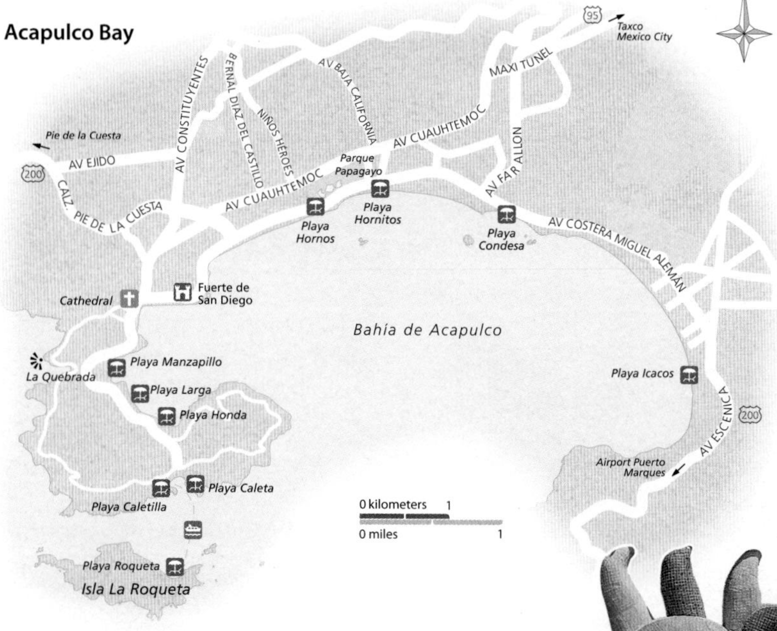

Exploring Acapulco

Acapulco can be divided into two distinct sections. To the west is the older, historic downtown area, or **Centro**; to the east is the "strip," which runs along the 11-km (7-mile) coastal road known as **La Costera Miguel Alemán**. This is lined with hotels, shops, restaurants, and nightclubs. The Centro is home to the 1930s, Moorish-style **cathedral**, which overlooks the main square, as well as the bullring, the docks, and **La Quebrada**, where the world-renowned cliff divers perform their daily routine. Two blocks east of La Quebrada is a house where artist Diego Rivera spent time toward the end of his life. His colorful mosaics adorn the house.

Señor Frog's, a popular restaurant overlooking the bay

The city boasts magnificent beaches and a worldwide reputation for the high life. It is also a working port and does not escape the environmental implications which that involves. The quality of the bay's water, for example, is not always perfect and drops noticeably in the rainy season (June–October) when litter is washed down from the hills.

Mosaic of Quetzalcoatl by Rivera, on a house near La Quebrada

Fuerte de San Diego

Calle Hornitos. **Tel** (744) 482 38 28.
Open 9am–6pm Tue–Sun.

Today, one of the few reminders of the city's history is the star-shaped Fuerte de San Diego, a 17th-century fort that houses the Museo de Acapulco. It details the city's history from pre-Columbian times to Independence, with special emphasis on its importance as a commercial center.

For hotels and restaurants see pp302–3 and pp325–6

Brightly colored hotels overlooking Playa Icacos

The Beaches

The city's main bay – 7 km (4 miles) wide – is broken up into a number of separate beaches. **Playa Caletilla** and **Playa Caleta** are situated on the peninsula south of the Centro. Smaller and more intimate than the other beaches, they are popular with local families who enjoy the calm, clean waters. Boats can be taken from here for the ten-minute trip to **Isla la Roqueta**, a small offshore island with thatched-roof restaurants, a small zoo, and several beaches.

Playa Honda, Playa Larga, and **Playa Manzanillo**, on the northern side of the same peninsula and just south of the main square, were popular in the 1930s and 40s, but now serve mainly as departure points for charter fishing trips. **Playa Hornos** and **Playa Hornitos** occupy a central position on the bay. They have a family atmosphere but can get busy on the weekends. They also have the advantage of several beachside restaurants and nearby Papagayo Park, which has boating, rides, and other children's activities.

Farther to the east is **Playa Condesa**, the best known and most crowded of all the beaches. It is considered by those in the know to be the resort's "hot-spot" and is a favorite with younger visitors. On the eastern side of the bay, **Playa Icacos** runs from the Presidente Hotel to the naval base and is often less crowded than the other beaches.

Environs

Pie de la Cuesta, 25 minutes' drive west of the city, is an attractive, broad, palm-fringed beach, but swimming here can be dangerous because of the powerful currents. The nearby **Laguna de Coyuca** is a large freshwater lake that featured in the early *Tarzan* films, as well as *The African Queen* and *Rambo II*. Fishermen and water-skiers share the lagoon with a wide variety of birds and wildlife. The sunsets here are superb. **Puerto Marqués** is a large bay to the east of the city, with a few luxury hotels, food stands on the beach, and safe swimming. Farther to the east is **Playa Revolcadero**, unsafe for swimming due to the strong undertow, but relatively free of crowds and perfect for sunset-watching, surfing, and riding horses (rentals available).

The palm-lined Laguna de Coyuca, west of the city

VISITORS' CHECKLIST

Practical Information
Guerrero. 700,000. Costera Miguel Alemán 4455, (744) 484 85 55. Festival Acapulco (late May), Virgen de Guadalupe (Dec 6–12).
visitmexico.com/en/acapulco

Transport
30 km (19 miles) SE. Av Cuauhtémoc 1605 (by Parque Papagayo), (744) 486 57 14.

La Quebrada Cliff Divers

The death-defying cliff divers of La Quebrada provide Acapulco's most famous and spectacular attraction. The performance starts with the young men climbing a 38-m (125-ft) cliff on the side of a narrow inlet. On reaching the top, they offer a prayer at a small altar before launching themselves into the shallow waters below. Each dive must coincide with an incoming wave if the diver is to avoid being dashed on the sharp rocks below. The five daily shows, one at 12:45pm and the rest in the evening, can be seen from a viewing platform or from Hotel El Mirador *(see p302)*. The last two shows are performed holding flaming torches.

❺ Monte Albán

Spectacularly situated on a mountain 400 m (1,315 ft) above the Oaxaca Valley, Monte Albán is the greatest of the Zapotec cities. In a triumph of engineering, the mountain top was leveled to allow for the creation of the ceremonial site. Its long history began with the Olmecs *(see p258)* around 500 BC. The city came to dominate the cultural, religious, and economic life of the region. Falling under the influence of Teotihuacán *(see p138–9)* during the height of its power, Monte Albán declined in later years and by AD 800 was largely abandoned. It was subsequently adopted by the Mixtecs, primarily as the site for some magnificent gold-laden burials.

★ Los Danzantes
This gallery of carvings shows humans in strange, tortured positions. Once identified as dancers, they are now thought to be prisoners of war.

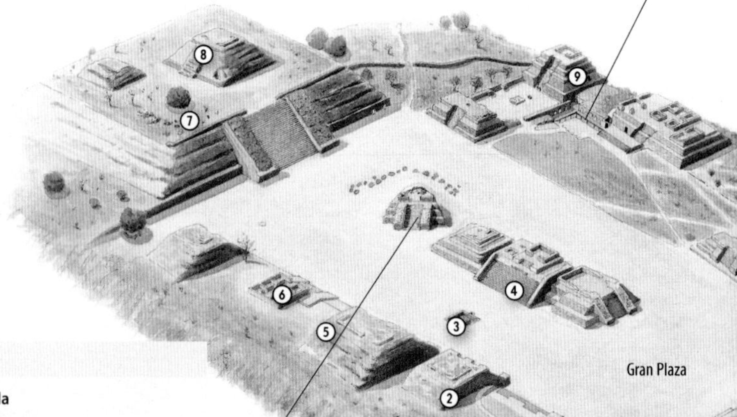

KEY

① **Stela**

② **Mound II**

③ **Altar**

④ **Buildings G, H, and I**, which served as temples, were found to contain several tombs. A tunnel leads from the Palace to Building H, possibly so that dignitaries could appear here as if by magic.

⑤ **Building P**

⑥ **Palace**

⑦ **The South Platform** has stelae at its northeast and northwest corners showing prisoners of war with their arms and legs bound.

⑧ **Mound III**

⑨ **Mound M**

⑩ **System IV** is almost identical to Mound M. Both are well-preserved pyramids that would once have been surmounted by one-room wooden temples.

⑪ **The Sunken Patio** has an altar at its center.

⑫ **Building B**

⑬ **Tomb 103**

Observatory
Thought to have been built as an observatory, or to celebrate victory in battle, this structure has glyphs carved on its walls. These may be the names of conquered tribes.

Ballcourt
A typical ballcourt, this I-shaped structure was used for playing the ceremonial ballgame *(see p281)*. There would originally have been a stone ring at the top of each sloping side to act as a "goal."

The enormous Gran Plaza, aligned on a north-south axis

VISITORS' CHECKLIST

Practical Information
Oaxaca. Off Mex 190, 8 km (5 miles) W of Oaxaca.
Tel (951) 516 12 15.
Open 8am–6pm daily.
inah.gob.mx

Transport
from Oaxaca.

0 meters 75
0 yards 75

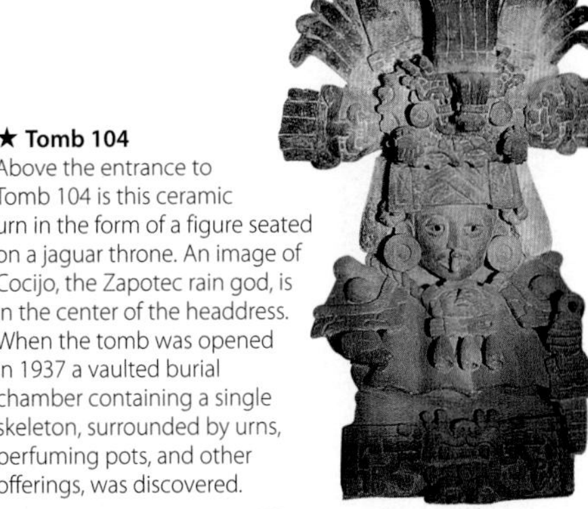

★ Tomb 104
Above the entrance to Tomb 104 is this ceramic urn in the form of a figure seated on a jaguar throne. An image of Cocijo, the Zapotec rain god, is in the center of the headdress. When the tomb was opened in 1937 a vaulted burial chamber containing a single skeleton, surrounded by urns, perfuming pots, and other offerings, was discovered.

11
12
13

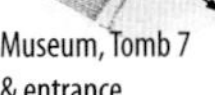

North Platform
A broad staircase leads up to the North Platform, the largest structure at Monte Albán. At the top of the steps are two rows of broken columns that would once have supported a flat roof.

6 Oaxaca

Set in a fertile valley 1,500 m (4,900 ft) up in the mountains of the Sierra Madre del Sur, the city of Oaxaca (pronounced "Wa-harker") is one of the best preserved and most charming of all Mexico's colonial cities. Laid out in 1529, in an area once dominated by the Mixtec and Zapotec cultures, the Spanish settlement quickly became the most important town in the south. Now a major commercial and industrial center, it still manages to retain a certain provincial feel. This is due, in part, to the cultural presence of a large indigenous population.

The main facade of the cathedral, with the Alameda de Léon in front

Central Oaxaca

The **Plaza de Armas**, or *zócalo*, is the geographical and social center of the city. Closed to traffic, it bustles instead with vendors, students, tourists, and colorfully dressed villagers from outside the city. It is a great place to relax and watch the world go by, especially from the many cafés situated around its perimeter. Just northwest of the *zócalo* is the **Alameda de León**, a lovely square with market stalls that specialize in arts and crafts.

Cathedral

The cathedral is on the north side of the *zócalo* but faces the Alameda de León. It was originally constructed in 1553, but a series of earthquakes meant that it had to be rebuilt in 1730, which explains its solid walls and asymmetrical towers. The attractive Baroque facade includes a fine relief of the Assumption of the Virgin Mary above the main door. Inside, the main feature is the splendid bronze altar, which was crafted in Italy.

Museo de Arte Contemporáneo

Alcalá 202. **Tel** (951) 514 10 55. **Open** Wed–Mon.
W museomaco.com

The city's contemporary art museum is housed in a carefully refurbished 16th-century building, called the Casa de Cortés (House of Cortés) after the conquistador who is reputed to have commissioned it. The museum displays works of note by local and international modern artists, including Francisco Toledo and Rodolfo Morales. It is also a popular venue for temporary exhibitions and other cultural events.

Iglesia de Santo Domingo

Of the many churches in the city, this is the one most likely to take your breath away. Begun in 1572, it was completed over 200 years later at a total cost of over 12 million pesos in gold. Its misleadingly simple facade hides an interior that dazzles with gilded plaster and colored stucco, in a sublime combination of Gothic, Romanesque, Baroque, and Moorish styles. On the south

Benito Juárez (1806–72)

A portrait of reformer Benito Juárez by the artist Ángel Bracho

Benito Juárez, one of Mexico's greatest liberal reformers, was born just north of Oaxaca. Of Zapotec Indian parentage, he was orphaned at the age of three, but was educated by priests and went on to become a champion of agricultural reform and Indian rights. He was made president in 1858 and, after defeating the French, personally oversaw the execution of Emperor Maximilian in 1867 *(see p57)*. He continued to pursue reform until his death.

Gold ornament in the Centro Cultural Santo Domingo

Main altar in the Iglesia de Santo Domingo

side is the gilt-covered Capilla del Rosario, where there are numerous paintings of saints and Madonnas in varying sizes. Another highlight is the unusual family tree of St. Dominic, painted on the low ceiling above the main entrance.

Centro Cultural Santo Domingo

Corner of Alcalá & Gurrión.
Tel (951) 51 62 991.
Open Tue–Sun.

Housed in a former monastery attached to the Iglesia de Santo Domingo, the Centro Cultural Santo Domingo has a museum, a botanical garden, a university library, and a bookstore. The museum is dedicated to pre-Columbian artifacts from the ancient cities of Oaxaca state. On display here are some of the remarkable treasures found at Monte Albán *(see pp224–5)*, in particular the extraordinary cache of Mixtec art and jewelry discovered in Tomb 7. This hoard includes beautifully crafted pieces in alabaster, obsidian, jade, and other precious materials, but is most famous for the objects in gold, regarded as the finest of their kind in the Americas.

VISITORS' CHECKLIST

Practical Information
Oaxaca. 300,000.
Murguia 206.
Tel (951) 516 01 23.
Guelaguetza (end Jul); Noche de Rábanos (Dec 23).
oaxaca.travel

Transport
8 km (5 miles) S.
Calz Niños Héroes 1036.

Casa de Juárez

García Vigil 609. **Tel** (951) 516 18 60.
Open Tue–Sun.

The house where Benito Juárez lived between 1818 and 1828 now contains a museum devoted to his life and times. Situated around a shady patio, the rooms have been kept almost exactly as they were when Juárez lived here, and provide fascinating insights into the lives of the middle classes in 19th-century Mexico.

Oaxaca City Center

1. Plaza de Armas *(zócalo)*
2. Alameda de León
3. Cathedral
4. Museo de Arte Contemporáneo
5. Iglesia de Santo Domingo
6. Centro Cultural Santo Domingo
7. Casa de Juárez
8. Basílica de la Soledad
9. Museo Rufino Tamayo
10. Iglesia de San Felipe Neri
11. Mercado Juárez
12. Mercado de Abastos

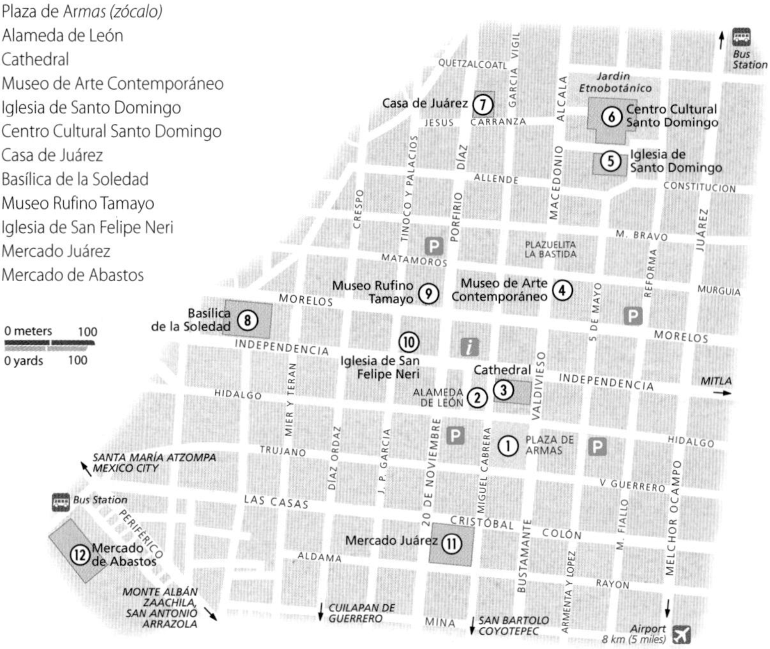

Exploring Oaxaca

Oaxaca has its fair share of interesting museums and colonial churches, all within walking distance of the center. However, its real charm lies in the rich blend of cultures on the streets themselves. Zapotec Indians, Mixtecs, and many other groups gather in force on Saturdays – the main trading day at the Mercado de Abastos, the country's biggest Indian market – to sell their traditional crafts. Techniques used to fashion textiles, ceramics, wood, and metal are passed down within families, and can be seen at workshops in villages around the city.

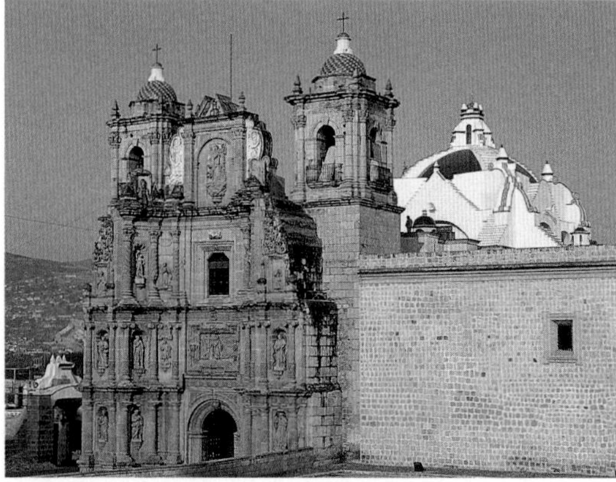

The impressive facade and dome of the Basílica de la Soledad

Preclassic female figure from Veracruz, in Museo Rufino Tamayo

Basílica de la Soledad

Avenida Independencia 107. **Tel** (951) 516 50 76.

The Basílica de la Soledad is noted for its 24-m (79-ft) high Baroque facade, which resembles a folding altarpiece, and for its gilded interior. It was built between 1682 and 1690 to house the image of the Virgin of Solitude, Oaxaca's patron saint. This figure can be seen inside, encrusted with 600 diamonds and topped with a 2-kg (4-lb) gold crown. There is a small religious museum attached to the church.

Museo Rufino Tamayo

Avenida Morelos 503. **Tel** (951) 516 76 17. **Open** Wed–Mon. reserve in advance.

This beautifully presented museum, housed in a charming 17th-century building, contains a collection of pre-Columbian art once owned by the artist Rufino Tamayo *(see p91)*. It was partly Tamayo's intention in collecting the pieces to stop them from falling into the hands of illicit artifact traders. He then left them to his native state to make his fellow Mexicans aware of their rich heritage. The fascinating displays are arranged according to aesthetic themes.

Iglesia de San Felipe Neri

This church also has a facade shaped like an altarpiece, but its highlight is the gilt altarpiece itself, in the Churrigueresque style *(see p31)*. Benito Juárez, Mexico's most celebrated president, was married here.

Mercado Juárez

Corner of 20 de Noviembre & Las Casas. **Open** daily.

Mercado Juárez was once the city's main market and is still a great place to pick up crafts made in surrounding villages. Traditional clothing, leather goods, and the famous Oaxaca pottery are all sold here.

Mercado de Abastos

Corner of Periférico and Las Casas. **Open** daily.

Most of the serious trading happens at this huge market, southwest of the center. Crafts such as ceramics, jewelry, and painted wooden animals are

Oaxaca's Black and Green Pottery

Distinctive black or dark green ceramics are seen all around Oaxaca. The black style, from San Bartolo Coyotepec, was popularized by Doña Rosa Real, who mastered and demonstrated the ancient art until her death in 1980. The green pottery, made in Santa María Atzompa, is beautifully decorated. It is best to buy both in the villages themselves.

Potter hard at work at the famous Doña Rosa Pottery in San Bartolo Coyotepec

Green-glazed pot with raised design from Santa María Atzompa

The Virgin of Solitude, draped in a cloak of black velvet, in the Basílica de la Soledad

sold here, but the real attraction is the chance to take in the noise, heat, smells, and color of one of the most vibrant markets in the country. The buyers and sellers chatter not in Spanish but mostly in the local Zapotec and Mixtec tongues, as they haggle at stalls laid out with the utmost care and attention. The liveliest day is Saturday.

Painted wooden carving

Environs

The village of **Santa María Atzompa**, 8 km (5 miles) north-west of the city, is home to hundreds of artisans dedicated to making green-glazed pottery. **San Antonio Arrazola,** close to Monte Albán *(see pp224–5)*, produces carved wooden figures of animals painted in vivid, multicolored designs.

The former convent at **Cuilapan de Guerrero**, 10 km (6 miles) southwest of the city on Mex 131, was established on the site of a Zapotec pyramid in 1550. It was abandoned two centuries later, but today still retains some impressive architectural features and murals. The roofless chapel has a Renaissance façade, an elegant columned nave, and thick earthquake-proof walls. Vicente Guerrero, hero of the War of Independence *(see p53)*, was imprisoned here before being executed on Valentine's Day 1831. A monument to his memory stands at the convent.

Zaachila, 16 km (10 miles) southwest of Oaxaca on the same road, is the site of the last Zapotec capital. A pyramid and two impressive tombs are open to the public.

San Bartolo Coyotepec, 10 km (6 miles) south of the city, is where the gleaming black pottery (*barro negro brillante*), so common in souvenir shops, is made.

Fiestas of Southern Mexico

Dancers performing at the Guelaguetza in Oaxaca

Guelaguetza *(last two Mondays of Jul)*, Oaxaca. Dancers from all over the state re-enact Zapotec and Mixtec ceremonies, wearing traditional outfits and feathered headdresses.

Easter Week *(Mar/Apr)*, San Juan Chamula and Zinacantán (Chiapas). Catholic ceremonies combine with pagan rituals in colorful festivals rated among the best in Mexico.

Feria de San Cristóbal *(Jul 25)*, San Cristóbal de las Casas. A torch-lit procession in honor of the town's patron saint finishes at the church of San Cristóbal, which opens its doors to the public only on this day.

Noche de los Rábanos *(Dec 23)*, Oaxaca. On the Night of the Radishes locals compete to carve the vegetables into people, animals, and plants.

The chapel of the former convent at Cuilapan de Guerrero, with the main church in the background

7 A Tour of the Tlacolula Valley

The area around Oaxaca, and in particular the Tlacolula Valley, has been an important cultural and historical center since the 7th century BC. Over 2,500 years of civilization have filled the 50-km (31-mile) valley with diverse attractions reflecting its Olmec, Zapotec, Mixtec, Aztec, and Spanish heritage.

Mexico City
Oaxaca
Tlalixtac
San Domingo Tomaltepec
Ocotlan

① Santa María del Tule Reputed to be over 2,000 years old, the Arbol del Tule in the churchyard here is one of the world's largest trees.

② San Jerónimo Tlacochahuaya The 16th-century church in this village was constructed as part of a Dominican monastery. It was decorated by Zapotec artisans and has an ornate bellows organ.

③ Dainzú Once a Zapotec city, Dainzú has a tiered pyramid, a ballcourt, several tombs, and a unique collection of carved stone reliefs depicting ballgame players. Parts of the site date from 350 BC.

④ Teotitlán del Valle The oldest town in the Tlacolula Valley, Teotitlán is known for its Zapotec rugs, made with natural dyes. It also has a small museum and some Zapotec ruins.

Key

Tour route

Highway

Other roads

8 Yagul

Oaxaca. Mex 190, 36 km (22 miles) SE of Oaxaca. **Tel** (951) 513 33 46. from Oaxaca. **Open** daily.

The city of Yagul was first inhabited by the Zapotecs in about 500 BC. However, it gained real religious and political influence in the region only after the decline of Monte Albán *(see pp224–5)*, at the end of the 8th century AD, and most of the buildings at the site date from this period. Yagul was subsequently taken over by the Mixtecs and was finally abandoned after the arrival of the Spanish.

Dramatically set on and around a rocky outcrop, the city had a good defensive position. It is divided into two main areas. The lower level, called the **Acropolis**, includes a large ballcourt, more than 30 tombs, and a labyrinthine complex of buildings known as the Palace of the Six Patios. On the summit of the outcrop is the **Fortress**, surrounded by a strong defensive wall and offering superb views.

Zapotec ruins on the lower level of the city of Yagul

9 Mitla

Oaxaca. Off Mex 190, 44 km (27 miles) SE of Oaxaca. **Tel** (951) 568 03 16. from Oaxaca. **Open** daily.

An important Zapotec city-state after the decline of Monte Albán *(see pp224–5)*, Mitla was home to approximately 10,000 people at its height. The city was later occupied by the Mixtecs, who had a significant influence on the architecture and decoration of its buildings. Many of Mitla's temples were destroyed by the Spanish when they invaded, and the stonework was used to build the Iglesia de San Pablo, the Catholic church that dominates the site.

Five main groups of buildings remain, two of which are accessible. The **Grupo de las Columnas**, in the east of the site, is a former palace. It consists of three large rooms set around tombs and a courtyard. The palace walls are decorated with the distinctive geometric mosaics that characterize Mitla's buildings. Each

For hotels and restaurants see pp302–3 and pp325–6

⑤ **Lambityeco** This small Zapotec site was settled around AD 700 after the decline of Monte Albán. The site has well-preserved stucco and stone carvings, and several tombs.

Tips for Drivers

Tour length: 88 km (55 miles), round-trip.
Stopping-off points: There are a few restaurants en route, including one in Teotitlán del Valle *(see p326)*, but hygiene standards vary. Visitors should carry their own water when exploring the sites.

④
San Miguel de Valle
Villa Diaz Ordaz
Santa Anna
⑤
⑥
⑦
⑧
San Pablo Villa de Mitla
Xaaga
Tehuantepec

⑥ **Tlacolula de Matamoros** This village has the area's main market, which sells pottery, woven goods, foodstuffs, and the local specialty, *mezcal (see p313).*

⑦ **Yagul** Perched on top of a rocky outcrop, the fortified city of Yagul was built by the Zapotecs and subsequently occupied by the Mixtecs.

⑧ **Mitla** Complex geometric stone mosaics adorn the facades of Mitla's fabulous pre-Columbian buildings. A Catholic church, constructed by Spanish colonists, also stands on the site.

0 kilometers 5
0 miles 5

Mitla's Catholic church, surrounded by pre-Columbian buildings decorated with distinctive geometric mosaics

frieze is made of up to 100,000 separate pieces of cut stone. One of the rooms, the Salón de las Columnas, houses six monolithic pillars that once supported the roof. To the north is the **Grupo de la Iglesia**, centered around the colonial Catholic church. The pre-Columbian buildings that survived its construction are of similar design to those in the Grupo de las Columnas, but on a smaller scale. They still retain traces of paintwork.

Housed in a typical Oaxacan building, the **Museo de la Filatelia** allows a closer look at all things postal, from stamps to post-office furniture.

Museo de la Filatelia
Reforma No. 504, Col. Centro.
Tel (951) 514 23 75. **Open** daily.
mufi.org.mx

The twelve apostles on the bell tower of the cathedral in Tuxtla Gutiérrez's main square

⑩ Tuxtla Gutiérrez

Chiapas. 553,000.
Corner of Avenida Central & Calle Central, (961) 617 05 50, 01800 280 3500. San Sebastián (Jan 15–23), San Marcos (Apr 20–25).
visitmexico.com

The capital of the state of Chiapas, Tuxtla Gutiérrez is a modern, working city, and a major gateway for visitors.

Plaza Cívica, the main square, bustles with life and is regularly used for music and street theater performances. On its south side is the **cathedral**, built at the end of the 16th century and refurbished in a more modern style in the 1980s. Twelve carved wooden figures of the apostles appear from the bell tower as the bells chime out the hour.

To the west, and just south of Avenida Central, is the impressive, if somewhat dilapidated, **Monumento a la Bandera** (Monument to the Flag), which celebrates the union of Chiapas and Mexico. Farther west on the same street is the Hotel Bonampak, which has reproductions of the Maya murals at Bonampak *(see p236)* in its lobby. The **Museo Regional**, northeast of the center, provides information on the geography and history of Chiapas. Nearby, the **Jardín Botánico** contains a range of plants native to the state, including beautiful orchids. On the outskirts of town, in the foothills of the Sierra Madre de Chiapas, is the excellent **Zoológico Miguel Alvarez del Toro**, opened to help prevent the extinction of the state's indigenous animals. A 1-km (0.5-mile) walk leads through a lush jungle environment in which over 150 species live in their natural habitats.

A street performer in Plaza Cívica

Museo Regional
Calzada de los Hombres Ilustres 885. **Tel** (961) 613 43 75. **Open** Tue–Sun. in advance.

Zoológico Miguel Alvarez del Toro
Corner of Calzada Cerro Hueco & Libramiento Sur. **Tel** (961) 614 47 00. **Open** Tue–Sun. Tue free.

The Zapatista Uprising

On January 1, 1994, the EZLN (Ejército Zapatista de Liberación Nacional), led by the masked "Subcomandante Marcos," seized the town of San Cristóbal de las Casas. Their aims – taken from those of Emiliano Zapata *(see p58)* – were a redistribution of power and the state's resources, from the wealthy few to the poor majority. The "Zapatistas," as they became known, were forced out of the town by the army and fled into the jungle. Although a ceasefire was agreed in 1995, the land the Zapatistas occupy is still heavily patrolled by government forces. So far, in spite of talks, the two sides have been unable to reconcile their differences.

Part of a mural in support of the Zapatista rebels of Chiapas

The dramatic Cañón del Sumidero, almost 1 km (half a mile) deep

⑪ Cañón del Sumidero

Chiapas. Tuxtlagutierrez. **Open** daily. by boat from Chiapa de Corzo or Cahuaré, (961) 616 15 72.

The breathtaking Sumidero Canyon forms the heart of a beautiful national park. Legend has it that in the mid-16th century several hundred Indians chose to hurl themselves down its precipitous sides after a defiant last stand, rather than submit to the invading Spanish forces.

Nearly a kilometer (half a mile) deep, and around 14 km (9 miles) in length, the canyon was carved by the Grijalva river over the course of millions of years. This important river stretches from Guatemala to the Gulf of Mexico.

Excellent views of the sheer-sided canyon are available from a series of five lookout points along its western rim. Alternatively, visitors can enjoy a two-hour boat trip along the river. Boats leave from two embarkation points, one at Cahuaré (on the west bank of the Grijalva, on Mex 190), and the other at the docks in Chiapa de Corzo. The trip passes caves and waterfalls. It also provides an opportunity to see a variety of unusual plants, and many animals and birds, including monkeys, crocodiles, iguanas, herons, and kingfishers.

◀ Ancient Zapotec city of Monte Albán, high above the Oaxaca Valley

⓬ San Cristóbal de las Casas

Chiapas. 186,000. Parque Manuel Velasco Suárez, (967) 678 65 70. Primavera y Paz (1 week before Easter), San Cristóbal (Jul 25).

Founded by the Spaniards in 1528 and marked by centuries of geographical isolation, San Cristóbal is still imbued with an atmosphere of sleepy colonial charm. However, it has a long and troubled history of conflict between the descendants of the Spanish and the local Indians. It was here that the Zapatista uprising began in 1994, and there is still a strong military presence in the town.

Situated at 2,300 m (7,550 ft) above sea level in the Chiapan highlands, San Cristóbal has a refreshingly cool climate. The town's main square, Plaza 31 de Marzo, is dominated by the **Palacio Municipal** and the **cathedral**. The latter was started in the 16th century, but construction and alterations continued until the beginning of the 19th century. Its lavish interior contains an elaborate gold-encrusted pulpit and several notable altarpieces. A few blocks to the north is the 16th-century Dominican **Templo de Santo Domingo**, the most impressive church in the city. It has an intricate pink facade, a gilded Baroque interior with several magnificent altarpieces, and a pulpit carved from a single piece of oak. Farther north, on General Utrilla, is the main market, where Indians from the surrounding hills come to trade.

Part of an elaborately gilded altarpiece in the Templo de Santo Domingo

The **Na Bolom** museum and research center, on the east side of the town, is devoted to studying and protecting the indigenous Lacandón Indians and their rainforest home. It was founded by a European couple in the 1950s, and is credited with having helped to stop the tribe from dying out.

The **Iglesia de San Cristóbal** to the west, and the **Iglesia de Guadalupe** to the east, offer excellent views over the city from their hilltop positions.

Crowds in front of the church in San Juan Chamula

Environs

There are several Indian villages 10 km (6 miles) or so from San Cristóbal, including **San Juan Chamula**, which has a beautiful church. A trip here provides an insight into the mix of Christian and pre-Columbian traditions of the Tzotzil-speaking inhabitants. The village's fiestas and markets are among the best in Mexico. Visitors are warned not to take photos, especially in religious buildings, as this may cause serious offense.

Some 84 km (52 miles) to the southeast of San Cristóbal is the charming border town of **Comitán de Domínguez**, a good base for exploring the ruins of **Chinkultic**, including several pyramids, a ballcourt, and a number of stelae. The **Lagos de Montebello** nearby is a chain of lakes, with lovely green and blue water.

Na Bolom
Avenida Vicente Guerrero 33. **Tel** (967) 678 14 18. **Open** daily (tours Tue–Sun at 11:30am, 4:30pm).
W nabolom.org

Chinkultic
Off Mex 190, 41 km (25 miles) SE of Comitán de Domínguez.
Open daily.

13 Agua Azul

Chiapas. Off Mex 199, 125 km (78 miles) NE of San Cristóbal de las Casas. from Palenque or San Cristóbal de las Casas.

A good stopping-off point on route from San Cristóbal de las Casas to Palenque, the Parque Nacional Agua Azul has some of the most beautiful waterfalls in Mexico. There are over 500 cascades in all, ranging from 3–30 m (10–100 ft) in height, together with a series of aquamarine-colored rock pools. It is possible to swim in some of these, which brings welcome relief from the heat and humidity of the lowlands, but do not swim where there are signs warning of dangerous currents. The falls are best visited outside of the rainy season (Jun–Sep), during which the waters become murky.

Environs

Some 22 km (14 miles) before the road from Agua Azul reaches Palenque is the spectacular, 30-m (100-ft) high waterfall at **Misol-Ha**. Set within the lush surroundings of a tropical rainforest, this is another good place at which to stop for a swim.

14 Palenque

See pp238–41.

One of the spectacularly beautiful waterfalls at Agua Azul

15 Bonampak

Chiapas. 153 km (95 miles) SE of Palenque. from Palenque. tours from Palenque. **Open** daily.

Discovered in the 1940s, the Maya site of Bonampak is of ancient origin but reached its apogee under Yahaw Chan Muwan (AD776–90). The subject of three fine stelae at the site, Yahaw Chan Muwan commissioned Bonampak's remarkable Temple of the Paintings. The walls and vaulted ceilings of the three chambers of this temple are covered with vividly colored murals. These give rich insights into the courtly life of the nobility of Bonampak and the pageantry surrounding Maya warfare. Murals in the two outer rooms (Rooms 1 and 3) show noblemen in fine clothes and elaborate headdresses. Below them are musicians and dancers, and on the ceiling animals and figures representing constellations of the Maya cosmos.

The two main paintings in the middle room (Room 2) depict a battle, in which Maya warriors are shown defeating their enemy.

As an alternative to making the trip to the site itself, giant reproductions of the murals can be seen in the lobby of Hotel Bonampak in Tuxtla Gutiérrez *(see p234)*.

Temple 33 at Yaxchilán, with its prominent roof comb

16 Yaxchilán

Chiapas. 130 km (80 miles) SE of Palenque. **Tel** (961) 612 28 24. from Palenque. tours from Palenque. **Open** daily.

The city of Yaxchilán, located 20 m (66 ft) above the Usumacinta River in the heart of the Lacandón rainforest, is one of the most dramatic of all Maya sites. It can only be reached by air or by taking first a bus and then a boat along the river.

Built between AD 350 and 800, it rose to prominence during the 8th century under the command of its most famous kings, "Shield Jaguar," and his son "Bird Jaguar." Yaxchilán is rich in glyphs, stelae, carved lintels, stucco roof combs, and temples. One of the best preserved buildings is Temple 33.

Yaxchilán is in the homeland of the small population of Lacandón Indians *(see p235)*, Mexico's last pagan native people, who live outside Hispanicized society.

The Art of the Maya

Of all Mesoamerican civilizations, the Maya produced the most enduring works of art, in the greatest quantity. Maya art is distinguished by its naturalistic approach which makes it more accessible to the modern eye than the art of other ancient Mexican cultures. The Maya used a variety of materials to decorate their buildings and to make sacred and functional objects: stone, wood, ceramics, stucco, shell, jade, and bone. Particularly striking are the Maya's portraits of themselves – as seen especially in the wall paintings of Bonampak and the carved bas-reliefs of Palenque – which give us an understanding of their way of life, methods of warfare, costumes, customs, and beliefs.

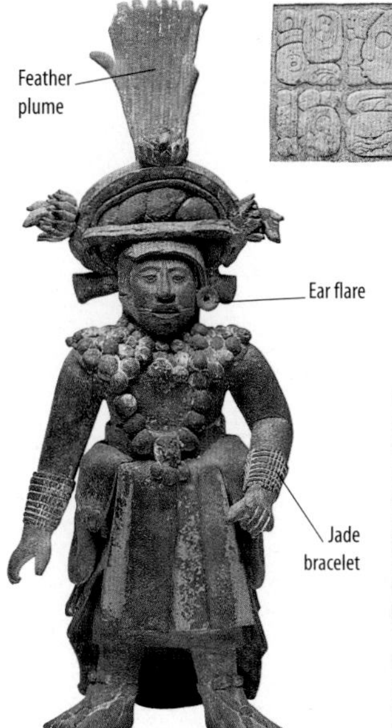

Ceramics were used to make delicate sculptures. This figurine, probably of a ruler, was found in a Maya tomb on the island of Jaina off the coast near Campeche *(see p264)*.

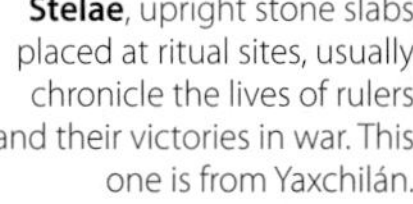

Glyphs *(see pp50–51)*, often recording royal biographies and events, were carved in stone or modeled in stucco.

Stelae, upright stone slabs placed at ritual sites, usually chronicle the lives of rulers and their victories in war. This one is from Yaxchilán.

Bas-reliefs show the Maya's skill in representing themselves, as seen in this detail from the Tablet of the Slaves in Palenque museum *(see p241)*.

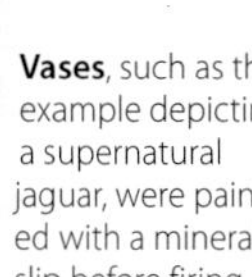

Vases, such as this example depicting a supernatural jaguar, were painted with a mineral slip before firing.

The murals of Bonampak depict scenes of Classic Maya life in vivid colors with an evocative sense of realism. This detail from the battle scene in Room 2 shows a warrior dressed in a jaguar skin seizing an enemy by the hair. Other remarkable frescoes believed to be by Maya artists can be seen at Cacaxtla *(see p160)*.

⓮ Palenque

Palenque is everything that an archaeological site should be: mysterious, solemn, well preserved, and imposing in its beautiful jungle setting. The Maya first settled here as early as 100 BC, and the city reached its apogee between AD 600 and 800, when it served as a regional capital. It fell into a precipitous decline in the early 10th century and was abandoned to the ever-encroaching jungle. Excavations have uncovered ruins emblazoned with fine sculpture and splendid stuccowork.

Central Palenque
The site's most important buildings, shown in the illustration, are known as the Principal Group.

Temple XIV
Although badly damaged, this temple has been largely reconstructed. It contains some well-preserved glyphs and carvings, among them this portrait of the ruler Ken Balam II, who is wearing a feathered headdress.

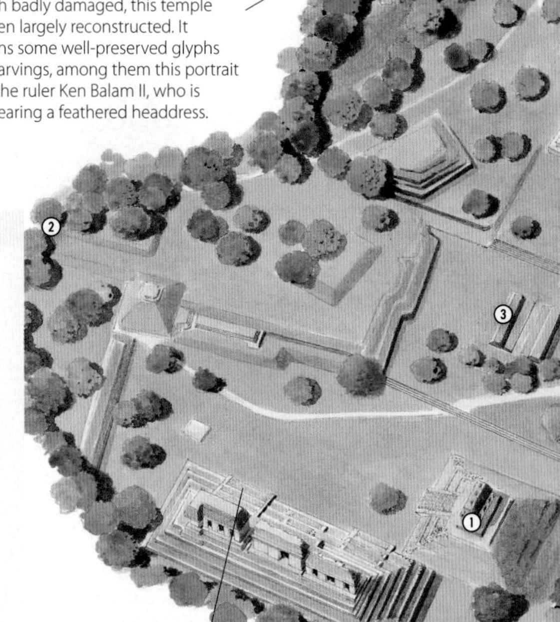

KEY

① **The Temple of the Count** was for two years in the 1830s the home of an eccentric European nobleman.

② **Path to Groups B and C, waterfalls, and museum** *(see p241)*

③ **Ballcourt**

④ **The Temple of the Cross** has a striking roof comb, and carvings inside.

⑤ **The Temple of the Foliated Cross** is named after a panel showing a cruciform corn plant.

⑥ **Water Channel**

⑦ **Path to Temple of the Jaguar** *(see p241)*

⑧ **Temple XIII**

⑨ **Temple of the Dying Moon**

⑩ **Tomb of Alberto Ruz Lhuillier** *(see p240)*

⑪ **Temple X**

North Group
This consists of five temples on a single platform. At the base of the platform is this carving of the god Tlaloc.

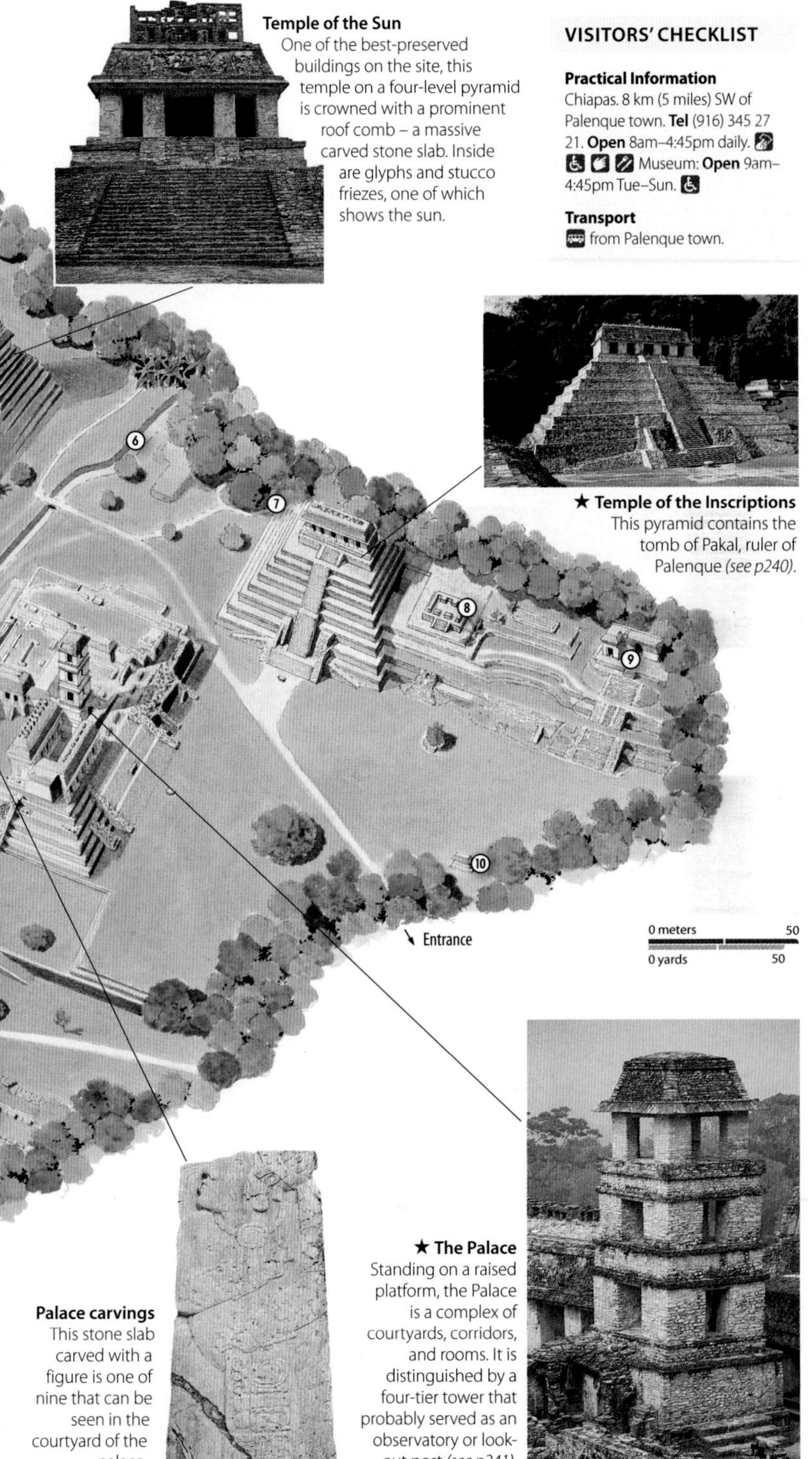

Temple of the Sun
One of the best-preserved buildings on the site, this temple on a four-level pyramid is crowned with a prominent roof comb – a massive carved stone slab. Inside are glyphs and stucco friezes, one of which shows the sun.

VISITORS' CHECKLIST

Practical Information
Chiapas. 8 km (5 miles) SW of Palenque town. **Tel** (916) 345 27 21. **Open** 8am–4:45pm daily. Museum: **Open** 9am–4:45pm Tue–Sun.

Transport
from Palenque town.

★ Temple of the Inscriptions
This pyramid contains the tomb of Pakal, ruler of Palenque *(see p240)*.

★ The Palace
Standing on a raised platform, the Palace is a complex of courtyards, corridors, and rooms. It is distinguished by a four-tier tower that probably served as an observatory or look-out post *(see p241)*.

Palace carvings
This stone slab carved with a figure is one of nine that can be seen in the courtyard of the palace.

The Temple of the Inscriptions

The tallest and most imposing building at Palenque is shown here as a reconstruction, complete with its roof comb. It was constructed during the 68-year reign of Pakal (AD615–83) and subsequently contained his funerary crypt, a fact that was revealed only by the dramatic discovery of his tomb by Alberto Ruz Lhuillier in 1952. Many of the artifacts and pieces of jewelry found in the tomb are now on display in the Museo Nacional de Antropología in Mexico City *(see pp94–9)*.

The steep climb of the main staircase at the front of the pyramid

The entrance to the tomb is by way of two flights of steep stone steps that descend 25 m (82 ft). When the staircase was discovered in 1949 it was filled with rubble, which took three years to remove before the tomb could be explored.

The roof comb would have been carved with deities and animal motifs.

The temple that surmounts the pyramid is divided into two halls.

Two shafts above the landing let in light and air from outside the pyramid.

Reconstruction of the Temple of the Inscriptions

In the time of the Classic Maya the temple would have been covered with plaster and painted a vivid red. The detailed carvings on the temple and the roof comb were picked out in other bright colors.

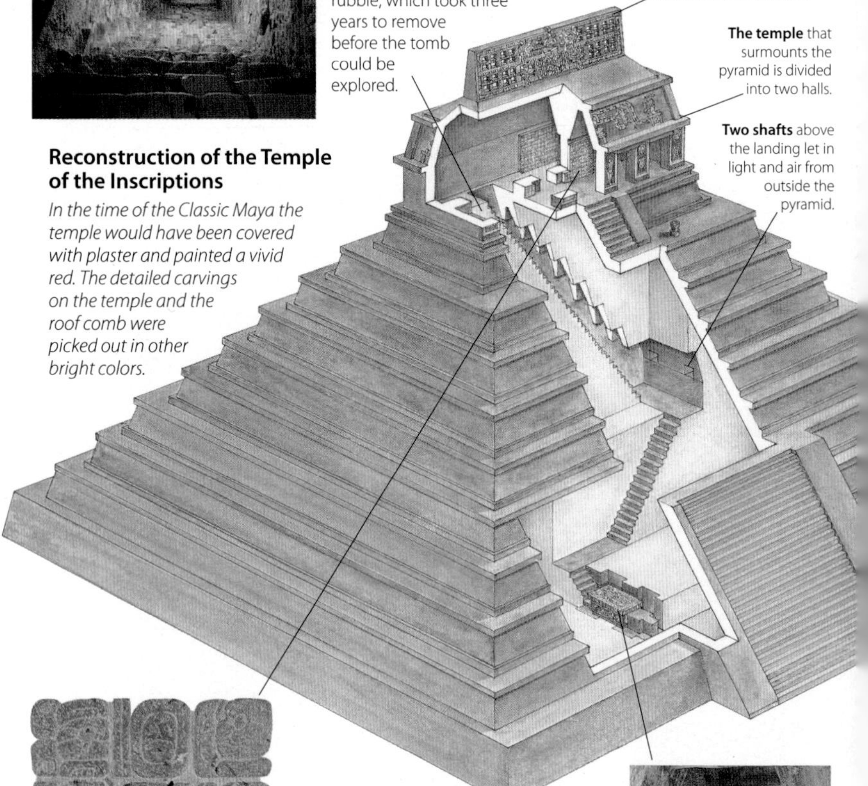

The inscriptions, which give the temple its name, can be seen on the temple walls. There are 617 carved glyphs in total, arranged on three stone slabs. To date, they have been only partially deciphered.

The Tomb of Pakal is a chamber measuring 9 m by 4 m (30 ft by 13 ft), with a vaulted ceiling almost 7 m (23 ft) high. Nine stucco figures, representing dynastic precursors, adorn the walls. The heavy stone lid of the sarcophagus is decorated with a symbolic scene of Pakal's resurrection from the jaws of the underworld. The tomb is permanently closed to the public.

Exploring Palenque

The most interesting and best preserved buildings are in the Principal Group (shown on the previous pages). A few lesser-known temples can be reached by easy paths through the jungle. Another path leads from the Principal Group past a series of waterfalls to the site museum.

Key

Principal Group *(see pp238–9)*

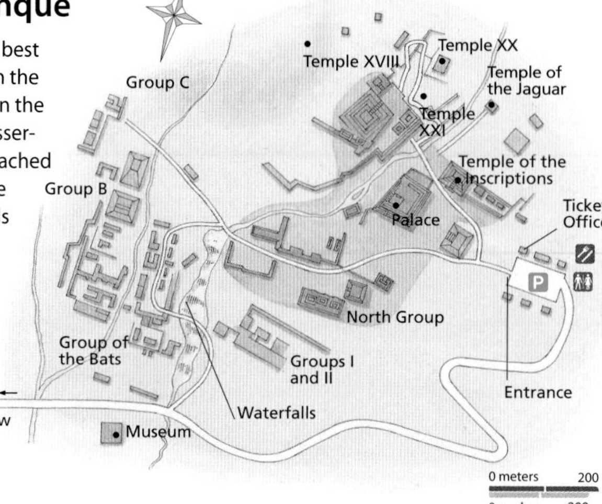

The Palace

Set on a platform some 100 m by 80 m (328 ft by 262 ft) and 10 m (33 ft) high, the palace complex is the product of many kings. The earliest buildings date to the time of Pakal, but the basal platform conceals earlier phases, some preserved as underground galleries. The palace was the home of the royal family and their immediate entourage. Carvings and stucco decorations can be seen in parts of the building. Particularly interesting are the sculptures of captives in the courtyard *(see p239)*, where visitors could be suitably impressed by the might of the Palenque kings. The Oval Tablet depicts the accession of Pakal, who receives the emblems of office from his mother, a short-reigning queen.

Oval Tablet in the Palace

Temple of the Jaguar

A short path behind the Temple of the Inscriptions leads to this ruined structure. Its name derives from the image of a king seated on a jaguar throne inside, now destroyed. Unexcavated and overgrown, it gives an idea of what the site must have been like when it was first explored in the late 18th century.

Outlying Temples

Two clearly marked paths that set off from in front of the Temple of the Sun lead to Temples XVIII and XXI, and other isolated buildings that are nearby but hidden by trees. More buildings can be reached by the path from the site to the museum, which passes through Group B and the Group of the Bats. Branches off this path lead to Group C, Group I, and Group II. There are hundreds of similar but less accessible structures at Palenque that are hidden by the surrounding jungle.

Temple of the Jaguar, one of many buildings in the jungle

The Museum

This modern building on the road between Palenque town and the archaeological site provides an overview of the development of the Maya city. Many artifacts found on the site are on display, including the so-called Tablet of the Slaves *(see p237)*.

The Palace, dominating the center of Palenque

THE GULF COAST

Tabasco · Veracruz

The lush, tropical plains fringing the Gulf of Mexico were once home to three major pre-Columbian cultures – the enigmatic Olmecs, the "mother culture" of ancient Mexican civilization; the Totonacs of Central Veracruz; and the Huastecs. Centuries later, this coast was once again at the fulcrum of Mexican history, when the first Spaniards set out on their historic conquest of the Aztec empire.

This green and fertile region stretches from Tampico and the Huasteca region in the north, to the steamy, low-lying jungle of the Istmo de Tehuantepec – Mexico's narrow "waist" – in the south. Much of Mexico's sugarcane, tropical fruits, cocoa, and coffee are produced on this coastal plain. Inland temperatures drop as the land rises toward the great heights of the Sierra Madre Oriental and the snow-capped Pico de Orizaba, Mexico's highest mountain at 5,747 m (18,856 ft).

The Olmec civilization arose in the southern part of this area in about 1000 BC. Later, the Maya people used the wide, meandering rivers that criss-cross Tabasco as their trading routes. Meanwhile, in the north of the region, other indigenous races built great cities, most notably at El Tajín. In 1519, the Spanish conquistador Hernán Cortés disembarked on the coast of Veracruz. He burnt his boats, before going into alliance with the Totonac Indians and setting off to conquer the Aztecs. Throughout the next three centuries, the port of Veracruz shipped endless quantities of gold and silver back to Europe. At the same time, colonial towns like Tlacotalpan grew and prospered. In recent decades, parts of Tabasco and the southern area of Veracruz have been transformed by another economic boom – this time stemming from the exploitation of oil.

A farmer with his crop of sugarcane, one of many plants grown in the humid Gulf Coast region

◀ Los Voladores, men jumping from the top of a pole and slowly descending to music, in an ancient ritual

Exploring the Gulf Coast

The humid Gulf Coast region has a rich hoard of pre-Columbian treasures. Artifacts from various cultures are preserved in Xalapa, in one of Mexico's best museums; in Villahermosa, meanwhile, an outdoor archaeological park exhibits the monumental art of the Olmec civilization. The ruined city of El Tajín, sacred to the god of thunder, should also not be missed. Other sights in the region include the vibrant port of Veracruz and the charming colonial towns of Tlacotalpan and Coatepec.

Macaque monkeys on Tanaxpillo Island in Laguna de Catemaco

Farmer working the fields, with the volcano of Pico de Orizaba in the background

Sights at a Glance

1. *El Tajín pp246–7*
2. Quiahuiztlan
3. *Xalapa pp250, 252–53*
4. Coatepec
5. Cempoala
6. El Puerto de Veracruz
7. Orizaba
8. Córdoba
9. Tlacotalpan
10. Santiago Tuxtla
11. Laguna de Catemaco
12. Comalcalco
13. Villahermosa

Fishing boats in the harbor of Veracruz

Key

- Highway
- Major road
- Minor road
- Main railroad
- Minor railroad
- State border
- International border

Getting Around

The region has two large airports, at Veracruz and Villahermosa, with Veracruz offering more international destinations. There is a smaller domestic airport at Minatitlán. The main towns in the area are linked by highways and regular bus services. However, the northern region is less visited and less well served – the easiest way to get to El Tajín is to fly to the domestic airport at Poza Rica. In the south, Villahermosa is a transportation hub offering road connections with the Yucatán Peninsula *(see pp260–91)* and convenient access to Palenque *(see pp238–41)*.

Brightly painted arches in the unspoiled town of Tlacotalpan

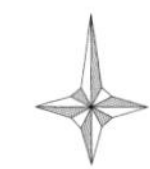

❶ El Tajín

Developed from an earlier settlement, the city of El Tajín was a political and religious center for the Totonac civilization. Many of its buildings date from the early Postclassic period, between AD 900 and 1150. Decorated with relief panels and sculptures, they would have been painted in strong colors such as red, blue, and black. The excavated nucleus of this spectacular ancient city covers about 1 sq km (0.4 sq miles), but the entire urban area once spread over 10 sq km (4 sq miles) and had a population of 25,000.

★ Pyramid of the Niches
Originally crowned by a temple, this pyramid has 365 niches, representing the days of the year. Each niche may have held an offering.

★ Southern Ballcourt
Six relief panels on the side walls of this ballcourt illustrate rituals of the game *(see p281)*, including the sacrifice of one or more players.

★ Statue of Dios Tajín
This small statue probably represents Tajín, god of thunder and lightning, an important deity to the people of El Tajín.

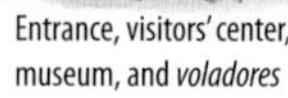

Entrance, visitors' center, museum, and *voladores*

Plaza del Arroyo
The four pyramids that surround this massive square stand at the cardinal points. They are some of the oldest structures in the city.

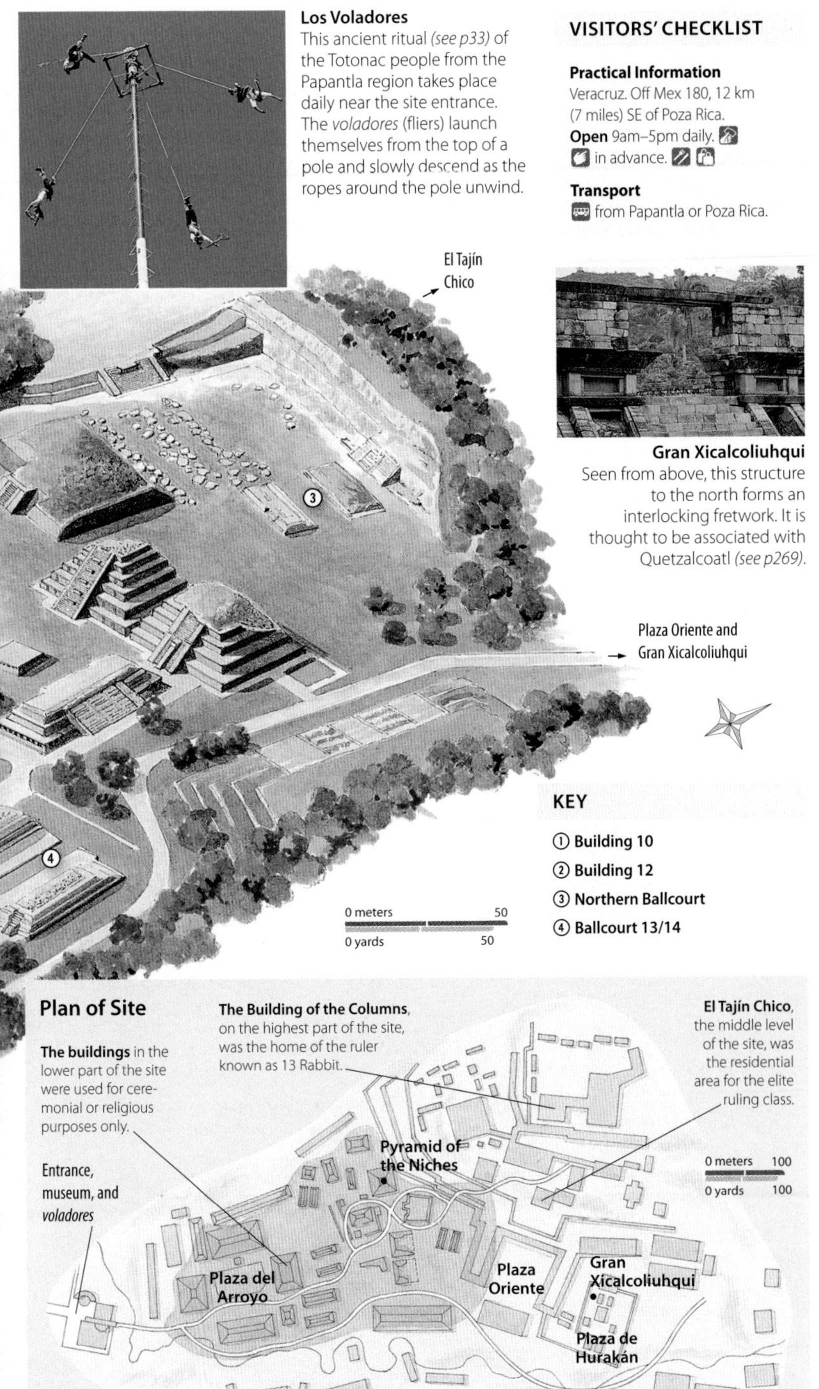

Los Voladores
This ancient ritual *(see p33)* of the Totonac people from the Papantla region takes place daily near the site entrance. The *voladores* (fliers) launch themselves from the top of a pole and slowly descend as the ropes around the pole unwind.

VISITORS' CHECKLIST

Practical Information
Veracruz. Off Mex 180, 12 km (7 miles) SE of Poza Rica.
Open 9am–5pm daily. in advance.

Transport
from Papantla or Poza Rica.

Gran Xicalcoliuhqui
Seen from above, this structure to the north forms an interlocking fretwork. It is thought to be associated with Quetzalcoatl *(see p269)*.

KEY

① Building 10
② Building 12
③ Northern Ballcourt
④ Ballcourt 13/14

Plan of Site

The buildings in the lower part of the site were used for ceremonial or religious purposes only.

Entrance, museum, and *voladores*

The Building of the Columns, on the highest part of the site, was the home of the ruler known as 13 Rabbit.

El Tajín Chico, the middle level of the site, was the residential area for the elite ruling class.

Key
Illustrated area

A stone carving at the UNESCO world heritage site, El Tajín ▶

Small stone tombs in the Totonac cemetery at Quiahuiztlan

❷ Quiahuiztlan

Veracruz Mex 180, 24 km (15 miles) N of Cempoala. to Cerro de los Metates then 2-km (1-mile) walk. **Open** 9am–5pm Tue–Sun.

Once inhabited by 15,000 people, the Totonac city of Quiahuiztlan was a hilltop stronghold. It was constructed in the late Classic period, when raids by warlike nomads from the north forced sites like El Tajín to be abandoned. Despite originally being ringed by defensive walls, it was twice conquered, first by the Toltecs in the 9th century and then by the Aztecs in the 13th century.

Today the only part of the terraced site that can be visited is the cemetery. Here some 100 tiny tombs were discovered, each resembling a pre-Columbian temple. Many had human bones and skulls in burial chambers in their bases. Small holes in the backs of the tombs may have been for relatives to communicate with the dead.

Across the main road (Mex 180) from Quiahuiztlan is Villa Rica de la Vera Cruz, the first Spanish settlement in Mexico, and now a fishing village.

❸ Xalapa

Veracruz. 525,000. Rio Tesechoacan 57, (228) 812 75 85. Feria de las Flores (Apr). **visit mexico.com/en/xalapa-veracruz**

The capital of Veracruz state, Xalapa (or Jalapa) is known for its university and cultural life, and has the second most important anthropology museum *(see pp252–3)* in Mexico. The city enjoys a beautiful setting: on a clear day there are splendid views of the 4,250-m (13,940-ft) Cofre de Perote peak from Parque Juárez, the main plaza. To one side of this square is the Neo-Classical **Palacio de Gobierno**, which has a mural by Mario Orozco Rivera (1930–98) on its stairs. Opposite the Palacio is the 18th-century **cathedral**. Uphill from the city center, brightly colored houses with sloping tiled roofs and wrought-iron balconies line the pretty, cobbled streets around the market.

Environs

The **Hacienda Lencero**, originally a 16th-century inn, was bought by the controversial General Santa Anna *(see p56)* in the 19th century. It is now a museum of furniture, utensils, and ornaments from that era.

The remote **Filobobos** consists of two archaeological sites 4 km (2.5 miles) apart, which date from AD 700–1200. Access to the site nearest to the road, El Cuajilote, is by an organized rafting trip along the River Bobos, or via an 8-km (5-mile) scenic walk. It is worth the effort of getting there, however, because the Filobobos ruins are truly spectacular.

Palacio de Gobierno
Avenida Enriquez. **Tel** (228) 841 74 00. **Open** Mon–Fri.

Hacienda Lencero
10 km (6 miles) E of Xalapa. **Tel** (228) 820 02 70. **Open** Tue–Sun.

Filobobos
Off minor road from Tlapacoyan to Plan de Arroyos, 110 km (68 miles) NW of Xalapa. **Open** Tue–Sun.

A charming cobbled street with colorful houses, near the market in Xalapa

Las Chimeneas, named after the hollow columns that line its upper tier

❹ Coatepec

Veracruz. 80,000. Miguel Rebolledo 1, (228) 816 09 64. San Jerónimo (Sep 29–30), Feria del Café (Apr 30–May 1).

A lovely town, Coatepec is famous for its coffee, fruit, liqueurs, orchids, and seafood restaurants. The town's elegant houses, with tiled roofs and ornate balconies, were built with the proceeds of the early 20th-century coffee boom. A converted hacienda in the center of the town is now one of Mexico's most charming hotels, the Posada Coatepec *(see p303)*. Near the Posada is the attractive Basílica Menor de Nuestra Señora de Guadalupe.

Environs

The area around Coatepec has a humid, semitropical climate with exuberant vegetation – in some places balls of grass even grow on telephone wires where birds have left traces of soil. The quiet colonial town of **Xico**, 9 km (6 miles) south of Coatepec, is worth a visit, especially on a Sunday (market day). From Xico, a path leads through coffee and banana plantations to the 40-m (131-ft) high **Texolo Waterfall**.

The Basílica Menor de Nuestra Señora de Guadalupe in Coatepec

❺ Cempoala

Veracruz. Mex 180, 44 km (27 miles) N of Veracruz. from Veracruz. **Open** daily.

Shortly after their arrival in Mexico in 1519 *(see p47)*, Cortés and his men sheltered in the Totonac city that stood on the site of modern-day Cempoala (or Zempoala). Like many other cities at the time, it was subjugated by the Aztecs, and the city's governor collaborated with Cortés in return for protection.

The walled archaeological site, which contains the ruins of the Totonac city, adjoins Cempoala town. Around a central plaza, buildings faced with smooth, rounded river stones show strong Aztec influences. Straight ahead from the entrance is the **Templo Mayor**, a 13-tier pyramid topped by a sanctuary, which was originally thatched with palm leaves. Nearby, in **Las Chimeneas** (The Chimneys), so-called because of its hollow columns, archaeologists found a *chacmool*-like figure *(see p48)*, suggesting the Maya were associated with the site. The east-facing **Gran Pirámide** was a temple dedicated to the sun.

Fiestas of the Gulf Coast

Carnival *(Feb/Mar)*. Celebrated in most parts of the Gulf Coast, but particularly in Veracruz, Villahermosa, and Tenosique (Tabasco), Carnival starts with the burning of a huge figure, representing "bad temper," who usually resembles an unpopular politician. There are also floats, parades, and dancing. Tenosique's Carnival is famous for its flour war, the Guerra de Pocho y Blanquitos.

Carnival in Veracruz

Candelaria *(week leading up to Feb 2)*. Celebrated throughout Mexico, the Christian festival of Candelaria (Candlemas) is particularly vibrant in the towns of Tlacotalpan *(see p256)* and Catemaco *(see p257)*. The festival traditionally features numerous street stalls, as well as dancing and music. In Tlacotalpan the local Virgin is taken on a river procession involving hundreds of boats.

Corpus Christi *(May/Jun)*. The religious festival of Corpus Christi is especially associated with Papantla. Here the renowned *voladores (see p33)* perform their spectacular ancient rite of twirling upside down from a towering pole, with the intention of invoking fertility and honoring the sun.

Feria de Santiago Tuxtla *(Jul 25)*, Santiago Tuxtla *(see pp256–7)*. In this saint's day celebration, gigantic *mojiganga* dolls are taken around the town. *Danzas de los liseres* (jaguar-mask dances) also take place.

Museo de Antropología de Xalapa

Second only in importance to the anthropology museum in Mexico City, this outstanding collection is displayed in spacious marble halls and open-air patios. It consists of sculptures and artifacts from the Gulf Coast's major pre-Columbian civilizations, found at various sites within the region. The first halls are dedicated to the Olmec civilization *(see p258)*. Central Veracruz and the Totonacs follow, and the final room exhibits the highly stylized sculptures of the Huastec culture.

The Olmec Patio, dominated by El Rey

Gallery Guide

The exhibits are displayed in a descending series of halls and patios with steps and wheelchair ramps linking each level. Beginning at the main entrance, the items are arranged chronologically. The gardens contain flora representative of different areas of Veracruz state.

Olmec Funerary Urn
When it was discovered in Catemaco, this huge terracotta urn held the remains of a small child, along with ritual offerings.

Exhibits from Remojadas

Totonac Patio I

Olmec room II

Olmec room I

El Señor de Las Limas
Found in Las Limas, this greenstone figure (900–400 BC) is thought to be an accession monument. It depicts a lordly figure holding the Werejaguar baby, an important Olmec symbol of divine power.

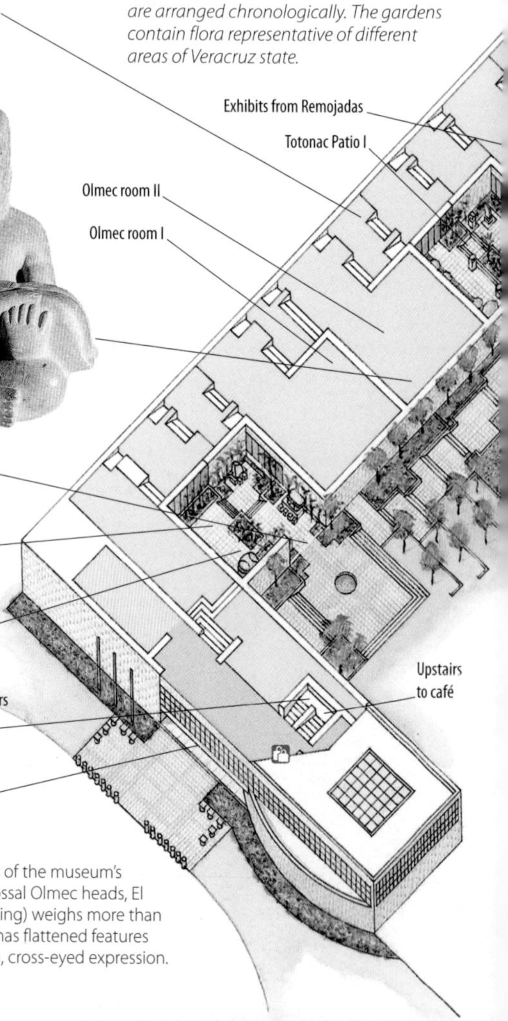

Entrance to gardens

Olmec Patio

Upstairs to café

Downstairs to toilets

Main entrance

★ El Rey
The largest of the museum's seven colossal Olmec heads, El Rey (The King) weighs more than 20 tons. It has flattened features and a stern, cross-eyed expression.

Mictlantecuhtli
Representing Mictlantecuhtli, the god of death, this extraordinary skeletal figure (AD 600–900) is made from terracotta and painted with tar.

Totonac Patio II

Rear entrance

Huastec room

Model of El Tajín

VISITORS' CHECKLIST

Practical Information
Avenida Xalapa, Xalapa. **Tel** (228) 815 49 52. **Open** 9am–5pm Tue–Sun. 11:30am (reserve in advance).
uv.mx/max

Transport
Avila Camacho, Centro, Tesorería.

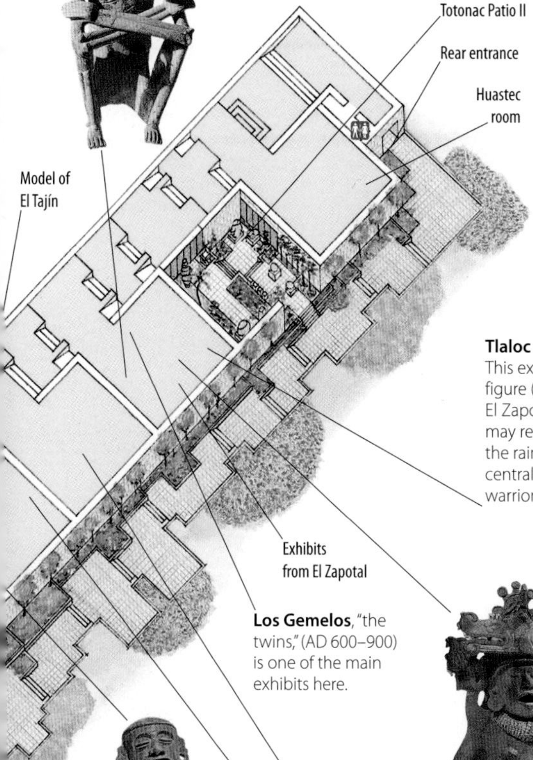

Key

- Permanent collection
- Temporary exhibitions
- Nonexhibition space

Tlaloc
This expressive terracotta figure (AD 600–900) from El Zapotal *(see p254)* may represent Tlaloc, the rain god of the central highlands, or a warrior or ballplayer.

Exhibits from El Zapotal

Los Gemelos, "the twins," (AD 600–900) is one of the main exhibits here.

Exhibits from El Tajín

Cihuateotl
This life-size figure (AD 600–900) depicts Cihuateotl, a woman deified after dying in childbirth. Her closed eyes and open mouth evoke the screaming faces of women sacrificed in her honor.

Smiling Figure from Veracruz
Characteristic of Central Veracruz culture, smiling figurines such as this one (AD 600–900) may have played a significant part in festive rituals.

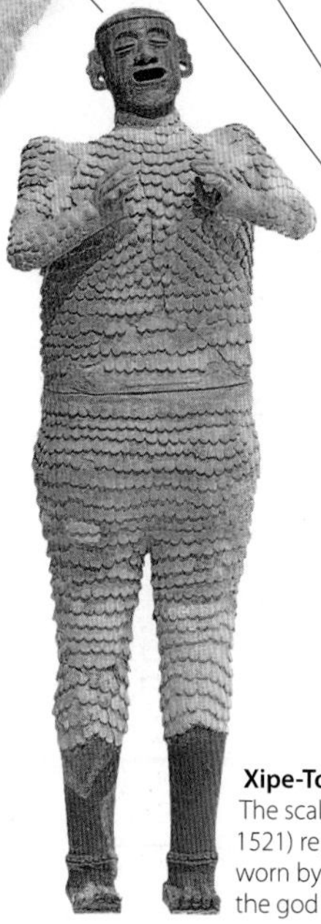

Xipe-Totec
The scaly skin of this terracotta figure (AD 1200–1521) represents the flayed skins of human sacrifices worn by priests during rites to honor Xipe-Totec, the god of spring.

❻ El Puerto de Veracruz

Veracruz. 552,000.
Palacio Municipal, (229) 841 74 00.
Carnival (Feb/Mar).

Veracruz is, more than anything else, a place of fun. The life of the city revolves around the Plaza de Armas and the *malecón* (waterfront promenade), an enjoyable place to stroll and watch the ships come and go. The tree-lined Plaza de Armas is flanked by the elegant 17th-century **Palacio Municipal** and the **cathedral**. The dome of the cathedral is covered with Puebla tiles *(see p157)* and crowned with a lantern and a small cross. Opposite the cathedral, the **Portales** (arcades) are filled with hotels and cafés. Musicians play here all day and most of the night, and most evenings there is dancing to watch, whether it is a frenetic *zapateo* or a poised, serene *danzón*. The entertainment reaches a peak during the city's famous carnival *(see p251)*.

Situated on the *malecón* is the Gran Café de la Parroquia *(see p327)*. This lively, convivial café opened in 1808 and is an institution. Farther south is the **Acuario de Veracruz**, said to be the largest and best aquarium in Latin America. Boat trips from the *malecón* run past the Isla de los Sacrificios and around the harbor to the fortress of **San Juan de Ulúa**. Fortified in 1692, it was home to the last Spanish garrison to accept Mexican Independence *(see p53)* and has since seen several foreign invasions, the last by the US in 1914. It also became the country's most notorious prison during the *porfiriato (see p57)*.

Palacio Municipal, with the busy harbor in the background

The tiny **Isla de los Sacrificios** was the first place the conquistadors landed *(see p47)*, and is named after the remains of human sacrifices they found.

The best of several museums in Veracruz, the **Museo Histórico Naval** is housed in the ex-Naval Academy in the city center. It tells the maritime history of the port. Exhibits include over 300 types of knots, and some intricate models of ships.

Sailors aboard a ship in Veracruz harbor

In 1880, the fortified wall around Veracruz was torn down leaving only one of the nine original bastions, the **Baluarte de Santiago**. This small fort, built in 1635, now houses a good collection of pre-Columbian gold jewelry.

The 17th-century fortress, San Juan de Ulúa

Environs

South of the town are the hotel-filled satellite suburbs of **Playa de Oro** and **Mocambo**. The beaches here are cleaner and less crowded than in Veracruz, but not very appealing. **Boca del Río**, farther along the coast, is famous for its seafood.

In the 1970s, excavations at **El Zapotal**, 75 km (47 miles) south, uncovered hundreds of clay sculptures – offerings to the god of the underworld, Mictlantecuhtli *(see p269)*. Most are in Xalapa's Museo de Antropología *(see pp252–3)*, but the central figure of Mictlantecuhtli, made of unfired clay, is still at El Zapotal.

Acuario de Veracruz
Blvd Manuel Avila Camacho.
Tel (229) 931 10 20. **Open** daily.
acuariodeveracruz.com

San Juan de Ulúa
Calle Pedro Sainz de Baranda.
Tel (229) 938 51 51. **Open** Jul–Aug: daily; Sep–Jun: Tue–Sun.
ground floor only.

Museo Histórico Naval
Calle Arista 418. **Tel** (229) 931 40 78.
Open Tue–Sun.

Baluarte de Santiago
Calle Francisco Canal. **Tel** (229) 931 10 59. **Open** Tue–Sun.

One of the cafés serving rich local coffee in Córdoba's Portal de Zevallos

❼ Orizaba

Veracruz. 117,000. El Palacio de Hierro, (272) 728 91 36. San Miguel (Sep 29).

Home to an Aztec garrison, and then to Spanish soldiers, Orizaba held a strategic position on the trading route between Veracruz and Mexico City in the 15th and 16th centuries. Dominated by the Cerro del Borrego hill, Orizaba today is an industrial city, but it still has some colonial character.

On the corner of the main plaza, Parque Apolinar Castillo, is the 17th-century church **Iglesia de San Miguel**. The **Ex-Palacio Municipal**, also on the plaza, is an ornate Art-Nouveau construction. Built in Belgium in the late 19th century, it was brought over in pieces and reassembled here.

The Neo-Classical **Palacio Municipal**, on Calle Colón, was the base for a workers' education center after the Revolution. It boasts a 1926 mural, *Reconstrucción*, by José Clemente Orozco. Orizaba's **Museo de Arte del Estado** has a fine collection of paintings housed in 10 beautifully restored rooms.

Environs

Pico de Orizaba, Mexico's highest mountain, lies 23 km (14 miles) northwest of Orizaba. A volcano that last erupted in 1546, it is 5,747 m (18,856 ft) high. The Aztecs gave it the name Citlaltépetl, "star mountain," for the way moonlight reflects off its snowy summit.

At the other extreme, the **Sierra de Zongolica**, south of Orizaba, has some of the world's deepest caves.

Museo de Arte del Estado

Corner of 4 Oriente & 23 Sur. **Tel** (272) 724 32 00. **Open** Tue–Sun. Sun free. Tue & Thu: 10am & 5pm.

❽ Córdoba

Veracruz. 197,000. Palacio Municipal, (271) 717 17 00. Expo Feria (May).

Córdoba is a busy, modern town, although traces of its colonial heritage are still to be found around the central Plaza de Armas. Viceroy Diego Fernández de Córdoba ordered the town's construction in 1618 to protect traders on the route between Veracruz and Mexico City from holdups by slaves.

Historically, Córdoba's most significant building is the 18th-century **Portal de Zevallos**, an arcade on the north side of the Plaza de Armas. The Treaties of Córdoba, endorsing Mexican Independence, were signed here in 1829. Also on the plaza are the Neo-Classical **Palacio Municipal** and the **Catedral de la Inmaculada Concepción**, which houses a lifelike image of the town's patron saint, the Virgen de la Soledad (Virgin of Solitude).

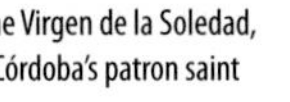

The Virgen de la Soledad, Córdoba's patron saint

Environs

West of Córdoba is the **Barranca de Metlac**, a spectacular gorge spanned by four bridges. One of these, a 19th-century railroad bridge, features in several paintings by artist José María Velasco.

Mexico's highest mountain, Pico de Orizaba, towering above the Gulf Coast

Colorful colonnade-fronted houses in the charming town of Tlacotalpan

❾ Tlacotalpan

Veracruz. 14,000. Palacio Municipal, Plaza Zaragoza, (288) 884 33 05. Candelaria (Feb 2), San Miguelito (Sep 29).

Exploring this delightful town is like turning the clock back 100 years. Its quiet streets are lined with striking houses fronted by colonnades and painted in a flamboyant range of colors. As the Mexican writer Elena Poniatowska puts it, "when we want to smile, we think of Tlacotalpan."

The town is on the banks of the Río Papaloapan ("River of Butterflies"), which is over 300 m (984 ft) wide. Most of the elegant houses, with their Mozarabic-style portals, date from the second half of the 18th century, when large sugar and cotton plantations were established here. Important shipyards were also moved here from Cuba as a direct result of an English blockade of Havana, another Spanish possession, in 1762. During this era, Tlacotalpan was the principal town in southern Veracruz and an important international port, often more in touch with Europe and Cuba than with the rest of Mexico. However, the building of railroad lines left Tlacotalpan without a commercial role. Paradoxically, the isolation that caused its decline has helped preserve this picturesque town.

The **Museo Jarocho Salvador Ferrando** is named after a local artist, and houses many of his portraits and landscapes, painted in the 19th century. Locally made furniture and crafts from the same period are also on display in the museum.

Museo Jarocho Salvador Ferrando
Manuel María Alegre 6. **Tel** (288) 884 24 95. **Open** Tue–Sun.

❿ Santiago Tuxtla

Veracruz. 55,000. San Juan (Jun 24), Santiago (Jul 22–7).

The town of Santiago Tuxtla is a gateway to the world of the ancient Olmecs *(see p258)*, who lived more than 3,000 years ago. A colossal stone head, typical of the Olmec culture, stands in the middle of the town's main square. The largest of the giant heads found so far, it is 3.4 m (11.2 ft) high and weighs around 50 tons. It is the only one of the heads yet discovered to have closed eyes and lacks the realism of the others.

The **Museo Tuxteco**, on one side of the plaza, has an interesting collection of pieces from nearby sites. They include a head called "El Negro," the legendary powers of which were formerly tapped by local witch doctors. Other exhibits include examples of the Olmec practices of skull deformation and tooth sculpting (probably expressions of beauty and class), another colossal head (this one from San Lorenzo Tenochtitlán), and ceremonial and domestic objects made out of jade and stone.

One pre-Columbian custom that lives on in Santiago Tuxtla is the *danza de los liseres*, in which the dancers don the mask of a jaguar deity. It is performed during summer fiestas.

Environs

A 20-km (12-mile) drive through lush, tropical vegetation, along a potholed road, leads to **Tres Zapotes**. This archaeological site was the center of Olmec culture around 400 BC, after

Giant Olmec head in the main square of Santiago Tuxtla

The Witch Doctors of Veracruz

Witch doctors still practice in the state of Veracruz, around San Andrés Tuxtla and Catemaco. Using an assortment of medicinal plants, potions, charms, effigies of saints and devils, dolls with pins stuck in them, and either black or white magic, they will undertake to cure their clients of diseases, help them find a better job, or resolve their marital problems. The practice is hereditary and can be traced back to a distant pre-Columbian past.

A witch doctor with the tools of his trade

Salto de Eyipantla waterfall, near San Andrés Tuxtla

La Venta *(see p258)* had been abandoned. The site itself is now just a series of mounds, but several of the finds are displayed in the museum in Tres Zapotes village nearby.

San Andrés Tuxtla, 14 km (9 miles) east of Santiago Tuxtla, is a sprawling commercial town famous for its cigars. There are fields of tobacco everywhere, and the roadside is lined with stalls selling the finished products.

A 3-km (2-mile) walk from San Andrés Tuxtla along a dirt track leads to the **Laguna Encantada** (Enchanted Lake), so-named because its water level mysteriously rises in the dry season and falls when it rains. Easier to reach, via a paved road that runs through mountains and fields of sugarcane, papaya, tobacco, and bananas, is the **Salto de Eyipantla**, a 50-m (164-ft) high waterfall. Local children act as guides, accompanying visitors down the 244 steps to the bottom of the falls.

Museo Tuxteco
Parque Juárez. **Tel** (294) 947 01 96.
Open Tue–Sun.

11 Laguna de Catemaco

Veracruz. Palacio Municipal, Av Carranza, Catemaco, (294) 943 02 58. Carmen (Jul 16).
catemaco.info

This picturesque lake lies in the crater of an extinct volcano. Its hot, humid climate suits many birds, including parrots and toucans, and its waters also contain a few crocodiles. Boat trips round the lake leave from the wharf in the town of Catemaco and circle the island of **Tanaxpillo**, which is home to a colony of macaque monkeys.

Two ecological parks on the north shore of the lake are accessible by boat or car. The more interesting of these, **Nanciyaga**, is a large swath of tropical rainforest. Visitors to the park can take part in pre-Columbian rituals, such as the *temazcal* (steam bath), or swim in spring-fed pools.

The town of Catemaco itself is dominated by the **Iglesia del Carmen**, a brightly painted church with twin bell towers. The statue of the Virgen del Carmen inside is dripping with jewelry and trinkets left by the many pilgrims who come here.

Environs

Ten of the 17 great Olmec heads so far discovered were found at **San Lorenzo Tenochtitlán**, 37 km (23 miles) southeast of Acayucan. This great Olmec ceremonial center flourished from 1200 BC to 900 BC, when it was destroyed. Most of the objects found here have been removed from the site. However, some of the pieces are on show in three small museums at **Potrero, El Azuzul**, and **Tenochtitlán**. Exhibits at El Azuzul include the sculpture known as *Los Divinos Gemelos* (The Divine Twins).

One of the Divine Twins from San Lorenzo

Nanciyaga
7 km (4.5 miles) NE of Catemaco.
Tel (294) 943 01 99. **Open** daily (Oct: Thu–Tue).

Boat trip around the islands of Laguna de Catemaco

⓬ Comalcalco

Tabasco. Off Mex 187, 58 km (36 miles) NW of Villahermosa. from Comalcalco town, Villahermosa, or Cardenas. **Open** Tue–Sun.

In the lush, green, cocoa-producing area northwest of Villahermosa are the Maya ruins of Comalcalco. Dating mainly from the late Classic period of Maya civilization (AD 700–900), the architecture differs quite markedly from that found at Palenque *(see pp238–41)*, which was occupied around the same time. Unlike Palenque, Comalcalco has structures built from bricks, held together with oyster-shell mortar. The bricks were sometimes incised with figures and glyphs when wet. Comalcalco's main structures are two pyramids, the Gran Acrópolis and the Acrópolis Este, and the North Plaza. Originally many of the site's structures would have been covered in high-relief stucco carvings. Of those that survive today, the most distinctive is a mask of the god El Señor del Sol, near the base of the Gran Acrópolis.

Mask of El Señor del Sol at the base of the Gran Acrópolis in Comalcalco

⓭ Villahermosa

Tabasco. 558,000. Avenida Juan Estrada, (993) 310 97 00. Río Usumacinta Nautical Marathon (Mar/Apr), Tabasco State Fair (Apr/May).

Now the capital of the state of Tabasco, Villahermosa was founded in the late 16th century by a community forced to move inland by repeated pirate attacks. Situated on the banks of the Grijalva River, Villahermosa today is a friendly, bustling city. It has two excellent museums, the **Parque-Museo de La Venta** and the **Museo Regional de Antropología Carlos Pellicer Cámara**. The latter has artifacts from the Olmec, Maya, and other Mesoamerican cultures, including pottery and jade carvings.

Environs

Yum-Ká, an ecological park a short drive east of Villahermosa, is named after a mythical Maya dwarf who protects the jungle. Animals, including the endangered ocelot, manatee, and howler monkey, are found in its 100 hectares (247 acres) of natural habitats.

La Venta, 117 km (73 miles) to the west of Villahermosa, is the site of the most important Olmec settlements. Its principal sculptures are now in the Parque-Museo de La Venta.

Museo Regional de Antropología Carlos Pellicer Cámara
Avenida Carlos Pellicer Cámara 511.
Tel (993) 312 63 44. **Open** Tue–Sun.

Yum-Ká
16 km (10 miles) E of Villahermosa.
Tel (993) 596 67 04. **Open** daily.
yumka.org

An ocelot, one of the endangered species in Yum-Ká ecological park

The Olmecs

Mexico's first notable culture, the Olmec, was established on the hot, humid Gulf Coast by 1200 BC. Often called the *cultura madre* (mother culture) because of their influence on later civilizations, the Olmecs are something of a mystery. Their main sites, at San Lorenzo and La Venta, wielded political, economic, and religious authority over big regions and large numbers of people. The earliest, San Lorenzo *(see p257)*, was systematically destroyed in about 900 BC, although why and by whom is a mystery. About the same time La Venta, farther east, reached the peak of its influence, becoming an important religious and political center and establishing far-flung trade routes. Around the beginning of the first millennium AD Olmec civilization gradually faded into obscurity. Today the most impressive reminders of the ancient culture are the colossal carved stone heads, of which the first to be discovered in modern times was found at Tres Zapotes *(see p256)*. They were fashioned from massive basalt blocks weighing up to 20 tons, which the Olmecs moved large distances, probably using river rafts.

Colossal Olmec head

Parque-Museo de La Venta

For nearly 600 years, from 1000 to 400 BC, the settlement at La Venta was the center of Olmec culture. In the 1950s its treasures were threatened by oil exploration nearby. Tabascan anthropologist Carlos Pellicer organized their rescue and had them installed on the shores of the Laguna de las Ilusiones in Villahermosa. To further protect the Olmec heads, altars, stelae, and mosaics, many pieces have been moved inside a museum and replaced by replicas along the winding jungle paths. Part of the park is a wildlife area, with some animals housed in the archaeological section.

VISITORS' CHECKLIST

Practical Information
Blvd Adolfo Ruíz Cortínes, Villahermosa. **Tel** (993) 314 16 52.
Open daily.

Transport
from Central Camionera or Mercado.

① La Abuela
This kneeling old woman holds a vessel as if in offering.

⑤ Gran Altar
The figure under this monument holds a rope binding the two men, probably captives, carved on its sides.

KEY

① La Abuela (The Grandmother)
② Jaula de Jaguar (Jaguar's Cage)
③ Personajes con Niños (People with Children)
④ Jaguar Humanizado (Human Jaguar)
⑤ Gran Altar (Great Altar)
⑥ Mosaico del Jaguar (Jaguar Mosaic)
⑦ El Rey (The King)
⑧ Cabeza Colosal 1 (Giant Head 1)
⑨ La Diosa Joven (The Young Goddess)

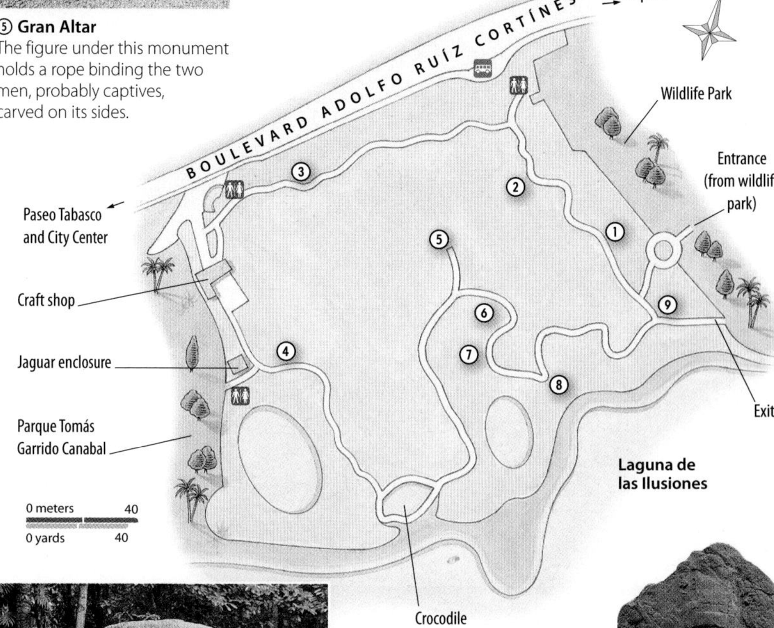

③ Personajes con Niños
Seated in front of this altar, or throne, is an adult figure holding an infant in his arms.

⑦ El Rey
Wearing a tall headdress and carrying a staff across his chest that signifies his power, the figure on this stela was clearly important. He is surrounded by six smaller figures, similarly attired and carrying staves.

Exploring the Yucatán Peninsula

Some of the finest archaeological sites in the Americas are situated on the Yucatán Peninsula. They include the sensational Chichén Itzá and Uxmal, as well as many lesser-known sites such as Cobá, Edzná, Tulum, and Ekbalam. The interior of the peninsula is jungle, some of which is conserved in its natural state, while the Mayan Riviera, on the east coast, has some of Mexico's best beaches. Many people come to the Yucatán to visit the offshore islands of Cozumel and Isla Mujeres and dive or snorkel over the superb coral formations of the Great Mesoamerican Reef, the world's second longest barrier reef. Attractive Spanish colonial architecture can be seen in Campeche, Mérida, Valladolid, and Izamal, and in the Franciscan churches of several towns south of Mérida.

The Ex-Templo de San José in the center of Campeche

Fishing boats on one of the beautiful white-sand beaches of Isla Mujeres

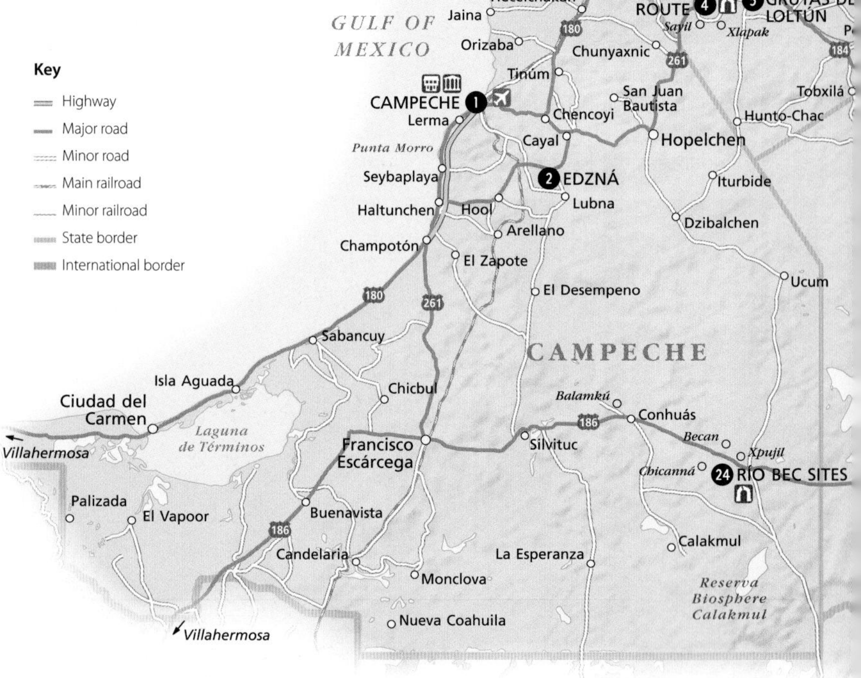

Key

- Highway
- Major road
- Minor road
- Main railroad
- Minor railroad
- State border
- International border

PROGRESO 10
Chicxulub Puerto
Dzidzantun
Sisal
Cansahcab
DZIBILCHALTÚN 9
Motul
Hunucma
MÉRIDA 7
CELESTÚN 8
Uman
Hoctún
Real de Salinas
Tecoh
Yaxcopoil
Mayapán
Maxcanu
Sotuta
Muna
Tekit
Halacho
UXMAL 3
Ticul
6 MANÍ
Kabah
Oxkutzcab
THE PUUC ROUTE 4
5 GRUTAS DE LOLTÚN
Hecelchakán
Jaina
Sayil
Xlapak
GULF OF MEXICO
Orizaba
Chunyaxnic
Tinúm
CAMPECHE 1
San Juan Bautista
Tobxilá
Lerma
Chencoyi
Hunto-Chac
Cayal
Hopelchen
Punta Morro
Seybaplaya
2 EDZNÁ
Iturbide
Haltunchen
Hool
Lubna
Dzibalchen
Arellano
Champotón
El Zapote
Ucum
El Desempeno
Sabancuy
CAMPECHE
Isla Aguada
Chicbul
Ciudad del Carmen
Balamkú
Conhuás
Laguna de Términos
Francisco Escárcega
Silvituc
Becan
Villahermosa
Xpujil
Chicanná
24 RÍO BEC SITES
Palizada
El Vapoor
Buenavista
Calakmul
Candelaria
La Esperanza
Monclova
Reserva Biosphere Calakmul
Nueva Coahuila
Villahermosa

For hotels and restaurants see pp304–5 and pp327–9

Sights at a Glance

1. Campeche
2. Edzná
3. *Uxmal pp266–8*
4. The Puuc Route
5. Grutas de Loltún
6. Maní
7. *Mérida pp274–5*
8. Celestún
9. Dzibilchaltún
10. Progreso
11. Izamal
12. *Chichén Itzá pp278–80*
13. Valladolid
14. Ekbalam
15. Río Lagartos
16. Cancún
17. Isla Mujeres
18. Cozumel
19. Xcaret
20. Cobá
21. Tulum
22. Sian Ka'an Biosphere Reserve
23. Chetumal
24. Río Bec Sites

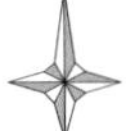

Getting Around

The Yucatán Peninsula has three international airports, Cancún, Mérida, and Campeche, and can be reached from other parts of Mexico by air or long-distance bus. The major roads within the peninsula are well maintained. A toll highway links Cancún and Mérida. Buses are the main form of public transportation in the region, but some of the most remote sights can be reached only by car or on an organized sightseeing tour. Regular car and passenger ferries run to Cozumel and Isla Mujeres.

Tulum, a magnificent late-Maya coastal settlement

For keys to symbols *see back flap*

Vivid exteriors of colonial houses in Campeche city center

❶ Campeche

Campeche. 259,000. Avenida Ruiz Cortines, (800) 226 73 24 or (981) 811 27 33. Carnival (Feb/Mar), Cristo Negro de San Román (Sep 15–30). **campeche.travel**

The Spanish settlement of Campeche was built on the site of a former Maya fishing village in about 1540. In colonial times it was the most important port on the Yucatán Peninsula, exporting timber and roots used to make dyes in European textile production.

Campeche's prosperity made it a frequent target for attacks by English, French, and Dutch pirates, who harassed ships in the area, and looted and destroyed the city several times. The worst attack, in 1663, resulted in the massacre of many of the city's inhabitants. As a consequence, thick walls were built around the town. These were strengthened by eight *baluartes* (bastions), seven of which have been put to other uses and can be visited. The largest of them, in the middle of the stretch of wall facing the sea, is the **Baluarte de la Soledad**. It is now a museum displaying an important collection of Maya stelae *(see p237)*, many of which were found at the Maya burial ground on the island of Jaina, 40 km (25 miles) to the north of Campeche. The **Baluarte de Santiago**, at the northwestern corner of the walls, has been transformed into a walled botanical garden containing over 200 species of subtropical plants. On the landward side of the walls, the **Baluarte de San Pedro** sells a small selection of regional handicrafts.

Jade mask, in Fuerte de San Miguel

Two gateways in the walls – the **Sea Gate** and the **Land Gate** – give access to the old part of the city. Between them runs Calle 59, on which stand several restored, single-story colonial houses, painted in bright blues, pinks, and ochers. One of the finest buildings is the **Casa de Teniente del Rey** (King's Lieutenant's House), the former residence of the Spanish king's military representative in the Yucatán. Transformed into offices, the house has a splendid courtyard, which can be visited.

The focal point of the old part of Campeche is the main square, the **Parque Principal**, which has elegant arcades and an elaborate, modern bandstand. Tours of the city in open-sided trams start from here. In the northern corner of the square is the **cathedral**, one of the first churches built on the Yucatán mainland, although much of the present building was constructed later, in the Baroque style. Behind it, on Calle 10, is the **Mansión Carvajal**, now divided into government offices. This building is a good example of 19th-century Spanish-Moorish architecture. Another attractive building in the city center is the **Ex-Templo de San José**, a former Jesuit church, now used as a cultural center, which has an elaborate façade of blue and yellow tiles.

Campeche's defenses were completed by two forts on hills outside the city, both now museums. Situated to the north is the **Museo Histórico Reducto**

Tiled doorway of the Ex-Templo de San José, now a cultural center

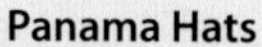

Panama Hats

The town of Becal, between Campeche and Mérida, is renowned for its production of Panama hats. Known locally as *jipis*, they received their common name when they became popular with workers building the Panama canal. The palm leaves used to make the hats are split and braided in caves, where the heat and humidity make the fibers more flexible. The finest hats *(finos)* have a smooth and silky feel and can be rolled up so tightly that they are able to pass through a man's wedding ring, and then regain their former shape.

Monument to the Panama hat in the main square of Becal

The Edificio de los Cinco Pisos (Building of the Five Levels) at Edzná

San José El Alto, with exhibits on colonial military history. To the south of the city is the **Fuerte de San Miguel**, begun in 1771 and protected by a moat crossed by a drawbridge. Exhibits inside this fort include distinctive jade masks from Calakmul *(see p291)*, and ceramic figurines from the island of Jaina.

On the way to the Fuerte de San Miguel is the **Iglesia de San Román**, the city's most popular shrine. It is famous for its large black ebony statue of Christ, which is believed to possess miraculous powers.

Stucco mask on the Templo de los Mascarones, Edzná

Baluarte de la Soledad
Calle 8 Circuito Baluartes (seaward side). **Tel** (981) 816 91 36. **Open** Tue–Sun.

Casa de Teniente del Rey
Calle 59 No. 40, corner of Calle 14. **Tel** (981) 816 91 11. **Open** daily.

Museo Histórico Reducto
Avenida Morazan. **Open** Tue–Sun.

Fuerte de San Miguel
Avenida Escénica. **Open** Tue–Sun.

❷ Edzná

Campeche. Mex 180 and 186, 60 km (37 miles) SE of Campeche. (981) 816 91 11. from Campeche. **Open** daily.

A sophisticated and extensive canal system radiates out from the center of this Maya settlement to the agricultural areas beyond. The canals were primarily used for the transportation of goods, but quite possibly also served a defensive purpose. Edzná may have been founded in around 600 BC, and in its heyday between AD 600 and 900 it is thought to have had a population of 25,000. The main structure is the Gran Acrópolis, which is dominated by the Edificio de los Cinco Pisos (Building of the Five Levels). Another building of interest is the Templo de los Mascarones (Temple of the Masks), named after its distinctive stucco mask.

Fiestas of the Yucatán

Equinoxes *(Mar 21 and Sep 21)*, Chichén Itzá. An optical illusion created by the ancient Maya can be seen when the sun casts a shadow on the north side of El Castillo *(see p280)*, making a "snake" move down the steps behind each of the two stone serpent heads at the base.

The stepped El Castillo pyramid, at Chichén Itzá

Carnival *(Feb/Mar)*, *(see p37)*. Celebrated in most parts of the Yucatán, but particularly in Campeche *(see p264)*. In many villages, a papier-mâché figure of "Juan Carnaval" is paraded through the streets, put in a coffin, and symbolically burned to conclude the festivities.

Cristo de las Ampollas *(Sep 27)*, Mérida. Festivities and processions in honor of "Christ of the Blisters," a wooden statue made in Ichmul and later moved to Mérida cathedral *(see p274)*. The statue is said to have blackened and blistered as skin would, rather than burned, in a fire at Ichmul's parish church.

Fuerte de San Miguel, once an integral part of Campeche's defenses against naval attack

❸ Uxmal

The late-Classic Maya site of Uxmal ("thrice built") is one of the most complex and harmonious expressions of Puuc architecture *(see p272)*. The city's history is uncertain, but most of the buildings date from the 7th–10th centuries AD, when Uxmal dominated the region. The real function of many of the structures is unknown, and they retain the fanciful names given to them by the Spanish. Unlike most Yucatán sites, Uxmal has no cenotes *(see p279)*, and water was collected in man-made cisterns *(chultunes)*, one of which can be seen near the entrance. The scarcity of water may explain the number of depictions of the rain god Chac on the buildings.

View of the Nunnery Quadrangle and Magician's Pyramid from the south

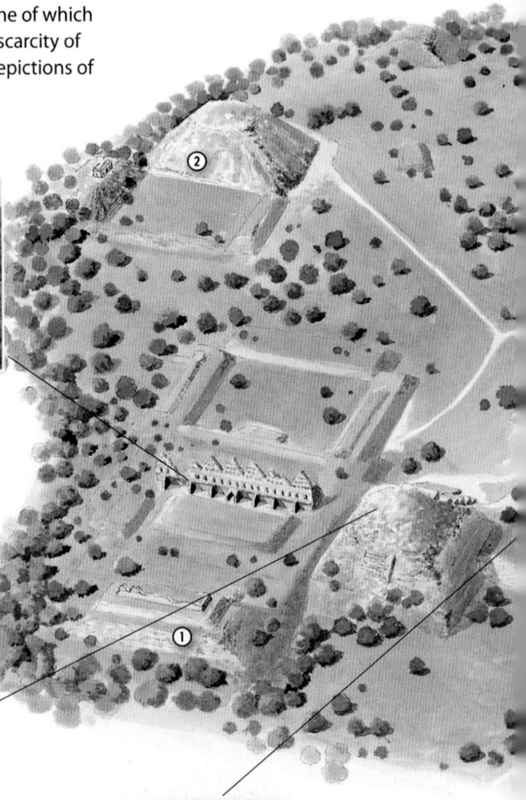

Dovecote
Named after its unusual roof comb, this ruined palace faces a rectangular garden and is one of Uxmal's most evocative and peaceful spots.

Great Pyramid
A stairway climbs the 30-m (100-ft) pyramid to a temple decorated with Chac masks and macaws, the latter associated with fire, suggesting it was a temple to the sun.

★ Governor's Palace
Regarded as the masterpiece of Puuc architecture, the 9th–10th-century palace is actually three buildings linked by Maya arches. The distinctive hooked noses of the Chac masks stand out against the mosaic frieze that runs the length of the structure.

KEY

① South Temple
② Cemetery Group
③ Ballcourt
④ Pyramid of the Old Woman

★ Nunnery Quadrangle
This impressive structure was given its unlikely name because the Spanish thought that the 74 small rooms set around a central courtyard looked like the cells of a nunnery. The stone latticework, ornate masks of Chac, and carved serpents on the walls are remarkable examples of closely fitting mosaic.

VISITORS' CHECKLIST

Practical Information
Yucatán. Mex 261, 78 km (48 miles) S of Mérida. (999) 944 00 43. **Open** 8am–5pm daily.

Transport
Tours from Mérida.

Entrance to site

★ Magician's Pyramid
The spectacular pyramid (seen here through an arch in front) is, at 35 m (115 ft), the tallest structure at Uxmal. Begun in the sixth century AD, it was added to over the next 400 years *(see p268)*.

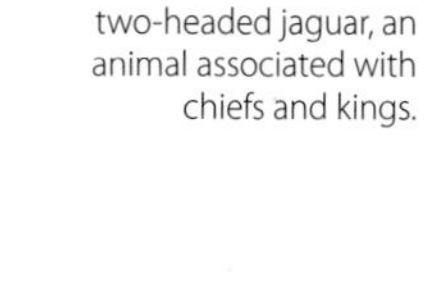

Jaguar Throne
This throne is carved as a two-headed jaguar, an animal associated with chiefs and kings.

0 meters 100
0 yards 100

House of the Turtles
The upper level of this elegant rectangular building is simply decorated with columns and, above them, a frieze of small turtles in procession around the building. Their presence suggests that it might have been dedicated to a water god.

The Magician's Pyramid

Tall, steep, and set on an unusual oval base, the Magician's Pyramid is the most striking of Uxmal's monuments. Legend tells that it was built in one night by a dwarf with supernatural powers – the magician – but, in fact, it shows five phases of construction from the 6th–10th centuries AD. At each phase a new temple was built, either on top of or obscuring the previous one. There are thus five temples on the pyramid. Unfortunately, visitors are no longer allowed to climb to the summit, to prevent further erosion.

View of the pyramid showing the west staircase and facades of Temples I and IV

The facade of Temple IV is actually an expressive Chac mask with large rectangular eyes and a curling moustache. Its wide-open, toothed mouth forms the entrance. Temple III is behind Temple IV.

Temple V is part of the final phase of construction – which took place around AD 1000 – and appears to be a small-scale reproduction of the nearby Governor's Palace *(see p266)*. It obscures the original roof comb on top of Temples II and III.

The east staircase provides access to Temple II, which is just a dark room today.

Entrance to Temple IV

Chac masks on facade of Temple I

Entrance to Temple I (now blocked)

Temple I was built in the sixth century AD, according to the results of radiocarbon dating, and is now covered by the pyramid. Partially collapsed, it is filled with rubble and cannot be visited.

Reconstruction of the Magician's Pyramid

This shows how the pyramid looked around AD 1000. The surface was probably painted red, with details in blue, yellow, and black. The colors and plaster have now eroded to reveal the limestone beneath.

The west staircase, at the front of the pyramid, is flanked by representations of Chac, the rain god. The staircase is extremely steep and ascends the pyramid at an angle of 60°, meaning that the climb to the summit was very difficult.

The Gods of Ancient Mexico

A vast array of gods and goddesses were worshiped by the civilizations of ancient Mesoamerica *(see pp 48–9)*. Some of them related to celestial bodies, such as the stars, sun, and moon. Some had calendrical significance. Others held sway over creation, death, and the different aspects of daily life. Frequently gods were passed from one civilization to another, usually changing their names in the process. These deities were feared as much as revered. If they had created the world, and ran it, they could just as easily destroy it. It was therefore essential to appease them as much as possible, often through human sacrifice.

Rain Gods

Abundant rainfall was vital to farming communities, and rain and lightning gods were venerated in all the civilizations of ancient Mexico.

Tlaloc was the central Mexican god of rain and lightning. He can be recognized by his goggle-like eyes and jaguar teeth, as in this sculpture from Teotihuacán *(see pp138–41)*.

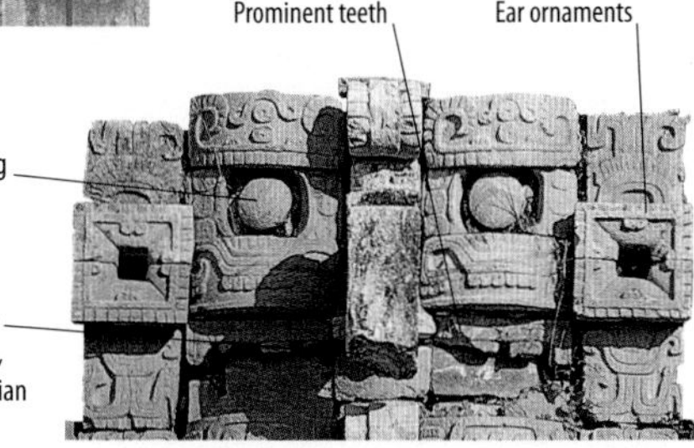

Chac, the Maya god of rain and lightning, was often represented on buildings. The mask seen here is from a palace at Kabah in the Yucatán *(see p272)*.

Quetzalcoatl

The most famous Mexican god was Quetzalcoatl (called Kukulcan by the Maya). A plumed or feathered serpent, he was a combination of quetzal bird and rattlesnake. The first carvings of him were made by the Olmecs. Subsequent representations of Quetzalcoatl/Kukulcan can be seen at many ancient sites; this bas-relief is on the Pyramid of the Plumed Serpent at Xochicalco *(see p149)*.

Tonacatecuhtli

Creator Gods

Mesoamerican societies had differing accounts of creation. According to one myth from central Mexico, Tonacatecuhtli resided in the 13th, or uppermost, heaven with Tonacacihuatl, his consort. From here they sent down souls of children to be born on earth.

The Sun God

This deity was associated with the jaguar in ancient Mexico, an animal that evoked the vigor and power of the rising sun. The Classic and Postclassic Maya venerated Kinich Ahau, the "great sun" or "sun-eyed" lord, seen here as a huge mask at Kohunlich *(see p291)*.

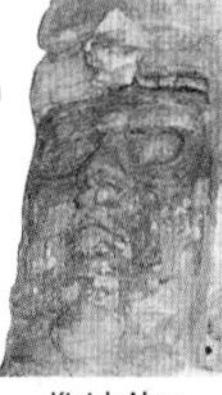

Kinich Ahau

Gods of the Underworld

Only those who suffered violent death went directly to one of the heavens. All other mortal souls were condemned to descend the nine levels of the underworld. In Aztec mythology, the soul had to pass through a series of hazards before reaching the deepest of these levels, the dreaded Mictlan, ruled over by Mictlantecuhtli and his consort Mictecacihuatl. The Aztecs depicted their god of death as a frightening skeletal figure, such as this one unearthed at the Templo Mayor in Mexico City *(see pp72–4)*.

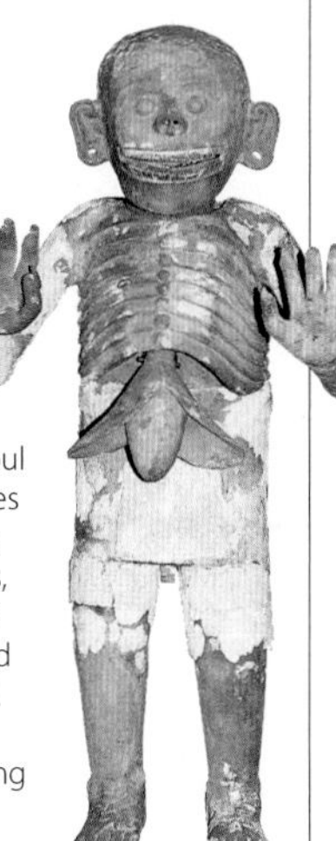

Mictlantecuhtli, Aztec god of death

Kabah's palace, the Codz Poop, ornamented with hundreds of Chac masks

❹ The Puuc Route

Yucatán. Starts from Mex 261, 20 km (12 miles) SE of Uxmal. tours from Mérida. All sites: **Open** daily.

Forming a low ridge across the western part of the Yucatán, about 100 km (62 miles) south of Mérida, the Puuc hills provide a welcome relief from the flat monotony of the rest of the peninsula.

Despite a lack of water, they offered a strong defensive position for the ancient Maya people, as well as good soil for cultivating maize, squash, and other vegetables. Several Maya settlements have been discovered in the region. All are believed to have reached their peaks from about AD 600 to AD 900 and they share the striking style of architecture and ornamentation that has become known as the Puuc style. This style is characterized by a façade which has plain walls at the base and detailed stone mosaic masks (often depicting gods) on its upper sections.

Some settlements are linked to each other and to the contemporary site of Uxmal *(see pp266–8)* by *sacbeob*, or "white roads," which were mainly used for ceremonial purposes.

The Puuc Route runs through four Maya sites, starting with **Kabah**. The main building here is the Codz Poop. The façade of this palace is decorated with more than 250 masks representing the rain god Chac *(see p269)*, with his distinctive hooked nose. Kabah was the closest settlement to the important Maya city of Uxmal. A single, undecorated arch straddles the entrance road.

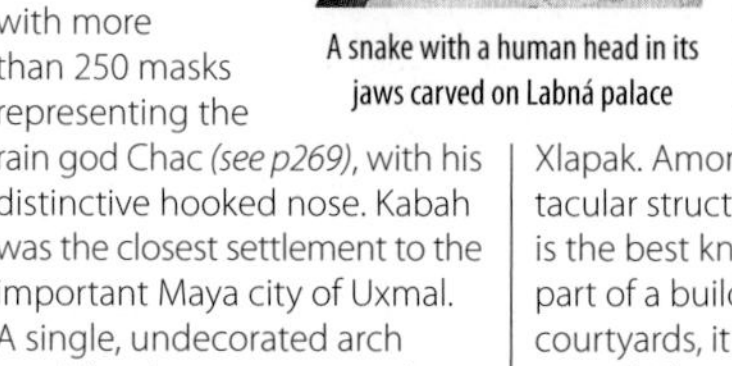

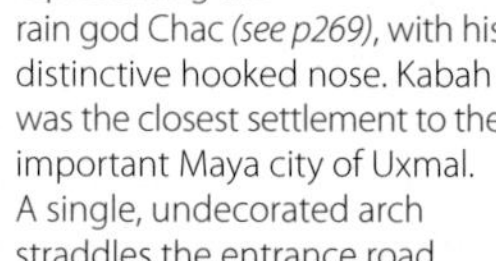

A snake with a human head in its jaws carved on Labná palace

Of all the Puuc sites, **Sayil**, around 10 km (6 miles) south of Kabah, is the one that provides most evidence of how the Maya in this area lived. Around the edge of the site, many of the ordinary dwellings have been excavated, as have the homes of the settlement's ruling elite, located in the central area. It is hard to envisage today, but the excavations suggest that Sayil was once populated by more than 8,000 people, with a similar number living in small, outlying communities surrounding the city. The huge three-tiered palace of Sayil's rulers is a splendid example of the rich Puuc style.

Sayil has no accessible supply of surface water, but several *chultunes*, large manmade cisterns for storing water, have been found at the site.

About 8 km (5 miles) east of Sayil is **Xlapak**. The best-preserved building here is the palace, which has masks of Chac, the rain god, above its entrances. Details such as a frieze of columns stand out on other buildings, but much of this site has yet to be cleared.

The last settlement on the Puuc Route is **Labná**, 5 km (3 miles) to the northeast of Xlapak. Among several spectacular structures here, the Arch is the best known. Originally part of a building between two courtyards, it is adorned with several Chac masks and two

The magnificent three-tiered palace in Sayil, with its frieze of small columns

◀ The beautiful stone friezes of the Uxmal Maya ruins in Yucatán

El Mirador (The Observatory) in Labná, crowned by a 4-m (13-ft) crest

representations of thatched Maya huts. Nearby is a structure with a high crest above its façade. Known as El Mirador (The Observatory), it may have been a temple.

At the other end of the site is the main two-story palace, which has a frieze of masks and latticework. On one corner of the palace is a powerful carving of a serpent's head with a human head in its jaws.

Another impressive structure is the Temple of Columns, which has a frieze around it, decorated with small columns.

5 Grutas de Loltún

Yucatán. Off Mex 180, 20 km (12 miles) SW of Maní. tours from Mérida. **Open** daily.

Visitors are taken on a tour that travels more than 1 km (half a mile) through the Grutas de Loltún, the longest cave system in the Yucatán. The earliest remains discovered here are bison, mammoth, and other animal bones, suggesting that Loltún was inhabited soon after the last Ice Age. The caves contain fascinating wall paintings from various periods of occupation. These include stylized humans and animals, and the superb Warrior of Loltún. However, the most striking features of the caves are the stalagmites and stalactites that give them the name Loltún, meaning "stone flowers."

6 Maní

Yucatán. 4,800. Fiesta tradicional (Aug 20).

From the fourth decade of the 16th century, Catholic priests, and in particular Franciscan friars, came from Spain to convert the Maya population of the Yucatán Peninsula. They constructed a network of huge, fortress-like churches and monasteries, often on the sites of earlier Maya temples. The most imposing of these is the **Iglesia de San Miguel Arcángel**, which dominates the town of Maní. It has a vast atrium, an open chapel, and a monastery with 114 cells. It was constructed by around 6,000 slaves on ground that was already holy to the Maya – a Maya cenote (natural well) is visible under the front of the church.

Part of the beautiful altarpiece in Maní's Franciscan church

Environs

Other Franciscan churches can be found in the towns all around Maní. Built in 1693–9, the church in Oxkutzcab, 10 km (6 miles) to the south, has a lovely Baroque altarpiece. The Iglesia de San Pedro Apóstol in Teabo, east of Maní, was begun in 1694, and traces of Franciscan murals can still be seen in its powder-blue interior. The road north out of Teabo leads through Tekit, which also has a Franciscan church, to Tecoh. The church here houses a huge red and blue wooden altarpiece and a beautiful wooden cross with the last hours of Christ's life painted on it.

Between Tekit and Tecoh is **Mayapán**, which became the Maya capital in the north of the peninsula after the fall of Chichén Itzá. Abandoned in the mid-15th century, Mayapán's most remarkable surviving feature is the pyramid of Kukulcan, which is built on nine levels and topped with a temple.

Iglesia de la Candelaria, Tecoh's Franciscan church

Mayapán

60 km (37 miles) N of Maní. **Tel** (999) 944 00 33. **Open** daily.

7 Mérida

The conquistador Francisco de Montejo the Younger founded this city in 1542 on the ruins of a large Maya settlement. He named it Mérida because it reminded him of the ruined Roman city of the same name in Spain. An important city during Spanish colonial rule, Mérida rose to prominence again at the turn of the 20th century when it enjoyed an economic boom, based on sales of locally grown sisal for rope-making. In the early 1900s, Mérida was said to have more millionaires per head of population than anywhere else in the world. This prosperity is reflected in its grand mansions, squares, parks, and statues. Modern Mérida is an important manufacturing city, and also a university, business, and cultural center.

The lofty interior of the grand Catedral de San Ildefonso

The Palacio Municipal on the Plaza Mayor

Exploring Mérida

Mérida is built on a grid system based around the main square, the Plaza Mayor (also known as the Plaza Grande or Plaza de la Independencia). In the evenings, and on Sundays, dancing and concerts take place outside the city hall, the **Palacio Municipal**. This building is in a mix of styles and has a notable 1920s clock tower.

The **Casa de Montejo** *(see p28)*, on the south side of the plaza, was built between 1543 and 1549 as the palace of the first Spanish governors. Now a bank, it still has its original portico, with the Montejo family coat of arms.

East of the Plaza Mayor lies Mérida's historic post office, now the **Museo de la Ciudad** with exhibits on the city's colonial past as well as contemporary artworks. Opposite the city hall is the **cathedral**, the oldest in the Americas. It was begun in the early 1560s, and finished in 1598. Three arched doors in the imposing façade lead to a soaring interior with a barreled roof and crisscross arches. There is a huge wooden sculpture of Christ behind the main altar.

Another wooden statue, *Cristo de las Ampollas* (Christ of the Blisters, *see p265)*, stands in a small chapel on the right. It is a copy of a statue that was brought to Mérida after miraculously surviving a fire. The original, which was later destroyed, is said to have developed blisters, as skin would, instead of burning.

The 19th-century **Palacio de Gobierno** houses the Yucatán state authorities. It is remarkable for the numerous large murals adorning its courtyard, stairs, and first-floor lobby. They were painted in the 1970s by Fernando Castro Pacheco, a local artist, and show his vision of Yucatán history from the time of the first Maya to the 19th century.

Just off Calle 60, one of the city's major roads, is **Parque Cepeda Peraza (Parque Hidalgo)**, a small but bustling square. Visitors can watch the many musicians and street merchants, or relax in one of the open-air cafés. The imposing Jesuit church, the **Templo de la Tercera Orden** (Temple of the Third Order), on the north side of the square, dates from the 17th century. It has a huge entrance and two narrow bell towers. Inside, the gold altar and friezes of biblical scenes are the only decoration.

Mérida prides itself on being the cultural capital of the Yucatán Peninsula, and the **Teatro José Peón Contreras** is one of its main showcases. Built at the turn of the 20th century, it is an extravagant Neo-Classical creation in beige and white, with elaborate chandeliers in its massive foyer.

The small **Iglesia de Santa Lucía**, one of the earliest and most harmonious of the city's churches, is where the local Maya Indians were encouraged to come and worship.

A mural by Fernando Castro Pacheco, in the Palacio de Gobierno

The Arco de San Juan, one of eight city entrances built by the Spanish

Across the street, the Parque Santa Lucía is used for dancing and cultural events, and has a flea market on Sundays. Bronze busts placed on tall, white columns lining one corner of the park honor *Yucateco* musicians and songwriters. Farther south, on Calle 64, the **Arco de San Juan** stands west of the Plaza Mayor, arguably the finest of eight arches, three of which remain today.

Farther north, the **Paseo Montejo** stretches for several kilometers. It is lined with the elegant town mansions of rich henequen or sisal plantation owners and the private banks that prospered in the late 19th century. Many of the houses were built by Italian architects and are a medley of Neo-Classical elements. One of the finest, the Palacio Cantón, houses the excellent **Museo Regional de Antropología**. Its pre-Columbian exhibits include a jaguar throne from Uxmal *(see pp266–8)*, a *chacmool* from Chichén Itzá *(see pp278–80)*, and fine examples of Mayan funerary offerings.

At the northern end of the Paseo Montejo is the **Monumento a la Patria** (Monument to the Fatherland), an elaborate 20th-century work by Colombian sculptor Rómulo Rozo. The striking monument shows historical figures and animal sculptures, and encloses an eternal flame, a symbol of Mexico's independence.

Detail, Monumento a la Patria

VISITORS' CHECKLIST

Practical Information
Yucatán. 1,000,000.
Calle 62, between calles 61 & 63 (Palacio Municipal). Cristo de las Ampollas (Sep 27).
yucatan.travel
merida.gob.mx/turismo

Transport
5 km (3 miles) S. Calle 70 No. 555, between calles 69 & 71, (999) 942 00 00.

Environs

Situated a short drive south-west of Mérida, **Hacienda Yaxcopoil**, a mansion surrounded by a henequen plantation, is now a museum providing a view into life on a hacienda *(see pp54–5)*.

Museo Regional de Antropología Palacio Cantón
Paseo Montejo 485. **Tel** (999) 923 05 57. **Open** Tue–Sun. in advance.

Hacienda Yaxcopoil
Yaxcopoil, 35 km (22 miles) SW of Mérida. **Tel** (999) 900 11 93. **Open** daily.
yaxcopoil.com

Mérida City Center

1. Palacio Municipal
2. Casa de Montejo
3. Museo de la Ciudad
4. Cathedral
5. Palacio de Gobierno
6. Parque Cepeda Peraza
7. Templo de la Tercera Orden
8. Teatro José Peón Contreras
9. Iglesia de Santa Lucía
10. Paseo Montejo
11. Museo Regional de Antropología

For keys to symbols *see back flap*

8 Celestún

Yucatán.  6,000.

The small fishing village of Celestún is situated on a spit of land almost entirely separated from the mainland. Several kilometers of palm-fringed beaches line the coast to the west of the village, but it is the flamingos on the estuary to the east that attract most of the visitors. Boats can be hired to get closer to the birds, which include pelicans and various waders, as well as flamingos. However, strict environmental laws now prohibit anyone from disturbing the birds, so it is a good idea to bring a pair of field glasses with you so that you can see their natural behavior up close.

Pink flamingos in the estuary

Other excursions on small launches are available, depending on weather conditions, including visits to the *bosque petrificado*, a forest of petrified wood. This surreal, desolate place, on the Isla de Pájaros to the south of Celestún, was created by prolonged salinization.

9 Dzibilchaltún

Yucatán. Off Mex 261, 15 km (9 miles) N of Mérida. (999) 944 00 43. from Mérida. **Open** daily.

Literally the "place with writing on flat stones," Dzibilchaltún was one of the most important centers in pre-Columbian Yucatán, and one of the earliest to be built. However, it was explored only in the 1940s, making it one of the latest to be rediscovered.

The site is arranged concentrically. A *sacbe*, or "white road," leads from the central plaza to the impressive Temple of the Seven Dolls. This building is named after the tiny clay dolls found buried in front of its altar. Several of the dolls have deformities, and are thought to be associated with rituals.

The cenote at Dzibilchaltún, a good place for a refreshing swim

Replicas are displayed in the ultra-modern and well laid-out museum. Other notable exhibits include the stelae and sculptures in the gardens leading up to the museum, ceramic figures, wooden altarpieces from the colonial era, and an attractive display on the pirates who plagued the seas around the Yucatán coast in the 16th and 17th centuries. Interactive screens and audio-visual commentaries provide information about the ancient Maya world view, the Maya today, and the history of the henequen industry.

The remains of a Franciscan chapel built of Maya masonry, probably at the end of the 16th century, are also worth seeing. This open chapel, where the monks preached to the local Indians, is still standing.

The Temple of the Seven Dolls in Dzibilchaltún

Dzibilchaltún's cenote, a natural turquoise pool more than 40 m (130 ft) deep, is a refreshing place for a swim after visiting the other sights. Many artifacts have been recovered from its depths.

10 Progreso

Yucatán. 37,000. Calle 80, between Calles 25 & 27, (969) 935 22 99.

Situated on the north Yucatán coast, Progreso was once an important port. With the construction of the railroad linking the port to Mérida in the 1880s, it experienced a boom that is hard to imagine now as one approaches the relaxed, low-lying town past mangrove swamps.

Progreso has probably the longest stone pier in the world, often bustling with people. Near its landward end is an attractive 19th-century lighthouse. On the town front, by the narrow sandy beach, are many good seafood restaurants. Several cruise liners stop in Progreso, and there are a number of ocean-front resorts, making the town popular with people from the north looking for a warmer winter.

Progreso's stone pier, thought to be the longest in the world

For hotels and restaurants see pp304–5 and pp327–9

Izamal's imposing Convento de San Antonio de Padua, built by Franciscan monks from Spain

⓫ Izamal

Yucatán. 24,400.
Cristo de Sitilpeth (Oct 18), Virgen de la Inmaculada (Dec 7–8).
yucatan.travel

Once as important a site as Chichén Itzá, Izamal is believed to have been founded around AD 300. The original village grew into an influential city-state and, by AD 800, it was governing the surrounding region. Modern Izamal is a fascinating combination of Maya remains and Spanish colonial buildings. There are around 20 Classic Maya structures still standing. Chief among these is the pyramid K'inich K'ak' Mo', named after the ruler "Great-Sun Fire Macaw." It is one of the largest pyramids in the Yucatán.

The importance of Izamal had declined by the time the Spanish arrived in the mid-16th century, but it retained enough religious influence for the Franciscan monks to construct the spectacular Convento de San Antonio de Padua here. They demolished a Maya temple and built the church on its massive platform base, giving it an elevated position. The huge atrium is surrounded by open cloisters, and contains some early Franciscan frescoes.

The church acquired even more importance when Bishop Diego de Landa installed in it a statue of the Virgen de la Inmaculada, which he had brought from Guatemala. This was immediately attributed with miraculous powers by the local Maya population, and in 1949 the Virgin was adopted as the patron saint of the Yucatán. A small museum in the church commemorates Pope John Paul II's visit to Izamal in 1993, the International Year of Indigenous People, when he pledged the Catholic Church's support for the Maya Indians. Adjacent to the church are two pretty arcaded squares. Here, and in the surrounding streets of low Spanish colonial houses, most of the buildings' façades are painted a glowing ocher color. This led to Izamal being nicknamed La Ciudad Amarilla, literally "The Yellow City."

The massive Maya pyramid, K'inich K'ak' Mo', in Izamal

Hammocks

Brightly colored hammocks are a common sight in the markets of Campeche, Mérida, and Izamal. Probably introduced to Mexico by Spanish colonists from the Caribbean, they are now used for sleeping by many Mexicans in the Yucatán region. The hammocks are traditionally made from twine produced from henequen, a type of fibrous agave plant that can be seen growing all over the Yucatán Peninsula (though modern hammocks tend to be made from cotton or silk). The leaves are cut from the spiky plants, shredded into long fibers, and then dried. The fibers can be dyed and braided, or woven into twine or rope. Other products made from henequen include mats and bags.

Traditional hammocks for sale in Mérida

⓬ Chichén Itzá

The best preserved Maya site on the peninsula, Chichén Itzá confounds historians. The date of first settlement in the southern part of the site is not certain, but the northern section was built during a renaissance in the 11th century AD. Similarities with Tula *(see p148)*, and myths that tell how exiled Toltec god-king Quetzalcoatl (Kukulcan) settled at Chichén Itzá, suggest that the renaissance was due to a Toltec invasion. However, other theories hold that Tula was influenced by the Maya, not vice versa. In its heyday as a commercial, religious, and military center, which lasted until about the 13th century, Chichén Itzá supported over 35,000 people. In 2007 it was voted one of the New Seven Wonders of the World.

★ Ballcourt
At 168 m (550 ft) in length, this is the largest ballcourt in Mesoamerica. Still in place are the two engraved rings that the ball had to pass through *(see p281)*.

Nunnery
So named because its small rooms reminded the Spaniards of nuns' cells, this large structure, built in three stages, was probably a palace. The facade of the east annex (seen here) has particularly beautiful stone fretwork and carvings.

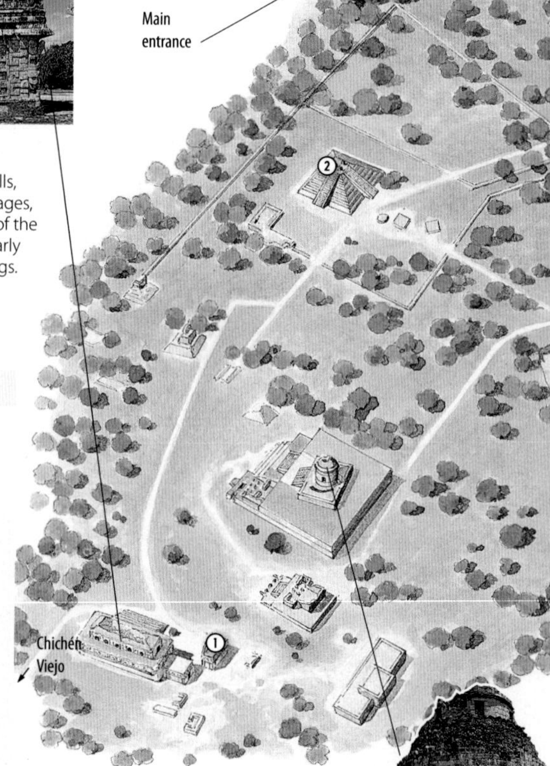

KEY

① **The Church**, or Iglesia, is decorated with fretwork, masks of the rain god Chac, and the *bacabs* – four animals who, in Maya myth, held up the sky.

② **Tomb of the High Priest**

③ **The Tzompantli** is a low platform whose perimeter is carved with grinning skulls. Archaeologists believe that it was used to display the heads of victims of human sacrifice, practiced during Chichén Itzá's late period.

④ **Platform of the Jaguars and Eagles**

⑤ **The Group of a Thousand Columns**, made up of carved stone colonnades on two sides of a huge plaza, may have been used as a market.

★ Observatory
Also called El Caracol (The Snail) for its spiral staircase, this building was an astronomical observatory *(see p51)*. The various slits in the walls correspond to the positions of certain celestial bodies on key dates in the Maya calendar.

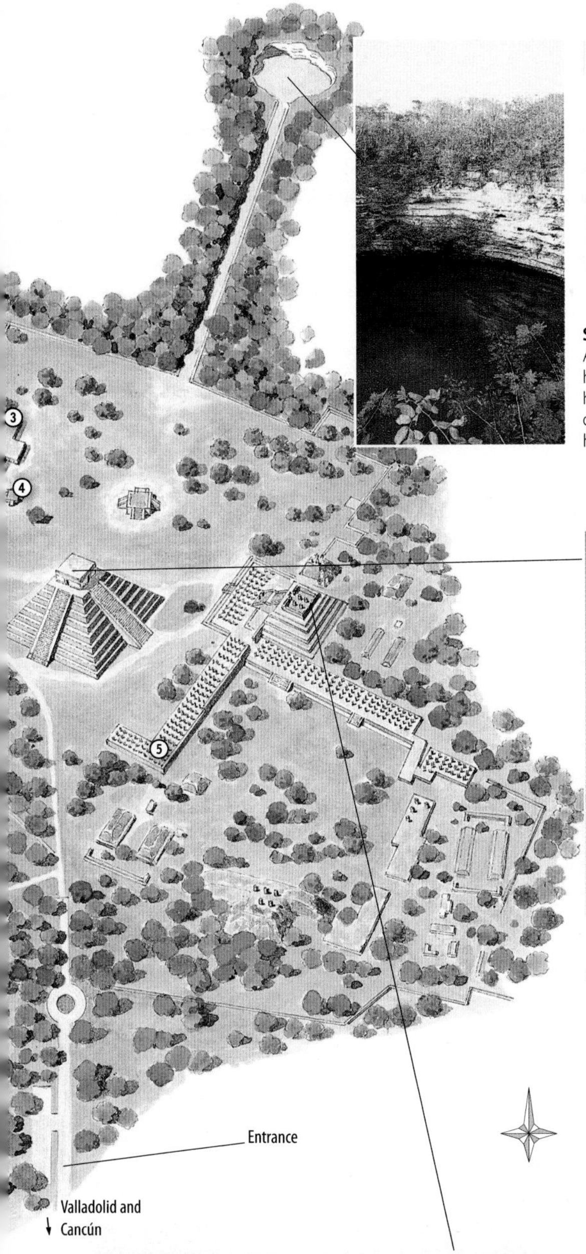

VISITORS' CHECKLIST

Practical Information
Yucatán. Off Mex 180, 40 km (25 miles) W of Valladolid. **Tel** (985) 851 01 37. **Open** daily. **chichenitza.inah.gob.mx**

Transport
from Valladolid, Mérida, Playa del Carmen, or Cancún.

Sacred Cenote
A *sacbe* (White road) leads to this huge natural well, thought to have been revered as the home of rain god Chac, and used for human sacrifice.

3

4

5

★ El Castillo
Built on top of an older structure, this 24-m (79-ft) high pyramid *(see p280)* was dedicated to Kukulcan, the Maya representation of the god Quetzalcoatl. Its height and striking geometric design dominate the whole site.

Entrance

Valladolid and Cancún

0 meters 150
0 yards 150

Temple of the Warriors
Set on a small pyramid, this temple is decorated with sculptures of the rain god Chac and the plumed serpent Kukulcan. A *chacmool (see p48)*, and two columns carved to represent snakes, guard the entrance.

El Castillo

The most awe-inspiring structure at Chichén Itzá is the pyramid known as El Castillo (The Castle), built around AD 800. It has a perfect astronomical design: four staircases face the cardinal points, various features correspond to aspects of the Maya calendar *(see pp50–51)*, and, twice yearly at sunrise, a fascinating optical illusion occurs on the north staircase *(see p265)*. Continuing excavations on the eastern side allow visitors to watch the painstaking process of archaeology as it reveals that the pyramid was built on the remains of a much older settlement.

View of El Castillo from beside the Platform of the Jaguars and Eagles

Reconstruction of El Castillo

This shows how the pyramid would have looked on completion. It was originally covered in plaster and painted a vivid red.

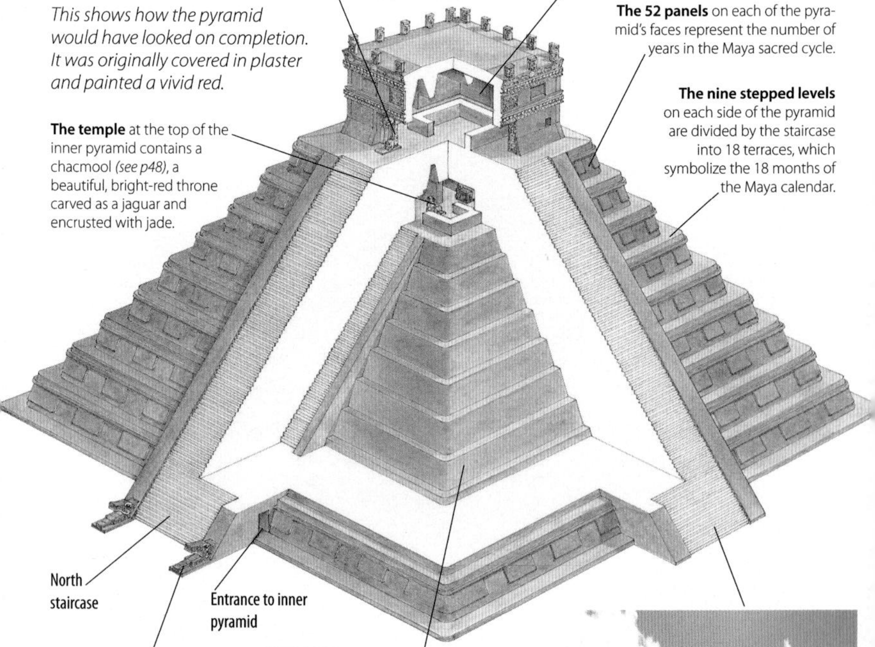

Temple entrance, divided by snake-shaped columns

Temple of Kukulcán

The 52 panels on each of the pyramid's faces represent the number of years in the Maya sacred cycle.

The nine stepped levels on each side of the pyramid are divided by the staircase into 18 terraces, which symbolize the 18 months of the Maya calendar.

The temple at the top of the inner pyramid contains a chacmool *(see p48)*, a beautiful, bright-red throne carved as a jaguar and encrusted with jade.

North staircase

Entrance to inner pyramid

Inner pyramid

Two serpents' heads at the foot of the north staircase are thought to represent the god Kukulcan, the Maya Quetzalcóatl. At the two yearly equinoxes, the play of light and shadow on the staircase makes them appear to crawl up the pyramid.

The four staircases of the pyramid are each made up of 91 steps. Together with the temple platform at the top, they make a total of 365 steps, the number of days in the year. Since the site was designated as one of the new seven wonders of the world, climbing the staircases is no longer permitted.

The Ballgame

More than a sport or a form of entertainment, the ballgame that was played throughout Mesoamerica had some kind of ritual significance. Two teams would compete against each other to manipulate a large rubber ball through a stone ring set high on the wall at the side of the court. It is thought that the losers of the game were subsequently put to death. Ballcourts have been found at all the main pre-Columbian sites, the largest being at Chichén Itzá. The cities of Cantona *(see p161)* and El Tajín *(see pp246–7)* each had a great number of ballcourts. A version of the game, called *hulama*, is still played today by Indians in the state of Sinaloa *(see p182)*.

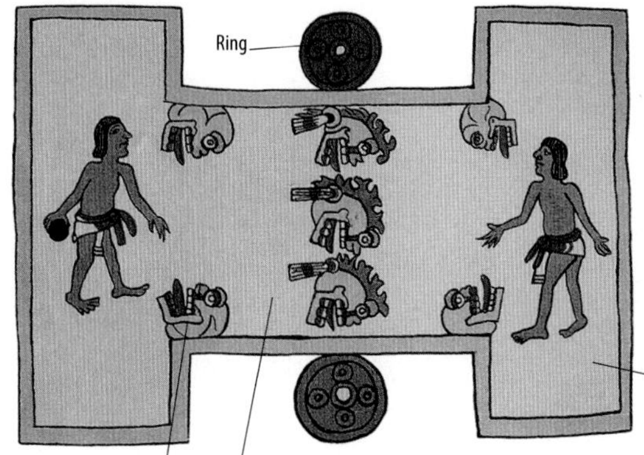

The Ballcourt

Although there were probably several versions of the game, it was always played on an I-shaped court, as seen in this Aztec codex illustration. Ballcourts varied in size, but early examples were usually aligned north-south, and later ones east-west.

Stone markers are thought to have been part of the normal system of scoring.

The aisle or central court had steeply sloping sides.

A heavy rubber ball, about as big as a man's head but shown here in exaggerated size, was used to play the game.

The ballgame player wore substantial body protection, as seen in this decoration on a Maya vessel. The ball had to be kept off the ground using only knees, elbows, or hips, never the hands or feet.

The ballcourt ring was a tiny "goal" that the ball had to pass through. This was just one way of scoring and would have been a rare event, as it clearly took a prodigious feat to achieve.

The Fate of the Losers

The losers were often sacrificed after the game, but this was considered an honorable way to die. This carved panel, one of six that decorate the South Ballcourt at El Tajín, shows two victors killing one of the losing team with an obsidian knife, while a third player looks on from the right. A savage looking death god descends from the skyband at the top of the panel to receive the human offering.

⓭ Valladolid

Yucatán. 69,000. Palacio Municipal, Calle 40 No. 200, (985) 856 25 29. Candelaria (Feb 2).
valladolid.com.mx

Lying almost exactly halfway between Mérida and Cancún, Valladolid is the third-largest city on the Yucatán Peninsula. It was founded by the Spanish on an earlier Maya settlement known as Zaci, and quickly became an important religious center. In 1552 the Franciscans built the Yucatán's first ecclesiastical buildings here, the **Iglesia de San Bernardino de Siena** and the adjoining **Ex-Convento de Sisal**. These have been restored, revealing original frescoes behind two side altars in the church. Also restored are the small Spanish colonial houses on Calle 41-A, the street from the town center to the church.

The *zócalo* (main square) is the focal point, and often the liveliest part, of this quiet and attractive city. Maya women sell *huipiles* (embroidered dresses) around its perimeter, and in the northeast corner small, inexpensive restaurants serve tasty local dishes and fruit juices late into the night. Overlooking the square is the **cathedral**, with its elegant façade, and the colonial hotel **El Mesón del Marqués**. Also on the square is the **Palacio Municipal** (City Hall). In the first-floor hallway are painted panels showing the history of the town from Maya times, and portraits of military leaders from Valladolid who helped initiate the Revolution *(see p58)*.

A little farther out from the main square, the churches of **Santa Ana** (four blocks east) and **Santa Lucía** (six blocks north), are fine examples of stark Franciscan architecture. These churches were originally used by Maya converts, and are still the most popular in the town.

Hanging stalactites and clear, turquoise water in the Cenote de Dzitnup

Statue on the main square in Valladolid

The intricately painted high altar of the Iglesia de San Bernardino de Siena, Valladolid

Environs

West of town is the **Cenote de Dzitnup**, a natural well, apparently unearthed by a pig in the 1950s. Visitors can climb down the steep steps to the underground pool, where a hole in the roof and electric lighting illuminate the dramatic setting. You can also swim here among the fish in the blue water.

West, near Chichén Itzá, are the **Grutas de Balankanché**, huge caves discovered in 1959. Maya artifacts found here suggest that this was a place of worship as early as 300 BC, dedicated to the rain god Chac. Guides point out some of the Maya objects still in situ, which include miniature corn-grinding stones, and decorated incense burners. There is a small museum on site.

Cenote de Dzitnup
7 km (4 miles) W of Valladolid. **Open** daily.

Grutas de Balankanché
Off Mex 180, 35 km (22 miles) W of Valladolid. **Open** daily.

⓮ Ekbalam

Yucatán. Off Mex 295, 25 km (16 miles) N of Valladolid. Temozón then taxi. **Tel** (988) 944 00 33. **Open** daily.

Ongoing excavation work has revealed Ekbalam ("Black Jaguar") as an important Maya city and religious center. It dates predominantly from AD 700–1000, is relatively compact, and has an unusual double perimeter wall for fortification. The main entrance is through a fine Maya arch, but the real highlight is the Tower – a 30-m- (98-ft-) high tiered pyramid that visitors can climb. On each of the pyramid's tiers, pits sunken into the structure are thought to be *chultunes* (Maya cisterns). From gaps in the surrounding walls at the cardinal points, Maya white roads, or *sacbeob (see p289)*, radiate out to a distance of over 1.5 km (1 mile).

⓯ Río Lagartos

Yucatán. Mex 295, 104 km (65 miles) N of Valladolid. from Valladolid and Mérida. **Open** daily.

The nature preserve of Río Lagartos, occupying brackish lagoons on the north coast of the peninsula, is a birdwatcher's paradise. It is home to over 260 species, including the huge colonies of pink flamingos that breed here in the summer. Between April and June, the flamingos' nests are protected, but at other times of the year, boat trips to see the elegant birds can be arranged in Río Lagartos village. Occasionally, snakes and turtles can also be seen.

The safe waters of Playa Langosta, Cancún

⓰ Cancún

Quintana Roo. 661,000. Avenida Yaxilan s/n, 17M Lote 6, (998) 881 90 00. **cancun.travel/en**

Before 1970, Cancún was little more than a sandy island and a fishing village of barely 100 inhabitants. The government decided to turn it into a resort, and in the late 1960s building began in earnest. Since then the population has soared to hundreds of thousands, and over 12 million (mainly non-Mexican) visitors flock here every year to enjoy the white-sand beaches and perfect weather.

Thatched shelters on Playa Marlín in Cancún

There are, in fact, two Cancúns. The downtown area, on the mainland, has very few hotels and no beaches, while the Cancún that most visitors see has plenty of both. The latter, known as **Isla Cancún** or the *zona hotelera* (hotel zone), is a narrow, 23-km (14-mile) L-shaped island connected to the mainland by two bridges.

Although many of the hotels appear to command private stretches of sand, all beaches in Mexico are public and can be enjoyed by anybody. The ones in front of the Hyatt Cancún and Sheraton hotels are particularly beautiful. If the resort beach scene and constant presence of hotel staff do not appeal, however, head for the equally attractive "public" beaches. **Playa Linda**, **Playa Langosta**, and **Playa Tortugas**, on the northern arm of the island, offer relaxed swimming in the calm Bahía Mujeres, while bigger waves and fine views can be found at **Playa Chac-Mool**, **Playa Marlín**, and **Playa Ballenas**, which face the open sea on the eastern side. The protected **Laguna Nichupté**, between Isla Cancún and the mainland, is perfect for watersports.

Toward the southern end of the island is the small Maya site of **El Rey** (The King), occupied from AD 1200 until the Conquest. Here, a low pyramid and two plazas provide a quiet, cultural retreat from the beachfront action.

Some ferries for Isla Mujeres *(see p285)* leave from a dock near Playa Linda, but the majority depart from Puerto Juárez or Punta Sam, both just to the north of Cancún.

The pyramid and other ruins of El Rey, echoed in the background by one of Cancún's many hotels

The Mayan Riviera

The development of Cancún *(see p283)*, and other smaller resorts, has brought profound changes to the Yucatán's east coast. Now known as the Mayan Riviera, it is a major tourist destination, and it is easy to see why. As well as idyllic sandy beaches and warm waters, the coast has the second longest coral reef in the world, providing ideal conditions for snorkeling and diving.

A dolphin, one of the animals that visitors can see at Xcaret *(see p288)*

Playa del Carmen is the second biggest resort on the coast after Cancún. The town has a relaxed atmosphere and Quinta Avenida, the main street, is lined with small shops, coffee bars, and traditional restaurants. Ferries to Cozumel leave from a pier close to the lively central square.

Akumal is an uncrowded resort based around what was once a coconut plantation. Its beautiful beach is a breeding ground for green turtles, and migrating whale sharks can sometimes be spotted swimming past in December and January. Since the 1990s, the sheltered bay has increasingly attracted windsurfers, divers, and snorkelers.

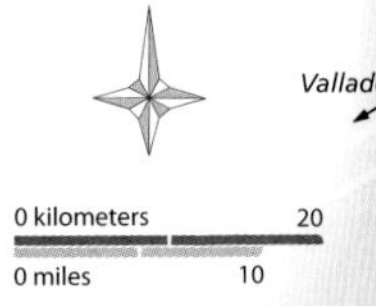

Xel-Ha nature preserve is a series of interconnecting lagoons set among spectacular rocks and caves. A huge variety of tropical fish swims in its beautifully clear waters. For years it was government-run and rather neglected, but it is now franchised to the same company that operates Xcaret. It has taken on a new lease of life, offering superb snorkeling and diving.

Xcaret *(see p288)* is a combination of zoo, beach resort, archaeological area, and theme park.

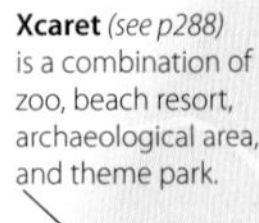

Tulum Playa, the most easy-going resort along the coast, is essentially a rapidly growing strip of beach huts and a handful of restaurants, bordering a magnificent sandy beach. Nearby is the late-Maya site of Tulum *(see pp288–9)*.

Puerto Aventuras is a purpose-built resort with a range of facilities, including an 18-hole golf course and a marina. It is popular for reef diving.

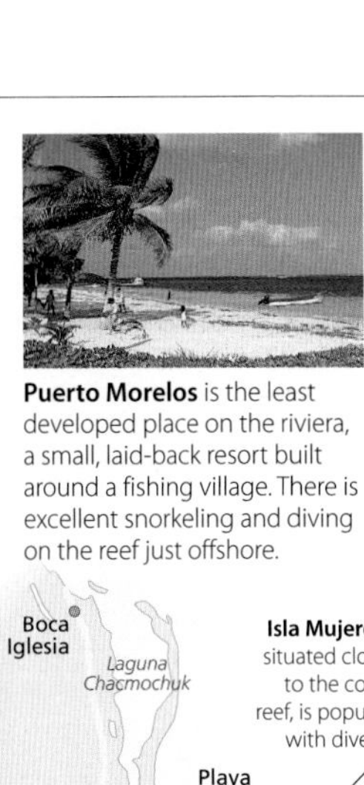

Puerto Morelos is the least developed place on the riviera, a small, laid-back resort built around a fishing village. There is excellent snorkeling and diving on the reef just offshore.

Isla Mujeres, situated close to the coral reef, is popular with divers.

Cancún is huge, attracting more visitors than any other resort in Mexico.

Cozumel *(see p286)* is one of the world's top diving sites.

A flotilla of small tour boats moored in the harbor on Isla Mujeres

⑰ Isla Mujeres

Quintana Roo. ⛴ passenger ferry from Puerto Juárez, car ferry from Punta Sam. ℹ Avenida Rueda Medina 130, (998) 877 07 67. **W isla-mujeres.net**

This small island is just 1 km (half a mile) wide by 8 km (5 miles) long. Its name, meaning "The Island of Women," probably derives from Maya female statuettes found here and destroyed by the Spanish. It has developed considerably since first becoming popular in the 1960s, but there are few high-rise buildings, and its small town is still quiet, especially in the evening when the day trippers from Cancún have left.

A lifeguard's lookout on Playa Los Cocos

The best way to explore the island is on a bike or scooter. Its middle part is taken up by a brackish lagoon and an airstrip for small planes from the mainland. Also in the center is the ruined **Mundaca Hacienda**, said to have been built by the pirate Fermín Mundaca to impress an island beauty.

Playa Los Cocos, located just to the north of the island's only town, has clean white sand and warm shallow water.

At Isla Mujeres' rather rugged southern tip are the **Garrafón National Park**, and **Playa de Garrafón**. The exciting diving afforded by the coral reef just offshore here is one of the main reasons for visiting the island. The snorkeling is also spectacular, but the beach gets very crowded in the middle of the day. Nearby are the ruins of what is said to be an old Maya lighthouse.

Environs

A popular day trip from Isla Mujeres is to **Isla Contoy**, a tiny island 30 km (19 miles) away, off the northern tip of the Yucatán Peninsula. It is located at the northernmost part of the barrier reef, where the waters of the Caribbean Sea and Gulf of Mexico meet. The mingling currents create ideal conditions for plankton – food for the many fish, which in turn support an abundant bird life. Over 90 species of birds, including large flocks of egrets, pelicans, frigate birds, and flamingos, nest on the island, which is now a protected nature preserve.

An intricate bas-relief carving on the entrance arch of the Mundaca Hacienda

For keys to symbols *see back flap*

⓲ Cozumel

Quintana Roo. ✈ ⛴ car ferry from Calica, passenger ferry from Playa del Carmen. ℹ Calle 15 Sur and 20 Av, (987) 869 02 12. W **cozumel.travel**

Situated off the east coast of the Yucatán Peninsula, Cozumel is Mexico's largest island, 14 km (9 miles) wide by 50 km (31 miles) long.

The Maya called the island Cuzamil, the "place of the swallows." It was an important center for the cult of Ixchel, goddess of fertility, pregnancy, and childbirth, and traces of Maya occupation can be found in several parts of the island. The ruins of two of the main settlements are at **El Cedral** and **San Gervasio**. Both are overgrown, but visiting them provides an opportunity to see some of Cozumel's varied birdlife in the jungle habitat that characterizes the interior of the island. San Gervasio, the larger site, has several restored buildings. **El Caracol** in the south of the island, is an isolated Maya shrine that is thought to have been used as a landmark for navigation. The Spaniards also came to Cozumel. The first Mass in Mexico was said here in 1518, and Hernán Cortés, warmly received by the local inhabitants, planned his conquest of mainland Mexico from the island.

Crystal-clear blue waters at the waterfront in Cozumel

Today, Cozumel is a tourist resort, and one of the world's foremost diving locations. Ferries from the mainland arrive at the pier in **San Miguel de Cozumel**, the island's only town. Near the dock are many tourist shops and restaurants, but a few blocks away, the town is quieter with a more traditional feel. The pretty **Iglesia de San Miguel Arcángel**, the town's only church, stands on the main square. Three blocks north of this square is the **Museo de la Isla**.

A pelican, one of many birds seen on Cozumel

Cozumel is ringed by stunning beaches, many of which are accessible only in a four-wheel drive vehicle. Those on the eastern, windward side are beautiful, but the sea here is dangerous, with heavy waves and a strong undertow. Safe swimming beaches are on Cozumel's sheltered western side. The best diving sites are here too, particularly around the **Colombia**, **Palancar**, **San Francisco**, and **Santa Rosa** reefs. Also on the west coast is **Chankanaab Park**, with hundreds of varieties of tropical plants.

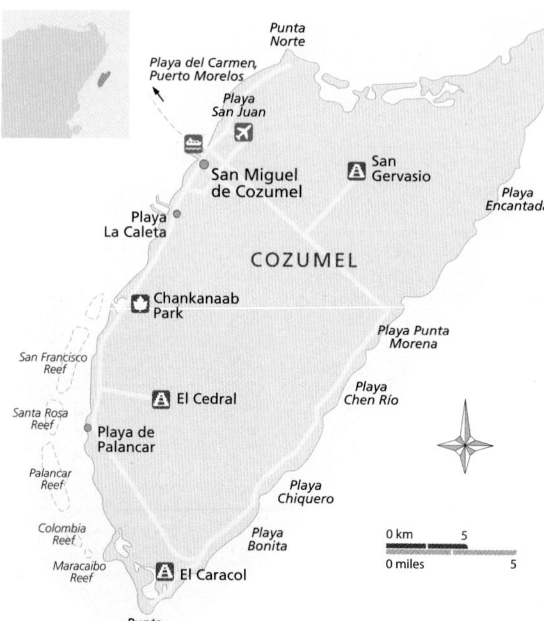

Museo de la Isla

Cnr of Av Rafael Melgar & Calle 6 Norte. **Tel** (987) 872 14 75. **Open** Mon–Sat. W **cozumelparks.com/eng/museo_isla.cfm**

The Iglesia de San Miguel Arcángel in Cozumel's only town

For keys to symbols *see back flap*

Diving in the Mexican Caribbean

The great Mesoamerican Reef System stretches for more than 1,000 km (620 miles) down the eastern coast of Yucatán to Belize, Guatemala, and Honduras. Home to an amazing variety of sea creatures, the crystal waters along the Yucatán coast are ideal for snorkeling and skindiving. There are diving sites on the reefs to suit every ability, from beginner to professional, the best known places being off the island of Cozumel. Equipment can be bought or rented from the many diving schools found on the coast. These also offer diving training, and lead groups of more experienced divers to explore the reef.

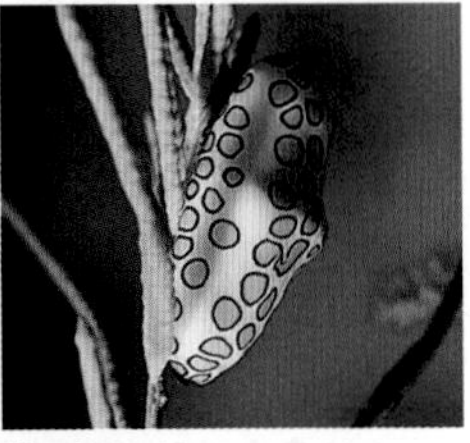

Flamingo tongue
Unlike most snails, this mollusk species extends its mantle over its shell as camouflage. It feeds and reproduces on soft corals.

Staghorn coral has stony, cylindrical branches and can appear in a variety of colours. The branches can grow up to 2 m (6.5 ft) in length.

Massive corals are the main basis of a reef. They grow only 3 mm (1/10 inch) a year, but can reach over 10 m (33 ft) in diameter.

Yucatán Coral Garden

The dramatic underwater landscape boasts abundant and colorful coral gardens, whose nooks and crannies teem with marine creatures in search of food and shelter.

Splendid toadfish
Active only at night, the pointed barbels and striped head of the splendid toadfish may give away its daytime hideaway.

Hawksbill turtle
These increasingly rare turtles nest along Cozumel's eastern coast. An endangered species, they are protected by law.

Basket star
Capable of reaching a diameter of up to 1 m (3 ft), basket stars can sometimes be seen when feeding at night.

⓳ Xcaret

Quintana Roo. Mex 307, 7 km (4 miles) S of Playa del Carmen. **Tel** (998) 251 65 60. from Cancún and Playa del Carmen. **Open** daily.
W **xcaret.com**

This large, well-planned "eco-archaeological" theme park is a combination of zoo, activity center, and beach resort. It is built around the ruins of Polé, an important Post-Classic Maya coastal settlement. A highlight for many visitors is a chance to float down the clear waters of the two naturally illuminated subterranean rivers that cross the park. Another popular activity is to swim with dolphins in a saltwater pool. The park's animal collection includes bats, butterflies, and turtles, as well as pumas and jaguars, kept on two Big Cat Islands. Other attractions are a re-created Maya village and a sound-and-light show about the Maya.

Beaches fringing a lagoon in Xcaret theme park

Puma, on Xcaret's Jaguar Island

⓴ Cobá

Quintana Roo. 47 km (29 miles) NW of Tulum. from Valladolid and Cancún. **Open** 8am–5pm daily.

Built around a group of lakes, Cobá is one of the most interesting archaeological sites in the Yucatán Peninsula. The city flourished from about AD 300 to AD 1000, and stood at the center of a network of *sacbeob*

㉑ Tulum

Spectacularly positioned on a cliff overlooking the Caribbean, Tulum is a late-Maya site that was at its height from around AD 1200 until the arrival of the Spanish. The name, which means "enclosure" or "wall," is probably modern. It is thought that the site was originally called Zama, or "dawn," reflecting its location on the east coast, and the west-east alignment of its buildings. Its inhabitants traded with Cozumel, Isla Mujeres, Guatemala, and central Mexico.

The House of the Cenote is so named because it stands above a cenote, a subterranean well.

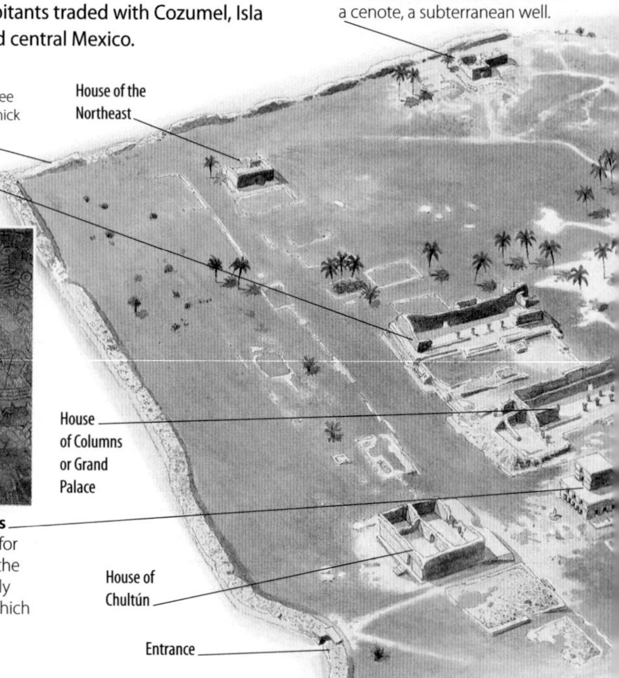

A perimeter wall runs along three sides of the site. It is 5 m (16 ft) thick and pierced by five gates.

House of the Northeast

House of the Halach Uinic, or Overlord

House of Columns or Grand Palace

The Temple of the Frescoes was used as an observatory for tracking the movements of the sun. Its interior walls are richly adorned with paintings in which supernatural serpents are a common motif.

House of Chultún

Entrance

For hotels and restaurants see pp304–5 and pp327–9

(meaning "white roads"): straight processional routes paved with limestone that connected Maya buildings or settlements to each other. More of these roads have been found here than anywhere else.

Up to 40,000 people are thought to have lived at this enormous site, thanks to the local abundance of water. However, only a small proportion of its area has been excavated so far. Much of it is still shrouded in jungle.

There are three principal clusters of buildings to visit. Be prepared for long walks between them, or rent a bike. Close to the entrance of the site is the **Cobá Group**. The main building in this group is a pyramid known as La Iglesia (the Church), because local people regard it as a shrine. Nearby is a ballcourt *(see p281)*. A trail beginning on the other side of Lago Macan-xoc leads to the **Macanxoc Group**, where a collection of stelae carved by the Maya as historical records can be seen. About 1.5 km (1 mile) to the north is the **Nohoch Mul Group**. Standing at 42 m (138 ft), Nohoch Mul is the highest pyramid in the Yucatán. It's a hard climb to the temple at the top, but once reached, there is an incomparable view of the lakes and jungle below.

The ballcourt, part of the extensive ruins of Cobá

The Temple of the Descending God has a carving over its door showing a swooping or falling figure. Similar carvings, of what is thought to be a deity associated with the setting sun, can be seen on El Castillo and in several other buildings on the site.

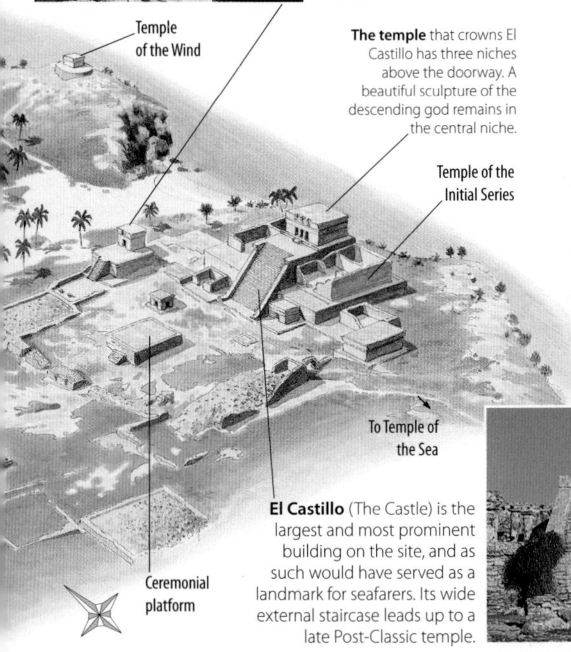

VISITORS' CHECKLIST

Practical Information
Quintana Roo. Mex 307, 128 km (80 miles) S of Cancún.
Open 8am–5pm daily.

Transport
from Cancún.

Temple of the Wind

The temple that crowns El Castillo has three niches above the doorway. A beautiful sculpture of the descending god remains in the central niche.

El Castillo, on its spectacular clifftop vantage point

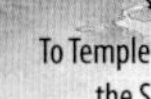

El Castillo (The Castle) is the largest and most prominent building on the site, and as such would have served as a landmark for seafarers. Its wide external staircase leads up to a late Post-Classic temple.

Ceremonial platform

㉒ Sian Ka'an Biosphere Reserve

Quintana Roo. tours from Tulum. Cesiak, Carretera 307, 68 Tulum, (984) 871 24 99. **cesiak.org**

Comprising over 4,500 sq km (1,700 sq miles) of low jungle and marshlands, and 110 km (69 miles) of coral reef, Sian Ka'an has a range of natural habitats that makes it one of the most important conservation areas in Mexico. It is run by a government agency and is not primarily geared toward tourism. Indeed, the poor roads within the preserve deter all but the most intrepid. However, the Amigos de Sian Ka'an (Friends of Sian Ka'an) run night tours for visitors, which focus on the crocodiles that inhabit the mangrove swamps. Lucky visitors may also see the flocks of local and migrating birds in the marshlands around Boca Paila, in the northern part of the preserve, including the rare Jabirú stork, or the elusive turtles and manatees that live in the waters off the coast.

The rare Jabirú stork, Sian Ka'an

Punta Allen, south of Boca Paila but still within the preserve, is a small fishing village. Lobsters, the main source of income here, are still caught using old Maya methods.

The Maya site of Kohunlich, near Chetumal

㉓ Chetumal

Quintana Roo. 245,000. Calzada del Centenario 622, (983) 835 08 60.

Founded on the estuary of the Río Hondo in 1898, Chetumal is now the capital of Quintana Roo state. It is situated near the frontier with Belize, and is a typical border town. There is a large naval base and a duty-free zone, with stores selling cut-rate luxury items from all over the world. Visitors from Belize and Guatemala come here for shopping, giving the city an exciting atmosphere. Most of the original wooden and tin-roofed buildings were destroyed in a hurricane in the 1950s, and the town has been rebuilt around wide avenues, some of which still end in undergrowth. Chetumal's spacious **Museo de la Cultura Maya** explores the Maya world, including astronomy, daily life, and Maya codices. Many of the exhibits are replicas, but there are good explanatory panels and interactive screens.

State emblem of Quintana Roo

Environs

Situated 40 km (25 miles) northwest of Chetumal, is the village of **Bacalar**. There is a natural pool here, over 60 m (200 ft) deep. Named **Cenote Azul** for its vivid blue color, it is perfect for a swim. Nearby **Laguna de Siete Colores**, overlooked by the Spanish fort in Bacalar, is also popular. West along Mex 186, farmed fields give way to jungle, the setting for the Maya site of

A pleasure boat plying the clear, blue waters of the Laguna de Siete Colores, near Chetumal

Kohunlich and its Temple of Masks. Dedicated to the Maya sun god, the steps of this 6th-century pyramid are flanked with masks facing the setting sun. About 29 km (18 miles) north of Kohunlich lie the attractive, if rather unremarkable, ruins of **Dzibanché**.

Museo de la Cultura Maya
Cnr of Avenida Héroes and Cristobal Colón. **Tel** (983) 832 68 38. **Open** Tue–Sat.

Kohunlich & Dzibanché
Open daily. **inah.gob.mx**

㉔ Río Bec Sites

Campeche. Mex 186, 120 km (75 miles) W of Chetumal. Xpujil. All sites: **Open** daily.

A group of stylistically similar Maya sites, situated in the lowlands west of Chetumal, are known collectively as the Río Bec sites. Many are hidden by jungle, but three of them, Xpujil, Becán, and Chicanná, are near enough to the main road (Mex 186) to be accessible to the casual visitor. These three can be visited on a day-trip from Chetumal, or en route to the city from Villahermosa *(see p258)* or Palenque *(see pp238–41)*.

The area may have been occupied from at least 550 BC, but the Río Bec style, which the sites share, was dominant between AD 600 and 900. The style is characterized by elongated platforms and buildings, flanked by slender towers with rounded corners. These towers are "fake" temple-pyramids – the steps are too steep to be used, and the structures seem to have no inner chamber and no special function apart from decoration. Representations of Itzamná, the creation god responsible for life and death, are the main ornamentation.

Coming from Chetumal, the first site is **Xpujil**, just across the border in the state of Campeche, and clearly visible from the road. Here, 17 building groups surround a central square, but the most remarkable structure is the main temple, whose three towers rise over 15 m (50 ft) from a low platform. These pointed towers, which are a classic example of Río Bec architecture, soar enigmatically above the surrounding jungle.

Structure X at Becán, its decorative stonework just visible at the top

Just 6 km (4 miles) farther west, a track north of the main road leads to **Becán**. The site dates from around 550 BC, and is thought to have been the principal Maya center in the Río Bec region. The substantial number of non-local artifacts found during excavations suggests it was an important trading center linking the two sides of the peninsula. Unusually, the main buildings here were surrounded by a trench or moat (now dry) that is up to 5 m (16 ft) deep and 16 m (52 ft) wide, and about 2 km (1 mile) in circumference.

Various Río Bec towers can be seen here, but Becán is also noted for the unusual rooms found inside Structure VIII. These chambers had no means of light or ventilation and may have been used for religious rituals that required darkness and isolation.

Chicanná, 3 km (2 miles) farther west, and south of the main road, has the most extraordinary architecture of the three sites. Its name means "house of the serpent's mouth," which refers to Structure II, whose façade is a snake's head formed by an intricate mosaic of stone. This striking zoomorphic shape represents the god Itzamná, while the snake's mouth forms the doorway. Structure XX, set apart from the main plaza, is a two-level building that echoes the design of Structure II. Its sides are decorated with masks of Chac, the rain god *(see p269)*.

Environs

Near the village of Conhuás, 60 km (37 miles) west of Xpujil, a minor road branches to the south and, after another 60 km, reaches **Calakmul**, one of the most important Maya cities in the Classic period. The 50-m (165-ft) high pyramid here is the largest in Mexico. Around a hundred stelae remain on site, but the jade masks found in the tombs are now on display in Campeche *(see p264)*.

Just west of Conhuás is the site of **Balamkú**, discovered by chance in 1990. Its most striking feature is a 17-m (55-ft) long stucco frieze on the building known as the House of the Four Kings. The frieze is thought to represent the relationship between Maya royalty and the cosmos.

The three Río Bec towers rising above the principal temple at Xpujil

TRAVELERS' NEEDS

WHERE TO STAY

As Mexico's tourist industry has grown over the years, so has the choice and variety of accommodation options for all types of traveler. As well as hotels, you will find guest houses, apartments, hostels, campgrounds, and even hammocks for rent. The hotels themselves range from budget motels to world-class luxury resorts in extraordinary settings. Room prices vary greatly, depending on the region, location of the hotel, season, and services provided. Visitors should be aware that inexpensive establishments may not always conform to the standards expected in the US or Europe.

Atmospheric foyer of Fiesta Americana Hacienda Galindo, Querétaro *(see p301)*

Hotel Grading

Room prices are often regulated by the state, and most hotels are classified into categories ranging from one to five stars or diamonds, plus a special Grand Tourism category. Many excellent hotels are not certified, but all rated hotels adhere to strict standards. Private bathrooms with showers, linen changes, and daily room cleaning are provided in all hotels from one-star upward. At the other end of the spectrum, the larger grand hotels are very luxurious and usually offer gym facilities, a gourmet restaurant, and sometimes even a nightclub.

Chain Hotels

Mexico has a number of hotel chains with varying services and prices. **Fiesta Americana** and **Presidente Intercontinental** are two local chains that offer reliable service, while **Camino Real** and **Quinta Real** have luxurious rooms. International chains, such as **Sheraton**, **Westin**, and **Marriott**, are also represented, and two good midrange options are the **Ostar Grupo** and **Howard Johnson**.

Historic Buildings

Mexico has plenty of old convents, mansions, and haciendas *(see pp54–5)* that have been converted into extraordinary hotels. Many have been declared national monuments and feature original furniture and decor. Those hotels housed in haciendas often have spacious gardens and modern amenities.

Budget Accommodation

There are many inexpensive hotels in the towns and villages across Mexico, but ask to have a look before committing to staying anywhere as the standards can vary hugely. The so-called *casas de huéspedes* (family-run guest houses) are one of the best forms of budget accommodation available in the country.

Camping is also very popular. There are numerous campgrounds scattered around the country, particularly in Baja California, on the Pacific coast, and on the Yucatán Peninsula. As beaches in Mexico are public property, camping is allowed on many of them. In the south, *cabañas* (beachside cabins) and hammocks can be rented and hung almost anywhere. These offer a low-cost way to spend the night right by the sea.

Booking and Paying

A number of online hotel booking services, among them **Hotels.com** and **Hotel Book**, provide lists of available quality lodgings all around the country.

In some hotels guests may be asked to sign a blank credit card slip on arrival. Travelers' checks are accepted in most hotels, and many will change or accept foreign currency, but not always at the best rate. Some budget hotels are cash only.

Rustic charm of Rancho San Cayetano, Zitacuaro *(see p302)*

◀ Traditional, colorful Mexican sombreros for sale

Most hotels have set prices that may vary according to the season, facilities, and the type of room. Hotels that depend on business travelers often have reduced rates for long stays and weekends. The normal 16 percent IVA tax is supplemented with a 3 percent lodging tax. These are not always included in the advertised rate. It is customary to tip porters and cleaning staff US$1–2. Checkout time is normally around noon.

Villas with *palapa* roofs near Careyes *(see p190)*

Apartment Rentals

Reasonably priced, comfortable apartments with well-equipped kitchens are available for rent all over the country. Some rental agencies, such as **Homeaway, Airbnb,** and **VRBO**, have properties in a number of locations. **Cozumel Vacation Rentals**, **Finca Sol**, and **Se Renta Luxury Villas** (Acapulco) concentrate on a particular region or a single resort. At the beach resorts there are also luxury villas and apartment hotels with resort-standard services.

Youth Hostels

Most of the country's youth hostels are attached to sports centers and have clean, single-sex dormitories. There are also a number of private hostels. Hostel listings can be found at **Mundo Joven** and **Hostelling International**.

Recommended Hotels

The lodging options featured on pages 296–305 have been selected across a wide price range for their excellent facilities, fine locations, and value for money. From family-owned inns and beachfront resorts to stylish boutique hotels, these places provide accommodation options for all budgets.

Befitting a massive country with a rich history, Mexico is awash in historic hacienda hotels. If you're after an intimate experience, consider one of the country's B&Bs. There are many properties centered around a courtyard pool. Luxury options also abound, offering service and amenities at world-class levels. Numerous properties provide rooms with spectacular views, whether overlooking a bustling city square or an endless white-sand beach. If you're traveling with a family, consider one of Mexico's resorts, many of which are all-inclusive.

For the best options, look out for those featured as "DK Choice." These establishments have been highlighted in recognition of an exceptional feature – a stunning location, notable history, or an inviting atmosphere. The majority of these are very popular, so be sure to book well in advance.

DIRECTORY

Chain Hotels

Camino Real
Tel (55) 52 27 72 00.
W caminoreal.com

Fiesta Americana
Tel (55) 53 26 69 00.
W fiestamericana.com

Howard Johnson
Tel (800) 221 58 01 (US and Canada).
W hojo.com

Marriott
Tel (800) 561 47 56.
W marriott.com

Ostar Grupo
Tel (55) 50 80 00 62.
W ostar.com.mx

Presidente Intercontinental
Tel (55) 53 27 77 77.
W ihg.com

Quinta Real
Tel (55) 11 05 10 00 (toll free within Mexico).
W quintareal.com

Sheraton
Tel (55) 52 42 55 55.
W starwoodhotels.com

Westin
Tel (55) 50 89 80 00.
W starwoodhotels.com

Hotel Booking Services

Hotel Book
Tel (800) 446 83 57 (US and Canada).
Tel 0208 604 8018 (UK).
W hotelbook.com

Hotels.com
Tel (877) 507 66 27 (US).
W hotels.com

Apartment Rentals

Airbnb
W airbnb.com

Cozumel Vacation Rentals
Tel (512) 541 41 46 (US).
W cozumel-vacation-rentals.com

Finca Sol
Tel (322) 222 04 77.
W fincasol.com.mx

Homeaway
W homeaway.com

Se Renta Luxury Villas (Acapulco)
Tel (744) 435 21 10.
W serenta.com

VRBO
W vrbo.com

Youth Hostels

Hostelling International
W hihostels.com

Mundo Joven
Insurgentes Sur 1510, Mexico City.
Tel (55) 54 82 82 82.
W mundojoven.com

Where to Stay

Mexico City

The Historic Center

Hotel Isabel $
Inn/B&B **Map** 4 D3
Isabel la Católica 63, Col Centro
Tel *(55) 55 18 12 13*
W hotel-isabel.com.mx
Elegant hotel, a longtime favorite with budget-conscious travelers. Simple, pleasant rooms, and a friendly, hostel-like atmosphere.

Best Western Hotel Majestic $$
Rooms with a view **Map** 4 E2
Francisco I. Madero 73, Col Centro
Tel *(55) 55 21 86 00*
W hotelmajestic.com.mx
Views of the Zócalo make up for the slightly old-fashioned rooms. Rooftop restaurant and bar.

Downtown $$
Historic **Map** 4 D2
Isabel la Católica 30, Col Centro
Tel *(55) 51 30 68 30*
W downtownmexico.com
Upscale hotel rooms and budget hostel accommodation housed in a grand 17th-century building.

Hampton Inn & Suites Mexico City – Centro Historico $$
Rooms with a view **Map** 4 E2
Calle 5 de Febrero 24, Col Centro
Tel *(55) 80 00 50 00*
W hamptonmexicocity.com
Modern, spacious rooms overlooking the Zócalo. Colonial courtyards with two restaurants.

Hotel Catedral $$
Rooms with a view **Map** 4 E1
Donceles 95, Col Centro
Tel *(55) 55 18 52 32*
W hotelcatedral.com
Well-located modern hotel with good views of the Zócalo and Catedral.

Hotel Gillow $$
Historic **Map** 4 E2
Isabel La Católica 17, Col Centro
Tel *(55) 55 18 14 40*
W hotelgillow.com
Historic building with a gleaming lobby, comfortable rooms, and a good restaurant. Old-fashioned charm and service.

Zócalo Central $$
Historic **Map** 4 E2
Av 5 de Mayo no. 61, Col Centro
Tel *(55) 51 30 51 30*
W centralhoteles.com
The former site of Moctezuma's palace and Hernán Cortés's residence. Modern amenities. Views from rooftop restaurant.

Reforma and Chapultepec

La Casa de la Condesa $$
Rooms with a view **Map** 2 F5
Plaza Luis Cabrera 16, Col Roma Sur
Tel *(55) 55 84 30 89*
W casadelacondesa.net
Colorful, well-appointed rooms, most with small kitchens, in a nice residential area.

Hotel Maria Cristina $$
Inn/B&B **Map** 2 E2
Río Lerma 31, Col Cuauhtémoc
Tel *(55) 55 66 96 88*
W hotelmariacristina.com.mx
Comfortable, Andalusian-style hotel with a garden restaurant. The rooms feature a blend of colonial and modern decor.

Sevilla Palace $$
Rooms with a view **Map** 2 F2
Paseo de la Reforma 105, Col Revolución
Tel *(55) 57 05 28 00*
W sevillapalace.com.mx
Large hotel with a soaring atrium and well-furnished guest rooms. Great views from the 23rd-floor bar. Live entertainment.

DK Choice

Las Alcobas Mexico DF $$$
Luxury **Map** 1 A2
Av Presidente Masarik 390A, Col Polanco
Tel *(55) 33 00 39 00*
W lasalcobas.com
An aesthetic marvel designed by renowned design firm Yabu Pushelberg, this plush hotel offers premier amenities such as custom designed furnishings, rain showers, and whirlpools in every room. Guests can enjoy state-of-the-art technology and personalized service as well as traditional Mexican food.

Price Guide
Prices are based on one night's stay in high season for a standard double room, inclusive of service charges and taxes.

$	up to $70
$$	$70 to $150
$$$	over $150

Four Seasons $$$
Luxury **Map** 1 C4
Paseo de la Reforma 500, Col Juárez
Tel *(55) 52 30 18 18*
W fourseasons.com/mexico
Serene property centered around a large interior garden and a lovely fountain. Elegant rooms. Business amenities.

Hotel Condesa DF $$$
Luxury **Map** 1 C5
Av Veracruz 102, Col Condesa
Tel *(55) 52 41 26 00*
W condesadf.com
This hip, minimalist hotel has clean white rooms, all with terraces. The rooftop restaurant offers excellent city views while the elegant El Patio restaurant serves French-Mexican fare.

Hotel Geneve $$$
Historic **Map** 2 E3
Londres 130, Col Juárez
Tel *(55) 50 80 08 00*
W hotelgeneve.com.mx
This legendary hotel built in 1907 has a *belle-époque* atmosphere, modern amenities, and first-class service. There is a lovely veranda as well.

Hyatt Regency $$$
Rooms with a view **Map** 1 A3
Campos Eliseos 204, Col Polanco
Tel *(55) 50 83 12 34*
W mexicocity.regency.hyatt.com
This stylish landmark hotel has well-appointed rooms that offer spectacular views of the Mexico City skyline. Expect luxurious amenities and an array of dining options.

The designer interior of Las Alcobas Mexico DF, Mexico City

Le Méridien $$$
Luxury **Map** 3 A2
Paseo de la Reforma 69, Col Tabacalera
Tel *(55) 50 63 30 00*
W starwoodhotels.com
This well-situated, glass-clad hotel is as elegant inside as it is out. French restaurant.

W Mexico City $$$
Luxury **Map** 1 A3
Campos Eliseos 252, Col Polanco
Tel *(55) 91 38 18 00*
W wmexicocity.com
Trendy hotel decorated with contemporary art. The restaurant is run by famous chef José Andrés.

Farther Afield

El Patio 77 $
Inn/B&B
Icazbalceta 77, Col San Rafael
Tel *(55) 55 92 84 52*
W elpatio77.com
An eco-friendly B&B housed in a colonial building. Service and breakfast are exceptional. Centrally located near the Metro.

Around Mexico City

CHOLULA: Villas Arqueológicas $$
Resort
2 Poniente 601, Zona Arqueológica
Tel *(222) 273 79 00*
W villasarqueologicas.com.mx
Centered around a lush garden, with views of the Great Pyramid. Rooms have beds in wall niches.

COCOYOC: Hacienda Cocoyoc $$$
Resort
Carretera Cuernavaca-Cuautla km 32.5
Tel *(735) 356 22 11*
W hcocoyoc.com
This resort, set amid expansive gardens, offers many amenities including golf and kids' activities.

CUERNAVACA: Hostería las Quintas $$$
Rooms with a view
Blvd Díaz Ordaz 9, Col Cantarranas
Tel *(777) 362 39 49*
W hosterialasquintas.com.mx
Individual rooms with stylish decor, many with balconies or private patios. Full-service spa.

CUERNAVACA: Las Mañanitas $$$
Luxury
Ricardo Linares 107
Tel *(777) 362 00 00*
W lasmananitas.com.mx
Stunning inn with a garden setting, and a superb restaurant serving French-inspired cuisine.

HUASCA: Hacienda San Miguel Regla $$
Historic
Calle las Carretas 1, Huasca de Ocampo
Tel *(771) 792 01 02*
W sanmiguelregla.com
Rooms with stone floors at this 17th-century hacienda. Offers horseback riding and hiking.

PACHUCA: Fiesta Inn $$
Inn/B&B
Carretera México-Pachuca km 85.5, Col Venta Prieta
Tel *(771) 717 07 00*
W fiestainn.com
Large, well-furnished rooms, and easy access to city attractions.

PUEBLA: Hotel Puebla Plaza $
Rooms with a view
5 Poniente 111, Centro Histórico
Tel *(222) 246 31 75*
W hotelpueblaplaza.com.mx
Comfortable downtown lodgings. All rooms have balconies.

PUEBLA: Hotel Colonial $$
Historic
Calle 4 Sur 105
Tel *(222) 246 46 12*
W colonial.com.mx
This hotel, once a 17th-century Jesuit monastery, has Colonial arches and Puebla Talavera tiles.

PUEBLA: Hotel Royalty $$
Rooms with a view
Portal Hidalgo 8
Tel *(222) 242 47 43*
W hotelr.com
Friendly colonial-style hotel in a prime location. Clean rooms. Popular streetside restaurant.

PUEBLA: Sacristía de la Compañia $$
Historic
Calle 6 Sur 304, Callejon de los Sapos
Tel *(222) 232 45 13*
W mesones-sacristia.com
This 18th-century mansion boasts stylishly furnished rooms adorned with antiques that are for sale.

PUEBLA: La Purificadora $$$
Historic
Callejón de la 10 Norte 802
Tel *(55) 52 82 21 99*
W lapurificadora.com
Built in a 19th-century water purification factory, this hotel has a rooftop pool with city views.

TAXCO: Los Arcos $
Historic
Juan Ruíz de Alarcón 4
Tel *(762) 622 18 36*
W hotellosarcostaxco.com
The central patio at Los Arcos is surrounded by arches. The rooms feature colonial-style furniture.

Bright and functional bedroom, Four Seasons, Mexico City

TAXCO: Hotel Victoria $$
Historic
Carlos J. Nibbi 5
Tel *(762) 622 00 04*
W victoriataxco.com
Offers a romantic glimpse of its fashionable 1930s heyday. Stellar views from most rooms.

DK Choice

TAXCO: Posada de la Mision $$$
Historic
Cerro de la Misión 32
Tel *(762) 622 00 63*
W posadamision.com
Built in 1940, this inn has been modernized while retaining the famous poolside mural by Juan O'Gorman. The rooms are spread over two areas: the old section has comfortable and simple rooms; the newer, multistory section offers large, more luxurious rooms. Popular restaurant on site and panoramic views of the town.

TEOTIHUACÁN: Villas Arqueológicas $$
Inn/B&B
Periférico Sur s/n, Zona Arqueológica
Tel *(555) 836 90 20*
W villasarqueologicas.com.mx
Pleasant rooms with rustic furnishings centered around a courtyard. Close to the entrance to the Teotihuacán ruins.

TEPOZTLÁN: Posada del Tepozteco $$$
Luxury
Paraíso 3, Barrio San Miguel
Tel *(739) 395 00 10*
W posadadeltepozteco.com.mx
Large rooms with tiled floors, loomed rugs, and wrought-iron furniture. Most have balconies with grand views. Refined service.

For more information on types of hotels *see p295*

TEQUESQUITENGO: Hacienda Vista Hermosa $$$
Inn/B&B
Km 7 Carretera Alpuyeca-Tequesquitengo, Puente de Ixtla
Tel *(734) 342 90 40*
W haciendavistahermosa.com.mx
Countryside hacienda with stone walls, turrets, and wrought-iron balconies. Antique-fitted rooms.

TLAXCALA: Hotel Alifer $
Inn/B&B
Morelos no. 11
Tel *(246) 462 30 62*
W hotelalifer.com.mx
A good choice close to the main plaza, with clean, pleasant rooms.

TULA: Hotel Sharon $
Inn/B&B
Callejón de la Cruz 1, Blvd Tula-Iturbe no. 1
Tel *(773) 732 09 76*
W hotelsharon.com.mx
Standard multistory hotel on the edge of town. Close to the archaeological site.

VALLE DE BRAVO: Avándaro Golf & Spa Resort $$$
Resort
Vega del Río s/n, Fracc Avándaro
Tel *(726) 266 03 70*
W hotelavandaro.com
Huge resort with an 18-hole golf course and a full spa. Every cabaña and villa has an open fireplace.

Northern Mexico

CABO SAN LUCAS: Los Milagros Hotel $$
Inn/B&B
Matamoros 3738
Tel *(624) 143 45 66*
W losmilagros.com.mx
A quiet place yet close to bars and restaurants. Gardens, sun terrace, and pool.

CABO SAN LUCAS: Siesta Suites $$
Inn/B&B
Calle Emiliano Zapata between Guerrero & Hidalgo
Tel *(624) 143 27 73*
W cabosiestasuites.com
Quaint, hospitable gem with colorful bedrooms and suites, all with fitted kitchens.

CABO SAN LUCAS: Casa del Mar $$$
Resort
Carretera Transpeninsular km 19.5
Tel *(624) 145 77 00*
W casadelmar.com.mx
Elegant rooms with either a balcony or terrace and views of the ocean. All-inclusive rates.

Luxurious suite and impressive views at Las Ventanas al Paraíso, San José del Cabo

CABO SAN LUCAS: Hotel Riu Palace $$$
Luxury
Camino Viejo a San José
Tel *(624) 146 71 60*
W riu.com
All-inclusive family-friendly hotel with a staggering amount of amenities, and lots of activities.

CABO SAN LUCAS: Pueblo Bonito Rose $$$
Resort
Playa El Médano
Tel *(624) 142 98 98*
W pueblobonito-rose.com
Hotel built around a palm-lined pool facing the beach. Every suite has a kitchen.

DK Choice

CABO SAN LUCAS: Sheraton Hacienda del Mar $$$
Resort
Carretera Transpeninsular km 10
Tel *(624) 145 80 00*
W starwoodhotels.com
This immaculate hotel looks like a perfect Mexican village. The rooms, set around a large pool, are decorated in cream and terracotta. Relax on the private beach or in the extensive gardens. Activities include sports fishing, horseback riding, sunset cruises, and watersports.

CHIHUAHUA: Quality Inn San Francisco $$
Hotel
Calle Victoria 409
Tel *(614) 439 90 00*
W qualityinnchihuahua.com
Stylish guest rooms with small lounge areas. Ideal option for both business and leisure travelers.

CIUDAD CUAUHTÉMOC: Tarahumara Inn $
Inn/B&B
Allende 373
Tel *(625) 581 19 19*
W tarahumarainn.com
This unpretentious two-story motel features simple yet comfortable rooms and suites. Guided tours of the local area can be arranged.

CREEL: Best Western The Lodge at Creel $$
Inn/B&B
Av Lopez Mateos 61
Tel *(635) 456 07 07*
W thelodgeatcreel.com
Classy hotel with one of the top restaurants of Creel. Log cabin-style rooms with wood-burning stoves.

CREEL: Copper Canyon Sierra Lodges $$$
Inn/B&B
22 km outside Creel
Tel *(635) 456 00 36*
W coppercanyonlodges.com
Located deep in Copper Canyon. Cabins feature log fires and kerosene lamps. Meals included.

EL DIVISADERO: Hotel Divisadero Barrancas $$$
Rooms with a view
Km 622 Ferrocarril Chihuahua
Tel *(614) 415 11 99*
W hoteldivisadero.com
The original hotel in the canyon, with a restaurant overlooking it all. Spectacular views from the rooms.

EL DIVISADERO: Mansión Tarahumara $$$
Rooms with a view
Av Juárez 1602
Tel *(614) 415 47 21*
W hotelmansiontarahumara.com.mx
Rock-walled cabins with pine furniture and fireplaces. Ask for one of the newer rooms.

DURANGO: Hotel Gobernador $$
Inn/B&B
20 de Noviembre Oriente 257
Tel *(618) 827 25 00*
W hotelgobernador.com.mx
One of the best hotels in town. Verdant grounds, Colonial touches, and an elegant restaurant.

Key to Price Guide *see p296*

ENSENADA: Estero Beach Resort $$
Rooms with a view
Playa del Estero, Ejido Chapultepec
Tel *(646) 176 62 25*
W hotelesterobeach.com
Beachfront hotel on its own estuary. Tastefully furnished rooms have either a balcony or terrace, both with water views.

HERMOSILLO: Araiza Hermosillo $$$
Rooms with a view
Blvd Eusebio Kino 353
Tel *(662) 109 17 00*
W araizahoteles.com
Lovely four-story, nicely landscaped hotel aimed at the business traveler but also good for vacationers. Rooms have wooden furniture.

LORETO: Oasis Loreto $$
Rooms with a view
Corner López Mateos and Baja California
Tel *(613) 135 02 11*
W hoteloasis.com
A tropical oasis on the beach. Rooms have either a patio or a balcony. Fishing and nature excursions can be arranged.

MAZATLÁN: Hotel Playa Mazatlán $$
Rooms with a view
Av Playa Gaviotas 202
Tel *(669) 989 05 55*
W hotelplayamazatlan.com
Highly rated beachfront hotel with an oceanside restaurant. Rooms have balconies.

MAZATLÁN: Pueblo Bonito $$$
Resort
Av Camarón Sabalo 2121
Tel *(669) 989 8900*
W pueblobonito-mazatlan.com
Chic and comfortable resort on Playa Sabalo. The suites all have balconies and kitchenettes.

MONTERREY: Gran Hotel Ancira $$$
Luxury
Ocampo 433 Oriente
Tel *(818) 150 70 00*
W hotel-ancira.com
Luxurious hotel in the heart of downtown, with a magnificent facade and elegant rooms.

MULEGÉ: Hotel Serenidad $$
Inn/B&B
El Cacheno
Tel *(615) 153 05 30*
W serenidad.com.mx
This cluster of accommodations includes rooms, cottages, luxurious villas, and RV hookups.

LA PAZ: Hotel Perla $$
Rooms with a view
Álvaro Obregón 1570
Tel *(612) 122 04 78*
W hotelperlabaja.com
Superb location fronting the bay. Some rooms have balconies. Popular restaurant and nightclub.

LA PAZ: Posada de las Flores $$$
Resort
Álvaro Obregon 440
Tel *(612) 122 74 63*
W posadadelasflores.com
Serene hotel with lovely views. Elegant rooms and deluxe suites with antiques. Great service.

SALTILLO: Camino Real $$
Resort
Blvd Los Fundadores 2000
Tel *(844) 438 00 00*
W caminoreal.com
Resort with modern, spacious rooms, set among gardens. Tennis courts and putting green, as well as a kids' playground.

SAN JOSÉ DEL CABO: El Delfin Blanco $
Inn/B&B
Calle Delfines, Pueblo la Playa
Tel *(624) 142 12 12*
W eldelfinblanco.net
Located on a hill overlooking the beach. Pleasant cabañas and casitas with shared patio areas.

SAN JOSÉ DEL CABO: Tropicana Inn $$
Inn/B&B
Blvd Mijares 30
Tel *(624) 142 15 80*
W tropicanainn.com.mx
Choose from a standard room, a suite or even a wooden cottage. Courtyard includes a pool.

Sunny terrace and inviting pool at Posada de las Flores, La Paz

SAN JOSÉ DEL CABO: One & Only Palmilla $$$
Resort
Carretera Transpeninsular km 7.5
Tel *(624) 146 70 00*
W palmilla.oneandonlyresorts.com
Exquisite resort set amid tropical gardens on the Sea of Cortez. Luxurious guest rooms.

SAN JOSÉ DEL CABO: Las Ventanas al Paraíso $$$
Resort
Carretera Transpeninsular km 19.5
Tel *(624) 144 28 00*
W rosewoodhotels.com
Elegant, all-suite hotel with tennis courts, golf courses, and a full service spa. All rooms have terraces.

SAN JOSÉ DEL CABO: Westin Resort & Spa $$$
Resort
Carretera Transpeninsular km 22.5
Tel *(624) 142 90 00*
W starwoodhotels.com
Huge, full-service resort offering large, tastefully furnished marble-floored rooms with balconies.

SANTA ROSALÍA: El Morro $
Rooms with a view
Carretera Transpeninsular km 1.5
Tel *(615) 152 04 14*
W santarosaliaelmorro.com
Located on a cliff 1 mile (1.6 km) south of Santa Rosalía. Simple rooms with patios. Stunning views.

TIJUANA: Hotel Ticuan $$
Rooms with a view
Av Miguel Hidalgo 8190
Tel *(664) 685 80 78*
W hotelticuan.com
Located in the safest part of the city near government offices, shopping, and attractions. Fine-dining restaurant on site.

The Colonial Heartland

AGUASCALIENTES: Hotel Francia Aguascalientes $$
Rooms with a view
Av Francisco I Madero 113
Tel *(449) 910 30 50*
W hotelfranciaaguascalientes.com
Business-friendly hotel located on the main square. The cozy guest rooms feature fireplaces.

AGUASCALIENTES: Quinta Real $$$
Luxury
Av Aguascalientes Sur 601
Tel *(449) 978 58 18*
W quintareal.com/aguascalientes
Elegant all-suite hotel with lovely gardens and an outdoor pool.

For more information on types of hotels *see p295*

AJIJIC: La Nueva Posada $
Rooms with a view
Donato Guerra 9
Tel *(376) 766 13 44*
W hotelnuevaposada.com
Romantic boutique hotel with an old-world style. Features garden villas and a rooftop terrace.

AJIJIC: Posada las Calandrias $
Inn/B&B
Carretera Chapala-Jocotepec 8 Poniente
Tel *(376) 766 10 52*
W hotelcalandrias.com
Family-owned motel on the outskirts of Ajijic, ideal for long stays. Rooms have fully equipped kitchenettes.

ANGANGUEO: Don Bruno $$
Inn/B&B
Morelos 92
Tel *(715) 156 00 26*
Rooms with pine furniture and tile floors. Popular with travelers focused on spotting birds and monarch butterflies.

CAREYES: Costa Careyes $$$
Resort
Km 53.5 Carretera, Barra de Navidad
Tel *(315) 351 03 20*
W careyes.com.mx
Exclusive hideaway in a private cove. Book a palm-roofed bungalow or go all-out on a cliffside castle. Dive, paddle board, or join in a round of polo.

COLIMA: Los Candiles $$
Inn/B&B
Blvd Camino Real 399
Tel *(312) 312 32 12*
W hotelloscandiles.com
Modern hotel-motel offering basic yet comfortable rooms with tile flooring.

Rural country charm of Hacienda El Carmen, Guadalajara

GUADALAJARA: Hacienda El Carmen $$$
Luxury
Díaz Ordaz 2–1, Ahualulco del Mercado
Tel *(386) 752 42 15*
W haciendaelcarmen.com.mx
Located in scenic countryside. Facilities include horseback riding and pyramid tours.

GUADALAJARA: Quinta Real $$$
Luxury
Av México 2727
Tel *(333) 669 06 00*
W quintareal.com
Fashionable hotel located within well-manicured gardens.

GUADALAJARA: Villa Ganz $$$
Historic
López Cotilla 1739
Tel *(333) 120 14 16*
W villaganz.com.mx
Boutique hotel housed in a 1930s mansion. Exceptional service.

GUANAJUATO: Posada Santa Fe $
Historic
Jardín de la Unión 12
Tel *(473) 732 00 84*
W posadasantafe.mx
Boasts a grand staircase, Mexican tiles, and elegant rooms decorated with colonial-style furniture.

GUANAJUATO: Hostería del Frayle $$
Historic
Sopeña 3
Tel *(473) 732 11 79*
Charming hotel in a 17th-century building. Rooms have hardwood floors. Can be noisy.

GUANAJUATO: Camino Real $$$
Luxury
Alhóndiga 100
Tel *(473) 102 15 00*
W caminoreal.com
This historic hotel was a colonial-era silver-processing hacienda. Rooms exude Mexican charm.

HUASTECA POTOSINA: Posada el Castillo $$
Historic
105 Calle Ocampo, Xilitla
Tel *(489) 365 00 38*
W elcastilloedwardjames.com
Edward James *(see p199)* once lived at this eclectic guesthouse now run by his niece. Offers naturalist-led hikes.

MORELIA: Hotel Casino $$
Rooms with a view
Portal Hidalgo 229
Tel *(443) 313 13 28*
W hotelcasino.com.mx
Faces Morelia's Plaza de Armas. Complimentary evening socials.

MORELIA: Hotel de la Soledad $$$
Historic
Zaragoza 90
Tel *(443) 312 18 88*
W hoteldelasoledad.com
Colonial-era hacienda dating back to the 17th century with patios, arches, and high ceilings.

MORELIA: Villa Montaña Spa $$$
Luxury
Patzimba 201
Tel *(443) 314 96 96*
W villamontana.com.mx
Spectacular location overlooking Morelia. Spacious, exquisitely outfitted casitas with fireplaces.

PÁTZCUARO: La Siranda $$
Inn/B&B
Dr. Coss 17, Centro
Tel *(434) 342 67 17*
W lasiranda.com
Pleasant rooms in a converted 18th-century colonial house.

PÁTZCUARO: Hacienda Mariposas Resort & Spa $$$
Resort
Carretera Pátzcuaro-Santa Clara del Cobre km 3
Tel *(434) 342 47 28*
W haciendamariposas.com
Eco-centered hotel surrounded by forest, orchards, and gardens. Offers tours and horseback riding.

PÁTZCUARO: Posada de la Basílica $$$
Inn/B&B
Árciga 6
Tel *(434) 342 11 08*
W posadalabasilica.com.mx
Charming 18th-century inn with rooms facing the Basilica.

DK Choice

PUERTO VALLARTA: Los Cuatro Vientos $$
Inn/B&B
Matamoros 520
Tel *(322) 222 01 61*
W cuatrovientos.com
A charming little hotel situated in the heart of the city. Rooms are spread around a small patio and pool, and folk art details dot the property. The rooftop bar provides great sunset views. Small, pretty pool.

PUERTO VALLARTA: Hacienda Buenaventura Hotel Spa $$
Rooms with a view
Blvd Francisco Medina Ascencio 2699
Tel *(322) 22 66 67*
W haciendaonline.com.mx
Set amid lush gardens close to the beach. Excellent amenities, including a kids' club.

Key to Price Guide *see p296*

PUERTO VALLARTA: Hacienda San Angel $$$
Luxury
Miramar 336
Tel *(322) 222 26 92*
W haciendasanangel.com
Luxurious boutique hotel overlooking the bay. Lush gardens, daily cocktail hour, and a highly regarded Mexican restaurant.

PUERTO VALLARTA: Velas Vallarta $$$
Resort
Paseo de la Marina Norte 585
Tel *(322) 226 86 73*
W velasvallarta.com
All-suite hotel featuring Mexican textiles, marble floors, and Huichol art. Full kitchens in some suites.

QUERÉTARO: Fiesta Americana Hacienda Galindo $$
Historic
Carretera a Amealco km 5.5
Tel *(427) 271 82 00*
W fiestamericana.com
One of the most visually stunning hacienda hotels in Mexico, dating back to the 16th century. Boasts a dazzling red facade.

QUERÉTARO: Hotel Río Querétaro $$
Inn/B&B
Matamoros 12
Tel *(442) 212 12 11*
W hotelesrio.com.mx
A modern, elegant hotel located near the historic center. Colonial and contemporary fittings.

QUERÉTARO: La Casa de la Marquesa $$$
Historic
Madero 41
Tel *(442) 227 05 00*
W hotelcasadelamarquesa.com
Opulent decor, lavish stonework, and antiques fill this 18th-century former private residence. All-suite luxury and unique furnishings.

REAL DE CATORCE: Mesón de la Abundancia $$
Historic
Lanzagorta 11
Tel *(488) 887 50 44*
W mesonabundancia.com
Rustic yet pleasant, with large rooms around an open patio. Some rooms have balconies. Good restaurant.

SAN BLAS: Garza Canela $$
Inn/B&B
Paredes 106 Sur
Tel *(323) 285 01 12*
W garzacanela.com
Spacious Colonial rooms and modern suites in leafy environs. Exceptionally hospitable service. Renowned restaurant on site.

The colonial house setting of Casa de Sierra Nevada, San Miguel de Allende

SAN LUIS POTOSÍ: Hotel Panorama $$
Inn/B&B
Av Venustiano Carranza 315
Tel *(444) 812 17 77*
W hotelpanorama.com.mx
Rooms with floor-to-ceiling windows. Piano bar in the lobby provides nightly entertainment.

SAN LUIS POTOSÍ: Hilton San Luís Potosí $$$
Luxury
Av Real de Lomas 1000
Tel *(444) 825 0125*
W starwoodhotels.com
Colonial-style hotel offering beautifully decorated rooms with high ceilings and top amenities.

SAN MIGUEL DE ALLENDE: Parador San Sebastián $
Historic
Mesones 7
Tel *(415) 152 70 84*
Welcoming hotel in a former colonial mansion. Comfortable guest rooms and a leafy patio.

SAN MIGUEL DE ALLENDE: Quinta Loreto $
Inn/B&B
Calle de Loreto 15
Tel *(415) 152 00 42*
W quintaloreto.com.mx
Top choice for budget travelers. Colorful decor, small pool, and a lush garden.

SAN MIGUEL DE ALLENDE: Mansión del Bosque $$
Inn/B&B
Calle de Aldama no. 65
Tel *(415) 152 02 77*
W mansiondelbosque.com
This charming guesthouse boasts a cozy library and a restaurant. Breakfast and dinner included.

SAN MIGUEL DE ALLENDE: Posada Carmina $$
Historic
Cuna de Allende 7
Tel *(415) 152 88 88*
W posadacarmina.com
Large colonial-era home with a sunny patio, located next to the Parroquia Church. Spacious, uniquely decorated rooms. On-site restaurant.

SAN MIGUEL DE ALLENDE: Casa de Sierra Nevada $$$
Luxury
Hospicio 35
Tel *(415) 152 70 40*
W casadesierranevada.com
Collection of colonial-era homes. Elegantly furnished rooms with city views. Offers cooking classes.

SAN MIGUEL DE ALLENDE: Casaluna $$$
Luxury
Quebrada 117
Tel *(415) 152 11 17*
W casaluna.com
Two Colonial-era guest houses, with lavishly decorated rooms. Pretty garden courtyard.

SIERRA GORDA: Misión Concá $$
Historic
Carretera Jalpan-Río Verde 57, km 32, Arroyo Seco
Tel *(487) 877 42 52*
W hotelesmision.com
Offers classic and modern hacienda rooms. Has spa facilities and a handicrafts shop.

TLAQUEPAQUE: Quinta Don José B & B Hotel $$
Inn/B&B
Calle Reforma 139
Tel *(333) 635 75 22*
W quintadonjose.com
Family-run boutique hotel with chic rooms, a sunny terrace, and a spa. Free door-to-door airport shuttle bus service.

TLAQUEPAQUE: Villa del Ensueño $$
Inn/B&B
Florida 305
Tel *(333) 635 87 92*
W villadelensueno.com
Welcoming B&B in a residential area, built around the gardens. Rooms are comfortable and tastefully decorated.

For more information on types of hotels *see p295*

URUAPAN: Hotel Mi Solar $$
Historic
Juan Delgado 10
Tel *(452) 524 09 12*
W hotelmisolar.com
Oldest hotel in Uruapan, restored as a homey but modern hotel. Spacious rooms with carved furniture.

URUAPAN: Hotel Mansión del Cupatitzio $$$
Resort
Rodilla del Diablo 20
Tel *(452) 523 21 00*
W mansiondelcupatitzio.com
Hacienda-style property with gorgeous grounds and pool. Access to the Parque Nacional.

ZACATECAS: Hotel Misión Argento Zacatecas $
Historic
Av Hidalgo 407
Tel *(492) 925 17 18*
W hotelesmision.com.mx/zacatecas.php
Housed in a former royal mint. Offers modern rooms with superb city views. Breakfast included. Excellent downtown location.

ZACATECAS: Mesón de Jobito $$
Historic
Jardín Juárez 143
Tel *(492) 924 17 22*
W mesondejobito.com.mx
Tastefully furnished rooms that exude old-world charm. Features plant-filled walkways and balconies.

ZACATECAS: Quinta Real Zacatecas $$$
Luxury
Av Ignacio Rayón 434
Tel *(492) 922 91 04*
W quintareal.com/zacatecas
This hotel on the site of a bullring looks the part. Lovely rooms and gardens.

ZITACUARO: Rancho San Cayetano $$$
Luxury
Hwy 51 to Huetamo km 2.3
Tel *(715) 153 1926*
W ranchosancayetano.com
This tranquil haven has rustic-chic rooms and cabins surrounded by manicured gardens. Canyon views.

Southern Mexico

ACAPULCO: Hotel Mirador $
Rooms with a view
Quebrada 74
Tel *(744) 483 12 60*
W miradoracapulco.com
Good option with great views of the bay. Located close to Old Acapulco restaurants and beaches.

ACAPULCO: Hotel Los Flamingos $$
Rooms with a view
Av López Mateos, Fracc Las Playas
Tel *(744) 482 06 90*
W hotellosflamingos.com
Cliffside hotel once popular with Hollywood stars. Charming rooms. Lovely sunset views from the bar.

ACAPULCO: Princess Mundo Imperial Acapulco $$
Resort
Costera de las Palmas, Fracc Granjas del Marquez
Tel *(744) 469 10 00*
W princessmundoimperial.com
Pyramid-shaped resort hotel. Pools, golf course, and spa.

ACAPULCO: Hotel Acapulco Malibu $$$
Rooms with a view
Av Costera Miguel Alemán 20
Tel *01800 712 91 42*
W acapulcomalibu.com
Waterfront hotel housed in two circular buildings. Octagonal rooms with refrigerators and balconies. Family friendly.

DK Choice

ACAPULCO: Hotel Elcano $$$
Rooms with a view
Av Costera Miguel Alemán 75
Tel *(744) 435 15 00*
W hotelelcano.com.mx
Stylish 11-story hotel set on a broad section of beach. Boasts a wonderful design combination of retro 50s and contemporary – awash with sea breezes, white tiles, and cerulean and navy blue decor. The pool area has four Jacuzzis, and the lobby bar often hosts live music.

Luxury pool and spa resort Princess Mundo Imperial Acapulco, Acapulco

ACAPULCO: Quinta Real $$$
Luxury
Paseo de la Quinta 6, Fracc Real Diamante
Tel *(744) 469 15 00*
W quintareal.com/acapulco
Cliffside location with stunning bay views from all rooms and an infinity pool overlooking the beach. Yellow accented rooms with marble floors.

HUATULCO: Camino Real Zaashila $$$
Luxury
Blvd Benito Juárez 5, Tangolunda
Tel *(958) 583 03 00*
W caminoreal.com/destinos/zaashila-huatulco
Bright-white buildings with bold blocks of color cover the hillside. The contemporary design continues inside the rooms. Most offer ocean views; some have private pools. Access to a secluded beach.

IXTAPA: Barceló Ixtapa Beach Resort $$$
Resort
Blvd Ixtapa
Tel *(755) 555 20 00*
W barceloixtapa.com
All-inclusive resort catering to families and groups. Chic rooms, spacious lobby area, and a beach.

IXTAPA: Las Brisas Ixtapa $$$
Luxury
Blvd Ixtapa, Playa Vistahermosa
Tel *(755) 553 21 21*
W brisas.com.mx/hotels/ixtapa
Oceanview rooms at this extensive hotel feature colorful Mexican decor and have terraces and hammocks.

OAXACA: Hotel Azucenas $
Inn/B&B
Calle Prof M. Aranda 203
Tel *(951) 514 79 18*
W hotelazucenas.com
Combines family hospitality with historic charm. Small, attractive rooms. Rooftop garden terrace.

OAXACA: Hotel Casa Cue $$
Inn/B&B
Aldama 103
Tel *(951) 516 77 84*
W hotelcasacue.com
Modest hotel opposite the market, with clean, comfortable rooms. The rooftop terrace has city views.

OAXACA: Hotel de la Parra $$
Inn/B&B
Guerrero 117
Tel *(951) 514 19 00*
W hoteldelaparra.com
This hacienda-style boutique hotel features tile floors and refined furnishings. Small garden pool.

Key to Price Guide *see p296*

Relax in a luxurious beach setting at Viceroy Zihuatanejo, Zihuatanejo

OAXACA: Casa Oaxaca $$$
Inn/B&B
Garcia Vigil 407, Centro
Tel *(951) 514 41 73*
W casaoaxaca.com.mx
A colonial-era building with bright, traditional decor. Guests can take regional cooking classes.

OAXACA: Quinta Real Oaxaca $$$
Luxury
Calle 5 de Mayo 300
Tel *(951) 501 61 00*
W quintareal.com/oaxaca
This elegant hotel, built as a convent in 1576, has tastefully furnished rooms. Garden views.

PALENQUE: Chan-Kah Resort Village $$
Resort
Carretera las Ruinas km 3
Tel *(916) 345 11 34*
W chan-kah.com.mx
Large wood and stone cottages in a jungle setting. Stunning stone-lined pool in lush gardens.

PALENQUE: Hotel Misión Palenque $$
Resort
Periferico Oriente s/n
Tel *(916) 345 02 41*
W hotelmisionpalenque.com
Modern hotel with tropical decor. Traditional *temazcal* spa treatments among the many services.

PUERTO ÁNGEL: Bahía de la Luna $$
Rooms with a view
Playa la Boquilla
Tel *(958) 589 50 20*
W bahiadelaluna.com
Hillside place with rustic-chic, cozy rooms. Breakfast, boat trips, and use of sea kayaks included in rates.

PUERTO ESCONDIDO: Villa Carrizalillo $
Rooms with a view
Camino Carrizalillo s/n
Tel *(954) 582 17 35*
W villacarrizalillo.com
A hillside boutique hotel with villas offering exceptional views of Carrizalillo Bay.

PUERTO ESCONDIDO: Hotel Santa Fé $$
Inn/B&B
Calle de Morro s/n
Tel *(954) 582 01 70*
W hotelsantafe.com.mx
Colonial hacienda-style hotel built around two pool-centered courtyards. Superb restaurant.

SAN CRISTÓBAL DE LAS CASAS: Hotel Don Quijote $
Inn/B&B
Cristóbal Colón 7
Tel *(967) 678 09 20*
W hoteldonquijote.com.mx
Simply furnished comfortable rooms with wood floors. Close to the central square.

SAN CRISTÓBAL DE LAS CASAS: Casa Mexicana $$
Historic
28 de Agosto 1
Tel *(967) 678 06 98*
W hotelcasamexicana.com
Centrally located colonial mansion with stylish rooms.

SAN CRISTÓBAL DE LAS CASAS: Hotel Rincón del Arco $$
Historic
Ejército Nacional 66
Tel *(967) 678 13 13*
W rincondelarco.com
Family-owned home-turned-hotel with high ceilings and late 19th-century Mexican atmosphere.

TUXTLA GUTIÉRREZ: Marriott Tuxtla Gutiérrez $$
Rooms with a view
Blvd Belisario Domínguez 1195
Tel *(961) 617 77 99*
W marriott.com
Modern hotel located on a hill. Has an atrium with a waterfall.

ZIHUATANEJO: La Casa Que Canta $$$
Luxury
Camino Escénico a Playa la Ropa
Tel *(755) 555 70 30*
W lacasaquecanta.com
Luxury hotel on a cliff. The rooms are elegant and come with lovely terraces.

ZIHUATANEJO: Viceroy Zihuatanejo $$$
Luxury
Playa la Ropa
Tel *(755) 555 55 00*
W viceroyhotelsandresorts.com
Luxurious and intimate with a beachfront location. Grounds feature waterfalls and lagoons.

The Gulf Coast

CATEMACO: La Finca $$
Resort
Carretera 180, km 147
Tel *(294) 947 97 00*
W lafinca.mx
Popular resort in a prime lakeside location. Large rooms with patios.

COATEPEC: Posada Coatepec $
Inn/B&B
Hidalgo 9
Tel *(228) 816 05 44*
W posadacoatepec.com.mx
Stylish, restored home with charming guest rooms.

CÓRDOBA: Villa Florida $$
Resort
Av 1, between Calles 30 & 32
Tel *(271) 716 33 33*
W villaflorida.com.mx/cordoba
Comfortable, pleasant rooms with mahogany furniture and large tiled bathrooms.

PAPANTLA: Hotel Tajín $
Rooms with a view
José de J. Nuñez y Dominguez 104
Tel *(784) 842 01 21*
W hoteltajin.com.mx
Rooms at this hotel feature pastel-hued walls, private baths, and deliberately mismatched fittings.

SANTIAGO TUXTLA: Gran Santiago Plaza $
Rooms with a view
Corner of Comonfort & 5 de Mayo
Tel *(294) 947 03 00*
W hotelgransantiagoplaza.com.mx
Prime location on the central plaza. Excellent restaurant.

TLACOTALPAN: Doña Lala $
Historic
Venustiano Carranza 11
Tel *(288) 884 24 55*
W hoteldonalala.mx
A 1932 national monument building, with rooms and suites.

VERACRUZ: Hotel Veracruz $
Inn/B&B
Av Independencia, s/n at Miguel Lerdo
Tel *(800) 292 33 00*
W hotelveracruz.com.mx
Most rooms have balconies. The seventh-floor sun room has spectacular city views.

For more information on types of hotels *see p295*

DK Choice

VERACRUZ: Hotel Mocambo $$
Resort
Calzada Adolfo Ruíz Cortines 4000
Tel *(229) 922 02 00*
W hotelmocambo.com.mx
This graceful, sprawling hotel with breezy, view-filled arches dates back to 1932 and retains its old-time charm. There are outdoor and indoor pools, gardens, a spa, a tennis court, as well as kids' activities. Great in-house café and restaurant serving local and international specialties.

VILLAHERMOSA: One Villahermosa Centro $
Rooms with a view
Calle General Ignacio Zaragoza no. 101, Centro
Tel *(993) 131 71 00*
W onehoteles.com
A minimalist hotel with simple yet comfortable rooms best suited for business and solo travelers.

VILLAHERMOSA: Villahermosa Marriott Hotel $$
Rooms with a view
Av Paseo Tabasco 1407
Tel *(993) 310 02 01*
W marriott.com
Located close to the city's key attractions, this hotel offers luxurious rooms and suites.

XALAPA: Posada del Cafeto $
Inn/B&B
Canovas 8 and 12
Tel *(228) 812 04 03*
W pradodelrio.com
Quiet guesthouse facing a tropical garden. Charming on-site café serves complimentary breakfast.

XALAPA: Mesón del Alférez $$
Inn/B&B
Sebastián Camacho 2
Tel *(228) 818 01 13*
W pradodelrio.com
Stately hotel offering a pleasant escape. Features rooms over two stories around a small central courtyard.

The Yucatan Peninsula

AKUMAL: Hotel Akumal Caribe $$
Resort
Hwy 307, km 104
Tel *(915) 584 35 52*
W hotelakumalcaribe.com
All-inclusive resort hotel in Half Moon Bay, with rooms, condos, and bungalows. Great for divers.

The large resort complex of Paradisus Cancún, Cancún

BACALAR: Casita Carolina $
Inn/B&B
Costera no. 15, X Calle 16 & 18
Tel *(983) 834 23 34*
W casitacarolina.com
Welcoming lakeside option with large rooms and a deluxe *palapa*. Kayaking, cycling, and diving.

BACALAR: Villas Ecotucan $$
Rooms with a view
Route 307 km 27.3
Tel *(983) 120 57 43*
W ecotucan.com/en
Tranquil little eco-hotel set beside the Cenote Azul. Kayaks and bikes available.

CAMPECHE: Hotel Francis Drake $$
Historic
Calle 12 no. 207, between Calles 63 & 65
Tel *(981) 811 56 26*
W hotelfrancisdrake.com
Well-located hotel in a converted house. Bright, comfortable rooms.

CAMPECHE: Hacienda Puerta Campeche $$$
Luxury
Calle 59 no. 71, between Calles 16 & 18
Tel *(981) 816 75 35*
W puertacampeche.com
Chic, deluxe rooms in an intimate colonial mansion. Lovely gardens, good restaurant, and a pool.

CANCÚN: Hotel Xbalamqué $$
Resort
Av Yaxchilán no. 31
Tel *(998) 193 27 20*
W xbalamque.com
Located on a lively street lined with restaurants. Rooms are bright and modern. Spa on site.

CANCÚN: El Rey del Caribe $$
Rooms with a view
Av Uxmal 24
Tel *(998) 884 20 28*
W elreydelcaribe.com
This eco-hotel in the heart of Cancún is a pleasant respite from the town's party atmosphere.

CANCÚN: Iberostar Cancun $$$
Resort
Blvd Kukulcán km 17
Tel *(998) 881 80 00*
W iberostar.com
This oceanfront luxury hotel has lots of activities, a water park, and a golf course. All-inclusive rates.

CANCÚN: Paradisus Cancún $$$
Luxury
Blvd Kukulcán km 16.5
Tel *(998) 881 11 00*
W paradisuscancunresort.com
Giant resort complex with lots of amenities such as pools, shops, 10 restaurants, golf, and watersports.

DK Choice

CANCÚN: The Ritz-Carlton $$$
Luxury
Retorno del Rey 36, Blvd Kukulcán km 14
Tel *(998) 881 08 08*
W ritzcarlton.com
This opulent resort hotel, set along the beach, boasts plush rooms with ocean views, two pools, a spa offering conventional and Mayan treatments, and six restaurants. There are two lounges and a culinary center with cooking classes.

CHETUMAL: Capital Plaza $$
Inn/B&B
Av Héroes 171
Tel *(983) 835 04 00*
W capitalplaza.mx
This simple former Holiday Inn boasts charming staff and a nice restaurant. Archaeological tours are available.

CHICHÉN ITZÁ: Hotel Dolores Alba $
Inn/B&B
Mérida-Cancún Hwy km 122
Tel *(985) 851 01 17*
W doloresalba.com
Bright rooms, two pools, and free transport to the ruins. Excellent value.

Key to Price Guide *see p296*

CHICHÉN ITZÁ: Villas Arqueológicas $$
Historic
Carretera Mérida Valladolid km 120
Tel *(987) 851 01 87*
W villasarqueologicas.com.mx
Rooms in cabins around a pretty garden. Good restaurant.

COZUMEL: Tamarindo Bed & Breakfast $
Inn/B&B
Calle 4 Norte no. 421
Tel *(987) 872 61 90*
W tamarindobedandbreakfast.com
Charming guesthouse with an open kitchen and a garden.

COZUMEL: Casa Mexicana $$
Inn/B&B
Av Rafael E. Melgar 457
Tel *(987) 872 90 80*
W casamexicanacozumel.com
Stylish waterfront hotel with chic, sunny, well-equipped rooms. Beautiful sunset views.

COZUMEL: Hotel Flamingo $$
Resort
Calle 6 no. 81
Tel *(987) 872 12 64*
W hotelflamingo.com
Attractive rooms and suites with plenty of extras. Excellent diving facilities and packages.

COZUMEL: Playa Azul Golf & Beach Hotel $$$
Rooms with a view
Carretera a San Juan km 4
Tel *(987) 869 51 60*
W playa-azul.com
Family-run resort with a pretty cove to itself. Offers diving, fishing, and golf. Lovely beachside pool.

ISLA MUJERES: Villa Kiin $$
Inn/B&B
Calle Zazil-Ha 129
Tel *(998) 877 00 45*
W villakiin.com
Friendly place set on a beach. Different facilities in each room, but all are comfortable.

ISLA MUJERES: Hotel Secreto $$$
Luxury
Punta Norte
Tel *(998) 877 10 39*
W hotelsecreto.com
Award-winning boutique hotel with stylish rooms, a pool, and a terrace. Excellent service.

MAJAHUAL: Balamku Inn on the Beach $
Rooms with a view
Carretera Mahahual-Xcalak km 5.7
Tel *(983) 732 10 04*
W balamku.com
Comfortable palm-roofed cabins. Free breakfast and use of kayaks. Great diving and fishing nearby.

MÉRIDA: Casa del Balam $$
Historic
Calle 60 no. 488, corner of Calle 57
Tel *(999) 924 88 44*
W casadelbalam.com
Pleasant rooms with some original 19th-century features and colonial-style decor.

MÉRIDA: Hotel Marionetas $$
Inn/B&B
Calle 49 no. 516, between Calles 62 & 64
Tel *(999) 928 33 77*
W hotelmarionetas.com
Small hotel with rooms around a garden patio. Superb breakfast.

MÉRIDA: Hacienda Xcanatún $$$
Luxury
Calle 20 s/n, Xcanatún Station, Carretera Merida Progreso km 12
Tel *(999) 930 21 40*
W xcanatun.com
Opulent all-suite property in an 18th-century hacienda. Two pools, a spa, and a fine restaurant.

MÉRIDA: Rosas y Xocolate $$$
Luxury
Calle Paseo de Montejo 480
Tel *(999) 924 29 92*
W rosasandxocolate.com
An elegant hotel housed inside a colonial-era estate. Each room has its individual outdoor bathtub.

Opulent bedroom in Hacienda Xcanatún, Mérida

PLAYA DEL CARMEN: La Tortuga Hotel & Spa $$
Historic
Av 10, by Calle 14
Tel *(984) 873 14 84*
W hotellatortuga.com
Palapa-style hideaway with unique rooms and all modern amenities. Courtyard with a pool, an outdoor bar, and patios.

PLAYA DEL CARMEN: Mahékal Beach Resort $$$
Resort
Calle 38 Norte
Tel *(984) 873 06 11*
W mahekalbeachresort.com
Hotel-village with spacious, beautifully decorated palm-roofed beach huts and superb penthouse cabins. All mod cons.

PUNTA BETE: Viceroy Riviera Maya $$$
Luxury
Riviera Maya Playa Xcalacoco, Fracc 7
Tel *(984) 877 30 00*
W viceroyhotelsandresorts.com
This spectacular beach retreat and spa has 41 villas, each with its own pool and dining room.

TULUM: Cabañas Copal Azulik $$
Rooms with a view
Beach Road km 5
Tel *01800 681 9537*
W ecotulum.com
Three eco-friendly cabaña-hotels. Azulik has villas made of natural materials; Copal has cabins; and Zahra is geared toward families.

TULUM: Piedra Escondida $$$
Inn/B&B
Carretera Tulum-Boca Paila km 3.5
Tel *(984) 100 14 43*
W piedraescondida.com
Set on a lovely sheltered beach. Palm-roofed villas with terraces or balconies and ocean views.

UXMAL: Flycatcher Inn $
Inn/B&B
Off Mex 261 in Santa Elena, 13 km E of Uxmal
Tel *(997) 978 53 50*
W flycatcherinn.com
Family-run B&B with welcoming owners. Spacious rooms with modern facilities and distinctive decor.

UXMAL: Hacienda Temozón $$$
Historic
Carretera Mérida-Uxmal km 182
Tel *(999) 923 80 89*
W haciendatemozon.com
Stunning luxury hotel in a 17th-century colonial hacienda. Rooms have high ceilings and huge bathrooms.

For more information on types of hotels *see p295*

WHERE TO EAT AND DRINK

Mexican cuisine is considered by many to be one of the world's richest and most creative. Chiefly a mix of Spanish and pre-Columbian elements, it has now been influenced by many European and Asian flavors. Dishes originating from all corners of the country are served in a wide variety of restaurants. Visitors will find authentic Mexican cuisine quite different from the "Tex-Mex" Mexican food they may be used to at home. For one thing, it is not necessarily as spicy. However, those who prefer their food milder can order meals without chili *(sin chile)*. Although vegetarian restaurants are rare, many traditional Mexican dishes, especially Spanish *tapas*-style meals like *antojitos* *(see p310)*, are meat-free.

Outdoor café at Parque Cepeda Peraza in Mérida *(see p274)*

Typical Restaurants and Bars

The cheapest places to eat good Mexican food are the small, family-run *fondas* where fixed-price menus *(menú del día* or *comida corrida)* are served at lunch time. These are generally four-course meals followed by coffee or tea.

The most common restaurants are the popular *taquerías*, small places serving tacos at a few tables around a cooking area, where the tortilla-makers can often be seen in action.

Cantinas *(see p120)* are rowdy establishments where heavy drinking is common, and women generally might not feel very comfortable.

In addition to native cuisine, international dining options are widely available, including Italian, Argentinean, Thai, and eclectic fusion fare.

The big cities also have a good selection of cafés, which generally serve light snacks rather than multi-course meals.

Regional Cuisine

First-time visitors are often surprised by the depth and complexity of classic Mexican cooking, which at its core combines indigenous techniques and ingredients with European imports, most of which arrived after the Spanish conquest of the Aztec Empire. Beyond the iconic staples of corn, beans, and chili peppers, diners can experience an assortment of flavors from the country's various regional cuisines. Northern Mexico features an endless array of grilled meats, while the Yucatán is famed for its Caribbean influences. Visitors to Veracruz can enjoy fiery Afro-Cuban flavors, and Oaxaca is famous for its rich *mole* sauces.

A rustic roadside café near Laguna de Chapala *(see p194)*

Chain Restaurants

All the principal American fast-food chains are conspicuous in Mexico, including McDonald's, Burger King, KFC, and Pizza Hut. There are also a number of good homegrown chains. One of the best is VIPS, which serves great breakfasts and international dishes. Other chains are more typically Mexican – Taco Inn serves tasty, original tacos, as well as a good range of vegetarian options, while El Fogoncito sells *tacos al carbon (see p311)*. Potzolcalli specializes in *pozole (see p310)* and *tostadas (see p310)*, while Pollos Río sells a selection of grilled chicken dishes.

Food Hygiene

Health standards are reasonably good in the main tourist hubs of Mexico, but it is still worth taking precautions. Outside of cities, drink only purified water, canned or bottled carbonated drinks, beer, wine, spirits, or hot drinks made from boiled water. In restaurants and bars, consider ordering drinks without ice *(sin hielo)*. Diners should avoid salads and uncooked vegetables in all but the best restaurants and remember to peel all fruit. Steer clear of unpasteurized milk and undercooked shellfish, meat, or fish. Open-air markets and street food stalls should also be treated with caution.

Interior of the charming Café Tacuba *(see p314)*, in the historic heart of Mexico City

Eating Hours

The streets are always full of food vendors because Mexicans eat at any time of day. They often have two breakfasts (*desayunos*). The first, eaten at home, is a light meal of fruit or pastries with milky coffee. A more substantial breakfast, or *almuerzo*, may follow between 10 and 11am and is usually available in restaurants until lunchtime. It may consist of spicy eggs with tortillas, or even a steak.

From about 1:30pm restaurants are ready to provide lunch *(comida)*, traditionally the main meal of the day. Mexicans take two to three hours for lunch, so restaurants are busy until 4 or 5pm.

Between 6 and 8pm is the *merienda*, a time for snacks, or *antojitos (see p310)*, and coffee, tea, or alcoholic drinks. A normal Mexican dinner *(cena)* at home is a light meal served between 8pm and 10pm.

Entertainment

Mexicans like their meals accompanied by music, and many restaurants have live acts performing at least once a week. The music ranges from classical piano to local styles such as festive *mariachi (see p32)* with dancers in colorful costumes, *jarocho* songs from Veracruz, and Mexican-style country music known as *música ranchera*.

Prices and Paying

Fixed-price menus such as *comida corrida* normally offer better value than the à la carte equivalent. Prices shown on menus do not include the mandatory 16 percent tax (IVA), but this will automatically be added to the bill. Service charge is not included, and the amount of tip is left to diners' discretion. It is usual to tip around 10 percent for good service. You are not obliged to leave a tip if the service has been poor.

Credit cards can be used in many restaurants in the larger cities, but in smaller places cash will definitely be required. Travelers' checks are rarely accepted now and, where they are, the exchange rate is poor.

Diners at a thatch-roofed beachside restaurant in Puerto Ángel *(see p221)*

Wheelchair Access

Some restaurants in Mexico make special provision for wheelchair users. The staff in most establishments will do their best to be helpful, and restaurants usually have a bathroom that can accommodate a wheelchair.

Children

Mexicans as a rule love children and most restaurants welcome them, especially family-run places. Few provide high chairs, however, and there is often little room for maneuvering strollers.

Smoking

Throughout Mexico smoking is prohibited in indoor public places such as hotels, restaurants, and airports, but is permitted in outdoor dining areas, and other spaces with special ventilation systems.

Recommended Restaurants

The restaurants featured in this guide have been selected to cover a comprehensive range of cuisine, styles, and price, chosen for their value, good food, atmosphere, and location. From authentic, no-frills snack shacks to pricey temples of gastronomy, these restaurants cross a range of price levels and cuisines. Diners can find a variation of cuisines from local and regional offerings to International tastes and flavors.

For the best of the best, look out for restaurants selected as "DK Choice." These establishments have been highlighted in recognition of a standout feature – be it for their exquisite food, a wonderful atmosphere, or exceptional service. The majority of these acclaimed restaurants are very popular among local residents and visitors alike, so be sure to make a reservation well in advance or you may have to wait for a table.

The Flavors of Mexico

In Mexico, each region's cuisine is distinctive, influenced by the soil, climate, and local produce. The Mexican diet is based on beans, corn, and chilies, and visitors are always amazed at the wide variety of dishes created from such simple foods. Tortillas (the soft, flat pancakes made from wheat or corn) may be tiny or huge, salsas mild to fiery, and beans, which might be red, pinkish-brown, or inky black, may be simply boiled, mashed ("refried"), or stewed with beer and spices. You can taste the rich heritage of the Aztecs, Maya, Olmecs, Mixtecs, and Zapatecs on your plate, along with that of Spanish and other settlers.

Cilantro (coriander)

Browsing the fruit stall at a Mexican street market

Northern Mexico

Baja (lower) California is a peninsula surrounded by sparkling sea, and well-known for its delicious fish tacos. It is also Mexico's vineyard.

El Norte (Chihuahua, Sonora, and Nuevo Leon) is a parched land of cowboys and cattle-raising. As a result, the most common meat is beef, usually cooked over an open fire or salted and dried. The cattle are also a source of dairy produce, and many dishes feature cheese. Beans are served spicy or cooked in beer, and tortillas are made from wheat instead of corn.

On the Pacific coast (from Mazatlan to Puerta Vallarta and Acapulco) shrimp, octopus, clams, oysters, squid, and crayfish are supremely good, and are served as *ceviche*, *antojitos*, or *tamales*, or grilled over an open fire.

Central Mexico

The verdant, lush Central Plains (Aguascalientes, Jalisco, Guanajato, Michoacán, Zacatecas, San Louis Potosi, and Hidalgo) are the source of a wealth of *antojitos* *(see p310)*, best enjoyed with a crisp, cool beer, or shots of tequila. *Pozole*, a stew of pork and hominy (a type of corn) is practically a cult, so beloved is it by the people of Jalisco.

Selection of luscious, ripe Mexican fruits

Mexican Dishes and Specialties

At nearly every meal, a plate of beans, rice, or tortillas will appear on the table. Tortillas are not only the bread of Mexico but also its knife and fork, the soft corn pancakes being torn into pieces and used to wrap up delicious morsels and transport them to the mouth. Salsa will always be on offer, freshly made and full of flavor, often with a hot kick to it. It can be a mixture of any number of ingredients, depending on the region you are in: tomatoes or tomatillos *(see p311)*, onions, chilies, garlic, avocado, citrus fruits, and cilantro (coriander) are all common. And, if that's not spice enough for you, a few bottles of Mexico's myriad hot sauces are usually to hand as well.

Red, black, and garbanzo beans

Huevos rancheros Strips of mixed peppers are sautéed, then eggs are broken into the pan and lightly cooked.

Stallholder's basket of mixed chili peppers

Mexico City is a place of many cultures, where Italian or French food, sushi, gaucho steaks, dim sum, and *cocina nuevo Mexicana* (new Mexican cuisine) can all be enjoyed. To the southeast lies Puebla, whose convents created the famous *mole poblano*, a thick sauce of puréed chilies, seeds, fruits, nuts, spices, and chocolate.

Southern Mexico

The Gulf coastline is rich with shrimp, red snapper, sea bass, crab, octopus, and crayfish. Veracruz is famous for its distinctive garnish of tomatoes, olives, capers, and long peppers.

The Isthmus (Tabasco, Chiapas, and Oaxaca) is a land of fertile soil, home of the Olmecs, Mixtecs, and Zapatecs. In Oaxaca you'll find hand-pounded chocolate, a rainbow of *moles*, and a range of white cheeses as well as delicacies such as fried grasshopper (eaten like popcorn) and crisp-dried maguet worms, ground with chilies as a seasoning.

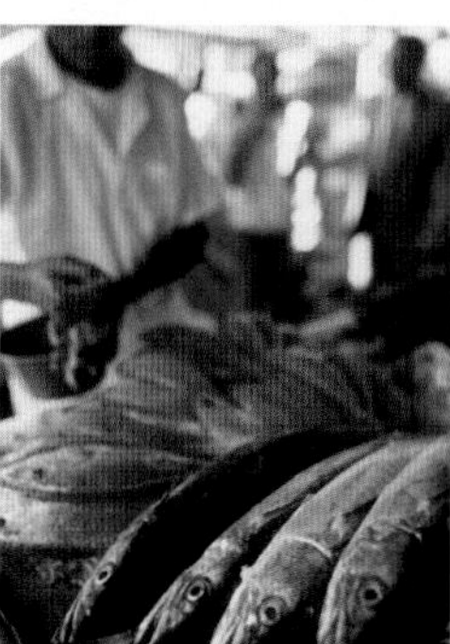

Ocean-fresh fish, straight from the Gulf of Mexico

The Yucatán peninsula (Merida, Cancun, and Cozumel) is the land of the Mayas, once cut off from the rest of Mexico by dense jungle. As well as fresh fish and seafood, try a bowl of *sopa de limon*, chicken soup with tiny yellow limes and crisp tortillas. The Yucatán offers myriad tortilla, bean, and egg dishes, often with pumpkin-seed sauces. Game is traditional, though pork and chicken are more common today. They are rubbed in spice pastes, then wrapped in leaves and baked. Spice pastes are the main flavorings of Yucatecan cuisine – you'll see them piled high in every market.

Street Food

Any number of delicious foods are sold in the street. For a sweet start to the day, find a stall selling *churros* or *buñuelos* (crisp fried pastries) along with coffee or hot chocolate in which to dip them. Walk down any street and inhale the aroma of barbecuing meat, then try some folded into a fresh tortilla. For a vitamin-rich and invigorating snack, buy a slab of fresh pineapple, a whole peeled orange, or a wedge of *jícama* *(see p311)* rubbed with fresh lime and sprinkled liberally with hot chili powder. And if you see a sign for *tortas* you must try one – it's a meal-in-a-roll, filled with meat, refried beans, avocado, salsa, and pickled onion.

Carne asada Spiced steak is barbecued with scallions, chilies, and peppers, and served with tortillas.

Ceviche Raw fish is diced and marinated in lemon juice, then mixed with chili, tomato, onion, and cilantro.

Tamales Corn husks are lined with corn dough and filled with shredded meat, then steamed.

Antojitos

Mexican appetizers are called *antojitos* and are similar to Spanish *tapas*. The name derives from the word *antojo* – "a craving" or "a whim" – and *antojitos* are literally "what you fancy." An *antojito* can be anything from decorative fruit to a substantial savory dish. These tasty little snacks are enjoyed everywhere in Mexico – in homes, bars, restaurants, markets, parks, and streets – at any time, day or night. An *antojito* can be ordered as an aperitif with drinks (when it is called a *botana*) or, in a restaurant, served as a first course.

Guacamole

Tostadas is a dish of crisp-fried tortillas topped with refried beans, chicken, salad, guacamole, and sour cream.

Tortas compuestas, tasty sandwiches made with small French-style loaves called *bolillos* or *terelas*, come with a choice of fillings.

Salsa can be served with *antojitos* as a fresh and spicy dip.

Flautas are tortillas filled with chicken or cheese, deep-fried and served with guacamole or salsa.

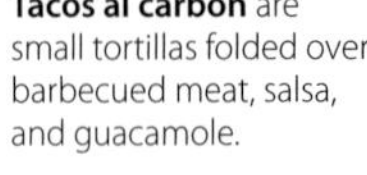

Tacos al carbon are small tortillas folded over barbecued meat, salsa, and guacamole.

Enchiladas, fried, filled, rolled tortillas with a sauce, can have a variety of fillings, such as cheese and onion or chicken.

Sopes are miniature fried corn-dough bowls filled with beans and sauce and topped with salad or cheese.

Street food stallholder preparing a variety of fresh *antojitos*

Popular Antojitos

If you were asked to describe the food of Mexico, the chances are that you would name dishes that are, in fact, *antojitos* – tacos, tostadas, enchiladas, quesadillas – things that you might find on a combination plate in a Mexican restaurant abroad. The most commonly available *antojitos* are dishes of tortillas and *masa* (corn flour), prepared in a variety of shapes and guises and topped or filled with the wide array of ingredients. Quesadillas (fried or grilled corn or wheat tortillas filled with melted cheese) are a delicious *antojito*. In addition to the cheese, they might contain *rajas* (sautéed mild chilies) or *carnitas* (long-simmered small pieces of pork). Tacos are popular *antojitos*, with a huge range of possible fillings, such as shrimp or fish with avocado, lobster with beans, stewed meat or simmered beans, or even strange ingredients such as the ants' eggs of Oaxaca.

Reading the Menu

General vocabulary likely to be useful when eating out is given in the Phrase Book on pages 389–92. The list below gives the main items and ingredients you will probably see on a Mexican menu, in alphabetical order. Not all regional variations of dishes are listed here. Some dishes commonly thought to be Mexican – burritos, fajitas, taco shells, and nachos – were actually invented in the United States. In Mexico, the main meal of the day is quite formal, starting with a soup or rice dish, followed by meat or fish, and ending with flan or a fruit dessert.

Chilies

achiote red paste made from annatto seeds.
adobo light version of *mole.*
albóndigas meatballs.
annatto small, dark red seed used by the Maya Indians to color and flavor food.
ate thick fruit jelly, typically made of quince or guava, often served with cheese.
atún tuna fish. Note that *tuna* is a fruit.
barbacoa lamb cooked in a pit.
buñuelos dessert of crispy, fried wheat pancakes.
cajeta de Celaya fudge sauce made with goat's milk.
caldo largo soup made with fish and seafood.
carne a la Tampiqueña thin strips of beef, grilled.
carnitas marinated fried pork.
cecina semi-dried, salted meat in thin slices.
chalupas boat-shaped, fried corn tortillas garnished with sauce, lettuce, and onions.
chicharrón pork scratchings.
chiles rellenos chilies stuffed with cheese or ground meat, battered, fried, and covered in tomato sauce.
chongos milky dessert of curds in syrup and cinnamon.
chorizo spicy pork sausage.

Dishes on a street food stall in the market at Oaxaca *(see p226–9)*

Street market in San Cristóbal de las Casas *(see p235)*

churros sugary, deep-fried batter sticks.
cochinita pibil Maya dish of suckling pig cooked in a pit.
cuitlacoche (or *huitlacoche*) fungus growing on corncobs; it is considered a delicacy.
dulce de calabaza stewed pumpkin in cinnamon syrup.
enchiladas suizas corn tortillas filled with chicken, covered in sauce, melted cheese and cream.
energético breakfast fruit salad with muesli and yogurt.
entomatada soft tortilla in a tomato sauce.
epazote aromatic herb used to flavor many dishes.
flor de calabaza pumpkin flower.
frijoles beans. Often eaten refried *(see p308)* or freshly cooked as *frijoles de olla*.
gorditas thick tortillas stuffed with cheese.
horno, al baked.
huevos a la mexicana scrambled eggs with tomatoes, chilies, and onions.
huevos motuleños tortilla topped with ham, fried eggs, and a sauce made with cheese, peas, and tomato.
huevos revueltos scrambled eggs.
jícama vegetable similar to a turnip; salted and sprinkled with lime and chili powder.
machaca sundried shredded beef from Nuevo León.
mole means "sauce" in Nahuatl. All *moles* are made using chilies, nuts, and spices. Green, red, and yellow *moles* are usually served with pork or chicken.
moros con cristianos rice dish made with black beans, garnished with fried plantain.
nopal the fleshy leaf of the prickly pear (paddle cactus).
panucho a Yucatecan dish of layered tortillas stuffed with beans.
pescado al mojo de ajo fish filet in a white, garlic sauce.
pipián pumpkin-seed sauce.
plátano macho frito fried plantain. Goes well with rice.
pollo verde almendrado chicken in green tomatillo and almond sauce.
pozole pork and corn soup.
puntas de filete quartered beef filet ends.
queso fresco a white cheese that is crumbled over some cooked dishes.
rajas chili strips and onion slices in tomato sauce.
sopa soup. Varieties include *de aguacate* (avocado), *de fideo* (chicken noodle), and *de lima* (chicken stock with lemon).
tacos al carbón soft corn tortillas wrapped around cooked meats.
tomatillo a berry related to the Cape gooseberry *(Physalis)*, which is used for flavoring sauces.
Veracruzana, a la fish cooked with tomatoes and onions.

What to Drink in Mexico

Mexico offers a wide variety of drinks, both alcoholic and nonalcoholic, but choose carefully if you don't want health problems. Outside of cities, don't drink tap water – buy bottled water from a supermarket or reputable shop. It is wise to avoid fruit juices, milkshakes, and other drinks sold at market and street stalls or in bars of dubious cleanliness. Soft drinks in bottles, cartons, and cans are all safe.

Los Danzantes bar in Mexico City *(see p316)*

Beer

Light and dark Mexican beers

Beer *(cerveza)* was introduced to Mexico by German immigrant miners. Much of the beer drunk is lager *(cerveza rubia)*, but there are also several good dark beers *(cerveza oscura)* available. Popular brands are Corona, Negra Modelo, and XX Dos Equis. *Michelada* is a refreshing drink made with beer and lime juice, and served with salt on the rim of the glass.

Wines

White wine by Domecq

Although Mexico is the oldest wine producer in the Americas, Mexicans are not big wine drinkers. The main vineyards are in the Valle de Guadalupe near Ensenada *(see p166)*, where the pioneer Bodega Santo Tomás is based, as is Monte Xanic. Other Baja California producers include Pinson and Cetto. Wine is made in Querétaro (by Cavas de San Juan, Freixenet, and Domecq), in Zacatecas (by Pinson), and in Coahuila (by Casa Madero). Imported wine is available too.

Other Alcoholic Drinks

Many other drinks are served in Mexican bars and restaurants, especially *kahlúa* (a coffee liqueur flavored with vanilla), *ron* (rum), and *rompope*, an eggnog made in Puebla, often offered to children or the elderly. *Aguardiente* is a fiery spirit, not for the faint hearted. Standard international cocktails include piña colada, a refreshing blend of pineapple juice, rum, and coconut, and daiquiri, made with rum, lime juice, and sugar.

Kahlúa *Rompope*

Cold Drinks and Fruit Juices

There are plenty of soft drinks available, but in a bar always make sure you drink from a bottle that has been opened in front of you. Water can be ordered still *(sin gas)* or fizzy *(con gas)*. Canned fizzy drinks are called *refrescos*. All the international varieties are available. A selection of freshly prepared fruit juices is also available, but try to choose those made with fruits that need to be peeled. Made like lemonade, *naranjada* is a refreshing orange juice drink. *Agua de Jamaica* is made from a hibiscus flower steeped in hot water and served chilled.

Agua de Jamaica Orange juice

Hot Drinks

Coffee is generally medium-strength filter coffee *(café americano)* which can be served with milk. For a strong, authentic Mexican coffee order *café de olla*, sweetened and flavored with cinnamon. Black coffee is *café negro, tinto,* or *solo*. Tea is not widely drunk but herb teas, such as camomile *(manzanilla)*, mint *(hierbabuena)*, and lemongrass *(té limón)*, are available. *Atole* is a nutritious drink of corn meal and milk, flavored with chocolate or fruits. Hot chocolate *(chocolate caliente)*, made with vanilla or cinnamon, is also popular.

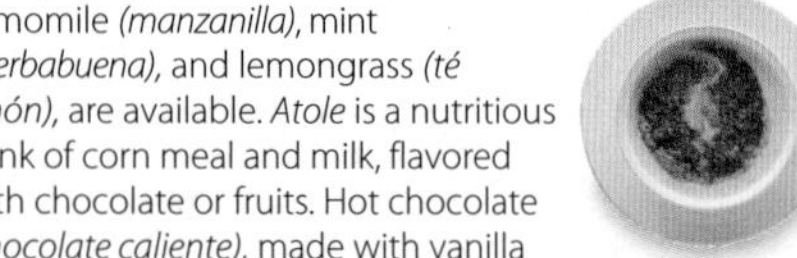

Atole

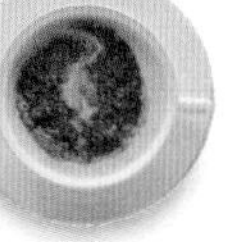

Café de olla

Hot chocolate

Tequila and Mezcal

Tequila and Mezcal are both internationally known Mexican aperitifs, distilled from the sap of different species of the agave plant. Tequila is to mezcal as Cognac is to brandy – a refined, connoisseur's drink. Both are made from similar ingredients by a similar process, but tequila can be produced only in a strictly defined region that centers on the town of Tequila near Guadalajara *(see p191)*. Both drinks are distantly derived from pulque, a low-alcohol, fermented beverage made from another species of agave, which was drunk by the people of ancient Mexico. If you stay any length of time in Mexico you will almost certainly be offered at least one glass of mezcal or tequila.

Pulque was first made as early as 200 BC. It was used by priests as a way of inducing a religious trance and given to sacrificial victims to ease their passage into the next world. Pulque, which is never bottled, is an acquired taste.

Buying Tequila and Mezcal

The best tequila is made from 100 percent blue agave: this is stated on the label to prove that sugar has not been added. Tequila comes in three varieties. *Blanco* (white) is unaged, clear, and colorless. *Reposado* and *añejo* are tequilas which have been aged in oak barrels (for up to a year and three years respectively), turning them an amber color. *Mezcal con gusano* is made near Oaxaca and Zacatecas. A caterpillar is placed in the bottle to prove that the mezcal is high enough in alcohol to preserve it.

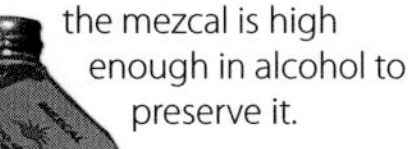

Mezcal con gusano

Tequila reposado

How Tequila Is Made

Tequila is made by fermenting the sap of the agave and distilling the resultant mixture twice before bottling.

Stage one The agave (Agave tequilana weber) is harvested after 8–10 years, before it flowers. The leaves are removed, leaving a compact heart or piña (literally "pineapple").

Stage two The *piñas* are steamed in an oven and crushed to release their sap, the raw material for tequila.

Stage three Yeast is added to the sap. After a period of fermentation the liquid is distilled twice to purify it. The tequila is then either bottled or aged in oak vats.

How to Drink Tequila

Tequila is usually served with lime and salt or as a *vampiro* with a tomato and orange chaser called a *sangrita*. *Tequila blanco* is often mixed with other drinks to make cocktails like tequila sunrise (with grenadine and orange juice), and margarita, made with lime juice and triple sec and served with salt around the rim of the glass.

Tequila with lime and salt

Where to Eat and Drink

Mexico City

The Historic Center

Café el Popular $
Regional Mexican **Map** 4 E2
Av de 5 de Mayo 50 & 52, Col Centro
Tel *(55) 55 18 60 81*
A crowd of regulars lend credence to the cafe's name. Fresh-baked goods at reasonable prices are the draw. Enjoy regional specialties and Oaxacan *tamales*.

Café Tacuba $
Regional Mexican **Map** 4 D1
Tacuba 28, Col Centro
Tel *(55) 55 21 20 48*
Dating back to 1912, this cafés interior walls are lined with paintings of historic scenes. Freshly baked goods, filling *tamales*, and regional food from all over Mexico is on offer.

Café Trevi $
Italian **Map** 3 B1
Colón 1, Col Centro
Tel *(55) 55 12 30 20*
A decades-old mainstay for Italian fare, Café Trevi is especially known for its homemade pastas and thin-crust pizzas. Attentive servers maintain a convivial atmosphere. The large picture windows face the scenic Alameda.

Churrería el Moro $
Regional Mexican **Map** 4 D2
Lázaro Cárdenas 42
Tel *(55) 55 12 08 96*
This institution near the Palacio de Bellas Artes specializes in fresh, hot *churros*. For an additional sugar fix, choose from the milk-shakes and four types of hot chocolate. Tiles walls and columns make for a lovely setting.

Azul Histórico $$
Modern Mexican **Map** 4 E2
Isabel la Católica 30, Col Centro
Tel *(55) 55 10 13 16*
Mexican regional cuisine gets a contemporary update at this restaurant. Enjoy sophisticated dishes of locally-sourced meat, fish, and vegetarian dishes.

Bar la Ópera $$
Spanish **Map** 4 D1
Av 5 de Mayo 10, Col Centro
Tel *(55) 55 12 89 59*
The most opulent of the city's turn-of-the-20th-century cantinas, Bar la Ópera provides a supreme visual and cultural treat for visitors. Try the house specialty – *pulpo a la castellana* (octopus in a tomato sauce).

El Cardenal $$
Regional Mexican **Map** 4 E2
Palma 23, Col Centro
Tel *(55) 55 21 30 80*
Reasonably priced, pre-Hispanic specialties as well as good comfort food served in a refined dining setting. Adventurous, authentic dishes on the menu include *escamoles al epazote* (ant eggs in a pungent herb sauce).

Casa de los Azulejos – Sanborns $$
International **Map** 4 D2
Francisco Madero 4, Col Centro
Tel *(55) 55 12 13 31*
The most famous Sanborns restaurant in Mexico is a supreme downtown meeting place with an international menu. The enchiladas are renowned – home cooking at its best.

Casa de las Sirenas $$
Modern **Map** 4 F1
República de Guatemala 32, Col Centro
Tel *(55) 57 04 32 73*
Housed in a 16th-century building, the main dining floor and colorful courtyard showcase a stunning rear view of the city's Catedral Metropolitana. Serves over 200 varieties of tequila along with nouvelle Mexican cuisine.

Casino Español $$
Spanish **Map** 4 D2
Isabel la Católica 29, Col Centro
Tel *(55) 55 10 29 67*
Casino Español has been serving delicious Spanish favorites like *paella* and roast baby pork for decades. There is a casual cantina-style eatery downstairs and an impressive elegant restaurant upstairs.

The elegant dining area of El Cardenal, Mexico City

Price Guide
Prices are based on a three-course meal for one, with a glass of house wine, including tax and service.

$	**up to $15**
$$	**$15 to $35**
$$$	**over $35**

Centro Castellano $$
Spanish **Map** 4 D2
Uruguay 16 & 18, Col Centro
Tel *(55) 55 18 60 80*
Close to the Zócalo, this restored house has a welcoming atmosphere. Savor authentic Spanish food with an emphasis on fresh seafood. The house specialty, *uachinango al perejil* (red snapper), is highly recommended.

Danubio $$
Seafood **Map** 4 D2
Uruguay 3, Col Centro
Tel *(55) 55 12 09 12*
Popular since 1936 for its well-prepared seafood recipes. Legions of waiters ferry platters of stuffed red snapper, smoked Norwegian salmon, and the specialty, *langostinos* (crayfish) in *mojo de ajo* (garlic sauce).

Fonda Don Chon $$
Modern Mexican **Map** 4 E3
Calle Regina 160, Col Centro
Tel *(55) 55 42 08 73* **Closed** *Dinner; Sun*
One of the city's most famous spots for pre-Hispanic food such as ant eggs, armadillo stew, roast *tepezquintle* (a type of rodent), and wild boar in mango sauce. Casual environs with mismatched furniture. Lunch only.

Los Girasoles $$
Regional Mexican **Map** 4 D1
Tacuba 8, Col Centro
Tel *(55) 55 10 06 30*
One of the neighborhood's few street-level restaurants, Los Girasoles offers French country decor indoors or views of the Museo Nacional de Arte outdoors. The menu ranges from pre-Hispanic specialties through nouvelle Mexican.

Hosteriá Santo Domingo $$
Regional Mexican **Map** 4 E1
Belisario Dominguez 72, Col Centro
Tel *(55) 55 26 52 76*
Dating back to 1860, this is one of the city's most lively, colorful, and popular restaurants. Try regional specialties such as *mole poblano* (chocolate-infused sauce) and *chiles en nogada* (stuffed peppers in walnut sauce).

La Terraza $$
Regional Mexican **Map** 4 E2
Francisco Madero 73, Col Centro
Tel *(55) 55 21 86 00*
Since 1937, the top-floor restaurant of the Hotel Majestic has offered excellent outdoor dining with views of the Zócalo. Although the menu is international, it has a number of Mexican specialties such as *chilaquiles* and *mole poblano.*

Reforma and Chapultepec

Fonda Mexicana $
Modern Mexican **Map** 1 A2
Homero 1910, Col Polanco
Tel *(55) 55 57 61 44*
Located in the chic Polanco neighborhood, hip Fonda Mexicana matches its well-dressed clientele. The menu focuses on specialties from Puebla, including *arrachera a la parrilla* (marinated flank steak) and *mole poblano.*

Los Almendros $$
Regional Mexican **Map** 1 A3
Campos Elíseos 164, Col Polanco
Tel *(55) 55 31 66 46*
Yucatecan food springs to life in this upscale branch of the Yucatán-based chain. Sample authentic renderings of *pollo* and *cochinita pibils* (slow-roasted chicken and pork) and *salbutes* (fried *masa* appetizer).

Bellinghausen $$
International **Map** 2 E3
Londres 95, Col Juárez
Tel *(55) 52 07 61 49*
Power-lunch spot where swarms of well turned-out waiters serve platters of meat and seafood in the stately dining room or outside on the patio. The house specialty is *filete chemita* (grilled beef steak).

La Bottiglia $$
Italian **Map** 1 B3
Edgar Allan Poe 8, Col Polanco
Tel *(55) 52 80 06 09*
Invitingly intimate spot, with cloth-covered tables and candles in Chianti bottles. The menu features innovative takes on Italian food such as red snapper in artichoke sauce.

Casa Portuguesa $$
Portuguese
Emilio Castelar 111, Col Polanco
Tel *(55) 52 81 00 75*
Located in a modern space with white walls and oversized windows. Offers delicious Portuguese dishes with a focus on seafood – try one of the numerous cod specials. Fine Portuguese wines and ports.

Stylish place setting at Dulce Patria, Reforma and Chapultepec

Dulce Patria $$
Modern Mexican
Anatole France 100, Col Polanco
Tel *(55) 33 00 39 99*
Classic Mexican dishes receive a modern treatment at this stylish restaurant. Flavor is rivaled only by presentation, which is creative and whimsical.

La Fonda del Recuerdo $$
Seafood **Map** 1 C2
Bahía de las Palmas 37, Col Verónica Anzures
Tel *(55) 91 12 74 76*
A rousing atmosphere, complete with live music, accompanies the mouthwatering fish and seafood *platillos* served here. Carnivores have plenty to choose from as well, including *carne Tampiqueña* (grilled beef).

Fonda del Refugio $$
Regional Mexican **Map** 2 E4
Liverpool 166, Col Juárez
Tel *(55) 52 07 27 32*
This small restaurant showcases Mexico's regional food. The decades-old interior features gleaming white walls, copper pots, and folk art. Mainstays on the menu include *chiles rellenos* (stuffed chilies) and *mole verde de pepita* (green *mole*).

Un Lugar de la Mancha $$
International
Esopo 11, Col Polanco
Tel *(55) 52 80 48 26*
Un Lugar de la Mancha, with a reference to *Don Quixote,* has a pretty floral garden. The varied international menu is dotted with Mexican favorites. There is also an attached bookstore.

Matisse $$
European
Amsterdam 260, Col Condesa
Tel *(55) 52 64 58 53*
Matisse is a delightful, cozy neighborhood restaurant in a restored 1930s house, filled with period furniture. The European menu includes hearty omelets, ratatouille, escargots, and homemade pastries. Tacos and other familiar Mexican treats available as well.

Máximo Bistrot Local $$
Mexican
Tonalá 133, Col Roma
Tel *(55) 52 64 42 91* **Closed** *Sun*
The menu changes daily at this popular restaurant, which is always teeming with guests. Local and seasonal ingredients are used to prepare simple yet delicious dishes.

Nautilus $$
Seafood **Map** 1 A2
Av Presidente Masarik 360, Col Polanco
Tel *(55) 52 80 22 83*
A casual yet trendy restaurant with an extensive menu that includes three kinds of *chilaquiles* at breakfast. Also on offer are delicious fish and seafood tacos, and main courses of meat, fish, and seafood using recipes from around the globe.

Rosetta $$
Italian
Colima 166, Col Roma
Tel *(55) 55 33 78 04* **Closed** *Sun*
Widely agreed to be Mexico City's best Italian restaurant, this pleasant, conveniently located restaurant is housed in an elegant townhouse. It serves delectable dishes such as handmade pastas and breads cooked by renowned chef Elena Reygadas.

For more information on types of restaurants *see p307*

Vibrant dining room of Contramar, Reforma and Chapultepec

Au Pied de Cochon $$$
French **Map** 1 A3
Campos Elisios 218
Tel *(55) 53 27 77 56*
One of the city's most popular French eateries, this bustling place is open until late. The chef turns out classic French dishes accompanied by an impressive, varied wine list.

Biko $$$
Spanish/Mexican
Av Presidente Masarik 407, Col Polanco
Tel *(55) 52 82 20 64* **Closed** *Sun*
Two inventive chefs, a Basque and a Mexican, bring the best of their countries' cuisines to this trendy, sophisticated restaurant. Biko features in Restaurant Magazine's list of the World's 50 Best Restaurants.

Contramar $$$
Seafood **Map** 2 D5
Calle Durango 200, Col Roma
Tel *(55) 55 14 31 69*
Unusual for a Mexico City restaurant, the menu at Contramar is almost exclusively made up of seafood dishes. Large, bright, and modern environs with an open kitchen. Consistently receives rave reviews, yet keeps prices reasonable.

DK Choice

Hacienda de los Morales $$$
Regional Mexican
Vázquez de Mella 525, Col del Bosque
Tel *(55) 52 83 30 29*
Housed in a spacious 16th-century hacienda, this restaurant's Spanish colonial decor includes wood furnishings and domed brick ceilings. Sit at one of the gardenside tables or in a romantic nook in one of the private salons. The diverse menu includes expertly prepared Mexican specialties and some nouvelle Mexican dishes.

El Lago $$$
Mexican **Map** 1 A4
Lago Mayor, 2a Sección
Tel *(55) 55 15 95 85*
Overlooking Chapultepec Park, this is one of the city's most stylish locations. The contemporary Mexican cuisine is served in a tiered dining room. The restaurant utilizes the best available ingredients including fresh fish along with local vegetables and herbs.

Les Moustaches $$$
French **Map** 2 D2
Río Sena 88, Col Cuauhtémoc
Tel *(55) 55 25 12 65*
This is considered one of the city's finest French options, thanks to its delectable cuisine and excellent wine list. Housed in a 20th-century mansion, the elegant dining area is filled with candlelit tables.

Pujol $$$
Modern Modern
Francisco Petrarca 254, Col Polanco
Tel *(55) 55 45 35 07* **Closed** *Sun*
Mexican star chef Enrique Olvera heads up the kitchen at this intimate, exceptional restaurant, where traditional Mexican ingredients are given contemporary treatments. Ranked among the world's top 50 restaurants.

Quintonil $$$
Regional Mexican
Newton 55, Col Polanco
Tel *(55) 52 80 16 60* **Closed** *Sun*
Quintonil offers imaginative interpretations of traditional Mexican cuisine. The acclaimed young chef uses regional ingredients to create modern dishes. The trendy crowd and decor would not be out of place in London or New York City.

Rincón Argentino $$$
Argentinian **Map** 1 A2
Av Presidente Masarik 177, Col Polanco
Tel *(55) 52 54 87 44*
Colorful Argentinian restaurant known for its exquisite cuts of beef served with authentic *chimichurri* sauce. The interior has a bar covered by a thatch roof, and the ceiling is painted to resemble the sky.

Specia $$$
European
Amsterdam 241, Col Hipódromo Condesa
Tel *(55) 55 64 95 76*
Dine with a view of Condesa through large picture windows. The wide European menu focuses on specialties from Poland and Hungary such as stuffed cabbage, baked lamb, and goulash.

Tezka $$$
Spanish **Map** 2 E3
Amberes 78, Col Juárez
Tel *(55) 91 49 30 00*
Located in the handsome Royal Zona Rosa Hotel, Tezka serves delightfully innovative Basque cuisine with nouvelle twists. The kitchen is a training ground for the city's brightest young chefs.

San Ángel and Coyoacán

Cantina La Coyoacána $$
Mexican
Higuera 14, Col Coyoacan
Tel *(55) 56 58 53 37*
This pleasing cantina has a well-stocked bar, and a varied menu of Mexican specialties such as *barbacoa* (meat cooked in an earth pit) and *tlacoyos* (stuffed masa cakes).

El Convento $$
Regional Mexican
Fernández Leal 96, Col Coyoacan
Tel *(55) 55 54 40 65* **Closed** *Sun*
Housed in a beautifully restored 16th-century convent, with garden seating along the cloister and colorful stained-glass windows. The menu includes contemporary Mexican dishes such as *pollo relleno de frutas secas* (chicken stuffed with sun-dried fruit).

Los Danzantes $$
Modern Mexican
Plaza Jardín Centenario 12, Col Coyoacan
Tel *(55) 55 54 12 13*
Oaxacan-Mexican specialties are served in this colonial-style restaurant. Dishes like *huitlacoche* (mushroom) ravioli and shrimp in coconut feature on the contemporary menu. The Mexican aperitif mezcal is made in Los Danzantes' own distillery.

Key to Price Guide *see p314*

Fonda San Ángel $$
Regional Mexican
Plaza San Jacinto 3, Col San Ángel
Tel *(55) 55 50 16 41*
Located near Bazaar Sábado, this place gets busy when the market does. Popular dishes include pork in plum sauce and cheese soup flavored with *poblanos*.

Restaurante San Ángel Inn $$$
Regional Mexican
Diego Rivera 50, Col San Ángel
Tel *(55) 56 16 22 22*
Housed in a 17th-century hacienda with spacious gardens, San Ángel Inn has served patrons since 1963. Delicious Mexican and international dishes on offer.

Farther Afield

Antigua Hacienda Tlalpan $$
International
Calzada de Tlalpan 4619, Col Tlalpan
Tel *(55) 56 55 78 88*
An 18th-century hacienda, tastefully resurrected into a quintessential Colonial-style destination, with scenic gardens filled with peacocks. The sophisticated international menu also includes Mexican specialties.

Casa Merlos $$
Regional Mexican
Victoriano Zepeda 80, Col Observatorio
Tel *(55) 52 77 43 60*
Specializing in Puebla cuisine, Casa Merlos is situated in a neighborhood south of Chapultepec Park. Colorful *mole* sauces are the big draw, along with other Puebla favorites including chicken *tinga* and *molotes* (empanadas).

Mazurka $$$
Polish
Nueva York 150, Col Nápoles
Tel *(55) 55 23 88 11*
The city's oldest Polish restaurant, Mazurka served Pope John Paul II on several occasions and offers a Degustación del Papa (Pope's menu). The casual environs mirror the hearty fare.

Around Mexico City

CHOLULA: Los Jarrones $
Regional Mexican
Portal Guerrero 7
Tel *(222) 247 10 98*
Los Jarrones is among the many restaurants under the *portales* facing the main square, with a popular terrace overlooking the plaza. The menu includes traditional Mexican fare plus a variety of soup, sandwiches, and pastries.

CUERNAVACA: Los Arcos $
Regional Mexican
Jardín de los Héroes 4
Tel *(777) 312 15 10*
For decades this plain but popular sidewalk restaurant opposite the Plaza de Armas has been a prime location for people-watching. The all-day menu has everything from morning coffee to late-night bites and cocktails.

CUERNAVACA: Armando's Pizzeria & Ristorante $$
Italian
Av Avila Camacho 500, Col Tlaltenango
Tel *(777) 317 19 55*
Popular spot for thin-crust pizzas with a wide selection of toppings; the menu also includes pasta dishes. Friendly service helps maintain the casual atmosphere. Many devotees opt to take their pizza to go.

CUERNAVACA: Gaia Bistro Wine Bar $$
International
Pabellón Vista Hermosa, Local 9/10, Av Río Mayo 1209, Col Vista Hermosa
Tel *(777) 316 00 00*
Part bistro, part wine bar, this romantic and casual spot is located in a strip mall. The contemporary dishes include delicious fusion sauces and are made with local ingredients. The lengthy international wine list is considered one of the city's best.

CUERNAVACA: La India Bonita $$
Modern Mexican
Dwight Morrow 15, Col Centro
Tel *(777) 312 50 21*
Cuernavaca's oldest restaurant is set in the lush courtyard of the former residence of Dwight Morrow, the American ambassador to Mexico from 1927 to 1930. La India Bonita serves traditional Mexican dishes including *chile en nogada* (*poblano* pepper in walnut sauce).

CUERNAVACA: El Madrigal $$$
Regional Mexican
Sonora 115, Col Vista Hermosa
Tel *(777) 100 77 00* **Closed** *Mon*
The inviting environs here feature colonial architecture and verdant gardens, and a choice of tables on the open or covered terrace. El Madrigal offers a sophisticated blend of Mexican and international dishes such as *filet mignon* and *arroz con leche brûlee* (baked rice pudding).

CUERNAVACA: Las Mañanitas $$$
Modern Mexican
Ricardo Linares 107, Col Centro
Tel *(777) 330 24 00*
One of the city's most popular fine-dining destinations, Las Mañanitas has a pretty garden setting complete with strolling peacocks. The international menu also boasts Mexican specialties such as *chile en nogada* (peppers in walnut sauce) and shrimp in tamarind sauce.

PACHUCA: Alex Steak $$
Steakhouse
Glorieta Revolución 102
Tel *(771) 713 00 56*
This handsome, award-winning restaurant is famed for huge portions and the excellence of its steaks. The house specialty is the *mar y tierra*, a combination platter of lobster (or other seafood) and the steak of your choice.

The entrance to the Restaurante San Ángel Inn, San Ángel and Coyoacán

For more information on types of restaurants *see p307*

PACHUCA: Don Horacio $$
Regional Mexican
Av Hidalgo 24, Col Centro Pachuquilla
Tel *(771) 716 05 25*
This temple of pre-Hispanic cuisine has won awards for the authenticity of its food. Great place to try *pulque* (fermented maguey juice) and *mixiotes* (steamed lamb in a sleaf pouch).

PUEBLA: Fonda de Santa Clara $
Regional Mexican
Av 3 Poniente 307
Tel *(222) 242 26 59*
Serving traditional seasonal specialties such as maguey worms and grasshoppers since the 1960s. For those who are less keen to experiment, the *mole poblano* and steamed *mixiotes* are safe bets.

PUEBLA: Tortas Meche $
Regional Mexican
Portal Juárez 111
Tel *(222) 232 86 28*
This casual eatery facing the main plaza is a handy spot for no-frills, comforting food, as well as fresh coffee and hot chocolate. Try the popular *consomeche* (chicken soup) and *torta de jamon* (ham sandwich).

PUEBLA: La Vaca Negra $
Regional Mexican
Av Reforma 106
Tel *(222) 246 20 51*
Located in a colonial-style building on the main square. Typical Mexican offerings are available, including local specialties such as *mole poblano* and *chalupas*, plus juicy hamburgers and giant hot dogs.

PUEBLA: Bola Roja $$
Regional Mexican
5 Poniente 2522-A
Tel *(222) 230 01 22*
Despite being one of the city's most well-regarded restaurants amongst locals, Bola Roja remains unknown to many toursists. Try the excellent *escamoles* (ant eggs prepared in a wine sauce) and fresh *mixiotes*.

DK Choice

PUEBLA: Mesón de Sacristía $$
Regional Mexican
Calle 6 Sur 304
Tel *(222) 232 45 13*
Located in the covered patio of the stylish small hotel of the same name. The kitchen specializes in traditional Pueblan cuisine and seasonal dishes such as *chiles en nogada, mole poblano,* and *chalupas*. Choose between the handsome dining room, the sunny courtyard patio, and the romantic piano room featuring live music at the weekends.

PUEBLA: El Mural de los Poblanos $$
Regional Mexican
16 de Septiembre 506
Tel *(222) 242 66 96*
Popular spot offering a wide range of delicious culinary options. Specialties include hearty seafood dishes along with traditional meals such as *mole poblano* or fish *mixiote*. Live *saltería* music on weekends.

TAXCO: El Adobe $
Regional Mexican
Plazuela San Juan 13
Tel *(762) 622 14 16*
Charming restaurant in the heart of Taxco, serving inexpensive dishes such as *cecina taxqueña* (thin strips of steak served with guacamole) and enchiladas. Live music at weekends.

TAXCO: La Hacienda $
Regional Mexican
Plaza Borda 4
Tel *(762) 622 11 66*
Located inside the Hotel Agua Escondida, this elegant restaurant is filled with colonial furniture and Mexican decor. The extensive menu of traditional local dishes includes hand-made tortillas and *cecina* steak with rice and beans, served with fresh guacamole.

Typical courtyard dining of Sotavento Restaurant Bar, Taxco

TAXCO: Restaurante Ethel $
Regional Mexican
Plazuela San Juan 14
Tel *(762) 622 07 88*
Casual eatery offering a standard Mexican menu containing some regional specialties such as *cecina* and *pozole*. The multi-course *comida corrida* (fixed-price meal) includes soup, main, rice, and dessert.

TAXCO: Del Angel Inn $$
International
Celso Muñoz 4
Tel *(762) 622 55 25*
This rooftop restaurant surrounded by colonial-era buildings is popular with tour groups due to its fantastic views. The varied menu includes international and Mexican dishes. Live *mariachi* bands often perform.

TAXCO: Sotavento Restaurant Bar $$
International
Juan Ruíz de Alarcón, Hotel Los Arcos
Tel *(762) 627 12 17* **Closed** *Mon*
Occupying a beautiful old home, Sotavento is decorated with colorful Mexican paintings. Additional seating is laid out on the front porch and plant-filled back patio. Choose from a varied menu of European and Mexican dishes.

TEOTIHUACÁN: Villas Arqueológicas $$
Regional Mexican
Periférico Sur s/n, Zona Arqueológica
Tel *(555) 836 90 20*
Villas Arqueológicas is a good place to relax after a walk around its manicured gardens or after exploring the adjacent archaeological ruins. Regional specialties are served up on the terrace or in the beautifully ornamented dining room.

TEPOTZOTLÁN: Los Colorines $
Regional Mexican
Av del Tepozteco 13
Tel *(739) 395 01 98*
The primarily Mexican menu at Los Colorines offers unusual delights at fair prices. Try the dish made from the red *colorín* flower that lends its name to the restaurant. Cozy interior decorated with festive banners.

TEPOTZOTLÁN: El Ciruelo $$
Modern Mexican
Zaragoza 17
Tel *(739) 395 25 59*
Enjoy innovative gourmet delicacies coupled with great views at this stylish dining venue. House specialties include *cilantro*

Key to Price Guide *see p314*

(coriander) soup with almonds and *chalupas* (taco shells) with goat cheese amongst a host of other fillings.

TEPOTZOTLÁN: Los Virreyes $$
Regional Mexican
Plaza Vierreinal 32
Tel *(555) 876 02 35*
One of several small restaurants on the shaded plaza opposite the main square, with a romantic atmosphere and nice views. Sample one of the soups or the *cabrito* (young goat) served with beans and rice.

TLAXCALA: Café Avenida $
Regional Mexican
Porfirio Díaz 14
Tel *(246) 466 36 69*
Café Avenida is the perfect choice for breakfast, with special egg dishes including *huevos Tarascos* (bathed in a green sauce with ham) and *huevos poblanos* (tomato sauce with corn and cream).

TLAXCALA: Los Portales $
Regional Mexican
Plaza de la Constitución 8
Tel *(246) 462 54 19*
Located under the colonial-era *portales*, amid the bustle of shops and restaurants, facing Tlaxcala's main square this is a great place for ice cream, coffee, soups, sandwiches, and full meals.

TLAXCALA: Pulquería la Tía Yola $
Regional Mexican
Plaza Xicotencatl 7
Tel *(246) 462 73 09* **Closed** *Mon*
The house specialty here is *pulque*, an alcoholic drink made from agave and one of Mexico's original spirits. The food menu focuses on regional delights.

TLAXCALA: Las Cazuelas $$
Regional Mexican
Km 20, Carretera San Martín Tlaxcala
Tel *(246) 462 50 02* **Closed** *Mon*
Las Cazuelas is an award-winning restaurant that emphasizes Tlaxcaltecan specialties. Try the soup, Tocatlán chicken steamed in maguey leaves, or the chicken in amaranth sauce made with a pre-Hispanic grain.

TOLUCA: La Vaquita Negra del Portal $
Regional Mexican
Portal Reforma 124, Int B
Tel *(722) 215 68 47*
This traditional eatery is a popular choice for fresh, over-stuffed sandwiches (the *toluqueña* contains chorizo, cheese, tomato, and *salsa verde*), and simple Mexican fare.

Modern decor and contemporary dining in Amaranta, Toluca

TOLUCA: Waffleria Shefali $
Vegetarian
José Vicente Villada 435
Tel *(722) 213 81 32*
A good place to take a break with a cup of tea or to indulge in the house specialty – delicious waffles. Casual decor with Mexican bric-a-brac.

TOLUCA: Nortesur $$
Regional Mexican
Ignacio Comonfort 302
Tel *(722) 199 44 24*
Try an assortment of regional Mexican specialties at this restaurant, which re-creates the ambience of an old train station. The terrace is the most coveted spot for a table.

TOLUCA: Amaranta $$$
Modern Mexican
Francisco Murguia 402, Col Universidad
Tel *(722) 280 82 65*
Thoroughly modern Mexican delights made with an eye towards authentic regional recipes. Not too far from the city's main commercial zone. Attentive service and an extensive wine list.

VALLE DE BRAVO: La Michoacana $
Regional Mexican
Calle de la Cruz 100
Tel *(726) 262 16 25*
Huge windows overlook the village, lake, and mountains, while diners sample food from the lengthy menu of Mexican and pre-Hispanic offerings. Large dining room and a welcoming lounge.

VALLE DE BRAVO: Da Ciro $$
Italian
Vergel 201
Tel *(726) 262 01 22* **Closed** *Mon–Thu*
Tempting aromas of wood-fired pizzas and other Italian specialties lure diners to Da Ciro, located a short walk from the town's central square. Choose to dine on the plant-filled patio or the comfortable interior. Also popular for takeout pizza.

Northern Mexico

CABO SAN LUCAS: Burrito Surf, Burrito Shop 1895 $
Regional Mexican
Corner of Niños Heroes y Matamoros
Tel *(624) 143 00 98*
Giant California-style burritos make for a fresh and fast meal at this no-frills spot. Healthy and vegetarian options abound, along with the usual Mexican staples. Look out for the daily specials, including cheap beer.

CABO SAN LUCAS: La Dolce $
Italian
Hidalgo and Zapata
Tel *(624) 143 41 22*
One of the region's most popular Italian options, with its authentic wood-oven pizzas and signature pasta specialties featuring fresh local seafood. A casual place, often packed out with locals and tourists alike.

CABO SAN LUCAS: El Coral Restaurant & Mesquite Grill $$
Regional Mexican
Intersection of Blvd Marina & Calle Hidalgo
Tel *(624) 143 01 50*
One of the area's oldest restaurants with open-air *palapa* dining since 1975. Typical Mexican and Tex-Mex offerings are served in a child-friendly atmosphere. The rustic decor features hand-carved chairs.

CABO SAN LUCAS: Hacienda Cocina y Cantina $$
Regional Mexican
Calle Gomez Farias s/n
Tel *(624) 163 31 44*
The signature restaurant of the Hacienda Beach Club serves traditional Mexican cuisine in a casual beachfront location. Dine on the outdoor terrace by the beachfront bar.

For more information on types of restaurants *see p307*

CABO SAN LUCAS: The Office on the Beach $$
Regional Mexican/American
Paseo Pescador at Médano Beach
Tel *(624) 143 34 64*
Idyllic beachfront restaurant serving seafood, sandwiches, and *cerveza* (beer). The shrimp fajitas sizzle, while the tacos come loaded with fish, shrimp, beef, or chicken. The juicy hamburgers and fries are always popular.

CABO SAN LUCAS: Pancho's $$
Regional Mexican
Corner of Hidalgo & Zapata
Tel *(624) 143 28 91*
Pancho's is a tequila bar renowned for its list of nearly 1,000 tequilas. Serves enormous platters of Mexican and seafood specialties. Colorful Mexican bric-a-brac adds to the festive atmosphere.

CABO SAN LUCAS: La Taverna Gastrobar $$
European
Waterside in the Cabo Marina
Tel *(624) 105 19 32*
Quaint place with a stylish but casual atmosphere where smooth jazz plays as diners enjoy the breeze from the sea. The varied menu ranges from steaks and seafood to tapas. Desserts flambéed tableside provide a theatrical finish.

CABO SAN LUCAS: Mi Casa $$$
Regional Mexican
Corner of Av Cabo San Lucas and Lázaro Cárdenas
Tel *(624) 143 19 33*
The vivid cobalt-blue exterior and colorful decor provide a lively backdrop for a meal at this lovely regional eatery. The menu, a combination of traditional and nouvelle Mexican specialties, features plenty of fresh seafood.

Enjoy a glass of sangria, whilst admiring the view at La Taverna, Cabo San Lucas

CHIHUAHUA: Degá $$
Regional Mexican
Calle Victoria 409
Tel *(614) 439 90 00*
A popular restaurant known for its reliably swift service and excellent food. The *plato* Mexicana includes a *tamale* and stuffed chili. The extensive breakfast menu includes several international and Mexican specialties.

CIUDAD CUAUHTÉMOC: Tarahumara Inn $$
International
Av Allende 373, Hotel Tarahumara Inn
Tel *(625) 581 19 19*
Located in a welcoming, popular inn, this casual restaurant opens early and closes late. The straightforward Mexican offerings include *filete barba* (grilled beef accompanied by chili and onion slices).

CREEL: La Cabaña $
International
López Mateos 36
Tel *(635) 456 09 15*
Wooden furniture and indigenous Tarahumara decorations lend plenty of atmosphere. The menu of familiar favorites ranges from fried chicken to taco platters with rice and beans.

CREEL: La Troje de Adobe $
Coffee shop
Av Francisco Villa 13
Tel *(635) 102 10 11*
Enjoy pastries, desserts, and smoothies made using local, organic ingredients at this charming café. It has received rave reviews for being one of the area's only spots for freshly roasted coffee and gourmet coffee drinks.

DURANGO: La Fogata $$
Steakhouse
Cuauhtémoc 200
Tel *(618) 817 03 47*
This pine-walled, thatched-roofed restaurant earned its fame decades ago for its meat dishes, prepared in a variety of ways. Beef is king, but there is also *cabrito* (young goat), ribs, and chicken.

ENSENADA: El Charro $
Regional Mexican
López Mateos 454
Tel *(646) 178 21 14*
This restaurant has been in operation since 1956. The marinated Mexican-style chicken, *carne asada*, grilled or roasted over an open flame, is a popular choice. Freshly made tortillas and salsas accompany all dishes.

ENSENADA: Deckman's en el Mogor $$$
Modern Mexican
Ensenada-Tecate Hwy km 85.5
Tel *(646) 188 39 60* **Closed** *Tue & Wed*
Committed to the principle of 'farm to table', this restaurant, situated on Mogor ranch, uses fresh, locally grown produce to prepare delightful Mexican dishes with a contemporary twist.

GUERRERO NEGRO: Malarrimo $$
Seafood
Emiliano Zapata s/n
Tel *(615) 157 01 00* **Closed** *Sat & Sun*
Widely considered the best restaurant in town, Malarrimo is decorated with nautical objects, colorful buoys, and noteworthy newspaper articles. The seafood-heavy menu has everything from lobster omelets to fresh prawns and giant scallops.

HERMOSILLO: Viva Sonora $$$
Regional Mexican/Steakhouse
San Pedro el Sauceto km 15
Tel *(662) 237 02 00*
Hungry diners drive 15 km (9 miles) from the city deep into cattle country for Viva Sonora's delicious beef specialties. Try the *cocido* (a hearty beef stew), *carne asada*, and *costillas* (pork ribs).

HIDALGO DEL PARRAL: Restaurant la Fuente $$
Regional Mexican
Calle 20 de Noviembre & Colegio
Tel *(627) 522 30 88*
The festively painted walls at Restaurant La Fuente create a lively ambience that draws guests. It has a varied menu of Mexican staples, from steak and chicken dishes to enchiladas.

LORETO: Café Olé $
Regional Mexican
Madero 14
Tel *(613) 135 04 96*
Café Olé is a little streetside place in the center of town that offers tasty, traditional Mexican dishes at reasonable prices. Travelers can often be seen starting their day with filling egg dishes under the *palapa* (palm frond) roof.

MAZATLÁN: Pura Vida $
Vegetarian
Bugambilia 18
Tel *(669) 916 1010*
At Pura Vida, vegetarian options abound from soy burgers to fruit plates. The menu also has chicken and fish sandwiches, soups, and wholewheat pancakes. Fresh local fruit appears in more than 100 blended juices.

Key to Price Guide *see p314*

Relaxed dining area at Caesar's, Tijuana

MAZATLÁN: Topolo $
Mexican / American
Constitución 629
Tel *(669) 136 06 60* **Closed** *Mon*
Mexican cuisine meets American flavors at this popular restaurant that also features a good selection of wines. Live music accompanies meals from Tuesdays to Saturdays.

MAZATLÁN: Jungle Juice $$
International
De las Garzas 101
Tel *(669) 913 33 15*
Enjoy fresh fruit smoothies and juices along with a variety of vegetarian, Mexican, and American offerings. There is a bar upstairs and an open-air patio downstairs.

MAZATLÁN: El Shrimp Bucket $$
Seafood
Av Olas Altas 126–11, Hotel Fiesta
Tel *(669) 981 63 50*
This restaurant has been serving local shrimp done many ways – breaded, beer-battered, barbecued, grilled, coconut crusted, or peel-and-eat – since 1963. Can get crowded during breakfast.

MULEGÉ: Los Equipales $
Regional Mexican
Moctezuma 70
Tel *(615) 153 03 30*
Breezy second-floor restaurant with a covered terrace, where the namesake leather *equipal* tables are adorned with colorful cloths and pottery. The menu highlights include Sonoran beef and seafood from the Sea of Cortez.

NUEVO CASAS GRANDES: Hacienda $
Regional Mexican
Av Benito Juarez 2603, Hotel Hacienda
Tel *(636) 694 10 48*
Located in one of the most popular inns in town, Hacienda serves Mexican and international specialties. The standards include soup, sandwiches, and platter meals with pork chops, grilled chicken, and enchiladas.

SALTILLO: El Tapanco $$
International
Allende Sur 225
Tel *(844) 414 43 39* **Closed** *Mon*
Set in an 18th-century mansion with an open patio. The international menu, which includes chateaubriand, almond-crusted salmon, and shrimp in garlic sauce, is dotted with Mexican favorites such as *mole poblano*, as well.

SAN JOSÉ DEL CABO: Mi Cocina $$
International
Blvd Mijares 4
Tel *(624) 146 71 00* **Closed** *Tue*
Nestled in the Casa Natalia hotel, this place is great for outdoor dining. The Mexican-Euro offerings include dishes such as beef medallions paired with Roquefort cheese in a chipotle chili sauce.

SAN JOSÉ DEL CABO: Tropicana $$
Regional Mexican
Blvd Mijares 30
Tel *(624) 142 15 80*
Tropicana offers convivial dining, an outdoor patio, and entertainment, amidst colorful hacienda decor. The international menu has something for everyone. Go for the shrimp fajita or steak.

DK Choice

SAN JOSÉ DEL CABO: Flora's Field Kitchen $$$
International
Las Animas Bajas
Tel *(624) 355 45 64* **Closed** *Mon*
Venture off the beaten track to experience this eco-conscious food emporium. Lengthy menus feature handmade dishes using farm-fresh ingredients as well as organic meat from a nearby ranch. The pizzas are cooked in a wood-burning oven. The adjacent Farm Bar serves unique takes on classic cocktails. Live music most nights.

SANTA ROSALÍA: El Muelle $
International
Corner of Constitución and the plaza
Tel *(615) 152 09 31*
Modern restaurant with seating both inside and on a palm-studded patio. Serves delicious grilled meats and seafood in large portions. The hamburgers and pizzas get rave reviews.

TIJUANA: Caesar's $$
Modern Mexican
Av Revolución 1927, Centro
Tel *(664) 685 19 27*
The original home of the Caesar salad sports a vintage feel with black and white tiled floors, dimmed lighting, and wood paneling. Upscale Mexican food and excellent service.

TIJUANA: Misión 19 $$$
Modern Mexican
Misión San Javier 10643, piso 2, VIA Corporativo, Zona Urbana Río
Tel *(664) 634 24 93*
One of the city's trendiest restaurants, serving innovative fare using local, organic ingredients. Perched on the second floor of a sleek office building with floor-to-ceiling windows.

The Colonial Heartland

AGUASCALIENTES: Antigua Hacienda La Noria $$
Regional Mexican
Hotel Hacienda de la Noria, Héroe de Nacozari Sur 1315
Tel *(449) 918 43 43*
Hacienda La Noria's restaurant is popular with locals and tourists for its Mexican specialties and polite service. Try the enchiladas in a red sauce, or the pork loin in a mild chili sauce.

AJIJIC: Manix $
International
Ocampo 57
Tel *(376) 766 00 61* **Closed** *Sun*
One of the town's oldest eateries, Manix is adorned with dark wood and bright accent walls. Several of the menu's Mexican dishes can be ordered as a family size to share.

AJIJIC: Restaurant 4 $$$
French
Donato Guerra 4
Tel *(376) 766 13 60* **Closed** *Mon & Tue*
This French-inspired restaurant still has a Mexican feel, thanks in part to the thatched *palapa* (dried palm) roof of the terrace dining area. It offers an extensive wine list.

For more information on types of restaurants *see p307*

ANGANGUEO: Los Geranios $
Regional Mexican
Hotel Don Bruno, Morelos 92
Tel *(715) 156 00 26*
Named for the geraniums that adorn the balconies in the charming Hotel Don Bruno, this restaurant overlooks a pleasant garden. The specials change daily but always feature regional Mexican favorites.

BUCERIAS: Mark's Bar & Grill $$$
Mediterranean/Asian
Lázaro Cárdenas 56
Tel *(329) 298 03 03*
Casual yet sophisticated dining in the town of Bucerias, north of Puerta Vallarta. Choose to eat at the black-granite bar, on the patio, or in the softly lit dining room. Homemade pizzas and fresh seafood are popular.

BUCERIAS: Mezzogiorno $$$
Italian/Regional Mexican
Av del Pacifico 33
Tel *(329) 298 03 50* **Closed** *Mon*
Relaxed eatery known for its fusion food and impeccable service. Beachfront location with stunning views across the Banderas Bay.

COLIMA: Los Naranjos $$
Regional Mexican
Gabino Barrera 34
Tel *(312) 312 00 29*
This restaurant has been feeding loyal locals since the 1960s. House specialties include *pollo los naranjos* (chicken in orange sauce) and clay pot chicken casserole.

GUADALAJARA: La Chata $
Regional Mexican
Av Corona 126
Tel *(333) 613 05 88*
Perennially popular since 1942 for its authentic Jalisco cuisine. The platters are centered around meat or enchiladas, with three variations of *pozole blanco* (white hominy broth with meat).

GUADALAJARA: Los Itacates $
Regional Mexican
Av Chapultepec Norte 110
Tel *(333) 825 11 08*
Los Itacates is renowned for its huge taco selection, *chiles rellenos*, and other regional specialties. Excellent breakfast buffet. Packed on weekdays with office workers.

GUADALAJARA: La Fonda de San Miguel $$
Regional Mexican
Donato Guerra 25
Tel *(333) 613 07 93*
The atmospheric central patio of the 17th-century convent Santa Teresa de Jesús is a popular spot. Fine regional fare such as favorites *mole poblano*, *chiles en nogada*, and *pozole*.

The bustling outdoor seating area at Sagrantino, Guadalajara

GUADALAJARA: La Trattoria $$
Italian
Av Niños Héroes 3051, Col Jardines del Bosque
Tel *(333) 122 18 17*
Sleek restaurant with natural wood and crisp linen covered tables. Visit here to sample some of the city's best Italian food, with homemade bread and pasta. It also features a fabulous salad bar.

GUADALAJARA: Sagrantino $$$
Italian/Modern Mexican
Golfo de Cortes 4152
Tel *(333) 813 13 79*
This busy spot caters to expats and adventurous locals with its fusion of Italian and Mexican flavors. Many items come straight off a charcoal grill or out of a wood-burning oven. Indoor and outdoor seating areas are available.

GUANAJUATO: Casa del Conde de Valencia $$
Modern Mexican
Valenciana km 5
Tel *(473) 732 25 50*
One of the most gracious restaurants in town, located in the charming, plant-filled courtyard of the former hacienda of the Count of Valenciana. Savor traditional Mexican food with nouvelle twists.

GUANAJUATO: El Gallo Pitagórico $$
Italian
Constancia 10 A
Tel *(473) 732 94 89*
This house-turned-restaurant sports a bright blue facade. Diners enjoy a superior view of the city while enjoying Italian specialties such as minestrone soup and lasagne.

GUANAJUATO: Quinta Las Acacias $$
International
Hotel Quinta Las Acacias, Paseo de la Presa 168
Tel *(473) 731 15 17* **Closed** *Sun*
With its classy service and ambience, this is the place for a special meal. The menu features Mexican overtones. Signature items include *poblana* soup with zucchini flowers, chili, corn, and mushrooms. Great views.

GUANAJUATO: Restaurante Las Mercedes $$
Regional Mexican
Calle de Arriba 6
Tel *(473) 733 90 59* **Closed** *Mon*
Savor delectable dishes and unusual regional fare such as *escamoles* (ant eggs) in a warmly lit dining room. Exceptional service.

GUANAJUATO: La Terraza $$$
Regional Mexican
Posada Santa Fe Hotel, Jardín Unión 12
Tel *(473) 732 00 84*
A prime location, with outdoor seating facing the main plaza and a beautiful indoor dining room. Specialties include beef skewers and chicken *mole*.

MORELIA: Fonda las Mercedes $$
International
León Guzmán 47
Tel *(443) 312 61 13*
Intimate courtyard dining room complete with gardens, exposed brick walls, art, and stone pillars. The international menu includes a variety of steaks, plus pastas, seafood, and savory crêpes.

MORELIA: Las Trojes $$
Regional Mexican
Juan Sebastián Bach 51
Tel *(443) 314 73 44*
Traditional Purépechan-carved log house offering Mexican and Michoacán specialties. Favorites include bean-based Tarasca soup and steak *poblano*.

Key to Price Guide *see p314*

MORELIA: Los Mirasoles $$$
International
Av Madero Poniente 549
Tel *(443) 317 57 75*
Private home converted into a sophisticated, art-filled restaurant. The beautifully decorated tables create a fine dining atmosphere. The menu includes delicious Argentinian-style grilled meat.

MORELIA: Villa Montaña $$$
International
Patzimba 201
Tel *(443) 314 00 18*
Located in a hotel at the top of a hill, this is a stylish international restaurant. Breakfast features a buffet of regional fare including *uchepos* and *corundas* (two different Michoacán *tamales*).

EL ORO DE HIDALGO: Vagón Expres Minero $
International
Angela Peralta 1, Centro
Tel *(711) 125 02 83* **Closed** *Mon*
A decommissioned train car that sits in front of the old railway station serves as this restaurant's dining room. Serves tasty food over breakfast, lunch and dinner.

PÁTZCUARO: Los Escudos $
Regional Mexican
Centro Hotel Los Escudos, Portal Hidalgo 73
Tel *(434) 342 12 90*
One of the town's central gathering places, located in the front section of the Hotel Los Escudos. Michoacán specialties such as fresh *tamales* and Tarascan soup are the main attractions.

PÁTZCUARO: Doña Paca $$
Regional Mexican
Portal Morelos 59
Tel *(434) 342 36 28*
Inviting hideaway on the first floor of a historic family-owned mansion. The menu includes a delightful mix of Mexican and Michoacán specialties, and over 30 options for breakfast.

PÁTZCUARO: Hostería de San Felipe $$
Regional Mexican
Av Lázaro Cárdenas 321
Tel *(434) 342 12 98*
One of the oldest restaurants in the city, with a history closely bound with that of the grand Michoacán families. Famous for its *botanas* (appetizers) and traditional Purépecha recipes.

PÁTZCUARO: El Primer Piso $$
Regional Mexican
Vasco de Quiroga 29
Tel *(434) 342 01 22* **Closed** *Tue*
From a charming old mansion, small balconies overlook the Plaza Grande. The menu puts a twist on familiar Mexican dishes.

PÁTZCUARO: El Viejo Gaucho $$
International
Iturbe 10
Tel *(434) 342 03 68* **Closed** *Sun & Mon*
The back section of the Hotel Iturbe houses a casual restaurant, only open for dinner. The menu comprises a fine mix of appetizers, salads, hamburgers, empanadas, pizzas, and pastas.

PUERTO VALLARTA: Fredy's Tucan $
Regional Mexican
Basillo Badillo 245, Col Emiliano Zapata Código
Tel *(322) 223 07 78*
Friendly staff and filling breakfasts with both Mexican and American offerings. Watch the colorful street life from the dining room or the covered patio.

PUERTO VALLARTA: Le Bistro Jazz Café $$$
International
Río Cuale 16-A
Tel *(322) 222 02 83*
Le Bistro Jazz Café has been providing a classy-yet-casual dining experience since 1979. Steak, chicken, seafood, pastas, and crêpes are prepared with flair. There is a lovely garden deck perched right over the river.

Stylish hill-top restaurant Villa Montaña, Morelia

DK Choice

PUERTO VALLARTA: Café des Artistes $$$
French
Guadalupe Sánchez 740
Tel *(322) 222 32 28*
Sophisticated cuisine served in several dining rooms filled with linen, crystal, candles, and art. The award-winning French chef's dinner-only menu features innovative fare with a focus on local, fresh ingredients. Signature dishes include king crab timbal with chipotle chili vinaigrette, and lamb medallions with wild mushroom and garlic sauce.

PUERTO VALLARTA: La Dolce Vita $$$
Italian
Calle Díaz Ordaz 674
Tel *(322) 222 38 52*
Popular Italian restaurant with a sister location in nearby Nuevo Vallarta. Serves pasta dishes and wood-fired pizzas. Great spot for people-watching and ocean views. Live jazz often featured.

PUERTO VALLARTA: Kaiser Maximillian $$$
European
Olas Altas 380-B
Tel *(322) 223 07 60* **Closed** *Sun*
Get a taste of Europe in bistro surroundings resembling a 19th-century Viennese café. The menu includes authentic Austrian dishes such as *wiener schnitzel*. Located in Los Muertos beach area.

PUERTO VALLARTA: La Leche $$$
International
Blvd Francisco Medina Ascencio km 2.5
Tel *(322) 293 09 00*
International cuisine with the occasional fusion surprise. Chef and former rock star Alfonso Cadena changes the menu nightly. All-white linens, crystal, and fine service set the upscale tone.

PUERTO VALLARTA: Trio $$$
International
Guerrero 264
Tel *(322) 222 21 96*
One of the city's most lauded restaurants, Trio is situated in a colonial town house with an open courtyard and roof-top terrace. Serves an ever-changing Mediterranean menu including creative presentations of seafood.

Brightly colored courtyard of Mesón de San José in San Miguel de Allende

QUERÉTARO: La Mariposa $
Regional Mexican
Angela Peralta 7
Tel *(442) 212 11 66*
Plainly furnished neighborhood restaurant, catering to both locals and tourists since 1940. Enjoy sandwiches, enchiladas, or tacos before heading over to the adjacent bakery to sample the acclaimed homemade ice cream and frozen yogurt.

QUERÉTARO: Orange $$
International
Pasteur Sur 17
Tel *(442) 212 00 46*
The eclectic flavors of different cuisines of the world are efficiently paired with Mexican favorites on the menu at this welcoming restaurant. Wine lovers will enjoy the impressive 500-bottle cellar.

REAL DE CATORCE: El Mesón de la Abundancia $
International
Lanzagorta 11
Tel *(488) 887 50 44*
This charming restaurant is located in the original home of the town treasury, dating back to 1863. The interior is filled with antique doors and furniture, old stone walls, and cast-iron gates. The varied menu includes Italian, Swiss, and Mexican options.

SAN BLAS: El Delfín $$
Mexican
Hotel Garza Canela, Paredes no. 106 Sur
Tel *(323) 285 01 12*
One of the few fine-dining options available in the area. Seafood dominates the sophisticated menu, which also includes dishes from all over the world. Try the delightful breakfast menu. International wine list.

SAN LUIS POTOSÍ: La Gran Via $$$
Spanish/Regional Mexican
Av Venustiano Carranza 560
Tel *(444) 812 36 33*
A real find among the otherwise nondescript offerings in this region. Excellent traditional Spanish and Mexican dishes served in a tranquil ambience. Live piano.

SAN MIGUEL DE ALLENDE: Mesón de San José $
International
Mesones 38
Tel *(415) 108 06 48* **Closed** *Dinner*
One of the city's most relaxing, beautiful settings – a tree-shaded courtyard surrounded by little boutiques. The lunch-only, contemporary menu spans the globe, from pastas to chicken curry.

SAN MIGUEL DE ALLENDE: El Correo $$
Regional Mexican
El Mesón Hotel, Correo 23
Tel *(415) 152 49 51* **Closed** *Tue*
A range of top Mexican regional food, such as *corundas* (a *tamale* from Michoacán) and *sopes* (the ubiquitous *masa* appetizer of central Mexico), is available here. The antique stone walls lend plenty of atmosphere.

SAN MIGUEL DE ALLENDE: Mama Mia $$
International
Umarán 8
Tel *(415) 152 20 63*
Mama Mia has a large open dining patio and regular live entertainment. The lengthy menu includes Italian, Mexican, and American fare. The extensive bar menu ensures a busy evening crowd.

SAN MIGUEL DE ALLENDE: El Pegaso $$
International
Corregidora 6
Tel *(415) 152 13 51* **Closed** *Wed*
This trendy, casual restaurant has three intimate dining rooms. The menu features soups, salads, and sandwiches along with specialty dishes from Mexico and Asia.

SAN MIGUEL DE ALLENDE: Moxi $$$
Modern Mexican
Aldama 53
Tel *(415) 152 10 15*
Housed inside Hotel Matilda, this restaurant dishes up culinary creations by Enrique Olvera, one of Mexico's most famous chefs. The menu features bold, contemporary interpretations of traditional Mexican dishes. Don't forget to try the tasting menu.

TLAQUEPAQUE: El Abajeño $$
Regional Mexican
Juárez 231
Tel *(333) 635 90 15*
Set in a large, plant-filled patio where musicians stroll while guests dine. The menu consists of regional and traditional Mexican food. Try the hearty *birria* (beef, goat, or lamb in a flavorful broth).

URUAPAN: La Mansión del Cupatitzio $$
Regional Mexican
Mansión del Cupatitzio Hotel, Corner of Rodilla del Diablo & Parque Nacional
Tel *(452) 523 21 00*
A bright and airy restaurant overlooking the Parque Nacional. Sit inside in the refined dining room or outside by the pool. This place is known for its regional dishes such as *trucha tarasca* (trout covered in almond sauce).

ZACATECAS: Los Dorados de Villa $$
Regional Mexican
Plazuela de García 314
Tel *(492) 922 57 22*
This unpretentious restaurant in the heart of the city's colonial area is filled with historical relics. Their enchiladas and *buñuelos* (fried dough balls) are widely considered the best in the area.

ZACATECAS: Garufa $$
Steakhouse
135 Jardin Juarez
Tel *(492) 924 29 10*
Popular Argentinian-style steakhouse that satisfies carnivores with chops and large cuts of fine steak. The menu also includes empanadas, pizzas,

Casual dining at El Pegaso, San Miguel de Allende

Key to Price Guide *see p314*

soups, and salads. A varied wine list and attentive service round out the experience.

ZITÁCUARO: San Cayetano $$
French/Regional Mexican
Carretera a Huetamo km 2.3
Tel *(715) 153 19 26*
Hotel restaurant in a quiet country setting. Perfect for relaxed dining, either inside the glass-walled dining room or out on the open patio with views of the manicured lawn and gardens. The menu of French and Mexican classics changes daily.

Southern Mexico

ACAPULCO: Bambuco $$
International
Hotel Elcano, Costera Alemán 75
Tel *(744) 435 15 00*
Hotel Elcano's terrace is a great setting for a restaurant, with delightful ocean views. The menu offers a number of staples including sandwiches, salads, pasta, seafood, and fish.

ACAPULCO: La Casa de Pasta $$
Italian
Blvd de las Naciones 504
Tel *(744) 466 26 83* **Closed** *Mon*
Enjoy filling, handmade pasta dishes, healthy salads, and sandwiches made with home-baked bread. Choose between the welcoming dining room or the breezy terrace tables. Takeout available.

ACAPULCO: Zolache $$
Modern Mexican
Fernando de Magallanes 19B
Tel *(744) 189 09 57*
A popular spot to indulge in food and people-watching. Zolache's upscale Mexican menu delights diners, as does the wine list, which specializes in Mexican varieties.

DK Choice

ACAPULCO: Su Casa/La Margarita $$$
International
Av Anahuac 110
Tel *(744) 484 43 50*
Open patio restaurant with a hot pink facade and panoramic views from its perch on a cliff overlooking Acapulco and the bay. The innovative menu changes frequently; try the *filete al Madrazo* (steak marinated in fruit juice and flambéed). A perfect place to sip on a margarita and enjoy the sunset.

ACAPULCO: Zibu $$$
Thai/Modern Mexican
Av Escénica, Fracc. Glomar
Tel *(744) 433 30 58*
Zibu has a constantly changing menu, but it never strays from its fusion base and the emphasis on delicious seafood dishes. A favorite with honeymooners for being unabashedly romantic with gorgeous views.

IXTAPA: Bistro Soleiado $$
International/Seafood
Paseo de Ixtapa
Tel *(755) 553 04 20*
Relish fresh seafood at this restaurant that features a lovely open-air dining terrace. It also serves good breakfasts and desserts. Well-chosen wine list.

IXTAPA: Beccofino $$$
Italian
Marina Ixtapa
Tel *(755) 553 17 70*
Enjoy top-notch Italian food at this alfresco restaurant on the marina. The owner brings family recipes and plenty of skill all the way from San Remo, Italy. Wide selection of pasta, much of it featuring seafood. Impressive wine list.

OAXACA: Don Juanito $
Regional Mexican
Valerio Trujano 203
Tel *(951) 514 81 60*
Casual eatery located in a colonial-era house with a covered patio. Choose from a wide array of tacos, plus traditional Oaxacan specialties such as *pozole* (pork and corn soup), *chapulines* (grasshoppers), and *tlayudas* (stuffed tortillas).

OAXACA: El Asador Vasco $$
Regional Mexican/Spanish
Portal de Flores 10 A
Tel *(951) 514 47 55*
A local favorite overlooking the Zócalo, El Asador Vasco offers a wide menu of Oaxacan dishes, flavorful Basque cuisine, and international favorites. Atmospheric tavern.

OAXACA: La Casa de la Abuela $$
Regional Mexican
Av Hidalgo 616
Tel *(951) 516 35 44*
Prime location overlooking both the Alameda and Zócalo. Enjoy well-prepared local specialties such as *tasajo* (thin pieces of salted beef with a rich cream sauce). Traditional colorful dining room and sunny balcony.

OAXACA: Casa Oaxaca $$
Regional Mexican
Constitucion 104A
Tel *(951) 516 85 31*
One of the city's most popular spots for special occasions, Casa Oaxaca pairs fine dining with indigenous recipes. Attentive servers explain the menu's many intricacies. The terrace has great views.

OAXACA: Restaurante La Olla $$
Regional Mexican
Av Reforma 402
Tel *(951) 516 66 68* **Closed** *Sun*
Small traditional Oaxacan restaurant, superbly located in the center of town. The dishes reveal a strong commitment to regional ingredients and the revival of colonial-era and pre-Hispanic cooking.

PALENQUE: Maya $
Regional Mexican
Corner of Independencia & Hidalgo
Tel *(916) 345 00 42*
Open since 1958, Maya faces the main plaza and serves a combination of Mexican standards and regional specialties such as *mole chiapaneco* (a dark red sauce like *mole poblano*, but less sweet) and *bolitas de masa* (corn dumplings).

Relaxed dining in the garden at San Cayetano, Zitácuaro

For more information on types of restaurants *see p307*

PALENQUE: La Selva $$
Regional Mexican
Carretera Palenque–Ruinas km 0.5
Tel *(916) 345 03 63*
One of the area's most upscale dining options. Linen-draped tables flicker with candlelight under an enormous *palapa* roof with jungle themed stained-glass panels. Try the regional enchiladas and *pigua*, a freshwater lobster.

PUERTO ÁNGEL: Villa Florencia $
Italian
Av Virgilio Uribe
Tel *(958) 584 30 44*
This casual, open-air restaurant is part of the Villa Florencia hotel. Reasonably priced menu of Italian and Mexican dishes. Popular spot for a bargain breakfast with beach views from the terrace.

PUERTO ESCONDIDO: Restaurant Sante Fe $$
Regional Mexican
Hotel Santa Fe, Calle de Morro s/n
Tel *(954) 582 01 70*
Open-walled, thatched roof restaurant right next to the beachside hotel of the same name. Enjoy ocean views while sampling the many seafood dishes on the menu. Numerous vegetarian and vegan items on offer.

SAN CRISTÓBAL DE LAS CASAS: Madre Tierra $
International
Av Insurgentes 19
Tel *(967) 678 42 97*
Housed in a one-story former residence with wooden floors and colorful ethnic textiles. The eclectic menu has plenty of vegetarian options. Breezy patio and welcoming dining room.

SAN CRISTÓBAL DE LAS CASAS: El Fogon de Jovel $$
Regional Mexican
Av 16 de Septiembre 11
Tel *(967) 678 11 53*
Located in a colonial-era home decorated with textiles, this is a top choice for experiencing Chiapan food and culture. The descriptive menu helps diners decide among the large selection of *tamales* and other specialties.

SAN CRISTÓBAL DE LAS CASAS: Tuluc $$
Regional Mexican
Av Insurgentes 5
Tel *(967) 678 20 90*
Hospitable eatery filled with Guatemalan textiles, serving delicious home cooking. The house specialty is *filete Tuluc*, a steak stuffed with spinach and cheese. Lighter fare includes Chiapan *tamales*.

Enjoy a traditional Maharachi band whilst you dine at Marganzo, Campeche

TEOTITLÁN DEL VALLE: Tlamanalli $$$
Regional Mexican
Av Juárez 39
Tel *(951) 524 40 06* **Closed** *Dinner; Mon*
One of the first restaurants in the area to truly celebrate the cuisine of Oaxaca. The lunch-only menu contains a varied menu of regional, pre-Hispanic recipes. Try the delicious *tamales*, *mole amarillo*, and *mole zapoteco*.

TUXTLA GUTIÉRREZ: La Huerta $$
International
Camino Real Tuxtla Gutiérrez, Blvd Belisario Dominguez 1195,
Tel *(961) 617 77 77*
The Camino Real Hotel's primary restaurant serves daily buffet breakfasts, plus a variety of desserts. Try the traditional *parillada* (mixed grill) at lunch. Popular for Sunday brunch.

TUXTLA GUTIÉRREZ: Las Pichanchas $$
Regional Mexican
Av Central Oriente 837
Tel *(961) 612 53 51*
Fine Chiapan food served in an enclosed patio, with live marimba music and traditional dancing adding to the convivial atmosphere. Menu highlights include local sausages, Chiapan *tamales*, and refreshing fruit drinks.

ZIHUATANEJO: Sirena Gorda $$
International
Paseo del Pescador 90
Tel *(755) 554 26 87* **Closed** *Wed*
The ever popular "Fat Mermaid" (as the name translates) offers a casual and pleasant dining experience. The bountiful breakfast menu has plenty of fresh yogurt and fruit. Try the seafood tacos and the juicy hamburgers.

The Gulf Coast

CATEMACO: Restaurante La Ola $
Regional Mexican
Paseo del Malecon S/N
Tel *(294) 943 00 10*
This lagoon-side café has been passed down over three generations. La Ola serves regional cuisine focusing on seafood and is famous for its *tegogolos* (shelled freshwater snails).

COATEPEC: Casa Bonilla $$
Seafood
Juárez 20
Tel *(228) 816 00 09*
Dine in the central courtyard of this spacious restaurant, which offers an extensive menu focused on seafood. Specialties include langoustines and sea bass wrapped in the fragrant *acuyo (hoja santa)* leaf.

COATEPEC: Restaurante el Tio Yeyo $$
Regional Mexico
Santos Degollado 4
Tel *(228) 816 36 45*
Sprawling restaurant set near verdant forest, a river, and a trout farm. Enjoy great views while sampling from the seafood-focused menu of regional specialties, including over a dozen different preparations of trout.

CÓRDOBA: Doña Lala $
Regional Mexican
Calle 7 325
Tel *(271) 712 71 11*
Located near the Palacio Municipal, in a colonial-style building, Doña Lala serves

Key to Price Guide *see p314*

inexpensive regional Mexican food. Specialties include *huevos motuleños* (eggs on tortillas with black beans and cheese) and *carne arrachera* (steak with garlic and lemon marinade).

PAPANTLA: Plaza Pardo $
Regional Mexican
Enriquez 105
Tel *(784) 842 00 59*
Aim for a table on the pleasant balcony, overlooking the plaza, and savor regional favorites, such as *tamales* and shrimp dishes while enjoying the city views.

PAPANTLA: Nakú Restaurante Papanteco $$
Regional Mexican
H. Colegio Militar s/n
Tel *(784) 842 31 12*
Local ingredients such as corn, beans, and chilies are used extensively to prepare the dishes at this rustic-style restaurant situated within driving distance of the El Tajín archaeological site.

TLACOTALPAN: Doña Lala $$
Regional Mexican
Hotel Posada Doña Lala, Carranza 11
Tel *(288) 884 25 80*
This restaurant is located in the 19th-century Hotel Posada Doña Lala. The emphasis here is on seafood and regional specialties. Try the barbecued meat wrapped in the fragrant *acuyo* leaf and rice mixed with seafood.

VERACRUZ: Gran Café de la Parroquia $
Café
Valentín Gómez Farias 34
Tel *(229) 932 25 84*
The city's most famous coffee house – it is also a favorite of visiting dignitaries – looks out on the port of Veracruz. Waiters circulate with kettles of steaming milk while delivering fresh pastries.

DK Choice

VERACRUZ: Villa Rica Mocambo $$
Seafood
Calzada Mocambo 527, Boca del Río
Tel *(229) 922 37 43*
A popular seafood restaurant, set in a relaxed space beneath a thatched roof. Located below the Hotel Mocambo, it attracts a mix of tourists and locals with authentic, Veracruz-style cooking. Try the *pompano al acuyo* (a sauce of green herbs) and *steak de camarón a la naranja* (shrimp cooked in orange sauce).

VERACRUZ: El Cacharrito $$$
Argentinian
Blvd Ruiz Cortinez 15
Tel *(229) 937 70 27*
Inviting, family-run steakhouse offering a proper Argentinian steak experience. Other specialties include grilled short ribs, authentic empanadas, and octopus dishes. Impressive wine list.

VILLAHERMOSA: Mero $$
Modern Mexican
Av Paseo Usumacinta s/n
Tel *(993) 139 78 44* **Closed** *Mon*
Creative interpretations of traditional Mexican flavors such as chilies and *cacao* (cocoa) are the specialties at this good-value seafood restaurant located in Plaza Cedros.

XALAPA: El Brou $
Mediterranean
Juan Soto 13
Tel *(228) 165 49 94*
This centrally located restaurant is renowned for its warm atmosphere, friendly staff, and reasonable prices. The menu focuses on Mediterranean fare and includes plenty of fresh seafood.

Dine in the tree-tops at La Buena Vida, Akumal

XALAPA: La Casona del Beaterio $$
International
Zaragoza 20
Tel *(228) 818 21 19*
Housed in a handsome colonial residence filled with historic photos and located near the main square. The lengthy menu includes top-notch steaks and local standards such as *sopa azteca* and enchiladas.

The Yucatán Peninsula

AKUMAL: La Buena Vida $$$
International
Calle Caleta Yalku Mz 7 Lt 41-G
Tel *(984) 875 90 61*
Large and lively restaurant on Half Moon Bay, with a busy bar and tables shaded by palm *palapas*. The menu has everything from burgers and salads to Yucatecan and Caribbean dishes.

CAMPECHE: Marganzo $$
Regional Mexican
Calle 8 no. 267
Tel *(981) 811 38 98*
Charming eatery housed in a fine old colonial building, just off the main square. A relaxed place in which to try local specialties like *pan de cazón* (dogfish in tomato sauce baked between tortillas).

CAMPECHE: La Pigua $$
Regional Mexican
Malecon Miguel Alemán 179-A
Tel *(981) 811 33 65*
This casual restaurant is considered a showcase for Campeche's distinctive cuisine, serving delicious versions of *arroz con pulpo* (octopus and rice salad) and *camarón al coco* (shrimp in coconut). Relaxed setting.

CANCÚN: 100% Natural $
Vegetarian
Av Sunyaxchén 62
Tel *(998) 884 01 02*
One of a chain of bright health food cafés delivering a welcome change from heavier local food. Plenty of vegetarian options, including imaginative salads refreshing fruit juices.

CANCÚN: La Parrilla $$
Regional Mexican
Av Yaxchilán 51
Tel *(998) 287 81 19*
A local favorite for its friendly atmosphere, and live *mariachi* bands. The menu includes traditional Mayan and Caribbean cuisine as well as many dishes prepared tableside.

For more information on types of restaurants *see p307*

CANCÚN: The White Box $$
International
Blvd Kukulcán km 16.5
Tel *(998) 881 70 00*
Chef Rafael Zafra brings his experience of working in various Michelin-starred restaurants all over the world to create an inventive menu of gastronomic delights at this restaurant housed in the Grand Oasis Hotel.

CANCÚN: La Dolce Vita $$$
Italian
Av Cobá 87, SM 3, Downtown Cancún
Tel *(998) 884 33 93*
Delectable Italian food served in a lovely, initmate setting. Try the signature snapper in puff pastry. The wine list is impressive. Friendly staff.

DK Choice

CANCÚN: La Habichuela $$$
Regional Mexican
Calle Margaritas 25
Tel *(998) 884 31 58*
One of downtown Cancún's longest-running restaurants, La Habichuela serves some of the city's best Mexican and Yucatecan food, adventurous dishes on the menu include richly flavored shrimp in tamarind sauce. Charming service and a lovely setting under the stars in a lush, romantic garden.

CANCÚN: La Joya $$$
International
Fiesta Americana Grand Coral Beach Hotel, Blvd Kukulcán km 9.5
Tel *(998) 881 32 00*
The Grand Coral Beach Hotel's elegant restaurant sports a striking interior with colorful artwork, stained-glass windows, and a fountain. Refined Mexican and international cuisine made with local ingredients.

CHETUMAL: Sergio's Pizza $$
Pizza
Av Alvaro Obregón 182
Tel *(983) 832 29 91*
This charming, casual restaurant is a local institution thanks to its thin-crust pizzas and excellent versions of local specialties like conch or red snapper with tropical fruit seasonings. Good wine list as well as cold beer.

CHICHÉN ÍTZA: Villas Arqueológicas $$
Regional Mexican/French
Mex 180, E of the archaeological site
Tel *(985) 851 01 87*
Tranquil hotel-restaurant, just a 10-minute walk from the ruins, with a colorful dining room and a bougainvillea-filled terrace. The menu features a mix of French and Mexican dishes.

COZUMEL: Casa Denis $$
Regional Mexican
Calle 1 Sur no.132, between Av 5 & 10
Tel *(987) 872 00 67*
Housed in a picturesque wooden house, Casa Denis has been open since 1945 and is still a popular meeting place. The terrace tables are ideal for people-watching. Reasonably priced mix of Yucatecan favorites and international dishes. Located on San Miguel's main square.

COZUMEL: La Choza $$
Regional Mexican
Av 10 no. 216 at Calle 3 Sur & A. Rosado Salas
Tel *(987) 872 09 58*
Popular open-air, hacienda-style restaurant. Extensive choice of Mexican dishes such as *poblanos* stuffed with shrimp, grilled *brochetas* (skewered meat), and homemade guacamole.

COZUMEL: Paprika $$
Caribbean/Regional Mexican
Carretera Costera Sur km 4.5
Tel *(987) 872 24 04*
This family-run restaurant south of town serves authentic and fresh Mexican-Caribbean food. Specialties include *xcatic* peppers stuffed with fresh fish, coconut shrimp, and the house special, *mariscada* (seafood) soup.

COZUMEL: Pepe's Grill $$$
International
Av Rafael E. Melgar, corner of Calle A. Rosado Salas
Tel *(987) 872 02 13* **Closed** *Mon*
Popular upscale place specializing in gourmet steaks, fresh fish, and lobster. The spacious, nautically themed room above the waterfront affords lovely sunset views.

ISLA MUJERES: Olivia $
International
Matamoros 11, Centro
Tel *(998) 877 17 65* **Closed** *Sun & Mon*
Romantic dinner spot serving homemade Mediterranean dishes with Turkish and Bulgarian influences. Try the authentic *moussaka* (a Greek meat dish) and Moroccan-style fish.

ISLA MUJERES: Pizza Rolandi's $$
Pizza
Av Hidalgo 110, between Av Madero & Abasolo
Tel *(998) 877 04 29*
Bright pizzeria located on one of the island's main streets. Delightful pastas, wood-fired

Dine in the garden setting at La Habichuela, Cancún

Key to Price Guide *see p314*

pizzas, and other Italian dishes feature on the menu. Try the lobster calzone.

ISLA MUJERES: Sunset Grill $$
International
Playa Norte, Av Rueda Medina, Condominios Nautibeach
Tel *(998) 274 55 88*
Sit either on the covered terrace or at the beach at this lovely restaurant. The varied menu features international fare and Mexican favorites. Free Wi-Fi.

IZAMAL: Kinich $$
Regional Mexican
Calle 27 no. 299, between Calle 28 & 30
Tel *(988) 954 04 89*
This delightful garden restaurant is one of the region's best bets for sampling traditional local dishes such as *pavo en relleno negro* (turkey in black chili sauce).

MÉRIDA: Los Almendros $$
Regional Mexican
Calle 50-A no. 493, on Parque de la Mejorada
Tel *(999) 928 54 59*
Well-known showcase for Yucatecan country cuisine; try the excellent *poc-chuc* (pork marinated in bitter oranges and garlic). Waitresses serve in traditional dress.

MÉRIDA: Hacienda Teya $$
Regional Mexican
Off Mex 180, 12.5 km E of Mérida
Tel *(999) 988 08 00*
Spacious dining room in a grand colonial hacienda, serving a lunch-only menu of refined Yucatecan dishes like *cochinita pibil* (pork marinated in bitter oranges and *achiote* spices).

MÉRIDA: Hennessy's Irish Pub $$
Irish
Paseo Montejo, Calle 56-A no. 486A, between Calle 41 & 43
Tel *(999) 923 89 93*
The preferred hangout of expats, Hennessy's Irish Pub has a wide range of drinks and reliably solid pub fare, with numerous vegetarian options. Live music.

MÉRIDA: Pancho's $$$
Modern Mexican
Calle 59 no. 509, between Calle 60 & 62
Tel *(999) 923 09 42*
Entertaining eatery with a Mexican bandit theme – waiters wear cartridge belts and big sombreros. The menu features contemporary spins on classics like enchiladas and quesadillas.

PLAYA DEL CARMEN: Kaxapa Factory $
Venezuelan
Calle 10, between Av 15 & 20
Tel *(984) 803 50 23* **Closed** *Mon*
This family-run café off the main road serves inexpensive, homemade Venezuelan food and fresh juices.

PLAYA DEL CARMEN: Glass Bar $$
Italian
Av 5 & Calle 12, Col Centro
Tel *(984) 803 12 70*
Sleek and stylish restaurant on one of the city's busiest corners, perfectly placed for people-watching. Serves refined modern Italian fare plus some global dishes. Brilliant wine list.

PROGRESO: Flamingo's $
Seafood
Malecón, corner of Calle 72
Tel *(969) 935 21 22*
Popular restaurant with a large terrace along the city's seafront. Specializes in fresh fish – choose between giant grilled fish platters or lighter *ceviches* made with fresh lime and coriander.

PUERTO MORELOS: John Gray's Kitchen $$
Modern Mexican
Av Niños Héroes, Lot 6
Tel *(998) 871 06 65*
The menu at John Gray's Kitchen changes daily. Adventurous cooking makes use of local ingredients from the nearby jungle. Elegant dining room.

PUERTO MORELOS: Los Pelícanos $$
Modern Mexican
Av Rafael E. Melgar
Tel *(998) 871 00 14*
This expansive, *palapa*-roofed restaurant sits right beside the beach, its wide terrace providing great sea views. Try the delicious grilled sea bass or *ceviche* of octopus or conch.

TULUM: Don Cafeto Centro $$
Regional Mexican
Av Tulum no. 64, Lot 12
Tel *(984) 871 22 07*
Lively spot with a large terrace. A great option at all hours, whether for traditional breakfasts, *tostadas*, and other snacks, or larger dishes such as grilled fish à la Veracruzana.

TULUM: Cetli $$$
Regional Mexican
Calle Polar Oriente
Tel *(984) 108 06 81* **Closed** *Wed*
The chef-owner prepares original, refined variations of traditional Mexican dishes. Candle-lit tables and a tropical garden create a romantic atmosphere. Wonderful views of the lagoon and the sea. Open for dinner only.

Beach side dining at Sunset Grill, Isla Mujeres

UXMAL: Hacienda San Pedro Ochil $$
Regional Mexican
Carretera Merida-Muná km 175
Tel *(999) 924 74 65*
A 17th-century hacienda converted into a restaurant, gift shop, and museum. Around the entrance are workshops, where local artisans make traditional hammocks, stone carvings, and jewelry. Refined versions of Yucatecan dishes.

UXMAL: Lodge at Uxmal $$
Regional Mexican
The Lodge at Uxmal, Carretera Merida Campeche km 78
Tel *(998) 887 24 95*
The Lodge at Uxmal is just a short walk from the entrance to the archaeological site. International classics and Mexican favorites served at breakfast, lunch, and dinner as well as regional specialties.

VALLADOLID: El Mesón del Marqués $
Regional Mexican
Calle 39 no. 203, between Calle 40 & 42
Tel *(985) 856 20 73*
Enjoy your meal surrounded by swaying palms and vividly colored flowers on the patio dining area. Excellent local specialties on the menu include *lomitos de valladolid* (diced pork with chili, garlic, and tomatoes) and Valladolid (pork loin), traditionally cooked.

For more information on types of restaurants *see p307*

SHOPPING IN MEXICO

For many people, shopping is one of the highlights of a trip to Mexico. Some enjoy the upscale boutiques or jewelry stores in big-city malls or beach resorts. (For shopping in Mexico City, see pp118–9.) Others prefer the excitement of a colorful, bustling street market piled high with unfamiliar fruits and vegetables, or of finding an isolated roadside stall selling beautiful earthenware pots or bright, handwoven rugs. Bartering is not appropriate everywhere. At craft stalls in tourist resorts, a certain amount of haggling is usually acceptable and even expected, but in most shops, prices are fixed. You can ask *Cuánto es lo menos?* (What is your best price?) but when buying from artisans, bear in mind that their profit is usually already pitifully low. Larger stores will ship your purchases home for you; it is illegal to export archaeological artifacts.

Roadside stall selling colorful souvenirs including rugs and bags

Opening Hours

Shops generally open from 9am through 7 or 8pm, Monday through Saturday. Bakeries and corner shops may open earlier, at 8am, and some stay open until 10pm. Boutiques and craft shops usually open at 10am. Sunday shopping is possible at supermarkets and in tourist areas.

Large American-style shopping malls have sprouted all over Mexico's cities in recent years. They open on Sundays, but some close on Mondays.

Outside Mexico City, most shops close for lunch between 2 and 4pm. Department stores and supermarkets everywhere stay open over lunchtime. Street markets usually pack up at about 2 or 3pm.

Paying

Cash and major credit cards (VISA, MasterCard, and, to a lesser extent, American Express and Diners Club) are acceptable forms of payment in most Mexican shops. Prices generally include 16 percent IVA (sales tax, or VAT). Credit card payments are usually subject to a small surcharge. Most places except the most touristy markets accept card payments.

General Stores

Glitzy department stores, modern malls, and expensive, trendy boutiques are the norm in certain parts of the capital and in a handful of cities and resorts around the country. In most big cities, there is at least one Sanborns *(see p119)*, which has a good selection of books, magazines, maps, gifts, chocolates, and toiletries. For everyday shopping, supermarkets like Superama or Comercial Mexicana are huge and well stocked with many familiar brand names.

Away from modern shopping centers, ordinary life in Mexico still revolves around the market and traditional shops in the surrounding streets: the *panadería* (bakery), *abarrotes* (grocery store), and *ferretería* (hardware store).

The bustling market in Tepoztlán, a lively jumble of people and products

Specialty Shops

León, Guadalajara, and Monterrey are all known for their fine-quality leatherware. Shoes, with designs ranging from trendy to classical, are particularly good value, and are sold in shops and markets all over the country. Belts and bags are also an excellent buy. The sturdy, rubber-soled *huarache* sandals are best bought in Guadalajara's *(see pp192–3)* San Juan de Dios market. In Jalisco, artisans also make *equipales*, the typically Mexican, rustic leather and wood armchairs.

Mexico is the world leader in silver production, and prices are well below those of Europe or the US. Silversmiths in Taxco *(see pp150–51)*, Guanajuato *(see pp206–8)*, and Zacatecas *(see pp196–7)* create modern designs, as well as those inspired by pre-Columbian jewelry. A 925 stamp will ensure that the silver is good quality. Alpaca, which is on sale all over Mexico, is a nickel alloy and contains no silver at all. Opals, jadeite, lapis lazuli, obsidian, onyx, and many other semi-precious stones, are relatively inexpensive to purchase.

Clothing

Casual clothing is available in all major tourist resorts and big cities. Imported designer labels, such as Gucci and Hermès, can be found in a few select boutiques and department stores. Less expensive clothes are on sale in smaller shops and markets everywhere. Any designer clothes and accessories that are for sale on cheap market stalls are almost certain to be fakes.

Villages in the south and southeast of Mexico are the best places to buy traditional, hand-embroidered Indian costumes. The more commercial designs – often using synthetic fabrics – are sold in craft shops everywhere.

Hats and scarves on a souvenir stall in a street market

Regional Products

The variety of crafts available in Mexico is vast *(see pp332–3)*. Every region has its specialties, and it is more interesting – and usually cheaper – to buy *artesanías* in the region where they are made. For an overview of what is available, most regional capitals have a Casa de las Artesanías, which houses exhibitions and sales of local craftwork. The most outstanding *artesanías* are found in those areas which have a significant Indian population, such as the states of Oaxaca, Puebla, Chiapas, Guerrero, Michoacán, and Nayarit.

Typical tourist shops in the resort of Playa del Carmen

Food and Drink

Fresh and dried chilies, spices, and pastes for preparing *mole* and other Mexican dishes are best bought from market stalls. Although not quite as good, *mole* is also found in jars or packages at supermarkets. Similarly, there are several varieties of chili bottled and in cans, which are more easily packed.

The best *añejo* tequilas *(see p313)* are made in Jalisco, and good brands, like Herradura or Centenario, can be bought at supermarkets and *vinaterías* (liquor stores) all over Mexico. Avoid non-labeled tequila, which may be contaminated with methanol. Mezcal, less widely sold, is best bought in its native Oaxaca.

Handmade sweets and candies are a specialty of central Mexico's colonial towns. Sweet-toothed visitors will want to try *cajeta* from Celaya, *chongos* from Zamora, *camote* from Puebla, and *cocada envinada* from Guadalajara. These, and more, can be found in Mexico City's Dulcería de Celaya *(see p118)*.

Markets

Every town in Mexico has at least one market. There is often a permanent indoor market, as well as a once-weekly street market, or *tianguis*, which is usually held in or around the main square. In large cities, each neighborhood has its *mercado sobre ruedas* (street market) on a different day of the week. These markets are a colorful array of fresh fruit, vegetables, fish and meat, and piles of herbs, spices, and chilies. Clothes, trinkets, and household items are also for sale. Prices are generally cheaper here than in supermarkets.

Markets are transformed at fiesta time. At Easter in Mexico City, there is an abundance of red papier mâché *diablos* (devils). Just before the Days of the Dead *(see pp38–9)*, stalls overflow with sugar skulls and dancing skeletons. And at Christmas, the usual decorations rub shoulders with typically Mexican nativity figures.

Vivid array of chilies, legumes (pulses), and spices for sale in a Mexican market

Folk Art of Mexico

Crafts in Mexico are an essential part of daily and ceremonial life, with techniques passed down from generation to generation. Contemporary folk art results from the fusion of Old and New World traits. After the Conquest, the impact of Spanish technology was widely felt. While some native arts such as feather working were lost, others were gained. Mission schools taught European skills, and Spanish methods for treating leather were introduced, together with treadle-loom weaving and the glazing of ceramics. Today, traditional methods and designs co-exist with recent innovations, producing a wide range of high-quality crafts for sale *(see pp334–5)*.

Spanish galleons, displaying the sign of the cross, brought Christianity to Mexico.

Religious festivals marked out the pre-Columbian year. Despite efforts by Spanish missionaries to ban the dance of the *voladores*, it is still performed today *(see p33)*.

The art of pottery goes back thousands of years in Mexico, and in other parts of the New World. Many ancient techniques are still in use today.

Pot making still utilises traditional methods. Tzeltal women, for instance, work without a wheel in Amatenango del Valle, Chiapas. Tubes of clay are coiled and pressed down with the fingers. The surfaces are burnished and decorated before being fired.

This weaver is using a backstrap loom. Textile skills in Tzotzil and other indigenous communities, are used primarily to make clothing. As in pre-Conquest times, weavers rely on techniques such as brocading to pattern cloth on the loom.

Corn (or maize) originated in the Americas, and formed part of the staple diet of Meso-american civilizations *(see p49)*. Then, as now, it was ground on a *metate* (grinding stone).

Silversmiths have practiced their art for many centuries in Mexico. After the Conquest, some processes like "lost wax casting" disappeared, but modern jewelers retain enormous skill. The above pieces were sand-cast.

Bark paper *(amate)* is still made in the Otomí village of San Pablito (Puebla), using an ancient, pre-Columbian method. Popular with collectors, the cut-out figures represent supernatural forces. They are used by Otomí shamans during rituals to encourage the growth of crops and to cure the sick.

The Meeting of Two Worlds

Metepec, outside Toluca, is famous for its exuberant pottery. Brightly painted "Trees of Life" are inspired by history, nature, and the Bible. The one pictured here, by Tiburcio Soteno, shows Spanish conquistadors discovering Aztec civilization in 1519.

Markets have always been good sources of local craft items. The vendors, who are often the makers, may travel long distances to sell their wares.

The Aztec calendar alluded to on the Sun Stone *(see p99)* combined a solar calendar of 365 days and a sacred calendar of 260 days, leading to cycles of 52 years *(see p51)*.

Human sacrifices took place in Aztec temples. The victims, regarded as the gods' messengers, had their hearts cut out on the sacrificial stone.

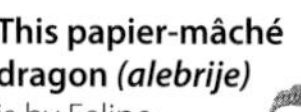

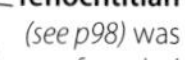

Tenochtitlán *(see p98)* was founded when the Aztecs entered the Valley of Mexico and saw the promised sign of an eagle on a prickly pear *(see p47)*.

This papier-mâché dragon *(alebrije)* is by Felipe Linares. European paper, introduced after the Conquest, is used in Mexico City and Celaya (west of Querétaro) to make fantastical papier-mâché figures of all shapes and kinds.

Glazed ceramics are decorative as well as functional. The pottery must be fired twice, and enclosed kilns have generally replaced pre-Columbian firing methods. The glaze is often transparent, but yellow, black, and green are used too.

Embroidery was practiced in Mexico before the Conquest but was given new impetus under Spanish rule. The blouse, here embroidered with flowers, was a garment introduced from Spain.

Tinsmiths are particularly prominent in Oaxaca City. The craftsmen use shears to cut through thin and flexible sheets of tin. Lanterns and decorative figures can be plain, or painted with bright, industrial colors.

Buying Mexican Crafts

Mexican folk art has a unique vitality. Good craft items are sold in street markets, as well as in shops and galleries. Work can also be bought directly from the makers. Artisans of various trades can be found in many villages and small towns by making inquiries on arrival. Although it is advisable to negotiate a fair price when buying crafts, purchasers should take into consideration the rising cost of materials, as well as the skill and time invested by the maker. Many folk artists now sign their work, aware that it is highly valued by an increasing number of museums and private collectors.

Tin-glazed earthenware dish from Guanajuato

Ceramics

Mexican ceramists practice a vast range of ancient and modern techniques. In Oaxaca, traditional firing methods produce pottery with a black, metallic lustre. Green glazes are popular in Michoacán. Puebla City is famous for its tin-glazed earthenware, and brightly-painted toys are produced in many places.

Painted pottery mermaid and animals

Pottery bandstand

Ceramic Adam and Eve

Papier-Mâché

Papier-mâché is used to create decorative figures and toys for seasonal festivities. Masks are made all year round, skeletons and skulls for the Days of the Dead *(see pp38–9)*.

Cockerel made of wire and papier-mâché

Jointed papier-mâché doll

Human and animal masks for children

Wooden Toys and Carvings

Inexpensive wooden toys are made in several states, including Michoacán, Guerrero, and Guanajuato. In the villages of Oaxaca, carved, painted figures and dance masks can fetch high prices.

Wooden tiger with sequin eyes

Fragile items

When transporting craft objects, any hollows should be padded out, and projecting features wrapped in paper.

Toy truck and passengers

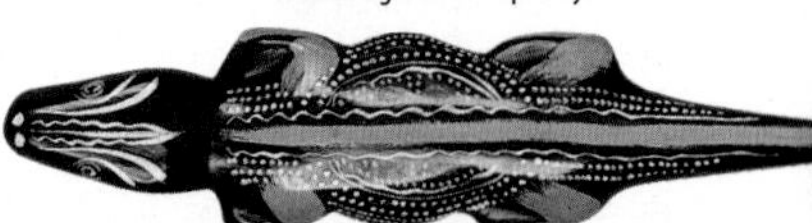

Lacquer-coated wooden lizard from Guerrero

Textiles

In some states, traditional garments such as sashes, shawls, wrap-around skirts, and *huipiles* (tunics) are woven on a backstrap loom from hand-spun wool or cotton. Treadle-loomed blankets and rugs are made in Oaxaca. Embroidered blouses can be found in many regions. The Huichol specialize in netted beadwork.

Woven cloth, patterned on the loom

Huichol netted beadwork bag

Otomí cloth with embroidery

Nahua embroidered blouse

Caring for textiles
Textiles should always be washed by hand in cold water. Even under these conditions, colors may run, so it is advisable to test-wash a small corner first.

Metalwork and Jewelry

Copper is worked only in Michoacán. It is hammered while red hot to form jugs, platters, and candlesticks. Taxco is world famous for its silverwork. In the Yucatán, gold- and silversmiths specialize in delicate earrings and necklaces.

Cockerel

Bull

Silver earrings from Puebla

Tin decorations
In Oaxaca City, the tinsmiths work with sheets of tin. The shapes are cut out and painted with translucent colors to form lamps, boxes, and shimmering figures. In central regions of Mexico, elegant candlesticks and Baroque mirror-frames are made from unpainted tin.

Mexican bird

Armadillo

Oaxacan woman

Other Crafts

In Mexico, there is hardly a substance that is not made to serve a functional, decorative, or ceremonial purpose. Fine and unusual work is done using sugar, bone, horn, vanilla, and gum. Pictures are often painted on tree-bark paper.

Lacquered gourd

Lacquered box

Lacquer work
Gourds and wooden items such as trays and boxes are given a hard, glossy coat. Archaeological remnants show that lacquer-working dates from pre-Columbian times.

Basketry
Beautiful yet sturdy, baskets are made in several regions of Mexico, including Oaxaca and Guerrero. Makers use palm, willow, cane, wheat-straw, and agave fibers.

ENTERTAINMENT IN MEXICO

One of Mexico's most fascinating features is its home-grown tradition in music, dance, and popular arts. The country has produced a huge range of uniquely Mexican musical styles, and equally distinctive, colorful dances. Cities and resorts offer buzzing nightlife, from salsa venues to trendy clubs. Mexico City and other big cities host quality classical music and theater. Sport is also hugely popular in Mexico – every Mexican soccer league game is shown live, and baseball is broadcast live on the radio. For a uniquely Mexican sporting event, nothing beats the exciting displays of horsemanship at a *charrería*. For annual events throughout Mexico, see pages 34–9.

Folk dancers performing to *jarana* music in the Yucatán

Traditional Music and Dance

Virtually every part of Mexico has its own style of music and dance. The most famous, *mariachi* music, originated in Jalisco state but can now be found all over the country. *Mariachis* are part of Mexico's wandering minstrel tradition, and can be heard in the street, or going from table to table in restaurants.

In many regions, though, the violins and trumpets of *mariachis* are less prominent than local styles and instruments: Caribbean *danzón* in Veracruz, *marimbas* in Chiapas, and the *jarana* music and dancers of the Yucatán.

The best occasions to experience other kinds of music and dance are local *fiestas*. Many cities, such as Mérida, also host smaller festivals with displays of local music and dance every week. In other towns, there are regular displays by folklore groups, and permanent theatrical shows. Some spectacular festivals celebrate a particular region's traditional dances, the most dazzling being Oaxaca's *La Guelaguetza*, every July *(see p35)*.

Pop, Rock, Latin Dance, and Clubs

Mexico also has a vibrant modern music scene, and artists such as Julieta Venegas and Paulina Rubio increasingly cross over to non-Latin audiences. Many performers mix Mexican styles with hip-hop, rock, and other international influences. Other stars from around the Hispanic world, as well as US and international artists, are also popular. Mexico City and other large cities have a big choice of live music venues. Concerts also feature in major *fiestas*, such as Carnival in Veracruz, or *Feria de Tabasco* in Villahermosa in April and May.

Julieta Venegas performing her own brand of accordion-based rock

Salsa, merengue, and other Latin dances are hugely popular, and every city and resort has a choice of Latin dance clubs, often with live bands. Clubs with international dance music are just as common, and vary from basic to dazzlingly chic and glamorous. Giant mega-clubs, with several different spaces and the latest technology, are the specialties of resorts like Cancún. For more intimate nightlife head for smaller resorts, like Puerto Escondido or Playa del Carmen.

Classical Music, Dance, and Theater

Mexico City has, by far, the largest classical music program, with three resident orchestras and regular visits by international orchestras, opera companies, and soloists. Guadalajara also has its own symphony orchestra, and Mérida has the Orquestra Sinfónica de Yucatán.

Classical ballet and contemporary dance can be seen in Mexico City at the Palacio de Bellas Artes *(see p84)* and Teatro de la Danza *(see p120)*. For Spanish-speakers there is a varied mix of live theater, especially in Mexico City and Guadalajara. Cultural festivals worth seeking out include the

International Chamber Music Festival in San Miguel de Allende (Aug), Guadalajara's October Festival, Zacatecas' Culture Festival (Semana Santa), and the Festival Internacional Cervantino in Guanajuato (Sep–Oct), with an international mix of music and theater.

Movies

Mexicans are eager moviegoers, and the country has a long movie-making tradition, producing a large number of films. In the 1930s and 1940s it produced hundreds of movies before falling into decline. The industry has since been revived with the emergence of actors such as Salma Hayek and Gael García Bernal, and movies like *Amores Perros* that have won international acclaim.

Cities offer a choice of modern, air-conditioned multiplex movie theaters. In multiplexes, Hollywood movies are often shown in English with Spanish subtitles on at least one screen.

The masked wrestlers of *lucha libre* – a popular sport in Mexico

Spectator Sports

Sports attract the biggest audiences of all in Mexico. Soccer (football) inspires the most passion – above all in central Mexico – with several teams in Mexico City, and one in each of the other major cities. TV provides constant coverage, but the best place to see a big game is Mexico City's vast Estadio Azteca *(see p121)*. Baseball is also popular, especially along the Pacific coast, the Gulf Coast, and on the Yucatán Peninsula, with two competitive professional leagues.

Two other sports are peculiarly Mexican. Mexico has produced many boxing champions, and there are matches every weekend in the capital and other cities. Even more popular is wrestling (*lucha libre*). Mexican wrestlers are popular idols. They often fight in masks and outrageous costumes and develop superhero-like personalities.

Charro riders in high-speed action in a *lienzo charro* (*charrería* ring)

Bullfighting

Spanish-style bullfights are held every Sunday at Mexico City's Plaza Mexico *(see p114)* – the largest bullring in the world – during the November–April season. This is the closed season for bullfighting in Spain, so many top Spanish *toreros* spend their winters in Mexico. Many other cities, and resorts like Cancún, also have bullrings with regular *corridas* throughout the year.

Smaller-scale bullfights are also part of many small town and village *fiestas*. These bullfights are much less formal, more raucous events, and often fairly chaotic as well – frequently though, the bull is not killed.

Charrerías

A uniquely Mexican event, a *charrería* is a rodeo in which cowboys *(charros)* in the traditional big *sombrero*, embroidered jacket, and trousers (and cowgirls – *charras*, riding side-saddle and wearing elaborate layered skirts) perform spectacular tests of horsemanship. There are *charrería* rings (*lienzos charros*), in every city, but the best are in the northern and western states – especially Jalisco, also home to *mariachi* music, which always accompanies a *charrería*. The annual Día del Charro (September 14) is the occasion for *charrería* displays throughout the country.

Ticket for a bullfight in Mexico City

Entertainment for Children

To entertain young visitors, there is the huge Six Flags Mexico theme park, just outside Mexico City. Closer to the center, Chapultepec Park houses an amusement park and zoo *(see p92)*. Resorts like Cancún and Acapulco have a choice of water parks, and on the Riviera Maya "eco-parks" like Xcaret *(see p288)* provide a child-friendly introduction to a tropical environment.

Young visitors are fascinated by the colors of local *fiestas*, which always include different events for children and temporary funfairs.

OUTDOOR ACTIVITIES & SPECIALIST HOLIDAYS

Mexico's enormously varied landscapes provide ideal settings for all kinds of activities. Along the coasts are long surf beaches, some of the world's richest sportfishing grounds, and coral reefs that are perfect for diving and snorkeling. Inland are fast-flowing rivers in spectacular gorges, and unforgettable forests, deserts, and mountains to explore by hiking, climbing, or on horseback. Other possibilities include discovering the country's wealth of wildlife, its special cuisines, or fascinating historic culture. Local tourist offices can provide the latest information on the ever-increasing number of activities available.

Diving and Snorkeling

The Great Maya Reef off Yucatán's Caribbean coast form one of the world's largest coral reef systems. Despite the growth in visitor numbers, huge areas are still vividly alive, with brilliantly colorful fish and coral gardens. There are reefs of every grade of diving difficulty, from novice dives to awesome wall dives. There are scuba diving centers all along the Riviera Maya, but for beginners and less experienced divers the best locations are Isla Mujeres, Puerto Morelos, Playa del Carmen, or Cozumel.

Snorkeling is an easier alternative, and some dive operators also offer snorkel tours. Off Cozumel, where reefs come close inshore, you can often see as much with a snorkel as with scuba tanks.

The waters of the Pacific coast are not as clear as those of the Caribbean, but there is still fine diving around Puerto Escondido, Ixtapa, and Zihuatanejo. The best Pacific diving and snorkeling is in the Sea of Cortéz, between Baja California and the mainland.

Thanks to the Yucatán's unique geology, riddled with limestone caverns, underground rivers, and open sinkholes called cenotes, this is also one of the world's foremost areas for cave diving. Operators in Akumal and Tulum such as **Aquatech** and **Diving Cenotes Tulum** specialize in cave dives, and **Hidden Worlds** in Tulum gives a great first taste of swimming in caves. You must have open-water diving certification to cave dive, but without this you can still snorkel in the upper levels of cenotes.

Surfing

The Pacific coast is lined with surfing beaches. Baja California has beaches almost along the whole of its length, and near its southern tip many companies like **Baja Wild** offer boat trips to remote surf beaches and islands. On the mainland, surfing centers include Mazatlán, Manzanillo, Troncones, Ixtapa and Zihuatanejo in Guerrero, and, the most popular, Puerto Escondido. Most surfers find their own way, but many agencies offer surf camps, courses, and trips to special locations.

Snorkeling in Chankanaab National Park Island, Cozumel

Fishing

Yucatán's Caribbean coast has fine deep-sea fishing for marlin, bonito, tuna, and more. Cozumel, Puerto Morelos, and Puerto Aventuras are all good fishing centers. **Captain Rick's Sportfishing** in Puerto Aventuras offers combined fishing and snorkeling trips.

Inshore fishing is just as popular: Ascension Bay, south of Tulum, has some of the richest fly-fishing grounds in the world, especially for bonefish, and there are fishing lodges scattered along the dirt road down to Punta Allen. **Cuzan Guest House** makes a good base and offers fly, offshore, and spin fishing trips.

On the Pacific, Mazatlán is the deep-sea fishing mecca, especially for marlin and billfish. **Bibi Fleet** in Mazatlán has well-organized trips. Freshwater fisheries are less developed, but there is good fishing for bass on Lago El Salto, inland from Mazatlán.

All fishing centers have agencies with boats for rent, and many US-based companies arrange fishing packages. Many dive shops, adventure tour agencies, and hotels also offer fishing trips, and in small towns these can be arranged informally with local fishermen.

A golf course in the grounds of a Cancún hotel resort

Licenses are required for deep-sea fishing; your boat agency will arrange this.

Other Water Sports

Sailing through the Sea of Cortéz off Baja California is a wonderful experience, with many rocky coves and islands to explore. There are excellent marinas at La Paz, San Carlos, Mazatlán, Puerto Vallarta, and Zihuatanejo, while on the Caribbean, Puerto Aventuras, and Cozumel are also sailing centers. The **Sonoran Sport Center** in San Carlos has a sailing school, while **The Moorings Boat Charters** offers the choice of crewed charters or boats to hire, supplied with a specially devised itinerary for your trip.

Windsurf boards can be rented in most resorts, but Mexico's windsurfing magnet is Los Barriles, in Baja California. In the bigger resorts you can also find Jet Skis, water skis, and banana boats (inflatables pulled along by a speedboat).

For more tranquil exploration, in Baja California, sea kayaking is one way of getting close to sea lions and whales. Around the southern Riviera Maya, many hotels offer kayaks for trips through the mangroves toward Ascension Bay, or around the exquisite lake at Bacalar. Recently there has been a huge expansion in freshwater kayaking and whitewater rafting on Mexico's many spectacular rivers. Popular routes include the Río Filolobos in Veracruz, the Amacuzac in Morelos, and the Huasteca Potosina region of San Luís Potosí. **Oaxaca Expediciones** takes kayak trips on the Lower Copalita River in Oaxaca. In Chiapas, **Explora** organizes trips of several days rafting down La Venta gorge or kayaking through the Lacandón rainforest.

White-water rafting

Golf

The number of golf courses in Mexico has grown fast, and there are now courses near all the main cities and resorts, especially Cabo San Lucás, Mazatlán, and Cancún. The **Cabo del Sol Golf Courses** in Cabo San Lucas has two large courses, and the **Cozumel Country Club** offers package deals with participating hotels. Some hotels have courses attached, and there's a growing number of golf resorts. Most are open to non-residents for an extra fee. For more on golfing in Mexico, check www.golfinmexico.net

Hiking, Climbing, and Adventure Sports

Mexico's rugged mountain ranges provide spectacular opportunities for outdoor sports. The awe-inspiring Copper Canyon of Chihuahua *(see pp180–81)* is the most popular area, with trekking and bike trails of every grade of difficulty, and dramatic gorges for more challenging activities like canyoneering and abseiling. Many US-based agencies like **Native Trails** and **Copper Canyon Trails** organize canyon treks, and local agencies, like **Expediciones Umarike**, provide equipment and Tarahumara Indian guides. Elsewhere, a popular trip from Mexico City is the climb up the massive 5,230-m (17,150-ft) volcano of Iztaccihuátl. You can also hike into tropical forest environments, like Los Tuxtlas in Veracruz or the Sierra Gorda mountains near Querétaro.

Many Mexican agencies offer adventure trips, such as **Tour by Mexico**. Information on adventure trips can be found on www.visitmexico.com/en/extreme-sports-and-adventure-in-mexico.

Taking a hike in Copper Canyon (Cañon del Cobre), Northern Mexico

Horseback Riding

Mexico has an ingrained horse culture, and there are plenty of opportunities to explore spectacular scenery on horseback. The best places are Copper Canyon, around Laguna de Chapala, Real de Catorce, and San Miguel de Allende and – along trails that lead to the migration-refuges of monarch butterflies – above Valle de Bravo. **El Caballo Rojo** in Laguna de Chapala has tours for riders of all abilities. In San Cristóbal, Chiapas, agencies offer horseback tours up to nearby Mayan villages.

Around coastal resorts, there are often horses to hire along beaches, and many hotels and eco-parks like **Xcaret** have horses to ride on well-organized trails.

Air Sports

The most exciting way to see Mexico's resorts must be to skydive onto their beaches. **SkyDive Cuautla** is based at Cuautla, outside Mexico City, but also has operations at Puerto Vallarta, Ixtapa, and Puerto Escondido. On the Riviera Maya, **SkyDive Playa** offers jumps over Playa del Carmen. Parasailing rides are available at most big resorts, but note that these operators are virtually unregulated, so check safety provisions carefully before trying any ride.

Globo Aventura and **Fly Volare** offer hot-air balloon tours of the Valley of Mexico and the Teotihuacán pyramids.

Whale and Shark Watching

The waters around Baja California contain one of the world's largest concentrations of whales and dolphins, from smaller species in the Sea of Cortez to giant whales that migrate along the Pacific coast from December to March. Guerrero Negro on the west coast is the best place to see larger whales, but whales can be found all around the peninsula, and all Baja-based dive shops and adventure sports agencies offer whale-watching trips. Whales and dolphins can also be seen off Puerto Vallarta, in the same season. **Discover Pacific Tours** based in Puerto Vallarta organizes enjoyable whale and dolphin spotting boat trips.

A much rarer phenomenon is the gathering of whale sharks, the world's largest fish, between July and September off Cabo Catoche, north of Cancún. Trips to see and swim with these huge – but entirely harmless – creatures are run by operators on Holbox island, such as the **Hotel Faro Viejo**.

Cycling

Bicycles are a universal means of transport in Mexico, and bikes can be rented in most resorts. For mountain biking, the most popular location is Copper Canyon, where local companies like **Expediciones Umarike** rent bikes and provide information, but there are countless other possibilities. **Ecocolors** and Canada-based **Bike Mexico** provide excellent guided bike tours.

Wildlife and Nature

Mexico has a wealth of wildlife in many different habitats – desert, mountain, rainforest, and the dry Yucatán woods. In the north, **Solipaso**, based near Copper Canyon, offers a range of excursions. Among the unmissable sights of central Mexico are the valleys that shelter millions of migratory monarch butterflies between November and March. Agencies in Morelia, Mexico City, and abroad run tours.

Farther south, trips are possible into the rainforests of Chiapas and Campeche, with the possibility of seeing jaguars, monkeys, and blue macaws. The Yucatán peninsula is exceptionally rich in birdlife, and Yucatán state hosts a bird festival, the Toh Festival, each November or December to coincide with the arrival of winter migrants from North America (www.yucatanbirds.com). The Yucatán's most famous birds are its flamingo colonies at Celestún and Río Lagartos, which are easy to reach. Longer guided trips around the region are available from specialists like **Ecoturismo Yucatán** or **Ecocolors**. Another destination not to be missed is Sian Ka'an reserve, home to forest animals and millions of birds. Tulum-based **CESiak** runs excellent one-day tours. For dedicated wildlife enthusiasts there are more gruelling options, such as the 10-day treks offered by the **Mesoamerican Tourism Alliance** into the vast El Triunfo reserve of southern Chiapas, the refuge of Mexico's rarest birds such as the Quetzal.

Specialist Holidays

One of the most rewarding ways to travel is to pursue a personal interest or a new skill, in ways that also give you extra insights into Mexico's culture. Food is one such field, and residential cooking courses – in English – are ever more popular. **Los Tamarindos**, **Alma de mi Tierra**, and **Los Dos Cooking School** are among the schools that give an enjoyable introduction to Mexico's culinary heritage.

Elsewhere, you can try photography workshops at **Aper Tours** in San Cristóbal de Las Casas, and there are several art workshops, especially in Baja California and San Miguel de Allende. If you want to know more about Mexico's past and cultural traditions than conventional tours may tell you, several agencies offer tours with archaeologists and experts as guides, such as US-based **Far Horizons** or **Academic Tours Oaxaca**.

Learning Spanish is another way of getting closer to Mexican life, and there are many schools that offer residential courses. Two good-value schools are **Becari** in Oaxaca and **Instituto Jovel** in San Cristóbal.

For more information on Spanish-language schools, workshops, and tours, you can browse the Internet for Mexico travel websites.

For an overview of spas and health retreats in Mexico, see pp342–3.

DIRECTORY

Diving and Snorkeling

Aquatech – Villas de Rosa
Aventuras Akumal, Akumal, Quintana Roo.
Tel (984) 875 9020.
W cenotes.com

Diving Cenotes Tulum
Cnr of Calle Polar and Calle Acuario, Tulum, Quintana Roo.
Tel (984) 140 6813.
W divingcenotes tulum.com

Hidden Worlds
Mex 307, north of Tulum, Quintana Roo.
Tel (998) 206 2507.
W hiddenworlds.com

Surfing

Baja Wild
San José del Cabo, Baja California Sur.
Tel (624) 122 0107.
W bajawild.com

Fishing

Bibi Fleet
Marina Puesta del Sol, Shop 8, Marina Mazatlán, Mazatlán, Sinaloa.
Tel (669) 913 1060.
W bibifleet.com

Captain Rick's Sportfishing
Puerto Aventuras, Quintana Roo.
Tel (984) 873 5195.
W fishyucatan.com

Cuzan Guest House
Punta Allen, Quintana Roo.
Tel (983) 834 0358.
W flyfishmx.com

Other Water Sports

Explora
Calle 1 de Marzo 30, San Cristóbal de Las Casas, Chiapas.
Tel (967) 631 7498.
W ecochiapas.com

Oaxaca Expediciones
Huatulco, Oaxaca.
Tel (958) 111 6588.
W oaxaca expediciones.com

The Moorings Boat Charters
Tel 1 888 952 8420 (US).
Tel 08444 636 879 (UK).
W moorings.com

Sonoran Sport Center
San Carlos, Sonora.
Tel (622) 226 0508.
W sailsancarlos.com

Golf

Cabo del Sol Golf Courses
Cabo San Lucas, Baja California Sur.
Tel (624) 145 8200.
W cabodelsol.com

Cozumel Country Club
Carretera Costera Norte, Cozumel, Quintana Roo.
Tel (987) 872 9570.
W cozumelcountry club.com.mx

Climbing, Hiking, and Adventure Sports

Copper Canyon Trails
Tel (520) 324 0209 (US).
W coppercanyontrails. org

Expediciones Umarike
Creel, Chihuahua.
Tel (635) 456 0632.
W umarike.com.mx

Native Trails
613 Querétaro Drive, El Paso, TX 79912, USA.
Tel (915) 833 3107.
W nativetrails.com

Tour by Mexico
Tel (999) 317 0220.
W tourbymexico.com

Horseback Riding

El Caballo Rojo
Ajijic, Laguna de Chapala, Jalisco. **Tel** (333) 473 7998.
W elcaballorojo. weebly.com

Xcaret
Quintana Roo. Mex 307, 4 miles (7 km) S of Playa del Carmen.
Tel (998) 251 6560.
W xcaret.com

Air Sports

Fly Volare
Tel (55) 5331 2460.
W flyvolare.com.mx

Globo Aventura
Tel (473) 734 7770.
W globoaventura.com

SkyDive Cuautla
Tel (55) 5517 8529.
W skydivecuautla.com

SkyDive Playa
Plaza Marina, Playa del Carmen, Quintana Roo.
Tel (984) 873 0192.
W skydive.com.mx

Whale and Shark Watching

Discover Pacific Tours
Puerto Vallarta, Jalisco.
Tel (322) 224 9027.
W discoverpacific tours.com

Hotel Faro Viejo
Holbox, Quintana Roo.
Tel (984) 875 2217.
W faroviejoholbox. com.mx

Cycling

Bike Mexico
344 Wycliffe Ave, Woodbridge, Ontario L4L 3N8, Canada.
Tel (416) 848 0265 (Can).
Tel (967) 678 0202 (Mex).
W bikemexico.com

Wildlife and Nature

CESiak – Centro Ecológico Sian Ka'an
Carretera 307, Tulum, Quintana Roo. **Tel** (984) 871 2499. **W cesiak.org**

Ecocolors
Calle Camarón 32, SM27, Cancún, Quintana Roo.
Tel (998) 884 3667.
W ecotravelmexico.com

Ecoturismo Yucatán
Calle 3 no. 235, Mérida, Yucatán. **Tel** (999) 920 27 72. **W ecoyuc.com**

Mesoamerican Ecotourism Alliance
4076 Crystal Court, Boulder, CO 80304, USA.
Tel 1 800 682 0584.
W travelwithmea.org

Solipaso
Calle Obregón 3, Alamos, Sonora. **Tel** (647) 428 1509.
W solipaso.com

Specialist Holidays

Academic Tours Oaxaca
Tel (951) 518 4728.
W academictours oaxaca.com

Alma de mi Tierra
Calle Pino Suárez 508, Oaxaca. **Tel** (951) 513 9211.
W almademitierra.net

Aper Tours Photography Workshop
Calle Tonalá 27, San Cristóbal de Las Casas, Chiapas. **Tel** (967) 678 5727. **W apertours.com**

Becari Language School
Calle M. Bravo 210, Plaza San Cristóbal, Oaxaca.
Tel (951) 514 6076.
W becari.com.mx

Los Dos Cooking School
Calle 68 no. 517, between 65 and 67, Mérida, Yucatán. **Tel** (999) 928 1116. **W los-dos.com**

Far Horizons
PO Box 2546, San Anselmo, CA 94979, USA.
Tel 1 800 552 4575.
W farhorizons.com

Instituto Jovel Language School
Francisco I. Madero 45, San Cristóbal de Las Casas, Chiapas.
Tel (967) 678 4069.
W institutojovel.com

Los Tamarindos
San José del Cabo, Baja California Sur.
Tel (624) 105 6031.
W huertalos tamarindos.com

SPA BREAKS IN MEXICO

Mexico's seductive climate, brilliant light and color, and laidback atmosphere have made it an ever popular destination for spa breaks, whether for a few days of pampering and deep relaxation or more spiritually oriented programs. Spas are enormously varied. Many are attached to hotels, but there are also "destination spas" where the spa experience is an essential reason to visit, and "day spas" where you can drop in for your choice of treatments. Most spas offer similar basic treatments – a wide range of massages, aromatherapy, reflexology, facials, body wraps, and more – but some focus more on beauty treatments or fitness, while others highlight yoga and holistic therapies. Many spas offer ancient local treatments such as the *temazcal* (traditional sweat bath), or Mayan healing and massage techniques.

Hotel and Resort Spas

The largest concentration of spas is in hotels and resort complexes, especially in and around the main beach resort areas like Baja California, Puerto Vallarta, Acapulco, and Yucatán's Riviera Maya. The use of the spa is generally an optional extra, charged for separately on the final bill.

Most high-end hotels and large resort complexes have some kind of spa, but they vary widely, ranging from just a few massage and beauty rooms to magnificent facilities with every kind of treatment. Major luxury hotels, such as the **Four Seasons** at Punta Mita, north of Puerto Vallarta, offer some of the finest spas. In Cancún, the **Ritz-Carlton**'s is perhaps the most sumptuous.

For a far more intimate experience, there are spas in stylish, seductive smaller resorts like the chic **Viceroy Riviera Maya**, as well as in exquisite beach retreats on their own isolated coves, like **Kinan Spa** at Maroma Resort and Spa. Here, restoring body and mind in an utterly tranquil tropical setting is an essential part of the luxury experience, and honeymoons are a specialty.

Less isolated but beautifully relaxing are the **Cabañas Copal, Azulik**, and **Zahra** hotels in their own patch of jungle on Tulum beach in the Riviera Maya. They share the Mayan Spa, offering massage and other therapies by the beach.

Away from the coasts, there are delightful spas combined with hacienda-style buildings and lush gardens in some hotels around Mexico's colonial cities, such as **Hostería Las Quintas** in Cuernavaca. One of the most sumptuous spas in the country is in **El Santuario**, a spectacular resort hotel with a fabulous view over the lake at Valle de Bravo, west of Mexico City.

A treatment room at the Maroma Resort and Spa, Riviera Maya, Mexico

Destination Spas

Spa treatments are the central purpose of a stay at a "destination spa." Most guests stay on packages that include their treatments and activities, accommodations, and meals. Some of these spas are as enticingly opulent as any small luxury hotel, and nearly all are in spectacular mountain or beach locations.

Several spas are in the hills around Cuernavaca, in Morelos state south of Mexico City, an area celebrated since Aztec times for its natural springs and fine mountain air. They include some of Mexico's most luxurious spa retreats, such as the **Hostal de la Luz** and **Misión del Sol**, which combine indulgent health and beauty treatments using natural materials with a range of therapies and practices from India, Japan, ancient Mexico and other countries. Other spas combine yoga and wellness programs with an energetic range of activities such as horseback riding or mountain biking. Two such spas are **Rancho La Puerta**, just south of the US border in Baja California, and **Armonia Spa**, an award-winning Cabo San Lucas spa in a secluded oceanfront location.

Tulum on the Riviera Maya has both the **Amansala** "bikini boot-camp" – an imaginative mix of fashionable beauty care, fitness training, and Mayan health treatments geared to women – and the **Maya Tulum**, with a program based on yoga and Indian beliefs. On the Pacific coast, in a wonderful location,

Mar de Jade is a remarkable center that offers a huge choice of activities from yoga and intensive spa health programs to water sports, gardening, dance, and Spanish classes, as well as workshops in cooking, arts, and music, in a relaxed, eco-friendly setting. There are also special programs for families and teens.

Day Spas

In all the main resorts there are small "day spas" where visitors can come for treatments. Many hotel spas are also open to non-guests on a pay-per-session basis. Day spas concentrate on massage, health, and beauty treatments, but two that also give casual visitors the opportunity to experience traditional pre-Hispanic *temazcal* baths and other treatments are the **Maya Spa**, in between the Copal, Azulik, and Zahra hotels in Tulum, and **Terra Noble**, in Puerto Vallarta.

Small-Group Retreats

Many groups (mostly US-based) organize small-group retreats around Mexico, lasting one to two weeks, with a wide range of emphases, from writing to intensive dance therapy in a variety of venues, from beachside *cabaña* hotels to remote mountain haciendas. Two popular permanent retreat centers are **El Santuario** in Baja California and **Present Moment** in Guerrero.

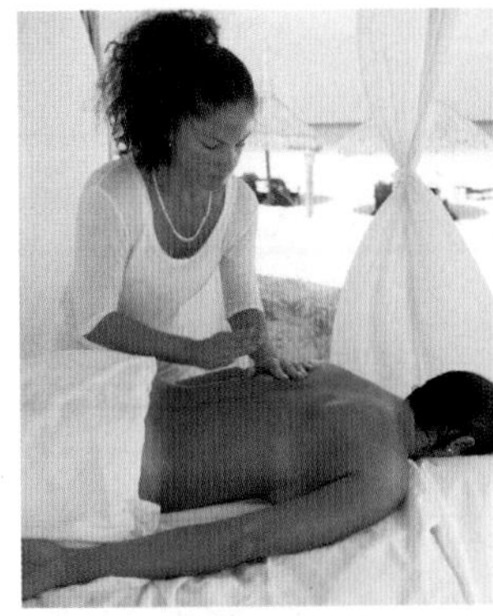

A relaxing massage treatment

Natural Springs

Several natural hot springs can be discovered around Mexico. Guadalupe Canyon, a short distance from the US border near Mexicali in Baja California, is famous for its hot pools. In central Mexico, as well as the hot springs at Río Caliente in Jalisco, are some scarcely developed springs in a beautiful mountain location at Los Azufres in Michoacán, with a charming, rustic *cabaña* hotel, **Balnearios Eréndira**.

Spas with Medical Facilities

Some spas cater for guests with specific medical problems. **Sanoviv**, in Baja California, is a fully equipped clinic with modern technology and a center for complementary medicine.

DIRECTORY

Hotel and Resort Spas

Cabañas Copal-Azulik-Zahra
Tulum, Quintana Roo.
Tel 1 800 681 9537.
W ecotulum.com

Four Seasons
Punta Mita, Bahía de Banderas, Nayarit. **Tel** (329) 291 6000. **W fourseasons.com/puntamita**

Hostería Las Quintas
Boulevard Díaz Ordaz 9, Cuernavaca, Morelos.
Tel (777) 362 3949.
W hlasquintas.com

Kinan Spa
Maroma Resort and Spa, Ctra Cancún–Tulum km 51, Solidaridad, Quintana Roo. **Tel** (998) 872 8200.
W maromahotel.com

Ritz-Carlton
Boulevard Kukulcán km14, Cancún, Quintana Roo. **Tel** (998) 881 0808.
W ritzcarlton.com

El Santuario
Carretera Colorines km 4.5, Valle de Bravo, Estado de México. **Tel** (726) 262 91 00. **W elsantuario.com**

Viceroy Riviera Maya
Off Mex. Hwy 307, Xcalacoco, Quintana Roo.
Tel (984) 877 3000.
W viceroyhotelsandresorts.com

Destination Spas

Amansala
Tulum, Quintana Roo.
Tel (984) 108 6583.
W amansala.com

Armonia Spa
Pueblo Bonito Pacifica, Av Cabo Pacifica, Cabo San Lucas, BCS. **Tel** (624) 142 9696. **W pueblobonitopacifica.com**

Hostal de la Luz
Amatlán, Morelos.
Tel (739) 395 3374.
W hostaldelaluzmexico.com

Mar de Jade
Chacala, Nayarit.
Tel (327) 219 4000.
W mardejade.com

Maya Tulum
Tulum, Quintana Roo.
Tel (984) 116 4495.
W rrresorts.com

Misión del Sol
Av. General Diego Díaz González 31, Cuernavaca, Morelos. **Tel** (777) 321 0999.
W misiondelsol.com

Rancho La Puerta
Tecate, Baja California Norte. **Tel** (665) 654 9155.
W rancholapuerta.com

Day Spas

Maya Spa
Tulum, Quintana Roo.
Tel (984) 807 7007.
W maya-spa.com

Terra Noble
Av Tulipanes 595, Puerto Vallarta, Jalisco.
Tel (322) 223 0308.
W terranoble.com

Small-Group Retreats

Present Moment
Troncones, Guerrero.
Tel (755) 103 0011.
W presentmomentretreat.com

El Santuario
Ensenada Blanca, Baja California Sur.
Tel (613) 104 4254.

Natural Springs

Balnearios Eréndira
Los Azufres, Michoacán.
Tel (786) 154 0169.
W mexonline.com/erendira

Spas with Medical Facilities

Sanoviv
Rosarito, Baja California Norte. **Tel** (661) 614 9200.
W sanoviv.com

SURVIVAL GUIDE

PRACTICAL INFORMATION

Mexico boasts a modern tourist infrastructure and is a relatively easy country to travel around, although tourist facilities in more remote areas may be limited. There are national tourist offices in all large cities and major resorts. In smaller towns, visitors can obtain information on hotels, restaurants, attractions, and activities in the area from the *palacio municipal* (town hall). Be prepared to slow down your pace of life in Mexico: everything tends to take a little longer. This may be desirable when embarking on a relaxing beach holiday, but it can become frustrating if you are up against bureaucracy. It helps to be patient and develop a philosophical outlook on life.

When to Go

The best time to visit inland sites is from February to June, before the rainy season begins *(see pp40–41)*. In Chiapas, Tabasco, and Veracruz, the rains are diluvial, but in most areas they are only a refreshing daily downpour.

November is ideal for the beach: the climate is fresh, and prices are lower than the mid-December high season. Mexicans also visit the coast during July, August, and on *puentes* (public holidays) *(see pp34–7)*. On the Caribbean coast, September and October may bring hurricanes. The smog in Mexico City is worst in December to February.

Visas and Passports

Residents of North America, the UK, Ireland, Israel, Japan, European countries under the Schengen agreement, and many other countries do not require visas to enter Mexico as tourists, but if going more than 30 km (19 miles) past the border or staying longer than 72 hours, they must obtain a *Forma Migratoria de Turista* (FMT). This carries a non-immigrant fee of around US$22, usually included in airfares, and permits visits of up to 180 days (on request). The law requires you to carry your FMT at all times.

To obtain the FMT visitors need a passport valid for six months from the travel date, proof of funds, and an onward ticket.

Anybody intending to cross into the US, including returning US citizens, must have a valid passport. Visa and passport requirements are prone to change – check before travel.

Mexican customs alcohol allowance

Customs Information

Customs searches are conducted randomly at all points of entry. After passing through passport control, each visitor must push a button which activates a traffic light system. A green light means you can pass; a red light means you must stop to have your luggage inspected.

Visitors over 18 have a duty-free allowance of 3 liters of spirits, 6 liters of wine, 25 cigars, and 20 packs of cigarettes or 200 grams of tobacco. All visitors are allowed two cameras (including a video camera), one laptop, one portable music player, and two mobile phones. If carrying prescription drugs bring the original prescription.

Anyone driving beyond the 30-km (19-mile) border zone will need a vehicle permit *(permiso de importación temporal de vehículos)* from customs or the Registro Federal de Vehículos *(see p362)*.

Archaeological artifacts may not be taken out of Mexico; the penalties for doing so are harsh. Good, certified reproductions are acceptable.

Aerial view of Palacio de Bellas Artes, one of the landmarks of Mexico City

Travel Safety Advice

Visitors can get up-to-date travel safety information from the Foreign and Commonwealth Office in the UK, the State Department in the US and the Department of Foreign Affairs and Trade in Australia.

Tourist Information

SECTUR (Secretaría de Turismo) offices are generally well

◀ Tour boats lined up along the beach at Isla Mujeres, Yucatán Peninsula

Sign for a tourist office

stocked with maps, brochures and English-speaking staff, but quality varies and some are not geared towards public visits at all, particularly those in rural areas. Most towns have at least two types of office with some degree of overlap. The municipal tourist office, usually located in the *palacio municipal* (town hall), offers information on local sights; the state tourist office can inform on wider attractions. You also may find small kiosks that hand out maps and flyers – Mexico City has them at all the major sights. Beware of time-share vendors or other commercial outfits posing as tourist information centers as they may try to sell you unwanted services.

Social Customs

Courtesy is appreciated in Mexico. On greeting, it is usual to shake hands or kiss on one cheek. When addressing people, use their relevant title *(señor, señora, señorita)*, or professional title according to their university degree, such as *Licenciado (Lic.)* for arts or law graduates.

Attire is casual, except when visiting churches. Shorts are rarely worn by Mexicans, except in resort areas.

Observe signs that forbid photography. Some indigenous people also do not like to be photographed, so ask first to avoid any confrontation.

Mexican *machismo* is world famous but generally harmless, although lone women should avoid isolated areas *(see p348)*.

Language

The official language of Mexico is Spanish, spoken by almost everyone. In the big tourist towns many locals will speak some English, but for anyone traveling off the beaten track, a smattering of Spanish is a great advantage.

There are some 62 indigenous groups in Mexico and each has its own language. In remote villages some people may speak little Spanish, although there are usually a few bilingual locals.

Admission Prices

Most of Mexico's museums and archaeological sites are governed by the state-run INAH (Instituto Nacional de Antropología e Historia) and art galleries are under the care of the INBA (Instituto Nacional de Bellas Artes). Entrance fees rarely exceed US$10; they are generally much lower in most places. Many museums and archaeological sites are technically free on Sunday, but in practice this may be reserved for Mexican nationals only. Children, seniors, and students can often expect a discount.

ISIC student card

Opening Hours

Opening hours vary between resorts, cities, and rural villages. City banking hours are generally 9am to 4pm, Monday to Friday; some open 9am to 1pm on Saturday. Most offices, including tourist offices, follow these hours, but some may work as late as 8pm with a lunch break between 2–4pm. In cities, stores are generally open 10am to 8pm, every day. In towns and villages they often open Monday to Saturday with an afternoon siesta. Many (but not all) museums open Tuesday to Sunday, 9am to 5pm. Major archaeological sites are open seven days a week. Nearly all businesses close on Christmas, Easter and public holidays.

Chichén Itzá, open seven days a week

Accessibility to Public Conveniences

Public toilets are few and far between in Mexico, and those that do exist are often badly equipped and unhygienic. It is advisable to carry some toilet paper, as this is often lacking. Soap or disinfectant hand wipes are a good idea too. In larger cities it is best to make for a Sanborns *(see p119)*, or another large department store, restaurant, or supermarket, as they provide better facilities.

Some enterprising people in Mexico City allow the public to use their toilets for a small fee; you will see signs around the Historic Center *(see pp65–85)*.

Taxes and Tipping

In Mexico, tips are generally unofficial, but appreciated. In restaurants, tip between 10 and 15 percent of the total bill. Taxi drivers do not expect to be tipped unless they have carried your luggage. Porters, however, especially those at airports or large hotels, expect a gratuity. It is usual to give small change to people who help you, such as chambermaids or gas station attendants, as tips are an essential part of their income. Parking attendants and children who help in supermarkets survive on tips.

Prices usually include 16 percent sales tax, or IVA, *(Impuesto al Valor Agregado)*. If a price is given as *más IVA* (plus sales tax) it means that 16 percent will be added to the bill.

Travelers with Special Needs

Most airports, upscale hotels, and good restaurants, particularly those in well-developed resort towns, usually have wheelchair access and adapted toilets, but always check in advance. Sidewalks can be difficult to negotiate and in bad repair, especially in the countryside, while long-distance buses are generally poorly equipped; consider traveling by air. Elsewhere, disabled facilities are scant but the situation is improving in big cities. Most Mexicans, ever helpful by nature, will be glad to assist if they can.

Traveling with Children

Facilities for children are most prevalent in and around major resorts, where you'll find theme parks with water slides, aquariums, and roller-coasters. Elsewhere, youngsters can try their hand at snorkeling, white-water rafting, rock-climbing, kayaking, horseback-riding, and surfing. Most mid-range and high-end hotels will arrange a cot or baby-sitter and make recommendations for family activities. The best resort complexes have family-sized apartments, playgrounds, and pools.

Mexicans are very family orientated, so expect lots of warm attention when traveling with young ones. Children are welcome at nearly all restaurants but not all offer high chairs and child menus. Major car rental agencies should be able to install a child safety seat.

Senior Travelers

Many foreign retirees have settled in Mexico – retirement communities are concentrated in San Miguel de Allende, Guanajuato, and around Lake Chapala, where you'll find no shortage of amenities. Elsewhere, major resorts offer the best services and comfort.

Getting around is not always straightforward in Mexico so it's worth using tour operators who specialize in senior activities. Elders are widely respected in Mexico, though foreigners are sometimes targeted by unscrupulous types. Expect reasonable discounts on admission costs, bus fares and, occasionally, hotel fees. Many travel agents also offer deals for senior clients.

Seniors taking in the pleasant view at Copper Canyon

Gay and Lesbian Travelers

Homosexuality is tolerated in Mexico, but public affection is generally frowned upon. Discrimination on the basis of sexual orientation has been officially outlawed but there is still prejudice and some locals may feel unnerved by unconventional sexual behavior. Gay scenes can be found in Puerto Vallarta, Guadalajara, Cancún, Mazatlán, Acapulco, Monterrey, Oaxaca, Veracruz, and especially in Mexico City, centered in the Zona Rosa neighborhood. Most big cities have gay-friendly bars and clubs, but few exclusively gay establishments.

Children and families enjoying an outdoor concert

Women Travelers

Women are respected in Mexico, but are not regarded as equals. Any woman who travels alone may get a stream of uninvited compliments. If the attention becomes too persistent, a firm *Déjeme en paz* ("Leave me be") should work. Mexican machismo can also be a help, since men will often come to your aid.

Women should avoid going to isolated beaches, or wandering through lonely streets at night. Nude or topless bathing is not generally acceptable.

Traveling on a Budget

Economical hotels can be found across the country, and are often more cost effective than youth hostels. The cheapest lodgings may lack windows, bathroom, television, or any charm whatsoever. Couples and groups can make good savings on accommodation, and in very warm areas a hammock may often suffice for the night.

Lunch-time rather than dinner is best for economical meals, with set menus, often described as *comida corrida*, served for a few dollars. The cheapest restaurants tend to be clustered around the markets, where you'll also find economical street food, but beware of bad hygiene (*see p350*). Head to a bakery for breakfast.

On the coast, prices may triple during high season, but good rates can often be negotiated at quieter periods. Outside the resorts, southern Mexico tends to be the cheapest region to travel. Allow US$70 per day for a comfortably modest trip; US$50 per day for a challenging one. Long-distance first-class bus travel can be expensive.

What to Take and What to Wear

If you intend to do a lot of traveling, it's worth investing in

Relaxing in a beach hammock at Quintana Roo

a good backpack. Pack hiking boots if you intend to do any serious walking or, at the very least, comfortable trainers. In the wet season *(see pp40–41)* take a lightweight, waterproof jacket, or a compact umbrella – also mandatory when visiting the rainforest. Light clothing is sufficient on the coast but a sweater is useful in the mountains, where evenings can be chilly.

It's wise to pack a small medical kit and insect repellent. Bring sufficient amounts of any prescribed medication. The sun is fierce in Mexico, so pack sunscreen with a protection factor of at least 25+, as well as a sunhat.

Time

Most of Mexico is in the Central Time Zone – six hours behind Greenwich Mean Time (GMT). Baja California Sur, Nayarit, Sinaloa, Sonora, and Chihuahua are in the Mountain Time Zone (seven hours behind GMT); and Baja California Norte is in the Pacific Time Zone (eight hours behind GMT).

Electricity

Electrical current is the same in Mexico as in the US and Canada. Three-prong, polarized, and European plugs will need adaptors.

Conversion Chart

US to metric
1 inch = 2.54 centimeters
1 foot = 30 centimeters
1 mile = 1.6 kilometers
1 ounce = 28 grams
1 pound = 454 grams
1 pint = 0.6 liter
1 gallon = 3.79 liters

Metric to US
1 millimeter = 0.04 inch
1 centimeter = 0.4 inch
1 meter = 3 feet 3 inches
1 kilometer = 0.6 mile
1 gram = 0.04 ounce
1 kilogram = 2.2 pounds
1 liter = 2.1 pints

Responsible Travel

Mexico has been slow to embrace ecotourism and many hotels and tour companies continue to act irresponsibly, damaging wild habitats and coral reefs. You can do your part by choosing local over corporate interests and using ethically minded companies such as members of **Tour Operators Initiative**, who are committed to responsible tourist development.

In 2008 the Mexican Tourism Secretariat allocated 500 million pesos (about US$37 million) to the development of ecotourism in Mexico. Meanwhile, dozens of government bodies and NGOs are involved in green tourism – although there is often poor communication between them.

The **Mesoamerican Reef Tourism Initiative (MARTI)** works to cut energy and waste in Caribbean resorts, as well as campaigning for sustainability and green legislation. Baja California has made great strides as a major eco- and adventure-tourism destination. Over 200 islands and islets are now protected, as well as breeding areas for migratory gray whales.

DIRECTORY

Embassies

A list of embassy contact details can be found here:
W sre.gob.mx/acreditadas/

Australia
Rubén Darío 55, Polanco, DF 11570.
Tel (55) 11 01 22 00.
W mexico.embassy.gov.au

Canada
Schiller 529,Polanco, DF 11580.
Tel (55) 57 24 79 00.
W canada.org.mx

United Kingdom
Río Lerma 71, Cuauhtémoc, DF 06500.
Tel (55) 16 70 32 00.
W gov.uk/government/world/mexico

US
Reforma 305, Cuauhtémoc, DF 06500. **Tel** (55) 50 80 20 00. **W mexico.usembassy.gov**

National Migration Institute of Mexico
Av Ejército Nacional 862, Col Los Morales Sección Palmas, Del Miguel Hidalgo, CP 11540.
Tel (55) 53 87 24 00.
W inm.gob.mx

Travel Safety Advice

Australia
W dfat.gov.au
W smartraveller.gov.au

United Kingdom
W gov.uk/foreign-travel-advice

US
W travel.state.gov

Tourist Office Websites

Mexico
W sectur.gob.mx
W visitmexico.com

Baja California Sur
W visitbajasur.travel

Campeche
W campeche.travel

Chihuahua
W chihuahua.gob.mx/turismoweb/
(Spanish only)

Guanajuato
W guanajuato.gob.mx/turismo.php
(Spanish only)

Mexico City
W mexicocity.gob.mx

Oaxaca
W oaxaca.travel

Querétaro
W queretaro.travel

San Luis Potosí
W visitasanluispotosi.com

Veracruz
W veracruz.mx
(Spanish only)

Green Organizations

Mesoamerican Reef Tourism Initiative (MARTI)
Tel (984) 859 22 34 .
W rivieramaya.org.mx/marti.html

Tour Operators Initiative
c/o World Tourism Organization (UNWTO), Capitán Haya 42, 28020 Madrid, Spain.
Tel (34) 91 567 81 00.
W toinitiative.org

Personal Security and Health

Mexico has a reputation for a high incidence of crime, but the overwhelming majority of foreign visitors have a trouble-free experience. Tourist areas are generally very safe and Mexico City is no more dangerous than most major American cities – stay alert and follow the usual big city rules. Areas affected by violence associated with organized crime, including some parts of the north, should be avoided. Check your government's travel advisory for an up-to-date assessment of the situation. Nasty tropical diseases are present in Mexico, but are rare and can be avoided by getting vaccinated prior to departure – check the latest information. Common ailments such as upset stomach can be prevented with sensible precautions. The sun's rays are very strong in Mexico, so wear sunscreen and a sunhat.

Police

It is best to avoid the police in Mexico; they are rarely helpful and can make difficult situations worse. Reporting a crime is often a slow, bureaucratic affair – consider contacting your embassy or **SECTUR** first. In the event of your arrest, always contact your embassy.

Police corruption is rife and many consider bribes or *mordidas* (literally "little bites") a supplement to their low income. Drivers should expect to be approached and "fined" at some stage; try explaining that you are a tourist or otherwise negotiate the fee downward.

The traffic police *(Policía de Tránsito)* are nicknamed *tamarindos* (tamarinds) in Mexico City for their dark brown uniforms. The auxiliary police *(Policía Auxiliar)*, dressed in dark blue, provide backup to the traffic police and work as security guards. Bank and industry police *(Policía Bancaria e Industrial)* also wear blue uniforms. Plain-clothed *Policía Judicial Federal* (PJF) have a sinister reputation and are best avoided. Outside the cities, the federal traffic police *(Policía Federal de Caminos)* patrol the highways in black and white cars. A few states have approachable tourist police *(Policía Turística)* and **Angeles Verdes** provide bilingual roadside assistance nationwide.

Insect repellent and a mosquito coil for protection against bites

Lost and Stolen Property

Only report lost or stolen property to the police if you need to file an official report *(levantar un acta)* for insurance purposes. Do this at the nearest police station *(delegación)* within 24 hours. Lost passports and traveler's checks should be reported to your embassy and the issuing bank.

What to Be Aware of

Petty theft is the greatest security threat to tourists. Beware of pickpockets, leave valuables in a hotel safe (never on the beach), and keep cash in a concealed money belt. Also, avoid driving at night. Park in hotel parking lots, and never leave possessions visible inside the car. Steer clear of isolated routes or beaches, and in the rare event of a mugging, always hand over your cash.

Stomach upsets, known locally as "Montezuma's revenge," are a common affliction. Outside resorts, drink purified or bottle water only and take care with salads, unpeeled fruits, ice and uncooked food, especially raw fish. Choose restaurants that look clean and be wary of unhygienic street food stalls.

Mosquitoes are rife in low-lying regions and have a ferocious appetite for tourists. DEET is the strongest insect repellent, but sensitive skin may prefer organic alternatives. Take care in the heat. Dehydration can lead to the potentially fatal condition of sun stroke, so always carry bottled water, sunscreen, and a hat when visiting archaeological sites, the beach or any exposed places. Snakes, such as the deadly fer-de-lance, can be a danger in the jungle. Watch where you step and wear long trousers and boots. If undertaking a lengthy trek, ensure your guide is packing antivenin. Mexico City's high altitude and air pollution can aggravate respiratory problems like asthma; seek medical advice before traveling.

In an Emergency

In case of emergency, the Red Cross has an ambulance service in most major cities and tourist centers. If you are in a remote area, it may be quicker to take a taxi to the nearest hospital. If you are not covered by medical insurance, go to the emergency room *(Emergencias)* of any state hospital.

SECTUR, the Mexican Ministry of Tourism, has a 24-hour telephone hotline. Although this is primarily for immediate assistance, it can also provide general, non-emergency health guidance.

Police car used by traffic police

Mexican ambulance

Hospitals and Pharmacies

There are three types of hospital in Mexico. Social Security (IMSS) hospitals are restricted to Mexican residents, and ISSSTE hospitals and clinics are for civil servants and university workers only. Everyone else, including visitors, must either pay for private treatment or rely on the local, and generally overcrowded, Centro de Salud (Civil Hospital) run by the state, or the Cruz Roja (Red Cross). Hotels have lists of English-speaking doctors.

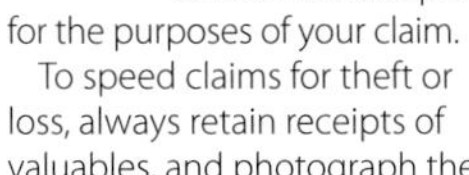

Sign for a Cruz Roja hospital

Mexicans pay for all drugs, except those patients on social security who receive basic drugs free of charge. Packets of oral rehydration salts are provided free at health centers for people suffering from diarrhea. Many tablets are sold individually, those with generic names are the cheapest. However, beware of fake or unlicensed medicines.

Minor Hazards

Coral cuts and jellyfish stings should be bathed in vinegar, then dabbed with antiseptic ointment. If the wound becomes infected, seek the advice of a doctor. The majority of visitors to Mexico are unlikely to come across any dangerous creatures, and it is rare for tourists to become seriously ill as a result of an insect bite. However, scorpions are common. Black or dark brown ones are quite harmless, but the light yellow ones, found in hot, dry places, will need an antidote (free from any Centro de Salud). Tarantulas look more intimidating than they are; far worse is the *capulina*, or black widow spider, found in western Mexico. Always check shoes and shake out clothing before putting them on, especially in more rural areas. Beware ticks when hiking in the jungle. If bitten, carefully extract them using tweezers.

Travel and Health Insurance

Travel insurance is essential in Mexico. Check the policy's small print and ensure you are covered for emergency flights, ambulance use, mugging, and any specialist activities you may require, such as trekking or diving. Private doctors and hospitals will require on-the-spot payment in cash, so retain all receipts for the purposes of your claim.

To speed claims for theft or loss, always retain receipts of valuables, and photograph the items before departure. Some general US health insurance policies extend to Mexico; check prior to travel.

Vaccinations

No specific vaccinations are required to enter Mexico, but you will need evidence of a Yellow Fever vaccination if coming from South America or other infected areas. All travelers are advised to seek immunization against hepatitis A, typhoid, tetanus, diphtheria, and for some, hepatitis B and rabies. Malaria is present in some rural parts of Mexico, so ask your doctor about anti-malarial medicines.

Serious Illness

Standard food and water precautions are the best forms of protection against cholera. Common parasitic infections include tapeworm as well as giardiasis, which is acquired by drinking contaminated water. It can cause chronic diarrhea, abdominal cramps, fatigue, nausea, loss of appetite, and weight loss. Treatment with the drug metronidazole is usually very successful.

Dengue fever is a viral illness spread by mosquitoes. The best protection is to use plenty of insect repellent, cover up well when outside, and sleep under mosquito nets. The onset of dengue is sudden, with fever, headache, joint pains, nausea, vomiting, and a rash. Outbreaks of swine flu (H1N1) in 2009 caused concern. The World Health Organization (WHO) provides up-to-date information on serious diseases.

Natural Disasters

In the event of an earthquake, move away from electricity poles, wires, or any high structure. Do not attempt to use elevators. If a hurricane hits, stay in your hotel, shut all windows, and stand as far away from them as you can. In all cases, follow the instructions given by staff.

Access to the area around Popocatépetl volcano *(see p153)* and Colima's Volcán de Fuego *(see p191)* is restricted because of seismic activity. If you plan to hike in the vicinity, check posted warnings and contact your embassy or **SECTUR** *(Secretaría de Turismo)* for the latest information.

Popocatépetl volcano

DIRECTORY

Emergency Numbers

Ambulance
Tel 065.

Angeles Verdes
Tel 078.

Fire Department and Earthquake Advice
Tel (55) 56 83 11 42.

Police
Tel 060; (55) 52 42 51 00.

Stolen Property
Tel 061.

SECTUR helplines
Tel 078; (55) 30 02 63 00; 01800 987 8224 (toll free).

Hospitals

ABC (American British Cowdray) Hospital
Mexico City. **Tel** (55) 52 30 80 00.

Banking and Currency

The unit of currency in Mexico is the peso, but US dollars are widely accepted in resorts and border towns. In order to support the local economy, visitors are advised to use pesos as their main currency. Most large hotels, shops, and restaurants accept major credit cards, and US dollars are readily exchanged in all banks. There are no restrictions on the import or export of peso notes and coins.

A typical ATM machine found all over Mexico

Banks and Bureaux de Change

The three largest banks in Mexico are **BBVA Bancomer**, **Banorte**, and **Banamex**, but there is a growing number of foreign banks which also operate branches in Mexico. Opening hours are normally from 9am to 4pm, weekdays only, although in the capital and other large cities, Banorte stays open until 7pm, and is open on Saturdays until 1pm. Many bank branches do not change foreign currency or travelers' checks after 2pm, so aim to go in the morning. Avoid the traditional monthly paydays of the 15th and 30th, as line-ups are often long. When entering a bank, ensure your appearance is unobscured by removing your hat and sunglasses.

Bureaux de change *(casas de cambio)* are open longer hours than banks, and offer a quicker service and better exchange rates, particularly compared to hotels and shops. The main international airports have at least one *casa de cambio* – useful for changing a small amount for taxis or buses. When changing money, you may be asked for your passport. Non-dollar currencies can sometimes be tricky to change.

ATMs

Cash dispensing machines *(cajero automático)* are widespread in Mexico and you should be able to draw cash in all but the most obscure places. Visa, MasterCard, plus, Cirrus debit and credit cards are all valid. Exchange rates on foreign ATMs are based on the equitable inter-bank lending rate. However, you will be charged a small transaction fee at the point of withdrawal, as well as by your own bank – rates vary with accounts, so check before departure. To protect against fraud, some banks require notification that you will be traveling, otherwise you will find your card temporarily frozen. Technical hitches happen, so keep an emergency supply of cash on you just in case.

As a precaution against theft, draw money from machines only during business hours, and in populated areas. Look out for any strange attachments to the machine that may be used to record card details.

Travelers' Checks

Travelers' checks drawn in US dollars are a safe way of carrying money, but are becoming less common. They can be changed at *casas de cambio* and at most banks. When cashing the checks you will need to show your passport. Fees are not charged, but the exchange rate is likely to

Customer using an enclosed ATM point at one of the largest banking groups, Banamex

DIRECTORY

Banks

Banamex
Isabel la Católica 44,
Mexico City.
Tel (55) 12 26 26 39.

Banorte
Calle 16 de Septiembre 57,
Mexico City.
Tel (55) 55 21 05 47.

BBVA Bancomer
Bolivar 38,
Mexico City.
Tel (55) 52 26 58 49.

Lost Cards and Travelers' Checks

American Express
Call hotline in country of origin.
Or:
Tel (55) 52 07 7049 (Mexico City) or 001800 504 04 00 (toll free).

MasterCard
Tel 001800 307 73 09 (toll free).

VISA
Tel 001800 847 29 11 (toll free).

Wiring Money

Western Union
Tel 1800 325 6000 (US only).
W westernunion.com

Queuing for tellers at the Spanish-owned BBVA Bancomer bank, Mexico City

be lower for checks than for cash. Keep the receipt and a record of the serial numbers separate from the checks, in case they are lost or stolen.

Wiring Money

Money can be wired safely and easily provided you are in possession of a passport or other official photo ID. Western Union "Dinero en Minutos" is the main service, available in most cities and resorts. Senders can arrange their transaction online or at a Western Union office and must designate an appropriate collection point. Recipients will be required to show ID and fees will be levied for the service. For US citizens, post offices also operate money transfers to Bancomer banks.

Currency

The Mexican peso is divided into 100 centavos. The symbol for the peso is $, and is easily confused with that of the US dollar. To solve this problem, prices are often printed with the letters MN after them, meaning moneda nacional (national currency). Some border towns and resorts will accept the US dollar, although using the peso will help to support the local economy, and will ensure you are not overcharged due to the application of a poor exchange rate on your purchase.

Always carry small amounts of cash around in both coins and small denomination bills, for tips and minor purchases. Beware that shops, taxis, and buses are often unable to give change for larger denomination notes, even in big cities.

Coins

Peso coins come in denominations of $1, $2, $5, and $10. All peso coins are colored silver and gold, and increase in size according to their value. Centavo coins are in denominations of 10¢, 20¢, and 50¢ and are silver in color. Older coins in the same denominations are gold in color. They are still in circulation and are legal tender.

Bank Notes

Mexican bank notes are issued in six denominations: $20, $50, $100, $200, $500, and $1,000. It can be hard to get change for larger denominations, particularly the $1,000 note, which should be avoided. The $20 note is blue polymer; the $50 is pink polymer. The higher value notes are paper: red for the $100, green for the $200, brown for the $500, and purple for the $1000. A red plastic version of the $100 note also circulates, as do older versions of the $100, $200 and $500, which are similar colors to the new ones, but slightly longer in size.

Coins for Tipping

There are a large number of people who work only for tips, for example the people who bag your groceries at the super market (often retired or students), car park attendants who help you in and out of your parking space, and the person who washes your car windscreen while your tank is being filled. It's always a good idea to have coins on hand to tip people providing this kind of service, and a $5 tip is usually more than sufficient and very gratefully received.

Imposing facade of the Bank of Mexico's main headquarters

Communications and Media

The telephone is the most popular means of communication in Mexico. The postal service is slow and unreliable – letters can take weeks to reach their destination. Public telephones are common, but are becoming less so as cell phones become ubiquitous. Most pay phones take phonecards, which can be bought at convenience stores such as OXXO, as well as at Sanborns stores. Mail boxes throughout the country are marked *Correos de Mexico*, although in Mexico City and tourist resorts most are bright red and marked *Buzón Expresso*. Internet cafés are widespread and cheap, while many mid-range and upscale hotels are equipped with Wi-Fi. For entertainment, Mexico has six television networks and two national radio stations. English-language visitors can catch up on events by reading *The News*.

Blue LADATEL telephone

International and Local Telephone Calls

Local telephone calls are cheap and many hotels will let you make them for free. Conversely, international calls from hotels are nearly always expensive, so instead use a *caseta de teléfono* (calling shop) or a long-distance phonecard, available at kiosks and grocery shops. You could also consider getting a Skype account, which allows international and video calls to other Skype users for free. Many Internet cafés have this facility, otherwise a reasonably modern Wi-Fi-enabled laptop should suffice. Collect calls can be made nationally and internationally, though these are expensive for the recipient.

Full numbers in Mexico are 10 digits long and comprise a 7-digit local number and 3-digit area code. If calling locally, simply enter the 7-digit number. If calling long-distance within Mexico, you will first need to enter 01, followed by the 3-digit area code, then the main 7-digit number. Exceptions are Mexico City, Monterrey, and Guadalajara. These cities have 2-digit area codes and 8-digit local numbers. To make an international call from Mexico, dial 00, then the country code, the area code, and the local number. To call a Mexican number from another country, dial your international access code, then 52, then the 10-digit number.

Cell Phones

If you want to use your cell phone in Mexico, you will need a roaming-enabled quad-band handset – consult your service provider for tariffs. Calls can be expensive for both caller and recipient, so consider purchasing a Mexican SIM card or phone once you've arrived.

Cell phone numbers have 10 digits, composed of an area code and main number. If calling a cell from a landline, add a prefix of 044 for local calls or 045 for long-distance calls. If calling from a cell phone, simply enter the whole 10-digit number.

Public Telephones

Local calls are inexpensive and can be made from pay phones in the street, and from coin-operated phones in stores and restaurants.

The blue LADATEL telephones, run by Teléfonos de México (TELMEX), take LADATEL phonecards, which are available in denominations of 30, 50, or 100 pesos from most newsstands and stores. Long-distance calls are cheapest on weekends and after 8pm on weekdays. A 50-peso LADATEL phonecard will get you a 5-minute transatlantic call, but not much more. Instead, use a long-distance phonecard. If no LADATEL phone is available, most towns and some villages have a *caseta de larga distancia*. These telephone booths charge higher rates than public phones but are cheaper than phoning from a hotel.

Internet and Email

High-speed Internet is generally widely available throughout many parts of Mexico, especially cities. Increasingly, cities are providing free Wi-Fi in public spaces, such as parks, and many cafés, restaurants, and businesses offer free Wi-Fi as an incentive to customers. Mexico City's Benito Juárez International Airport has free Wi-Fi hotspots, as do many other airports around Mexico. The free service may be limited

Dialing Codes

- Operator/directory service: 040
- Collect call / reverse charges: 020 (domestic) or 090 (international)
- Long-distance: 01 – area code – number
- Landline to cell phone (local): 044 – area code – number
- Landline to cell (long-distance): 045 – area code – number
- International: 00 – country code – area code – number
- Country codes: Australia 61; Ireland 353; New Zealand 64; South Africa 27; UK 44; USA and Canada 1.

to 30 minutes, however. Many hotels impose a daily charge for in-room Internet use; ask at the front desk if the policy is not clear.

Logo for a Wi-Fi ZONE

Internet cafés are widely available across nearly all Mexican towns, cities, and villages. Rates tend to be very reasonable and the better equipped places have CD burners and memory card readers, should you need to make CDs of your photos. Some are also equipped with Skype facilities.

Postal Services

Sending (and receiving) parcels by regular mail service in Mexico is not recommended. Registering both letters and parcels improves the odds against pilfering. Conventional mail times from Mexico to Europe are 1 to 2 weeks; from Mexico to Canada/USA, 4 days to 2 weeks. Mark all air mail *Vía Aérea*. However, the safest way to send anything abroad is through one of the international courier services such as DHL.

The main post offices *(oficinas de correos)* are open from 8am to 8pm on weekdays, and from 8am to 3pm on Saturdays. Smaller post offices usually have shorter opening hours. Stamps for postcards can usually be purchased from the larger hotels.

A mail holding service is available at most main post offices. *Poste restante* letters should be addressed to the *Lista de Correos*, followed by the name of the town and state. You will need to show ID when collecting letters.

American Express also provides a free holding service for their customers. You can have your mail sent directly to one of their offices, from where you can then collect it.

Mexican Addresses

Mexican addresses list the house number after the name of the street. Sometimes the street number is followed by a hyphen and then the number or letter of the apartment. The next line of the address may indicate the name of the *Fraccionamiento (Fracc.)* if the house is in a private community. The *colonia (col.)* refers to the area within the city. Include the *Código Postal* (zip code) if you can.

Newspapers and Magazines

The News, published in the capital, covers mostly Mexican and US news, and has listings pages for cultural activities in Mexico City. For Spanish-speaking visitors, the listings in *Time Out México*, *Donde Ir*, and *Chilango* are more complete. Outside Mexico City, English-language newspapers are published in areas with English-speaking communities, such as Guadalajara and San Miguel de Allende.

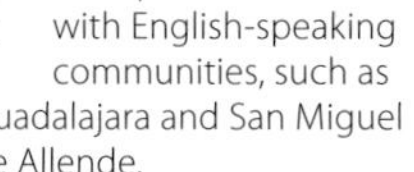

Mail box

Sanborns *(see p119)* is a good place to pick up English-language publications, while online discussion groups are an alternative way to keep up with the latest happenings in Mexico. *The International Herald Tribune* and *New York Times* are usually on newsstands the day after publication. News magazines such as *Time* and *Newsweek* are also available.

The widely read national broadsheet newspapers are *Reforma*, *El Universal*, *La Jornada*, and *Excelsior*. The tabloids, such as *La Prensa*, have a far larger readership. A number of local dailies, such as *Más por Más* and *24 Horas*, are available for free.

TV and Radio

Not all of Mexico's television channels can be seen across the whole country, and some regions broadcast local programs at certain times of the day. Channels 11, 22, and 40 broadcast programs of cultural and scientific interest.

The largest television companies are Televisa and TV Azteca; Cablevisión and Sky are the two principal cable television companies. Digital television services are being rolled-out across the country.

Foreign programs are generally dubbed into Spanish, but movies are occasionally shown in their original language with Spanish subtitles. Most hotels provide cable television, with programs in both Spanish and English. Satellite TV is often available at the more upscale hotels throughout the country.

Almost every city in Mexico has a local radio station, and some, particularly in the more touristy areas, play English-language songs and also have daily slots for English programs. In northern areas it is possible to pick up US radio stations.

English-language and local newspapers for sale in Querétaro

TRAVEL INFORMATION

Mexico is a huge country, but getting around is easy and reasonably priced, thanks in part to domestic budget airlines and an extensive bus system. There are airports within reach of all the major cities, and flights from the US and around the world arrive at more than a dozen international airports. Sadly, privatization of the railroad system has eliminated passenger services, except for the "El Chepe" route *(see p180 and p3601)*, and a few tourist trains running on disused lines *(see p361)*. There is, however, a bus network that reaches the most remote areas, and the first-class coaches are comfortable. Driving offers most flexibility, but it can be hair-raising, with road conditions not always good and lacking signage. Ferries connect the mainland with Baja California and the Caribbean islands of Cozumel and Isla Mujeres.

Arriving by Air

There are 62 airports in Mexico. Of these, 51 are classified as "international"; 15 operate international flights for tourists. The remainder either service towns on the US border or operate only limited flights to foreign destinations. The other 11 airports are for domestic flights only *(see p359)*.

Green Travel

Mexico's extensive bus system provides a viable low-carbon alternative to internal flights, but may not be feasible for traveling long distances if you have only limited time. If you intend to focus your trip in southern Mexico, consider flying into Cancún so you do not have to travel to and from the capital. Alternatively, if you wish to follow the classic route from Oaxaca to Quintana Roo via Chiapas, fly into Mexico City and out of Cancún.

You can do your part to improve air quality in the capital by using the Metro system instead of buses, taxis, and *peseros (see p364)*. An exception is the Metrobús, which runs on clean diesel and covers 105 km (65 miles) of the city. The route will continue to expand up to 200 km (124 miles).

Mexico City has launched a campaign to promote cycling in the capital as part of a wider plan to clean up the city's air and water, but considering how busy the roads are, you will need nerves of steel for that *(see p364)*. For more on responsible travel see p349.

Cancún's international airport

Airports

Mexico City's Aeropuerto Benito Juárez is the key arrival point for international flights into Mexico, closely followed by Cancún, with scheduled flights to the capital from over 20 US cities. Additionally, travelers can fly direct from numerous cities in the US to Acapulco, Cozumel, Guadalajara, Guaymas, Huatulco, Loreto, La Paz, Manzanillo, Mazatlán, Puerto Vallarta, San José del Cabo, Veracruz, and Zihuatanejo. Flying times from New York and Los Angeles to Mexico City are approximately five and three-and-a-half hours respectively. **Air Canada** flies daily from Toronto to Mexico City in around five hours.

From Europe, some international airlines still fly via the USA, although **Aeroméxico**, **British Airways**, **Iberia**, **Air France**, **KLM**, and **Lufthansa** operate direct flights, cutting travel time considerably. British Airways (BA) operates four direct flights

AIRPORT	INFORMATION	DISTANCE TO TOWN OR RESORT	AVERAGE TIME BY ROAD FROM AIRPORT
Mexico City	(55) 24 82 24 00	Zócalo 15 km (9 miles)	45 minutes
Acapulco	(744) 435 20 60	Downtown 30 km (19 miles)	30 minutes
Cancún	(998) 848 72 00	Cancún City 20 km (12 miles)	30 minutes
Cozumel	(987) 872 20 81	Cozumel town 6 km (4 miles)	5 minutes
Guadalajara	(33) 36 88 52 48	Downtown 16 km (10 miles)	20 minutes
La Paz	(612) 124 63 36	Downtown 14 km (9 miles)	10 minutes
Puerto Vallarta	(322) 221 15 37	Calle Madero 7 km (4 miles)	10 minutes
Tijuana	(664) 607 82 00	Downtown 7 km (4 miles)	15 minutes
Veracruz	(229) 934 90 08	Downtown 18 km (11 miles)	15 minutes

from London to Mexico City each week, with a flying time of 12 hours. There is also a weekly BA scheduled flight to Cancún. Air France and Aeroméxico fly direct from Paris; KLM from Amsterdam; Lufthansa from Frankfurt; and Iberia and Aeroméxico from Madrid (a flight time of just over 11 hours). Some chartered flights travel direct from Europe to the major beach resorts. Visitors transferring in Mexico City must claim their baggage before boarding their onward domestic flight.

There are no direct flights from New Zealand or Australia, but you can transfer in LA or San Francisco to a connecting flight. The total flying time from Sydney to Mexico City, via LA, is 16.5 hours.

Central and South American airlines **Avianca** and **Copa** run flights into Mexico City. **Aeroméxico** also offers connections between Central and South American cities and Mexico City.

Sign to the airport

Tickets and Fares

Air fares vary greatly, depending on travel agencies and seasons. Christmas, summer, and to a lesser extent, Easter, tend to be the most expensive times. Fixed-date returns are always cheaper than open returns and international air tickets are comparatively expensive to buy in Mexico.

Inclusive packages for major resorts are available at travel agencies worldwide and through major travel websites. These are increasingly popular and tend to be cheaper than independent travel. There are also companies, both in Mexico and abroad, that focus in regions of particular interest, such as the archaeological sites of Yucatán, or specialist activities like horseback riding, scuba diving, white-water rafting, and bird-watching *(see pp338–43)*.

Infants under two often travel free on domestic flights, provided they do not have a seat of their own. Children over two, but under 12, pay roughly two thirds of the full fare, and are entitled to a seat and standard baggage allowance. Certain airlines also offer discounts for students and senior citizens (ID required).

Modern interior of Mexico City's international airport

To and from the Airport

From Mexico City's international airport, tickets for set-price taxis (called *sitios*) can be bought from kiosks near the exit. These are safe, authorized taxis whose fares are based on zones. You prepay your fare at the kiosk. Avoid the taxi touts.

Direct Metro links connect with the city center. The Metrobús *(see pp364–5)* conveniently pulls up just outside the terminal door, but may take longer than a taxi or the Metro (about an hour to the Zócalo or the terminus, the Buenavista station). You'll need to purchase a fare card and pre-load the fare – about 30 pesos – at a kiosk inside the terminal.

Bus connections are also available from Mexico City airport to nearby cities, including Toluca and Cuernavaca. Finally, a number of rental car kiosks are located inside the terminal and reservations can be made on the spot.

From Cancún's international airport, a shuttle bus runs to the downtown area every 10 to 15 minutes.

DIRECTORY

International Airlines

Aeroméxico
Tel 01800 02 14 000 (toll free) or (55) 51 33 40 00.
W aeromexico.com

Air Canada
Tel (55) 91 38 02 80.
W aircanada.com

Air France
Tel 01800 024 03 72 (toll free).
W airfrance.com

British Airways
Tel 001 866 835 4133.
W britishairways.com

Iberia
Tel (55) 11 01 15 15.
W iberia.com

KLM
Tel 01800 266 00 49 (toll free).
W klm.com

Lufthansa
Tel (55) 52 30 00 00.
W lufthansa.com

Central and South American Airlines

Avianca
Tel 01800 123 31 20 (toll free).
W avianca.com

Copa
Tel 01800 265 26 72).
W copaair.com

Arriving from the US

US citizens who are entering from the US are free to enter Mexico's border zone (including the Baja California peninsula and the Sonora Free Trade Zone) without passing through immigration control. To re-enter the US however a passport is required. If you wish to travel beyond the free zone or stay for more than 72 hours, you must obtain an FMT tourist card *(Forma Migratoria de Turista)* or visa *(see p346)*.

Several international bus companies, including **Greyhound**, offer connections from major US border towns into Mexico. Alternatively, many visitors choose to cross the border on foot and pick up one of the cheaper Mexican buses on the other side. At present, there are no international rail crossings. Cruise ships offer connections by sea, docking at locations in Baja California, the Yucatán Peninsula and all along the Pacific Coast. Ships usually stay a couple of days in port and passengers tend to disembark for short periods of time only.

Vehicle entry into Mexico is strictly regulated, and drivers bringing their cars across the border from the US need to obtain a temporary import permit *(a permiso de importación temporal)*, as well as separate car insurance *(see pp362–3)*. Note that rental companies do not allow their vehicles to be driven across the border.

The border crossing between Tijuana and San Diego

Arriving from Central America

The official immigration procedure is the same as when entering from the USA, although it is invariably less efficient and occasionally subject to dubious "fees". Visitors traveling south of the border must hand in their tourist card; on returning to Mexico, a new FMT will be issued. Direct bus services run between Guatemala City and Mexico City (stopping in Chiapas en-route); Belize City and Chetumal; and Flores and Chetumal. Otherwise, you can simply cross the border on foot and catch a frequent shuttle to the nearest local transport hub. There are no ferry or rail connections with Central America, although some adventurous souls may want to cross the Mexico–Guatemala border by *lancha* (high-speed motorboat) on the Usumacinta River.

Border Crossings

Exactly where you cross the US–Mexico border will depend much on your intended destination. If heading to Baja California, San Diego–Tijuana is the most popular crossing, which can be very crowded if heading into the US; get there early or expect to queue for up to 3 hours. Alternatively, try one of the quieter crossings, such as Tecate or Calexico–Mexicali. Nogales is the main crossing for those heading to the Pacific northwest. Laredo–Nuevo Laredo – and a string of quiet crossings east on the Río Grande – offer access to the northeast and gulf coast.

Crossings in and out of Central America can be hectic; take care with money changers particularly. Chetumal is the main crossing into Belize with buses running direct to Belize City a few times daily. There are also buses to Flores, Guatemala from here. There are three conventional crossings into Guatemala. Ciudad Cuauhtémoc–La Mesilla connects with San Cristóbal de las Casas in Chiapas. El Carmen–Talismán and Ciudad Hidalgo–Tecún

Aerial view of the runway at Cozumel airport, served by both international and domestic flights

Small, domestic planes at Palenque Airport

Umán provide access to Tapachula in Chiapas. In Guatemala, all crossings offer highway access to the capital. The Río Usumacinta crossing is an interesting adventure involving a 30-minute motorboat ride. In Mexico, head to Corozal in eastern Chiapas and visit immigration, then take a *lancha* to Bethel, which connects with Flores.

Domestic Air Travel

In a country the size of Mexico, internal flights can be a convenient alternative to long bus journeys. Standard fares for domestic flights are usually at least double the equivalent trip by bus, but special deals are often available, so it is worth shopping around. The domestic network is extensive, but not all routes are direct.

In order to get these special deals, reservations should be made as far in advance as possible, especially during peak seasons. Tickets can be reserved online, by telephone, or through a travel agent. A small airport departure tax, payable either in US dollars or pesos, is levied on all flights in Mexico. This may be included in the price of your ticket.

For longer trips to small towns, airlines occasionally partner with bus companies to offer combination deals, especially around the holidays, Holy Week, and school vacations. There are often further discounts for students and older travelers but tickets must be reserved in advance.

The baggage allowance for domestic flights is usually 23 kg (50.6 lbs). Be sure to arrive for check in at least two hours before takeoff for domestic flights, and up to three hours before takeoff for all international flights.

Aeroméxico is the country's largest airline, and it serves most national destinations as well as many international ones. **Aeromar** operates primarily in north and central Mexico and has its own terminal at Aeropuerto Benito Juárez in Mexico City. It serves all major Mexican coastal cities; border cities with the United States, such as Piedras Negras, Nuevo Laredo, Reynosa, and Matamoros; and the Texan cities of Austin and McAllen. **Interjet** and **VivaAerobus** are popular low-cost carriers that serve airports such as Campeche, Cancún, Ciudad Juárez, Huatulco, Mazatlán, Mérida, Monterrey, Oaxaca, Puerto Escondido, Tuxtla Gutiérrez, Veracruz, and Villahermosa. VivaAerobus flies only to Houston, Texas, in the US. Interjet flies to the American destintations of Las Vegas, Orange County (CA), Miami, New York, and San Antonio, plus numerous Latin American capitals such as Bogotá, Havana, Guatemala City, and San José in Costa Rica. **Volaris** flies to many Mexican destinations and numerous US cities. **Magnicharters** focuses on the domestic tourism market and mainly serves the major beach resorts. However, it also offers a wide range of charter flights, as well as all-inclusive vacations. **MAYAir** serves Mexico's south-eastern cities, including Cancún and Villahermosa.

DIRECTORY

International Coaches

Greyhound
Tel 01800 231 2222.
greyhound.com.mx

Domestic Airlines

Aeromar
Tel 01800 237 6627 (toll free) or (55) 51 33 11 11 (Mexico City).
aeromar.com.mx

Aeroméxico
Tel 01800 021 4000 (toll free) or (55) 51 33 40 00.
aeromexico.com

Interjet
Tel 01800 322 50 50 (toll free) or (55) 11 02 55 55.
interjet.com

Magnicharters
Tel (55) 53 36 01 51.
magnicharters.com.mx

MAYAir
Tel 01800 962 92 47 (toll free).
mayair.com.mx

VivaAerobus
Tel (55) 40 00 01 80.
vivaaerobus.com

Volaris
Tel 01800 122 8000 (toll free) or (55) 11 02 80 00.
volaris.com

The international airport at Puerto Vallarta

Traveling Around

Buses are the best and most economical form of public transportation between the various cities and towns in Mexico. Although second-class buses can provide quite a bone rattling experience for visitors, the luxury bus services are extremely comfortable. Tickets are significantly cheaper than domestic air travel *(see p359)*, but expect slower journeys.

A long-distance luxury bus for direct intercity services

Buses and Coaches

Mexico's numerous private bus companies can make a typical bus terminal – known as the *Central Camionera* or *Terminal de Autobuses* – busy and initially confusing. These are usually located on the outskirts of town, sometimes with separate buildings for first- and second-class services. Mexico City has four bus terminals serving places to north, south, east, and west.

There are three types of intercity bus *(camión)*, offering luxury, first-class, or second-class services. For long-distance travel, luxury or first-class is recommended. These services are more reliable, more comfortable, safer, and less likely to break down. Top-of-the-range luxury *(de lujo)* buses offer direct intercity services, with air-conditioning, fully reclining seats, hostesses, refreshments, video screens, and on-board toilets, although fares are between 30 and 50 percent more than first-class tickets. First-class *(primera)* buses are air-conditioned, with semi-reclining seats, video, and a toilet. On shorter trips, less reliable second-class buses may be the only option. Services marked *directo* or *sin escalas* (nonstop) are faster than those that make stops.

Bus Tickets

Generally, you should expect to pay US$3–5 per hour of first-class travel. For long-distance journeys of over four hours it is advisable to book in advance, especially at Christmas or Easter. At other times, just turning up at the station should be sufficient. Timetables, fares, and routes are posted at the terminals, but information and advance bookings are also sometimes available from travel agents. Many large companies have their own booking offices in town centers and some have websites to check timetables and book online. If traveling in the south of the country, the **ADO** website is useful and will let you book your journey to many different locations. **Bamba Experience** offers a backpacker multi-pass that lets you hop on and off at major destinations. Tickets are usually refundable if they are canceled at least three hours before departure. Some buses give student discounts to travelers who can show an International Student Identification Card (ISIC).

Local Buses

The local bus, also known as a *camión*, is the cheapest and easiest way to get around the provincial towns of Mexico. Apart from taxis, they are also the principal means of getting between the bus station and downtown area. Fares rarely exceed US$0.30; buy your ticket on the bus, then pull the cord or shout "*Baja*" when you want to get off. Supplementing this service are *colectivos* – vans or minibuses that follow fixed routes but charge a flat rate, regardless of distance. They can often be cramped and uncomfortable, but offer an authentic opportunity to rub shoulders with the locals. They often stop on request rather than at designated points, so just tell the driver when you want to get off. Central plazas and market places are usually the main hubs of local transport.

Ferries

Passenger and car ferries leaving from Santa Rosalía and La Paz connect the Baja California peninsula to Guaymas, Topolobampo, and Mazatlán on the Pacific mainland. Two standards of cabin are offered – a *turista*, with bunkbeds and a washbasin, or a more expensive *especial*, which has an entire suite of rooms. Schedules often

Luxury ADO buses at the Cancún bus depot

change at random and should always be confirmed in advance. The Santa Rosalía–Guaymas ferry may sometimes operate sporadically in low season.

On the Caribbean coast, ferries leave from Puerto Morelos (car ferry) and Playa del Carmen (passenger only) to the island of Cozumel *(see p286)*. Ferries from Puerto Juárez (passenger only) and Punta Sam (car ferry), both north of Cancún, travel to Isla Mujeres *(see p285)*. Another, more expensive ferry leaves for Isla Mujeres from Playa Linda, in Cancún, four times every day.

Boarding an island passenger ferry destined for Playa del Carmen

Trains

Mexico's train lines are used for freight and – beyond the suburban rail services in Mexico City – there are no passenger rail lines in the country. The **Tequila Express** in Jalisco is one of just two notable tourist train services remaining. It offers a fun day trip to a tequila-producing hacienda. The Chihuahua al Pacífico Railroad (nicknamed "El Chepe") runs through the Cañón del Cobre region *(see pp180–81)*. Considered one of the world's great railroad journeys, it covers 670 km (415 miles) over 13 hours, traversing some of Mexico's most spectacular landscapes. It departs at 6am daily from Los Mochis on the Pacific coast, and at the same time from Chihuahua in the north.

Tickets for El Chepe

First-class tickets for "El Chepe are available up to a week in advance from Los Mochis and Chihuahua stations. Economy-class tickets are available 24 hours in advance. Same-day tickets can also be purchased from Los Mochis, Chihuahua, and Creel stations; get there early to avoid queues or disappointment. Advance reservation is really only necessary during high season and public holidays. For a list of travel agents that sell tickets for El Chepe, check the **Ferrocarril Mexicano Railroad** website. You can also simply purchase your ticket on the train.

The cost of accomplishing the journey in staggered sections is exactly equal to completing it in one go, meaning it's quite feasible to stop off for excursions. While second-class tickets are roughly half the price of first class, you are still advised to travel first class for the best comfort and views. Children under 12 pay a reduced adult fare, and children under 5 travel free.

DIRECTORY

Bus Terminals in Mexico City

Norte
Eje Central Lázaro Cárdenas 4907.
M Autobuses del Norte.
Tel (55) 55 87 15 52.
W **centraldelnorte.com**

Destinations:
Aguascalientes, Baja California, Chiapas, Chihuahua, Coahuila, Colima, Durango, Guanajuato, Hidalgo, Jalisco, Michoacán, Nayarit, Nuevo Leon, Oaxaca, Puebla, Querétaro, San Luis Potosí, Sinaloa, Sonora, Tamaulipas, and Veracruz, as well as some destinations in the US.

Oriente TAPO
Calz Ignacio Zaragoza 200.
M San Lázaro.
Tel (55) 55 22 93 81.
Destinations: Campeche, Chiapas, Oaxaca, Puebla, Quintana Roo, Tabasco, Tlaxcala, Veracruz, and the Yucatán.

Poniente
Sur 122, corner of Río Tacubaya.
M Observatorio.
Tel (55) 52 71 01 49.
Destinations: Guerrero, Jalisco, Michoacán, Nayarit, Querétaro, State of Mexico, Sinaloa, and Sonora.

Sur
Av Taxqueña 1320.
M Tasqueña.
Tel (55) 56 89 97 45.
Destinations: Chiapas, Guerrero, Morelos, Puebla, Oaxaca, Tabasco, and Veracruz.

Bus Tickets

ADO
Tel 01800 369 4652.
W **ado.com.mx**

Bamba Experience
Tel 01800 462 2622.
W **bamba experience.com**

Ferry Services

Baja Ferries
Tel 01800 337 74 37.
W **bajaferries.com**

Santa Rosalía Ferries
Tel (615) 152 12 46.
W **ferrysanta rosalia.com**

Train Services

Ferrocarril Mexicano Railroad
Corner of Mendez & 24, Chihuahua.
Tel (614) 439 72 12.
Prolongación Bienestar, Los Mochis.
Tel (668) 824 11 67.
W **chepe.com.mx**

Tequila Express
Vallarta Av 4095, Jalisco.
Tel (33) 38 80 90 99 (toll free).
W **tequilaexpress.mx**

Driving in Mexico

Traveling around by car at your own pace is the most practical and flexible way to explore Mexico (the only exception being Mexico City). Driving is generally safe, but motorists need to take some precautions. Robberies do occur, and it is advisable not to drive at night and to avoid overnight street parking. In Mexico City, drive with the doors locked and the windows rolled up. Try to plan your trip in advance, take a good road map, and know where your stops are likely to be. Hitchhiking is not recommended.

Lonely highway in Northern Mexico

Rules of the Road

Mexicans drive on the right-hand side of the road, and distances are measured in kilometers rather than miles. Most traffic regulations and warnings are represented by internationally recognized symbols and signs, but some signs are unique to Mexico.

Parking, which can often be a problem in the big cities, is permitted where you see a sign with a black E (for *estacionamiento*) in a red circle. The same E with a diagonal line through it means no parking. A white E on a blue background indicates a parking lot.

The wearing of seat belts is compulsory. Normal speed limits are 40 km/h (25 mph) in built-up areas, 70 km/h (45 mph) in rural areas, and 110 km/h (68 mph) on freeways. Traffic must stop completely at *Alto* (halt) signs.

Slow down when approaching villages, where there are often speed bumps *(topes)*. Beware that these can be very high, and are not always marked. Take extreme care at rail crossings, both in cities and in the open country, as there is often no system to warn that a train is coming, and accidents can occur. Avoid driving at night when there is increased risk of robbery, and animals roam freely. Potholes are often unmarked, and it is hard to spot obstacles on the road.

What You Need

Regulations for bringing cars into Mexico are very strict. Obtain a *permiso de importación temporal* (temporary import permit) from Banjercito banks at border crossings, various Mexican consulates in the United States, or online from the Banjercito website. Online applications can be made up to 60 days or a minimum of seven days prior to arrival. Expect to be charged a fee of US$50 for the six-month, multiple-entry permit, plus a deposit of US$200–400 depending on the year of your car.

Rows of rush hour traffic in Mexico City

Several other original documents are also needed, and these should all be photocopied once or twice. These include an authorized immigration form (FMT) or visa; a valid driver's license (US, Canadian, British, Australian, and New Zealand licenses are valid); a passport (or other compliant document for North American residents); vehicle registration papers; and a credit card (Visa, MasterCard, or American Express) in the same name as the car registration papers.

It is rare for rental firms to allow their vehicles over the border, but if you manage to find one who will comply you'll need at least their written permission. If driving a company car, you'll need proof of employment and proof of the company's ownership of the vehicle.

If you wish to cross the border several times, you may do so for the period specified on your FMT. Ask officials for a *tarjetón de internación*, which you can exchange for a *comprobante de retorno* when you leave, and again for a *tarjetón* when you return. Don't forget to cancel your import permit when you leave Mexico for the final time. This can be done as you enter the border zone. Failure to do this can result in fines to your credit card.

Note that US car insurance does not cover driving south of the border, so separate coverage must be arranged. Insurance is sold in most cities and towns on both sides of the border.

Mexican Road Signs

End of surfaced road

Public convenience

Medical assistance

Car parking available

Road Classification

There are three main kinds of highway in Mexico: four-lane *super carreteras*, ordinary *cuota* (toll) roads, and *libre* (free) roads.

The cost of the tolls on the *super carreteras* is much higher than the ordinary *cuota* roads. As a result, there is less traffic, no trucks, and few buses. Beware that there aren't many service stations on the *super carreteras*.

Cuota highways range from fast, four-lane roads, to those that are little better than *libre* (free) roads. Tolls are charged according to distance and the number of axles on the vehicle. If there is a choice of toll payment booth, opt for the lane marked *autos*. On *cuotas*, drivers are insured against accident or breakdown.

Two-lane *libre* (free) roads are often very busy with local traffic, trucks, and buses, and are not ideal for long-distance or inter-city travel. For shorter trips, however, they can provide a scenic alternative to the main roads.

Fuel and Gas Stations

Since the privatization of Mexico's oil industry in 2014, gas prices are prone to fluctuations. However, it has been predicted that the price of gas may be on par with that of the US in the near future.

Priced by the liter, *Gasolina* is unleaded. It is graded either *Magna Sin* (standard) or *Premium*.

Gas stations are plentiful in towns but are less common in rural areas. In some regions it is possible to drive for 100 km (62 miles) without seeing a gas station. Gas stations are open 7am–10pm daily and are not self-service. The attendant asks *¿cuánto?* (how much?), to which you reply *lleno por favor* (fill the tank please), or specify an amount.

One of the many PEMEX gas stations found across the country

Accidents and Breakdown

In the event of an accident, stay with your vehicle. Inform the insurance companies immediately, and file a claim before leaving the country. If anyone has been hurt, you may be detained by the police until fault can be established. If nobody is hurt, it is best to resolve the situation without involving the police *(see p350)*.

The *Angeles Verdes* (Green Angels) are a fleet of pickup trucks that patrol major tourist routes, helping motorists in difficulties. The service is provided free of charge by Mexico's Ministry of Tourism (SECTUR). The mechanics speak English and can administer first aid. They only charge for spare parts or fuel, although tips are appreciated.

Maps

A selection of reliable city, regional, and national road maps are published by Guía Roji. These maps can be bought at bookstores, supermarkets, branches of Sanborns *(see p119)*, newsstands, and gas stations. SECTUR offices can provide free maps. The American Automobile Association (AAA) also publishes a map of Mexico, which is available to AAA members.

Car, Bicycle, and Motorbike Rental

Car rental is expensive in Mexico. International car rental companies, such as Hertz and Budget, have offices in main airports, and large towns, but local companies may offer the cheapest deals. When pre-booking, make sure the price incorporates the 16 percent tax, and full insurance. It is important that the insurance includes theft and collision damage waiver. Some policies provide only nominal coverage, and additional insurance cover may be necessary. To rent a car in Mexico you must be 21 or over (25 for some agencies) and have held a valid driver's license for at least one year. Rental must be paid for with a major credit card. Companies often require customers to sign a blank credit card slip, which is then torn up when the car is returned intact.

Traveling by moped

Bicycles, mopeds, and motorbikes can be rented in resorts. Before setting out, make sure that the vehicle is in good condition and that your insurance cover is adequate. Also check that your personal travel insurance covers motorbike accidents.

Hitchhiking

For safety reasons, hitchhiking is not recommended. Robberies and worse have occurred near the US border, and banditry exists in some regions, such as Sinaloa. Many Mexican landscapes are harsh and remote with sparse passing traffic. The north and Baja California are particularly unforgiving.

However, in some isolated areas hitching is the only way to get around and tends to be quite common among locals over short distances. A small fee may be expected in such cases where individual drivers serve as the local transportation. Truck drivers may also demand a fee.

Getting Around Mexico City

Traffic congestion in Mexico City is appalling and driving is not practical. Walking is the easiest way to negotiate certain areas in the center or south of the city, but elsewhere distances are so vast that some form of transport is necessary. The extensive Metro and Metrobús systems cover most of the city; both are affordable and are generally clean and safe. In the south, an electric train connects the subway at Tasqueña to Embarcadero in Xochimilco. Taxis are inexpensive, and *peseros* (collective taxis) are even cheaper. Traffic is worst during rush hours (6:30–9am and 4–7pm).

Crowd in front of the Basílica de Guadalupe *(see p112)*

Walking

Walking is a great way to explore the historic center, as well as areas like San Ángel, Coyoacán, and the Zona Rosa. Allow time to adjust to the altitude and pollution *(see pp350–51)* before long walks.

Those on foot generally take second place to vehicles. Do not assume that a car will automatically stop at a pedestrian crossing, and be prepared for uneven road surfaces and sidewalks. Look both ways when crossing one-way streets, as on some, buses are allowed to travel in both directions. Keep to busy, well-lit streets at night and avoid underpasses. Carry valuables in a money belt.

Taxis

Mexican taxis are good value, and it is possible to hire one by the hour for sightseeing. Due to incidences of robbery and assault on passengers, it is considered unsafe to flag down a taxi in the street. However, a free smart phone app called "taxiaviso," can help by providing instant verification of whether a car and driver are registered with the city.

White-and-beige *sitios* (radio taxis) are a much safer option. As a precaution, ask the dispatcher for the driver's name and the cab's license plate number.

Turismo sedans, with hooded meters and English-speaking drivers, tend to park outside big hotels. They are more expensive for short trips but can be hired by the hour. Check with the hotel that the driver is genuine.

The taxi service Uber is now very popular in the capital. It is considered reliable and cost-effective, and drivers are subject to rigorous background checks. From the airport, it is essential to take a prepaid, official taxi *(see pp357)*.

Driving

Driving in Mexico City can be a nerve-racking experience and is best avoided if possible. If you do decide to drive, keep calm and take nothing for granted. A green traffic light does not necessarily mean the road is clear. Check in your mirror before stopping at an amber light, as the driver of the car behind may not think you are going to stop. Car theft is rife, so remove or hide all possessions and be sure your hotel has safe night-parking. Signs on the city's freeways are erratic at best. If it is hard to get on them, it is harder to know where to exit. There are two main ring roads: an inner one, *El Circuito Interior*, and an outer one, the *Anillo Periférico*. A third freeway, *Viaducto Miguel Alemán*, cuts across from west to east *(see map on p123)*. Invest in a good map, such as the *Guía Roji* guide.

Cycling

A network of dedicated bike lanes is being developed, but cycling in Mexico City is still not recommended due to poor quality roads and the volume of traffic. Chapultepec Park is one exception. You can hire bicycles from outside the Museo de Antropología. Ask at the tourist office for good routes, including the one that follows the old Cuernavaca railroad.

Buses and Peseros

Buses are cheap but crowded, especially at rush hour. They run from 5am to midnight, and fares are paid to the driver on entering the bus. Route maps are available at tourist offices. *Peseros* (sedans, vans, or minibuses) use the same routes as the buses, but charge a flat rate.

Turibús (www.turibus.com.mx) runs hop-on, hop-off buses that pass most of the city's notable sights.

Metrobús

In 2005 Mexico City built its first Metrobús line along Avenida Insurgentes and down to Coyoacán and San Ángel – the service has grown exponentially ever since. Using articulated buses and dedicated lanes, the system follows five set routes and is well connected to the Metro system.

A single fare is 6 pesos, except on the airport route, where the full fare is 30 pesos. First-time riders will need the rechargeable fare card, which is 16 pesos and includes a free ride. Metrobús cards can be purchased and topped-up at machines located at each station. Transfers between lines are free. Hours of service vary by line, so consult the Metrobús website (www.metrobus.df.gob.mx) for current schedules.

The Metro

The subway system in Mexico City is one of the cheapest, cleanest, and busiest in the world. Lines are represented by numbers and colors; stations are identified by their name and a pictographic representation.

There are usually metro maps on display at the stations, occasionally on the platforms, and inside the trains as well.

Tickets *(boletos)* are sold at metro stations, singly or in strips of five. Bulk-buying saves standing in line but is no cheaper. Tickets must be validated in the machine at the entrance to the platforms. Each flat-rate ticket is valid for one trip, including transfers to other metro lines.

At peak times, the metro can be unbearably crowded and hot. People with large or bulky luggage may not be allowed on the metro at busy times. There are special carriages designated for women and children only during the rush hours.

Some of the central subway stations are worth visiting in their own right, even if you do not plan to use the metro to travel. The Zócalo station has interesting models of the city center, before and after the Spanish conquest. Inside Pino Suárez station there is a small Aztec pyramid, discovered during construction of the subway. Replicas of archaeological pieces are displayed at Bellas Artes station; and contemporary art exhibitions are often organized at Copilco station.

COPILCO 3

Sign outside Copilco station

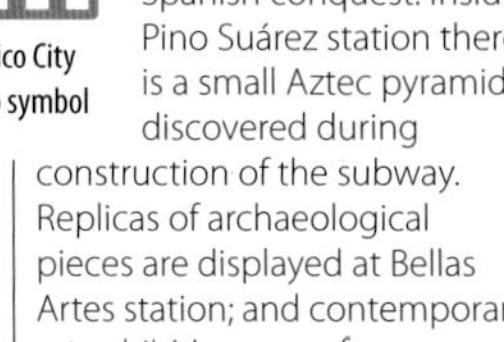

Mexico City Metro symbol

Useful Mexico City Metro Routes

Most visitors will only use sections of lines 1, 2, and 3.
The electric train from Tasqueña is shown as a dotted line.

General Index

Page numbers in **bold** refer to main entries.

B

C

N

O

Acknowledgments

Dorling Kindersley would like to thank the following people whose contributions and assistance have made the preparation of this book possible.

Contributors and Consultants

Antonio Benavides has worked as an archaeologist in the Yucatán Peninsula since 1974. He has written several books on the Maya and the colonial history of the Yucatán.
Nick Caistor, a specialist on Latin American literature, is a writer, translator, and broadcaster. He works for the BBC World Service.
Maria Doulton is a freelance writer who has been involved with Mexico for many years.
Petra Fischer is a writer and television producer working in Mexico. German born, she has spent much of her life in Mexico.
Eduardo Gleason, a former tour guide, is a writer and researcher based in Mexico City.
Phil Gunson is a journalist and naturalist. He is the former Latin America correspondent for *The Guardian* newspaper.
Alan Knight is Professor of Latin American history at St Anthony's College, Oxford.
Felicity Laughton, a freelance writer, has lived and worked in Mexico for many years.
Simon Martin is an epigrapher at the Institute of Archaeology, University College London, and specializes in ancient Maya inscriptions.
Richard Nichols is half-Mexican and has had a life-long connection with Mexico. He is a former businessman turned writer.
Chloë Sayer has written numerous books about Mexico, worked on television documentaries about the country, and made ethnographic collections in Mexico for the British Museum.

Additional Contributors

Marita Adair, Andrew Downie, David Maitland, Nick Ryder, Rosa Rodríguez.

Proofreader

Stewart J Wild.

Indexer

Hilary Bird.

Revisions Team

Ashwin Adimari , Emma Anacootee, Richard Arghiris, Tessa Bindloss, Sam Borland, Julie Schwietert Collazo, Neha Chander, Caroline D'Cruz , Surya Deogun, Stephanie Driver, Ellen and James Fields, Joy Fitzsimmons, Fay Franklin, Eva Gleason, Geoffrey Groesbeck, Lydia Halliday, Emily Hatchwell, Carolyn Hewitson, Shobhna Iyer, Claire Jones, Elly King, Priya Kukadia, Kathryn Lane, Maite Lantaron, Francesca Machiavelli, Stewart Mandy, Sue Metcalfe-Megginson, Rebecca Milner, Sonal Modha, George Nimmo, Scarlett O'Hara, Helen Partington, Animesh Pathak, Susie Peachey, Naomi Peck, Helen Peters, Adrian Potts, Rada Radojicic, Marisa Renzullo, Ellen Root, Zoë Ross, Sands Publishing Solutions, Avijit Sengupta, Jaynan Spengler, Helen Townsend, Richa Verma, Paul Whitfield.

Maps

Michael Bassett, Sharon O'Reilly, Richard Toomey (ERA-Maptec Ltd) (BIMSA Cartosistemas, S.A. de C.V.).

Photographers

Demetrio Carrasco, Linda Whitwam, Peter Wilson, Francesca Yorke.

Additional Photography

Paul Franklin, Eva Gleason, Stewart Mandy, Ian O'Leary, Rough Guides/Sarah Cummins, Clive Streeter.

Illustrators

Gary Cross, Richard Draper, Isidoro González-Adalid Cabezas (Acanto Arquitectura y Urbanismo S.L.), Paul Guest, Stephen Guapay, Claire Littlejohn, John Woodcock

Additional Illustrations

José Luis de Andrés de Colsa, Javier Gómez Morata (Acanto Arquitectura y Urbanismo S.L.).

For Dorling Kindersley

Fay Franklin, Louise Bostock Lang, Annette Jacobs, Vivien Crump, Gillian Allan, Douglas Amrine, Marie Ingledew, David Proffit

Special Assistance

Arq. Humberto Aguirre; Emilia Almazán; Margarita Arriaga; Juan Francisco Becerra Ferreiro; Patricia Becerra Ramírez (Posada Coat2epec); Sergio Berrera; Lic. Marco Beteta; Giorgio Brignone; Rosa Bugdud; Fernando Bustamante (Antropólogo); Libby Cabeldu; Canning House (London); Lic. Laura Castro; Santiago Chávez; Josefina Cipriano; Ana Compean; María Eugenia Cruz Terrazas (INEGI); Greg Custer; Jane Custer; Mary Lou Dabdoub; Avery Danziger; Lenore Danziger; Areli Díaz (Instituto Nacional de Antropología, Mexico); Lucía Díaz Cholico; Fernando Díaz de León; Lic. Roberto Durón Carrillo; Peter McGregor Eadie; Ana María Espinoza; Ludwig Estrada; José Falguera; Lic. Lincoln Fontanills (Secretaría de Turismo, Mexico); Elena Nichols Gantous; Robert Graham; Ma. del Carmen Guerrero Esquivel; Lic. José Luis Hernández (Secretaría de Turismo del Estado de Puebla); Ing. Guillermo Hidalgo Trujillo; Ariane Homayunfar; Jorge Huft; Instituto Nacional Indigenista (Nayarit); Carlos Jiménez; Lourdes Jiménez Coronel; Ursula Jones; Eric Jordan; La Mexicana Quality Foods Ltd; Marcela Leos (Mexican Embassy to the UK); Kevin Leuzinger (Cozumel Fan Club); Sol Levin Rojo (Instituto Nacional de Antropología, Mexico); Oscar López; Carlos Lozano de la Torre; Alan Luce; Arq. Alfredo Lugo; Berta Maldonado; Gabriel Martínez; Manuel Mata; Cathy Matos (Mexican Tours); Fabián Medina; Enrique Mendoza; Meteorological Office; Mexico Ministry of Tourism, London; Ivalu Mireles Esparza; Silvia Niembro (Antropóloga, Museo de Antropología de Xalapa); María Novaro; Diego de la O Peralta; Magdalena Ordóz Estrada; Dolores Ortuño Araiza; Margarita Pedraza; Ma. Irma del Peral; Ma. del Pilar Córdoba; Margaret Popper; Petra Puente; Bertha Alicia Ramírez; José Rangel Navarro; Jesus Rodríguez Morales; Anita Romero de Andrade; Celia Romero Piñón; Elena de la Rosa; Idalia Rubio; Paulina Rubio; Carlos Salgado; Alejandro Sánchez Galván; Alejandro Santes García (Antropólogo); Marta Santos; David Saucedo; Gloria Soledad González; Lisette Span; Pablo Span; Turismo del Estado de Aguascalientes (Dirección); Turismo del Estado de Colima (Secretaría); Turismo del Estado de Guanajuato (Secretaría); Turismo del Estado de Hidalgo (Dirección General); Turismo del Estado de Jalisco (Secretaría); Turismo del Estado de Michoacan (Secretaría); Turismo del Estado de Nayarit (Secretaría); Turismo del Estado de Querétaro (Secretaría); Turismo del Estado de San Luis Postosí (Dirección General); Turismo del Estado de Veracruz-Llave (Dirección); Turismo del Estado de Zacatecas (Dirección); Juan Carlos Valencia; Gilberto Miguel Vázquez; Josefina Vázquez; Luis Antonio Villa; Jesús Villafaña; Helen Westwood; John Wiseman.

Special Photography
© INAH, Cambridge Museum of Archaeology and Anthropology, Philip Dowell, Neil Mersh, Stephen Whitehorne, Jerry Young, Michel Zabé.

Mexico's Cultural Heritage

Photography Permissions
The Publisher would like to thank all the cathedrals, churches, museums, restaurants, hotels, shops, galleries, and others sights, too numerous to thank individually, for their co-operation and contribution to this publication.

Key:
a-above; b-below/bottom; c-centre; f-far; l-left; r-right; t-top.

Some of the following photographs form part of the Cultural Heritage of Mexico, which is protected by the Instituto Nacional de Antropología e Historia, Mexico.

Works of art have been reproduced with the permission of the following copyright holders: Ex-Aduana de Santo Domingo (west wall) *Patriots and Parricides* David Alfaro Siqueiros (1945) © Instituto Nacional de Bellas Artes (INBA) – Sala de Arte Público Siqueiros 76br.

The publisher would like to thank the following individuals, companies, and picture libraries for their kind permission to reproduce their photographs in this publication:

123RF.com: csp 54bl.

Las Alcobas: 315tr, Evan Dion 296br; **Pablo De Aguinaco**, Mexico: 21b, 27c,35c, 35br, 36c, 38br, 38–9, 39tl, 143cr, , 169cra, 229b 231b, 241bl; A.P. Giberstein 168clb, Carlos Puga 174cb,183crb, 251cr, 339c; **AKG Photo**, London: 52tl; Erich Lessing 57tl; **Alamy Images**: Agencja Fotograficzna Caro 363bl; Dorothy Alexander; 29br Sue Clark 309tl; dbimages 356clb; Danita Delimont 167bl; Danita Delimont/Cindy Miller Hopkins 348c; Danita Delimont 336cla, 338bl; Diana Bier Puebla Carnival 350crb; Eagle Visions Photography/Craig Lovell 18; Tony Gale 357c; Geogphotos 308cla; Bill Gorum 24cb; Steve Hamblin 355br; imageBROKER 250tl; incamerastock 287cl; Jon Arnold Images Ltd 317br; Frans Lemmens 349tl; Lightworks Media 71c, 82br; CJ Middendorf 349tl; John Mitchell 360br; Moreleaze Tropicana 350br; Luc Novovitch 14tr; M.Sobreira 86; Ollie Weait 354cra; Janusz Wrobel 339br; **Amaranta Restaurant:** 319tr; **Ardea London Ltd**: Piers Cavendish 25br; **The Art Archive**: Archaeological and ethnological Museum Guatamala City/Dagli Orti 8-9; **AWL Images:** Demetrio Carrasco 260; Danita Delimont Stock 162, 170-1.

Banco Nacional De Mexico SA: Fomento Cultural 47tc; **Sandro Bestmann:** 209tr; **La Buena Vida:** 327br; **John Brunton**: 32t, 33cla, 222bl, 223bl, 259bl.

Michael Calderwood: 220tr; **Cambridge Museum of Archaeology and Anthropology:**95tc; **Demetrio Carrasco**:352tl; **Casa de Sierra Nevada**: 301tr; **Bruce Colleman Collection**: John Shaw 24c; **Corbis**: Lynsey Addarid 309c; Atlantide Phototravel 96tr, 220cr; Jan Butchofsky-Houser 310bl; Randy Faris 67cr; William Henry Jackson 52cr; Danny Lehman 70c; Robert Harding World Imagery/Wendy Connett 12bl; Erich Schelgel 25cb; David H. Wells 311bl; Stuart Westmorland 15bc.

Dreamstime.com: Aquanaut4 25tr; Lukas Blazek 25bl; Francesca Braghetta 280br; Rafał Cichawa 270-1; Maciej Czekajewski 25bc; Uli Danner 100; 346bl; Dplphoto 184; Emattil 10bc; Alexandre Fagundes De Fagundes 242; Ginosphotos 286tr, 336bc; Jonathan Hugo Jiménez Gómez 37c; Javarman 60-1; Javarman 261b; Jerl71 134, 232-3; Jesús Eloy Ramos Lara 93tl; Lali Kacharava 24bl; Grzegorz Kielbasa 2-3; Patryk Kosmider 221cl; Chao Kusollerschariya 130-1; Mellisandre 344-5; Mgkuijpers 24bc; Borna Mirahmadian 80-1; Kaye Eileen Oberstar 25tl; Svx94 14bl; Phoebezzf 63crb; Glenn Price 24crb; Speshilov Sergey 96c; Siempreverde22 25crb; Tomstox 13bl; Martyn Unsworth 216; Joao Virissimo 175cr.

Tor Eigeland: 26clb; **Embajada De Mexico, London**: 33br.

Fairmont Acapulco Princess: 302bc; **Fiesta Americana**

Hacienda Gallindo: 294cl; **Luis Felix** © 1979: 199bc; **Four Seasons Mexico City:** 297tr; **Robert Fried Photography**: 24br.

Getty Images: AFP/Omar Torres 351cr; Bloomberg via Getty Images 352bl, 353b; **Eva Maria Gleason, Mexico**: 68all, 69br, 145tl, 145bc, 146ca, 146br, 147ca, 147bl, 351t, 355c, 360cla, 365t; **Andreas Gross, Germany**: 38tr, 265cra; **Grupo Aeroportuario Del Pacífico:** 359br; **Grupo Contramar**: 316tl; **Grupo Plascencia**: 321tl
La Habichuela: 328b; Hacienda Mariposas Resort & Spa: 300bl; **Hacienda Xcanatun:** 305bl; **Dave G. Hauser**: 168cr, 175c, 223cr, 225br; John Elkins 132tl; Susan Kaye 251bl; **Hutchison Library**: 222tr, 236bl.

Fototeca Del Inah Fondo Casasola: 54tl, 54br; **Index, Barcelona**: 43b, 53bc; Mithra *El Feudalismo Porfirista* Juan O'Gorman 57crb.

Justin Kerr: 281crb.

David Lavender: 33cl, 33cr, 39cra, 39crb, 332–3, 332bl, 333bl, 333cra, all 334-5; **Lonely Planet Images**: Richard I'Anson 42; John Neubauer 70bl.

Maroma Resort and Spa: 342bl, 343tr; **Enrico Martino**: 22t, 23cl, 28cb, 34cl, 34br, 36tl, 167cr, 179tl, 180bc, 266cla; **Jose Luis Moreno**: 287bl, 287bc.

Juan Negrin: 26–7; **NHPA**: John Shaw 215br.

G. Dagli Orti: 50cl, 237cra, 237crb.

Paradisus Cancun Resort: 304tr; **El Pegaso**: 324br
Planet Earth Pictures: Mary Clay 25crb; Brian Kenney 25clb; Ken Lucas 24clb; ; Claus Meyer 290ca; **Posada de las Flores:** 299bc.

Rancho San Cayetano: 294br, 325br; **Restarante Marganzo:** 326tr; **Restaurant El Cardenal:** 314bc; **Restaurante Sunset Grill:** 329tr; **Restaurante Trio:** 324tl; **Rex Features**: 59crb, 358tc; KD/Keystone USA 353tl; Sipa Press/L. Rieder 59bc; **Robert Harding Picture Library:** age fotostock/Remedios Valls Lopez 13tl; Robert Freck/Odyssey 55cra, 55cr.

Sagrantino Restaurant: 322tr; **Chloe Sayer:** 21cr, 26ca, 26bc, 29cl, 29cra, 31cb, 33b, 32bl, 32br, 33tr, 33crb, 39bl, 199tr, 199cl, 332ca, 332br, 333br; **Sexto Sol, Mexico**: 24cra, 26tr, 180tr, Edn 38ca; Adalberto Rios Szalay 37bl, 56crb 121tr, 174t, 174bl, 175bl, 183tl, 188tc, 229tr, 357tr, 358b; Adalberto Rios Lanz 36bl; A.M.G. 22c, 337clb; Ernesto Rios Lanz 25cl, 175cra; **Bob Schalkwijk**: 27br, 53cb, *Padre Hidalgo* O'Gorman 53tr, 95cl; **Sotavento Restaurant:** 318bl; **South American Pictures**: 58tl, 85b, 114t; Tony Morrison 225tl; Chris Sharp 45t, 247tl; **Heri Stierling**: 51crb, 237bc.; **SuperStock:** age fotostock 204-5, Prisma 15tr, 248-9.

Terraqua: 287cr, 287br; **La Taverna, Cabo San Lucas**: 320bl; **Tony Stone Images**: 240tr, Richard During 223tl.

Mireille Vautier: 20t, 26cl, 27bc, 30tr, 33tl, 33bc, 35tl, 37tr, 38clb, 39cla, 39c, 44clb, 46bl, 46br, *The Conquest* O'Gorman 47crb, 48tl, 48br, 49tr, 55tl, 56bl, 58crb, 58bc, 59tc, 97tl, 97crb, 98b, 166tl, 166cb, 189cr, 239cra, 268br, 269clb, 281cla, 337tr, **Las Ventanas al Paraiso/Nike Communications, INC:** 298tr; **Viceroy Zihuatanejo/P & G Communications**: 303tl; **Villa Montana Hotel and Spa:** 323bl.

Werner Formen Archive: Museo Nacional de Antropología, Mexico 48ca; **Elizabeth Whiting Associates**: 54clb; Peter Wilson: 22bl; **www.wi-fi.org**: 355tc; **WYSE Travel Confederation**: 347c.

Alejandro Zenteno: 191bl, 252c, 253tl, 281br.

Front endpaper: **Alamy Images**: M.Sobreira Lcb; **AWL Images:** Demetrio Carrasco Rtr; Danita Delimont Stock Ltl; **Dreamstime.com**., Uli Danner Lbl; Dplphoto Lbr; Alexandre Fagundes De Fagundes Rtc; Jerl71 Rtl; Martyn Unsworth Rc.

Jacket Front main and spine top - **Photoshot:** Gary Withey.

Cover images: **Front:** Alamy Images: Hans Delnoij; **Spine:** Alamy Images: Hans Delnoij

All other images © Dorling Kindersley.
For further information see: www.dkimages.com

Phrase Book

Mexican Spanish is essentially the same as the Castilian spoken in Spain, although there are some differences in vocabulary and pronunciation.

The most noticeable are the use of *ustedes* (the plural version of "you") in both informal and formal situations, and the pronunciation of the soft "c" and the letter "z" as "s" rather than "th."

Mexicans use *carro* (instead of *coche*) for a car, and often call buses, as well as trucks, *camiones*. Words of indigenous origin are common. A word for market used only in Mexico is *tianguis*, for example, although *mercado* is also employed. Mexicans tend to be fairly formal, and it is good manners to use *usted* (rather than *tú*) for "you," unless you know the person well. Always say *buenos días* or *buenas tardes* when boarding a taxi, and address both male taxi drivers and waiters as *señor*.

If you wish to decline goods from street vendors, a polite shake of the head and a *muchas gracias* will usually suffice. Adding *muy amable*, literally "very kind," will help to take the edge off the refusal. A term to be handled with care is *madre* (mother), as much bad language in Mexico is based on variants of this word. When referring to someone's mother, use *tu mama* (your mom), or the formal version *su señora madre*, just to be safe.

In an Emergency

Help!	**¡Socorro!**	*soh*-**koh**-*roh*
Stop!	**¡Pare!**	**pah**-*reh*
Call a doctor!	**¡Llame a un médico!**	**yah**-*meh ah* **oon meh**-*dee-koh*
Call an ambulance!	**¡Llame una ambulancia!**	**yah**-*meh ah* **oonah** *ahm-boo*-**lahn**-*see-ah*
Call the fire department!	**¡Llame a los bomberos!**	**yah**-*meh ah lohs bohm*-**beh**-*rohs*
Where is the nearest telephone?	**¿Dónde está el teléfono más cercano?**	**dohn**-*deh ehs*-**tah** *ehl teh*-**leh**-*foh-noh* **mahs** *sehr*-**kah**-*noh*
Where is the nearest hospital?	**¿Dónde está el hospital más cercano?**	**dohn**-*deh ehs*-**tah** *ehl ohs-pee*-**tahl mahs** *sehr*-**kah**-*noh*
policeman	**el policía**	*ehl poh-lee*-**see**-*ah*
Could you help me?	**¿Me podría ayudar?**	*meh poh*-**dree**-*yah ah-yoo*-**dahr**
I've/we've been mugged	**Me/nos asaltaron**	*meh/nohs ah-sahl*-**tahr**-*ohn*
They stole my …	**Me robaron el/la…**	*meh roh*-**bahr**-*ohn ehl/lah*

Communication Essentials

Yes	**Sí**	*see*
No	**No**	*noh*
Please	**Por favor**	*pohr fah*-**vohr**
Thank you	**Gracias**	**grah**-*see-ahs*
Excuse me	**Perdone**	*pehr*-**doh**-*neh*
Hello	**Hola**	**oh**-*lah*
Good morning	**Buenos días**	**bweh**-*nohs* **dee**-*ahs*
Good afternoon (from noon)	**Buenas tardes**	**bweh**-*nahs* **tahr**-*dehs*
Good night	**Buenas noches**	**bweh**-*nahs* **noh**-*chehs*
Bye (casual)	**Hasta luego**	*ah*-**stah** *loo*-**weh**-*goh*
Goodbye	**Adiós**	*ah-dee*-**ohs**
See you later	**Hasta luego**	*ah*-**stah** *loo*-**weh**-*goh*
Morning	**La mañana**	*lah mah*-**nyah**-*nah*
Afternoon/ early evening	**La tarde**	*lah* **tahr**-*deh*
Night	**La noche**	*lah* **noh**-*cheh*
Yesterday	**Ayer**	*ah*-**yehr**
Today	**Hoy**	*oy*
Tomorrow	**Mañana**	*mah*-**nyah**-*nah*
Here	**Aquí**	*ah*-**kee**
There	**Allí**	*ah*-**yee**
What?	**¿Qué?**	**keh**
When?	**¿Cuándo?**	**kwahn**-*doh*
Why?	**¿Por qué?**	*pohr*-**keh**
Where?	**¿Dónde?**	**dohn**-*deh*
How are you?	**¿Cómo está usted?**	**koh**-*moh ehs*-**tah** *oos*-**tehd**
Very well, thank you	**Muy bien, gracias**	*mwee bee*-**ehn grah**-*see-ahs*
Pleased to meet you	**Mucho gusto**	**moo**-*choh* **goo**-*stoh*
See you soon	**Hasta pronto**	*ahs-tah* **prohn**-*toh*
I'm sorry	**Lo siento**	*loh see*-**ehn**-*toh*

Useful Phrases

That's fine	**Está bien**	*ehs*-**tah** *bee*-**ehn**
Great/fantastic!	**¡Qué bien!**	**keh** *bee*-**ehn**
Where is/are …?	**¿Dónde está/están …?**	**dohn**-*deh ehs*-**tah**/*ehs*-**tahn**
How far is it to …?	**¿Cuántos metros/ kilómetros hay de aqui a …?**	**kwahn**-*tohs* **meh**-*trohs/kee*-**loh**-*meh-trohs* **eye** *deh ah*-**kee** *ah*
Which way is it to …?	**¿Por dónde se va a …?**	*pohr* **dohn**-*deh seh* **vah** *ah*
Do you speak English?	**¿Habla inglés?**	**ah**-*blah een*-**glehs**
I don't understand	**No comprendo**	*noh kohm*-**prehn**-*doh*
Could you speak more slowly, please?	**¿Puede hablar más despacio, por favor?**	**pweh**-*deh ah*-**blahr mahs** *dehs*-**pah**-*see-oh pohr fah*-**vohr**
I want	**Quiero**	*kee*-**yehr**-*oh*
I would like	**Quisiera/ Me gustaría**	*kee-see*-**yehr**-*ah meh goo-stah*-**ree**-*ah*
We want	**Queremos**	*keh*-**reh**-*mohs*
Do you have change (for 50 pesos)?	**¿Tiene cambio (de cincuenta pesos)?**	*tee*-**eh**-*neh* **kahm**-*bee-yoh deh seen*-**kwehn**-*tah* **peh**-*sohs*
(It's) very kind of you	**Muy amable**	**mwee** *ah*-**mah**-*bleh*
There is/there are	**Hay**	*eye*
Do you have/is there/are there?	**¿Hay?**	*eye*
Is there any water?	**¿Hay agua?**	**eye ah**-*gwah*
It's broken	**Está roto/a**	*ehs*-**tah roh**-*toh/tah*
Is it far/near?	**¿Está lejos/cerca?**	*ehs*-**tah leh**-*hohs/***sehr**-*kah*
Take care/be careful!	**¡Ten cuidado!**	**tehn** *koo-ee*-**dah**-*doh*
We are late	**Estamos atrasados**	*ehs*-**tah**-*mohs ah-trah*-**sah**-*dohs*
We are early	**Estamos adelantados**	*ehs*-**tah**-*mohs ah-deh-lahn*-**tah**-*dohs*
OK, all right	**De acuerdo**	**deh** *ah*-**kwehr**-*doh*
Yes, of course	**Claro que sí**	**klah**-*roh keh* **see**
Of course!/with pleasure	**¡Cómo no!/con mucho gusto**	**koh**-*moh* **noh**/*kohn* **moo**-*choh* **goo**-*stoh*
Let's go	**Vámonos**	**vah**-*moh-nohs*

Useful Words

big	**grande**	**grahn**-*deh*
small	**pequeño/a**	*peh*-**keh**-*nyoh/nyah*
hot	**caliente**	*kah-lee*-**ehn**-*the*
cold	**frío/a**	**free**-*oh/ah*
good	**bueno/a**	**bweh**-*noh/nah*
bad	**malo/a**	**mah**-*loh/lah*
enough	**suficiente**	*soo-fee-see*-**ehn**-*teh*
well	**bien**	*bee*-**ehn**
open	**abierto/a**	*ah-bee*-**ehr**-*toh/tah*
closed	**cerrado/a**	*sehr*-**rah**-*doh/dah*
full	**lleno/a**	**yeh**-*noh/nah*

empty	**vacío/a**	vah-**see**-oh/ah
left	**izquierda**	ees-key-**ehr**-dah
right	**derecha**	deh-**reh**-chah
(keep) straight ahead	**(siga) derecho**	(**see**-gah) deh-**reh**-choh
near	**cerca**	**sehr**-kah
far	**lejos**	**leh**-hohs
up	**arriba**	ah-**ree**-bah
down	**abajo**	ah-**bah**-hoh
early	**temprano**	tehm **prah** noh
late	**tarde**	**tahr**-deh
now/very soon	**ahora/ahorita**	ah-**ohr**-ah/ah-ohr-**ee**-tah
more	**más**	**mahs**
less	**menos**	**meh**-nohs
very	**muy**	**mwee**
a little	**(un) poco**	**oon poh**-koh
very little	**muy poco**	**mwee poh**-koh
(much) more	**(mucho) más**	(**moo**-choh) **mahs**
too much	**demasiado**	deh-mah-see-**ah**-doh
too late	**demasiado tarde**	deh-mah-see-**ah**-doh **tahr**-deh
farther on/ahead	**más adelante**	**mahs** ah-deh-**lahn**-teh
farther back	**más atras**	**mahs** ah-**trahs**
opposite	**frente a**	**frehn**-teh ah
below/above	**abajo/arriba**	ah-**bah**-hoh/ ah-**ree**-bah
first, second, third	**primero/a segundo/a tercero/a**	pree-**meh**-roh/ah seh-**goon**-doh/ah tehr-**sehr**-oh/ah
floor (of a building)	**el piso**	ehl **pee**-soh
ground floor	**la planta baja**	lah **plahn**-tah **bah**-hah
entrance	**entrada**	ehn-**trah**-dah
exit	**salida**	sah-**lee**-dah
elevator	**el ascensor**	**ehl** ah-sehn-**sohr**
toilets	**baños/sanitarios**	**bah**-nyohs/ sah-nee-**tah**-ree-ohs
women's	**de damas**	deh **dah**-mahs
men's	**de caballeros**	deh kah-bah-**yeh**-rohs
sanitary napkins	**toallas sanitarias/ higiénicas**	toh-**ah**-yahs sah-nee-**tah**-ree-yahs/hee-**hyeh**-nee-kahs
tampons	**tampones**	tahm-**poh**-nehs
condoms	**condones**	kohn-**doh**-nehs
toilet paper	**papel higiénico**	pah-**pehl** hee-**hyen**-ee-koh
(non-)smoking area	**área de (no) fumar**	**ah**-ree-ah deh (**noh**) foo-**mahr**
camera	**la cámara**	lah **kah**-mah-rah
batteries	**las pilas**	lahs **pee**-lahs
passport	**el pasaporte**	**ehl** pah-sah-**pohr**-teh
visa	**el visado**	ehl vee-**sah**-doh

Health

I feel ill	**Me siento mal**	meh see-**ehn**-toh **mahl**
I have a headache	**Me duele la cabeza**	meh doo-**eh**-leh lah kah-**beh**-sah
I have a stomach-ache	**Me duele el estómago**	meh doo-**eh**-leh ehl ehs-**toh**-mah-goh
I need to rest	**Necesito descansar**	neh-seh-**see**-toh dehs-kahn-**sahr**
The child is/the children are sick	**El niño está/los niños están enfermo(s)**	ehl **nee**-nyoh ehs-**tah**/lohs **nee**-nyos ehs-**tahn** ehn-**fehr**-moh(s)
We need a doctor	**Necesitamos un médico**	neh-seh-see-**tah**-mohs **oon meh**-dee-koh
thermometer	**el termómetro**	ehl tehr-**moh**-meh-troh
drug store	**la farmacia**	lah fahr-**mah**-see-ah
medicine	**la medicina/ el remedio**	lah meh-dee-**see**-nah/ehl reh-**meh**-dee-oh
pills	**las pastillas/ píldoras**	lahs pahs-**tee**-yahs/ lahs peel-**doh**-rahs

Post Offices and Banks

Where can I change money?	**¿Dónde puedo cambiar dinero?**	**dohn**-deh **pweh**-doh kahm-bee-**ahr** dee-**neh**-roh
What is the dollar rate?	**¿A cómo está el dólar?**	ah **koh**-moh ehs-**tah** ehl **doh**-lahr
How much is the postage to…?	**¿Cuánto cuesta enviar una carta a…?**	**kwahn**-toh **kweh**-stah ehn-vee-**yahr oo**-nah **kahr**-tah ah
and for a post-card?	**¿y una postal?**	ee **oo**-nah pohs-**tahl**
I need stamps	**Necesito estampillas**	neh-seh-**see**-toh ehs-tahm-**pee**-yahs
cashier	**cajero**	kah-**heh**-roh
ATM	**cajero automático**	kah-**heh**-roh ahw-toh-**mah**-tee-koh
withdraw money	**sacar dinero**	sah-**kahr** dee-**neh**-roh

Shopping

How much does this cost?	**¿Cuánto cuesta esto?**	**kwahn**-toh **kwehs**-tah **ehs**-toh
I would like …	**Me gustaría …**	meh goos-tah-**ree**-ah
Do you have?	**¿Tienen?**	tee-**yeh**-nehn
I'm just looking, thank you	**Sólo estoy mirando, gracias**	**soh**-loh ehs-**toy** mee-**rahn**-doh **grah**-see-ahs
What time do you open?	**¿A qué hora abren?**	ah **keh** oh-rah **ah**-brehn
What time do you close?	**¿A qué hora cierran?**	ah keh oh-rah see-**ehr**-rahn
Do you take credit cards/ traveler's checks?	**¿Aceptan tarjetas de crédito/ cheques de viajero?**	ahk-**sehp**-tahn tahr-**heh**-tahs deh **kreh**-dee-toh/ **cheh**-kehs deh vee-ah-**heh**-roh
I am looking for…	**Estoy buscando…**	**ehs**-tohy boos-**kahn**-doh
Is that your best price?	**¿Es su mejor precio?**	ehs soo meh-**hohr**-**preh**-see-oh
discount	**un descuento**	**oon** dehs-koo-**ehn**-toh
clothes	**la ropa**	lah **roh**-pah
this one	**éste**	**ehs**-the
that one	**ése**	**eh**-she
expensive	**caro**	**kahr**-oh
cheap	**barato**	bah-**rah**-toh
size, clothes	**talla**	**tah**-yah
size, shoes	**número**	**noo**-mehr-oh
white	**blanco**	**blahn**-koh
black	**negro**	**neh**-groh
red	**rojo**	**roh**-hoh
yellow	**amarillo**	ah-mah-**ree**-yoh
green	**verde**	**vehr**-deh
blue	**azul**	ah-**sool**
antique store	**la tienda de antigüedades**	lah tee-**ehn**-dah deh ahn-tee-gweh-**dah**-dehs
bakery	**la panadería**	lah pah-nah-deh **ree**-ah
bank	**el banco**	ehl **bahn**-koh
bookstore	**la librería**	lah lee-breh-**ree**-ah
butcher's	**la carnicería**	lahkahr-nee-seh-**ree**-ah
cake store	**la pastelería**	lah pahs-teh-leh-**ree**-ah
department store	**la tienda de departamentos**	lah tee-**ehn**-dah deh deh-pahr-tah-**mehn**-tohs
fish store	**la pescadería**	lah pehs-kah-deh-**ree**-ah
greengrocer's	**la frutería**	lah froo-teh-**ree**-ah
grocer's	**la tienda de abarrotes**	lah tee-**yehn**-dah deh ah-bah-**roh**-tehs
hairdresser's	**la peluquería**	lah peh-loo-keh-**ree**-ah
jeweler's	**la joyería**	lah hoh-yeh-**ree**-yah
market	**el tianguis/**	ehl tee-ahn-goo-

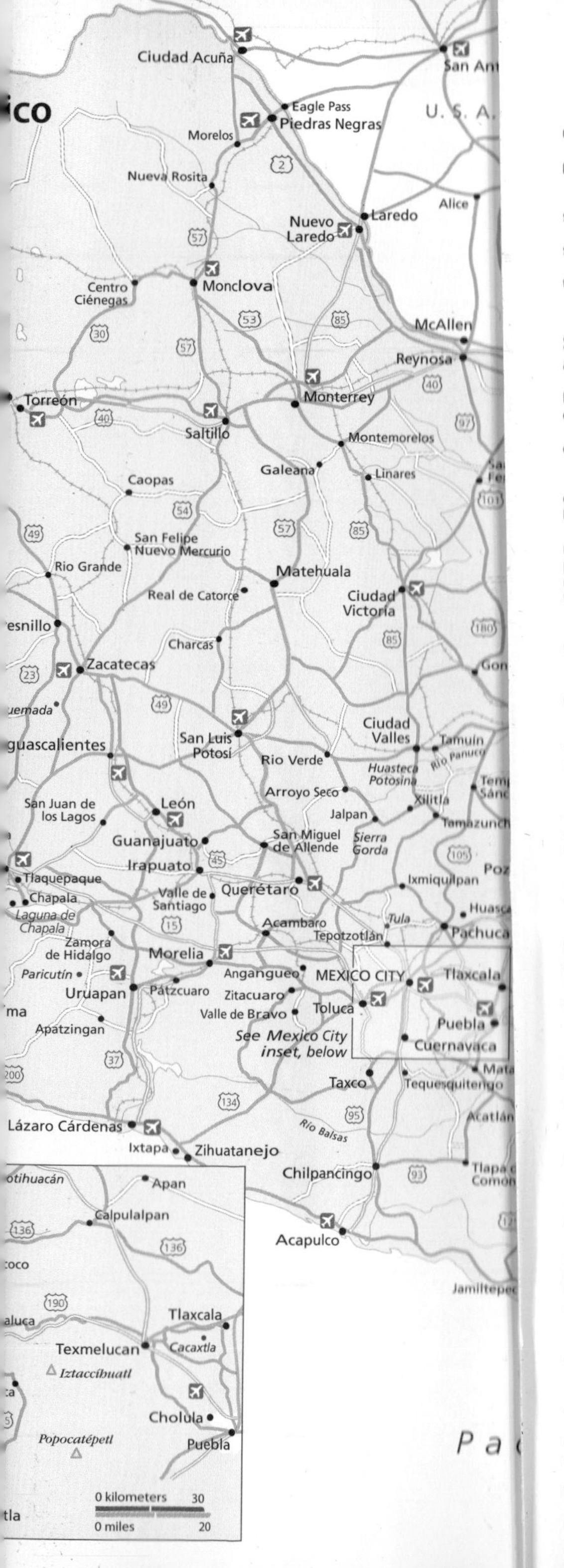

	mercado	ees/mehr-kah-doh
newsstand	**el puesto de periódicos**	ehl poo-es-toh deh pe-rio-dee-kohs
post office	**la oficina de correos**	lah oh-fee-see-nah deh kohr-reh-ohs
shoe store	**la zapatería**	lah sah-pah-teh-ree-ah
supermarket	**el supermercado**	ehl soo-pehr-mehr-kah-doh
travel agency	**la agencia de viajes**	lah ah-hehn-see-ah deh vee-ah-hehs

Sightseeing

art gallery	**galería de arte**	ehl moo-seh-oh deh ahr-teh
beach	**la playa**	lah plah-yah
cathedral	**la catedral**	lah kah-teh-drahl
church	**la iglesia/ la basílica**	lah ee-gleh-see-ah/ lah bah-see-lee-kah
garden	**el jardín**	ehl hahr-deen
library	**la biblioteca**	lah bee-blee-oh-teh-kah
museum	**el museo**	ehl moo-seh-oh
pyramid	**la pirámide**	lah pee-rah-meed
ruins	**las ruinas**	lahs roo-ee-nahs
tourist information office	**la oficina de turismo**	lah oh-fee-see-nah deh too-rees-moh
town hall	**el palacio municipal**	ehl pah-lah-see-oh moo-nee-see-pahl
closed for holidays	**cerrado por vacaciones**	sehr-rah-doh pohr vah-kah-see-oh-nehs
ticket	**la entrada**	lah ehn-trah-dah
how much is the entrance fee?	**¿Cuánto vale la entrada?**	kwahn-toh vah-leh lah ehn-trah-dah
guide (person)	**el/la guía**	ehl/lah gee-ah
guide (book)	**la guía**	lah gee-ah
guided tour	**una visita guiada**	oo-nah vee-see-tah gee-ah-dah
map	**el mapa**	ehl mah-pah
city map	**el plano de la ciudad**	ehl plah-noh deh lah see-oo-dahd

Transportation

When does the… leave?	**¿A qué hora sale el…?**	ah keh oh-rah sah-leh ehl
Where is the bus stop?	**¿Dónde está la parada de autobuses?**	dohn-deh ehs-tah lah pah-rah-dah deh ow-toh-boo-sehs
Is there a bus/train to…?	**¿Hay un camión/ tren a…?**	eye oon kah-mee-ohn/trehn ah
the next bus/train	**el próximo camión/tren**	ehl prohx-ee-moh kah-mee-ohn/trehn
bus station	**la central camionera/ de autobuses**	lah sehn-trahl kah-mee-ohn-ehr-ah/deh aw-toh-boo-sehs
train station	**la estación de trenes**	lah ehs-tah-see-ohn deh treh-nehs
subway/metro	**el metro**	ehl meh-troh
platform	**el andén**	ehl ahn-dehn
ticket office	**la taquilla**	lah tah-kee-yah
round-trip ticket	**un boleto de ida y vuelta**	oon boh-leh-toh deh ee-dah ee voo-ehl-tah
one-way ticket	**un boleto de ida solamente**	oon boh-leh-toh deh ee-dah soh-lah-mehn-teh
airport	**el aeropuerto**	ehl ah-ehr-oh-poo-ehr-toh
customs	**la aduana**	lah ah-doo-ah-nah
departure lounge	**sala de embarque**	sah-lah deh ehm-bahr-keh
boarding pass	**pase de abordar**	pah-seh deh ah-bohr-dahr
taxi stand/rank	**sitio de taxis**	see-tee-oh deh tahk-sees
car rental	**renta de automóviles**	rehn-tah deh aw-toh-moh-vee-lehs
motorcycle	**la moto (cicleta)**	lah moh-toh(see-kleh-tah)
mileage	**el kilometraje**	ehl kee-loh-meh-trah-he
bicycle	**la bicicleta**	lah bee-see-kleh-tah
daily/weekly rate	**la tarifa diaria/ semanal**	lah tah-ree-fah dee-ah-ree-ah/ seh-mah-nahl
insurance	**los seguros**	lohs seh-goo-rohs
gas station	**la gasolinería**	lah gah-soh-leen-er-ee-ah
garage	**el taller mecánico**	ehl tah-yehr meh-kahn-ee-koh
I have a flat tire	**Se me ponchó la llanta**	seh meh pohn-shoh lah yahn-tah

Staying in a Hotel

Do you have a vacant room?	**¿Tienen una habitación libre?**	tee-eh-nehn oo-nah ah-bee-tah-see-ohn lee-breh
double room	**habitación doble**	ah-bee-tah-see-ohn doh-bleh
with a double bed	**con cama matrimonial**	kohn kah-mah mah-tree-moh-nee-ahl
twin room	**habitación con dos camas**	ah-bee-tah-see-ohn kohn dohs kah-mahs
single room	**habitación sencilla**	ah-bee-tah-see-ohn sehn-see-yah
room with a bath	**habitación con baño**	ah-bee-tah-see-ohn kohn bah-nyoh
shower	**la ducha**	lah doo-chah
Do you have a room with a view (of the sea)?	**¿Hay alguna habitación con vista (al mar)?**	eye ahl-goo-nah ah-bee-tah-see-ohn kohn vees-tah (ahl mahr)
I have a reservation	**Tengo una habitación reservada**	tehn-goh oo-nah ah-bee-tah-see-ohn reh-sehr vah-dah
The … is not working	**No funciona el/la…**	noh foon-see-oh-nah ehl/lah
I need a wake-up call at … o'clock	**Necesito que me despierten a las …**	neh-seh-see-toh keh meh dehs-pee-ehr-tehn ah lahs
Where is the dining-room/bar?	**¿Dónde está el restaurante/ el bar?**	dohn-deh ehs-tah ehl rehs-toh-rahn-teh/ehl bahr
hot/cold water	**agua caliente/ fría**	ah-goo-ah kah-lee-ehn-teh/ free-ah
soap	**el jabón**	ehl hah-bohn
towel	**la toalla**	lah toh-ah-yah
key	**la llave**	lah yah-veh

Eating Out

Have you got a table for …	**¿Tienen una mesa para …?**	tee-eh-nehn oo-nah meh-sahpah-rah
I want to reserve a table	**Quiero reservar una mesa**	kee-eh-roh reh-sehr-vahr oo-nah meh-sah
The bill, please	**La cuenta, por favor**	lah kwehn-tah pohr fah-vohr
I am a vegetarian	**Soy vegetariano/a**	soy veh-heh-tah-ree-ah-no/na
waiter/waitress	**mesero/a**	meh-seh-roh/rah
menu	**la carta**	lah kahr-tah
fixed-price menu	**menú del día/comida corrida**	meh-noo dehl dee-ah/koh-mee-dah koh-ree-dah
wine list	**la carta de vinos**	lah kahr-tah deh vee-nohs
glass	**un vaso**	oon vah-soh
bottle	**una botella**	oo-nah boh-teh-yah
knife	**un cuchillo**	oon koo-chee-yoh
fork	**un tenedor**	oon teh-neh-dohr
spoon	**una cuchara**	oo-nah koo-chah-

		rah
breakfast	**el desayuno**	*ehl deh-sah-***yoo***-noh*
lunch	**la comida**	*lah koh-***mee***-dah*
dinner	**la cena**	*lah* **seh***-nah*
main course	**el plato fuerte**	*ehl* **plah***-toh foo-***ehr***-teh*
starters	**las entradas**	*lahs ehn-***trah***-das*
dish of the day	**el plato del día**	*ehl* **plah***-toh dehl* **dee***-ah*
rare	**termino rojo**	**tehr***-mee-noh* **roh***-hoh*
medium	**termino medio**	**tehr***-mee-noh* **meh***-dee-oh*
well done	**bien cocido**	*bee-***ehn** *koh-***see***-doh*
Could you heat it up for me?	**¿Me lo podría calentar?**	*meh loh pohd -***ree***-ah kah-lehn-***tahr**
chair	**la silla**	*lah* **see***-yah*
napkin	**la servilleta**	*lah sehr-vee-***yeh***-tah*
tip	**la propina**	*lah proh-***pee***-nah*
Is service included?	**¿El servicio está incluido?**	*ehl sehr-***vee***-see-oh ehs-***tah** *een-skloo-***ee***-doh*
Do you have a light?	**¿Tiene fuego?**	*tee-***eh***-nee foo-***eh***-goh*
ashtray	**cenicero**	*seh-nee-***seh***-roh*
cigarettes	**los cigarros**	*lohs see-***gah***-rohs*

Menu Decoder *(see also pp311)*

el aceite	*ah-***see***-eh-teh*	*oil*
las aceitunas	*ah-seh-***toon***-ahs*	*olives*
el agua mineral	**ah***-gwa mee-neh-***rahl**	*mineral water*
sin gas/con gas	*seen gas/kohn gas*	*still/sparkling*
el ajo	**ah***-hoh*	*garlic*
el arroz	*ahr-***rohs**	*rice*
el azúcar	*ah-***soo***-kahr*	*sugar*
la banana	*bah-***nah***-nah*	*banana*
una bebida	*beh-***bee***-dah*	*drink*
el café	*kah-***feh**	*coffee*
la carne	**kahr***-neh*	*meat*
la cebolla	*seh-***boh***-yah*	*onion*
la cerveza	*sehr-***veh***-sah*	*beer*
el cerdo	**sehr***-doh*	*pork*
el chocolate	*choh-koh-***lah***-teh*	*chocolate*
la ensalada	*ehn-sah-***lah***-dah*	*salad*
la fruta	**froo***-tah*	*fruit*
el helado	*eh-***lah***-doh*	*ice cream*
el huevo	*oo-***eh***-voh*	*egg*
el jugo	*ehl***hoo***-goh*	*juice*
la langosta	*lahn-***gohs***-tah*	*lobster*
la leche	**leh***-cheh*	*milk*
la mantequilla	*mahn-teh-***kee***-yah*	*butter*
la manzana	*mahn-***sah***-nah*	*apple*
los mariscos	*mah-***rees***-kohs*	*seafood*
la naranja	*nah-***rahn***-hah*	*orange*
el pan	**pahn**	*bread*
las papas	**pah***-pahs*	*potatoes*
las papas a la francesa	**pah***-pahs ah lah frahn-***seh***-sah*	*French fries*
las papas fritas	**pah***-pahs* **free***-tahs*	*potato chips*
el pastel	*pahs-***tehl**	*cake*
el pescado	*pehs-***kah***-doh*	*fish*
picante	*pee-***kahn***-teh*	*spicy*
la pimienta	*pee-mee-***yehn***-tah*	*pepper*
el pollo	**poh***-yoh*	*chicken*
el postre	**pohs***-treh*	*dessert*
el queso	**keh***-soh*	*cheese*
el refresco	*reh-***frehs***-koh*	*soft drink/soda*
la sal	**sahl**	*salt*
la salsa	**sahl***-sah*	*sauce*
la sopa	**soh***-pah*	*soup*
el té	**teh**	*herb tea (usually camomile)*
el té negro	**teh neh***-groh*	*tea*
la torta	**tohr***-tah*	*sandwich*
las tostadas	*tohs-***tah***-dahs*	*toast*
el vinagre	*vee-***nah***-greh*	*vinegar*
el vino blanco	**vee***-noh* **blahn***-koh*	*white wine*
el vino tinto	**vee***-noh* **teen***-toh*	*red wine*

Numbers

0	**cero**	**seh***-roh*
1	**uno**	**oo***-noh*
2	**dos**	*dohs*
3	**tres**	*trehs*
4	**cuatro**	**kwa***-troh*
5	**cinco**	**seen***-koh*
6	**seis**	*says*
7	**siete**	**see***-eh-teh*
8	**ocho**	**oh***-choh*
9	**nueve**	**nweh***-veh*
10	**diez**	*dee-***ehs**
11	**once**	**ohn***-seh*
12	**doce**	**doh***-seh*
13	**trece**	**treh***-seh*
14	**catorce**	*kah-***tohr***-seh*
15	**quince**	**keen***-seh*
16	**dieciséis**	*dee-eh-see-***seh-ees**
17	**diecisiete**	*dee-eh-see-see-***eh***-teh*
18	**dieciocho**	*dee-eh-see-***oh***-choh*
19	**diecinueve**	*dee-eh-see-***nweh***-veh*
20	**veinte**	**veh***-een-teh*
21	**veintiuno**	*veh-een-tee-***oo***-noh*
22	**veintidós**	*veh-een-tee-***dohs**
30	**treinta**	**treh***-een-tah*
31	**treinta y uno**	*treh-een-tah ee* **oo***-noh*
40	**cuarenta**	*kwah-***rehn***-tah*
50	**cincuenta**	*seen-***kwehn***-tah*
60	**sesenta**	*seh-***sehn***-tah*
70	**setenta**	*seh-***tehn***-tah*
80	**ochenta**	*oh-***chehn***-tah*
90	**noventa**	*noh-***vehn***-tah*
100	**cien**	*see-***ehn**
101	**ciento uno**	*see-***ehn***-toh* **oo***-noh*
102	**ciento dos**	*see-***ehn***-toh* **dohs**
200	**doscientos**	*dohs-see-***ehn***- tohs*
500	**quinientos**	*khee-nee-***ehn***-tohs*
700	**setecientos**	*seh-teh-see-***ehn***-tohs*
900	**novecientos**	*noh-veh-see-***ehn***-tohs*
1,000	**mil**	*meel*
1,001	**mil uno**	**meel oo***-noh*

Time

one minute	**un minuto**	**oon** *mee-***noo***-toh*
one hour	**una hora**	**oo***-nah* **oh***-rah*
half an hour	**media hora**	**meh***-dee-ah* **oh***-rah*
half past one	**la una y media**	*lah* **oo***-nah ee* **meh***-dee-ah*
quarter past one	**la una y cuarto**	*lah* **oo***-nah ee* **kwahr***-toh*
ten past one	**la una y diez**	*lah* **oo***-nah ee dee-***ehs**
quarter to two	**cuarto para las dos**	**kwahr***-toh pah-rah lahs* **dohs**
ten to two	**diez para las dos**	*dee-***ehs** *pah-rah lahs* **dohs**
Monday	**lunes**	**loo***-nehs*
Tuesday	**martes**	**mahr***-tehs*
Wednesday	**miércoles**	*mee-***ehr***-koh-lehs*
Thursday	**jueves**	*hoo-***weh***-vehs*
Friday	**viernes**	*vee-***ehr***-nehs*
Saturday	**sábado**	**sah***-bah-doh*
Sunday	**domingo**	*doh-***meen***-goh*
January	**enero**	*eh-***neh***-roh*
February	**febrero**	*feh-***breh***-roh*
March	**marzo**	**mahr***-soh*
April	**abril**	*ah-***breel**
May	**mayo**	**mah***-yoh*
June	**junio**	**hoo***-nee-oh*
July	**julio**	**hoo***-lee-oh*
August	**agosto**	*ah-***gohs***-toh*
September	**septiembre**	*sehp-tee-***ehm***-breh*
October	**octubre**	*ohk-***too***-breh*
November	**noviembre**	*noh-vee-***ehm***-breh*
December	**diciembre**	*dee-see-***ehm***-breh*
Two days ago	**Hace dos días**	**hah***-seh* **dohs dee***-ahs*
In two day's time	**En dos días**	*ehn* **dohs dee***-ahs*
May 1	**El primero de mayo**	*ehl pree-***meh***-roh deh* **mah***-yoh*

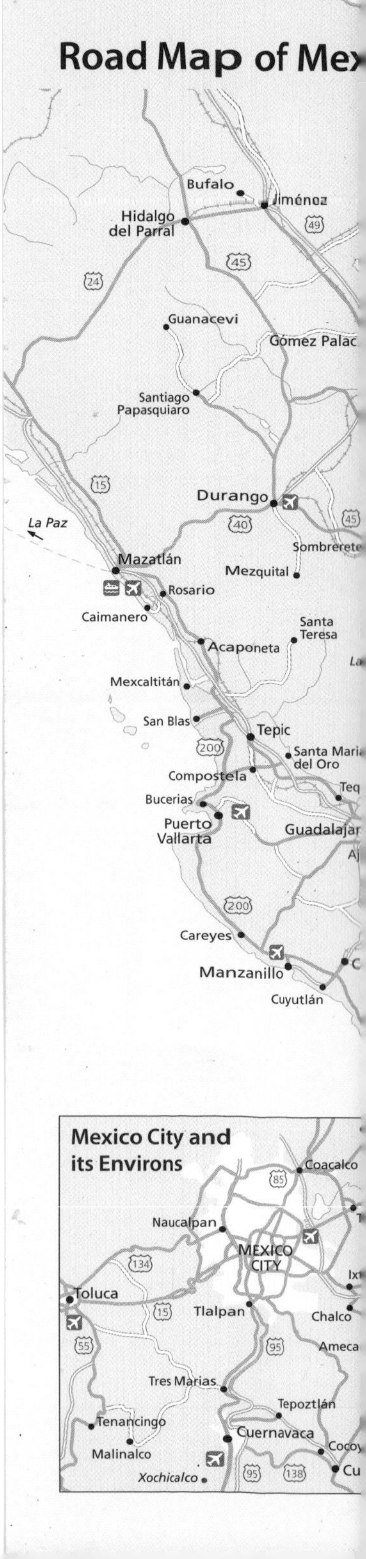